T0227493

Accountable Care Organizations

Value Metrics and Capital Formation

Accountable Care Organizations

Value Metrics and Capital Formation

Robert James Cimasi, MHA, ASA, FRICS, MCBA, AVA, CM&AA

Foreword by Peter A. Pavarini, Esq.

CRC Press is an imprint of the
Taylor & Francis Group, an **informa** business
A PRODUCTIVITY PRESS BOOK

CRC Press
Taylor & Francis Group
6000 Broken Sound Parkway NW, Suite 300
Boca Raton, FL 33487-2742

International Standard Book Number-13: 978-1-4665-8183-8 (Hardback)

Library of Congress Cataloging-in-Publication Data

Cimasi, Robert James, author.
Accountable care organizations : value metrics and capital formation / Robert James Cimasi.
p. ; cm.
Includes bibliographical references and index.
ISBN 978-1-4665-8183-8 (hardcover : alk. paper)
I. Title.
[DNLM: 1. Accountable Care Organizations--economics--United States. 2. Accountable Care Organizations--organization & administration--United States. 3. Capital Financing--United States. 4. Delivery of Health Care, Integrated--economics--United States. 5. Managed Competition--United States. 6. Quality Assurance, Health Care--economics--United States. WA 540 AA1]

362.1068'1--dc23 2013001454

Visit the Taylor & Francis Web site at
http://www.taylorandfrancis.com

and the CRC Press Web site at
http://www.crcpress.com

To my wife

Laura M. Baumstark, MBA, CAE

Contents

List of Figures

List of Exhibits

List of Tables

Disclaimer

This work includes information regarding the basic characteristics of various statutes and regulations related to the healthcare industry. It is intended to provide only a general overview of these topics. This information is provided with the understanding that the author and publisher are not rendering legal advice and services. The author has made every attempt to verify the completeness and accuracy of the information; however, neither the author nor publisher can guarantee, in any way whatsoever, the applicability of the information found herein. Further, this work is not intended as legal advice or a substitute for appropriate legal counsel.

Foreword

On June 28, 2012, the U.S. Supreme Court largely upheld the constitutionality of the Patient Protection and Affordable Care Act of 2010 (ACA) and in so doing removed one of the impediments to a number of reforms that had gained growing support within the healthcare industry. While very few correctly predicted how the Roberts Court would reach its decision, there was as much relief as surprise knowing that the Constitution would not stand in the way of implementing major sections of ACA that were never in dispute. One part of the 2010 law that was rarely the subject of partisan bickering consisted of four pages (out of nearly 2,000) promoting the development of accountable care organizations (ACOs). Despite its brevity, this portion of the legislation has been widely viewed as one facet of reform that could result in a sustainable solution to the nation's healthcare cost conundrum.

Although many authors, including the one writing this foreword, have previously attempted to explain the ACO concept in practical terms, virtually no one thought to thoroughly analyze the financial underpinnings of this model until Bob Cimasi decided to write this book. What an ambitious work it is. Even though most existing ACOs remain gestational or in their earliest years of operation, Cimasi and his associates at Health Capital Consultants have managed to assemble an authoritative body of information on this rapidly evolving subject and to present their findings in an easily understood manner.

Together with many of my colleagues in the American health law bar, I have long respected Bob Cimasi's passion and talent for unraveling complex healthcare equations and objectively assigning value to all or part of a business or relationship. That was difficult enough to do in a traditional fee-for-service environment; it will be much harder as the nation transitions to shared savings, bundled payments, and other new methods of value-based purchasing. With the publication of *Accountable Care Organizations: Value Metrics and Capital Formation,* readers will now have insight on the principles and methods Cimasi and his team of experts carefully use to appraise transactions within a changing healthcare payment and delivery system. This text is much more than a compilation of educational resources on a currently hot topic. Rather, it could become a seminal work relied upon by all stakeholders in a transformed healthcare marketplace. I cannot think of anyone more qualified than Bob Cimasi to take on such a daunting task.

It is always a privilege to be asked to read a manuscript before it becomes publicly available. This time, however, I found reading *Accountable Care Organizations: Value Metrics and Capital Formation* to be like looking through a window on a brave new world. I found myself asking: Is this finally the way Americans will learn how to assure quality, efficiency, and fairness in one of the most important aspects of their daily lives? I hope the readers of this book will be challenged to ask that same question as they seek to understand the ins and outs of ACOs.

Peter A. Pavarini, Esq.
Partner, Squire Sanders (US) LLP

Foreword

Preface

The only thing new in this world is the history that you don't know.

Harry S. Truman

This year the consulting firm I started in 1993 will celebrate its twentieth anniversary. Over that period, Health Capital Consultants has developed a diverse clientele, first offering services to solo and small group medical practices, then participating in the consolidation accompanying the managed care boom of the 1990s, and, most recently, directing our focus to the economic and financial challenges of yet another iteration of healthcare reform. As both a healthcare consultant and small business owner (providing employee health benefits), I have witnessed the continuous transformation of the healthcare delivery landscape. In the past three years, however, I have noticed a policy movement that, while similar in many characteristics, may portend, in scope, a heretofore unseen paradigm shift. As I write this preface, the U.S. Supreme Court recently upheld the constitutionality of the Patient Protection and Affordable Care Act (ACA), in two consolidated opinions: *National Federation of Independent Business v. Sebelius* and *Florida v. Department of Health and Human Services.*[1] President Obama has just been reelected to a second term, as the primary driver and namesake for the historic healthcare form known as "Obamacare." These two landmark events will most certainly shape his presidency, as well as dramatically change the course of events in U.S. health policy.

However, regardless of the current level of political relevance, achieving cost and quality is not a new pursuit. For more than 80 years, there has been an effort to improve the cost and quality of healthcare.[2] The year 1946 brought the Hill–Burton Act that offered federal funding to hospitals that didn't discriminate and that covered a reasonable volume of patients. The year 1965 saw the advent of Medicare and Medicaid, the first universal (though limited) coverage for vulnerable populations. Then, in 1999, the Institute of Medicine's seminal work, *To Err is Human: Building a Safer Health System*, boosted public awareness of deficiencies in care for perhaps the first time; a harbinger of change for transparency and disclosure within an industry that had operated behind an opaque veil comprised of patients' often uninformed, and most always, trustful belief in the physicians and healthcare institutions on which they relied.[3]

Today the face of healthcare reform efforts toward a more accountable system of care is symbolized by, and has its foundation in, the ACA and related legislation on both federal and state levels. The Medicare Shared Savings Program (MSSP), which promulgates Accountable Care Organizations (ACO), is set forth on a mere four pages in the ACA.[4] It has created waves throughout the entire industry and public discourse, by seeking to provide the accountability for quality and cost that the healthcare market has sought for decades. The ACA advances the movement toward universal coverage within a framework of existing federal, state, and private insurance models, in contrast to moving to a single payor system. The debate across every sector of healthcare begs the question: Given such high expectations, can ACOs deliver?

The United States attains lower global health ratings and spends nearly 50% more in per capital health expenditures than the next highest nation. At the same time, the percentage of GDP (gross national product) spent on U.S. healthcare is nearing 18%, 5% higher than any other country.[5] As healthcare expenditures continue to rise, the economy has been suffering through the Great Recession.[6] Although technically on the road to recovery, unemployment and the prevalence of uninsured and under-insured citizens have approached an all-time high.

Republicans and Democrats alike have agreed that the cost of healthcare is too high and quality must improve. More importantly, the discussion of quality and costs in healthcare has moved past politics and business into the homes of patients, resulting in a consensus that a change, of some sort, is needed, albeit the definition of that change is in volatile dispute. The incentives created by ACOs (a type of value-based purchasing) have the potential to shift the way healthcare is delivered to affect cost and quality issues.

Note that, *accountable care* is not a new concept, with roots in the past failed efforts of both *managed care* and *managed competition*. Despite the deep-seated history of accountable care, the newly proposed models of ACOs represent a renewed, and perhaps enhanced, opportunity to succeed in shifting the way healthcare services are delivered. Accountable care, transparency, and value-based purchasing are already making a foothold in healthcare through federal programs and private payors. The current economic environment of slowed growth, high unemployment, and record federal deficit and debt may be the perfect storm that drives lasting change. Whether ACOs are the ultimate answer, the aims of lower costs and better quality are the change which patients, payors, and the healthcare industry have pursued.

This text is designed to examine what ACOs may potentially offer, how feasible their promise is, and what value they create within the current healthcare environment. To provide a probative understanding of ACOs, requisite for any informed investment decision, we examine the history from which the accountable care concept evolved into the current manifestation of ACOs as conceived within the ACA of 2010. Without this background, a knowledgeable distinction between ACOs and the failed efforts at managed competition, through the managed care plans of the 1990s, cannot be made, dooming ACOs to result in a similar failed outcome.

To make an educated investment decision, the activities of capital and financial feasibility must be based on a thorough understanding of the structure and history of healthcare delivery. Once this foundation is laid, this book, through the looking glass of the *Four Pillars of Healthcare Industry Value* (i.e., regulatory, reimbursement, competition, and technology), addresses the following questions: what are ACOs; under what circumstances and capital structures might they represent a sound investment; what value might they offer; and, are they the cost containment and quality improvement answer for which we have been searching?

Robert James Cimasi, MHA, ASA, FRICS, MCBA, AVA, CM & AA
Health Capital Consultants

ENDNOTES

1. *National Federation of Independent Business v. Sebelius,* Certiorari to the United States Court of Appeals for the Eleventh Circuit, S.C. Slip Opinion No. 11-393, June 28, 2011.
2. The committee on the cost of medical care reports. 1932. *The American Journal of Nursing* 32 (12): 1286.
3. *To err is human: Building a safer health system.* 1999. The Institute of Medicine, November.
4. Patient Protection and Affordable Care Act. Public Law 111-148, Section 3032, 124 STAT 395 (March 23, 2010).
5. OECD health data 2011—Frequently requested data. 2011. The Organization for Economic Co-operation and Development, November. Online at: http://www.oecd.org/document/16/0,3343,en_2649_34631_2085200_1_1_1_1,00.html (accessed January 1, 2012).
6. Becker, G. S. 2011. The great recession and government failure. *The Wall Street Journal*, September 2. Online at: http://online.wsj.com/article/SB10001424053111904199404576536930606933332.html (accessed April 26, 2012).

Acknowledgments

Anne P. Sharamitaro, Esq., HCC's executive vice president and general counsel, was central to the development of the book, both in conducting and directing the research and coordinating the efforts of all those who contributed to the project.

Todd A. Zigrang, MBA, MHA, FACHE, ASA, HCC's president, who has excelled for over 18 years in representing HCC throughout numerous healthcare industry client engagements, greatly assisted in the development of the underlying concepts, as well as contributing the benefit of his experience and the specific background issues in this book.

Other HCC colleagues who contributed significantly to this book include Kyle F. Krahl, MBA, vice president; Matthew J. Wagner, MBA, vice president; and John R, Chwarzinski, MSF, MAE, vice president, who assisted greatly with their reviews and comments.

HCC's research and library staff, in particular, Jessica C. Burt, Esq., MHA and senior research associate, as well as members of HCC's consulting and administrative support team were of great help.

Also, many thanks to our professional colleagues and clients who served as reviewers and commentators of the various drafts of this work along the way, including Peter Pavarini, Esq. for his comments and contributing the Foreword; Fred Geilfuss, Esq. of Foley & Lardner, LLP; and David Grauer, Esq. of Squire Sanders, LLP.

About the Author

Robert James Cimasi, MHA, ASA, FRICS, MCBA, AVA, CM&AA, is chief executive officer of Health Capital Consultants (HCC), a nationally recognized healthcare financial and economic consulting firm headquartered in St. Louis, Missouri, since 1993. Cimasi has more than 25 years of experience in serving clients, with a professional focus on the financial and economic aspects of healthcare service sector entities including valuation consulting and capital formation services; healthcare industry transactions including joint ventures, mergers, acquisitions, and divestitures; litigation support and expert testimony; and certificate-of-need and other regulatory and policy planning consulting.

Cimasi holds a master's in health administration from the University of Maryland and holds several professional designations: Accredited Senior Appraiser (ASA–American Society of Appraisers), Fellow Royal Intuition of Chartered Surveyors (FRICS–Royal Institute of Chartered Surveyors), Master Certified Business Appraiser (MCBA–Institute of Business Appraisers), Accredited Valuation Analyst (AVA–National Association of Certified Valuators and Analysts), and Certified Merger & Acquisition Advisor (CM&AA–Alliance of Merger & Acquisition Advisors). He has served as an expert witness in numerous court cases and has provided testimony before federal and state legislative committees. He is a nationally known speaker on healthcare industry topics, the author of several books, including *The Adviser's Guide to Healthcare* (AICPA. 2010) and *Healthcare Valuation: The Financial Appraisal of Enterprises, Assets, and Services in the Era of Reform* (Wiley, 2005), as well as numerous chapters, published articles, research papers and case studies, and is often quoted by healthcare industry press. In 2006, Cimasi was honored with the prestigious Shannon Pratt Award in Business Valuation conferred by the Institute of Business Appraisers. Cimasi serves on the editorial board of *Business Appraisals Practice* of the Institute of Business Appraisers, of which he is a member of the College of Fellows. In 2011, he was named a Fellow of the Royal Institution of Chartered Surveyors (RICS) and serves on the editorial board of the RICS *Modus Americas* journal. Cimasi is also the current chair of the American Society of Appraisers Healthcare Special Interest Group (ASA HSIG) subcommittee.

Introduction

Whereof what's past is prologue, what to come, in yours and my discharge.

William Shakespeare
The Tempest

While the concept of accountable care has existed for some time, it was given new life and renewed vigor by the March 23, 2010 passage of the Patient Protection and Affordable Care Act (ACA), which established the Medicare Shared Savings Program (MSSP) and drove the continued evolution of the Accountable Care Organization (ACO) from its early inceptions, e.g., the Medicare Healthcare Quality Demonstration (2003), the Medicare Physician Group Practice Demonstration (2005), and similar models adapted by provider organizations, such as Kaiser Permanente and Healthcare Partners Medical Group. The promise of lower healthcare costs and higher quality of care has precipitated a national fascination with ACOs throughout every level of healthcare, from government agencies, academic research institutes, and large provider delivery systems to individual physicians. As the nature and structure of both federal and commercial ACOs continue to be defined and distinguished, the question remains: Do ACOs, as a model, provide a sustainable solution to the nation's rising healthcare spending or will these emerging healthcare organizations follow the ascendency and ultimate demise of previous managed care models of the 1990s?

The term *managed care* generally refers to a collaborative effort between health services delivery and benefit design utilizing management and financing to influence cost, quality, or other specific outcomes.[1] Similarly, an ACO is an organized network of providers that coordinates care in order to lower costs and increase quality to achieve financial incentives established through a contract with an associated payor. Just as a square is a rectangle, but a rectangle is not a square, ACOs are a form of managed care, but the two concepts are not interchangeable.

Managed care took off in the 1990s through the advent of the health maintenance organization (HMO), a prepaid health plan model that used designated provider networks to increase efficiency of care for enrolled members. Distinctions between HMOs and ACOs are illustrated below, in Table I.1.

The widespread acceptance of managed care led to a consumer backlash. Providers and insurers were accused of lowering costs in an effort to enrich themselves, resulting in poor quality care and little to no impact on the continual rise in premiums for coverage.[3] Even though some of the managed care initiatives were considered notorious by the end of the decade, the model evolved and still exists in, perhaps, a different form in numerous markets. In line with that historical path, ACOs are now being touted as the means to address a seemingly intractable healthcare budget, quality, and access/coverage issues.

It may be that now, at this present point in time, the U.S. healthcare system has reached a tipping point where either costs will continue to increase until healthcare is unmistakable as a luxury good, available only to those that can afford adequate quality and access or, the triple aim of healthcare reform (i.e., access, cost, and quality) and some stability will be attained through the promotion of evidence-based medicine and value-based purchasing—both key concepts of ACOs. That this essential healthcare debate has polarized political parties and permeated every level of our society is self-evident to anyone who reads a daily paper, watches television, listens to the radio, or follows a blog. The Clinton-era attempt at universal employer healthcare showed that, without public demand and alignment of stakeholder interests, change is not likely to be adopted.[4] As healthcare industry spending nears 18% of the U.S. gross domestic product (GDP) and the prevalence of the uninsured

TABLE I.1
Differentiating HMOs from ACOs[2]

	HMOs	ACOs
Accountability	Accountable for patients signed up through insurer	Accountable for patients based on payment method (e.g., Medicare or a specific commercial insurer)
Providers	Providers offer specified services for predetermined payment (premiums)	Providers integrate and coordinate care to meet evidence-based targets set by CMS or insurer
Risk	Some plans bear risk, but not a requirement	Risk based on reimbursement for outcomes and value-based payments
Reimburstment	Reimbursement primarily based on financial performance	Reimbursement based on quality and cost measures

and under-insured patients reaches an all-time high, the calls for change are resounding. ACOs are one of the current methods of implementing value-based purchasing toward the goal of meeting these demands.

Especially within the commercial market, ACOs are revitalizing coordinated care and episode-of-care payment ideals to further their success. There has been a growing acknowledgment that traditional fee-for-service reimbursement models are leading providers down the wrong path, toward volume incentives, instead of value incentives.[5] The variety of financial incentives utilized by ACOs covers many of the episode-of-care payment models that have been associated with the transition to a focus on the value of care provided, including pay-for-performance, bundled payments, population payments, and any other model that rewards care coordination and efficiency.[6]

ACOs are often compared to the mythical unicorn, i.e., "everyone has heard of one, but no one has ever seen one."[7] At the time of publication of this book, over 200 ACOs have come into being across federal and commercial markets and, unlike unicorns, their existence and performance can now be observed and evaluated.[8] Yet, despite growing health policy support of the accountable care concept, tangible evidence of ACO feasibility and sustainability related to their monetary or nonmonetary success is lacking. Practitioners, providers, and policy makers outside already clinically integrated health systems (e.g., Kaiser Permanente) are especially weary of investing the time and capital required in chasing what may prove to be yet another unicorn. Even as ACOs continue to evolve and spread, the question remains as to whether ACOs can avoid the fate of the 1990s HMO model.

In developing an understanding of the forces and stakeholders that drive healthcare markets, it is useful to examine the Four Pillars of Healthcare Industry Value, i.e., regulation, reimbursement, competition, and technology. A visual depiction of the Four Pillars is set forth below, in Figure I.1.

These four elements shape the value metric of healthcare delivery and serve as a framework for analyzing the viability, efficiency, efficacy, and productivity of healthcare enterprises. A comparison of the potential value of ACOs to their necessary capital requirements and financial feasibility is requisite to understanding the likelihood of success for this emerging model.

It is not the intent of this book to declare whether the ACO model will ultimately prevail. Rather, in Chapter 1 through Chapter 5, we seek to lay out the historical background and evolution of the ACO model as the basis for the development of the value metrics and capital formation analyses that are foundational to accessing the current efficacy and capacity for change, which may result from pursuing the development of an ACO, both to their potential for nonmonetary as well as monetary value. The discussion of nonmonetary value is focused on a review of aspects of population health within the context of such objectives as improved quality outcomes and access to care.

In Chapter 6 and Chapter 7, this book addresses the value metrics of ACOs, including the requirements for capital formation, financial feasibility, and economic returns.

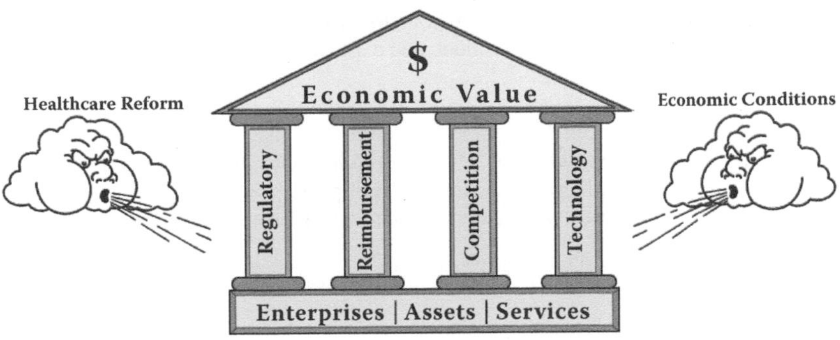

FIGURE I.1 The four pillars of healthcare industry value.

It has long been held that all financial value is the expectation of future economic benefit.[9] Accordingly, part of any investment analysis involves a forecast of the most probable future economic outcomes. In developing these forecasts, a concise and clear understanding of historical market conditions that represent the setting from which those outcomes spring is required. Otherwise providers, patients, and policy makers may fall victim to the failures of history, as "those who cannot remember the past are condemned to repeat it."[10] Therefrom arises the concern surrounding the development of ACOs repeating the failures of the past. To discourage this counterproductive outcome, there must be a discussion of the foundation and roots of managed competition from the earliest efforts of care integration to the current attempt at accountable care.

In Chapter 8, this book examines the positive externalities of the ACO model, including results for third parties outside the basic construct of the ACO contracts shared savings payments.

Finally, in Chapter 9, this book presents a brief discussion of (1) the potential role of consults in assisting providers in the consideration, development, implementation, and operation of an ACO; (2) the various modalities and specific types of consulting engagements typically utilized in such endeavors; and (3) the respective benefits, drawbacks, and opportunities to be derived from each.

Also included are some concluding remarks, a brief epilogue, a review of significant literature, and a compendium of bibliographic sources.

In applying the lessons from the past to today's rapidly evolving healthcare environment, this work seeks to present the requisite analytical exercise to facilitate decisions as to whether ACOs are feasible and have the potential to overcome decades of failed efforts at managed competition. These decisions and their outcomes may well impact the entire healthcare industry, now one-fifth of the U.S. economy, and growing.

ENDNOTES

1. Marcinko, D. (ed.) 2006. Managed care. In *Dictionary of health insurance and managed care,* p. 174. New York: Springer Publication.
2. Aon Hewitt. 2011. Integrated health care delivery/ACO's: What does it all mean to employers? Paper presented at the National Accountable Care Organization Congress, November 1, p.13.
3. Kaiser Family Foundation. 2006. The public, managed care, and consumer protections. *Kaiser Public Opinion Spotlight*, January, p. 1.
4. Bok, D. 2003. Leadership in the great health care debate of 1993–1994. In *Public discourse in America: Conversation and community in the twenty-first century*, p. 97. Philadelphia,: University of Pennsylvania Press.
5. Institute of Medicine. 2006. *Rewarding provider performance: Aligning incentives in Medicare.* Washington, DC: National Academies Press, p. 4.
6. Davis, K. 2007. Paying for care episodes and care coordination. *The New England Journal of Medicine* 356 (11): 1166.

7. Morrison, I. 2011. *Leading change in health care: Building a viable system for today and tomorrow.* (Concept attributed to Mark Smith, president and CEO of the California Healthcare Foundation). Chicago: Health Forum, Inc., p. 184.
8. Muhlestein, D., et al. 2012. *Growth and dispersion of accountable care organizations: June 2012 update.* Salt Lake City: Leavitt Partners, p. 2.
9. Pratt, S. P., Reilly, R. F., and Schweihs, R. P. 2001. *Valuing a business: The analysis and appraisal of closely held companies*, 4th ed. New York: McGraw Hill, p. 40.
10. Santayana, G. 1998. *Life of reason: The phases of human progress.* New York: Prometheus Books, p. 82. (Republication of 1905 text)

1 Background and the Path to ACOs

INTRODUCTION

Driven by the current healthcare environment and the passage of healthcare reform legislation, healthcare professionals and policy makers have been considering new ways to increase efficiency and quality, while decreasing the cost of providing healthcare services, including the creation of accountable care organizations (ACOs). ACOs are healthcare organizations in which a set of providers, usually physicians and hospitals, are held accountable under a contract with payor(s) for the cost and quality of care delivered to a specific local population.[1] There is no set model for ACOs, nor is their success completely assured. Ideally, ACOs will help shift the current healthcare payment system from its present emphasis on achieving revenue solely by generating high volumes of procedure-driven services to a system emphasizing quality and efficiency of care leading to lower overall costs.[2]

Key Term	Definition	Citation
Accountable Care Organization (ACO)	A healthcare organization where a set of otherwise independent providers, usually physicians and hospitals, willingly integrate to become responsible for the cost, quality, and overall care delivered to a specified patient population.	*Can Accountable Care Organizations Improve the Value of Health Care by Solving the Cost and Quality Quandaries?* By Kelly Devers and Robert Berenson, Urban Institute, (October 2009) p. 1.

HISTORY OF ACCOUNTABLE CARE

While the term ACO has recently captured the imagination of the healthcare industry, the Patient Protection and Affordable Care Act (ACA) was not the first iteration of the accountable care concept. ACOs are merely the latest version in a dialog that has been evolving for generations as to how to manage the rising cost of healthcare in a manner that addresses both *cost* and *quality*. Specifically, the concept of *accountable care* has existed in the U.S. healthcare industry for decades—long before the emergence of ACOs, beginning with the very origins of managed care.

Key Concept	Definition	Citation
Accountable Care	A strategy for managing the rising cost of healthcare in a manner that addresses both *cost* and *quality*	*Health Capital Consultants*

History of Managed Care

Managed care plans were designed to integrate the financing and provisions of health services through a Managed Care Organization (MCO) in an effort to contain costs. MCOs attempt to hold providers accountable for providing care to a population through clinical practice standardization, selective contracting, low-cost settings, reduced discretionary hospital admissions, and effective use of staff.[3]

Factoid 1.1

Five major recommendations of the 1932 Committee on the Costs of Medical Care: (1) organize medical service by groups of physicians, nurses, pharmacists, etc., centered around a hospital; (2) make all basic public health services available to the entire public; (3) implement group payment, such as insurance or taxation, for costs of medical care; (4) state focus on coordination of care and creation of agencies that further such actions; and (5) make professional medical education stricter with emphasis on prevention and expansion of primary care physicians. (Source: I. S. Falk, the Committee on the Costs of Medical Care, and the Drive for National Health Insurance. By Milton I. Roemer, *American Journal of Public Health*, vol. 75, no. 8 (1985), p. 842.)

The discourse related to accountable care began as early as 1932 with the Committee on the Costs of Medical Care (CCMC), which issued a report in 1932 that marked the culmination of a five-year survey and an intensive study of the organization and cost of medical services. The report is not unanimous, and a wide divergence of viewpoints exists between the main body of the committee representing institutions, social interests, public health, social sciences and the public, and a minority group effectively representing the American Medical Association.[4] Seventeen of the 25 physicians on the committee, and 35 of the committee's total membership of 48, signed the majority report. Eight of the nine who approved the minority report were physicians.[5] The committee was established under the auspices and with the financial backing to the extent of almost $1 million of several of the great educational and eleemosynary (charitable) institutions of the United States, including the Rockefeller and the Carnegie Foundations and the Julius Rosenwald and Milbank Memorial Funds.[6]

Although the members never reached complete agreement, they issued five major recommendations for the healthcare community:

1. Organize medical service by groups of physicians, nurses, pharmacists, etc. centered around a hospital
2. Make all basic public health services available to the entire public
3. Implement group payment, such as insurance or taxation, for costs of medical care
4. State focus on coordination of care and creation of agencies to further such actions
5. Make professional medical education stricter with emphasis on prevention and expansion of primary care physicians.[7]

The committee's members supported an increased governmental and organizational presence and control over medical care.[8] A two-volume set was produced, presenting some of the committee's theories and efforts during meetings. The first of the volumes, *The Cost of Medical Care*, reported the data collected during the committee's research, and the second volume, *Medical Care for the American People*, expressed the committee's recommendations.[9]

Factoid 1.2

The term "accountable care organizations" was first coined in 2006 during an exchange between Elliott Fisher, a physician and professor of medicine at Dartmouth Medical School and arguably the creator of the ACO idea, and Glenn Hackbarth, the chairman of the Medicare Payment Advisory Commission (MedPAC). (Source: Creating Accountable Care Organizations: The Extended Hospital Medical Staff. By Elliott S. Fisher, et al., *Health Affairs*, vol. 26, no. 1 (2007), p. 56, note 7.

The committee's report was based on a majority consensus rather than requiring unanimous agreement. While the minority and majority factions agreed on the overall direction of healthcare and both emphasized the importance of community evaluation in order to appropriately care for a population, they differed on focus areas.[10] Specifically, the majority highlighted "cooperative planning" whereas the minority "stress[ed] individualism in medical practice."[11]

The committee minority also produced a report emphasizing the maintenance of a "personal relationship between physician and patient, and the free choice of physician by the patient," and provided suggestions to aid in such efforts without commercialization or increased monitoring and regulation.[12] The minority report suggested that the government should emphasize public health and public service efforts comparable to those associated with the army and navy, the provision of medical services to indigent individuals should be viewed as a community issue, and the costs associated with providing care to low-income populations should be distributed throughout the community. Writers at the time suggested that, while the committee majority would not likely disagree with the minority report, they would have prioritized these issues differently.[13]

The committee majority recommended that large, organized groups of providers oversee and deliver all medical care. The report also provided suggestions for organizational structure standards to ensure protection of the physician–patient relationship. Unlike the minority report, the majority report was centered on the increased role of organizational regulation and maintenance. The committee majority proposed the establishment of comprehensive community medical centers with hospitals. Branches and medical stations were to be included in the comprehensive centers to allow for a delivery and payment of services within the proposed organizational structure.[14]

Of note is the theme of accountability expressed in both the majority and minority opinions, with numerous aspects of each report foreshadowing elements of the modern concept of ACOs. Historians monitoring the progress of the CCMC's recommendations have noted that four of the five major recommendations have been essentially fulfilled in the modern healthcare marketplace; only the fourth recommendation to achieve better coordination of care is left to accomplish.[15] Notwithstanding the extraordinary changes in the healthcare industry as it developed since 1932, the common aspirations to reduce waste, decrease cost, and provide quality care set forth in the report of the Committee on the Costs of Medical Care are still significant today.

Prior to the establishment of Blue Cross and Blue Shield, insurance was not purchased as a set of benefits. Instead, individuals could purchase accident or casualty insurance, which would replace income in the case of an illness or accident, but did not offer coverage for medical services. The first insurance company, which provided casualty insurance for rail and steamboat accidents, started in 1847. By the end of the 1800s, 47 companies existed and offered insurance for nearly every type of accident.[16] This type of coverage protecting against catastrophic risk remained prevalent until the 1930s, when "The Blues," as they were commonly referred to, entered the insurance market.[17]

The Blue Cross Blue Shield Association (BCBSA) started as two separate entities, with Blue Cross covering hospital services and Blue Shield providing coverage for physician services.[18] The Blue Cross Organization was created first in 1929 as a nonprofit, prepaid hospital plan for Dallas-area teachers developed by Justin Ford Kimball, a vice president of the University Hospital at Baylor University.[19] The plan initially covered 1,500 teachers who paid $6 per year for 21 days of hospital care at the University Hospital.[20] At that time, the Great Depression resulted in a growing number of patients who could not afford to pay their bills, and prepaid plans similar to the Baylor Plan quickly began to develop at hospitals across the country.[21] These plans providing hospital coverage were called Blue Cross and gained formal recognition in 1934 when the American Hospital Association and the American College of Surgeons expressed their approval of hospital group plans.[22]

Blue Shield developed in response to the public's desire to have prepaid coverage for physician services, comparable to what Blue Cross offered for hospital services. Beginning in 1933, Dr. Sidney Garfield offered prepaid physician services to 5,000 aqueduct workers in California, each of whom paid a nickel per day.[23] Admiring this success, Henry J. Kaiser adopted Dr. Garfield's approach in the late 1930s to provide his employees with physician services. The Kaiser Foundation Health Plan prospered and thrives today as the Kaiser Permanente plan.[24]

Since their formation, Blue Cross and Blue Shield have remained strong forces in the insurance market, but they did experience some issues in development. In the 1960s and 1970s, the government began challenging Blue Cross and Blue Shield plans across the country to use their market power to hold down hospital and medical costs, while their for-profit competitors challenged their tax-exempt status (which was later partially revoked by the Tax Reform Act of 1986).[25] The plans also were hampered by a dual structure and a lack of a clear, coherent viewpoint.[26] In response to these challenges, Blue Cross and Blue Shield merged into one organization—BCBSA—in 1977 that allowed the new organization to become a "*more efficient and effective network*."[27] BCBSA currently provides insurance to more than 100 million individuals.[28] The companies with BCBSA offer many forms of insurance plans, including managed care and one of the first commercial ACO contracts.

Blue Cross and Blue Shield were two of the earliest widespread versions of managed care. The prepaid, group practice plan models associated with Blue Cross and Blue Shield continued to expand in the 1930s and 1940s and several new plans were formed, including Kaiser Permanente in Los Angeles, Group Health Association in Washington, D.C., Group Health Cooperative of Puget Sound in Seattle, and the Health Insurance Plan (HIP) of Greater New York. These plans were the precursors to today's health maintenance organization (HMO).[29]

In his 1904 address, *The Doctor's Duty to the State*, John Roberts, the then president of the American Academy of Medicine, noted the unethical pitfalls that may ensnare the medical profession:

> The professional coward and the commercial coward have aided efficiently, if perchance unwittingly, the present degradation of the body politic and the body medical. Moral cowardice is a characteristic of both corporations and individuals in this twentieth century, and is the result of the worship of the "Almighty Dollar," which has usurped the place of "Self-Respect" in men's minds.[30]

The moral dangers associated with the seductive *nostrums of ill-gotten financial incentives,* were perceived and condemned by many patients during the managed care boom in the 1990s.

Key Term	Definition	Citation
Health Maintenance Organization (HMO)	An organization providing an agreed-upon set of basic and supplemental health maintenance and treatment services that are reimbursed through a predetermined fixed, period prepayment made by each person or family unit that is voluntarily enrolled.	Glossary of Terms Commonly Used in Health Care. *AcademyHealth,* 2004 Edition.

HMOs are a prepaid health plan model that use provider networks with a system of *primary care gatekeepers* and capitated provider reimbursement incentivizing decreases in utilization and increases in the efficiency of care for HMO members. When issues of cost containments and coverage for the uninsured became topics of political contention, Congress passed the Health Maintenance Organization Act of 1973, which funded the development and spread of HMOs. The HMO Act originally promised some of the same major fundamental objectives of accountable care, i.e., lower costs and higher quality outcomes for patients. Although the federal government did not meet its stated goals of increasing the number of HMO plans from 30 in 1970 to 1,700 by 1976 and covering 90% of the population by 1980, managed care plans flourished throughout the 1970s and 1980s, maintaining prominence into the 1990s. There were over 600 HMOs in operation by 1996 with almost 65 million enrollees—almost one fourth of the U.S. population at the time.[31]

The significant shift to HMOs was not without controversy. The American Medical Association (AMA) staunchly opposed any form of nonphysician control over the medical profession, including the types of prepaid health plans that grew out of the managed care movement.[32] Along with the AMA's misgivings, individual providers resisted dramatic changes to reimbursement models. To promote provider acceptance, the HMO Act allowed for the formation of independent physician associations (IPAs), which were less restrictive and allowed physicians to maintain a level of control with less loss of autonomy than traditional group practices of similar size. Many providers, in choosing the IPA model as a less restrictive form of integration, were acting as resistors, which led to the failure to fully achieve desired goals of the HMO Act.[33] Public fear regarding the loss of their chosen physician providers' control over their patient care ultimately led to a backlash against the cost containment models of many managed care plans, HMOs in particular.

During the 1990s, a significant consumer backlash followed the rapid and widespread incursion of managed care plans, as both providers and patients turned against the model. The capitation form of payment in many plans, originally hailed as a means for reducing health costs, instead caused physicians and hospitals to underprovide services for fear of surpassing their spending thresholds. Patients accused HMO gatekeeper providers and insurers of being more focused on managing the cost of care for their own financial benefit, rather than the interests of their patients.[34] By 1997, 52% of U.S. citizens were in favor of the government stepping in to regulate managed care companies, even if it resulted in increased cost. Further, 54% believed the continued use of managed care plans would harm the quality of medical care.[35]

The public discontent with managed care plans was heavily publicized, adding fuel to the eventual consumer backlash, despite surveys indicating overall satisfaction with the level of medical care received from HMO providers.[36] Since the 1990s, HMOs have continued to be utilized as a means of controlling costs; however, reports suggest that restrictions on provider preferences have been relaxed.[37] The boom in HMO enrollment in the late 1990s, its subsequent decline, and its ultimate staying power, is illustrated in Figure 1.1.

The resistance to change that has affected the implementation of new provider reimbursement models is not a novel phenomenon. Prominent philosopher John Dewey has suggested that this type of resistance has happened in different industries throughout history, notably in the scientific community during the sixteenth century:

> Take, as an outstanding example, the difficulties experienced in getting a hearing for the Copernican astronomy a few centuries ago. Traditional and customary beliefs, which were sanctioned and maintained by powerful institutions, regarded the new scientific ideas as a menace. Nevertheless, the method which yielded propositions verifiable in terms of actual observations and experimental evidence maintained themselves, widened their range, and gained continually in influence.[39]

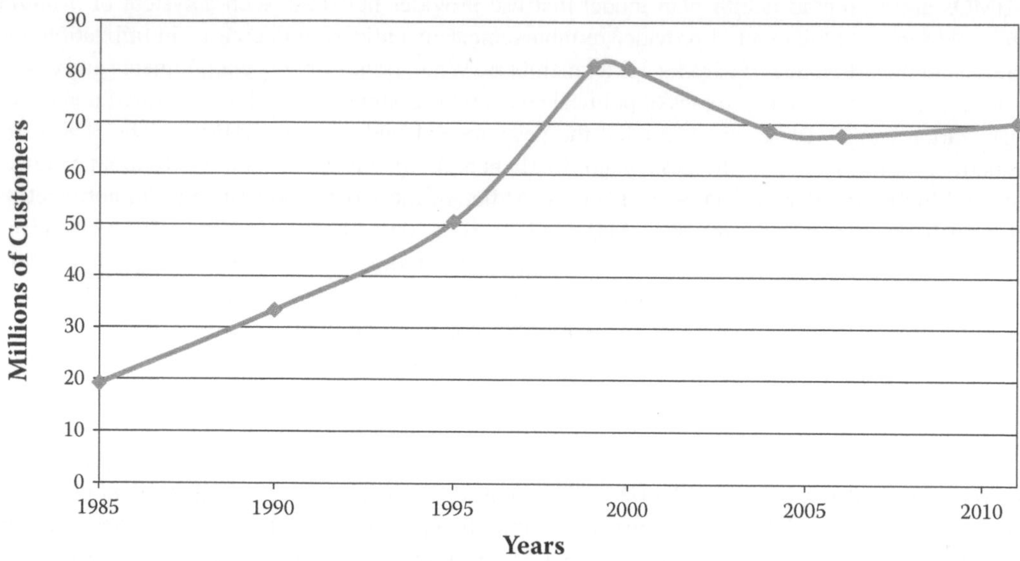

FIGURE 1.1 National HMO enrollment: 1987–2010. (Adapted from Endnote 38.)

Eventually, verified evidence supporting Copernicus' theories allowed his supporters to overcome the resistance of those clinging to traditional beliefs. It has yet to be determined whether new reimbursement models are as effective as some predict or whether they will eclipse traditional methods, as Copernicus' theories eventually did; in the meantime, the healthcare industry will continue to monitor the outcomes of these new models.

Although managed care plans are still prevalent today, most states have laws ensuring wider public choice and access, (e.g., "any willing provider" laws).[40] More recently, volume-focused reimbursement models, (e.g., fee-for-service (FFS)), and alternative access models, (e.g., preferred provider organizations (PPOs)), have gained popularity and, along with various environmental drivers (discussed further below in section Setting the Stage for ACOs), have rekindled the cost-containment and access debates that were so prevalent in the 1970s.

Key Concept	Definition	Citation
"Willing Provider" Laws	State laws regulating public choice and access to healthcare services	Understanding the Managed Care Backlash by Robert J. Blendon, et al., *Health Affairs,* Vol. 17, No. 4, July/August 1998, p. 80.

Resistance to most aspects of the HMO Act, and to managed care plans in general, highlights the fact that physicians have historically been fiercely independent and autonomous by nature and averse to change.[41] In light of these patterns, physicians are more likely to prefer an ACO model that permits a greater level of independence and self-governance. The architects of the new ACO guidelines and regulations are aware of existing concerns that ACOs may operate in a manner that is perceived by physicians as being too similar to HMOs and other 1990s-era managed care plans, and have shaped the development of ACO policies accordingly.[42]

At its essence, managed care is the use of incentives to reach a desired outcome. The concept of accountable care, as manifested by ACOs, evolved from the ideals of managed care—first expressed through Blue Cross/Blue Shield, and later through the development of HMOs throughout the 1980s and 1990s. However, both the managed care models and the accountable care concept are examples of a larger theory of healthcare delivery—managed competition.

ACO: Another Name for Managed Competition

Key Concept	Definition	Citation
Managed Competition	Dominant theory of 1990s healthcare reform, devised by Alain Enthoven of Stanford University. Competing healthcare entities, particularly payors, were to be monitored by a supervisory structure that established equitable rules, created price-elastic demand, and avoided uncompensated risk selection.	The History and Principals of Managed Competition by Alain C. Enthoven, *Health Affairs*, Vol. 12, No. Supp. 1, 1993, p. 24.

While ACOs, still in their design phase, have certain tenets similar to managed care, (e.g., to contain healthcare costs and integrate health systems), they are more akin to the theory of managed competition.

Managed competition was a dominant theory of 1990's healthcare reform.[43] As envisioned by Alain Enthoven of Stanford University, competing healthcare entities, particularly payors, were to be monitored by a supervisory structure that established equitable rules, created price-elastic demand, and avoided uncompensated risk selection; not a far cry from the emerging structure of the ACO/payor relationships as set forth in the Final ACO Rule.[44] Enthoven's model represented a combination of competitive and regulatory strategies that he suggested must seek to co-exist in the healthcare industry as an aim to achieve maximum value for both consumers and providers.[45] Several commentators viewed this compromise as springing from a belief that healthcare is both a *right* and an *obligation,* heralding the individual mandate of the current healthcare reform, i.e., that people have a right to access and an obligation to pay for their portion.[46] Some, like healthcare futurist Ian Morrison, see this compromise as potentially leading to universal coverage, with ACOs being a stepping stone on this path.[47] An illustration of the comparative features of the evolution of models of managed competition, from managed access to managed outcomes (e.g., ACOs), is set forth in Figure 1.2.

1st Generation	2nd Generation	3rd Generation	4th Generation
Managed Access	**Managed Benefits**	**Managed Care**	**Managed Outcomes**
• Emphasis on managing/restricting patient access • Administrative burdens (e.g., pre-certification, significant co-pays) • Reliance primarily on non-clinical reviewers • Physician totally outside system	• Emphasis on managing benefits • Pre-certification primary and treatment planning secondary • Cost containment emphasized over clinical management • Traditional treatment models employed • Physicians "*included*," but their care delivery "*inspected*"	• Greater emphasis on treatment planning and quality management • Focus on most appropriate care in most appropriate setting • Patients managed through continuum of care • Clinical management of network; provider–care manager collegiality • Shift toward improving access and benefits to reduce costs	• Operational, clinical, and financial integration • Locally responsive delivery systems and services based on national standards and capabilities • Mutually beneficial partnerships with physician community • Effective use of technology to measure, report, and enhance quality and outcomes • Proof of value for patients • Full accountability for costs and quality

FIGURE 1.2 The four phases of managed competition.

The Path to Accountable Care Organizations

The current federal ACO model is based on the perceived success of a demonstration project comprised of 10 large physician group practices that utilized financial incentives to lower costs and improve quality of care.

Key Term	Definition	Citation
Medicare Physician Group Practice (PGP) Demonstration Project	Five-year demonstration project beginning in April 2005. Medicare's first physician pay-for-performance initiative. Designed to assess if care management initiatives would improve quality in order to ultimately lower cost for providers.	*Report to Congress: Physician Group Practice Demonstration First Evaluation Report*, By Michael O. Leavitt, (2006) p. 1, 11.

Key Term	Definition	Citation
Centers for Medicare and Medicaid Services (CMS)	An agency within the U.S. Department of Health and Human Services responsible for the administration of Medicare, Medicaid, and other programs.	*Centers for Medicare and Medicaid Services- CMS,* U.S. Department of Health and Human Services, 2011, http://www.healthfinder.gov/orgs/HR0033.htm (Accessed on 5/25/2012).

In 2000, Congress requested that the Department of Health and Human Services (HHS) examine and evaluate incentive-based payment methods for physicians with the intent of encouraging Medicare to consider methods for process improvements, care coordination, and quality outcomes.[48] As a response to Congress's request, the Centers for Medicare and Medicaid Services (CMS) created the Medicare Physician Group Practice (PGP) demonstration project to assess if care management initiatives could reduce avoidable hospitalizations, readmissions, and emergency department visits; improve quality of care provided; and, ultimately, lower costs for providers.[49] Mandated under §412 of the Medicare, Medicaid, and SCHIP Benefits Improvement and Protection Act of 2000,[50] the five-year demonstration began in April 2005.[51] The PGP demonstration's stated goals included:

1. Testing the use of incentives for health care groups
2. Encouraging coordination of healthcare furnished under Medicare Parts A and B
3. Encouraging investment in care management infrastructure and processes for efficient service delivery
4. Rewarding physicians for improving health care processes and outcomes.[52]

The PGP demonstration was Medicare's first physician pay-for-performance initiative.[53] Although participants were primarily reimbursed through the standard Medicare FFS model, the demonstration also used financial incentives, provided by CMS, to physician groups who could successfully improve patient outcomes and decrease overall medical costs through the coordination of care and implementation of new care management strategies into daily operations. Care management strategies included proper anticipation and planning of patient needs, reducing complications and errors, and preventing avoidable hospitalizations.[54] Through the demonstration, CMS was able to assess incentives within a wide range of environments with the goal of eventually identifying which models to implement throughout the healthcare system.[55]

The PGP demonstration included 10 large physician group practices that were "large physician-driven organizations with diverse organizational structures including free-standing multispecialty group practices, faculty group practices, integrated delivery systems," and had "a physician network made up of small and individual physician practices."[56] Collectively, the PGP demonstration included over 220,000 Medicare beneficiaries and over 6,000 physicians from faculty group practices with academic medical centers (two); integrated delivery systems (five); and freestanding physician group practices (two). The final participant was a physician network composed of 60 small, individual physician practices, which, unlike the larger group practice participants, was structured as a management services organization. A majority of the demonstration's participants had experience working with capitated managed care (a reimbursement model that shares many of the strategic methods being assessed): seven of the PGPs owned or had owned an HMO at some point, and managed care insurers had previously given management responsibility to some of the demonstration participants.[57] The 10 participants are further described in Table 1.1.

Key Term	Definition	Citation
Physician Quality Reporting Initiative (PQRI)	A quality reporting incentive program authorized by the Medicare Improvements and Extensions Act of 2006.	*Physician Quality Reporting System,* Centers for Medicare and Medicaid Services, http://www.cms.gov/Medicare/Quality-Initiatives--Patient-Assessment-Instruments/PQRS/index.html?redirect=/PQRS/, (Accessed on 5/25/2012).

Any incentive payments were given in conjunction with CMS's Physician Quality Reporting Initiative (PQRI). Participants received payments by achieving quality targets, uniquely developed for their organization, for each of the demonstration's quality metrics. Quality targets were established in concurrence with national benchmarks and measurement/reporting methods created by both CMS and the participating physician groups.[58] While performance was evaluated annually, only measures associated with diabetes mellitus were reported during the first performance year. Measures for congestive heart failure and coronary artery disease were added during the second performance year. Throughout the third, fourth, and fifth performance years, measures focusing on hypertension and cancer screenings were included as well.[59] The quality measures reported to achieve financial incentives for the PGP demonstration are further described in Table 1.2.

The participants' diversity as to organizational structure and access to capital resources in relation to their size aided CMS's ability to assess the feasibility of implementing various strategic models in different settings.[60]

Within the constructs of the demonstration, the PGP participants had the ability to redesign care processes and invest in care management initiatives for efficient and appropriate care delivery, strategically designed for each sites specific characteristics.[61]

Overall, the participants' strategic efforts emphasized the implementation of evidence-based care in order to improve quality and reduce costs.[62] Individually, each participant redesigned workflows to decrease gaps in provided care and increase patient-centered care.[63] Some participants' strategies included implementing evidence-based, standardized policies and improving their information technology infrastructure.[64] Other efforts focused specifically on certain medical conditions, such as "heart failure care management," which multiple participants noted as an area for substantial cost reduction.[65] Some participants (e.g., Everett Clinic and University of Michigan Faculty Group Practice) made efforts to improve the delivery of care to specific populations, such as seniors, by providing patient reports and dashboards, patient education techniques, and clinical follow-up procedures.[66] Others (e.g., Forsyth Medical Group) focused on those patients at high risk for adverse events and readmissions (i.e., the frail and elderly, chronic disease patients, and those participating in multiple therapies) by working with third-party services, such as COMPASS Disease Management Navigators and Safe Med Pharmacists.[67] The Middlesex Health System looked beyond their own organization with community assessments.[68] All efforts centered on increasing care coordination.

TABLE 1.1
Summary of PGP Participants

Participant	Organizational Model	Organizational Structure	Includes Hospital	Not for Profit	Number of Providers	Region	Service Area	Urban/Rural Characteristics
Dartmouth–Hitchcock Clinic	Academic Medical Center	Faculty/Community Group Practice	Yes	Yes	907	Northeast	NH/Eastern VT	Rural (small city)
University of Michigan Faculty Group Practice	Academic Medical Center	Faculty Practice	Yes	Yes	1291	Midwest	Southeastern MI	Suburban (small city)
Marshfield Clinic	Freestanding Group Practice	Group Practice	No	Yes	1039	Midwest	North–Central WI	Rural (small city)
The Everett Clinic	Freestanding Group Practice	Group Practice	No	No	250	West	West–Central WA	Suburban (small city)
Billings Clinic	Integrated Delivery System	Group Practice	Yes	Yes	232	West	South–Central MT/ Northwestern WY	Rural (small city)
Geisinger Clinic	Integrated Delivery System	Group Practice	Yes	Yes	833	Northeast	Central–Northeast PA	Rural (small city)
Forsyth Medical Group	Integrated Delivery System	Group Practice	Yes	Yes	250	South	Northwest NC	Small Urban City
Park Nicollet Clinic	Integrated Delivery System	Group Practice	Yes	Yes	648	Midwest	South–Central MN	Suburban (large metropolitan)
St. John's Clinic	Integrated Delivery System	Group Practice	Yes	Yes	522	Midwest	South–Central MO/ Northwest AR	Rural (small city)
Middlesex Health System	Network Model	Network Model	Yes	Yes	293	Northeast	South–Central CT	Suburban (small city)

TABLE 1.2
PGP Demonstration Quality Measures

Diabetes Mellitus	Congestive Heart Failure	Coronary Artery Disease	Preventative Care
HbA1c management	Left ventricular function assessment	Antiplatelet therapy	Blood pressure screening
HbA1c control	Left ventricular ejection fraction testing	Drug therapy for lowering LDL cholesterol	Blood pressure control
Blood pressure management	Weight measurement	Beta-blocker therapy-prior MI	Blood pressure control plan of care
Lipid measurement	Blood pressure screening	Blood pressure	Breast cancer screening
LDL cholesterol level	Patient education	Lipid profile	Colorectal cancer screening
Urine protein testing	Beta-blocker therapy	LDL cholesterol level	
Eye exam	Ace inhibitor therapy	Ace inhibitor therapy	
Foot exam	Warfarin therapy for patients HF		
Influenza vaccination	Influenza vaccination		
Pneumonia vaccination	Pneumonia vaccination		

Key Concept	Definition	Citation
Evidence-Based Care	A strategy for providing healthcare that uses data to improve the quality and reduce the cost of healthcare services.	The Medicare Physician Group Practice Demonstration: Lessons Learned on Improving Quality and Efficiency in Health Care: The Commonwealth Fund, February 2008.

Whether through implementation of a specific model, e.g., a medical home (The Geisinger Clinic) or more general practice efforts, strategic initiatives focused on increasing accountability and team-based, patient-centered care. Program enhancements, especially in information technology, were meant to work in conjunction with several initiatives to amplify clinical and administrative efficiencies (Marshfield Clinic).[69]

To evaluate the strategic initiatives of each participant independently from other potential service area spending patterns, CMS created comparison groups for each participant.[70] Similarly, to ensure that expenditure changes among participants could be compared to other participants, CMS included risk adjustments to patient status during evaluation. The risk adjustments ensured that changes in spending could be associated with actual changes, rather than differences in patient status or diagnosis.[71] Quality considerations were also a part of CMS's evaluation, independent of any impact on methods of cost saving.[72]

Over the course of a five-year program, on average, the PGP participants improved their quality scores 11 percentage points for the diabetes measures; 12 percentage points for the heart failure measures, 6 percentage points for coronary artery disease measures, 9 percentage points for cancer screening measures, and 4 percentage points for the hypertension measures.[73] Each participant collected incentive payments from the Medicare PQRI based on their overall quality performance under the demonstration, and four of the participating physician groups—Dartmouth-Hitchcock Clinic, Marshfield Clinic, St. John's Health System, and University of Michigan Faculty Group Practice—received significant (amounts over 10 million) incentive payments for reaching Medicare savings targets. Everett Clinic, Geisinger Clinic, and Park Nicollet Clinic also received incentive payments, but amounts considerably below the other successful participants ($1 million, $3.8 million, and $5.7 million, respectively).[74] Overall, CMS paid more than $100 million to 7 of the 10 participants for meeting quality treatment measures and achieving cost savings.[75] The participant's successes in each performance year of the PGP demonstration project are summarized in Table 1.3.

TABLE 1.3
Performance Summary of PGP Participants

	Percentage of Quality Goals Attained					Shared Savings Payments (in millions)					
PGP Participants	**Year 1**	**Year 2**	**Year 3**	**Year 4**	**Year 5**	**Year 1**	**Year 2**	**Year 3**	**Year 4**	**Year 5**	**Overall**
Billings Clinic	91%	98%	98%	92%	100%						
Dartmouth-Hitchcock Clinic	95%	98%	92%	94%	96%		$6.7	$3.6	$0.3		$10.6
Everett Clinic	86%	96%	94%	94%	100%		$0.1				$0.1
Forsyth Medical Group	100%	100%	96%	96%	100%						
Geisinger Clinic	73%	100%	100%	100%	100%			$2.0	$1.8		$3.8
Marshfield Clinic	82%	100%	98%	100%	98%	$4.6	$5.8	$13.8	$16.1	$15.8	$56.1
Middlesex Health System	86%	96%	92%	94%	100%						
Park Nicollet Clinic	95%	98%	100%	100%	100%					$5.7	$5.7
St. John's Clinic	100%	100%	96%	98%	100%			$3.1	$8.2	$2.3	$13.6
University of Michigan Faculty Group Practice	95%	100%	94%	96%	98%	$2.8	$1.2	$2.8	$5.2	$5.3	$17.3
Total Shared Savings Achieved by PGP	$7.4	$13.8	$25.3	$31.6	$29.1	$107.2					
Total Medicare Program Savings	**$9.5**	**$17.4**	**$32.3**	**$38.7**	**$36.2**						

Some participants experienced external praise for their achievements. The effects of Billings Clinic's efforts with diabetes care were so successful that a majority of the eligible physicians were included in the NCQA's Diabetes Physician Recognition Program for excellence in diabetes care.[76]

Despite their overall success, following the PGD demonstration, the participants expressed discontentment with CMS; specifically, with the timeliness of CMS feedback on data (e.g., utilization patterns and resource monitoring). Participants explained that delays prevented timely incentive payments, which may have impacted overall performance. Prompt payments would have allowed for additional program funding and developments, thus improving outcomes.[77] Participants also expressed concern with differences among local markets, and that CMS may not have properly adjusted for market differences during evaluation. Further criticism concerned differences in beneficiaries, especially the prevalence of specialists between various participants.[78]

The PGP demonstration provided insight into successful quality improvement initiatives and pointed to the importance of committed physician leadership as well as the need for central health information technology.[79] Further, the demonstration targeted the optimal healthcare entities for such initiatives—large integrated organizations. The 10 participants represented large groups of physicians and integrated delivery systems, which is not representative of the nation's physician population. The physician community is mostly comprised of smaller group practices or solo practitioners, with less than 1% of U.S. physician practices having more than 150 physicians.[80] The PGP participants had several advantages due to their large size, including (1) access to both financial and management capital; (2) increased likelihood of obtaining, implementing, and/or updating an Electronic Health Record (EHR) system; (3) associations with an integrated delivery system, hospital, or health insurance organization; and (4) the ability to adjust to the new incentive structures due to increased likelihood of experience with pay-for-performance initiatives.[81] U.S. GAO's (General Accounting Office) evaluation of the PGP demonstration project indicated that smaller practices might have difficulties implementing the strategies used, primarily due to their size and the initial and continuing costs of an EHR system and care coordination programs.[82]

Key Term	Definition	Citation
Medicare Shared Savings Program (MSSP)	Healthcare providers and suppliers have the ability to be eligible for additional payments if they meet specific quality and savings requirements.	*Medicare Program; Medicare Shared Savings Program: Accountable Care Organizations,* Federal Register, 2011, http://www.federal register.gov/articles/2011/11/02/2011-27461/medicare-program-medicare-shared-savings-program--accountable-care-organizations (Accessed 11/3/11).

The PGP demonstration also provided some appreciation for the likely costs associated with large-scale implementation of such a program (e.g., the current Medicare Shared Savings Program (MSSP)). In the demonstration's first year, participants invested an average of $1.7 million. Over the full five years, the average investment neared $737 per PGP patient, with a 13% margin required to break even.[83] These numbers led to CMS's predicted three-year minimum performance period requiring a 20% margin to break even within the proposed MSSP rule. Of note is that, even if a small practice could handle the initial investment, the large margin would likely be insurmountable.[84] Further, the PGP demonstration indicated that even for large organizations, incentive payments to help offset the initial investment might be difficult to achieve (see Table 1.3).[85]

Factoid 1.3

The PGP demonstration's goals included "(1) testing the use of incentives for healthcare groups, (2) encouraging coordination of health care furnished under Medicare Parts A and B, (3) encouraging investment in care management infrastructure and processes for efficient service delivery, and (4) rewarding physicians for improving health care processes and outcomes." (Source: *Physician Group Practice Demonstration First Evaluation Report.* Michael O. Leavitt, Report to Congress (2006) p. 1.)

The PGP demonstration also indicated the importance of information technology and the method of Medicare beneficiary assignment. The demonstration showed that an EHR system was a critical component in electronic communication, tracking trends, identifying gaps in care, process improvement, and helping with overall quality improvement and waste reductions. Another barrier to smaller practices would be the larger per physician cost for EHR acquisition and implementation in contrast to the ability of larger practices to amortize the fixed costs over a greater number of physicians.[86] In determining the patient population for which each participant would be accountable, comparison groups were assigned retroactively.[87] The U.S. GAO's 2008 Report to Congress indicated that the level of perceived success of these comparison groups might be "impractical for more widespread use beyond this demonstration because physician groups cannot accurately predict on an ongoing basis whether they would be able to generate cost-savings and receive bonus payments."[88] This concern was echoed by practitioners in response to the MSSP Proposed Rules' retroactive assignment of Medicare beneficiaries to federal ACOs.

Factoid 1.4

In the demonstration's first year, participants invested an average of $1.7 million. Over the full five years, the average investment neared $737 per PGP patient, with a 13% margin required to break even. These numbers led to CMS's predicted three-year minimum performance period requiring a 20% margin to break even within the proposed MSSP rule. (Source: The ACO Model—A Three-Year Financial Loss? Trent T. Haywood and Keith C. Kosel, *New England Journal of Medicine*, April 7, 2011, p. e27(1)–e27(2). Online at: http://www.nejm.org/doi/pdf/10.1056/NEJMp1100950 (Accessed March 23, 2011).)

Ultimately, the PGP demonstration suggested that care coordination is effective in improving Medicare beneficiary patient outcomes and may result in financial savings.[89] The GAO's 2008 analysis of the demonstration noted that although the demonstration's design was acceptable, additional years of analysis might be required for CMS to fully evaluate the effectiveness and potential savings of its programs.[90] Further, the GAO suggested that alternative methods be used for evaluation and incentive payments, as physician groups are unable to make program adjustments on a "real-time basis" when being provided "performance feedback and bonus payments to participants more than 12 months after the end of the measurement period."[91] Despite GAO concerns, there is a clear correlation between Congress's request in 2000 that created the PGP demonstration and ACO goals, and the MSSP Final Rule, as each emphasized increasing quality and efficiency while controlling costs—all through accountability of a defined population.

Factoid 1.5

Further, the GAO suggested that alternative methods be used for evaluation and incentive payments, as physician groups are unable to make program adjustments on a "real-time basis" when being provided "performance feedback and bonus payments to participants more than 12 months after the end of the measurement period." (Source: *Medicare Physician Payment: Care Coordination Programs Used in Demonstration Show Promise, But Wider Use of Payment Approach May Be Limited.* United States Government Accountability Office, Report to Congressional Committees (February 2008) p. 37.)

Although the general idea and implementation of managed care models began several decades ago, the discussion of ACOs specifically began more recently. The term *accountable care organizations* was first coined in 2006 during an exchange between Elliott Fisher, a physician and professor of medicine at Dartmouth Medical School and arguably the creator of the ACO idea, and Glenn Hackbarth, the chairman of the Medicare Payment Advisory Commission (MedPAC).[92] The ACO idea was further solidified in various publications by Dr. Fisher and his colleagues, particularly *Fostering Accountable Heath Care: Moving Forward in Medicare.*[93] Dr. Fisher is also part of the collaboration between Dartmouth's Institute for Public Health Policy and Clinical Practice and the Engelberg Center for Health Care Reform at the Brookings Institution, which is responsible for implementing ACO pilot programs in various regions of the country. (Various ACO pilot programs are discussed in more detail in Chapter 2, Federal ACOs.) The first substantial notion of a Medicare ACO was introduced in a 2009 MedPAC report to Congress.[94]

Factoid 1.6

Over the course of four years, on average, the PGP participants improved their quality scores 10 percentage points for the diabetes measures, 13 percentage points for the heart failure measures, 6 percentage points for coronary artery disease measures, 9 percentage points for cancer screening measures, and 3 percentage points for the hypertension measures. (Source: Medicare Physician Group Practice Demonstration Project Racks up $38.7 Million in Savings. Chris Anderson, *Healthcare Finance News*, December 13, 2010. Online at: http://www.healthcarefinancenews.com/news/medicare-physician-group-practice-demonstration-project-racks-387-million-savings (Accessed 4/4/2012).

As previously discussed, ACOs did not originate with the Patient Protection and Affordable Care Act (ACA). Rather, various factors, such as increased emphasis on quality and efficiency of the provision of healthcare services, shifts in the healthcare environment, and the responses to these factors, have contributed to the development of ACOs.

In June 2009, MedPAC issued the *Report to Congress: Improving Incentives in the Medicare Program*, including an entire chapter on ACOs. The chapter discusses the PGP program, in addition to publications by Dr. Fisher, the differences between voluntary and mandatory ACOs, how a Medicare ACO should be structured, as well as the likelihood of projected savings in an ACO.[95] The MedPAC vision for an ACO included primary care physicians, specialists, and at least one hospital, whereby the providers would "accept joint responsibility for the quality of care and the cost of care received by the panel of patients."[96] Ultimately, the report notes that the payment bonus incentives of ACOs should not be the only tool to overcome volume incentives created by fee-for-service reimbursement models. The MSSP, signed into law within the ACA, incorporated many of the suggestions set forth in the MedPac Report. However, the test of mobilizing such a massive transformation in healthcare, like the creation of ACOs, both in legislation and implementation, requires an environment demanding such change, not just legislation for its implementation.

Key Term	Definition	Citation
Patient Protection and Affordable Care Act (ACA)	Landmark healthcare reform legislation passed on March 23, 2010.	Patient Protection and Affordable Care Act Public Law 111-148 (March 23, 2010).

Factoid 1.7

Ultimately, MedPAC's *Report to Congress: Improving Incentives in the Medicare Program* notes that the payment bonus incentives of ACOs should not be the only tool to overcome volume incentives created by fee-for-service reimbursement models. (Source: Chapter 2: Accountable Care Organizations. MedPAC, in *Report to Congress: Improving Incentives in the Medicare Program,* June 2009, p. 39–40.)

Factoid 1.8

When issues of cost containments and coverage for the uninsured became topics of political contention, Congress passed the Health Maintenance Organization Act of 1973, which funded the development and spread of HMOs. (Source: *A Brief History of Managed Care.* Tufts Managed Care Institute, 1998. Online at: http://www.thci.org/downloads/briefhist.pdf (Accessed 12/28/2011).)

Setting the Stage for ACOs: An Environment Demanding Change

It requires a certain political and economic environment to focus attention on a single issue and initiate change, as well as shift the societal perspective as to the value of the proposed change. Wilbur Marshall Urban, a philosopher, posited that:

Fundamental changes in the actual values of mankind, giving rise to what has been well called "our anxious morality," with its characteristic talk of creating and conserving values, have brought with them what may, without exaggeration, be described as a gradual shifting of the philosophical centre of gravity from the problem of knowledge to the problem of values.[97]

Key Concept	Definition	Citation
Value	The present work of all the rights to future benefits arising from ownership of the thing valued (i.e., the expectation of future benefit).	*Dictionary of Health Insurance and Managed Care* by David E. Marcinko, Springer Publishing Company, 2006, p. 293.

The current turbulent state of U.S. healthcare delivery was not unexpected. Costs, access, and the impact of an aging baby boomer generation are all factors that have been on alarming paths for some time. Yet, when the Clinton healthcare reforms attempted to deal with these concerns, the political or public demand was not feverish enough to motivate change.[98]

In this more recent decade, having reached such a state of concern regarding healthcare, the U.S. government passed the ACA on March 23, 2010. Several issues have brought healthcare to the forefront of both political and consumer debates: the ever-rising cost of healthcare, the breakdown of healthcare costs across the industry, the disparities between classes in access and quality, the falling health status of the United States as compared to other developed nations, and the budget threat related to the cost of care of the baby boomer generation entering the Medicare population. The following exhibits demonstrate the environment of healthcare today that has allowed for ACOs to become a realistic option. A visual depiction of the rising trend of national health expenditures is set forth in Figure 1.3.

From 2000 to 2010, national health expenditures per capita have increased more than 72%. In addition, more than half of healthcare spending today is spent on hospital care and physician/clinical services. Another visual representation of healthcare expenditures is depicted in Figure 1.4.

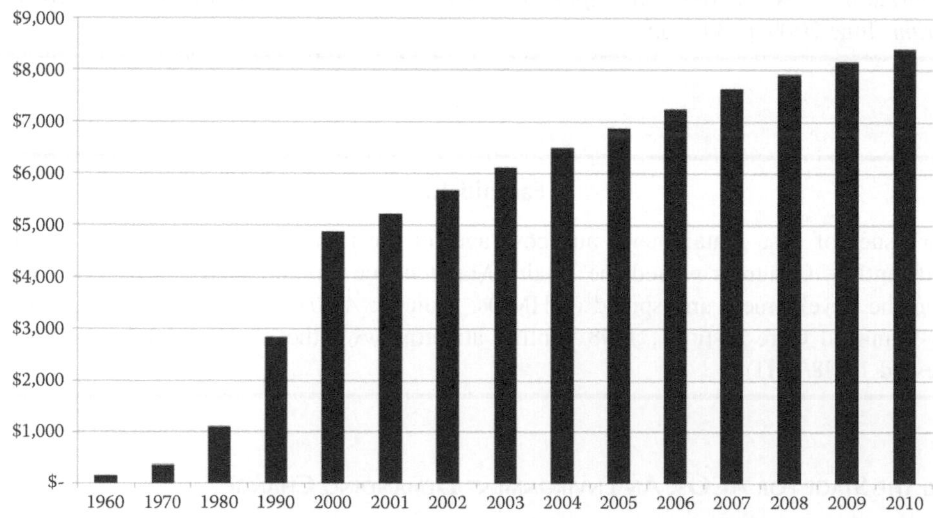

FIGURE 1.3 National health expenditures per capita, 1960–2010. (From Endnote 99.)

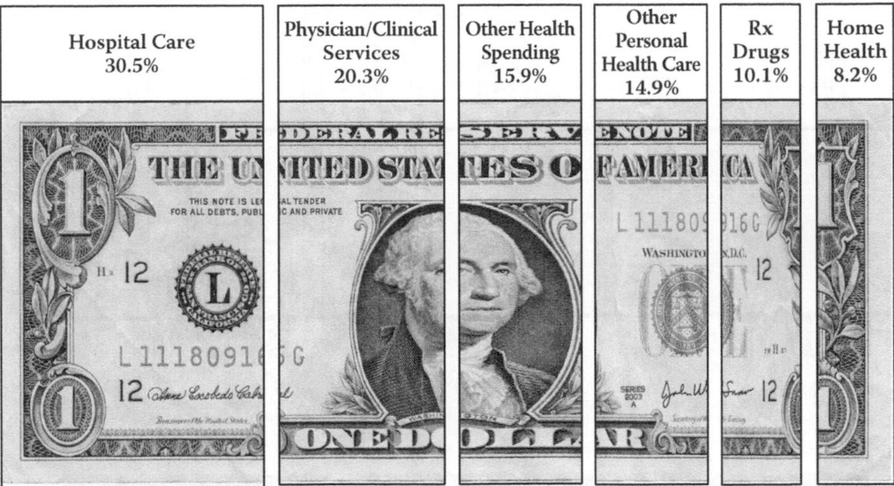

FIGURE 1.4 Breakdown of 2010 healthcare expenditures. (From Endnote 100.)

Factoid 1.9

From 2000 to 2010, national health expenditures per capita have increased more than 72%. In addition, more than half of healthcare spending today is spent on hospital care and physician/clinical services. (Source: *National Health Expenditures Aggregate, Per Capita Amounts, Percent Distribution, and Average Annual Percent Change: Selected Calendar Years 1960–2010.* Centers for Medicare and Medicaid Services, Office of the Actuary, National Health Statistics Group. Online at: https://www.cms.gov/NationalHealthExpendData/downloads/tables.pdf (Accessed 2/1/2012).)

Relative to other developed countries, the United States spends far more—over 16% of GDP (gross national product)—on healthcare, yet the United States is ranked very low in terms of health status, due to record-level access and quality disparities. A comparison of the total health expenditures as a share of GDP to the percentage of healthcare that is publicly funded for several developed countries (presented in order of health status) is seen in Figure 1.5.

Interestingly, the United States has the highest percent of its GDP going toward healthcare, yet it has the lowest health status (as measured by mortality rate). Further, as of 2009, the United States publicly financed only 47.7% of the country's total expenditure on healthcare, which is far below the 69.9% average of comparable countries for that year (this average was calculated without including the United States).[102]

While all of these statistics may be on an alarming trajectory, further strains on the cost and quality of healthcare loom on the horizon, most significantly, the addition of the baby boomer population to Medicare eligibility. The effect on Medicare enrollment from this population and their progeny is demonstrated in Figure 1.6.

As costs and disparities continue to tarnish the global ranking of U.S. health status and strain both family and governmental budgets, both political parties seem to agree that something must be done to change the current direction of healthcare delivery. ACOs are one of the several options that have been presented to implement change in the healthcare industry.

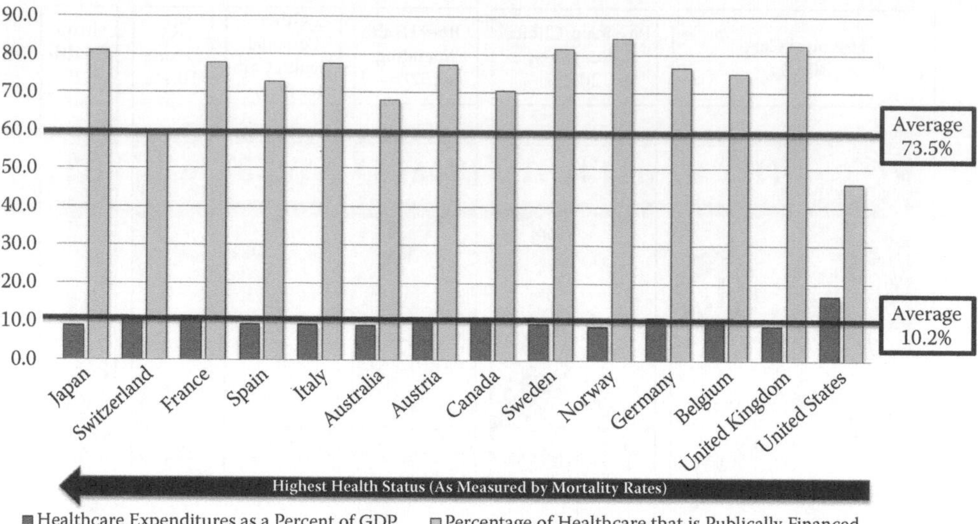

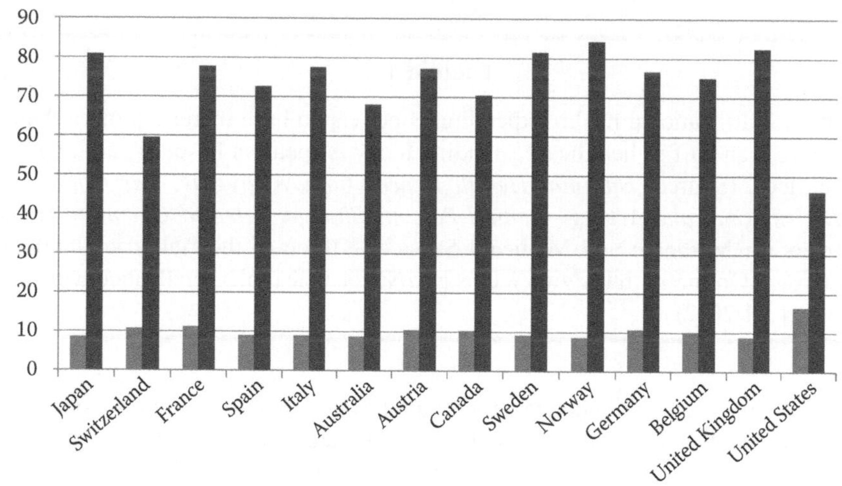

FIGURE 1.5 Total health expenditures as a share of GDP compared to percentage of healthcare publicly financed, in order of health status (mortality), 2008. (Adapted from Endnote 101.)

CHAPTER SUMMARY

Though the concept of accountable care is not entirely new, the inclusion of ACOs in the Patient Protection and Affordable Care Act of 2010 has led to renewed emphasis on this model as a potential solution for addressing issues of cost, quality, and access within the healthcare system.

The discussion of accountable care began in 1932, when the Committee on the Costs of Medical Care conducted a five-year study of the healthcare system in which they made five major recommendations involving the organization of medical services and coordination of care in order to reduce waste, decrease cost, and improve quality of and access to care. As the healthcare industry continued to evolve, managed care developed as a new approach to limit healthcare costs while

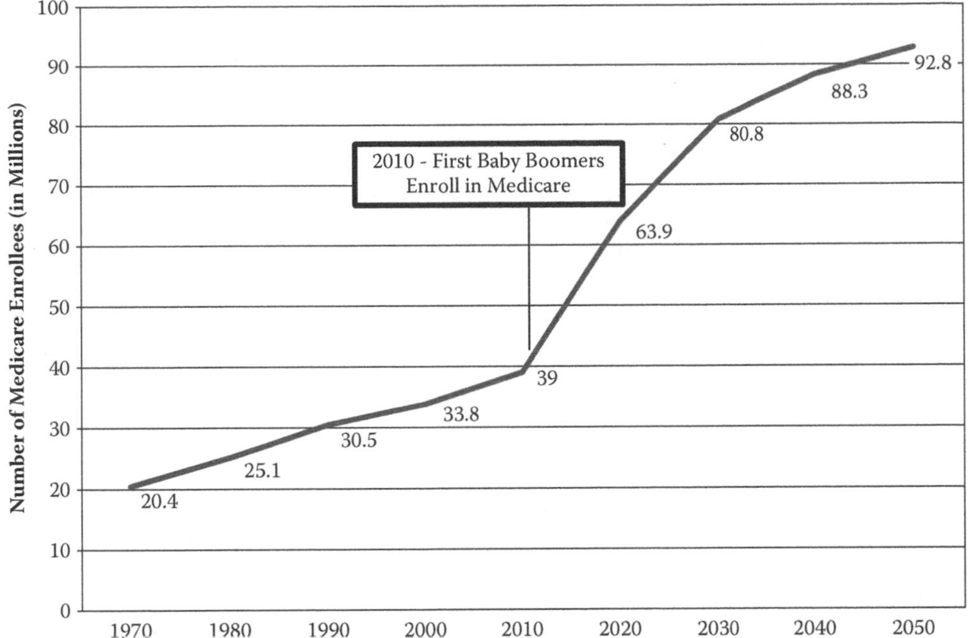

FIGURE 1.6 Historical and projected Medicare population (not including disabled persons), 1970–2050.

maintaining and improving quality. Blue Cross and Blue Shield plans were some of the earliest versions of managed care, followed by the development of HMOs in the 1980s and 1990s, which used provider networks with a system of primary care gatekeepers to attempt to control utilization and promote efficiency. In the late 1990s, there was public and media backlash against managed care plans, especially their gatekeeper provisions, fueled by the perception that the system was overly focused on cost control at the expense of patient care.

Managed care and *accountable care* are both models that evolved out of Alain Enthoven's larger theory of *managed competition*, the dominant theory of 1990s healthcare reform, which involves blending competitive and regulatory strategies in order to achieve maximum value for both consumers and providers.

The current federal ACO model is based on the outcomes of Medicare's first physician pay-for-performance initiative, the Medicare Physician Group Practice (PGP) demonstration project. The PGP demonstration, which included 10 large physician group practices, ran from 2005 to 2010 and offered incentive payments for improving patient outcomes and decreasing medical costs. All PGP participants collected incentive payments for improving their overall quality performance and four received incentive payments for reaching cost-savings targets, suggesting that care coordination might be an effective means of improving patient outcomes and achieving financial savings. However, concerns were raised regarding the feasibility of the PGP as a model for Federal ACOs, including the necessity for a large initial investment. Despite reservations, MedPAC suggested in its 2009 Report to Congress that ACOs be developed within the U.S. healthcare delivery systems.

As further strains on the U.S. healthcare system loom on the horizon including the aging baby boomer population, the U.S.'s falling health status as compared to other developed nations, the effect of the Great Recession on the availability of capital, economic conditions, and a rising concern over Federal deficits, the current healthcare environment may be leading up to a "perfect storm" that may be able to, for the first time, fuel real changes to the current system of healthcare delivery. However, to succeed, ACOs must seek to avoid the issues associated with the perceived failure of managed care plans in the 1990s, instead facilitating public understanding, payor support, partnerships between physicians and hospitals, necessary capital resources, and both clinical and administrative integration.

ENDNOTES

1. *Can Accountable Care Organizations Improve the Value of Health Care by Solving the Cost and Quality Quandaries*? By Kelly Devers and Robert Berenson, Robert Wood Johnson Foundation, Urban Institute, October 2009. Online at: http://www.rwjf.org/files/research/acosummaryfinal.pdf (Accessed 1/19/12), p. 1.
2. A National Strategy to Put Accountable Care into Practice. By Mark McClellan, et al., *Health Affairs*, vol. 29, no. 5, May 2010, p. 982.
3. *A Guide to Consulting Services for Emerging Healthcare Organizations*. Robert James Cimasi, New York: John Wiley & Sons, 1999, p. 12.
4. The Committee on the Costs of Medical Care—25 Years of Progress. I. S. Falk, *American Journal of Public Health,* vol. 48, no. 8, August 1958, pp. 979–982.
5. *Medical Care for the American People. Committee on the Costs of Medical Care*, Chicago: The University of Chicago Press, 1932, p. xi.
6. The Committee on the Costs of Medical Care—25 Years of Progress, pp. 979–982.
7. *Medical Care for the American People. Committee on the Costs of Medical Care*, Chicago: The University of Chicago Press, 1932, p. xvi; I. S. Falk, The Committee on the Costs of Medical Care, and the Drive for National Health Insurance. By Milton I. Roemer, *American Journal of Public Health,* vol. 75, no. 8, 1985, p. 842.
8. *The Costs of Medical Care: A Summary of Investigations on the Economic Aspects of the Prevention and Care of Illness*. I. S. Falk, et al., Chicago: The University of Chicago Press, 1933, p. 589–591.
9. The Committee on the Costs of Medical Care Reports. *The American Journal of Nursing*, vol. 32, no. 12, December 1932, p. 1286.
10. Report of the Committee on the Costs of Medical Care. Arthur C. Christie, *California and Western Medicine*, vol. XXXVIII, no. 5, May 1933, p. 341–342.
11. The Committee on the Costs of Medical Care Reports, p. 1286.
12. Report of the Committee on the Costs of Medical Care. Arthur C. Christie, *California and Western Medicine,* vol. XXXVIII, no. 5, May 1933, p. 341; *Medical Care for the American People*. Committee on the Costs of Medical Care, Chicago: The University of Chicago Press, 1932, p. xvi.
13. Ibid.
14. *Medical Care for the American People*. Committee on the Costs of Medical Care, Chicago: The University of Chicago Press, 1932, p. 109–110; Report of the Committee on the Costs of Medical Care. Arthur C. Christie, *California and Western Medicine*, vol. XXXVIII, no. 5, May 1933, p. 343.
15. I. S. Falk, The Committee on the Costs of Medical Care, and the Drive for National Health Insurance. Milton I. Roemer, *American Journal of Public Health*, vol. 75, no. 8, 1985, p. 844.
16. *The U.S. Health System: Origins and Functions*. Marshall W. Raffel, New York: John Wiley & Sons, 1980, p. 394.
17. Ibid., p. 395.
18. *The Blues: A History of the Blue Cross and Blue Shield System*. Robert Cunningham III and Robert M. Cunningham Jr., DeKalb, IL: Northern Illinois University Press, 1997, p. viii.
19. Ibid., p. 3–4.
20. *The Social Transformation of American Medicine: The Rise of a Sovereign Profession and the Making of a Vast Industry*. Paul Starr, New York: Basic Books, 1982, p. 295.
21. Ibid., pp. 295–296.
22. *The Blues: A History of the Blue Cross and Blue Shield System*, p. 19
23. *The Blues: A History of the Blue Cross and Blue Shield System*, p. 39.
24. Ibid.
25. Ibid, pp. 173–176, 215.
26. Ibid., p. 195.
27. Ibid., p. 197, 199.
28. About the Blue Cross and Blue Shield Association. Blue Cross Blue Shield Association, 2011. Online at: http://www.bcbs.com/about-the-association/ (Accessed 12/27/2011).
29. A Brief History of Managed Care. Tufts Managed Care Institute, 1998. Online at: http://www.thci.org/downloads/briefhist.pdf (Accessed 12/28/2011).

30. *The Doctor's Duty to the State: Essays on the Public Relations of Physicians*. John B. Roberts, Chicago: American Medical Association, 1908, p. 9.
31. A Brief History of Managed Care.
32. Ibid.
33. *Accountable Care Organizations: Will They Deliver*? Marsha Gold, Mathematica Policy Research, Inc., January 2010, p. 5.
34. *The Public, Managed Care, and Consumer Protections*. Kaiser Family Foundation, Kaiser Public Opinion Spotlight (January 2006), p. 1; Understanding the Managed Care Backlash. Robert J. Blendon, et al., *Health Affairs*, vol. 17, no. 4, July/August 1998, pp. 87–88.
35. Understanding the Managed Care Backlash. Robert J. Blendon, et al., *Health Affairs*, vol. 17, no. 4, July/August 1998, pp. 83–84.
36. Ibid., pp 90–91.
37. The Managed Care Backlash: Did Consumers Vote With Their Feet? Susan Marquis, et al., *Inquiry*, vol. 41, No. 4, Winter 2004/2004, p. 387.
38. *Timeline*. Managed Care Museum: Modesto, CA, February 2011. Online at: http://www.Managedcaremuseum.com/timeline.htm (Accessed 4/10/12); *Total HMO Enrollment*, July 2010. Kaiser Family Foundation, July 2010. Online at: http://www.statehealthfacts.org/comparetable.jsp?ind=348&cat=7&sub=85&yr=208&typ=1&sort=a&o=a&sortc=1 (Accessed 4/10/12).
39. *Theory of Valuation*. John Dewey, Chicago: The University of Chicago Press, 1966, p. 62.
40. Understanding the Managed Care Backlash, p. 81.
41. *The Social Transformation of American Medicine: The rise of a sovereign profession and the making of a vast industry*. Paul Starr, New York: Basic Books, 1982, p. 25.
42. *Administration Releases Proposed Rules for Medicare Accountable Care Organizations*. Ceci Connolly, et al., McKinsey Center for U.S. Health System Reform, April 1, 2011, p. 1.
43. The New American Compromise. Ian Morrison, *Trustee*, vol. 61, No. 8, September 2008, p. 32.
44. The History and Principles of Managed Competition. Alain C. Enthoven, *Health Affairs*, vol. 12, no. suppl 1, 1993, pp. 30–33; Medicare Program; Medicare Shared Savings Program: Accountable Care Organizations, *Federal Register*, vol. 76, no. 212, November 2, 2011.
45. The History and Principles of Managed Competition. Alain C. Enthoven, *Health Affairs*, vol. 12, no. suppl 1, 1993, pp. 24, 29.
46. The New American Compromise. Ian Morrison, *Trustee*, vol. 61, no. 8, September 2008, p. 32.
47. Ibid.; Chasing Unicorns: The Future of ACOs. Ian Morrison, *HHN Magazine*, January 3, 2011.
48. Consolidated Appropriations Act, Pub. L. 106-554, 114 Stat 2763A-509 (2000); Medicare Physician Group Practices: Innovations in Quality and Efficiency. Michael Trisolini, et al., RTI International, Posted on The Commonwealth Fund (February 2008), p. 2. Online at: http://www.commonwealth-fund.org/~/media/Files/Publications/Fund%20Report/2008/Feb/The%20Medicare%20Physician%20Group%20Practice%20Demonstration%20%20Lessons%20Learned%20on%20Improving%20Quality%20and%20Effici/1094_Trisolini_Medicare_phys_group_practice_demo_lessons_learned%20pdf.pdf (Accessed 4/6/12).
49. Assessing an ACO Prototype—Medicare's Physician Group Practice Demonstration. John K. Iglehart, *New England Journal of Medicine,* vol. 364, no. 3, January 20, 2011, p. 198.
50. Medicare Program; Solicitation for Proposals for the Physician Group Practice Demonstration. *Federal Register* vol. 67, no. 188 (September 27, 2002), p. 61116; Consolidated Appropriations Act. Pub. L. 106-554, 114 Stat 2763A-509-15 (2000).
51. *Medicare Physician Group Practice Demonstration: Physicians Groups Continue to Improve Quality and Generate Savings under Medicare Physician Pay-for-Performance Demonstration. Centers for Medicare and Medicaid Services* (July 2011), p. 1. Online at: https://www.cms.gov/DemoProjectsEvalRpts/downloads/PGP_Fact_Sheet.pdf (Accessed 7/31/2011); Medicare Physician Group Practices: Innovations in Quality and Efficiency. Michael Trisolini et al., RTI International, Posted on The Commonwealth Fund (February 2008), p. vi. Online at: http://www.commonwealthfund.org/~/media/Files/Publications/Fund%20Report/2008/Feb/The%20Medicare%20Physician%20Group%20Practice%20Demonstration%20%20Lessons%20Learned%20on%20Improving%20Quality%20and%20Effici/1094_Trisolini_Medicare_phys_group_practice_demo_lessons_learned%20pdf.pdf (Accessed 4/6/12).
52. *Physician Group Practice Demonstration First Evaluation Report*. Michael O. Leavitt, Report to Congress (2006) p. 1.
53. Ibid., p. 11.

54. *The Medicare Physician Group Practice Demonstration: Lessons Learned on Improving Quality and Efficiency in Health Care*. Michael Trisolini, et al., The Commonwealth Fund, February 2008, p. 2.
55. *Physician Group Practice Demonstration Evaluation Report*. Kathleen Sebelius, Report to Congress (2009), p. 28.
56. *Physician Group Practice Demonstration First Evaluation Report*, pp. 1–2.
57. *Physician Group Practice Demonstration Evaluation Report*, pp. 25–26.
58. *Medicare Physician Group Practice Demonstration*, pp. 2–3.
59. Ibid.; *Physician Group Practice Demonstration Evaluation Report*, p. 39
60. *Medicare Physician Group Practice Demonstration*, pp. 3–4.
61. *The Medicare Physician Group Practice Demonstration: Lessons Learned*, pp. 1, 20.
62. Ibid., p. 9.
63. *Physician Group Practice Demonstration First Evaluation Report*, p. 79.
64. *The Medicare Physician Group Practice Demonstration: Lessons Learned*, p. 9.
65. Ibid., p. 16.
66. *Medicare Physician Group Practice Demonstration*, p. 8.
67. *Contemplating the ACO Opportunity*. Healthcare Financial Management Association, An HFM Compendium, November 2010, p. 60.
68. *Medicare Physician Group Practice Demonstration*, pp. 6–9.
69. *Contemplating the ACO Opportunity*, p. 61.
70. *Medicare Physician Payment: Care Coordination Programs Used in Demonstration Show Promise, But Wider Use of Payment Approach May Be Limited.* United States Government Accountability Office, Report to Congressional Committees (February 2008) p. 26.
71. Ibid., p. 27.
72. Ibid.
73. *Medicare Physician Group Practice Demonstration*, p. 5.
74. Ibid., pp. 4–6.
75. Physician Group Practice Demonstration Succeeds in Improving Quality and Reducing Costs: All Participating Practices to Continue in 2-Year PGP Transition Demonstration. Centers for Medicare and Medicaid Services, *Medicare News* (August 8, 2011). Online at: https://www.cms.gov/DemoProjectsEvalRpts/downloads/PGP_PR.pdf (Accessed 3/29/12).
76. *Billings Clinic Enhances Quality of Care under Federal Demonstration Project*. Billings Clinic, July 11, 2007. Online at: http://www.billingsclinic.com/body.cfm?id=568 (Accessed 3/28/12).
77. *Medicare Physician Payment*, p. 29..
78. Ibid., pp. 31–32.
79. The ACO Regulations—Some Answers, More Questions. John K. Iglehart. *NEJM* (April 13, 2010), p. 2.
80. *Physician Group Practice Demonstration Evaluation Report*, p. 69; *Medicare Physician Payment: Care Coordination Programs Used in Demonstration Show Promise, But Wider Use of Payment Approach May Be Limited.* U.S. Government Accountability Office, Report to Congressional Committees (February 2008) p. 6.
81. *Medicare Physician Payment*, p. 33.
82. Ibid., pp. 35–36, 38.
83. The ACO Model—A Three-Year Financial Loss? Trent T. Haywood and Keith C. Kosel, *New England Journal of Medicine,* April 7, 2011, p. e27(1)– e27(2). Online at: http://www.nejm.org/doi/pdf/10.1056/NEJMp1100950 (Accessed March 23, 2011).
84. Ibid.
85. Ibid.
86. *Medicare Physician Payment*, pp. 35–36.
87. Ibid., p. 37.
88. Ibid.
89. *Medicare Touts Success of Demonstrations That Paved the Way for ACOs*. Jane Norman, The Commonwealth Fund, August 8, 2011. Online at: http://www.commonwealthfund.org/Newsletters/Washington-Health-Policy-in-Review/2011/Aug/August-15-2011/Medicare-Touts-Success-of-Demonstrations.aspx (Accessed 4/4/2012); *Physician Group Practice Demonstration.*
90. *Medicare Physician Payment*, p. 37.
91. Ibid.
92. Creating Accountable Care Organizations: The Extended Hospital Medical Staff. Elliott S. Fisher, et al., *Health Affairs*, vol. 26, no. 1 (2007), p. 56, note 7.

93. Fostering Accountable Health Care: Moving Forward in Medicare. Elliott Fisher, et al., *Health Affairs*, vol. 28, no. 2, March/April 2009, pp. w219–w231.
94. Accountable Care Organizations (Chapter 2). MedPAC, in *Report to Congress: Improving Incentives in the Medicare Program*, June 2009.
95. Ibid., pp. 39–58.
96. Ibid., p. 39.
97. *Valuation: Its Nature and Laws, Being an Introduction to the General Theory of Value*. Wilbur Marshall Urban, New York: The Macmillan Co, 1909, p. 3.
98. *Public Discourse in America: Conversation and Community in the Twenty-First Century*. Judith Rodin and Stephen P. Steinberg, Philadelphia: University of Pennsylvania Press, 2003, p. 97.
99. *National Health Expenditures Aggregate, Per Capita Amounts, Percent Distribution, and Average Annual Percent Change: Selected Calendar Years 1960–2010*. Centers for Medicare and Medicaid Services, Office of the Actuary, National Health Statistics Group. Online at: https://www.cms.gov/NationalHealthExpendData/downloads/tables.pdf (Accessed 2/1/2012).
100. *National Health Expenditures, by type of service and source of funds, CY 1960–2010*. Centers for Medicare and Medicaid Services, Table 4. Online at: http://cms.hhs.gov/Research-Statistics-Data-and-Systems/Statistics-Trends-and-Reports/NationalHealthExpendData/NationalHealthAccountsHistorical.html (Accessed 6/6/12).
101. Health status can be measured by several means. This list used mortality by measuring life expectancy at birth of the total population. *OECD Health Data 2011—Frequently Requested Data*. The Organization for Economic Co-operation and Development, November 2011. Online at: http://www.oecd.org/document/16/0,3343,en_2649_34631_2085200_1_1_1_1,00.html (Accessed 1/1/2012).
102. Ibid.
103. *Medicare Enrollment: National Trends 1966–2010*. Centers for Medicare and Medicaid Services. Online at: https://www.cms.gov/MedicareEnRpts/Downloads/HI2010.pdf (Accessed 1/1/2012); *Medicare Spending and Financing*. Kaiser Family Foundation, September 2011. Online at: http://www.kff.org/medicare/upload/7305-06.pdf (Accessed 1/1/2012); Latest Medicare Projections Renew Alarm on Long-Term Sustainability. Doug Trapp, *American Medical News*, April 14, 2008. Online at: http://www.ama-assn.org/amednews/2008/04/14/gvl10414.htm (Accessed 1/1/2012).

Acronyms

Acronym	Definition
ACA	Patient Protection and Affordable Care Act
ACO	Accountable Care Organization
MCO	Managed Care Organization
BCBSA	Blue Cross Blue Shield Association
HIP	Health Insurance Plan
HMO	Health Maintenance Organization
AMA	American Medical Association
IPA	Independent Physician Associations
FFS	Fee-For-Service
PPO	Preferred Provider Organizations
HHS	U.S. Department of Health and Human Services
CMS	Centers for Medicare and Medicaid Services
PGP	Medicare Physician Group Practice demonstration
PQRI	Physician Quality Reporting Initiative
EHR	Electronic Health Record
MSSP	Medicare Shared Savings Program
GAO	Government Accountability Office
MedPAC	Medicare Payment Advisory Commission
ACA	Patient Protection and Affordable Care Act
GDP	Gross Domestic Product

2 Federal ACOs

Federal ACOs are those governed by the Medicare Shared Savings Program (MSSP), where the program has gone through several variations and generated much public debate. The public response to the regulation of federal ACOs has fluctuated between various degrees of support and outright rejection. This evolving public reaction has significantly affected the ultimate structure and operation of these emerging healthcare organizations (EHO). The timeline associated with the development of federal ACOs is set forth in Figure 2.1.

Key Term	Definition	Citation
Medicare Shared Savings Program (MSSP)	The MSSP is one form of value-based purchasing linking shared savings incentive payments to ACO participants that achieve quality metrics for Medicare beneficiaries.	Medicare Program; Medicare Shared Savings Program: Accountable Care Organizations. *Federal Register* vol. 76 no. no. (November 2, 2011).

PURPOSE OF ACCOUNTABLE CARE ORGANIZATIONS

ACOs are designed to increase healthcare quality while decreasing cost. To support an increase in the quality, in contrast to the quantity, of services provided within an ACO, physicians will receive financial bonuses for meeting resource use and quality targets over the course of a year, and penalties for failing to meet these requirements.[2] These financial incentives must be substantial enough to overcome the reimbursement yield that physicians obtain from existing models that encourage a high volume of services, e.g., the fee-for-service (FFS) reimbursement system utilized by Medicare, in order to achieve a decrease in the growth of Medicare spending.

Key Term	Definition	Citation
Accountable Care Organization (ACO)	A healthcare organization where a set of otherwise independent providers, usually physicians and hospitals, willingly integrate to become responsible for the cost, quality, and overall care delivered to a specified patient population.	*Accountable Care Organizations in Medicare and the Private Sector: A Status Update.* Robert A. Berenson and Rachel A. Burton, The Robert Wood Johnson Foundation and The Urban Institute (November 2011). Online at: http://www.rwjf.org/files/research/73470.5470.aco.report.pdf (Accessed 1/28/12), p. 5.

In addition to minimizing healthcare costs, ACOs are designed to deliver integrated care to patients, in contrast to the sporadic and uncoordinated delivery of patient care that characterizes today's fragmented U.S. healthcare system. Strategies utilizing vertical integration, which involves incorporating providers from all stages of healthcare, e.g., primary care physicians (PCPs), specialists, hospitals, and outpatient providers, have been touted as a means of improving the quality of care delivery. However, early results have demonstrated that vertical integration in an ACO will only be effective if the infrastructure is sufficiently interconnected through an electronic health record system and robust communication among the various levels of providers. In that manner, the success of an ACO as a business, as well as an integrated system of care, is largely dependent on (1) its formal structure, (2) the degree of its interconnectedness, and (3) the extent to which it achieves financial incentives, as defined in the MSSP,[3] each of which needs to be superior to those available under the current FFS system.

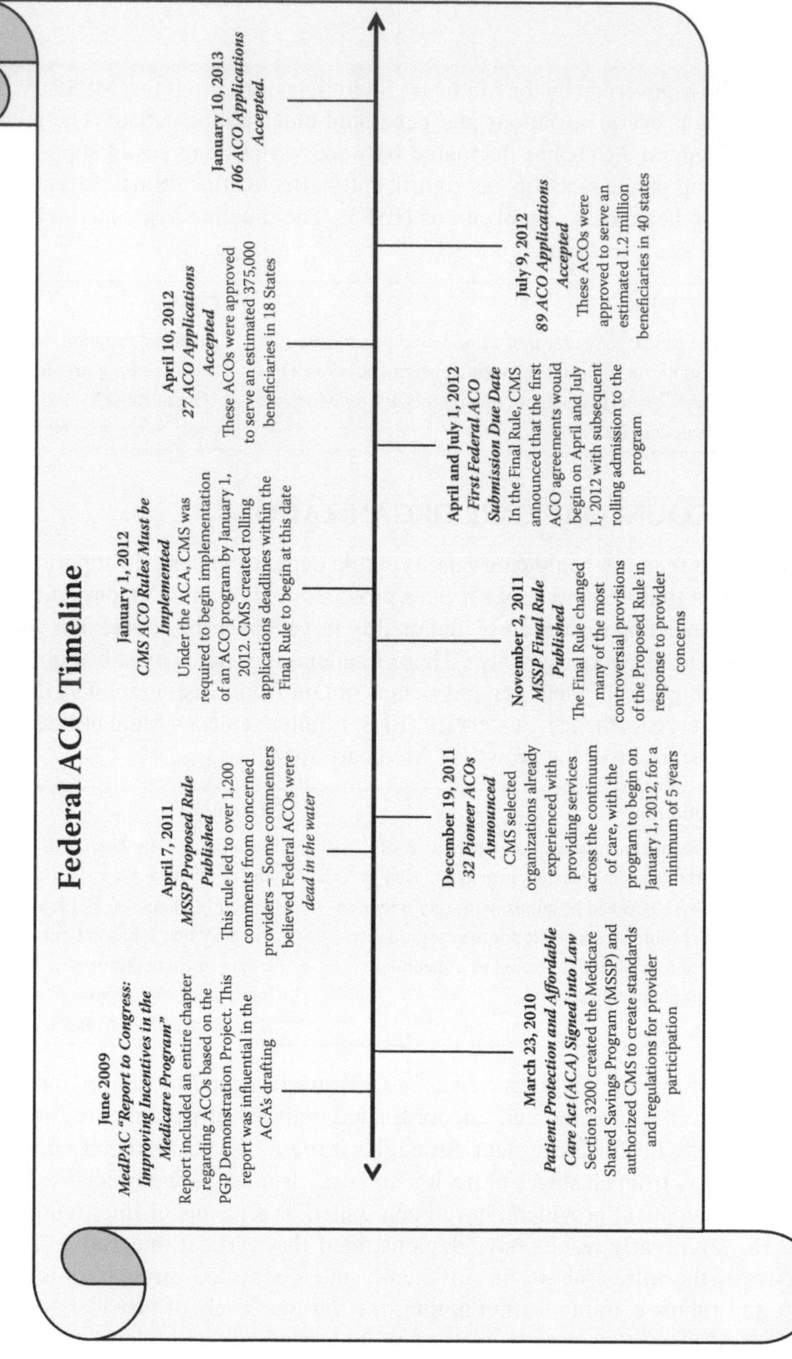

FIGURE 2.1 Timeline of federal ACO development. (From Endnote 1.)

Factoid 2.1

What sets ACOs apart from other integrated health systems is the degree of autonomy given to physicians and the flexibility afforded to physician groups, hospitals, and other networks of providers for the implementation of ACOs. (Source: *Accountable Care Organizations: A New Model for Sustainable Innovation.* Paul H. Keckley and Michelle Hoffman, Deloitte Center for Health Solutions, 2010, p. 11.)

OVERVIEW OF VALUE-BASED PURCHASING

The definition of value-based purchasing (VBP) encompasses any model of provider payments that links reimbursement or incentive bonus payments to the quality and the cost of care, which a provider can achieve for a defined patient population. Most often, these rewards are offered to providers who meet established standards for patient health outcomes and set percentage reductions in actual annual Medicare beneficiary expenditures.[4] The MSSP is one program implementing the theory of value-based purchasing, which links shared savings incentive payments to ACO participants who achieve quality metrics and expenditure reduction targets for Medicare beneficiaries.[5] While some VBP programs were able to achieve statistically significant reductions in expenditures, e.g., the Medicare Participating Heart Bypass Center Demonstration[6] (which indicated a 10% reduction), there is some recent evidence that results from past VBP demonstrations have been inconclusive, with most demonstrations indicating that no significant reductions in healthcare expenditures were achieved.[7]

Key Term	Definition	Citation
Value-Based Purchasing	The notion that purchasers hold healthcare providers accountable for both the quality and cost of care.	Glossary of Terms Commonly Used in Health Care. *AcademyHealth*, 2004 Edition.

There has been a growing general industry consensus that one way to decrease costs is to move away from fee-for-service payment systems. This change may be difficult given that the current incentives for fee-for-service payments do not engender or favor robust or consistent communication among providers. In order to decrease costs and improve the quality of care delivered,[8] a major restructuring of payment systems may be required to develop and implement care coordination programs. The Centers for Medicare and Medicaid Services (CMS) is supporting and funding these types of restructurings through its Hospital Value-Based Purchasing (VBP) program, which is set to distribute approximately $850 million to hospitals based on reported quality performance measurements beginning in October 2012.[9] A visual depiction of the value-based purchasing arrangements used for ACOs, as compared to the Hospital VBP program, is outlined in Figure 2.2.

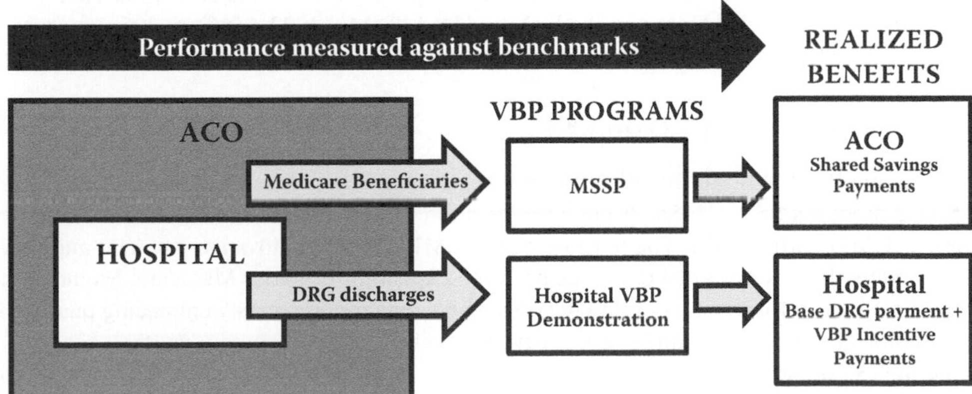

FIGURE 2.2 Diagram of value-based purchasing programs under the ACA. (From Endnote 10. With permission.)

THE PATIENT PROTECTION AND AFFORDABLE CARE ACT (ACA) AND THE MEDICARE SHARED SAVINGS PROGRAM

The ACA was signed into law on March 23, 2010, and was amended on March 30, 2010, by the Health Care and Education Reconciliation Act. Combined, these two laws are commonly referred to as healthcare reform or popularly, as "Obamacare." Many of the reform initiatives, introduced within the ACA, are designed to enhance the delivery of U.S. healthcare by focusing on a three-part aim: (1) better care for individuals, (2) better health for populations, and (3) decreased growth in healthcare expenditures.[11] The ACA, §3022, formally introduced the federal ACO model, i.e., the Medicare Shared Savings Program (MSSP), which amends Title XVIII of the Social Security Act[12] (SSA) by adding §1899 to the end of the Title.[13]

Overview and Intent of the MSSP

The intent of the MSSP was to encourage the development of ACOs for specific Medicare populations. The MSSP creates a program "that promotes accountability for a patient population and coordinates items and services under parts A and B, and encourages investment in infrastructure and redesigned care processes for high quality and efficient service delivery."[14] While the ACA lays out some foundational information on the structure of ACOs and set January 1, 2012 as the date for the start of their implementation, most of the law provides for the Secretary of Health and Human Services (HHS) to later develop the substantive regulatory framework for ACOs. Under this direction, CMS released the Proposed Rule for ACOs on April 7, 2011, and the Final Rule on November 2, 2011, both of which are discussed below. While the MSSP was a direct predecessor to ACOs, many other provisions within the ACA have aided and continue to aid in the development of these quality enhancing, cost controlling EHOs.

Key Term	Definition	Citation
Federal Accountable Care Organization (ACO)	ACO where the contracting payor is CMS. These ACOs are monitored and regulated through the MSSP and general healthcare laws.	Health Capital Consultants

Factoid 2.2

The MSSP creates a program "that promotes accountability for a patient population and coordinates items and services under parts A and B, and encourages investment in infrastructure and redesigned care processes for high quality and efficient service delivery." (Source: *Patient Protection and Affordable Care Act.* Public Law 111–148 (March 23, 2010), p. 395.)

Related Affordable Care Act Provisions

Center for Medicare and Medicaid Innovation

ACA §2012 modifies SSA §1115A through the creation of the Center for Medicare and Medicaid Innovation (CMI) within CMS. The purpose of the CMI is to test innovative payment and service delivery models that are designed to reduce program expenditures under Medicare, Medicaid, and the Children's Health Insurance Program (CHIP), while contemporaneously enhancing quality. The CMI is authorized to expand, through the development of further regulations, the scope of any model being tested, including ACOs.[15] CMS aims to develop multiple ACO models and support systems that offer "providers new options and incentives to participate in ACOs"[16] utilizing the CMI.

Value-Based Purchasing Demonstrations

While VBP is discussed above as a reimbursement scheme integral to the development of ACOs, several VBP demonstration programs have been established under the ACA for specific groups of providers, including hospitals (§3001), home health agencies (§3006), ambulatory surgery centers (§10301), and others.[17] Some of these provisions are not voluntary and contain distinct time frames for participation and quality reporting that, if not followed, may result in financial losses for entities that fail to meet quality standards.[18]

Medical Home Model

Key Term	Definition	Citation
Patient-Centered Medical Home (PCMH)	A patient-centered medical home (PCMH) model approaches the delivery of healthcare services through coordinated, centralized patient care, with an emphasis on the primary care physician as manager of the patient's treatment.	*Joint Principles of the Patient-Centered Medical Home.* American Academy of Family Physicians, American Academy of Pediatrics, American College of Physicians, and American Osteopathic Association, February, 2007, Online at: http://www.aafp.org/online/etc/medialib/aafp_org/documents/policy/fed/jointprinciplespcmh0207.Par.0001.File.dat/002107medicalhome.pdf (Accessed 12/14/11).

A Patient-Centered Medical Home (PCMH) model approaches the delivery of healthcare services through coordinated patient care, centered on a PCP who accepts responsibility for managing the patient beneficiary across the continuum of care and the spectrum of services he or she may require.[19] Similar to an ACO, a PCMH is designed to improve the quality of patient care through the incorporation of a value-based payment model.[20] An essential difference between a PCMH and an ACO lies in the scale of their respective operation. A PCMH is limited to a single physician practice setting, with one PCP coordinating the patient's care (similar to the gatekeeper function), whereas an ACO typically operates as an entire organization, within which providers coordinate care and are accountable for patient health outcomes and costs.[21] However, PCMH providers may be an essential component of an ACO, by utilizing the function of the PCP to improve health outcomes for ACO patients. An illustration of the hypothetical relationship between an ACO and a PCMH is seen in Figure 2.3.

The PCMH concept first appeared in federal legislation as a demonstration project included in the Tax Relief and Health Care Act of 2006 (TRHCA).[22] The Medicare Medical Home Demonstration Project was established to "redesign the healthcare delivery system to provide targeted, accessible, continuous and coordinated, family-centered care to high-need populations."[23] High-need populations are defined in TRHCA as individuals with chronic conditions. The project provided "care management fees" to a patient's personal physician, and incentive payments to providers participating in a medical home.[24] The demonstration project was to be conducted in eight states, in urban, rural, and underserved areas, over a three-year period.[25]

Eventually, initiatives developed by CMI superseded the Medicare Medical Homes Demonstration Project.[26] CMS credits two CMI initiatives in particular for the discontinuance of the TRHCA medical homes model: (1) the Multipayer Advanced Primary Care Practice Demonstration (Comprehensive Primary Care Initiative), and (2) the Federally Qualified Health Centers (FQHC) Advanced Primary Care Practice Demonstration (APCP).[27]

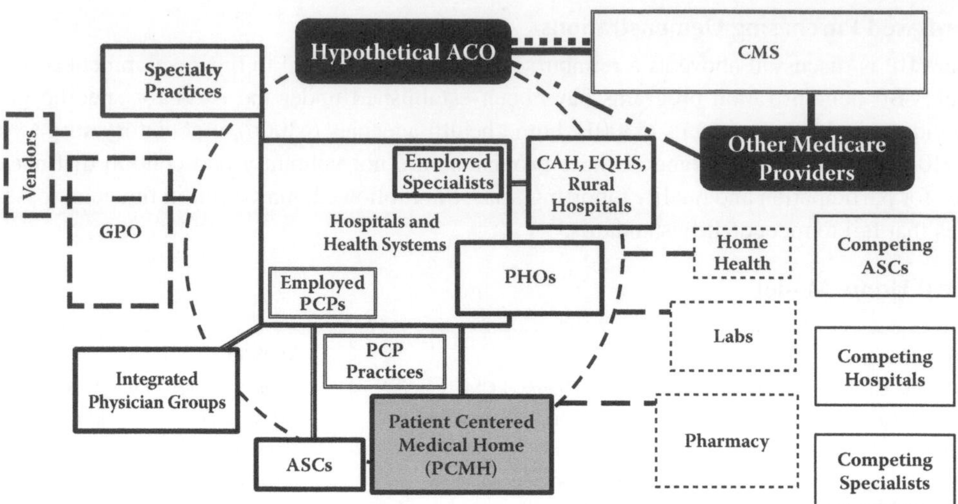

FIGURE 2.3 ACO with a PCMH.

In April 2011, CMI announced the seven markets selected to participate in the September 2011 implementation of the Comprehensive Primary Care Initiative, which mimics successful financial incentives used by large employers and other private healthcare enterprises (e.g., commercial ACOs). These seven markets, in eight states, were chosen as representative of major U.S. regions, and include:

1. Arkansas
2. Colorado
3. New Jersey
4. New York
5. Ohio and Kentucky
6. Oklahoma
7. Oregon

The selected applicants for this Comprehensive Primary Care Initiative contract with a variety of payors, including private health plans, state Medicaid agencies, and employers.[28]

The Comprehensive Primary Care Initiative follows a dual-phase payment schedule. In the first two years, CMS will pay providers a "risk adjusted, monthly care management fee" for all Medicare FFS patients, which is designed to average $20 per beneficiary, per month (PBPM).[29] Then, in years three and four, that monthly management fee will be reduced to approximately $15 PBPM; participating PCPs will have the opportunity to supplement their base management fee by sharing in any patient expenditure savings generated in their market after the second year.[30] These shared savings act as a bonus payment for PCPs who "better coordinate" their Medicare patient's care. Further, those PCP practices participating in the Comprehensive Primary Care Initiative will have access to resources that may increase the probability that physicians will achieve improved care coordination, i.e., "enhanced support above and beyond visit based fee-for-service payments (e.g., care management fees, or other nonvisit-based and nonvolume-based compensation, shared savings or similar incentives for effective stewardship of resources) for comprehensive primary care."[31]

In October 2011, CMS published a list of the 500 FQHC applicants chosen to participate in another distinct program, the Medicare Federally Qualified Health Center Advanced Primary Care

Practice (FQHC APCP), a three-year demonstration project intended to "evaluate the impact of the advanced primary care practice model, also known as the patient-centered medical home."[32] Participating FQHCs will receive a $6 "monthly management fee" per eligible Medicare patient, to assist the FQHC in making the transition to a "person-centered, coordinated, seamless primary care practice."[33] The FQHC APCP receives additional funding through various provisions of the ACA designed to support the implementation and development of FQHCs.[34]

Similar to the intent of the FQHC APCP, ACA §3502, Establishing Community Health Teams to Support the Patient-Centered Medical Home, stipulates that CMS will establish a program to spur national use of the PCMH model through grants and/or contracts with states and/or state-designated entities, and Indian tribes and/or tribal organizations.[35] Entities accepted into the program must use the funds to develop contracts to create "health teams" that support primary care practices, including obstetrics and gynecology.[36] Under the program's design, these interdisciplinary and interprofessional health teams should incorporate care management resources into programs for prevention and patient education.[37]

The ACA also includes provisions supporting PCMH providers within state specific populations. ACA §2703, State Option to Provide Health Homes for Enrollees with Chronic Conditions, focuses on implementing medical homes for state Medicaid populations beginning in January 1, 2011. The program provides funding for states to reimburse PCMH providers who treat Medicaid beneficiaries with chronic medical issues.[38] Eight states including Maine, Vermont, Rhode Island, New York, Pennsylvania, North Carolina, Michigan, and, Minnesota have been chosen as participants in established demonstration projects to evaluate 1,200 PCMHs, serving over 1.8 million individuals in Michigan alone.[39] To further support PCMH initiatives in community-based primary care practices, the Primary Care Extension Program, detailed under ACA §5405, funds state-organized programs to educate PCPs on preventative care and health literacy.[40] The purpose of this program is to assist providers in incorporating what they learned into their practices in order to ultimately reach and benefit their communities.[41]

Bundling Demonstration Project

Bundling is a means of furthering cost efficiency in healthcare reimbursement by combining payments for medical services that are generally performed together. Bundling programs are designed to lessen administrative strain, prevent fraudulent claims, and associate reimbursements with the whole episode of care,[42] in contrast to multiple individual procedures,[43] reimbursed separately. CMS has already executed several programs implementing bundling for specific medical specialties, separate from the ACA provisions, through the Medicare program (e.g., orthopedics),[44] and plans for more widespread implementation with the ICD-10 conversion. Section 3023 of the ACA supports the prevalence of bundling in the healthcare industry by providing the secretary of HHS the ability to institute a bundling demonstration project for PCPs.[45]

The bundling demonstration project for PCPs provides bundled payments to PCPs who treat specified conditions as chosen by the secretary of HHS. These conditions must be chosen to include a range of criteria, e.g., a mix of chronic and acute conditions and a mix of surgical and medical conditions. As mandated by the ACA, this program was implemented January 1, 2013 and may last up to five years.[46] The secretary of HHS also has the discretion to choose who participates in the program; however, participants must represent a range of healthcare providers, including "a hospital, a physician group, a skilled nursing facility, and a home health agency[47]

PCPs are imperative to the success of federal ACOs, as they are typically the first stop on a patient's journey through the continuum of care. Further, beneficiary assignment, i.e., the determination of those beneficiaries whose health outcomes and expenditures an ACO is accountable for, is directly tied to those patients receiving care from a participating ACO PCP (or a specialist acting as a PCP). Therefore, any provision of the ACA that incentivizes, or otherwise impacts, the use of a

PCP in the coordination of patient care or the improvement of patient outcomes, will likely support ACO development. None of the provisions of the ACA are as significant to the furtherance of ACOs as the MSSP, which has its foundation in the ACA, but was expanded within the Proposed Rule and Final Rule released by CMS.

MSSP PROPOSED RULE

The Proposed Rule for ACOs, released on March 31, 2011 and published on April 7, 2011, expanded on the basic ACO structure laid out in §3022 of the ACA.[48] The Proposed Rule represented an important step in the development of federal ACOs, without which providers may not have had the opportunity to comment on the Rule and express which provisions most concerned them. Many of the provisions of the Proposed Rule were not ultimately implemented due, in part, to negative industry feedback. This section will briefly discuss the main provisions of the Proposed Rule and the industry response, before explaining the eventual regulations released under the Final Rule.

Overview of the Main Provisions of the MSSP Proposed Rule

An overview of the main provisions included in the Proposed Rule is presented in Table 2.1.

Industry Response

Despite receiving initial praise based on the introduction of ACOs presented in §3022 of the ACA, the Proposed Rule received negative overall commentary from the healthcare industry. In a letter to the director of CMS, the American Hospital Association (AHA) wrote that its members were "disappointed with" the proposed ACO program design, and that since the release of the proposed regulations, "excitement about Medicare ACOs [had] dwindled dramatically."[50]

The American Medical Association (AMA) also expressed distaste for the Proposed Rule, stating that it made physician participation in ACOs "difficult, if not impossible."[51] The insurance industry's trade group, America's Health Insurance Plans (AHIP), asserted that the proposed ACO program: (1) lacked a novel reimbursement structure; (2) that the current Medicare payment model "provides few disincentives for overuse, underuse, or misuse of care, and does not reward efficiency;" and (3) that use of this payment model in the ACO program results in a program that "offers far fewer incentives to deliver value-based care than models in the private sector."[52]

An Intermountain Healthcare representative stated that their health system had decided not to participate in the ACO Pioneer program (an alternative ACO program discussed further below in section Subsequent ACO Model/Pioneer Model) because "the ACO regulations fell short of the goals that had been set, especially as it pertains to institutions that already are organized to coordinate care."[53] Even the Physician Group Practice (PGP) demonstration participants, whose outcomes from the demonstration project were a significant driver and template for ACOs inclusion in the ACA, and who were assumed to participate in the MSSP, expressed frustration with the Proposed Rule, publicly stating they would not apply for ACO status.[54]

Significant Changes between the MSSP Proposed and Final Rule

Most commentators expected the Proposed Rule and Final Rule to mirror each other, but in response to negative industry feedback, CMS incorporated numerous concessions in an attempt to render federal ACOs as more appealing to providers.[55] In the Final Rule, published nearly seven months after the Proposed Rule, CMS allowed for more lenient participation requirements, greater flexibility within the shared savings contract, and higher and more probable financial incentives.[56] The most significant changes between the Proposed Rule and Final Rule are enumerated in Table 2.2.

TABLE 2.1
Main Provisions of the MSSP Proposed Rule

	Provision/Topic	Description	Proposed Rule Citation
1	Eligible Entities or Participants	(1) ACO professionals in group practice arrangements, (2) networks of individual practices of ACO professionals, (3) partnerships or joint venture arrangements between hospitals and ACO professionals, and (4) hospitals employing ACO professionals. Lastly, other eligible entities may be detailed by the Secretary of HHS.	(Vol. 76, No. 67 II.B.1)
2	Assignment of Beneficiaries	In the one-step assignment process, beneficiaries will be "assigned on the basis of a plurality of allowed charges for primary care services rendered by primary care physicians."	(Vol. 76, No. 67 § 425.6)
3	Track 1 Transition to Risk	ACOs can choose from either Track 1 or Track 2. Track 1 should comprise two years of one-sided shared savings with a required change in the third year to a similar performance-based initiative detailed under Track 2. Track 2 would consist of three years performing in regards to the two-sided model. Both Track 1 and Track 2 will have a three-year agreement.	(Vol. 76, No. 67 II.G.2)
4	Prospective or Retrospective Assignment	Utilization of primary care services would determine which patients are *retrospectively* assigned to the ACO. Furthermore, a *prospective* identification of a benchmark population would determine which of the ACO patients are counted toward shared savings.	(Vol. 76, No. 67 II.D)
5	Beneficiary Claims Data	Beneficiaries can decline to participate at initial visit and patients seen by the ACO's primary care physician during the performance year are the only patients subjected to shared claims data.	(Vol. 76, No. 67 II.C.6)
6	Reports and Preliminary Prospective List	Information provided for the ACOs at start of all performance years and contain the following beneficiary information: name, date of birth, sex, and health insurance claim number.	(Vol. 76, No. 67 § 425.19)
7	Utilization of Electronic Health Records (EHR)	Fifty percent of primary care physicians must be "meaningful users" by the second performance year.	(Vol. 76, No. 67 § 425.11)
8	Marketing Guidelines for ACOs	The Centers for Medicare and Medicaid Services must give seal of approval to all ACO marketing materials.	(Vol. 76, No. 67 II.B.11)
9	Shared Savings among ACO Participants	One-sided risk model: 2% savings triggers sharing amongst ACO, (small, physician-only and rural ACOs will have some exceptions compared to normal ACOs). Two-Sided Risk Model: Shared savings from the beginning with no 2% savings required to trigger savings.	(Vol. 76, No. 67 II.F)
10	Potential Start Date	Three-year agreements with same annual start date; performance year coincides with calendar year.	(Vol. 76, No. 67 II.C.1)
11	Quality Measures	Five domains with 65 measures of quality and payment for acceptable reporting the first year, with a transition to pay-for-performance in later years. Proposed measures would eventually reflect traditional quality measures.	(Vol. 76, No. 67 II.E.c)

Factoid 2.3

Initially, the Proposed Rule suggested a retroactive assignment process, but after vivid disagreement from industry groups, the Final Rule implemented a prospective assignment method. (Source: Medicare Program; Medicare Shared Savings Program: Accountable Care Organizations. *Federal Register* vol. 76 no. 212, (November 2, 2011), p. 67862, 67.)

TABLE 2.2
Substantive Changes between the MSSP Proposed Rule and Final Rule

Provision/Topic	Proposed Rule	Final Rule
Quality Measures	(1) Five categories with 65 measures of quality; (2) Payment for acceptable reporting the first year, with a transition to pay-for-performance in later years; (3) Proposed measures would eventually reflect quality goals currently utilized on the healthcare market. (Vol. 76, No. 67 II.E.c)	Reduced to 4 categories with 33 quality measures, and a lax transition period for the ACO; full reimbursement in the initial year for *reporting*, with a mix of *reporting* and *performance* in the next two years for reimbursement. (Vol. 76, No. 212 II.F.2.c)
ACO Reports	Information provided for the ACOs at start of all performance years and contains the following information of assigned Medicare beneficiaries: name, date of birth, sex, and health insurance claim number. (Vol. 76, No. 67 § 425.19)	According to the Centers for Medicare and Medicaid Services, "[a]dditional reports will be provided quarterly." (Vol. 76, No. 212 § 425.702)
Beneficiary Assignment	In the one-step assignment process, beneficiaries will be "assigned on the basis of a plurality of allowed charges for primary care services rendered by primary care physicians." (Vol. 76, No. 67 § 425.6)	The assignment process will occur over two steps: (1) "use plurality of allowed charges for primary care services rendered by primary care physicians" for those "beneficiaries who have received at least one primary care service from a physician," and (2) for those who have not received primary care services, "use plurality of allowed charges for primary care services rendered by any other ACO professional." (Vol. 76, No. 212 § 425.402)
Utilization of Electronic Health Records (EHR)	Fifty percent of primary care physicians must be "meaningful users" by the second performance year. (Vol. 76, No. 67 § 425.11)	EHRs and "meaningful users" is no longer a requirement, but is still utilized for quality measures, and carries significant weight. (Vol. 76, No. 212 § 425.506)
Potential ACO Participation Start Date	Three-year agreements with same annual start date; performance year same as calendar year. (Vol. 76, No. 67 II.C.1)	According to CMS, "[p]rogram established by January 1, 2012"; first round of applications are due in early 2012. First ACO agreements start 4/1/2012 and 7/1/2012. ACOs will have agreements with a first performance "year" of 18 or 21 months. ACOs starting 4/1/2012 and 7/1/2012 have option for an interim payment if they report quality measures for CY 2013 to qualify for first-performance year shared savings. (Vol. 76, No. 212 II.C.1)
Beneficiary ACO Assignment	Primary care services utilization would determine which patients are *retrospectively* assigned to the ACO. Furthermore, a *prospective* identification of a benchmark population would determine which of the ACO patients are counted toward shared savings. (Vol. 76, No. 67 II.D)	Initially, prospective assignment will identify participating Medicare patients each quarter. Lastly, "final reconciliation after each performance year based on patients served by the ACO." (Vol. 76, No. 212 § 425.400)
One-Sided Shared Savings Disbursement Model and Conversion to Risk	ACOs can choose from either Track 1 or Track 2. Track 1 should comprise two years of one-sided shared savings with a required change in the third year. Track 2 would consist of three years performing in regards to the two-sided model. Three-year agreement for both tracks. (Vol. 76, No. 67 II.G.2)	Two-sided risk eliminated from Track 1, but two tracks are still available for ACOs depending on where they fall on the spectrum of preparedness. Track 2 allows for greater reward and greater risk. (Vol. 76, No. 212 § 425.600)

TABLE 2.2 (continued)
Substantive Changes between the MSSP Proposed Rule and Final Rule

Provision/Topic	Proposed Rule	Final Rule
Marketing Guidelines for ACOs	The Centers for Medicare and Medicaid Services must acknowledge and approve all ACO marketing materials. (Vol. 76, No. 67 II.B.11)	CMS will provide feedback on acceptable and "approved language," and the ACO can utilize marketing materials five days after they file materials with CMS, and "after certifying compliance with marketing guidelines." (Vol. 76, No. 212 § 425.310)
ACO Shared Savings	One-sided risk model: 2% savings triggers sharing amongst ACO, (small, physician-only and rural ACOs will have some exceptions compared to normal ACOs). Two-Sided Risk Model: Shared savings from the beginning with no 2% savings required to trigger savings. (Vol. 76, No. 67 II.F)	When the minimum savings rate is achieved, participating ACOs will have shared savings from the "first dollar." (Vol. 76, No. 212 II.G.2.a)
Eligible ACO Entities or Participants	(1) ACO professionals in group practice arrangements, (2) networks of individual practices of ACO professionals, (3) partnerships or joint venture arrangements between hospitals and ACO professionals, and (4) hospitals employing ACO professionals. Lastly, other eligible entities detailed by the secretary of HHS. (Vol. 76, No. 67 II.B.1)	Aside from those detailed in the ACA, eligibility is extended to "Federally Qualified Health Centers (FQHCs) and Rural Health Clinics (RHCs)." The only stipulation is FQHCs and RHCs need to detail primary care providers in their facilities who provide services to beneficiaries. (Vol. 76, No. 212 II.B.d.2)
Beneficiary Claims Data	Beneficiaries can decline to participate at initial visit. During the first performance year, patients seen by the primary care physician of the ACO are the only ones subjected to shared claims data. (Vol. 76, No. 67 II.C.6)	Participating beneficiaries will be offered an opportunity to decline after the ACO contacts them to detail the potential impact. (Vol. 76, No. 212 § 425.708)

Source: Endnote 57.

MSSP FINAL RULE

Released on October 28, 2011, and published on November 2, 2011, the MSSP Final Rule represented a strategic effort by CMS to increase provider interest in Federal ACOs by decreasing certain burdens, risks, and costs within the Proposed Rule that many providers had previously identified as disincentives for participation.[58]

Key Concept	Definition	Citation
MSSP: Operational Terminology	CMS has outlined 30 terms within the Final Rule to ensure quasi-uniformity for healthcare organizations participating in the MSSP. A portion of the operational terminology includes (1) accountable care organization (ACO), (2) ACO participant, (3) ACO provider, (4) ACO supplier, and (5) ACO professional.	Medicare Program; Medicare Shared Savings Program: Accountable Care Organizations. *Federal Register* vol. 76 no. 212, (November 2, 2011), pp. 67974–67978.

Operational Terminology

CMS has outlined 31 terms within the Final Rule to ensure quasi-uniformity for healthcare organizations participating in the MSSP. These terms are set forth in Exhibit 2.1.

Five terms of the operational terminology, which are integral to defining the stakeholders of an ACO, include

1. Accountable care organization (ACO)
2. ACO participant
3. ACO provider
4. ACO supplier
5. ACO professional[59]

While the definitions for these five terms may overlap, each describes a vital component of an ACO, and are defined below.

Accountable Care Organization

An ACO is defined as a legal entity "recognized and authorized under applicable State, Federal, or Tribal Law, … identified by a Taxpayer Identification Number (TIN), and is formed by one or more ACO participant(s)…"[60] Under the Final Rule, only specified organizations are eligible to gain ACO status (these organizations will be set forth later in this section). Even if a healthcare organization is not identified or listed as eligible within the Final Rule, it can still participate in the MSSP through several types of separate agreements with an existing ACO participant, as will be discussed below.[61]

Factoid 2.4

An ACO Participant is "an individual or group of ACO provider(s)/supplier(s), that is identified by a Medicare-enrolled TIN [Tax Identification Number], that alone or together with one or more other ACO participants comprise(s) an ACO. An ACO is a collection of one or more ACO Participants. As part of their application to CMS, an ACO must provide CMS with a list of participants or providers/suppliers participating in the program. (Source: Medicare Program; Medicare Shared Savings Program: Accountable Care Organizations. *Federal Register* vol. 76 no. 212, (November 2, 2011).)

ACO Participant

An ACO Participant is defined as "an individual or group of ACO provider(s)/supplier(s), that is identified by a Medicare-enrolled TIN [Tax Identification Number], that alone or together with one or more other ACO participants comprise(s) an ACO.[62] In other words, an ACO is a collection of one or more ACO participants. As part of their application to CMS, an ACO must provide CMS with a list of participants or providers/suppliers to be included within the organizational structure of their specific ACO, and their specific ACO contract.[63]

ACO Provider/Supplier

The Final Rule defines an ACO provider/supplier as any individual or entity that: "(1) is a provider or a supplier [of medical goods or services], (2) is enrolled in Medicare, (3) bills for items and services it furnishes to Medicare fee-for-service beneficiaries, and (4) is included on the list of ACO providers/suppliers."[64] According to §400.202 of the Medicare program, a provider is any

EXHIBIT 2.1
Operational Terminology of the MSSP

Term	Definition
Accountable care organization (ACO)	A legal entity that is recognized and authorized under applicable State, Federal, or Tribal law, is identified by a [TIN], and is formed by one or more ACO participants(s) that is (are) defined at [43 CFR] § 425.102(a) and may also include any other ACO participants described at [43 CFR] § 425.102(b).
ACO participant	An individual or group of ACO provider(s)/supplier(s) that is identified by a Medicare-enrolled TIN that alone or together with one or more other ACO participants comprise(s) an ACO, and that is included on the list of ACO participants that is required under [42 CFR] § 425.204(c)(5).
ACO professional	An ACO provider/supplier who is either of the following: (1) A physician legally authorized to practice medicine and surgery by the State in which he performs such function or action; (2) A practitioner who is one of the following: (i) A physician assistant (as defined at [42 CFR] § 410.74(a)(2)); (ii) A nurse practitioner (as defined at [42 CFR] § 410.75(b)). (iii) A clinical nurse specialist (as defined at [42 CFR] § 410.76(b)).
ACO provider/supplier	An individual or entity that (1) Is a provider (as defined at 42 CFR § 400.202) or a supplier (as defined at [42 CFR] § 400.202); (2) Is enrolled in Medicare; (3) Bills for items and services it furnishes to Medicare fee-for-service beneficiaries under a Medicare billing number assigned to the TIN of an ACO participant in accordance with applicable Medicare regulations; and (4) Is included on the list of ACO providers/suppliers that is required under [42 CFR] § 425.204(c)(5).
Agreement period	The term of the participation agreement, which begins at the start of the first performance year and concludes at the end of the final performance year.
Antitrust Agency	The Department of Justice (DOJ) or Federal Trade Commission (FTC).
Assignment	The operational process by which CMS determines whether a beneficiary has chosen to receive a sufficient level of the requisite primary care services from a physician who is an ACO provider/supplier so that the ACO may be appropriately designated as exercising basic responsibility for that beneficiary's care.
At-risk beneficiary	A beneficiary who (1) Has a high risk score on the CMS–HCC risk adjustment model; (2) Is considered high cost due to having two or more hospitalizations or emergency room visits each year; (3) Is dually eligible for Medicare and Medicaid; (4) Has a high utilization pattern; (5) Has one or more chronic conditions; (6) Has had a recent diagnosis that is expected to result in increased cost; (7) Is entitled to Medicaid because of disability; or (8) Is diagnosed with a mental health or substance abuse disorder.
Continuously assigned beneficiary	A beneficiary assigned to the ACO in the current performance year who was either assigned to or received a primary care service from any of the ACO's participant during the most recent prior calendar year.
Covered professional services	Services for which payment is made under, or is based on, the fee schedule established under this section and which are furnished by an eligible professional, (citing 42 U.S.C. § 1395w-4(k)(3)(A)).
Critical access hospital (CAH)	A facility designated by HFCA as meeting the applicable requirements of [Social Security Act § 1820] and of [42 CFR § 485], (citing 42 CFR § 400.202).
Eligible professional	(i) A physician; (ii) [a] practitioner described in 42 U.S.C § 1395u(b)(18)(C); (iii) [a] physical or occupational therapist or a qualified speech-language pathologist; or (iv) a qualified audiologist (as defined in 42 U.S.C. § 1395x(ll)(3)(B)), (citing 42 U.S.C. § 1395w-4(k)(3)(B)).
Federally qualified health center (FQHC)	Same meaning given to this term under [42 CFR] § 405.2401(b) of this chapter.
Hospital	A hospital subject to the prospective payment system specified in [42 CFR] § 412.1(a)(1).

continued

EXHIBIT 2.1 (continued)
Operational Terminology of the MSSP

Term	Definition
Marketing materials and activities	General audience materials, such as brochures, advertisements, outreach events, letters to beneficiaries, Web pages, data sharing opt out letters, mailings, social media, or other activities conducted by or on behalf of the ACO, or by ACO participants, or ACO providers/suppliers participating in the ACO, when used to educate, solicit, notify, or contact Medicare beneficiaries or providers and suppliers regarding the Shared Savings Program, *but does not include* Certain informational materials customized or limited to a subset of beneficiaries; materials that do not include information about the ACO, its ACO participants, or its ACO providers/suppliers; materials that cover beneficiary-specific billing and claims issues or other specific individual health related issues; educational information on specific medical conditions (for example, flu shot reminders), written referrals for healthcare items and services, and materials or activities that do not constitute "marketing" under 45 CFR 164.501 and 164.508(a)(3)(i).
Medicare fee-for-service beneficiary	An individual who is (1) [e]nrolled in the original Medicare fee-for-service program under both parts A and B; and (2) [n]ot enrolled in any of the following: (i) a MA plan under part C; (ii) an eligible organization under section 1876 of the Act; or (iii) a PACE program under section 1894 of the Act.
Medicare Shared Savings Program (MSSP)	Means the program, established under section 1899 of the Act and implemented in this part.
Newly assigned beneficiary	A beneficiary that is assigned in the current performance year who was neither assigned to nor receives a primary care service from any of the ACO's participants during the most recent prior calendar year.
One-sided model	A model under which the ACO may share savings with the Medicare program, if it meets the requirements for doing so, but is not liable for sharing any losses incurred under subpart G of this part.
Performance year	The 12-month period beginning on January 1 of each year during the agreement period, unless otherwise noted in the ACO's agreement. For an ACO with a start date of April 1, 2012 or July 1, 2012, the ACO's first performance year is defined as 21 months and 18 months, respectively.
Physician	A doctor of medicine or osteopathy (as defined in section 1861(r)(1) of the Act).
Physician Quality Reporting System (PQRS)	The quality reporting system established under section 1848(k) of the Act.
Primary care physician	A physician who has a primary specialty designation of internal medicine, general practice, family practice, or geriatric medicine, or for services furnished in an FQHC or RHC, a physician included in an attestation by the ACO as provided under § 425.404.
Primary care services	The set of services identified by the following HCPCS codes: (1) 99201 through 99215; (2) 99304 through 99340, and 99341 through 99350, G0402 (the code for the Welcome to Medicare visit), G0438 and G0439 (codes for the annual wellness visits); and (3) Revenue center codes 0521, 0522, 0524, 0525 submitted by FQHCs (for services furnished prior to January 1, 2011), or by RHCs.
Quality measures	The measures defined by the Secretary, under section 1899 of the Act, to assess the quality of care furnished by an ACO, such as measures of clinical processes and outcomes, patient and, where practicable, caregiver experience of care and utilization.
Reporting period	The calendar year from January 1 to December 31.
Rural health center (RHC)	"same meaning given to this term under § 405.2401(b)"
Shared losses	A portion of the ACO's performance year Medicare fee-for-service Parts A and B expenditures, above the applicable benchmark, it must repay to CMS. An ACO's eligibility for shared losses will be determined for each performance year. For an ACO requesting interim payment, shared losses may result from the interim payment calculation.

EXHIBIT 2.1 (continued)
Operational Terminology of the MSSP

Term	Definition
Shared savings	A portion of the ACO's performance year Medicare fee-for-service Parts A and B expenditures, below the applicable benchmark, it is eligible to receive payment from CMS. An ACO's eligibility for shared savings will be determined for each performance year. For an ACO requesting interim payment, shared savings may result from the interim payment system calculation.
Taxpayer Identification Number (TIN)	A federal taxpayer identification number or employer identification number as defined by the IRS in 26 CFR 301.6109–1.
Two-sided model	A model under which the ACO may share savings with the Medicare program, if it meets the requirements for doing so, and is also liable for sharing any losses incurred under subpart G of this part.

Source: Medicare Program; Medicare Shared Savings Program: Accountable Care Organizations, *Federal Register*, vol. 76, no. 212 (November 2, 2011), pp. 67974–67975; Quality Reporting System, 42 U.S.C. § 1395w-4(k)(3)(A); Definitions Specific to Medicare, 42 C.F.R. § 400.202 (2012).

healthcare organization that participates in Medicare for inpatient or outpatient services, "or a community mental health center that … only … furnish[s] partial hospitalization services."[65] Similarly, a supplier is "a physician or other practitioner, or an entity other than a provider, that furnishes healthcare services under Medicare."[66] While an ACO participant is construed as a legal part of the whole ACO, an "ACO provider/supplier" must only meet the requirements above and, therefore, can indirectly participate in the MSSP. Each individual physician or other practitioner practicing within an ACO is known as an *ACO professional.*

ACO Professional

An ACO professional is defined as a licensed professional that provides healthcare services within an ACO. This term is further defined under §425.20 of the MSSP as: "(1) a physician legally authorized to practice medicine and surgery by the State in which he performs such function or action, or (2) a practitioner who is one of the following: a physician assistant, a nurse practitioner, a clinical nurse specialist."[67] Any of these physicians or midlevel providers can participate in an ACO, either directly through involvement in the ACO contract between the ACO and CMS or indirectly through a separate contract with the ACO entity. The various types of eligible entity combinations that integrate, or contract, to form an ACO will be a significant factor influencing how a specific ACO may develop.

Development

Eligible Entities

Key Concept	Definition	Citation
Eligibility to participate in ACOs	The MSSP Final Rule lists those entities that are eligible to participate in a Federal ACO, based on those entities listed in §1899(b)(1) of the SSA. While the Proposed Rule only included the listed entities and arrangements, the Final Rule expanded ACO eligibility to include critical access hospitals (CAH).	Medicare Program; Medicare Shared Savings Program: Accountable Care Organizations. *Federal Register* vol. 76 no. 212, (November 2, 2011), p. 67812.

TABLE 2.3
Potential ACO Participants: The Eligible Entities

Eligible Entities	Potential Provider Organizations	Definition
ACO professionals in group practices	Primary Care Physician Practices	Practice that provides the patient with services, including health promotion, disease prevention, health maintenance, counseling, etc., beginning at the first point of entry.
Networks of individual practices of ACO professionals	Independent Practice Associations (IPA)	Legal entities of independent physicians that contract with health insurance companies to provide medical services.
	Multispecialty Physician Groups (MSPG)	Group practice with physicians practicing in more than one specialty.
Partnerships or joint venture arrangements between hospitals and ACO professionals	Integrated Delivery Networks (IDN)	A network of facilities and providers working together in order to provide a continuum of care to a market or geographic area.
	Clinical Integrated Networks (CIN)	Physicians, hospitals, and care delivery resources collaborate as an integrated unit to increase care quality and coordination.
Hospitals employing ACO professionals	Hospital Medical Staff Organizations (MSO)	A legal entity owned by physician, hospitals, or lay investors that provide an array of practice management services. In some cases, the hospital owns the entity that may sell management services to medical staff.
	Physician Hospital Organizations (PHO)	An enterprise that unites a hospital or group of hospitals with a physician organization through a contractual relationship.
	Extended Hospital Medical Staff	A multispecialty group associated with a hospital that provides the hospital with direct and indirect referrals.
Critical Access Hospital (CAH)	Critical Access Hospital (CAH)	A rural hospital providing both inpatient and outpatient services located more than 35 miles from the nearest facility. The hospital must provide emergency services 24 hours a day, contain fewer than 25 inpatient beds, and have an average length of stay of less than 96 hours.

Such other groups of providers of services and suppliers as the secretary determines appropriate.

Source: Endnote 71.

The MSSP Final Rule lists those entities that are eligible to participate in a federal ACO, based on §1899(b)(1) of the SSA.[68] Originally, critical access hospitals (CAH) were not included as an eligible entity under the Proposed Rule. However, the Final Rule includes CAHs due to their role in providing healthcare services to underserved and low-income populations, which traditionally have high Medicare populations.[69] Policy makers expressed concern that CAHs would be unable to meet the necessary criteria to become an ACO, despite their eligibility. To address this concern, CAH eligibility is limited under the Final Rule, so that only those CAHs that bill directly to Medicare for both facilities and professional services are eligible to be an ACO.[70] The potential integrated models that encompass the eligible entities for ACO participation, along with definitions of each type of entity are provided in Table 2.3.

Key Term	Definition	Citation
Critical Access Hospital (CAH)	A rural hospital providing both inpatient and outpatient services located more than 35 miles from the nearest facility. The hospital must provide emergency services 24 hours a day, contain fewer than 25 inpatient beds, and have an average length of stay of less than 96 hours.	*Critical Access Hospitals Centers for Medicare & Medicaid Services.* Rural Health Fact Sheet Series, January 2012, p. 2. [Definition for CAH]

Of note, to lessen any anticipated administrative reimbursement hassles, the definition of Hospitals, under the MSSP Final Rule, is limited to: "only acute care hospitals paid under the hospital inpatient prospective payment system (IPPS)."[72]

Key Term	Definition	Citation
Primary Care Physician Practices	Practice that provides the patient with services, including health promotion, disease prevention, health maintenance, counseling, etc., beginning at the first point of entry.	*Primary Care*. American Academy of Family Physicians, 2012. Online at: http://www.aafp.org/online/en/home/policy/policies/p/primarycare.html#Parsys0003 (Accessed 1/24/2012).

Key Term	Definition	Citation
Independent Practice Association (IPA)	Legal entities of independent physicians that contract with health insurance companies to provide medical services.	*Health Care Glossary Stoney Brook Medicine*, 2012. Online at: http://stoneybrookmedicine.edu/patientcare/healtheducation/glossary#i (Accessed 06/12/2012). [Definition for IPA]

Key Term	Definition	Citation
Multispecialty Physician Groups (MSPGs)	Group practice with physicians practicing in more than one specialty.	*Cost Survey for Primary Care Practices: 2010 Report Based on 2009 Data.* Medical Group Management Association, 2009, p. 369. [Definition for MSPG]

Key Term	Definition	Citation
Integrated Delivery Networks (IDN)	A network of facilities that provides working together in order to provider a continuum of care to a market or geographic area.	*Integrated Delivery Network (IDN.* Glen McDaniel, GLG Research, Gerson Lehrman Group, Inc. 2011. Online at: http://www.glgresearch.com/Dictionary/HC-Integrated Delivery-Network-(IDN).html (Accessed 1/24/2012). [Definition for IDN]

Key Term	Definition	Citation
Hospital Medical Staff Organizations (MSO)	A legal entity owned by physician, hospitals, or lay investors that provide an array of practice management services. In some cases, the hospital owns the entity that may sell management services to medical staff.	*The Advisor's Guide to Health Care: Professional Practices.* Robert James Cimasi, American Institute of Certified Public Accountants, Inc., New York, 2011, p. 477; *Accountable Care Organizations: A Roadmap for Success: Guidance on First Steps*, 1st ed. Bruce Flareau and Joe Bohn,Virginia Beach, VA: Convergent Publishing, LLC, 2911, p. 45. [Definition for MSO]

Key Term	Definition	Citation
Physician Hospital Organization (PHO)	An enterprise that unites a hospital or group of hospitals with a physician organization through a contractual relationship.	*Accountable Care Organizations: A Roadmap for Success: Guidance on First Steps.* Bruce Flareau and Joe Bohn, Virginia Beach, VA: Convergent Publishing, LLC, p. 10. [Definition for PHO]

Key Term	Definition	Citation
Extended Hospital Medical Staff	A multispecialty group associated with a hospital that provides the hospital with direct and indirect referrals.	*Creating Accountable Care Organizations: The Extended Hospital Medical Staff.* Elliot S. Fisher et al., Health Affairs, 2007. [Definition for Extended Hospital Medical Staff]

The same reimbursement and compliance concerns that resulted in CMS limiting CAH eligibility also led to the intentional exclusion of both Federally Qualified Health Centers (FQHCs) and Rural Health Centers (RHCs) from the list of eligible entities.[73] However, the Final Rule does allow for the indirect inclusion of both FQHCs and RHCs through increased shared savings payments under an eligible ACO's contract.[74] Those FQHCs and RHCs and other Medicare enrolled providers who are unable to formally transition to an ACO may still participate in the MSSP by establishing, through a contracting process, indirect collaborations with legally permitted ACOs (see definition of ACO provider/supplier and ACO Professional above).[75] Mergers or integration contracts involving the above listed eligible entities, as well as indirectly included participants, also are regulated under the MSSP Final Rule.

Structural Requirements

ACOs may form through any state permitted organizations, e.g., corporation, limited liability corporation (LLC), partnership, foundation, etc., with the limitation that their legal structure must be capable of the following: (1) receiving and distributing shared savings to both ACO participants and providers/suppliers; (2) repaying shared losses;[76] (3) establishing, reporting, and ensuring the compliance of ACO participants and ACO providers/suppliers with program requirements, including quality performance standards;[77] and (4) performing any ACO function identified in the statute.[78] A key structural requirement, unique to ACOs, is that it must include a mechanism for shared governance, i.e., the establishment of a governing body.[79]

Governance

Key Concept	Definition	Citation
CMS Requirement for Federal ACO Formation	Each individual ACO participant must have a representative on the governing body to ensure that the governing body is provider-driven, while still allowing nonproviders to have a voice. To demonstrate patient centeredness, ACOs also are required to have Medicare beneficiary representation within the ACO governing body, although ACOs are afforded the option to implement innovative methods of involving beneficiaries in ACO governance.	Medicare Program; Medicare Shared Savings Program: Accountable Care Organizations *Federal Register* vol. 76 no. 212, (November 2, 2011), pp. 67819–67820.

Only ACO applicants that have "established a mechanism for shared governance" are eligible to participate in the MSSP.[80] The MSSP includes several standards for an established governing mechanism to be compliant with the MSSP, e.g., the governing body must contain a management structure that includes both clinical and administrative systems to facilitate the coordination of patient care between providers.[81] However, these specific standards do not apply to all ACOs. In order to allow greater flexibility and to prevent disincentives to ACO formation, the Final Rule does not require a specific structure for the formation of the governing body, e.g., the formation of a board of directors or a board of managers, for not-for-profit or community-based healthcare organizations. Even if an ACO chooses not to create a governing board, the MSSP encourages it by noting that a governing board "… help[s] insulate [an ACO] against conflicts of interest that could potentially put the interest of an ACO participant (in an ACO formed among otherwise independent ACO participants) before the interest of the ACO."[82]

Factoid 2.5

The leadership and management of an ACO has the ability and authority to affect the three aims of the MSSP (i.e., quality of care for patients, health of populations, and lower growth in expenditures) for both administrative and clinical systems. (Source: Medicare Program; Medicare Shared Savings Program: Accountable Care Organizations. *Federal Register* vol. 76, no. 212 (November 2, 2011), p. 67822.)

Control of the day-to-day operations of an ACO by an outside or third party entity would likely hinder vertical integration and clinical coordination. Therefore, the MSSP requires that ACO participants must control at least 75% of an ACO's governing body.[83] Further, each individual ACO participant must have a representative within the governing body to ensure a provider presence, while still allowing nonproviders to be part of management decisions.[84] To demonstrate patient-centeredness, ACOs also are required to have some level of Medicare beneficiary representation within the ACO governing body, although ACOs are afforded the option to implement innovative methods to involve beneficiaries in ACO governance.[85] In situations where a preexisting healthcare entity has transitioned into an ACO, but also maintains a preexisting board, a new governance body does not need to be established, so long as the remaining board is able to meet the criteria listed above.[86]

The MSSP also establishes guidelines for management at lower levels in the ACO organization. The Final Rule sets forth basic guides for the leadership and management of an ACO, including management hierarchy and systems criteria, which must be met under the MSSP:

1. The ACO's operations should be managed by an executive officer manager, or general partner, whose appointment and removal are under control of the organization's governing body, and whose leadership team has demonstrated the ability to influence or direct clinical practice to improve efficiency processes and outcomes.
2. Clinical management and oversight should be managed by a senior level medical director who is a board-certified physician, licensed in the state in which the ACO operates, and is physically present on a regular basis in an established location of the ACO.
3. ACO participants and ACO providers/suppliers should have a meaningful commitment to the ACO's clinical integration program to ensure its likely success.
4. The ACO should have a physician-directed quality assurance and process improvement committee to oversee an ongoing quality assurance and improvement program.[87]

5. The ACO should develop and implement evidence-based medical practice or clinical guidelines and processes for delivering care consistent with the three-part aim of health-care reform, i.e., (a) better care for individuals, (b) better health for populations, and (c) lower growth in expenditures.
6. The ACO should have a health information technology infrastructure that enables the ACO to collect and evaluate data and provide feedback to the ACO providers/suppliers across the entire organization, including providing information to influence care at the point of service.[88] Of note, within the Final Rule, the specific requirement for the implementation of an electronic health record system was removed and replaced with the vague requirement listed above.
7. Prior to approval from CMS, ACOs must submit documents proving that each of the above listed requirements has been achieved and that the leadership and management in place within the ACO has the ability and authority to impact both administrative and clinical systems.[89]

Implementation

Before a prospective ACO is allowed to contract with CMS for shared savings payments, it must apply for the federal ACO program, i.e., the MSSP. To date, there have been two application deadlines: April 1, 2012, and July 1, 2012, in addition to rolling admissions after these dates.[90] From the 50 applications received on April 1, 2012, 27 enterprises were accepted and entered the federal ACO program on April 10, 2012. CMS reviewed another 150 applications for the July 1st application deadline, which resulted in another 89 new organizations entering the program on July 9, 2012. From the rolling admission period from August 1, 2012 to September 6, 2012, an additional 106 applications were accepted to join the MSSP. In total, there are currently 222 Federal ACOs in operation. The next application period to evaluate organizations to join the MSSP in January 2014 was set to begin in summer 2013.

Factoid 2.6

In the Final Rule, CMS requires a "compliance plan." The compliance plan is a means by which an employee, contractor or other ACO member may anonymously report suspected fraud or abuse to law enforcement. (Source: Medicare Program; Medicare Shared Savings Program: Accountable Care Organizations *Federal Register* vol. 76 no. 212, (November 2, 2011), p. 67952.)

The application process to become an ACO involves the following steps:

- Submit a Notice of Intent (NOI) to CMS
- Submit the complete application package
- Respond to any requests for additional information
- Receive an acceptance or denial
- If denied, appeal the decision through a CMS reconsideration review.[93]

As mentioned above, all applications must be accompanied by supporting documentation that confirms an ACO is compliant with all MSSP structural and operational requirements. A description of the documents needed for an application is provided in Table 2.4.

Once an ACO has been accepted into the federal MSSP program, the regulation and monitoring of the ACO is controlled through the terms of a contract, also known as the *ACO agreement*, between the ACO and CMS.

TABLE 2.4
Required Documents and Evidence to Apply for ACO Status

Requirement	Definition
ACO Documents	ACO documents (for example, participation agreements, employment contracts, and operating policies) that describe the ACO participants' and ACO providers/suppliers' rights and obligations in the ACO, how the opportunity to receive shared savings will encourage ACO participants and ACO providers/suppliers to adhere to the quality assurance and improvement program and the evidenced-based clinical guidelines.
Scope and Scale Documents	Describes the scope and scale of the quality assurance and clinical integration program systems and processes.
Organization and Management Documents/Evidence	Supporting materials documenting the ACO's organization and management structure, including an organizational chart, a list of committees (including the names of committee members) and their structures, and job descriptions for senior administrative and clinical leaders.
Staffing Documents/Evidence	Evidence that the ACO has a board-certified physician as its medical director who is licensed in the state in which the ACO resides and that a principal CMS liaison is identified in its leadership structure.
Governing Body Documents/Evidence	Evidence that the governing body includes persons who represent the ACO participants, and that these ACO participants hold at least 75% control of the governing body.

Source: Endnote 94.

The ACO Agreement

The MSSP stipulates that an ACO must contract with the secretary of HHS (through CMS) to participate in the MSSP for no less than a three-year period.[95] This ACO agreement specifies the method of determining shared savings payments and an ACO's evaluation timeline.

In response to concerns regarding the Proposed Rule, the Final Rule offers flexibility for ACOs in terms of the timeline under which their performance will be assessed to determine a benchmark by which to calculate shared savings amounts.[96] For those ACOs that applied by April 1, 2012, the first performance period will be for 21 months ending on December 31, 2013, with the three-year ACO contract period ending on December 31, 2015.[97] For those ACOs that applied by July 1, 2012, the first performance period will be 18 months and end on December 31, 2013, with the three-year ACO contract period for this start date also ending on December 31, 2015.[98] The Final Rule states that: "ACOs will begin receiving data immediately upon entry into the program." Therefore, an ACO may receive performance period data in the form of historical and aggregate reports, along with rolling information as it is being collected by CMS.[99] The data gathered during a performance period will be used to establish a benchmark for each ACO. Annual reports of quality metrics and Medicare patient expenditures will be compared to this benchmark to determine the amount of shared savings payments to be distributed to the ACO. The specific calculation of shared savings is discussed in more detail below.

If quality and expenditures targets are achieved, an ACO will receive a shared savings payment for each year of the ACO contract period.[100] The expenditure and utilization data that is compared to the CMS established benchmark is assembled from the claims submitted to CMS, which are based on the "claims run-out period," i.e., the time between the date when a Medicare-covered service has been furnished to a beneficiary, and the date when the final payment is actually issued.[101] The Final Rule utilizes a three-month claim run-out period, which balances the need for timely feedback (favoring a shorter period) with the need for accurate and precise data (favoring a longer period).[102]

Accountability: The Assignment of Medicare Beneficiaries

The ACO is required to detail its intent to be accountable for the healthcare of assigned Medicare beneficiaries in its application to CMS. Beneficiary accountability entails accepting responsibility and accountability for the "quality, cost, and overall care of the Medicare fee-for-service beneficiaries assigned to the ACO."[103] CMS prospectively defines the Medicare beneficiary population for which an ACO will be accountable by determining which patients are likely to receive a majority of their primary care services from the ACO (not necessarily limited to the care received from primary care physicians) throughout the participation period.

Key Concept	Definition	Citation
Assignment of Medicare Beneficiaries	Secretary determines an appropriate method of assignment for beneficiaries based on their location and other characteristics to suitable ACO.	Medicare Program; Medicare Shared Savings Program: Accountable Care Organizations *Federal Register* vol. 76 no. 212, November 2, 2011, p. 67851.

CMS has described the assignment of beneficiaries to an appropriate ACO as more akin to an "alignment of benefits" to appropriate beneficiaries.[104] CMS recognized that, in addition to the utilization of healthcare services, there are four elements that are necessary to consider when assigning a fee-for-service Medicare beneficiary, including:

1. An operational definition of an ACO
2. The definition of primary care services for the purposes of identification and appropriate beneficiary placement
3. The decision to either *assign beneficiaries prospectively*, i.e., based on services rendered during the year prior to an ACOs establishment within the MSSP, or *retrospectively*, i.e., based on services rendered during the first year an ACO is operating within the MSSP
4. A determination to consider the proportion of the services that are necessary to be received from the ACO[105]

The issues related to the assignment of beneficiaries were one of the most significant changes between the MSSP Proposed Rule and Final Rule. Initially, the Proposed Rule suggested a retrospective assignment process, but following notable disapproval from industry groups, the Final Rule implemented a prospective assignment method.[106] Provider preference for prospective assignment focused on their ability to know which patients they are accountable for, while services are being performed. Providers noted in their criticism of the Proposed Rule that this information was essential, given the cost and expenses associated with ACO formation and implementation. Critics of the prospective assignment model have expressed concerns that ACO providers might treat assigned patients differently from patients that do not influence the ACO's shared savings payments.[107] However, monitoring and beneficiary updates may assuage this concern.

Under the prospective method, Medicare beneficiaries are assigned to an ACO based on the most recent data available at the beginning of a performance year.[108] These assignments are updated quarterly, with a final assignment to be determined at the end of a performance year.[109] In assigning beneficiaries, CMS utilizes a stepwise process: (1) identification of beneficiaries who have received at least one primary care service from an ACO provider or supplier, and (2) confirmation that the total charges billed for services from the beneficiary's ACO provider exceed the total charges billed for services from other non-ACO providers. Though this process is most directly applicable to primary care providers, the Final Rule also applies the beneficiary assignment process to specialists acting as primary care providers. For example, an elderly patient who receives the majority of his care from a cardiologist also may receive traditional primary care services, e.g., blood pressure readings and annual wellness visits, from that cardiologist. In this way, CMS has adopted "a more balanced assignment process that simultaneously maintains the primary care-centric approach of our proposed approach to beneficiary assignment, while recognizing the necessary and appropriate role of specialists in providing primary care services."[110] The inclusion of specialists into the methodology utilized for the assignment of beneficiaries employs a "stepwise" process, i.e., if a patient receives no services from any primary care providers affiliated with an ACO, then any primary care services that patient receives from a specialist are considered when determining whether the patient will be assigned to that ACO, assuming that the patient receives the requisite amount of primary care services from specialists within the specific ACO.[111] CMS also clarified that the Final Rule in no way restricts the rights of beneficiaries to choose from which provider(s) they will ultimately receive their healthcare services.[112]

In addition to this method of Medicare beneficiary assignment, comments on the Proposed Rule also presented concerns regarding which patient populations were eligible to be included in the assigned Medicare beneficiaries population.[113] In the Final Rule, traditional Medicare beneficiaries, as well as dual-eligibles (patients enrolled in both Medicare and Medicaid programs) were included.[114] CMS noted a particular interest in the care provided to the dual eligible cohort, and further stated that the policies concerning Medicare assignment of beneficiaries to an ACO under the MSSP is "consistent with the definition of [a] Medicare fee-for-service beneficiary."[115] As an ACO's market share changes over time, the patient population for which the ACO is accountable may be redefined, impacting the operation of the ACO and its ACO participants.

Operation

Prior to being approved by CMS, an ACO must identify all individual ACO participants (i.e., separate participating entities) and, as part of its ongoing operation, ACOs must update this identification of participants as needed throughout the life of the ACO.[116] ACO participants that may impact an ACO's beneficiary assignment must follow "required exclusivity," meaning these participants may only be involved in a single ACO as defined by an individual tax identification number (TIN).[117] However, providers may participate in multiple ACOs if they have multiple TINs. Therefore, "exclusivity of an ACO participant leaves individual [National Provider Identifiers] NPIs free to participate in multiple ACOs if they bill under several different TINs." [118] Even though the MSSP identifies participants through an NPI, as described above, Medicare providers are only issued one NPI, which characteristically drives the decision that ACO billing cannot be linked to the NPI and still allow providers to participate in multiple ACOs.

Participants that do not affect beneficiary assignment are not limited by the MSSP and may participate in numerous ACO arrangements.[119] However, limitations are applied to participating FQHCs, RHCs, and any "ACO participants that include NP [nurse practitioners], PAs [physician assistants], and specialists upon which beneficiary assignment" is determined.[120] For that beneficiary population for which an ACO is accountable, the organization must monitor and report various quality and cost metrics.

Quality and Other Reporting Requirements

Factoid 2.7

In order to receive shared savings payments, ACOs must meet quality and performance standards described earlier in the final rule as well as demonstrate that it has "achieved savings against a benchmark of expected average per capita Medicare FFS expenditures." (Source: Medicare Program; Medicare Shared Savings Program: Accountable Care Organizations *Federal Registry* vol. 76 no. 212, November 2, 2011, pg. 67904.)

The MSSP requires ACO participants to collect expenditure information and quality data to be submitted to CMS.[121] CMS requires reporting for 33 quality metrics, divided into four domains of care, including (1) patient/caregiver experience [7 measures], (2) care coordination/patient safety

[6 measures], (3) preventive health [8 measures], and (4) at-risk population [11 measures].[122] These quality measures, as well as the reporting methods required of providers, are listed by category in Exhibit 2.2.

ACOs are responsible for collecting and submitting data for those quality measures listed above as utilizing the Group Practice Reporting Option (GPRO) Web interface as the method of submission. This Web interface is utilized for reporting the 22 clinical quality measures, and provides ACOs with examples for how to assign vulnerable populations to care categories (e.g., diabetes, heart failure[123]). This design of the GPRO is nearly identical to the Physician Quality Reporting System (PQRS)[124] recently implemented by the Medicare program.[125] To promote the continued incorporation of the PQRS system, even though the MSSP and the PQRS are entirely separate programs, CMS has, since 2012, included GPRO measures within the PQRS, indirectly merging the two programs for those particular metrics.[126]

For those quality measures that utilize survey reporting methods, CMS will bear the administrative and financial burden of collecting survey data for the first two years of the ACO contract, at which point ACOs must assume the responsibility of acquiring and paying for a CMS-certified survey vendor to continue reporting on these metrics.[127] Any measures associated with claims-based reporting methods are monitored by CMS independent of ACO quality data submission, therefore, ACO providers are not required to monitor or track these measures. In addition to monitoring an ACO's achievement of the above quality metrics, CMS also monitors general ACO compliance under the MSSP.

Key Concept	Definition	Citation
Quality and Other Reporting Requirements	The MSSP requires ACO participants to collect clinical information and quality data and submit this information to CMS. CMS requires reporting under 33 quality criteria, divided into four domains of care: (1) patient/caregiver experience (7 measures), (2) care coordination/patient safety (6 measures), (3) preventive health (8 measures), and (4) at-risk population (11 measures).	Medicare Program; Medicare Shared Savings Program: Accountable Care Organizations. *Federal Register* vol. 76 no. 212, (November 2, 2011), pp. 67899–90.

Monitoring and Termination

In the Final Rule, CMS requires each ACO to create a formal "compliance plan." The compliance plan is a means by which an employee, contractor, or other ACO member may anonymously report suspected fraud or abuse to law enforcement.[128] Section 425.300 of the MSSP requires that the ACO designate a compliance official, as well as implement various training and reporting provisions.[129] Section 425.302 of the MSSP requires that ACOs submit accurate and complete certified data reports at the end of each performance year, so that CMS may confirm compliance.[130]

An entity's ACO status may be revoked (thereby terminating the ACO) for any of the following reasons:

- The ACO is not in compliance with eligibility and other requirements.
- The ACO is sanctioned by a federal, state, or local accrediting organization, which creates a situation by which an ACO is unable to comply with the Final Rule.
- The ACO violates any relevant Medicare laws, e.g., antikickback or self-referral laws.[131]
- The ACO does not meet the established quality performance measures.[132]
- The ACO avoids providing care for high-risk beneficiaries.[133]

CMS is responsible for providing notice to an ACO, in writing, of its decision to terminate an ACO's participation in the program.[134] An ACO also may terminate its own participation in the program voluntarily, provided it issues a 60-day notice to all of its participants, including: ACO

EXHIBIT 2.2
Metrics and Methods to Establish Quality Performance

Measure	Domain	Measure Title	Method of Data Submission	Pay for Performance Phase in R = Reporting P = Performance Year 1	Year 2	Year 3
		AIM: Better Care for Individuals				
1	Patient/Caregiver Experience	CAHPS: Getting Timely Care, Appointments and Information	Survey	R	P	P
2	Patient/Caregiver Experience	CAHPS: How Well Your Doctors Communicate	Survey	R	P	P
3	Patient/Caregiver Experience	CAHPS: Patients' Rating of Doctor	Survey	R	P	P
4	Patient/Caregiver Experience	CAHPS: Access to Specialists	Survey	R	P	P
5	Patient/Caregiver Experience	CAHPS: Health Promotion and Education	Survey	R	P	P
6	Patient/Caregiver Experience	CAHPS: Shared Decision Making	Survey	R	P	P
7	Patient/Caregiver Experience	CAHPS: Health Status/Functional Status	Survey	R	R	R
8	Care Coordination/ Patient Safety	Risk-Standardized, All Condition Readmission	Claims	R	R	P
9	Care Coordination/ Patient Safety	Ambulatory Sensitive Conditions Admissions: Chromic Obstructive Pulmonary Disease	Claims	R	P	P
10	Care Coordination/ Patient Safety	Ambulatory Sensitive Conditions Admissions: Congestive Heart Failure	Claims	R	P	P
11	Care Coordination/ Patient Safety	Percent of PCPs Who Successfully Qualify for an HER Incentive Program Payment	EHR Incentive Program Reporting	R	P	P
12	Care Coordination/ Patient Safety	Medication Reconciliation: Reconciliation after Discharge from an Inpatient Facility	GPRO Web Interface	R	P	P
13	Care Coordination/ Patient Safety	Falls: Screening for Fall Risk	GPRO Web Interface	R	P	P
		AIM: Better Health for Populations				
14	Preventive Health	Influenza Immunization	GPRO Web Interface	R	P	P
15	Preventive Health	Pneumococcal Vaccination	GPRO Web Interface	R	P	P
16	Preventive Health	Adult Weight Screening and Follow-Up	GPRO Web Interface	R	P	P
17	Preventive Health	Tobacco Use Assessment and Tobacco Cessation	GPRO Web Interface	R	P	P
18	Preventive Health	Depression Screening	GPRO Web Interface	R	P	P
19	Preventive Health	Colorectal Cancer Screening	GPRO Web Interface	R	R	P

continued

EXHIBIT 2.2 (continued)
Metrics and Methods to Establish Quality Performance

Measure	Domain	Measure Title	Method of Data Submission	Pay for Performance Phase in R = Reporting P = Performance		
				Year 1	Year 2	Year 3
20	Preventive Health	Mammography Screening	GPRO Web Interface	R	R	P
21	Preventive Health	Proportion of Adults 18+ who had their Blood Pressure Measured within the preceding 2 years	GPRO Web Interface	R	R	P
22	At Risk Population–Diabetes	Diabetes Composite (All or Nothing Scoring): Hemoglobin A1c Control (<8%)	GPRO Web Interface	R	P	P
23	At Risk Population–Diabetes	Diabetes Composite (All or Nothing Scoring): Low Density Lipoprotein	GPRO Web Interface	R	P	P
24	At Risk Population–Diabetes	Diabetes Composite (All or Nothing Scoring): Blood Pressure < 140/90	GPRO Web Interface	R	P	P
25	At Risk Population–Diabetes	Diabetes Composite (All or Nothing Scoring): Tobacco Non Use	GPRO Web Interface	R	P	P
26	At Risk Population–Diabetes	Diabetes Composite (All or Nothing Scoring): Aspirin Use	GPRO Web Interface	R	P	P
27	At Risk Population–Diabetes	Diabetes Mellitus: Hemoglobin A1c Poor Control (>9 percent).	GPRO Web Interface	R	P	P
28	At Risk Population–Hypertension	Hypertension (HTN): Blood Pressure Control	GPRO Web Interface	R	P	P
29	At Risk Population–Ischemic Vascular Disease	Ischemic Vascular Disease (IVD): Complete Lipid Profile and LDL Control < 100 mg/dl	GPRO Web Interface	R	P	P
30	At Risk Population–Ischemic Vascular Disease	Ischemic Vascular Disease (IVD): Use of Aspirin or Another Antithrombotic	GPRO Web Interface	R	R	P
31	At Risk Population–Heart Failure	Heart Failure: Beta-blocker therapy for Left Ventricular Systolic Dysfunction (LVSD).	GPRO Web Interface	R	R	P
32	At Risk Population–Coronary Artery Disease	Coronary Artery Disease (CAD) Composite: All or Nothing Scoring: Drug Therapy for Lowering LDL Cholesterol	GPRO Web Interface	R	R	P
33	At Risk Population–Coronary Artery Disease	Coronary Artery Disease (CAD) Composite: All or Nothing Scoring: Angiotensin-Converting Enzyme (ACE) Inhibitor or Angiotensin Receptor Blocker (ARB) Therapy for Patients with CAD and Diabetes and/or Left Ventricular Systolic Dysfunction (LVSD)	GPRO Web Interface	R	R	P

Source: Medicare Program; Medicare Shared Savings Program: Accountable Care Organizations, Federal Register vol., 76, no. 212, November 2, 2011, pp. 67899–67890.

participants, provider/suppliers, and others that perform services for the ACO.[135] However, the ACO is not required to notify beneficiaries of its termination of participation, a provision that was included within the Final Rule to reduce administrative burdens on an ACO.[136] The rules regulating the termination of an ACO for noncompliance are set forth under § 425.216 of the MSSP.[137] Under this section, in lieu of full termination, CMS may opt to: (1) provide a warning to the noncompliant ACO, (2) request a corrective action plan (CAP) from the noncompliant ACO, or place the noncompliant ACO on a special monitoring plan.[138]

Reimbursement

Section 1899(d)(1)(A) of the SSA, as modified by §3022 of the ACA, provides that ACOs will be reimbursed under a fee-for-service (FFS) model as previously established for Medicare Part A and Part B.[139] However, providers in an ACO have some discretion as to the method of disbursement for incentive bonuses, i.e., shared savings payments, based on the amount of risk they choose to assume.[140] Under the MSSP, participating physicians will receive bonuses for achieving resource use and quality targets over the course of a year, as well as being subject to penalties, i.e., shared losses, for failing to meet these requirements.[141] The Final Rule sets out two risk models for ACOs to receive share savings payments or pay shared losses: the one-sided risk model and the two-sided risk model. These two models are discussed further below.

Shared Savings Payments

Based on comments received on the Proposed Rule regarding the uncertainty and insufficiency of potential shared savings payments, the Final Rule set forth a more financially attractive program to encourage broader participation by small- and medium-sized entities. As mentioned above, in order to receive shared savings payments, an ACO must achieve quality and performance standards (described above in Quality and Other Reporting Requirements), as well as demonstrate that the ACO has "achieved savings against a benchmark of expected average per capita Medicare FFS expenditures."[142] An illustration of the various scenarios resulting in shared savings or losses for both the one-sided and the two-sided distribution models is set forth in Figure 2.4 and Figure 2.5.

Calculating Shared Savings

Shared savings payments are determined by calculating: (1) a CMS established benchmark that estimates the total expenditures for the assigned Medicare beneficiary population, and (2) the actual annual Medicare beneficiary expenditures for the assigned Medicare beneficiary population. Section §425.602 of the Final Rule establishes the methodology that CMS uses to establish this benchmark based on previous Medicare beneficiary expenditures, defined as "... expenditures of beneficiaries who would have been assigned to the ACO in any of the three years prior to the start of an ACO's agreement period."[143]

In order to receive the shared savings, an ACO's actual annual Medicare beneficiary expenditure must be below the applicable benchmark. However, §425.602 of the MSSP allows for expenditures to be risk adjusted based on characteristics, chosen at the discretion of the secretary of HHS, of the assigned beneficiary population.[144] The following groups of patients within an assigned beneficiary population will result in a risk adjustment for the ACO:

1. End stage renal disease
2. Disabled
3. Aged/dual eligible Medicare and Medicaid beneficiaries
4. Aged/nondual eligible Medicare and Medicaid[145]

The Final Rule, §425.602, also requires CMS to "risk adjust an ACO's historical benchmark expenditures using the CMS-HCC [CMS-Hierarchical Condition Category] model," as a means of risk adjusting the benchmark to which actual annual Medicare beneficiary expenditures are compared.[146]

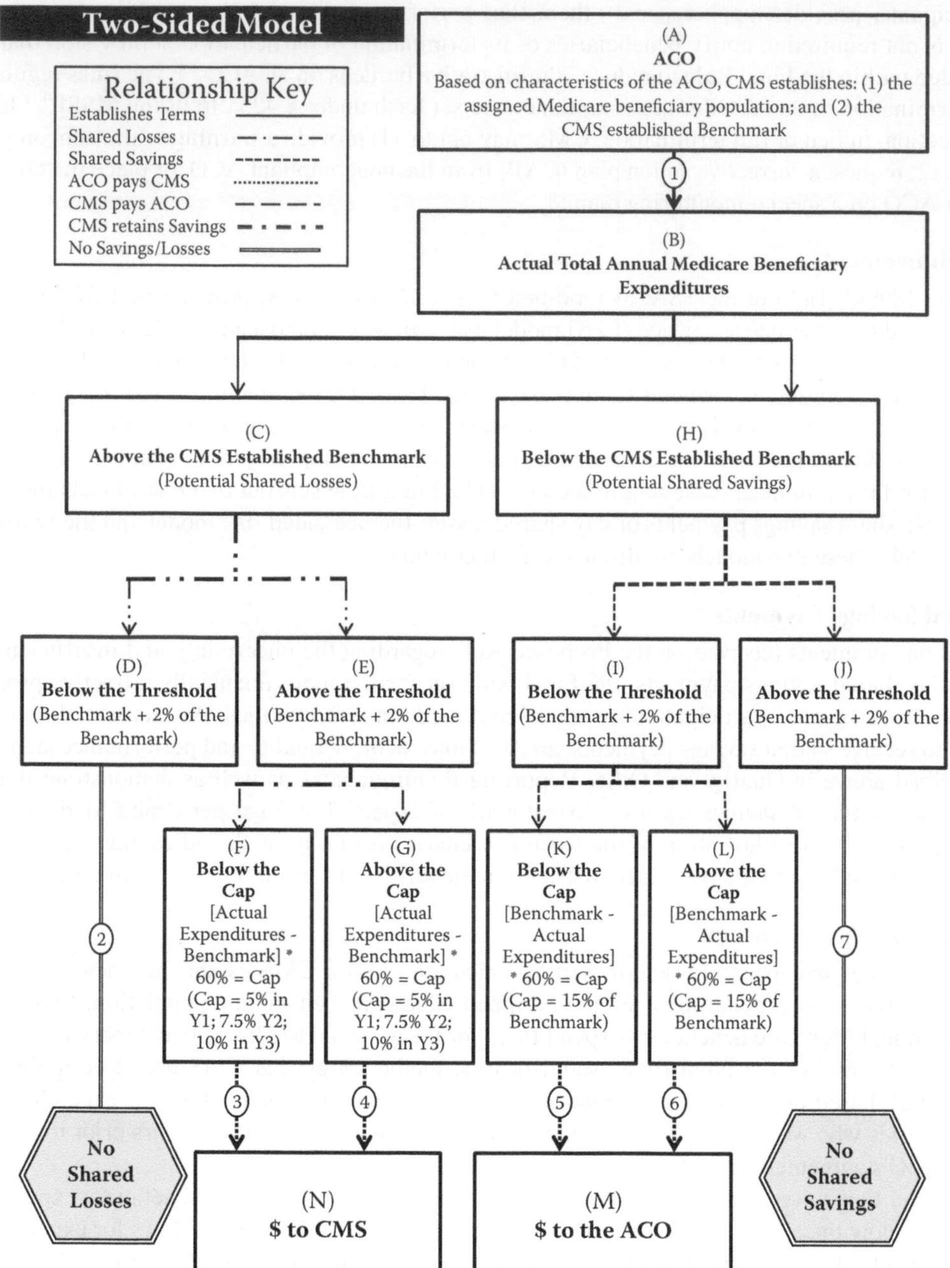

FIGURE 2.4 Relationship between an ACO and CMS resulting in shared savings or shared losses under the two-sided model.

Additionally, the Final Rule removes from the benchmark calculation any Indirect Medical Education (IME) and Disproportionate Share Hospital (DSH) payment adjustments used to compensate hospitals for patient care costs incurred from teaching activities and the treatment of low income populations.[147] These payments are not included in order to allay concerns regarding the nonparticipation by academic facilities and rural facilities.[148]

To receive shared savings payments, ACOs must reduce Medicare patient expenditures to a level below a threshold percentage amount of the prescribed CMS established benchmark.[149] Although an

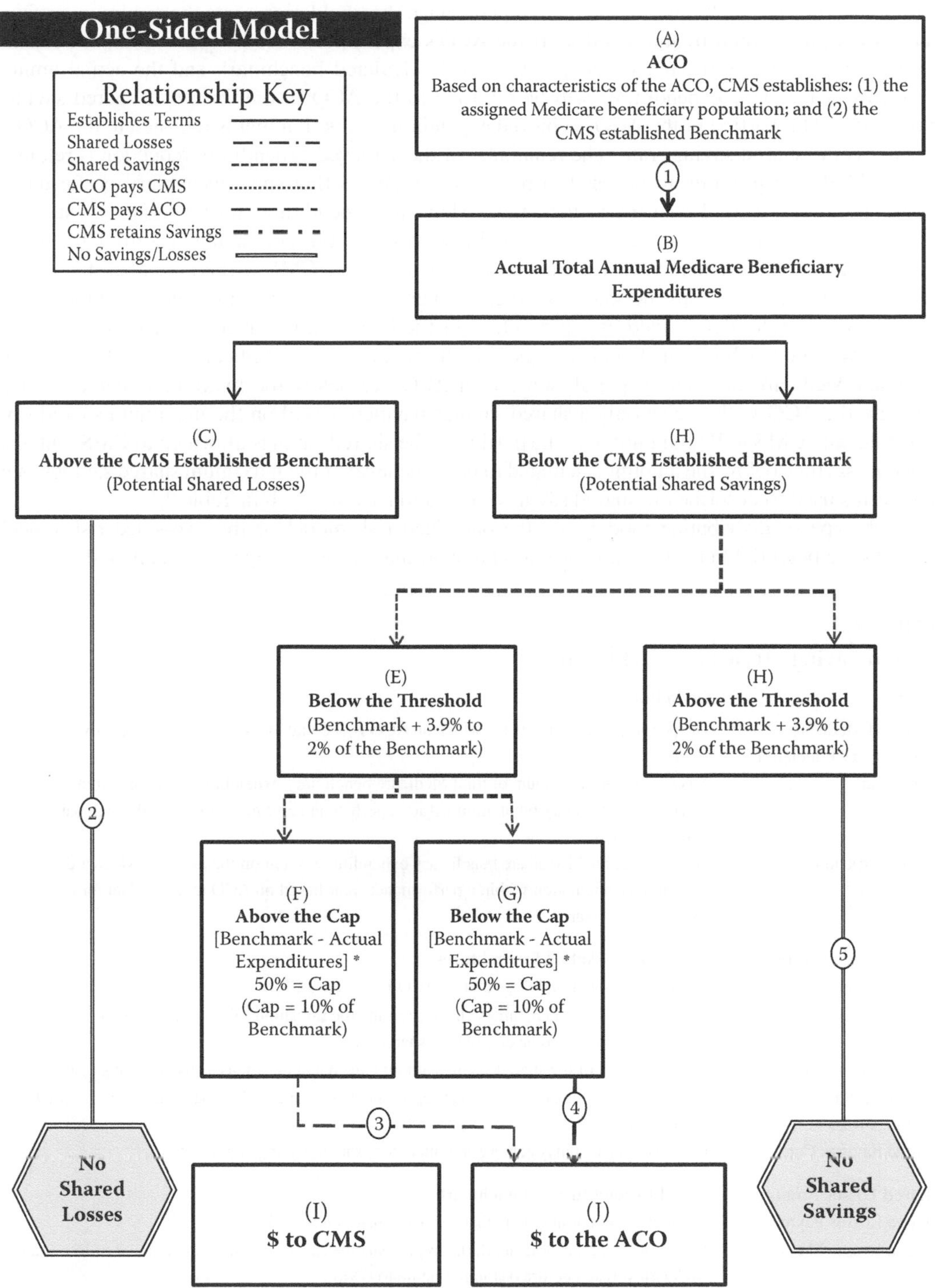

FIGURE 2.5 Relationship between an ACO and CMS resulting in shared savings under the one-sided model.

ACO that achieves sufficient expenditure reductions will receive a shared savings payment based on the first dollar under the CMS established benchmark, the ACO is only eligible for shared savings if their expenditures reach this threshold. This percentage threshold represents the minimum savings rate (MSR), as defined by the MSSP.[150] If the ACO's expenditures are below the MSR threshold, then a portion of the difference between the CMS calculated benchmark and the actual annual Medicare beneficiary expenditures will be returned to the ACO in the form of a shared savings payment.[151] The portion of the ACOs achieved expenditure reduction that is returned to the ACO is known as the shared savings rate. The remainder of the achieved expenditure reduction is retained by the Medicare program to be used to reward those ACOs that show exemplary performance under the rule.[152] Note that, if the actual annual Medicare expenditures for the assigned Medicare beneficiary population for an ACO are below the benchmark, but not enough to satisfy the MSR, the ACO is not eligible to receive a shared savings payment, and CMS will retain all cost savings.

The Final Rule also caps the shared savings payments that an ACO can achieve at a maximum shared savings rate, determined as a percentage of the benchmark that represents the maximum that an ACO may achieve in shared savings.[153] If the actual annual Medicare expenditures for the assigned Medicare beneficiary population for an ACO are below the maximum shared savings amount, the ACO will receive only a shared savings payment based on the maximum shared savings rate, and CMS will retain not only the portion of the shared savings allocated to CMS, but also any cost savings below the amount calculated to be at the level of the maximum shared savings rate. The terms used to describe the shared savings calculation are set forth in Table 2.5.

Each type of distribution model, i.e., the one-sided risk model or the two-sided risk model, changes the potential benefits (shared savings amount) that an ACO may achieve, and risks (shared

TABLE 2.5
Shared Savings Terms and Definitions

Term	Definition
Assigned Medicare Beneficiary Population	The population of patients for which an ACO is accountable as assigned prospectively by CMS.
Benchmark	An estimate of the amount of total Medicare beneficiary expenditures for the assigned Medicare beneficiary population within a performance year, set by CMS through past Medicare data.
Actual Expenditures	The actual annual Medicare beneficiary expenditures spent on the assigned Medicare beneficiary population within a performance year based on ACO reported data for a performance year.
Shared Savings Amount	**Benchmark—Actual Expenditures**
Shared Savings Payment	The actual amount in dollars that an ACO is given by CMS.
Minimum Savings Rate (MSR)	A percentage of the benchmark that represents the threshold minimum amount of savings an ACO must achieve to be eligible for shared savings.
Shared Savings Rate	The proportion of the shared savings amount an ACO is given as a shared savings payment.
Maximum Shared Savings Rate	A percentage of the benchmark that represents the most an ACO may achieve as a shared savings payment.
Shared Savings Cap	The most an ACO may achieve in dollars as a shared savings payment.
Shared Losses Amount	**Actual Expenditures—Benchmark**
Shared Losses Payment	The actual amount in dollars that an ACO must pay to CMS.
Shared Losses Threshold	A percentage of the benchmark that represents the threshold minimum amount of losses an ACO must reach before becoming liable to CMS.
Shared Losses Cap	The most an ACO must pay to CMS.

Source: Endnote 154.

losses) that an ACO may incur. Generally the one-sided model provides lower risks, and lower rewards, while the two-sided model provides higher risks and higher rewards. These risk factors are varied based on the model chosen in that each respective model is afforded a different defined percentage for each of the following: the MSR, the shared savings rate, and maximum shared savings rate.

Factoid 2.8

Track 1 is a shared savings only model that may be appropriate for entities that are new ACOs, whereas Track 2 is an option that may be more attractive for more experienced ACOs "willing and able to take on performance-based risk in exchange for higher reward." (Source: Medicare Program; Medicare Shared Savings Program: Accountable Care Organizations. *Federal Registry* vol. 76 no. 212, November 2, 2011, pg. 67907.)

One-Sided Risk Model—The one-sided model is a "shared savings only" model in that ACOs are not exposed to potential risk (i.e., shared losses) if actual annual Medicare beneficiary expenditures are above the CMS established benchmark. Therefore, the one-sided model may be most appropriate for entities that are smaller and less mature in terms of their level of integration and coordination of care. Section 425.604 of the MSSP provides for the calculation of shared savings under the one-sided model.[155] As mentioned above, an ACO will only receive shared savings payments if they achieve a level of actual annual Medicare beneficiary expenditures that is below the CMS established benchmark, as adjusted by the MSR.

Key Term	Definition	Citation
One-Sided Risk Model	Savings determination is calculated on whether the ACO's expenditures from the performance are below the benchmark determined by § 425.602.	Medicare Program; Medicare Shared Savings Program: Accountable Care Organizations. *Federal Register* vol. 76 no. 212, (November 2, 2011), p. 67986.

The one-sided model utilizes a sliding scale, based on the size of the ACO's assigned Medicare beneficiary population, to determine the MSR for each specific ACO.[156] Under the one-sided model, the MSR ranges from 3.9% for small ACOs to 2% for large ACOs. Therefore, a small ACO must achieve actual annual Medicare beneficiary expenditures below the CMS established benchmark minus 3.9% of the benchmark to be eligible for shared savings. An identical calculation would be applied to ACOs of any size, substituting the given MSR that is defined by the MSSP by the number of beneficiaries included in their specific assigned Medicare beneficiary population.

An ACO's shared savings payment is determined as a percentage (i.e., the shared savings rate) of the total amount of actual annual Medicare beneficiary expenditures below the CMS established benchmark (benchmark—actual expenditures), assuming the MSR threshold has been reached. In exchange for the lower risk associated with the one-sided model, the potential incentive payments are lower than could be achieved by an ACO under the two-sided model (discussed in the next section). Under the one-sided model, an ACO that meets all threshold and quality requirements will receive 50% of the total shared savings amount. ACOs under the one-sided model also are limited in the total amount of shared savings they can receive. The MSSP caps one-sided shared savings payment distributions at 10% of the CMS established benchmark. Optimally, under the one-sided model, the 10% maximum shared savings rate would equal an ACO's 50% shared savings proportion. CMS retains any portion of the ACO's 50% shared savings payments that is over the 10% cap, creating a disincentive to achieve any cost reductions over this amount. While the two-sided model has similar caps and thresholds, it allows ACOs to experience greater shared shavings payments.

Two-Sided Risk Model—The two-sided model may be more attractive for more experienced ACOs that are willing to take on higher risks for potentially higher rewards. Section 425.606 of the MSSP provides for the calculation of shared savings under the two-sided model.[157] The two-sided model uses a flat 2% threshold requirement for the MSR, in contrast to the sliding scale utilized under the one-sided model.[158] The flat MSR is equal to the one-sided rate set for large ACOs, because the two-sided model caters to those ACOs more able to avoid potential shared losses (i.e., larger organizations). ACOs under the two-sided model are allowed a larger percentage of the shared savings amount, with a shared savings rate of 60% for an ACO that achieves the quality requirements, but with a shared savings payment cap equal to 15% of the CMS established benchmark.[159] In contrast to the one-sided model, which does not subject an ACO to the responsibility for shared losses, an ACO under the two-sided model, in exchange for greater possible shared savings payments, also are responsible for their portion of any shared losses resulting from actual annual Medicare beneficiary expenditures in excess of the CMS established benchmark, assuming the 2% threshold is surpassed.

Key Term	Definition	Citation
Two-Sided Risk Model	Each performance year, CMS will determine whether the ACO's expenditures are above or below the appropriate benchmark previously calculated under §425.602. In order to receive savings payments or be responsible for losses, the expenditures must be above (to receive shared payment) or below (to share in losses) by at least the minimum savings or loss rate.	Medicare Program; Medicare Shared Savings Program: Accountable Care Organizations. *Federal Register* vol. 76 no. 212, (November 2, 2011), p. 67986.

The calculations for shared losses mirror that for shared savings under the two-sided model. An ACO, whose actual annual Medicare beneficiary expenditures exceed their CMS established benchmark, will be responsible for paying 60% of the total overage to CMS.[160] Although the amount an ACO is liable for is based on all expenditures from the first dollar over the CMS established benchmark, the 2% MSR threshold is applied to shared losses as well. Therefore, the actual annual Medicare beneficiary expenditures associated with an ACOs assigned Medicare population must be an amount that is 102% (or more) above the benchmark before they become liable to CMS for any shared losses. The total amount an ACO may have to pay to CMS also is capped. In contrast, to shared savings under the two-sided model, the cap for shared losses is phased in, whereby an ACO is gradually exposed to risk over the course of its initial three-year contract: 5% of the CMS established benchmark in the first performance year, 7.5% in the second performance year, and 10% in the third and any subsequent performance year.[161] Within the three-year initial contract, ACOs also have an additional safety net provision under §425.202(a), whereby an ACO that experiences a net loss may resubmit, for the consideration of CMS, expenditure data identifying any events that may have resulted in the net loss and demonstrating that procedures have been put in place to prevent further poor performance.

Initially, the MSSP allows ACOs to choose which distribution model is best suited to their organization; however, following the initial three-year contract, all ACOs must operate under the two-sided model. In light of this requirement, an organization that chooses to continue as a federal ACO after the initial contract must be able to accommodate some level of shared risk.

SUBSEQUENT ACO MODELS UNDER DEVELOPMENT

In order to attract more providers to participate in the ACO model, the Centers for Medicare and Medicaid Innovation (CMI) created three alternative inducement programs as extensions of the basic MSSP:[162] the Pioneer ACO Model, the Advanced Payment ACO Initiative, and the Accelerated Development Learning Series. Each of these three programs is described below.

Key Concept	Definition	Citation
Subsequent ACO Models under Development	In order to help attract more providers to participate in the ACO model, the Centers for Medicare and Medicaid Innovation (CMI) created several extensions of the ACO Medicare Shared Savings Program (MSSP). These three extensions include the Pioneer ACO Model, the Advanced Payment ACO Initiative, and the Accelerated Development Learning Series.	Medicare ACO Options Added After Criticism. Charles Fiegl, *American Medical News,* May 30, 2011. Online at: http://www.ama-assn.org/amednews/2011/05/30/gv110530.htm (Accessed 7/15/11).

Pioneer ACO Model

The Pioneer ACO Model is intended for "mature ACO"[163] organizations that have already begun coordinating care efforts.[164] Paralleling the traditional MSSP ACO model, the Pioneer Model is designed to incentivize the reduction of healthcare expenditures and increased quality outcomes.[165] Though the Pioneer Model is separate and distinct from the MSSP model, the two programs are designed to work cooperatively and be complementary.[166] Some primary differences between the structures of the Pioneer Model program and the MSSP are set forth in Table 2.6.[167]

The Pioneer ACO Model program consists of 32 healthcare institutions,[169] including: integrated delivery systems, medical group practices, independent practice associations, and partnerships of healthcare systems.[170] HHS estimates that the Pioneer ACO Model participants could save up to $1.1 billion over five years through better, more coordinated care for Medicare beneficiaries.[171] The participants of the Pioneer ACO Model are seen in Exhibit 2.3.

In allowing for flexibility to meet the differing organizational needs of the various Pioneer ACO Model program participants, CMI created several payment options to be utilized within the program.[172] The options for the core payment arrangement available to Pioneer ACO Model participants are shown in Table 2.7.[173]

In addition to flexibility within the core payment arrangement, after the first two years of its contract term with CMS, Pioneer ACO Model participants are given the option to transition from a volume-based FFS reimbursement model to a population-based payment model for their Medicare beneficiaries. Further, by performance year two, at least 50% of a Pioneer ACO Model participant's revenue must be generated by alternative Value Based Purchasing (VBP) arrangements with non-Medicare payors (either commercial or public).[175] By the end of their second performance year,

TABLE 2.6
Pioneer ACO Model versus MSSP ACO Model: Program Structure

Measure	MSSP ACO Model	Pioneer ACO Model
Contract length	3 year	3 to 5 years
Minimum patients	5,000	15,000[a]
Initial start date	January 1, 2012	January 1, 2012
Application due date	April 1 and July 1, 2011 (then rolling admissions)	Aug. 19, 2011
Number of participants	116	32
Quality measures	33	33
Projected Medicare savings	$940 million	$430 million

Source: Endnote 168.

[a] Pioneer ACOs with a majority of physicians in rural areas need a minimum of 5,000 patients.

EXHIBIT 2.3
Pioneer ACO Model Participants

Name	Institution Type	Description	Service Area
Allina Hospitals & Clinics	Integrated Delivery System	11 hospitals, 90 clinics and specialty care centers	Minnesota and Western Wisconsin
Atrius Health Services	Medical Group Practice	1,000 physicians and over 1,425 other healthcare professionals	Eastern and Central Massachusetts
Banner Health Network	Integrated Delivery System	13 acute-care hospitals	Phoenix, Arizona Metropolitan Area (Maricopa and Pinal Counties)
Bellin-ThedaCare Healthcare Partners	Integrated Delivery System	8 healthcare facilities and nearly 700 physicians	Northeast Wisconsin
Beth Israel Deaconess Physician Organization	Network of Independent Practice Associations	Over 1,600 physicians, over 125 primary care locations	Eastern Massachusetts
Bronx Accountable Healthcare Network (BAHN)	Partnership of integrated delivery system and independent practice association	4 hospitals, 22 primary care sites, and home care agency	New York City (the Bronx) and lower Westchester County, NY
Brown & Toland Physicians	Independent Practice Association	Over 1,500 physicians serving over 335,000 HMO and PPO patients	San Francisco Bay Area, CA
Dartmouth-Hitchcock ACO	Integrated Delivery System	Composed of a hospital and clinic	New Hampshire and Eastern Vermont
Eastern Maine Healthcare System	Integrated Delivery System	Nearly 8,000 employees, 7 member hospitals, 3 affiliated hospitals, number of other organizations	Central, Eastern, and Northern Maine
Fairview Health Systems	Integrated Delivery System	Over 40 primary care clinics, 7 hospitals, additional services	Minneapolis, MN Metropolitan Area
Franciscan Health System	Integrated Delivery System	14 hospitals	Indianapolis and Central Indiana
Genesys PHO	Partnership of hospital system and medical practices	160 primary care physicians, 400 specialist physicians	Southeastern Michigan
Healthcare Partners Medical Group	Independent Practice Association	Over 1,200 physicians in 900 locations	Los Angeles and Orange Counties, CA
Healthcare Partners of Nevada	Independent Practice Association	Over 203 primary care physicians in 102 locations with over 1,700 specialists	Clark and Nye Counties, NV
Heritage California ACO	Independent Practice Association	2,300 primary care physicians, 30,000 specialists, over 100 hospitals	Southern, Central, and Coastal California
JSA Medical Group, a division of HealthCare Partners	Independent Practice Association	184 primary care physicians in 96 locations	Orlando, Tampa Bay, and surrounding South Florida
Michigan Pioneer ACO	Partnership of hospital system and medical practices	Partnership of The Detroit Medical Center and its physicians	Southeastern Michigan

EXHIBIT 2.3 (continued)
Pioneer ACO Model Participants

Name	Institution Type	Description	Service Area
Monarch Healthcare	Independent Practice Association	Over 2,300 independent, private-practice physicians	Orange County, CA
Mount Auburn Cambridge Independent Practice Association (MACIPA)	Independent Practice Association	Over 500 physicians	Eastern Massachusetts
North Texas Specialty Physicians	Partnership of health system and Independent Physician Association	Nearly 600 family and specialty doctors, 24 acute-care hospitals	Tarrant, Johnson, and Parker counties in North Texas
OSF Healthcare System	Integrated Delivery System	Over 650 member physicians in 90 locations	Central Illinois
Park Nicollet Health Services	Integrated Delivery System	Over 1,000 physicians	Minneapolis, MN Metropolitan Area
Partners Healthcare	Integrated Delivery System	2 academic medical centers, community and specialty hospitals, physicians network, other services	Eastern Massachusetts
Physician Health Partners	Network of Independent Practice Associations	Over 260 primary care physicians	Denver, CO Metropolitan Area
Presbyterian Healthcare Services—Central New Mexico Pioneer Accountable Care Organization	Integrated Delivery System	3 acute-care hospitals with over 600 licensed beds	Central New Mexico
Primecare Medical Network	Medical Groups and Independent Practice Associations`	Over 200 primary care providers, 1,000 specialists	Southern California (San Bernadino and Riverside Counties)
Renaissance Medical Management Company	Independent Practice Association	IPA owned and managed by primary care physicians	Southeastern Pennsylvania
Seton Health Alliance	Partnership of hospital system and medical practices	13 hospitals, 21 primary and specialty care outpatient clinics,	Central Texas (11 county area, including Austin)
Sharp Healthcare System	Integrated Delivery System	Serving nearly 33,000 Medicare beneficiaries in San Diego County	San Diego County
Steward Health Care System	Integrated Delivery System	Over 16,000 employees serving over 1 million patients annually	Eastern Massachusetts
TriHealth, Inc.	Integrated Delivery System	Acute-care hospital, community health center, rural health clinics, medical group, home health agency	Northwest Central Iowa
University of Michigan	Integrated Delivery System	Over 1,600 faculty physicians, 40 U-M health centers	Southeastern Michigan

Source: Pioneer Accountable Care Organization Model: General Fact Sheet, Center for Medicare and Medicaid Services, December 19, 2011.

TABLE 2.7
Optional Variations on the Core Payment Arrangement Available to Pioneer ACO Model Participants

Arrangement/Option	Performance Period 1	Performance Period 2	Performance Periods 3, 4, and 5
Core Arrangement, OR	Up to 60% shared savings Shared losses 10% maximum	Up to 70% shared savings Shared losses 15% maximum	Population-based payment Up to 70% shared savings Shared losses 15% maximum
Option A, OR	Up to 50% shared savings Shared losses 5% maximum	Up to 60% shared savings Shared losses 10% maximum	Population-based payment as in Core Payment Arrangement
Option B	Up to 70% shared savings Shared losses 15% maximum	Up to 75% shared savings Shared losses 15% maximum	Population-based payment Up to 75% shared savings Shared losses 15% maximum

Source: Endnote 174.

the VBP models within Pioneer ACO Models may more closely resemble some of the reimbursement models utilized within the commercial ACO market than those VBP models used in traditional federal ACOs.

In order to participate in the Pioneer ACO Model, an organization must have submitted a letter of intent to participate by June 30, 2011.[176] The Pioneer ACO Model participants are comparable to those eligible for MSSP participation, with two significant differences: Federally Qualified Health Centers (FQHC) are eligible for participation, and there is a deviation in the definition of the term *hospital*, whereby, some non-Prospective Payment System (PPS) hospitals may participate, e.g., specific pediatric hospitals, cancer hospitals, and critical access hospitals.[177]

Advanced Payment ACO Model Initiative

The Advanced Payment ACO Model is designed to encourage healthcare providers to create ACOs and participate in the MSSP. As the name suggests, the Advanced Payment Model (APM) provides certain participating ACOs with advanced payments of the potential shared savings they may achieve in the future. Advanced payments are designed to facilitate the development and the initial establishment of each participant's ACO, and provide the necessary capital to make investments for coordinating care.[178] The purpose of the APM is two-fold: (1) to test whether the program's system of advance payments will increase participation in the MSSP,[179] and (2) to test whether advance payments will improve the quality of care and increase the amount of, and speed at which, ACOs achieve shared savings.[180]

Participation in the APM is available to only a select few participants of the MSSP. In order to be eligible for the APM, an ACO must be classified in one of the following categories: (1) large organizations with limited risk of not repaying the money, i.e., ACO does not include inpatient facilities that have less than $50 million in total revenue annually; or (2) small organizations that may present significant risk, but that CMS wishes to incentivize to participate in the MSSP to improve patient access, i.e., the ACO's inpatient facilities are for critical access hospitals and/or Medicare low-volume, rural hospitals and have less than $80 million in total annual revenue.[181] ACOs between these two classifications are not eligible to participate in the APM.

Those ACOs that are chosen to participate in the APM choose between one of three options to receive advanced payments, dependent upon the size of the ACO:

1. A fixed up-front payment
2. An up-front payment that varies year-to-year based on the number of historically assigned beneficiaries
3. Two payments, in two monthly installments

Participating ACOs must enter into a contract with CMS that details their repayment obligations. The program is designed so that these payments will be recouped by CMS from the shared savings that the participant would have otherwise received. If the participating ACO does not achieve sufficient shared savings to cover their debt to CMS, CMS will continue to offset shared savings payments or pursue recoupment by other means. Each round of ACO applications is accompanied by an application timeline to participate in the APM.[182]

Factoid 2.9

The Advanced Payment ACO Model is intended to encourage healthcare providers to create ACOs, participate in the MSSP, and allow participants to build up their ACOs and provide the necessary capital to make necessary investments for coordinating care. (Source: *Advanced Payment Model—OFR*. Department of Health and Human Services, 2011. Online at: http://www.ofr.gov/OFRUpload/OFRData/2011-27458_PI.pdf (Accessed 10/26/11).)

Accelerated Development Learning Sessions

To encourage ACO formation, CMI developed a series of ACO Accelerated Development Learning Sessions (ADLS). The ADLS provided lessons for MSSP participants on establishing and implementing core functions of an ACO in order to improve quality while maintaining lower costs. The material was presented by senior members of already established ACOs.[183] These programs were available to both existing and newly formed ACOs, and consisted of four components: (1) presession planning; (2) a main session, in which the ADLS faculty member and MSSP participant identify the goals and challenges of forming the participant's ACO; (3) postsession webinars presenting additional information and guidance; and (4) implementation tracking.

The main sessions were designed for attendance by two to four senior leaders who were in the process of forming ACOs, including leaders with financial/management responsibility and clinical responsibilities. Both the session and postsession webinars provide follow-up support to improve healthcare delivery by increasing quality and reducing costs, effectively use health information technology (HIT), and develop strategies for dealing with performance-based financial risk. Further, participants received resources and toolkits to assist them in implementing their ACO.[184] It is unclear whether this type of learning session will be repeated by CMS.

PROPOSALS FOR STATE PAYORS: MEDICAID ACOS

The federal Medicaid program is a joint venture between states and the federal government to provide healthcare to low income individuals and dual-eligibles[185] in the Medicare and Medicaid programs. As the largest payor for long-term care in the United States, the Medicaid program could benefit from the coordinated care efforts and cost containment program designs that exist in the MSSP.

Even though the federal government currently provides relatively few incentives to adopt an ACO model into the Medicaid program, some states have passed legislation for Medicaid savings based on the ACO archetype. In March 2011, the New Jersey state legislature passed a bill to create

TABLE 2.8
State Medicaid ACO Programs

State	Program	Date Enacted
Colorado	Accountable Care Collaborative	Spring 2011
Oregon	Coordinated Care Organizations	June 2011
Maine	MaineCare Accountable Communities Initiative	January 2010
Minnesota	The Minnesota Accountable Health Model	August 2012
New Jersey	Medicaid ACO Demonstration Project	August 2011
Utah	Early Stages	
Massachusetts	Early Stages	
Texas	Early Stages	
Vermont	Early Stages	

Source: Endnote 192.

"demonstration projects" focused on Medicaid ACOs over three years.[186] The New Jersey legislature's stated intent was to increase access, improve quality, and provide more cost-efficient care to state Medicaid recipients.[187] The new law's objective was to achieve these goals without impacting Medicaid availability for patients or access to Medicaid reimbursement for providers.[188] The New Jersey Medicaid ACO Demonstration Project facilitates and incentivizes participation through a gainsharing model that provides incentive payments for cost savings achieved. To date, it has yet to be seen whether the program will prove to be successful.[189]

As of March 2011, there were 49 bills in 21 states relating to ACOs. These new state laws address issues including the study of ACOs, Medicaid participation, a retreat from FFS payment systems, and other payment issues.[190] Glen Stream, president of the American Academy of Family Physicians (AAFP), categorizes the state attempts into two categories: (1) "introducing enabling legislation for ACOs at the state level" and (2) "looking for cost savings from ACOs."[191] However, as of October 2012, only five states had established Medicaid ACO programs, with four others being in the early stages of implementation, all of which are seen in Table 2.8: State Medicaid ACO Programs.

INDUSTRY FEEDBACK AND AGENCY RESPONSE

CMS issued several requests for feedback on the MSSP Proposed Rule and received over 1,300 public comments from various healthcare industry stakeholders.[193] Based on these comments, CMS made "significant modifications to reduce [the] burden and cost for participating ACOs," and outlined 13 changes to the Proposed Rule, discussed above.[194] The overall goal of CMS's proposed changes was to remove potential barriers to the formation of ACOs. After the publication of the Final Rule, industry stakeholders again released comments on that Final Rule. However, in comparison to the comments submitted following publication of the Proposed Rule, the central theme of the new comments submitted following publication of the Final Rule were significant expressions of appreciation for the changes made by CMS, accompanied by expressions of continued cautiousness regarding uncertainty as to the probability for success of the program. Several of the more notable items of industry and stakeholder feedback are discussed below.

American Hospital Association (AHA)

Initially, the American Hospital Association (AHA) expressed several concerns with the CMS Proposed Rule, regarding flexibility, management structure,[195] and upfront costs.[196] The AHA found the changes made by CMS in response to public comments regarding the Proposed Rule to be promising, particularly with both the increased control given to potential ACO participants, as well as the increased coordination between federal agencies toward better care for patients.[197] Notably, the AHA praised the CMS decision to remove its original antitrust pre-approval requirement for every organization applying to form an ACO, calling the removal of this pre-approval regulatory burden "essential" for working toward the acceptance and more widespread adoption of the ACO model.[198] Although many of the AHA's initial concerns were resolved with the publication of the Final Report, the organization noted that some obstacles still exist, including already established legal and regulatory barriers to clinical integration within the healthcare system.[199]

American Medical Group Association (AMGA)

The American Medical Group Association's (AMGA) initial reaction to the ACO Proposed Rule noted the "overly prescriptive" nature of the proposal, and how it would make voluntary participation within the program unappealing.[200] Further, 93% of AMGA members stated they "would not enroll as an ACO under the current regulatory framework," and that substantial changes to the Final Rule were necessary to incentivize more providers to enroll as ACOs.[201] In its letter to CMS, the AMGA thanked CMS for acting on the public comments generated by the Proposed Rule.

American Medical Association (AMA)

The American Medical Association (AMA) applauded the CMS Final Rule, especially focusing on the financial incentives and the lowered risk for physicians interested in pursuing the ACO model. AMA President Peter M. Carmel commented that the Proposed Rule's financial risk discouraged physicians from pursuing ACO formation, but that the Final Rule "limits financial risk, which is important for practicing physicians".[202] Essentially, the CMS prepayment initiative allocates approximately $170 million for small physician practices and gives rural communities the chance to receive loans to help with the cost of undertaking ACO formation.[203] In addition to lowering financial risk, the AMA applauded CMS for removing the requirement that 50% of ACO primary care providers must "meaningfully use" electronic health records (EHR),[204] as well as lowering the number of quality measures for reporting from 65 to 33 measures.[205] The AMA also echoed other industry stakeholders in highlighting the removal by CMS of the pre-application antitrust screening for ACOs, which, they explained, "will significantly lower the administrative burden and cost for potential ACOs to comply with the antitrust rules." [206]

American Academy of Family Physicians (AAFP)

The American Academy of Family Physicians (AAFP) praised the CMS Final Rule, pointing to new initiatives that allow physicians greater flexibility to participate in Medicare ACOs and lower burdens that would be experienced by small practices. Like the AMA, the AAFP also referenced the reduction in quality measures, noting that these would "enable small- to medium-sized practices" to change internal "procedures and other functions over a manageable time frame."[207]

America's Health Insurance Plans (AHIP)

The health insurance industry trade group, America's Health Insurance Plans (AHIP), highlighted the benefit of potential financial incentives provided under the Final Rule, but also touched on lingering legal and reimbursement concerns. Unlike provider groups, AHIP presented a concern regarding the decision by CMS to divest the ACO "antitrust screening mechanism," citing its potential impact on increasing healthcare costs.[208] Eliminating antitrust screening, AHIP argued, would not dampen the market power of potentially powerful ACOs that would ultimately increase healthcare costs for both the consumer and competing healthcare organizations.[209] AHIP has urged both the Department of Justice (DOJ) and the Federal Trade Commission (FTC) to inquire into potential lingering antitrust issues embedded in the Final Rule.[210]

Physician Group Practice Demonstration Project Participants

The Physician Group Practice (PGP) Demonstration Project was a main contributor to the design of the Proposed Rule; however, of the various PGP participants, none stated that they would participate in the MSSP due to perceived insufficiencies within the Proposed Rule. All 10 PGP participants began the PGP Transition Demonstration project on January 1, 2011, which was designed to facilitate the PGP participants transition into either the MSSP or the Pioneer ACO Model. This transition is slated to end in December 2012,[211] at which time all 10 PGP participants will have the option of transitioning into the MSSP at the conclusion of the PGP Transition Demonstration.[212] Further, three PGP participants have chosen to forgo the Transition Demonstration and are already participating in the Federal Pioneer ACO Model.[213]

Medicare Payment Advisory Commission

In its response to the Proposed Rule, the Medicare Payment Advisory Commission (MedPAC) noted several desired changes for CMS to investigate prior to the release of the Final Rule in the fall of 2011. MedPAC noted six areas of the Proposed Rule that would be "crucial" to the success of the MSSP, including:

1. Prospective assignment for Medicare beneficiaries
2. Risk adjustment
3. Quality measures
4. Assessing benchmarks for operation
5. Inclusion of FQHCs and RHCs
6. Expanding the one-sided risk model and decreasing risk[214]

While MedPAC has consistently expressed general approval of the ACO concept, following publication of the Final Rule, they have expressly stated their support for the MSSP.[215]

CHAPTER SUMMARY

Federal ACOs are those governed by the Medicare Shared Savings Program (MSSP) and are defined as legal entities that are "recognized and authorized under applicable State, Federal, or Tribal Law, … identified by a Taxpayer Identification Number (TIN), and … formed by one or more ACO participant(s)." The MSSP, as introduced within the ACA, is one form of value-based purchasing, which offers rewards to providers for supplying high quality, efficient clinical care. The MSSP was expanded upon in the Proposed Rule, published by CMS on April 7, 2011. In response to negative feedback to that proposed rule, the Final Rule, published by CMS on November 2, 2011, expanded provider flexibility as well as the probability of reaching quality and cost targets when developing and operating an ACO.

Under the MSSP Final Rule, a Federal ACO's legal structure must provide both the basis for its shared governance, as well as the mechanism for it to receive and distribute shared savings payments to federal ACO participants and provider/suppliers. To be included in the MSSP, a federal ACO is required to detail its intent to be accountable for the healthcare needs and services of assigned Medicare beneficiaries in a formal application submitted to CMS. The requirement for beneficiary accountability entails accepting the responsibility and liability for the "quality, cost, and overall care of the Medicare fee-for-service beneficiaries assigned to the ACO." Once approved, ACOs sign a three-year initial contract with CMS.

The MSSP requires federal ACO participants to collect clinical information and quality data and submit this information to CMS throughout each performed year. CMS requires that federal ACOs meet the "established quality performance standards" for 33 quality metrics, or risk termination.[216] Further, the Final Rule requires the implementation of a "compliance plan" to be used as a means by which an employee, contractor or other federal ACO member may anonymously report suspected fraud or abuse to law enforcement.

For shared savings distributions, the MSSP provides one-sided and two-sided risk models for eligible federal ACO participants. The one-sided risk model is characterized by decreased risk (i.e., no shared losses in the initial ACO contract) and decreased reward (i.e., only eligible for 50% of shared savings). In contrast, the two-sided risk model has increased risk (i.e., potential payments to CMS for any losses) and increased reward (i.e., 60% of shared savings). Shared savings payments are determined by the amount of Medicare beneficiary expenditure reductions an ACO achieves, in comparison to established CMS benchmarks, calculated on a per beneficiary basis. Federal ACOs that fail to meet quality standards may experience lower than expected shared savings. Shared losses, under the two-sided model, are calculated as a percentage (60%) of the expenditures over the ACOs' established benchmark.

ENDNOTES

1. *Improving Incentives in the Medicare Program.* Medicare Payment Advisory Commission, June 2009, pg. 39-57; *Proposed Rule versus Final Rule for Accountable Care Organizations (ACOs) In the Medicare Shared Savings Program.* Centers for Medicare & Medicaid Services. Online at: https://www.cms.gov/ACO/Downloads/Appendix-ACO-Table.pdf (Accessed 12/28/11); Medicare Program; Medicare Shared Savings Program: Accountable Care Organizations. *Federal Register* vol. 76 no. 67 (April 7, 2011); Medicare Program: Medicare Shared Savings Program: Accountable Care Organizations. *Federal Register* vol. 76 no. 212, (November 2, 2011); Patient Protection and Affordable Care Act. 124 Stat. 119, March 23, 2010; *Pioneer Accountable Care Organization Model: General Fact Sheet.* Center for Medicare and Medicaid Services, December 19, 2011; *HHS Announces 89 New Accountable Care Organizations.* Health and Human Services, July 9, 2012. Online at: http://www.hhs.gov/news/press/2012pres/07/20120709a.html (Accessed 10/23/2012).
2. *Accountable Care Organizations.* David Glass and Jeff Stensland, MedPAC, (April 9, 2008), p. 4.
3. Vertical Integration and Organizational Networks in Healthcare. James Robinson and Lawrence Casalino, *Health Affairs*, vol. 15, no. 1, (1996).
4. *Lessons from Medicare's Demonstration Projects on Disease Management, Care Coordination and Value-based Payment.* Lyle Nelson, Congressional Budget Office, January 2012, p. 1.
5. Medicare Program; Medicare Shared Savings Program: Accountable Care Organizations. *Federal Register* vol. 76 no. 212, (November 2, 2011).
6. *Lessons from Medicare's Demonstration Projects on Disease Management, Care Coordination and Value-Based Payment*, p. 1. (The Medicare Participating Heart Bypass Center Demonstration utilized bundled payments for all inpatient hospital care for coronary artery bypass graft surgeries at seven hospitals to lower the amount spent on each patient.)
7. Ibid., p. 2.
8. Ibid.
9. *CMS Final Rule Implements $850 Million Hospital Value-Based Purchasing Program.* Nathaniel Weixel, Health Law Reporter, May 5, 2011. Online at: http://healthlawrc.bna.com/hlrc/display/batch_print_display.edp (Accessed 6/16/2011).
10. *Accountable Care Organizations: A Roadmap for Success: Guidance on First Steps*, 1st ed. Bruce Flareau and Joe Bohn, Virginia Beach, VA: Convergent Publishing, LLC, 2011, p. 22.
11. *Patient Protection and Affordable Care Act.* Public Law 111-148, (March 23, 2010)/ (42 U.S.C. 1395 et. seq.)
12. *Shared Savings Program.* 42.U.S.C. 1395jjj Sec 1899 (March 23, 2010); *Patient Protection and Affordable Care Act.* Public Law 111-148, (March 23, 2010).
13. *Patient Protection and Affordable Care Act*, p. 395.
14. Ibid., p.393.

15. *Affordable Care Act Gives Providers New Option to Better Coordinate Health Care.* Centers for Medicare and Medicaid Services. Online at: http://www.healthcare.gov/news/factsheets/accountablecare05172011a.html (Accessed 6/6/2011)
16. *Patient Protection and Affordable Care Act*, pp. 353, 372, 936. "Others" include: §3002—Improvements to the Physician Quality Reporting System; §3007—Value-Based Payment Modifier under the Physician Fee Schedule; §10326—Pilot Testing Pay-for-Performance Programs for Certain Medicare Providers; and §3022—Medicare Shared Savings Program.
17. The Cost of Confusion: Healthcare Reform and Value Based Purchasing. Trent Haywood, *Healthcare Financial Management*, vol. 64, no. 10, (October, 2010).
18. *Joint Principles of the Patient-Centered Medical Home.* American Academy of Family Physicians, American Academy of Pediatrics, American College of Physicians, and American Osteopathic Association, February 2007. Online at: http://www.aafp.org/online/etc/medialib/aafp_org/documents/policy/fed/jointprinciplespcmh0207.Par.0001.File.dat/022107medicalhome.pdf (Accessed 12/14/11).
19. Ibid.
20. *Medical Homes and Accountable Care Organizations: If We Build It, Will They Come*? Academy Health, 2009 Annual Research Meeting Brief. Online at: http://www.academyhealth.org/files/publications/RschInsightMedHomes.pdf (Accessed 1/4/12).
21. The Medicare Medical Home Demonstration Project, in *Tax Relief and Health Care Act of 2006*. Pub. L. 109-432, 120 STAT 2987, Section 204 (December 20, 2006).
23. Ibid.
24. Ibid.
25. Ibid.
26. *Medicare Demonstrations: Details for Medicare Medical Home Demonstration.* Centers for Medicare and Medicaid Services. Online at: https://www.cms.gov/DemoProjectsEvalRpts/MD/itemdetail.asp?itemID=CMS1199247, (Accessed 1/4/12).
27. Ibid.
28. *Fact Sheet: Comprehensive Primary Care Initiative.* U.S. Department of Health and Human Services, September 28, 2011. Online at: http://innovations.cms.gov/initiatives/cpci/index.html, (Accessed 1/4/12); *Comprehensive Primary Care Initiative.* Center for Medicare and Medicaid Innovation. Online at: http://www.innovations.cms.gov/initiatives/Comprehensive-Primary-Care-Initiative/index.html (Accessed 6/11/12).
29. *Fact Sheet: Comprehensive Primary Care Initiative.*
30. Ibid.
31. *FAQ: The CPC Initiative and Participation in Other CMS Initiatives.* Center for Medicare and Medicaid Innovation. Online at: http://www.innovations.cms.gov/Files/x/Comprehensive-Primary-Care-Initiative--Frequently-Asked-Questions.pdf (Accessed 11/5/2012).
32. *Fact Sheet: Medicare Federally Qualified Health Center Advanced Primary Care Practice.* U.S. Department of Health and Human Services, October 24, 2011, Online at: http://www.fachc.org/pdf/legislative/FQHC_Demo_Fact_Sheet_Oct_24_2011.pdf (Accessed 11/5/2012).
33. Ibid.
34. *Patient Protection and Affordable Care Act.* Public Law 111-148 (March 23, 2010), p. 676–677.
35. Ibid., p. 513.
36. Ibid.
37. Ibid.
38. Ibid., p. 156.
39. Center for Medicare and Medicaid Selects Michigan for Demonstration Project to Improve Patient Care. James McCurtis, *Community Health*, November 16, 2010. Online at: http://www.michigan.gov/mdch/0,1607,7-132-2939-247191—,00.html (Accessed 6/11/2012).
40. *Patient Protection and Affordable Care Act*, p. 649.
41. Ibid.
42. Opportunities and Challenges for Episode-Based Payment. Robert E. Mechanic, *The New England Journal of Medicine*, vol. 365, no. 9, September 1, 2011, p. 777. (Bundled payments fall under the umbrella of Episode-of-Care Payments, which refers to one reimbursement payment made to providers for at least a portion of the medical services provided within a particular course of treatment.)
43. *Patient Protection and Affordable Care Act*, pp. 399–403.
44. *Medicare Acute Care Episode Demonstration for Orthopedic and Cardiovascular Surgery.* Centers for Medicare and Medicaid Services, p. 1. Online at: http://www.cms.hhs.gov/DemoProjectsEvalRpts/downloads/ACE_web_page.pdf (Accessed 6/3/09).

45. *Patient Protection and Affordable Care Act*, p. 399.
46. Ibid., pp. 399–400.
47. Ibid., p 401.
48. *Summary of Proposed Rule Provisions for Accountable Care Organizations under the Medicare Shared Savings Program.* Centers for Medicare and Medicaid Services, Medicare Fact Sheet, March 31, 2011.
49. *Proposed Rule versus Final Rule for Accountable Care Organizations (ACOs) in the Medicare Shared Savings Program.* Centers for Medicare & Medicaid Services. Online at: https://www.cms.gov/ACO/Downloads/Appendix-ACO-Table.pdf (Accessed 12/28/11); Medicare Program; Medicare Shared Savings Program: Accountable Care Organizations. *Federal Register* vol. 76 no 67, (April 7, 2011); *Patient Protection and Affordable Care Act.* 124 Stat. 119, March 23, 2010.
50. Letter from AHA to CMS Regarding Medicare Program; Medicare Shared Savings Program; Accountable Care Organizations. Rick Pollack, American Hospital Association, June 1, 2011. Online at: http://www.aha.org/advocacy-issues/letter/2011/110601-cl-acoprprule.pdf, (Accessed 1/5/12).
51. Letter from AMA to CMI Regarding Advanced Payment Initiative for Accountable Care Organizations. Michael D. Maves, CEO American Medical Association, to Richard J. Gilfillan, Acting Director of Center for Medicare and Medicaid Innovation, June 16, 2011, p.1.
52. Letter from AHIP to CMS Regarding CMS-1345-P; Proposed Rule Regarding Medicare Program; Medicare Shared Savings Program: Accountable Care Organizations. Carmella Bocchino, Executive Vice President, Clinical Affairs & Senior Counsel Strategic Planning, to Donald M. Berwick, CMS Administrator, June 16, 2011, p. 6.
53. *Poster Boys Take a Pass on Pioneer ACO Program.* Jenny Gold, Kaiser Health News, September 14, 2011. Online at: http://www.kaiserhealthnews.org/Stories/2011/September/14/ACO-Pioneers-Medicare-hospitals.aspx, (Accessed 1/6/11).
54. Letter from PGP Demonstration Program to CMS. PGP Group Participants to Dr. Berwick, May 12, 2011.
55. Making Good on ACOs' Promises—The Final Rule for the Medicare Shared Savings Program. Donald M. Berwick, *The New England Journal of Medicine*, vol. 365 no. 19, November 10, 2011, p. 1755.
56. Medicare Program; Medicare Shared Saving Program: Accountable Care Organizations. *Federal Registrar*, vol. 76, no. 212 (November 2, 2011), p. 67804.
57. *Proposed Rule versus Final Rule for Accountable Care Organizations (ACOs) in the Medicare Shared Savings Program.* Centers for Medicare & Medicaid Services. Online at: https://www.cms.gov/ACO/Downloads/Appendix-ACO-Table.pdf (Accessed 12/28/11); Medicare Program; Medicare Shared Savings Program: Accountable Care Organizations. *Federal Register* vol. 76 no. 67 (April 7, 2011); Medicare Program: Medicare Shared Savings Program: Accountable Care Organizations. *Federal Register* vol. 76 no. 212, (November 2, 2011); *Patient Protection and Affordable Care Act.* 124 Stat. 119, March 23, 2010.
58. Medicare Program; Medicare Shared Saving Program: Accountable Care Organizations. *Federal Registrar*, vol. 76, no. 212 (November 2, 2011), p. 67804.
59. Ibid., pp. 67974–67978.
60. Ibid., p. 67974.
61. Ibid., p. 67975.
62. Ibid., p. 67974.
63. Ibid., p. 67978.
64. Ibid., p. 67974.
65. *Definitions Specific to Medicare.* 42 C.F.R. §400.202 (2010).
66. Ibid.
67. Medicare Program; Medicare Shared Savings Program: Accountable Care Organizations. p. 67974.
68. Ibid., p. 67812.
69. Ibid.
70. Ibid., pp. 67812–67813.
71. Medicare Program; Medicare Shared Savings Program: Accountable Care Organizations and Medicare Program: Waiver Designs in Connection with the Medicare Shared Savings Program and the Innovation Center; Proposed Rule and Notice. *Federal Register*, vol. 76, no. 67 (April 7, 2011), p. 19537; *Accountable Care Organizations: A Roadmap for Success: Guidance on First Steps.* Bruce Flareau and Joe Bohn, Virginia Beach, VA: Convergent Publishing, LLC, 2011, p. 45; *Primary Care.* American Academy of Family Physicians, 2012. Online at: http://www.aafp.org/online/en/home/policy/policies/p/primarycare.html#Parsys0003 (Accessed 1/24/2012). [Definition for Primary Care Physician Practices]; *Health Care Glossary.* Stoney Brook Medicine, 2012. Online at: http://stoneybrookmedicine.edu/patientcare/

healtheducation/glossary#i (Accessed 06/12/2012). [Definition for IPA]; *Cost Survey for Primary Care Practices: 2010 Report Based on 2009 Data.* Medical Group Management Association, 2009, p. 369. [Definition for MSPG]; *Integrated Delivery Network (IDN).* Glen McDaniel, GLG Research, Gerson Lehrman Group, Inc. 2011. Online at: http://www.glgresearch.com/Dictionary/HC-Integrated-Delivery-Network-(IDN).html (Accessed 1/24/2012). [Definition for IDN]; *Accountable Care Organizations: A Roadmap for Success: Guidance on First Steps*, 1st ed. Bruce Flareau and Joe Bohn, Virginia Beach, VA: Convergent Publishing, LLC, 2011, pp. 10, 45, 53. [Definition for CIN]; *The Advisor's Guide to Health Care: Professional Practices.* Robert James Cimasi, American Institute of Certified Public Accountants, Inc., New York, 2011, p. 477; Creating Accountable Care Organizations: The Extended Hospital Medical Staff. Elliot S. Fisher et al., *Health Affairs*, 2007. [Definition for Extended Hospital Medical Staff]; *Clinical Access Hospitals.* Centers for Medicare & Medicaid Services, Rural Health Fact Sheet Series, January 2012, p. 2. [Definition for CAH].

72. *Medicare Program; Medicare Shared Savings Program: Accountable Care Organizations*, p. 67812.
73. Ibid., p. 67814.
74. Ibid., p. 67812.
75. Ibid.
76. Ibid., p. 67814.
77. Ibid
78. Ibid.
79. Ibid.
80. Ibid., p. 67812.
81. Ibid., p. 67816.
82. Ibid., p. 67817.
83. Ibid., pp. 67819–67820.
84. Ibid.
85. Ibid., p. 67821.
86. Ibid., pp. 67816–67817.
87. Ibid., p. 67822.
88. Ibid.
89. Ibid.
90. Ibid., p. 67836.
91. *Fact Sheet: CMS Names 89 New Medicare Shared Savings Accountable Care Organizations.* CMS Office of Public Affairs, July 9, 2012. Online at: http://www.cms.gov/apps/media/press/factsheet.asp?Counter=4405&intNumPerPage=10&checkDate=&checkKey=&srchType=1&numDays=3%20500&srchOpt=0&srchData=&keywordType=All&chkNewsType=6&intPage=&showAll=&pYear=&year=&desc=&cboOrder=date (Accessed on 7/12/12).
92. *Shared Savings Program Application.* Centers for Medicare and Medicaid Services, August 8, 2012. Online at: http://www.cms.gov/Medicare/Medicare-Fee-for-Service-Payment/sharedsavingsprogram/Application.html (Accessed 10/22/2012).
93. *Medicare Shared Savings Program: Application Process and Overview of the Advance Payment Model Application.* Kelly Hall, CMS Innovation Center, Baltimore, MD.
94. *Medicare Program; Medicare Shared Savings Program: Accountable Care Organizations*, p. 67822.
95. Ibid., p. 67807.
96. Ibid., p. 67836.
97. Ibid.
98. Ibid.
99. Ibid.
100. Ibid., p. 67837.
101. Ibid.
102. Ibid.
103. Ibid., p. 67977.
104. Ibid., p. 67851.
105. Ibid.
106. Ibid., pp. 67862, 67867.
107. Prospective or Retrospective Beneficiary Assignments to Calculate Eligibility for Shared Savings. Lisa Han, Squire Sanders, April 3, 2011. Online at: http://www.accountablecareforum.com/payment-methodologies/how-prospective-and-retrospective-beneficiary-assignments-will-help-acos-to-calculate-eligibility-fo, (Accessed 6/11/2012).

108. Medicare Program; Medicare Shared Savings Program: Accountable Care Organizations, p. 67867.
109. Ibid.
110. Ibid., p. 67855.
111. Ibid., p. 67853.
112. Ibid., p. 67867.
113. Ibid., p. 67852.
114. Ibid.
115. Ibid.
116. Ibid., p. 67811.
117. Ibid.
118. Ibid., p. 67809.
119. Ibid., p. 67811.
120. Ibid.
121. Ibid., p. 67870.
122. Ibid., pp. 67899–90.
123. Chronic heart failure is currently the only major cardiovascular disorder that is continuing to increase in prevalence and incidence. This condition affects approximately 5 million people in the U.S., primarily the elderly. Cited in Preoperative Management of Chronic Heart Failure. Leanne Groban and John Butterworth, *International Anesthesia Research Society*, vol. 103, no. 3, September 2006. p. 557.
124. The Physician Quality Reporting System is a voluntary program instituted within the Medicare program that allows providers to submit quality outcomes data for certain medical conditions to CMS in exchange for potential financial incentives. *2012 Physician Quality Reporting System: Electronic Health Record (EHR) Reporting Made Simple*. Centers for Medicare and Medicaid Services, January 2012, p. 1.
125. *Accountable Care Organization 2012 Program Analysis: Quality Performance Standards Narrative Measure Specifications: Final Report*. RTI International, Quality Measurement & Health Assessment Group, Office of Clinical Standards & Quality, Centers for Medicare & Medicaid Services, Waltham, MA, December 12, 2011, p. 3.
126. Ibid., p. 2.
127. Ibid., p. 3.
128. Medicare Program; Medicare Shared Savings Program: Accountable Care Organizations, p. 67952.
129. Ibid., p. 67980.
130. Ibid.
131. Ibid.
132. Ibid., p. 67951.
133. Ibid., p. 67960.
134. Ibid., p. 67980.
135. Ibid., p. 67960.
136. Ibid.
137. Ibid., p. 67979.
138. Ibid., p. 67980.
139. Ibid., p. 67904.
140. *Accountable Care Organizations: A New Model for Sustainable Innovation*. Paul H. Keckley and Michelle Hoffman, Deloitte Center for Health Solutions, 2010, p. 11.
141. *Accountable Care Organizations*. David Glass and Jeff Stensland, MedPAC, April 9, 2008, p. 4.
142. Medicare Program; Medicare Shared Savings Program: Accountable Care Organizations, p. 67904.
143. Ibid., p. 67916.
144. Ibid., p. 67918.
145. Ibid., p. 67916.
146. Ibid., p. 67919.
147. Indirect Medical Education and Disproportionate Share Adjustments to Medicare Inpatient Payment Rates. Nguyen Xuan and Steven Sheingold, U.S. Department of Health and Human Services, *Medicare and Medicaid Research Review*, vol. 1, no. 4, 2011, p. E1.
148. Medicare Program; Medicare Shared Savings Program: Accountable Care Organizations, p. 67922.
149. Ibid., p. 67927.
150. Ibid.
151. Ibid.
152. Ibid.
153. Ibid., p. 67929.

154. Ibid., pp. 67916–67929.
155. Ibid., p. 67985.
156. Ibid., p. 67929.
157. Ibid., p. 67986.
158. Ibid., p. 67987.
159. Ibid.
160. Ibid.
161. Ibid.
162. Medicare ACO Options Added after Criticism. Charles Fiegl, *American Medical News*, May 30, 2011. Online at: http://www.ama-assn.org/amednews/2011/05/30/gv110530.htm (Accessed 7/15/11).
163. *Affordable Care Act Gives Providers New Options to Better Coordinate Health Care*. U.S. Department of Health and Human Services, May 17, 2011. Online at: http://www.healthcare.gov/news/factsheets/accountablecare05172011a.html (Accessed 7/15/11).
164. Ibid.
165. *CMS Announces ACO "Pioneer" Program and Advanced Payment Initiative*. Henry J. Kaiser Family Foundation, May 17, 2011. Online at: http://healthreform.kff.org/Scan/2011/May/CMS-Announces-ACO-Pioneer-Program-and-Advanced-Payment-Initiative.aspx (Accessed 7/15/11).
166. *Pioneer ACO Model*. Healthcare Financial Management Association, 2011. Online at: http://www.hfma.org/PioneerACOModel/ (Accessed 7/15/11).
167. Medicare ACO Options Added after Criticism, 2011; Pioneer ACO Deadline Extended. Margaret Dick Tocknell, *HealthLeaders Media*, June 10, 2011. Online at: http://www.healthleadersmedia.com/print/TEC-267205/Pioneer-ACO-Deadline-Extended (Accessed 7/15/11).
168. Medicare ACO Options Added after Criticism; Pioneer ACO Deadline Extended; *Pioneer ACO Model: Overview*. Center for Medicare and Medicaid Innovation. Online at: http://innovations.cms.gov/initiatives/aco/pioneer/ (Accessed 5/22/12); *Quality Measures and Performance Standards*. Centers for Medicare and Medicaid Services, August 2, 2012. Online at: http://www.cms.gov/Medicare/Medicare-Fee-for--Service-Payment/sharedsavingsprogram/Quality_Measures_Standards.html (Accessed 11/12/12); HHS_Names_Pioneer_ACOs._Jessica Zigmond and Rich Daly, *Modern Healthcare*, December 19, 2011. (Accessed 5/22/12); *HHS Announces 89 New Accountable Care Organizations*. Health and Human Services, July 9, 2012. Online at: http://www.hhs.gov/news/press/2012pres/07/20120709a.html (Accessed 10/23/2012); *Pioneer Accountable Care Organization Model: General Fact Sheet*. Centers for Medicare and Medicaid Services, December 19, 2011.
169. Selected Participants in the Pioneer ACO Model. *Modern Healthcare*, December 19, 2011. Online at: http://www.modernhealthcare.com/assets/pdf/CH768931219.DOC (Accessed 12/27/11).
170. HHS Names Pioneer ACOs.
171. *Affordable Care Act Helps 32 Health Systems Improve Care for Patients, Saving Up to $1.1 Billion*. U.S. Department of Health and Human Services, December 19, 2011. Online at: http://www.hhs.gov/news/press/2011pres/12/20111219a.html (Accessed 12/27/11).
172. *Pioneer ACO Model*.
173. *Pioneer ACO Model*.
174. Ibid.
175. *Pioneer Accountable Care Organization Model: Fact Sheet*, pp. 6–7.
176. Pioneer ACO Deadline Extended; *Pioneer ACO Application*. Center for Medicare and Medicaid Innovation. Online at: http://innovations.cms.gov/area-of-focus/seamless-and-coordinated-care-models/pioneer-aco-application (Accessed 7/15/11).
177. *CMMI Announces Pioneer ACO Model*. Illinois Hospital Association, May 2011; *The "Pioneer" Model: CMS's Alternative Shared Savings Program for ACOs*. McDermott Will and Emery, 2011. Online at: http://www.mwe.com/index.cfm/fuseaction/publications.nldetail/object_id/e9bf1179-043c-479d-badb-56a9874e4246.cfm (Accessed 7/29/11).
178. *Advanced Payment Model—OFR*. Department of Health and Human Services, 2011. Online at: http://www.ofr.gov/OFRUpload/OFRData/2011-27458_PI.pdf (Accessed 10/26/11).
179. *Advance Payment Accountable Care Organization (ACO) Model*. Centers for Medicare and Medicaid Innovations, October 20, 2011. Online at: http://innovations.cms.gov/documents/payment-care/AdvancePaymentsFactSheet_10_20_2011.pdf (Accessed 10/26/11).
180. *Advanced Payment Solicitation*. Centers for Medicare and Medicaid Innovations, 2011. Online at: http://innovations.cms.gov/documents/payment-care/APACO_Solicitation_10_20_11_Compliant1.pdf (Accessed 10/26/11); *Advanced Payment Model—OFR*.
181. Advance Payment Accountable Care Organization (ACO) Model.

182. Ibid.
183. Frequently Asked Questions (FAQs). Centers for Medicare and Medicaid Innovations, 2011. Online at: https://acoregister.rti.org/index.cfm?fuseaction=dsp_faq (Accessed 10/27/11).
184. Ibid.
185. Dual eligibles are those beneficiaries that are eligible for benefits under both the Medicare and Medicaid programs.
186. Establishes Medicaid Accountable Care Organization Demonstration Project in DHS. N.J. S. Bill No. 2443 (December 6, 2010). Online at: http://www.njleg.state.nj.us/2010/Bills/S2500/2443_I1.HTM (Accessed 11/7/2011), p. 14.
187. Ibid., p. 2.
188. Ibid.
189. Ibid., p. 9.
190. 27 States Debate ACO-Related Bills, but Just 10 Enact Laws. Judy Packer Tursman, *AIS Health*, vol. 2, no. 8, August 2011.
191. Ibid.
192. Accountable Care Explained: An Experiment in State Health Policy. Christine Vestal, Stateline, *Kaiser Health News*, October 18, 2012. Online at: http://www.kaiserhealthnews.org/Stories/2012/October/18/aco-accountable-care-organization-states-medicaid.aspx (Accessed 10/22/2012); *State "Accountable Care" Activity Map*. National Academy for State Health Policy, 2012. Online at: http://nashp.org/state-accountable-care-activity-map (Accessed 10/22/2012); *Maine*. National Academy for State Health Policy, August 2012,. Online at: http://www.nashp.org/med-home-states/maine (Accessed 10/22/2012); *Oregon*. National Academy for State Health Policy, October 2012. Online at: http://www.nashp.org/aco/oregon (Accessed 10/22/2012); *Colorado*. National Academy for State Health Policy, October 2012. Online at: http://www.nashp.org/aco/colorado (Accessed 10/22/2012); *Minnesota*. National Academy for State Health Policy, October 2012. Online at: http://www.nashp.org/aco/minnesota (Accessed 10/22/2012); *New Jersey*. National Academy for State Health Policy, October 2012. Online at: http://www.nashp.org/aco/new-jersey (Accessed 10/22/2012).
193. Medicare Program; Medicare Shared Savings Program: Accountable Care Organizations, p. 67804.
194. Ibid.
195. Letter from AHA to CMS Regarding ACO Recommendations. Linda E. Fishman, AHA (November 17, 2010), p. 3.
196. Letter from AHA to CMS Regarding Advanced Payment Initiative. Linda E. Fishman, senior vice president of Public Policy Analysis and Development, AHA, to CMS, June 17, 2011.
197. Statement of Final ACO Rule. Rich Umbdenstock, American Hospital Association, October 20, 2011. Online at: http://www.aha.org/presscenter/pressrel/2011/111020-st-acorule.pdf (Accessed November 10, 2011).
198. Ibid.
199. Ibid.
200. Letter from AMGA to CMD Regarding Medicare Shared Savings Program: Accountable Care Organizations. Donald W. Fisher to Donald M. Berwick, Centers for Medicare and Medicaid Services, 5/11/2011.
201. Ibid.
202. AMA: Final ACO Rule Offers Promise to Improve Care Delivery. American Medical Association: CMS Final Rule on ACOs (October 20, 2011). Online at: http://www.ama-assn.org/ama/pub/news/news/final--aco-rule.page (Accessed 11/14/2011).
203. CMS Spotlights Physician-Friendly Changes in Final ACO Rule. Charles Fiegl, American Medical News, October 20, 2011. Online at: http://www.ama-assn.org/amednews/2011/10/17/gvsf1020.htm (Accessed 11/14/2011).
204. AMA: Final ACO Rule Offers Promise to Improve Care Delivery.
205. CMS Spotlights Physician-Friendly Changes in Final ACO Rule.
206. AMA: Final ACO Rule Offers Promise to Improve Care Delivery.
207. AAFP Statement: AAFP Commends CMS for Improving Medicare ACO Final Rule, Announcing the Advance Payment Model. American Academy of Family Physicians, Press Release (October 21, 2011). Online at: http://www.aafp.org/online/en/home/media/releases/2011newsreleases-statements/aco-final-rule.html (Accessed 11/14/2011).
208. AHIP Statement on ACO Regulations. America's Health Insurance Plans, Press Release (October 20, 2011). Online at: http://www.ahipcoverage.com/2011/10/20/ahip-statement-on-aco-regulations/ (Accessed 11/14/2011).

209. Ibid.
210. Ibid.
211. Physician Group Practice Transition Demonstration. Centers for Medicare and Medicaid Services, August 2012. Online at: http://www.cms.gov/Medicare/Demonstration-Projects/DemoProjectsEvalRpts/Downloads/PGP_TD_Fact_Sheet.pdf (Accessed 10/1/12), p. 1.
212. Ibid., p. 3.
213. Selected Participants in the Pioneer ACO Model. Center for Medicare and Medicaid Innovation, Baltimore, MD, September 12, 2012, p. 10.
214. Letter from Medicare Payment Advisory Commission to Dr. Donald M. Berwick, Centers for Medicare & Medicaid Services, RE: File Code CMS-1345-P. Glenn M. Hackbarth, June 6, 2011.
215. Report to the Congress: Medicare and the Health Care Delivery System. Medicare Payment Advisory Commission, Washington, D.C., June 2012, pp. 34–35, 51–52.
216. Medicare Program; Medicare Shared Savings Program: Accountable Care Organizations, p. 67951.

Acronyms

Acronym	Description	Acronym	Description
AAFP	American Academy of Family Physicians	HHS	U.S. Department of Health and Human Services
ADLS	Accelerated Development Learning Sessions	HIT	Health Information Technology
AHA	American Hospital Association	IME	Indirect Medical Education
AHIP	America's Health Insurance Plans	IPPS	Inpatient Prospective Payment System
AMA	American Medical Association	LLC	Limited Liability Corporation
AMGA	American Medical Group Association	MedPAC	Medicare Payment Advisory Commission
APCP	Advanced Primary Care Practice Demonstration	MSR	Minimum Savings Rate
APM	Advanced Payment Model	MSSP	Medicare Shared Savings Program
CAH	Critical Access Hospital	NOI	Notice of Intent
CAP	Corrective Action Plan	PBPM	Per Beneficiary, Per Month
CHIP	Children's Health Insurance Program	PCMH	Patient-Centered Medical Home
CMI	Center for Medicare and Medicaid Innovation	PCP	Primary Care Physicians
DOJ	Department of Justice	PGP	Physician Group Practice Demonstration
DSH	Disproportionate Share Hospital	PPS	Prospective Payment System
EHO	Emerging Healthcare Organizations	PQRS	Physician Quality Reporting System
EHR	Electronic Health Records	RHC	Rural Health Centers
FFS	Fee-For-Service	SSA	Social Security Act
FQHC	Federally Qualified Health Centers	TIN	Taxpayer Identification Number
FTC	Federal Trade Commission	TRHCA	Tax Relief and Health Care Act
GPRO	Group Practice Reporting Option	VBP	Value-Based Purchasing

Program Abbreviations

Program	Abbreviation	Brief Description	Date of Enactment	Citation
Accelerated Development Learning Series	ADLS	The ADLS provided lessons for new and established ACO MSSP participants on establishing and implementing core functions of an ACO in order to improve quality while maintaining lower costs.	January 13, 2011–July 28, 2011	*Accountable Care Organizations Accelerated Development Learning Program: Webinars*. Centers for Medicare and Medicaid Innovations, 2011. Online at: https://acoregister.rti.org/index.cfm?fuseaction = dsp_web (Accessed 10/22/12).

Program Abbreviations (continued)

Program	Abbreviation	Brief Description	Date of Enactment	Citation
Advanced Payment ACO Initiative	APM	Available to a select few MSSP participants, advanced payments are designed to facilitate the development and the initial establishment of each participant's ACO, and provide the necessary capital to make investments for coordinating care. This initiative will test whether advance payments increase MSSP participation or improve quality of care to achieve shared savings.	November 2, 2011	Medicare Program; Medicare Shared Savings Program: Accountable Care Organizations. *Federal Register,* vol. 76 no. 212 (November 2, 2011).
Bundling Demonstration Project		Provides bundled payments to PCPs who treat a mix of chronic/acute and surgical/medical conditions.	March 23, 2010	*Patient Protection and Affordable Care Act, Sec. 3023.* Pub. Law 111–148, 124 Stat. 119 (March 23, 2010), p. 399-400.
Children's Health Insurance Program	CHIP	A program under which CMS matches state Medicaid expenditures for children and pregnant women, primarily.	August 5, 1997	*Balanced Budget of 1997, Sec. 4901 et seq.* Pub. Law 105-33, 111 Stat. 251 (August 5, 1997), pp. 552–573.
Establishing Community Health Teams to Support the Patient-Centered Medical Home		Spurs national use of the patient centered medical home (PCMH) model through grants and/or contracts with state entities and tribal organizations in order to create "health teams" that support primary care practices, including obstetrics and gynecology as well as prevention and patient education.	March 23, 2010	*Patient Protection and Affordable Care Act, Sec. 3502.* Pub. Law 111–148, 124 Stat. 119 (March 23, 2010), pp. 513–515.
Federally Qualified Health Centers Advanced Primary Care Practice Demonstration	FQHC-APCP	A three-year program that employs a "monthly management fee" per eligible Medicare patient to assist the FQHC in making the transition to a "person-centered, coordinated, seamless primary care practice"	October 1, 2011	*Medicare Demonstrations: Details for Medicare Medical Home Demonstration.* Centers for Medicare and Medicaid Services. Online at: https://www.cms.gov/DemoProjectsEvalRpts/MD/itemdetail.asp?itemID = CMS1199247 (Accessed 1/4/12).

continued

Program Abbreviations (continued)

Program	Abbreviation	Brief Description	Date of Enactment	Citation
Group Practice Reporting Option	GPRO	A Web interface for submitting data for quality measures, which can provide examples for how to assign vulnerable populations to care categories.	January 1, 2010	*Satisfactory reporting measures for group practices.* 42 U.S.C. § 1395w-4(m)(3)(C) (2010).
Hospital Value-Based Purchasing Program	Hospital VBP	A federal initiative under the ACA that is set to distribute approximately $850 million to hospitals based on reported quality performance measurements beginning in October 2012.	October 1, 2011	*Patient Protection and Affordable Care Act, Sec. 3001, 10335.* Pub. Law 111-148, 124 Stat. 119 (March 23, 2010), p. 353, 974.
Medicaid ACO Demonstration Project		A New Jersey Medicaid ACO Demonstration Project that facilitates and incentivizes participation through a gainsharing model that provides incentive payments for cost savings achieved.	December 6, 2010	*Establishes Medicaid Accountable Care Organization Demonstration Project in DHS.* N.J. S. Bill No. 2443 (December 6, 2010). Online at: http://www.njleg.state.nj.us/2010/Bills/S2500/2443_I1.HTM (Accessed 11/7/2011), p. 2.
Medicare Medical Home Demonstration Project		Provided "care management fees" to a patient's personal physician, and incentive payments to providers participating in a medical home, and was to be conducted in eight states, in urban, rural, and underserved areas, over a three-year period. However, it was superseded by programs developed by the Center for Medicare and Medicaid Innovation (CMI).	December 20, 2006	*Tax Relief and Health Care Act of 2006, Sec. 204.* Pub. Law 109-432, 120 Stat. 2922 (December 20, 2006), p. 2987.
Medicare Participating Heart Bypass Center Demonstration		A value-based purchasing program that achieved a 10% reduction in expenditures by utilizing bundled payments for all inpatient hospital care for coronary artery bypass graft surgeries at seven hospitals to lower the amount spent on each patient.	1991–1996	*Medicare Participating Heart Bypass Center Demonstration.* Health Care Financing Administration, September 1998, pp. 3–4, 11.

Program Abbreviations (continued)

Program	Abbreviation	Brief Description	Date of Enactment	Citation
Medicare Shared Savings Program	MSSP	The MSSP is one form of value-based purchasing linking shared savings incentive payments to federal ACO participants that achieve quality metrics for Medicare beneficiaries.	November 2, 2011	*Patient Protection and Affordable Care Act, Sec. 3022, 10307.* Pub. Law 111-148, 124 Stat. 119 (March 23, 2010), pp. 395, 940; Medicare Program; Medicare Shared Savings Program: Accountable Care Organizations. *Federal Register* vol. 76 no. 212, (November 2, 2011).
Multipayer Advanced Primary Care Practice Demonstration	MAPCP Demonstration	A program under which Medicare will participate with existing state-level multipayor health reform initiatives employing a dual-phase payment schedule to contract with various payors (e.g., private health plans, Medicaid, and employers).	July 1, 2011	*Multipayer Advanced Primary Care Practice (MAPCP) Demonstration Fact Sheet.* Centers for Medicare and Medicaid Services, April 5, 2012. Online at: www.cms.gov/Medicare/Demonstration.../mapcpdemo_Factsheet.pdf (Accessed 10/22/12).
PGP Transition Demonstration		A program designed to facilitate the transition of former PGP participants into either the MSSP the Pioneer ACO Model.	January 1, 2011	*Physician Group Practice Transition Demonstration.* Centers for Medicare and Medicaid Services, August 2012. Online at: http://www.cms.gov/Medicare/-Demonstration-Projects/DemoProjectsEvalRpts/Downloads/PGP_TD_Fact_Sheet.pdf (Accessed 10/1/12), p. 1.
Physician Group Practice Demonstration	PGP Demonstration	A demonstration program to assess if care management initiatives could reduce avoidable hospitalizations, readmissions, and emergency department visits; improve quality of care provided; and, ultimately, lower costs for providers. The outcomes of this program were an impetus for the inclusion of ACOs in the ACA.	April 1, 2005	*Consolidated Appropriations Act.* Pub. Law 106-554, 114 Stat 2763 (December 21, 2000), pp. 2763A–509.

continued

Program Abbreviations (continued)

Program	Abbreviation	Brief Description	Date of Enactment	Citation
Physician Quality Reporting System	PQRS	A voluntary program instituted within the Medicare program that allows providers to submit quality outcomes data for certain medical conditions to CMS in exchange for potential financial incentives.	December 20, 2006	*Tax Relief and Health Care Act of 2006, Div. B, Title I, Sec. 101*. Pub. Law 109-432, 120 Stat. 2922 (December 20, 2006), pp. 2975–2981.
Pioneer ACO Model	Pioneer	Intended for well-established ACOs that have already begun coordinating care efforts. Pioneer parallels and complements the traditional MSSP program.	January 1, 2012	*Affordable Care Act Gives Providers New Options to Better Coordinate Health Care*. U.S. Department of Health and Human Services, May 17, 2011. Online at: http://www.healthcare.gov/news/factsheets/accountablecare05172011a.html (Accessed 7/15/11); *The Pioneer ACO Model.* Healthcare Financial Management Association, 2011. Online at: http://www.hfma.org/PioneerACOModel/ (Accessed 7/15/11).
Primary Care Extension Program		Supports PCMH initiatives in community-based primary care practices by funding state organized programs to educate primary care physicians (PCPs) on preventative care and health literacy and incorporating the program into their practice to benefit their communities.	March 23, 2010	*Patient Protection and Affordable Care Act, Sec. 5405*. Pub. Law 111-148, 124 Stat. 119 (March 23, 2010), p. 649.
State Option to Provide Health Homes for Enrollees with Chronic Conditions		Focused on implementing medical homes for state Medicaid populations, the program provides funding for states to reimburse PCMH providers who treat Medicaid beneficiaries with chronic medical issues.	January 1, 2011	*Patient Protection and Affordable Care Act, Sec. 2703*. Pub. Law 111-148, 124 Stat. 119 (March 23, 2010), p. 319.

3 Commercial ACOs

Even prior to the publication of the Final Rule, the ACO concept had evolved beyond the restraints of the Medicare Shared Savings Program (MSSP) and entered the commercial healthcare market. As of May 2012, there were approximately 160 established or developing commercial ACOs.[1] Despite the less strict requirements in the Final Rule, as compared to the Proposed Rule, many providers were still not satisfied with the Centers for Medicare and Medicaid Services (CMS) regulations,[2] and many opted to create ACOs through value-based purchasing contracts with private payors that emphasize increased quality of care and lower costs. In a less mature form, the commercial ACO market has existed in the healthcare industry long before the MSSP. Some of the largest and most well-known health systems in the United States have been on the path to creating functional ACOs for many years, e.g., Kaiser, Geisinger, Mayo, Cleveland Clinic, large medical groups in California, and several health maintenance organizations (HMO).[3]

Factoid 3.1

Some of the largest and most accepted health systems in the United States have been on the path to creating functional ACOs for many years, without prodding by the CMS. These entities include Kaiser, Geisinger, Mayo, Cleveland Clinic, medical groups in California, and even several HMOs. (Source: *Leading Change in Health Care: Building a Viable System for Today and Tomorrow*. Ian Morrison, Chicago: Health Forum, Inc., 2011, pp. 184–185.)

WHAT ARE COMMERCIAL ACOS?

Key Term	Definition	Citation
Commercial ACOs	An ACO where the contracting payor is a private insurer. These are monitored and regulated through general healthcare laws.	*Federal Trade Commission, Department of Justice Issue Statement of Antitrust Policy Enforcement Regarding ACOs*. Federal Trade Commission, 10/20/2011. Online at: http://www.ftc.gov/opa/2011/10/aco.shtm, (Accessed on 5/25/2012).

In contrast to federal ACOs, which contract with CMS, commercial ACOs assume risk and realize financial incentives by means of contractual ACO arrangements made with private payors. Similar to the federal market, commercial ACOs accept the accountability and responsibility for the health outcomes and cost containment of an established patient population by offering coordinated, high quality care.[4] In the absence of the type of regulatory guidelines imposed on federal ACOs, commercial ACOs may develop any number of operational and governance structures depending on the nature and terms of the contract negotiated with the chosen private payor, as well as the resources available to the ACO based on its scale. Although commercial ACOs and federal ACOs share a common policy goal, i.e., higher quality of care at lower costs, the two organizations are very different.

TABLE 3.1
Distinguishing between Federal ACOs and Commercial ACOs through the Four Pillars

4 Pillars	Federal ACOs	Commercial ACOs
Regulatory	Regulated by the MSSP	Must be compliant with the same rules as non-ACO providers
	Waivers for Stark Law, Anti-Kickback, and CMP	As of yet not eligible for CMS, DOJ, FTC waivers
	Guidelines and policies available for antitrust	
	Accredited by NCQA Standards	Accredited by NCQA Standards
Reimbursement	Reimbursed through FFS	Reimbursements range from FFS to single capitation models
	Shared Savings under two disbursement two options.	Any number of value-based purchasing agreements (to be negotiated between ACO and payor)
	Shared risk based on whether benchmarks are met (only for two-sided option) leading to possible shared losses	Shared risk located within overall reimbursement (i.e., capitated payment) or as shared losses (less common for commercial)
	Shared savings only for Medicare population	Shared savings for negotiated population
Competition	Medicare beneficiaries not required to stay within the ACO, leading to competition	Population may or may not go outside of the ACO depending on the payor contract.
Technology	Doesn't require EHR, but requires sophisticated data gathering	Doesn't require EHR, but requires sophisticated data gathering
		Some payors help implement telecommunications within the ACO

Distinguishing between Federal ACOs and Commercial ACOs

Key Concept	Definition	Citation
The Four Pillars of the Healthcare Industry	Regulatory, reimbursement, competition, and technology	Health Capital Consultants

The distinct characteristics of the two types of ACOs, i.e., federal ACOs and commercial ACOs, can be distinguished through the conceptual lens of the Four Pillars of Healthcare, i.e., (1) regulatory, (2) reimbursement, (3) competition, and (4) technology, as shown in Table 3.1.

Factoid 3.2

Commercial ACOs are financially invested in meeting quality and cost goals without being subject to the heightened financial risks caused by the uncertain outcomes of the federal MSSP. (Source: *An ACO Overview*. Toshiba American Medical Systems, Inc., Tustin, CA, 2011, p. 2.)

Regulatory

Commercial ACOs experience greater flexibility in terms of participating entities, allowable organizational structures, and possible reimbursement methodologies, because they are not hindered by the provisions of the MSSP. Conversely, without the compliance waivers and safeguards granted to federal ACOs by CMS, the Department of Justice (DOJ), and the Federal Trade Commission (FTC), commercial ACOs may have to limit certain collaboration/integration arrangements that may violate federal and state referral and competition laws, i.e., Stark Law, Anti-Kickback Statute, and Antitrust. The impacts of these various compliance issues are discussed in Chapter 5. While the above mentioned regulatory agencies did not specifically provide waivers for commercial ACOs, CMS has stated that "avenues exist to provide flexibility for ACOs participating in commercial plans."[5] CMS also has identified several means by which a commercial ACO may maintain compliance while still achieving the ACO objective of coordinating care:

1. Participation Waiver: Available for certain transactions undertaken by providers participating in a commercial ACO.
2. Stark Exceptions: Commercial ACOs are able to structure their shared savings plans to fit within any of the current Stark Exceptions.
3. Federal Anti-Kickback Safe Harbors: Commercial ACO arrangements may also fit into certain antikickback safe harbors, e.g., the managed care safe harbors.
4. Fraud and Abuse Laws: Commercial ACOs that do not meet the regulatory threshold of the current fraud and abuse laws will not need any special treatment in maintaining compliance.[6]

Factoid 3.3

In the Stark and antikickback interim final rules, CMS did not specifically provide waivers for commercial ACOs. However, the agency opined that "avenues exist to provide flexibility for ACOs participating in commercial plans." (Source: Medicare Program; Final Waivers in Connection with the Shared Savings Program. *Federal Register* vol. 76, no. 212 (November 2, 2011), p. 68006.)

Reimbursement

While federal ACOs are reimbursed under a traditional fee-for-service (FFS) model, commercial ACOs may implement other types of value-focused reimbursement models (e.g., partial capitation) that are designed to incentivize quality of care.[7] Commercial ACO contracts may address financial incentives through reimbursement models incorporating shared risk, shared savings bonus payments (similar to federal shared savings payments), or value-based compensation arrangements. Each of these options has benefits and barriers that should be considered based on the particular circumstances of the ACO. Further, the reimbursement model selected could fall anywhere on the spectrum between FFS (a separate payment for each service) and global capitation (a single payment per member per month).[8] Several common reimbursement options will be discussed further later in this chapter.

Factoid 3.4

Commercial ACOs can fall anywhere on the spectrum between FFS and global capitation, although some commercial ACOs are aiming to share more upfront costs through partially capitated models. (Source: Global Cap Dominates Some Private-Sector Payment Models; Others Seek Partial Cap. *ACO Business News,* vol. 1, no. 1, November 2010, p. 1.)

Competition

One difference between a federal ACO and an HMO is that ACOs allow their member beneficiaries to choose a physician outside of the ACO. However, that may not always be true for commercial ACOs, particularly for those ACOs formed by a health system with its own health plan, e.g., Kaiser

Permanente.[9] The level of competition between an ACO and others in the market will likely be significantly affected by whether its beneficiaries are limited in this way. ACOs that do limit beneficiaries in their choice of physicians to those within the ACO may compete with non-ACO providers in a similar manner as any larger health entity. However, ACOs that do not limit beneficiary access may experience added concerns from being accountable for patients who may seek care from non-participating providers outside of the governance and quality control ACO, while the ACO retains the responsibility for quality and cost targets related to these patients. Of note, in areas where an ACO has the majority of the market share in the community, the ACO may have a virtual monopoly on healthcare even if it does not limit beneficiaries' access.[10]

Technology

Both federal ACOs and commercial ACOs are required to gather, process, and report quality and cost data. Although electronic health records (EHRs) are not required by CMS or commercial payors, the implementation of ACOs is still likely to necessitate the use of sophisticated health information technology (HIT) in order to meet date reporting requites. Larger healthcare entities may have an advantage over smaller entities, as these organizations will likely already have HIT systems in place that are interoperable with satellite and outpatient locations. Many commercial payors, including Aetna, Blue Cross Blue Shield (BCBS), and Anthem/WellPoint, are providing support for their providers to help them overcome issues related to insufficient IT (Information Technology), as discussed further below.[11]

DEVELOPMENT

A commercial ACO's development is dependent on the type of ACO contract it can negotiate with the commercial payor. Most commercial ACOs will likely have a similar structure to a federal ACO, although this structure can vary in scope between an independent service line and an integrated health system.

Eligible Entities

A commercial ACO creates a contractual relationship between entities that coordinate services in order to benefit from financial incentives set out under a contract with a private payor. While some entities may not possess the necessary infrastructure to coordinate care effectively, none are inherently prevented from participation so long as they possess a "strong foundation of patient-centered primary care"[12] based on standards set by the National Committee for Quality Assurance (NCQA), which provides accreditation for both commercial ACOs and federal ACOs. Accreditation guidance from the NCQA may provide insight in determining which organizations are best suited to integrate and function as an ACO.

Structural Requirements

An ACO contract with a private payor outlines both the scope of the entire ACO and the goals for quality improvement and cost reduction. In turn, organizational scope and goals, based on the contract, will determine what internal structure is needed to achieve the targeted delivery of care.[13]

Many large integrated health systems may not need to make significant changes to develop into an ACO. For example, Geisinger Health System and Kaiser Permanente have already significantly achieved an integrated delivery system model, with their own hospitals, physicians, and insurance plans that offer the coordination of care to achieve many of the goals sought by ACOs. For entities that have not already developed the structure necessary for ACO status, stakeholders should, as recommended by the American Hospital Association (AHA), prepare a well-developed business plan that answers foundational questions, several examples of which are shown in Table 3.2.

TABLE 3.2
AHA Recommendations for Structural Decisions

What are the key competencies required of ACOs?
The AHA recommends that every ACO should establish competencies in the following areas: "leadership; organizational culture of teamwork; relationships with other providers; IT infrastructure for population management and care coordination; infrastructure for monitoring, managing, and reporting quality; ability to manage financial risk; ability to receive and distribute payments or savings; and resources for patient education and support."
How will ACOs address physician barriers to integration?
How and in what capacity will data from outside providers be considered by the ACO? What reimbursement model will best meet the needs of the ACO and its physicians? How will the ACO associate between the various entities: mergers and acquisitions, joint ventures, contracts?
What are the legal and regulatory barriers to effective ACO implementation?
What structures and regulations need to be in place to ensure the ACO can coordinate care while remaining compliant with Stark Law, Anti-Kickback Statutes (state and federal), IRS regulations, antitrust laws, etc.? How will existing provider contracts need to be amended to be in compliance with the new regulations?
How can ACOs maintain patient satisfaction and engagement?
For which patients will the ACO be accountable? How will the ACO inform its patients of the new ACO model and its impact on them? How will patient satisfaction be measured and reported? Will there be any restrictions on member beneficiaries' access to providers outside the ACO?
How will quality benchmarks be established?
What quality measures must the ACO report? Will they be the same as those required of federal ACOs by CMS?
How will savings be shared among ACOs?
How will the ACO manage financial risk? What will the benchmarks be for determining shared savings and losses and how will they be determined?

Source: Adapted from Endnote 14.

As an ACO proceeds with the analysis and determination of its optimal structural components, it also should be considering the requisite capital requirements for its formation, implementation, and operation, which are often the most limiting constraint to ACO development. To determine the cost of formation, implementation, and operation,[15] ACOs should look to capital and operational estimates of currently successful ACOs or other healthcare providers that have already achieved a high level of integration.[16] The interaction between each organizational component (e.g., providers, suppliers, and outside contracted parties) of the ACO should be considered as well during the structural development and capital formation phase. In addition to the main ACO contract between the ACO and the private payor, ACOs may find it appropriate to consider establishing clarifying contracts between ACO participants to clearly illustrate expectations and specific responsibilities.[17]

Coordination of Care

To attain the goals of any ACO, achieving high levels of coordinated care among participating entities is crucial. There are three basic ways by which an ACO can structure the coordination between participating entities: (1) fully integrated structures, (2) virtual or partially integrated structures, or (3) contractual structures.[18] The benefits and limitations of these options are described in Table 3.3.

In addition to the level of coordinated care, commercial ACOs also must seek to determine the scope of their coordinated care. Scope is customarily ascertained by determining the types of patient services for which the providers within the ACO are accountable. For example, an organization may opt to slowly transition to an ACO by testing its ACO contract terms within a single service

TABLE 3.3
Levels of ACO Integration

	A	B	C	D
	Level of Integration	**Types of Organizations**	**Benefits**	**Limitations**
1	Fully Integrated	Common ownership and common employment	Greater ability to invest in coordination tools; tighter decision making; clear hierarchy for control to drive quality and cost-efficiency; better legal protection (i.e., antitrust, stark, anti-kickback)	Legal scrutiny under antitrust if organization too big; cost limitations; charter restrictions, willingness of provider acquisition.
2	Partially Integrated	Joint ventures; joint operating agreements; virtual parent governing bodies (Some financial integration, but mostly clinical)	Maintain some individual control	Greater burden to prove quality and cost benefits; higher scrutiny of financial arrangements (referrals).
3	Contractual	contract language contains elements of integration—physician-hospital organization (PHO)	Can be short term or long term.	May not be strong enough to achieve sufficient integration. Less likely to be used by large health systems.

Notes: "Constructing Accountable Care Organizations: Some Practical Observations at the Nexus of Policy, Business, and Law" By Douglas A. Hastings, Bureau of National Affairs, Health Law Reporter, Vol. 19, No. 25, June 24, 2010.

line. Perhaps the easiest service lines to test an ACO are those with limited physician–patient interaction, e.g., laboratory services, because financial incentives designed to increase efficiency are not complicated by patient satisfaction or care sought outside of the ACO.[19]

In most commercial ACOs, the type of patient care services the ACO is accountable for also may be limited by payor-type, e.g., the ACO contract with Aetna provides incentives that only apply to those patients covered by Aetna insurance. Thus, the largest ACO contracts (and possibly the easiest to employ) may be those contained within a commercial ACO that does not segment the assigned beneficiary population. The feasibility of the various scopes of commercial ACOs will be discussed further in Chapter 4.

Technology

As mentioned above, while neither federal ACOs nor commercial ACOs have specified technology requirements, a modernized HIT system is essential to gather and manage the requisite data for both coordination between providers and reporting of quality metrics. In addition, to these HIT benefits, there are also programs offering financial incentives for HIT that have already begun, e.g., the American Recovery and Reinvestment Act (ARRA) of 2009 provides funding for the meaningful use of EHRs. ACOs with established EHR systems may be positioned to reap the most benefit from the incentives offered through the ARRA, both by achieving the payments offered until 2014, and avoiding the penalties that go into effect in 2015 for those providers who do not adopt a compliant EHR system. Many large institutions primed for ACO formation, have had functioning HIT for some time, e.g., the Mayo Clinic replaced paper records with an EHR system in 2005.[20] Similarly, Kaiser Permanente's EHR system, HealthConnect®, has been in place since 2010, and currently covers 8.6 million people, 454 medical offices, and 36 hospitals.[21] The NCQA suggests that ACOs use EHRs extensively for at least 50% of their patients.[22] While HIT may be necessary, smaller or

TABLE 3.4
ACO Contracts with HIT Components

Contracting Method	Payor Example	HIT Contract Description
Data-Sharing Systems	Model Practice	Payor supports provider through a member health data sharing system and advanced technology systems for patients to communicate with providers.
Payor Driven Data Collection	Medica Health Plan	Providers receive patient cost data from payor.
Capital Infusion	MaineGeneral	Payor assists its providers with health information technology needs.

Source: Adapted from Endnote 24.

less sophisticated health entities may find the capital requirement for implementation of HIT systems burdensome.

Factoid 3.5

A modernized health information technology (HIT) system is essential to gather and manage data for both delivery coordination and quality assurance. Indeed, the American Recovery and Reinvestment Act (ARRA) of 2009 has already implemented incentives for the meaningful use of EHRs. (Source: *Standards and Guidelines for the Accreditation of Accountable Care Organizations*. National Committee for Quality Assurance, Washington, D.C.: 2011, pp. 6–7, 97–108.)

To lessen the potential capital and technological barriers for smaller entities to transition to an ACO, some payors are providing financial and other types of support for their providers to help them overcome issues related to insufficient HIT. Three examples of methods by which ACO contracts include support for HIT include

1. Supplying access to data-sharing systems
2. Payor-driven collection burdens
3. Direct capital infusion[23]

Examples of ACO contracts that utilize these HIT components are illustrated in Table 3.4.

Governance

Although commercial ACOs do not have federal mandates for leadership and management structures, "a successful ACO will have a governing board."[25] While federal ACOs are required to populate their governance boards with physicians, as well as to maintain some representation of Medicare beneficiaries, commercial ACOs are not controlled by such regulations. Nevertheless, it may be beneficial for commercial ACOs to incorporate physician leaders and other stakeholder representatives into their governance boards. A greater diversity of representatives within the governance board may assist ACOs in reaching a higher degree of coordination. While there is no current "best practice" for how to structure physician participation in governance, e.g., governance committees, contracted employment responsibilities, or management boards,[26] governance diversity may bolster physician buy-in and acceptance of new reimbursement and productivity strategies, all of which will be essential to the ACO's success.

IMPLEMENTATION

For more mature institutions, implementation may consist of simply signing an ACO contract, because their internal structure already includes the necessary components for a functioning ACO. Less integrated entities will have to develop an implementation strategy that addresses internal conflicts, timeliness, and capital requirements.

Several consulting companies have created models and strategies to aid healthcare entities in forming and organizing their own ACOs. For example, in 2010, Premier Consulting Solutions, a subsidiary of Premier, Inc., started the ACO Implementation Collaborative, which provides models and strategies for hospitals to develop and organize a functioning ACO. Premier's models are based on seven elements that it asserts will drive ACO success:

1. Establish goals and a mission: Define areas of issue and outline steps to achieve the organization's mission.
2. Define consistent measures of success: ACO payers and providers collaborate on and commit to define preferred outcomes and measures for improvement.
3. Data collection and normalization: Establish a standardized approach to analyzing patient data for comparison purposes/quality and cost measurement.
4. Transparency: Commitment by providers to share performance data and learn from/implement the success of top performers.
5. Drive analysis and collaborative execution: Utilize the collected data to determine sources of poor patient outcomes and then pinpoint opportunities for improvement.
6. Share best practices: Disseminate lessons learned to other members to further increase quality and cost metrics.
7. Performance improvement analysis: Continue to monitor performance metrics in order to identify trends and further opportunities for improvement.[27]

The ACO Agreement

Each individual ACO contract is negotiated between the ACO and a private payor, many of which have created unique prepackaged ACO contracts to offer providers. A selection of these contracts is detailed in Table 3.5.

One of the first, and, therefore, most publicized, ACO contracts was launched by Blue Cross Blue Shield of Massachusetts (BCBSMA) in 2009, before both the ACA and the MSSP.[29] The current movement toward accountable care has given added emphasis and market power to BCBSMA's Alternative Quality Contract (AQC). While the federal ACO model was still evolving within the legislation, the AQC implemented a modified global payment connected to an organization's achievement of quality goals, and, by 2010, all participating groups had earned significant quality bonuses.[30]

BCBSMA spokeswoman Jenna McPhee differentiated the AQC's modified global payment from historic capitation models, which were critically underfunded, noting the BCBS global payment is based on actual costs, adjusted for health status and inflation. Under this model, groups that have implemented the AQC since its launch in 2009 saw "substantial improvements" in many clinical quality measures over the first year, as compared to the non-AQC networks.[31] Under the AQC, some participants saw improvements in their patients covered under other payors. For example, Hampden County Physician Associates, a Multispecialty Group Practice with a management services component, formed an integrated network under the AQC, and was able to lower Medicare expenditures by 22 to 24%, including reductions in unnecessary hospitalizations, testing, and medications as well as similar expenditure reductions for commercial payors in the amount of 5%.[32]

TABLE 3.5
List of Insurers Offering ACO Contracts

Name of Organization	Scope	Prepackaged ACO Contract
Aetna	National	Aetna offers providers who wish to participate in ACO-like arrangements three models to choose from, based on the provider's needs: (1) ***Population-Specific Collaboration***: Manages the transition of patients between member providers by utilizing interoffice EHRs for clinical needs and quality reporting. This model is beneficial for providers who need to increase Medicare savings and overall revenue by reducing hospital readmissions. (2) ***Enhanced Clinical Capabilities:*** Manages clinical integration, patient population risk, and access to evidence-based quality measures via health information exchanges. This model is useful to providers who need to optimize workflow and efficiency. (3) ***Private Label Health Plans:*** Allows the development of a private label or co-branded health plan by partnering with Aetna, which will manage risk and basic insurer operations (e.g., process claims, customer services). This model is best suited for providers seeking growth in their brand and market share.
Blue Cross Blue Shield of Massachusetts	State	***Alternative Quality Contract:*** Aims to align financial and clinical goals by tying together fixed payments per patient and performance-based payments related to quality benchmarks. The goal is to create a flexible payment structure to allow for better quality of care.
Blue Cross Blue Shield of Minnesota	State	***Shared Incentive Payment Model:*** Providers initially receive a base payment rate. Over the agreement term, the payment method shifts from a fixed amount to variable payments based on quality and efficiency benchmarks. This approach aims to improve patient outcomes, reduce costs, and curb patient premium increases.
CIGNA Health Group	International	***Collaborative Accountable Care (CAC)***: This model offers CAC contracts to large provider groups or organizations. Providers are reimbursed only if they meet or exceed quality standards for evidence-based medicine. The goals of this model are to increase care coordination, engage patients, and utilize reported performance data.
UnitedHealth	National	UnitedHealth offers a variety of ACO-like models to providers, including: (1) ***Performance-Based Incentive Contracts:*** Providers can contract to meet negotiated quality benchmarks. Meeting or exceeding these standards could lead to an increase in future reimbursement rates. (2) ***Risk-based Compensation/Delivery System Configuration:*** Provider groups specify a patient population for which they will assume responsibility for patient experience and quality and cost of care as the basis of shared savings and losses.
Wellpoint, Inc.	State	***Northwest Metro Alliance:*** The model has three components: coordinated care management, payer-based data models, and electronic health information sharing. It also employs best practice contracting models and performance measures based on Triple Aim. The overall goals are to increase provider collaboration and a cultural commitment to supporting this model.

Source: Endnote 28.

Accountability

Key Term	Definition	Citation
Accountability	In the context of ACOs, the treatment outcomes of a patient population for which data are gathered determines whether the ACO is eligible for shared savings. Commercial ACOs have the flexibility to adjust the scope of accountability to either a specific patient population or all patients seen by the ACO.	*Accountable Care Organizations in Medicare and the Private Sector: A Status Update.* Robert A. Berenson & Rachel A. Burton, The Robert Wood Johnson Foundation and The Urban Institute (November 2011) Online at: http://www.rwjf.org/files/research/73470.5470.aco.report.pdf (Accessed 1/28/12), p. 5.

Accountability refers to the patient population for which data are gathered and used to determine whether the ACO is eligible for financial incentives. For federal ACOs, this population consists of the Medicare beneficiaries, who do not opt out of the program, and are prospectively assigned to an ACO by CMS.[33] Commercial ACOs have the flexibility to adjust the scope of accountability to either a specific patient population or to all patients seen by the ACO. Greater accountability escalates the opportunity for more financial incentives, but also increases risk in both liability and financial exposure.[34]

Various ranges of accountability offer distinct benefits for ACOs and payors. Typical avenues for tailoring the population for which an ACO is accountable include patients, services, and payment methods. Some ACO contracts exclude patients at higher risk for bad debt (e.g., patient populations covered under self-employment contracts), while others exclude patient populations that require specialized services (e.g., pediatric patients). Commercial ACOs also have the ability to exclude certain services from their accountability population, or exclude some services from being included in the determination of financial incentives based on the uneven administration of benefits (a common critique of the MSSP). For example, if an employer typically sends his/her employees to outside providers or vendors for prescriptions, an ACO may have contracted for such services to be excluded from financial incentive calculations. ACO contracts commonly exclude the following from the calculation of financial incentives: patient payments not directly related to patient services, outlier high patient care costs, and, occasionally, outlier low patient care costs.[35]

Factoid 3.6

ACO accountability may be tailored further to account for uncertain payments. ACO contracts commonly exclude the following from shared savings calculations: patient payments not directly related to patient services, outlier high patient care costs, and, occasionally, outlier low patient care costs. (Source: Key Design Elements of Shared-Savings Payment Arrangements. Michael Bailit and Christine Hughes, *The Commonwealth Fund*, vol. 20, no. 1539 (August 2011), pp. 2–4. Online at: http://www.commonwealthfund.org/Publications/Issue-Briefs/2011/Aug/Shared-Savings-Payment-Arrangements.aspx (Accessed 11/17/11).)

OPERATION

As there are no official standard operating procedures to which all commercial ACOs must conform, commercial ACOs have the flexibility to define their own operations. A commercial ACO can base its operational structure upon its individual participant contracts. In addition to the typical healthcare operations, protocols, procedures, and systems for the delivery of care, ACOs also must construct infrastructure to ensure efficient quality and cost reporting, and monitor ACO operations.

Quality and Other Reporting Requirements

Even though the current size of the emerging ACO market may now be considered marginal in comparison to the size of the overall provider market, the demand for uniform methods of reporting for quality and costs, outside of ACOs, within individual practices and across the entire network of participating practices is continuing to grow.[36] The Cleveland Clinic has successfully implemented a Quality and Patient Safety Institute that coordinates and monitors seven departments dedicated to "reconnecting quality and patient safety with clinical care."[37] While acknowledging that quality varies between providers within the organization, the Institute is able to monitor and assess each of its member hospitals and medical centers through Quality Performance Reports to "support the organizational mission to provide high quality care and to continuously improve our performance."[38]

In addition to improving quality of care and reducing costs, organizations may boost their credibility through national recognition by independent third-party accrediting entities, which generally require high-quality reporting in order to maintain accreditation. For example, The Joint Commission, a nonprofit organization dedicated to improving healthcare quality,[39] accredited Geisinger Medical Center, an entity within the overall Geisinger Health System.[40] As a requirement of maintaining program accreditation, Geisinger must submit to periodic quality reviews by The Joint Commission and publish any resulting reports on the Geisinger Web site.[41]

In the absence of set standards in the commercial market, the NCQA released its Standards and Guidelines for the Accreditation of Accountable Care Organizations in November 2011.[42] Within two months of the programs initiation, six provider groups had sought and obtained ACO accreditation through the NCQA: Billings Clinic, Children's Hospital of Philadelphia, Crystal Run Healthcare, Essential Health, HealthPartners, and Kelsey-Seybold Clinic.[43]

Monitoring

Monitoring of an ACO occurs at many levels of ACO development, beginning at the implementation stage of the ACO, with a review of the established patient base, and continuing through the life of the ACO contract. The NCQA's accreditation standards require that organizations have established methods for collecting, recording, monitoring, and disseminating clinical data among providers and ancillary health services.[44] In Michigan, for example, Metro Health[45] employed college students to sort through the records of the ACO's patients and identify those with chronic conditions; the ACO then developed a disease registry to monitor six chronic conditions. In New York, Catholic Medical Partners established disease management programs to monitor and to support those participating beneficiaries suffering from chronic conditions, such as asthma, diabetes, or pediatric obesity.[46] Medication is another area that an ACO regularly monitors for its beneficiary population. Catholic Medical Partners[47] employs full-time pharmacists to assist participating physicians in monitoring their patients' prescription data, and incorporates registered nurses into participating primary care practices to monitor and coordinate patient follow-up care.[48]

Reimbursement

Without the specified reimbursement format of the MSSP, which is established by laws and regulatory edict, commercial ACOs have the flexibility to include quality and cost incentives into their reimbursement structures, in addition to the shared savings offered through the ACO contract. The NCQA accreditation standards require that some portion of provider payments be based on the "performance of the ACO as a whole, using clinical quality, cost, and patient experience indicators."[49] As mentioned above, ACO contracts may use differing methods to incentivize achievement of the ACOs goals, including: a basic reimbursement model, with shared savings bonus payments; incentives created through the reimbursement model; and incentives through provider compensation arrangements.

Factoid 3.7

It is less common to find shared losses contracted in the commercial ACO market; instead, commercial ACOs use a variety of methods to accommodate risk within the general reimbursement scheme. (Source: *Promising Payment Reform: Risk-Sharing with Accountable Care Organizations.* Suzanne F. Delbanco, et al., The Commonwealth Fund, July 2011, p. 5. Online at: http://www.commonwealthfund.org/~/media/Files/Publications/Fund%20Report/2011/Jul/1530Delbancopromisingpaymentreformrisksharing%202.pdf (Accessed 11/17/11).)

The best option for a given ACO will depend on the level of risk sharing the ACO and the payor are comfortable establishing. There is neither a common definition nor a uniform program design for "risk-sharing" among the organizations that have initiated a contracted arrangement for shared losses.[50] Some examples of risk-sharing models and ACOs who employ them include:

1. Bonus Payment at Risk: Providers risk losing their bonus based on quality and/or efficiency of performance (e.g., BCBS of MN[51]).
2. Market Share Risk: This is based on patient incentives created by the payor (lower co-pays or premiums) to choose certain providers, so providers who are less appealing to the payor risk loss of market share (e.g., Minnesota Health Action Group[52]).
3. Risk of Baseline Revenue Loss: Providers risk financial loss if they fail to meet cost or quality expectations, and/or if the actual cost exceeds a set target cost (e.g., BCBS of MA[53] AQC, BCBS of Illinois/Advocate[54]).
4. Financial Risk for Patient Population: A partially/fully capitated, global budget model, where the providers manage all the healthcare services provided to a patient, episode, etc., and are responsible for any costs that exceed the predetermined payment for that patient, e.g., State Employees Health Commission,[55] Anthem/WellPoint,[56] both of which are still in the planning process.[57]

The various reimbursement models available to commercial ACOs each offer varying distributions of risk between provider and payor, which is illustrated in Figure 3.1.

Each of these models is described in more detail in the sections below.

Key Term	Definition	Citation
Case-Based Payment	A case-based payment system reimburses the healthcare entity based on a predetermined and fixed rate per case treated by the entity.	Case-Based Hospital Payment Systems. Sheila O'Dougherty, et al., in *Designing and Implementing Health Care Provider Payment Systems: How-To Manuals.* Washington, D.C.: The International Bank for Reconstruction and Development/ The World Bank, 2009, p. 126.

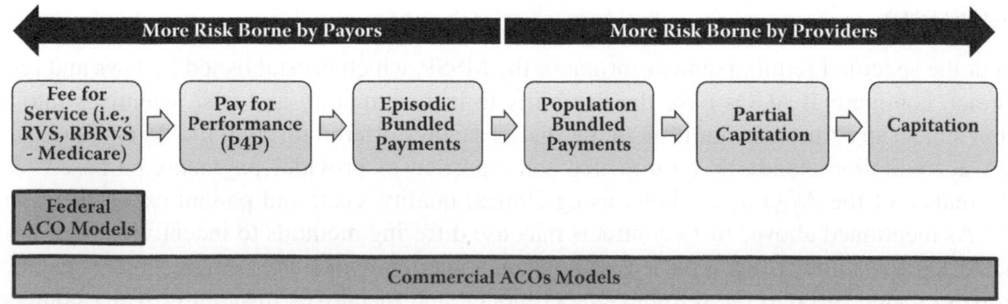

FIGURE 3.1 Models of reimbursement.

Fee-for-Service

A fee-for-service payment method is one of the most common and oldest methods of healthcare payment, whereby healthcare providers receive separate compensation for each service they provide, such as an office visit or procedure. Those critical of this method contend that it incentivizes the over-use of services and can lead to "duplicative or conflicting treatments" if the providers are not properly coordinated. ACOs have the potential to resolve these issues by offsetting the incentive to over-treat, by means of providing financial incentives (in the form of bonuses) for lower cost care and higher quality care.[58] In order to provide benefits for both parties to the ACO contract, these financial incentives are typically shared between the provider and the payor.[59]

Key Term	Definition	Citation
Fee-for-Service	A method of billing for health services where each patient is charged differently from the physician or other practitioner.	Glossary of Terms Commonly Used in Health Care. *AcademyHealth,* 2004 Edition.

Under the MSSP, financial incentives, i.e., shared savings payments, are calculated based on reductions in costs and 33 specific quality metrics. Commercial ACOs can negotiate these terms with a private payor, which allows them more control over the process.[60] Negative incentives, in the form of shared losses, also may be incorporated into an ACO contract. However, it is less common to find shared losses contracted in the commercial ACO market. Instead, commercial ACOs use a variety of methods to accommodate risk within the general reimbursement scheme.[61]

Pay-for-Performance

Pay-for-performance (P4P) is a healthcare payment method whereby compensation is based on the providers' performance based on achieving beneficial health outcomes. For example, a physician with a high performance may receive a bonus in addition to his or her usual fee-for-service payment. Although a P4P system can be structured in several ways, the common elements to all systems include:

Key Term	Definition	Citation
Pay-for-Performance (P4P)	A payment system that incentivizes healthcare organizations and professions to achieve healthcare quality objectives.	*Pay for Performance.* American Medical Association. Online at: http://www.ama-assn.org/ama/pub/physician-resources/practice--management-center/claims-revenue-cycle/managed-care-contracting/evaluating-payment-options/pay-for-performance.Pay_For_Performance_AMA_12.2011.pdf (Accessed 12/28/11).

- A set of targets or objectives for quality and cost outcomes that define what metrics will be evaluated
- Measures and performance standards for establishing whether the target criteria were met
- Rewards (typically financial incentives) that are at risk, including the amount and the method for allocating the payments among those who meet or exceed the reward threshold(s)[62]

Proponents of P4P remuneration systems argue that they have the potential to improve the quality of care and slow the growth in healthcare costs through improvements in quality and provider efficiency.[63]

For ACOs, common factors considered when deciding P4P compensation include administrative or claims data that measures "quality and/or cost of care," and patient satisfaction.[64] According to the Agency for Healthcare Research and Quality (AHRQ), P4P is designed "to offer financial incentives to physicians and other healthcare providers to meet defined quality, efficiency, or other targets."[65]

Bundled Payment

Key Term	Definition	Citation
Bundled Payment	Often based on a specific episode of care or over a specific period of time. A bundled payment may include a single payment for multiple provider entities. This method apportions the bundled payment to each entity that provided service.	*Bundled Payments.* American Medical Association. Online at: http://www.ama-assn.org/ama/pub/physician-resources/practice-management-center/claims-revenue-cycle/managed-care-contracting/evaluating-payment-options/bundled-payments.Bundled Payments_AMA_2011.pdf (Accessed 12/28/11).

A bundled payment (also referred to as an episode-based payment) occurs when payments for multiple related procedures or diagnoses are combined, or bundled, to reimburse for the entirety of one episode of care. Under this payment scheme, a provider that performs cardiac surgery, for example, receives one payment that covers all of the services provided for that surgery, including the surgery itself, and preceding patient preparation, including diagnostics. An ACO may employ this method to receive the bundled payment and then apportion the payment to each entity that provided service.[66] Similar to the goals of ACOs, there are currently bundling initiatives in place that are designed to lower costs and promote efficient and high-quality care.

On August 23, 2011, as mandated by the ACA (Patient Protection and Affordable Care Act, 2010), CMS announced the Bundled Payments for Care Improvement Initiative (Bundled Payments Initiative).[67] The Bundled Payments Initiative includes four approaches to bundled payments. One model is based on a single prospective payment for all services provided during a single inpatient stay, while the remaining three models are based on a retrospective payment system that sets a target cost for an established episode of care.[68] The Bundled Payments Initiative aims to improve patient care through a patient-centered approach, emphasizing care coordination and quality.[69] A description of several characteristics of each of the four bundling options is set forth in Exhibit 3.1.

Partial Capitation

Capitated payments, along with quality incentives, are methods for improving quality and slowing rising costs. A capitated payment system offers providers a fixed price for a defined range of services, making providers responsible for care decisions as well as losses due to costs exceeding the fixed price. Some commercial ACOs are pursuing partial capitation with the aim of sharing some of the initial investment costs,[71] and also because the full capitation model causes the risk of loss to fall too heavily on the provider, and fear that full capitation provides incentives for low-quality care in order to cut costs. Some industry commentators have suggested that partial capitation reimbursement models should only be practiced by those organizations that already have highly integrated systems in place when implementing an ACO.[72]

Key Term	Definition	Citation
Capitation	Method of payment for health services in which an individual or institutional provider is paid a fixed amount for each person served.	*Pay-for-Performance.* American Academy of Family Physicians, 2012. Online at: http://www.aafp.org/online/en/home/policy/policies/p/payforperformance.html (Accessed on 5/25/2012).

Full Capitation

A full capitation payment system provides reimbursement based on the number of patients registered to be cared for by the healthcare entity. The amount paid per member per month (PMPM) is determined in advance and is considered to be prospective reimbursement. The full capitation model may encourage providers to treat a larger number of patients than they would otherwise attempt to treat in order to increase revenue, which could lead to a higher workload and shorter consultations.[73]

EXHIBIT 3.1
Key Features of Bundled Payment Models Compared

Model Feature	Model 1 Inpatient Stay Only	Model 2 Inpatient Stay plus Postdischarge Services	Model 3 Postdischarge Services Only	Model 4 Inpatient Stay Only
Eligible Awardees	Physician group practices; Acute care hospitals paid under the IPPS; Health systems Physician–hospital organizations; and, Conveners of participating healthcare providers	Physician group practices; Acute care hospitals paid under the IPPS; Health systems Physician–hospital organizations; Postacute providers; and Conveners of participating healthcare providers	Physician group practices; Acute care hospitals paid under the IPPS; Health systems Long-term care hospitals Inpatient rehabilitation facilities; Skilled nursing facilities; Home health agency; Physician-owned hospital organizations; and Conveners of participating healthcare providers	Physician group practices; Acute care hospitals paid under the IPPS; Health systems; Physician–hospital organizations; and Conveners of participating healthcare providers
Payment of Bundle and Target Price	Discounted IPPS payment; no separate target price	Retrospective comparison of target price and actual FFS payment	Retrospective comparison of target price and actual FFS payment	Prospectively set payment
Clinical Conditions Targeted	All MS-DRGs	Applicants to propose based on MS-DRG for inpatient hospital stay	Applicants to propose based on MS-DRG for inpatient hospital stay	Applicants to propose based on MS-DRG for inpatient hospital stay
Types of Services Included in Bundle	Inpatient hospital services	Inpatient hospital and physician services; Related postacute care services; Related readmissions; and Other services defined in the bundle	Postacute care services; Related readmissions; and Other services defined in the bundle	Inpatient hospital and physician services; and Related admissions
Expected Discount Provided to Medicare	To be proposed by applicant CMS requires minimum discounts increasing from 0% in first 6 mos. to 2% in Year 3	To be proposed by applicant; CMS requires minimum discount of 3% for 30–89 days postdischarge episode; 2% for 90 days or longer episode	To be proposed by applicant	To be proposed by applicant; subject to minimum discount of 3%; larger discount for MS-DRGs in ACE Demonstration

continued

EXHIBIT 3.1 (continued)
Key Features of Bundled Payment Models Compared

Model Feature	Model 1 Inpatient Stay Only	Model 2 Inpatient Stay plus Postdischarge Services	Model 3 Postdischarge Services Only	Model 4 Inpatient Stay Only
Payment from CMS to Providers	Acute care hospital: IPPS payment less predetermined discount; and Physician: Traditional fee schedule payment (not included in episode or subject to discount)	Traditional fee-for-service payment to all providers and suppliers, subject to reconciliation with predetermined target price	Traditional fee-for-service payment to all providers and suppliers, subject to reconciliation with predetermined target price	Prospectively established and bundled payment to admitting hospital; hospitals distribute payments from bundled payment
Quality Measures	All hospital IQR measures and additional measures to be proposed by applicants	To be proposed by applicants, but CMS will ultimately establish a standardized set of measures that will be aligned to the greatest extent possible with measures in other CMS programs		

Source: Endnote 70.

One benefit of the capitated model is that PMPM payments may incentivize capital expenditures by the ACO. For example, a provider in a capitated payment model may be more inclined to pursue a significant capital expenditure to invest in the technology request to decrease costs, amortized over the life of the asset, because lower costs derived from the investment translate to higher earnings achieved from the predetermined PMPM. In contrast, a provider in a FFS payment model may be less inclined to make the same capital expenditure because the income yield achievable from FFS reimbursement is less likely to be significantly enhanced, whether the provider did or did not make the capital investment.

Global Budget

Global budgets in healthcare delivery are meant to contain the total amount of money spent on services. A global budget is determined by the entity responsible for funding the services to patients "and will act as a cap on that agent's exposure in the overall system."[74] The global budget is often decided in advance and set for a period of time, and services to be covered and not covered should be defined in the global budget payment schematic, which is negotiated.[75] A benefit of a global payment model of reimbursement is that value-based purchasing strategies can be applied to all payments, not only shared savings.

Key Concept	Definition	Citation
Global Budget	Global budgets in healthcare delivery are meant to contain the total amount of money spent on services.	*Hospital Global Budgeting*. Robert Dredge; *Designing and Implementing Health Care Provider Payment Systems: How-To Manuals*. Washington, D.C.: The International Bank for Reconstruction and Development/The World Bank, 2009, p. 215.

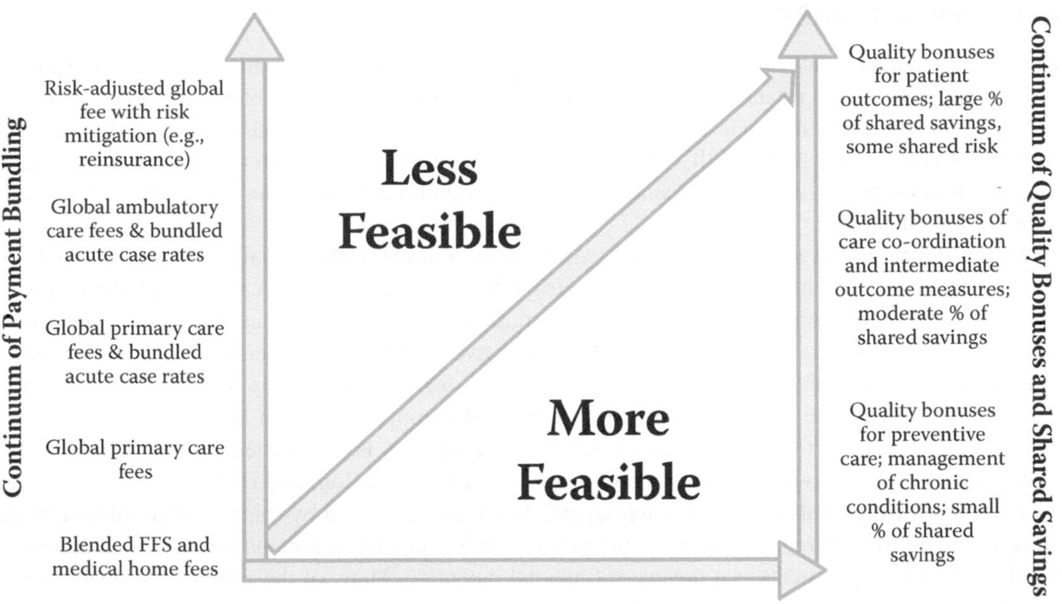

FIGURE 3.2 Mix and match reimbursement strategies and outcomes. (Adapted from Endnote 77.)

Tiered Payment Models

Some ACOs may consider a tiered provider implementation strategy, which provides for different levels of financial risk through different modes of payment.[76] Commercial ACOs can use different reimbursement models for different providers and mix and match reimbursement strategies may complicate administrative functions; they also allow an ACO to incentivize different groups for different results. A visual depiction of multiple reasons why an ACO may choose to implement different types of reimbursement methods are set forth in Figure 3.2.

Shared Savings and Losses

Shared savings are determined by a combination of actual savings and those achieved through satisfying payer-defined quality measures. These quality measures usually include a combination of measures under these categories:

- Beneficiary access to care
- Patient experience
- Quality of care
- Utilization of services

Some ACOs take a "gate" approach, meaning the provider must first meet the quality measures in order to qualify for the savings reward. Alternatively, other ACOs use a "ladder" approach, whereby the provider's percentage of the shared savings correlates with his/her score on the quality measurement scale.[78]

It should be noted, that almost universally, shared savings accompany shared risk, in that commercial ACO providers share in the savings, but they also share in the losses. *The Commonwealth Fund* describes them as "payment models in which providers share in a portion of the savings they achieve … but, are also at risk for a portion of spending that exceeds a target."[79]

CHAPTER SUMMARY

Commercial ACOs have more flexibility in design and operation than their federal counterparts. As commercial ACOs establish contracts with private payors, they are able to negotiate a wider range of reimbursement models, patient populations, service lines, and savings disbursement methods than federal ACOs with CMS contracts. The structural and operational choices in the aforementioned areas may vary depending on the commercial insurer, the size of the ACO, and contract specifications.

In the development stages, commercial ACOs can contract with virtually any payor, but it is imperative that a sufficient infrastructure and strong foundation in primary care be established prior to ACO implementation. Large health systems may not require significant changes to their normal operations when transitioning into an ACO. However, smaller organizations require a business plan to manage the substantial restructuring necessary for ACO formation. Organizations of any size should address the following key areas in their ACO implementation strategies: governance, key competencies, barriers to integration, legal and regulatory issues, patient satisfaction, quality benchmarks, shared savings, implementation costs, care coordination, and HIT.

In contrast to federal ACOs, commercial ACOs are not restricted by traditional reimbursement structures and, therefore, may explore alternative reimbursement options outside of, or in addition to, shared savings payments as a means of financial incentive. Many of these options transfer some or all of the reimbursement risk from the payor to the provider, while also allowing for increased reimbursements to be achieved under agreed upon metrics. Commercial ACO reimbursement models may range from traditional fee-for-service to partial and full capitation.

The commercial ACO market has no clear uniform standards regarding ongoing operations comparable to the fixed regulations for federal ACOs. In response, the NCQA launched its own ACO accreditation program, which contains several core components of precursor ACOs, such as requirements for quality metrics, monitoring performance, reporting data, reimbursement, and savings and loss distribution. While NCQA accreditation is for all ACOs, associated guidelines may be more critical in the commercial market, as it lacks a formal regulatory source.

ENDNOTES

1. Are You Ready for an ACO? Margaret Dick Tocknell, *HealthLeaders Magazine*, May 2012, p. 1.
2. ACOs: Tailoring Your Own Solution. Philip Betbeze, *HealthLeaders Media*, 2011, p.2.
3. *Leading Change in Health Care: Building a Viable System for Today and Tomorrow*. Ian Morrison, Chicago: Health Forum, Inc., 2011, pp. 184–185.
4. *An ACO Overview*. Toshiba American Medical Systems, Inc., Tustin, CA, 2011, p. 2.
5. Medicare Program; Final Waivers in Connection with the Shared Savings Program. *Federal Register* vol. 76, no. 212 (November 2, 2011), p. 68006.
6. Ibid.
7. *Value in Health Care: Current State and Future Directions*. Healthcare Financial Management Association, HFMA's Value Project, June 2011, p. 24; *Accountable Care Organizations in Medicare and the Private Sector: A Status Update*. Robert A. Berenson and Rachel A. Burton, The Robert Wood Johnson Foundation and The Urban Institute, November 2011, pp. 3, 4. Online at: http://www.rwjf.org/files/research/73470.5470.aco.report.pdf (Accessed 11/16/11).
8. Global Cap Dominates Some Private-Sector Payment Models; Others Seek Partial Cap. *ACO Business News*, vol. 1, no. 1, November 2010, p. 1.
9. Patients' Role in Accountable Care Organizations. Anna D. Sinaiko and Meredith B. Rosenthal, *The New England Journal of Medicine*, vol. 363, no. 27, December 30, 2010, p. 2583.
10. CMS Seeks Input Mainly on ACO Structure, But Market Power Issues Remain a Concern. *ACO Business News,* vol. 1 no. 2, December 2010. Online at: http://www.snrdenton.com/pdf/ABN1210_a-Funk.pdf (Accessed 1/27/2012).

11. *Promising Payment Reform: Risk-Sharing with Accountable Care Organizations*. Suzanne F. Delbanco, et al., The Commonwealth Fund, July 2011, pp. 10–27. Online at: http://www.commonwealthfund.org/~/media/Files/Publications/Fund%20Report/2011/Jul/1530Delbancopromisingpaymentreformrisksharing%202.pdf (Accessed 11/17/11).
12. *NCQA Accountable Care Organization Accreditation*. The National Committee for Quality Assurance, 2011. Online at: http://www.ncqa.org/LinkClick.aspx?fileticket=Mv2IW8SCCvI%3D&tabid=1312 (Accessed 1/27/12).
13. Contracts Should Spell Out Everyone's Role in an ACO. Steven M. Harris, McDonald Hopkins, *American Medical News*, May 9, 2011. Online at: http://www.ama-assn.org/amednews/2011/05/09/bicb0509.htm (Accessed 11/18/11).
14. *Accountable Care Organizations*. American Hospital Association Committee on Research, AHA Research Synthesis Report, June 2010, pp. 8–11.
15. Capital considerations, both as to feasibility and value metrics, are discussed at length in Chapter 7: Financial Feasibility Analysis for ACO Investments and Chapter 8: Considerations of Value for the Positive Externalities of ACOs.
16. *Accountable Care Organizations*, pp. 8, 11.
17. Contracts Should Spell Out Everyone's Role in an ACO.
18. Constructing Accountable Care Organizations: Some Practical Observations at the Nexus of Policy, Business, and Law. Douglas A. Hastings, *Bureau of National Affairs Health Law Reporter*, vol. 19, no. 25, June 24, 2010, pp. 1–2.
19. Healthcare Innovation: How Plans and Providers are Driving Change, Improving Care, and Achieving Value in a Post Reform World. Craig E. Samitt, Paper presented at the Active Communications International ACO Summit: Cutting Costs and Raising Quality in Healthcare through Accountable Care Organizations: Chicago, September 16, 2011, pp. 32, 36; *The Role of Laboratory Medicine in Accountable Care Organizations*. Joe Miles and Ronald L. Weiss, ARUP Laboratories, August 2011, pp. 5–6.
20. The Electronic Medical Record at Mayo Clinic. Mayo Clinic. Online at: http://www.mayoclinic.org/emr/ (Accessed on 5/23/12).
21. *About Kaiser Permanente: Kaiser Permanente HealthConnect® Electronic Health Record*. Kaiser Permanente. Online at: http://xnet.kp.org/newscenter/aboutkp/healthconnect/index.html (Accessed on 11/18/11).
22. *Standards and Guidelines for the Accreditation of Accountable Care Organizations*. National Committee for Quality Assurance, Washington, D.C.: 2011, pp. 6–7, 97.
23. *Promising Payment Reform: Risk-Sharing with Accountable Care Organizations*, p. 9
24. Ibid., pp. 19–27.
25. Contracts Should Spell Out Everyone's Role in an ACO.
26. Hospitals, Docs are Assuming Leadership in Majority of ACO Governance Structures. *ACO Business News*, vol. 3, no. 3, March 2012, pp. 1, 9–11.
27. *Premier Accountable Care Collaboratives: Driving to a Patient-Centered Health System*. Premier, Inc., White Paper, 2011. Online at: https://www.premierinc.com/quality-safety/tools-services/ACO/ACO_WhitePaper_011410.pdf (Accessed 10/30/12).
28. *Models of Collaboration*. Aetna Inc. Online at: http://www.aetnaacs.com/models-of-collaboration.html (Accessed 6/7/12); *The Alternative QUALITY Contract*. Blue Cross Blue Shield of Massachusetts (May 2010), p. 2–3. Online at: http://www.bluecrossma.com/visitor/pdf/alternative-quality-contract.pdf (Accessed 6/7/12); *Minnesota's Largest Health Plan Signs "Total Cost of Care" Agreement with Park Nicollet Health Services*. Blue Cross Blue Shield of Minnesota, News Release, February 24, 2011. Online at: http://www.bluecrossmn.com/bc/wcs/idcplg?IdcService=GET_DYNAMIC_CONVERSION&RevisionSelectionMethod=Latest&dDocName=POST71A_159803 (Accessed 6/7/12); *Collaborative Accountable Care: CIGNA's Approach to Accountable Care Organizations*. CIGNA, White Paper (April 2011), pp. 3–5. Online at: http://newsroom.cigna.com/images/9022/media_gallery/knowledge_center/CollaborativeCare_WhitePaper_2011.pdf (Accessed 6/7/12); *Value-Based Contracting and Accountable Care Organizations*. United HealthCare Services, Inc., Viewpoint: ACOs, December 2011. Online at: http://www.uhc.com/live/uhc_com/Assets/Documents/ViewpointACO.pdf (Accessed 1/25/12); Minnesota and the Emerging ACO. George J. Isham, *MetroDoctors,* March/April 2011, p. 23–25.

29. *Blue Cross Blue Shield of Massachusetts: The Alternative QUALITY Contract*. Blue Cross Blue Shield of Massachusetts, May 2012, p. 2.
30. Private-Payer Innovation In Massachusetts: The "Alternative Quality Contract." Michael E. Chernew, et al., *Health Affairs*, vol., 30, no., 1, January 2011, p. 51.
31. Global Cap Dominates Some Private-Sector Payment Models; Others Seek Partial Cap, p. 2.
32. Ibid., p. 3.
33. Medicare Program; Medicare Shared Savings Program: Accountable Care Organizations. *Federal Register* vol. 76 no. 212, (November 2, 2011), p. 67851.
34. *Payment Reform: Current and Emerging Models*. Paul N. Casale , et al., American College of Cardiology, July 2011, p. 10; *Accountable Care Organizations in Medicare and the Private Sector: A Status Update*, pp. 34.
35. Key Design Elements of Shared-Savings Payment Arrangements. Michael Bailit and Christine Hughes, *The Commonwealth Fund*, vol. 20, no. 1539 (August 2011), pp. 2–4. Online at: http://www.commonwealthfund.org/Publications/Issue-Briefs/2011/Aug/Shared-Savings-Payment-Arrangements.aspx (Accessed 11/17/11).
36. Can Accountable Care Organizations Improve the Value of Health Care by Solving the Cost and Quality Quandaries? Kelly Devers and Robert Berenson, Urban Institute, October 2009. Online at: http://www.rwjf.org/files/research/acosummaryfinal.pdf (Accessed 1/19/12), p. 2.
37. *About the Quality & Patient Safety Institute*. Cleveland Clinic. Online at: http://my.clevelandclinic.org/about-cleveland-clinic/quality-patient-safety/about-quality-safety-institute.aspx (Accessed 1/19/12).
38. Ibid.
39. The Joint Commission was founded in 1951 and today "accredits and certifies more than 19,000 health-care organizations and programs in the United States." Online at: http://www.jointcommission.org/; *About the Joint Commission*, The Joint Commission, 2012. Online at: http://www.jointcommission.org/about_us/about_the_joint_commission_main.aspx (Accessed 10/22/2012); *History of the Joint Commission*, the Joint Commission. Online at: http://www.jointcommission.org/about_us/history.aspx (Accessed 10/22/2012).
40. *Geisinger Medical Center Quality Report: Summary of Quality Information*. The Joint Commission. Online at: http://www.qualitycheck.org/qualityreport.aspx?hcoid=6048# (Accessed 2/15/12).
41. *Facts about Hospital Accreditation*. The Joint Commission, Nov. 4, 2011. Online at: http://www.jointcommission.org/assets/1/18/Hospital_Accreditation_1_31_11.pdf (Accessed 1/19/12); *Geisinger Quality Measures*. Geisinger Health System, December 1, 2011, Online at: http://www.geisinger.org/quality/chooseHospital.html (Accessed 1/19/12).
42. *Standards and Guidelines for the Accreditation of Accountable Care Organizations*. National Committee for Quality Assurance, Washington, D.C.: 2011.
43. *Early Adopters Are First to Seek ACO Accreditation from NCQA*. National Committee for Quality Assurance, News Release (January 12, 2012). Online at: http://www.ncqa.org/tabid/1476/Default.aspx (Accessed 6/7/12); *Accrediting Highly-Qualified Accountable Care Organizations*. National Committee for Quality Assurance, August 15, 2012. Online at: http://www.ncqa.org/portals/0/Public%20Policy/Accrediting_ACO_8.15.12.pdf (Accessed 10/22/2012).
44. *Standards and Guidelines for the Accreditation of Accountable Care Organizations*, pp. 97–108, 121–127.
45. Metro Health is an integrated health system with a 208-bed acute-care osteopathic teaching hospital located in Michigan. *About Metro Health*. Metro Health. Online at: http://metrohealth.net/about-metro/ (Accessed 10/22/2012).
46. *The Work Ahead: Activities and Costs to Develop an Accountable Care Organization*. Keith D. Moore and Dean C. Coddington, American Hospital Association, April 2011, p. 7, http://www.aha.org/content/11/aco-white-paper-cost-dev-aco.pdf (Accessed 1/19/12).
47. Catholic Medical Partners is a not-for-profit "partnership between Catholic Health, Mount St. Mary's Hospital and a network of associated physicians" located in Buffalo, NY. *Catholic Medical Partners*. Catholic Medical Partners. Online at: http://www.chsbuffalo.org/ForPhysicians/CIPA (Accessed 10/22/2012).
48. *The Work Ahead*, pp. 8, 12.
49. *Standards and Guidelines for the Accreditation of Accountable Care Organizations*, p. 52.
50. *Promising Payment Reform: Risk-Sharing with Accountable Care Organizations*. Suzanne F. Delbanco, et al., *The Commonwealth Fund*, July 2011, p. 5. Online at: http://www.commonwealthfund.org/~/media/Files/Publications/Fund%20Report/2011/Jul/1530Delbancopromisingpaymentreformrisksharing%202.pdf (Accessed 11/17/11).

51. Online at: https://www.bluecrossmn.com
52. Minnesota Health Action Group, formally known as Buyers Health Care Action Group, is a group purchasing organization in Bloomington, Minnesota. Minnesota Health Action Group. Online at: http://mnhealthactiongroup.org/ (Accessed 10/22/2012).
53. Online at: http://www.bluecrossma.com/
54. *Advocate Health Care, Blue Cross and Blue Shield of Illinois Sign Agreement Focusing on Improving Quality, Bending the Health Care Cost Curve.* Blue Cross Blue Shield of Illinois, October 6, 2010. Online at: http://www.bcbsil.com/company_info/newsroom/news/advocate_announcement.html (Accessed 10/22/2012).
55. State insurance program for employee health in Maine. State Employees Health Commission, 5 ME. Re.S 13 Sec. 285-A (2009).
56. Online at: http://www.anthem.com
57. *Promising Payment Reform*, p. 6.
58. Accountable Care Organizations. Mark Merlis, *Health Affairs*, July 27, 2010 (updated August 13, 2010), p. 1. Online at: http://www.healthaffairs.org/healthpolicybriefs/brief.php?brief_id=23 (Accessed 12/28/11).
59. *Key Design Elements of Shared-Savings Payment Arrangements*, p. 1.
60. *Accountable Care Organizations in Medicare and the Private Sector*, pp. 3, 6.
61. *Promising Payment Reform*, p. 5.
62. *Pay-for-Performance in Health Care.* Jim Hahn, Congressional Research Service, November 2, 2006, p. CRS-4.
63. Ibid., pp. CRS-1, CRS-13.
64. Pay-for-Performance Programs. Steve Ellwing, in *Evaluating and Negotiating Emerging Payment Options*, American Medical Association, Chicago: 2012, p. 1.
65. *Pay for Performance (P4P): AHRQ Resources.* Agency for Healthcare Research and Quality, March 2006. Online at: http://www.ahrq.gov/qual/pay4per.htm (Accessed 12/28/11).
66. Bundled Payments. Edgar ("Jed") C. Morrison, Jr., in *Evaluating and Negotiating Emerging Payment Options,* American Medical Association, Chicago: 2012, p. 1.
67. *Affordable Care Act Initiative to Lower Costs, Help Doctors and Hospitals Coordinate Care*. U.S. Department of Health and Human Services, August 23, 2011. Online at: http://www.hhs.gov/news/press/2011pres/08/20110823a.html (Accessed 10/24/2011*); Bundled Payments for Care Improvement Initiative.* Centers for Medicare and Medicaid Services, August 23, 2011. Online at: http://www.innovations.cms.gov/areas-of-focus/patient-care-models/bundled-payments-for-care-improvement.html (Accessed 10/24/2011), p. 1.
68. *Bundled Payments for Care Improvement Initiative*, pp. 34; *Affordable Care Act Initiative to Lower Costs.*
69. *Bundled Payments for Care Improvement Initiative*, p. 1; *Affordable Care Act Initiative to Lower Costs.*
70. *Bundled Payments for Care Improvement Initiative*, p. 5–6.
71. Global Cap Dominates Some Private-Sector Payment Models; Others Seek Partial Cap. *ACO Business News*, vol. 1, no. 1, November 2010, p. 1.
72. *Accountable Care Organizations*, pp. 3–4.
73. *Capitation, Salary, Fee-for-Service, and Mixed Systems of Payment: Effects on the Behavior of Primary Care Physicians (Review).* T. Gosden, et al., The Cochrane Library, No. 3, 2006, p. 2.
74. Hospital Global Budgeting. Robert Dredge, jn *Designing and Implementing Health Care Provider Payment Systems: How-To Manuals.* Washington, D.C.: The International Bank for Reconstruction and Development/The World Bank, 2009, p. 215.
75. Ibid.
76. *Accountable Care Organizations*, p. 4.
77. *Organizing the U.S. Health Care Delivery System for High Performance*. A. Shih, et. al., New York: The Commonwealth Fund, August 2008, p. xi.
78. *Key Design Elements of Shared-Savings Payment Arrangements*, p. 9
79. *Promising Payment Reform*, p. 2.

Acronyms

Acronym	Definition
ACO	Accountable Care Organization
AHA	American Hospital Association
AHRQ	Agency for Healthcare Research and Quality
AQC	Alternative Quality Contract
ARRA	American Recovery and Reinvestment Act
BCBS	Blue Cross Blue Shield
BCBSMA	Blue Cross Blue Shield of Massachusetts
DOJ	Department of Justice
EHR	Electronic Health Records
FFS	Fee-For-Service
FTC	Federal Trade Commission
HIT	Health Information Technology
HMO	Health Maintenance Organizations
NCQA	National Committee for Quality Assurance
P4P	Pay-for-Performance
PMPM	Per Member Per Month

4 Hypothetical Models for the Development and Operation of ACOs

Following the release by the Centers for Medicare and Medicaid Services (CMS) of the Proposed Rule for the Medicare Shared Savings Program (MSSP) on April 7, 2011, despite it being negatively reviewed by numerous stakeholders, 64% of healthcare organizations reported plans to form an ACO.[1] Over a year later, with 32 Pioneer ACOs selected (on December 19, 2011),[2] 116 federal applications accepted (on April 10, 2012, July 9, 2012, and January 10, 2013),[3] and the continued development of commercial ACOs, the number and variety of potential features associated with these emerging organizations as related to their structural, operational, and reimbursement, has dramatically grown.

Factoid 4.1

Even after the release of CMS Proposed Rule, 64% of healthcare organizations reported plans to form an ACO. (Source: *The Leap to Accountable Care Organizations*. Jim Molpus, HealthLeaders Media Intelligence, HcPro, April 2011, p. 13.)

STRUCTURAL FEATURES

Within both the federal ACO and commercial ACO markets, there have been numerous methods by which providers have chosen to integrate and/or collaborate in order to form an ACO. To some extent, the regulatory environment related to, e.g., antitrust, antikickback, and other areas of the law, combined with the typical effect of leverage and market position on the direction of contract negotiations to govern how these entities ultimately combine, collaborate, and interact, as regards to their respective capital resources and competitive strategy decisions. In 2011, a majority of the existing ACOs (32%) were structured around a hospital-based core.[4] While ACOs sponsored[5] by hospital systems have remained the majority model (53%), ACOs formed around physician groups have experienced the largest amount of growth from June 2011 to June 2012, nearly doubling in number to account for 32% of all ACOs.[6] ACOs may be categorized by the types of entities that participate in the creation of the ACO entity and accept responsibility for the health outcomes and costs associated with the patient populations for which the ACO is accountable. Four such categories include: Insurer ACO, Insurer-Provider ACO, Single Provider ACO, and Multiple Provider ACOs, each of which is described in Table 4.1.

Key Term	Definition	Citation
Clinical Integration	The confidential, sure, and correct union of patient electronic medical information with all appropriate healthcare parties or decision makers: physicians, facilities, laboratories, and payers.	*Dictionary of Health Information and Technology and Security*. David Edward Marcinko, Springer Publishing Company, New York, 2007, p. 55.

TABLE 4.1
ACOs by Participating Provider Type

Provider Type	Description	Percent of ACO Market
Insurer ACO	An insurance company that accepts responsibility and accountability for the care provided to a patient population.	8%
Insurer Provider ACO	An insurance company and a provider organization are equally responsible and accountable for the care provided to a patient population.	6%
Single Provider ACO	Typically, an integrated delivery system that accepts responsibility and accountability for the care provided to a patient population while the payors involvement is limited to providing reimbursement under a risk-based reimbursement model.	67%
Multiple Provider ACOs	Two, or more, providers, e.g., a hospital and a physician group, partner to be responsible and accountable for the care provided to a patient population while the payors involvement is limited to providing reimbursement under a risk-based reimbursement model.	19%

Source: Adapted from Endnote 7.

Key Term	Definition	Citation
Merger	The combination of a single firm, from two or more existing firms.	*Dictionary of Health Economics and Finance.* David Edward Marcinko, Springer Publishing Company, New York, 2007, p. 238.

Key Term	Definition	Citation
Joint Venture	When two or more companies enter into a business enterprise together sharing investment, risks, and profits.	*Dictionary of Health Insurance and Managed Care.* David Edward Marcinko, Springer Publishing Group, New York, 2006, p. 165.

Irrespective which entity serves as the central organization, or the main driver of ACO formation, successful ACOs require the integration of provider entities, each combination of which creates a unique ACO structure. The key parties that may be included in the development of several ACO models, and the possible relationships between those parties, is discussed below.

Federal ACOs

Key Term	Definition
Federal ACO	ACO where the contracting payor is CMS. These ACOs are monitored and regulated through the MSSP and general healthcare laws.

The MSSP limits the types of organizations that are eligible to form an ACO and the relationships that may exist between participating entities. A full examination of those entities eligible to participate in the MSSP, and the rules that govern their integration, was provided in Chapter 2, Federal ACOs. A hypothetical model for the structure of a federal ACO (with a key describing each entity and the relationships between them), where all or some of the illustrated entities may participate, is shown in Figure 4.1.

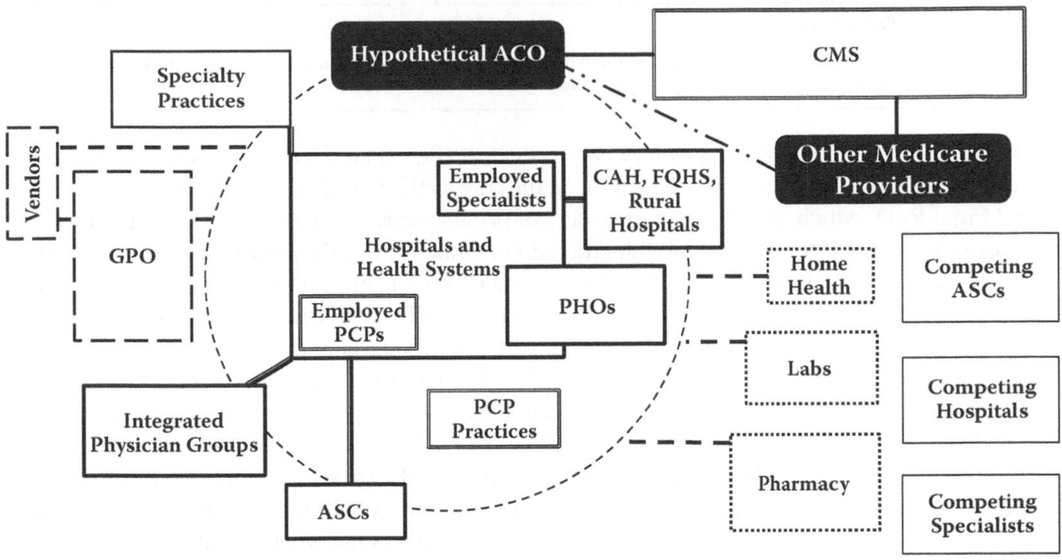

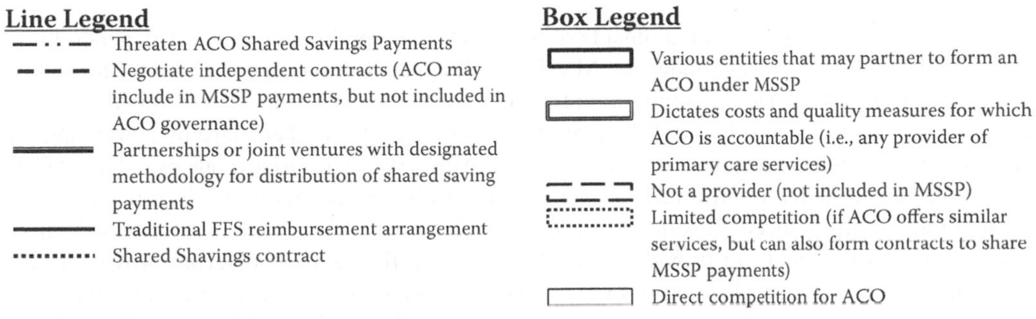

FIGURE 4.1 Potential federal ACO structure and key.

Within this figure, the size of the box representing each entity illustrates that entity's proportionate effect on the potential success of an ACO. The entities located within or on the circular dotted ring labeled "Hypothetical ACO" are those that have been approved to receive a portion of shared savings payments as a participant in the legal entity that operates as a federal ACO. The Final Rule specifies that only these ACO participants be a party in the MSSP contract between the CMS and an ACO (indicated by the dashed line marked as "Shared Savings contract" in the key). While other entities are prohibited from direct participation in the MSSP, approved federal ACOs may negotiate with these entities (e.g., vendors, group purchasing organizations (GPOs), home health services organizations, labs, and pharmacies) to create independent, value-based contracts, indicated by the long dashed line labeled "Negotiate independent contracts" in the key, allowing for further distribution of shared savings payments.[8] Third-party participating entities are distinguished by whether the entity is a provider or supplier, although both may utilize independent contracts with the ACO. For example, vendors and GPOs (enclosed in a long dashed box and labeled as "Not a provider" in the key) are suppliers to providers and, as such, do not threaten an ACO's competitive market position in regards to patient volumes directly, while home health, lab, and pharmacy entities (enclosed in a square-dashed box and labeled "Limited competition" in the key) involve a more approximate degree of direct-to-patient care, which may affect the ACO's achievement of quality and cost goals.

Key Concept	Definition
Types of Federal ACOs	While there may be variation in the types of entities or the size, a federal ACO is formed by a contract between a single legal entity and CMS.

On the federal ACO diagram, primary care providers (PCPs) are placed firmly within the ACO (the dotted ring), while specialists are located on the ring itself. This distinction is descriptive of the MSSP Final Rule, which specifies that providers of primary care services are restricted to offering services only within one ACO per tax identification number (TIN) they possess, while specialists may provide services in or out of their ACO contract.[9] This restriction is founded on the MSSP provision that the CMS will prospectively assign Medicare beneficiaries based on the use of primary care services, by Medicare patients, at the ACO. Therefore, any providers (e.g., PCPs, nurse practitioners, physician assistants, or even specialists), where the total charges billed for primary care services from that provider exceed the total charges billed for primary care services from other non-ACO providers,[10] are included in the determination of which patients are prospectively assigned to an ACO, and are restricted to bill for services only in that ACO per TIN. Note that this limitation is tied to the TIN under which the provider bills and, as such, a PCP (or any provider of primary care services) who has multiple TINs would be able to practice outside of the ACO (even in other ACOs), as long as they bill under a separate TIN. This regulation also will apply to specialists that offer primary care services, but for the purposes of Figure 4.1, this option is not explored. Those entities that do influence beneficiary assignments (i.e., PCPs and CMS) are noted by double-lined boxes within the figure.

Those Medicare providers located outside of the ACO that may threaten the ACO's general revenue, as well as, shared savings under the MSSP, are designated in the figure above with a single solid line box (labeled as "Direct competition for ACO" on the key). Similar to traditional competitive scenarios, providers outside the ACO may threaten the ACO's market share by competing for patient volumes, which the quantity of services provided directly relates to revenue as federal ACOs are still reimbursed under a traditional Fee-for-Service (FFS) model. Additionally, a federal ACO is accountable for all Medicare beneficiaries prospectively assigned to it, even if those beneficiaries seek care from other Medicare providers not affiliated with the ACO. If external providers provide subquality care, the ACO's quality or cost goals and, subsequently, their shared savings payment, may be affected, as indicated by the intermittent dashed box labeled "Threaten ACO Shared Savings Payments" in the key. Note that this was a particularly unpalatable aspect of federal ACOs for participants, which was addressed in the Final Rule under provisions by which ACOs might gain relief under various circumstances. (For further information, see Chapter 2.)

It is important to note that the only payor relevant to a federal ACO contract is the CMS, because only Medicare beneficiaries are included in the quality and cost metrics that dictate the ACO's shared savings payments. The solid black line (labeled "Traditional FFS reimbursement arrangement" in the key) represents the ACO contract between the ACO and the CMS that governs this payor relationship. While Federal ACOs are restricted in their structure, nothing in the MSSP prohibits a federal ACO from entering into commercial ACO contracts with private payors. In this way, an ACO could be both commercial and federal.

Commercial ACOs

Key Term	Definition	Citation
Commercial ACO	An ACO where the contracting payor is a private insurer. These are monitored and regulated through general health care laws.	*Federal Trade Commission, Department of Justice Issue Statement of Antitrust Policy Enforcement Regarding ACOs.* Federal Trade Commission, 10/20/2011. Online at: http://www.ftc.gov/opa/2011/10/aco.shtm. (Accessed on 5/25/2012).

Commercial ACOs are not constrained by federal regulation (other than those that apply to all healthcare entities), which allows for more flexibility when determining their structure. In contrast to the limitation on the types of entities that are eligible to participate in a federal ACO (resulting in specific types of interactions between ACO payors and ACO providers/suppliers), a commercial ACO may have analogous relationships between any array of entities. For example, a commercial ACO may function based on a set of integration and risk sharing agreement(s) between providers and payor(s), without any single provider, or group of providers, operating as the central entity, in contrast to the requirement under the MSSP that a central collection of providers be legally organized as an ACO. The following describes several hypothetical models that illustrate the range of options a commercial ACO may choose to pursue, although it is important to note that within each model, ACOs will likely vary in their scope and degree of clinical and legal integration. It should be noted that while commercial ACOs have the benefit of not being constrained by federal regulation, they do not share in the benefits of regulatory safeguards and waivers applied to the federal ACO market for antikickback, stark law, and the civil monetary penalty. (For more information on federal ACOs and the CMS-established waivers, see Chapter 2 and Chapter 5.)

Key Concept	Definition
Types of Commercial ACOs	An ACO may function based on a set of integration and risk-sharing agreement(s) between providers, without any single provider, or group of providers, operating as the central entity. This allows for a Traditional Model, a Single Healthcare Organization Structure, and a service line ACO.

Traditional Structure

The commercial model, which most parallels federal ACOs, is developed from the integration of discrete entities. A hypothetical model for the structure of a traditional commercial ACO (with a key describing each entity and the relationships between them), where all or some of the illustrated entities may participate, is seen in Figure 4.2.

As with the hypothetical model for federal ACO structure, Figure 4.1, the size of the box representing each entity within the figure indicates that entity's proportionate effect on the potential success of an ACO. The primary distinguishing characteristic of commercial ACOs is that they comprise and operate through independently negotiated commercial ACO contracts, which are sometimes referred to as "ACO-like" contracts, denoted above by the square-dashed line and labeled "ACO/value-based purchasing contract." The specifics of commercial ACO contracts, including the various value-based purchasing models utilized were further explained in Chapter 3 and later in this chapter, in the section Operational Challenges.

Commercial ACOs may coordinate care through any number of independent, distinct arrangements, as demonstrated in Figure 4.2 by the double lines radiating from the Hypothetical ACO circle's center and labeled "Clinical integration and/or risk sharing agreement" (INTEGRATION AGREEMENT) in the key. It is important to remember that commercial ACOs are not required to integrate as a single legal organization. Therefore, any level of clinical integration, financial integration, and risk sharing arrangements that are agreed upon, may exist anywhere on the spectrum of potential intraprovider/supplier contracts, ranging from a full merger to a simple contract. Additionally, agreements between entities within a single commercial ACO need not be identical. For example, a hospital may fully merge with a physician group, while, at the same time, only entering into a value-based purchasing contract with a group purchasing organization (GPO) or home health provider. However, all of these entities still may share in the potential benefits and financial incentives offered by the ACO contract with the commercial payor, as long as that ACO contract is negotiated in a manner that accommodates that structure of the provider/supplier INTEGRATION AGREEMENT.

Similar to federal ACOs, commercial ACOs also may negotiate independent agreements with entities outside the ACO that may or may not contain value-based purchasing language, as

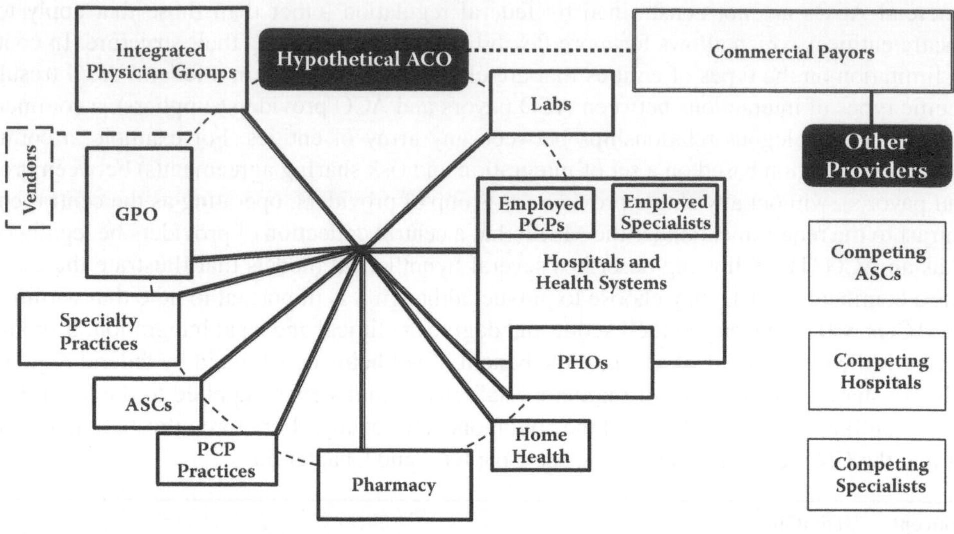

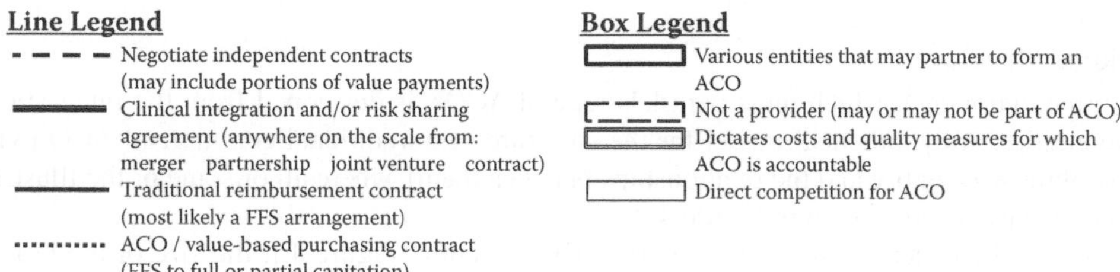

FIGURE 4.2 Potential commercial ACO structure and key.

demonstrated in Figure 4.2 by the long dashed line labeled "Negotiate independent contracts" in the key. As reflected above, by the illustrated relationship between outside vendors and the ACO, not every entity in a commercial ACO is a party in the ACO commercial payor contract. These separate agreements may exist as well between the ACO and nonprovider entities, e.g., suppliers, represented in the figure as enclosed in long dashed boxes and labeled "Not a provider" in the key.

Single Healthcare Organization Structure

The scope of a commercial ACO may be confined within a single healthcare provider entity, as long as that healthcare provider entity includes all of the organizational components requisite for an ACO. Accordingly, commercial ACOs have the ability to fully exist within a single healthcare entity. In this model, the ACO arrangement or a value-based purchasing agreement, may be constructed either;

- Between a single health system and an external payor, i.e., health system ACO—external payor
- Between the providers and payors that exist under the legal umbrella of a single health system, i.e., health system ACO—internal payor or
- Between the services lines of a single organization and a similarly owned payor, i.e., service line ACO

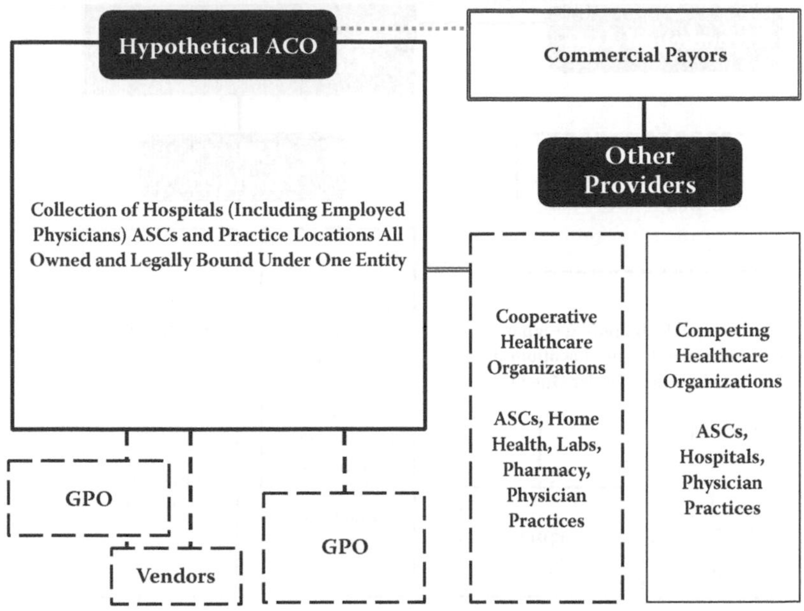

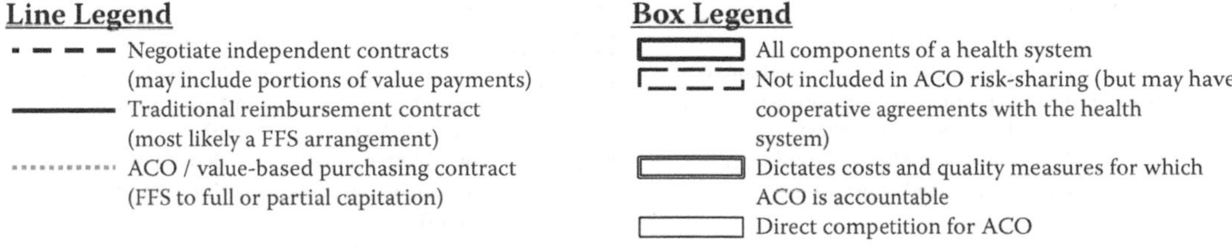

FIGURE 4.3 Potential commercial health system ACO: External payor structure and key.

Health System ACO

The structure of a commercial health system ACO depends on whether the contracting payor is external or internal to the health system. A health system ACO that contracts with an external commercial payor has a structure similar to a federal ACO, whereby the ACO is a central legal entity that forms contractual relationships with payors outside the ACO that may or may not include a value-based purchasing component. A hypothetical model for the structure of a commercial health system ACO with an external payor (with a key describing each entity and the relationships between them) is illustrated in Figure 4.3.

Health system ACOs also can be formed between the providers of a health system and a system-run payor, i.e., both the health system clinical operations and the payor are owned by the same legal organization. Many large health systems, e.g., Kaiser Permanente, have developed health plans to maximize profits through lower administrative costs associated with billing and claim submissions. A hypothetical model for the structure of a commercial health system ACO, between a health system provider and its internal payor (with a key describing each entity and the relationships between them), is seen in Figure 4.4.

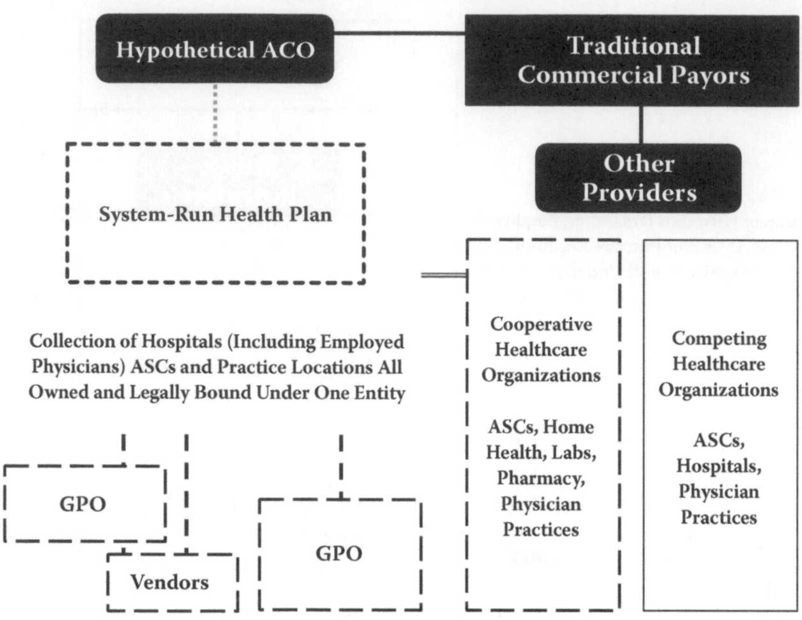

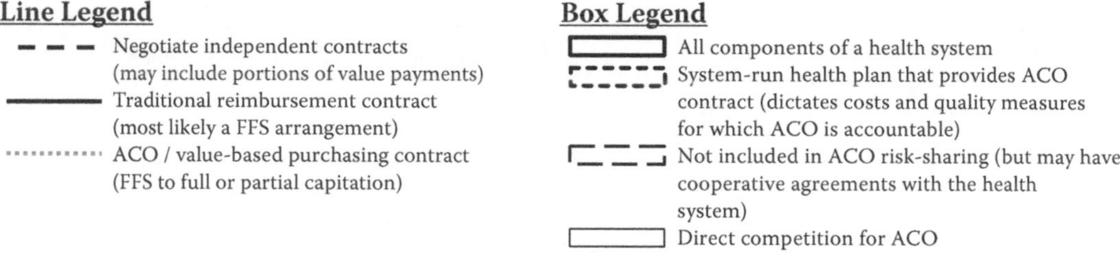

FIGURE 4.4 Potential commercial health system ACO: Internal payor structure and key.

In contrast to the traditional commercial ACO structure, commercial health system ACOs with an internal payor are organized around a value-based purchasing agreement (not necessarily a formal ACO contract) between the health system and a system-run health plan, represented by the dashed box labeled "System-run health plan" in the key, and enclosed in a solid box labeled "All components of a health system" in the key. Similar to other value-based purchasing models, the commercial health system ACO agreement may utilize risk-sharing incentives, reflected in Figure 4.4 by the square-dashed line labeled "ACO/value-based purchasing contract" in the key, to improve quality and lower costs within the targeted patient population of the health systems.

As with any ACO, those entities that are not directly included in the ACO's agreement with the payor may still benefit from shared savings by negotiating independent contracts with the commercial ACO, as demonstrated by the long dashed lines labeled "Negotiate independent contracts" in the key. These entities, where the ACO provider and payor are part of the same overall parent health system, may be more apt to implement pay-for-performance (P4P) initiatives and other provider compensation incentive programs to improve cost and quality outcomes, as the parent organization is more able to target the individual providers by incorporating physician compensation into the incentive programs. Internal payors also allow parent commercial health system organizations to control the scope of their ACO, focusing either on all providers or a single service line.

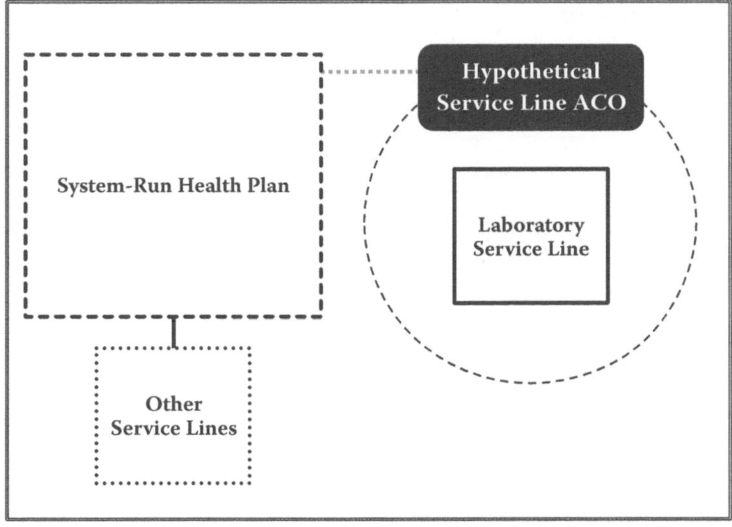

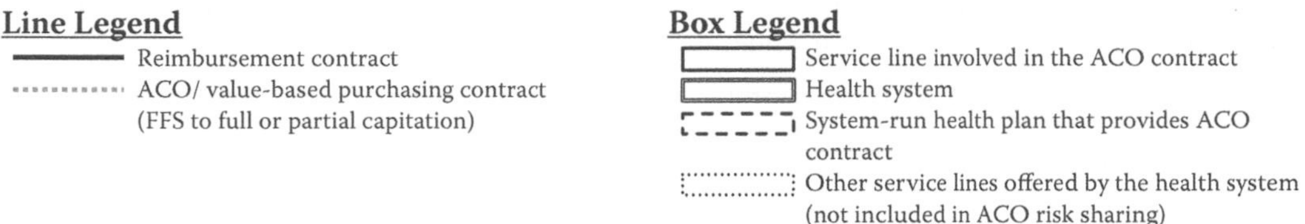

FIGURE 4.5 Potential commercial service line ACO structure and key.

Service Line ACO

The second type of single healthcare organization commercial ACO is created when there is an ACO agreement between providers within a specific service line of a health system and a payor operated by same parent health system. Because individual service lines do not typically contract with third party payors, service line ACOs will likely only exist within large health systems that are capable of sustaining health plans as an internal payor. The hypothetical structure of a service line ACO (with a key describing each entity and the relationships between them), is shown in Figure 4.5.

Figure 4.5 illustrates a hypothetical service line ACO model where an ACO agreement is formed between a commercial health system's internal health plan and the health system's laboratory service line (the entity within the ACO dotted ring enclosed in a thick black box labeled "Service line involved in the ACO contract"). Note that in the figure, only the health system is displayed, as an individual service line specifically does not contract with outside providers or vendors. While independent ACO contracts could exist with vendors that supply the materials needed for a specific service line, it would be difficult to correlate any benefits or negative impacts of these vendor contracts to the ACO contract between the health system's service line and the health plan. Therefore, the main focus of a service line ACO is the quality and cost of the services provided by the particular service line. While a service line ACO arrangement could potentially be set up for any service line, departments, such as pharmacology or laboratory, may be best suited to achieve desired ACO outcomes for several reasons:

1. There is little overlap in staff.
2. There is limited direct competition with other providers.
3. These departments have fairly standard through-put as to the type and volume of care services provided.

For these reasons, less complicated service lines also may act as a beneficial starting point for providers who aim to eventually transition to a full commercial health system ACO.[11]

Similar to a health plan ACO with an internal payor (denoted in the key by a square-dashed transactional line labeled "ACO/value-based purchasing contract" in the key), the ACO contract between the health plan and a service line ACO typically uses reimbursement models to incentivize service line staff to lower costs and increase quality. Additionally, as the staff of the service line will generally be a mix of employed physicians, midlevel providers, and technicians (depending on the type of service line), the health system may incentivize better outcomes and costs with various risk-based compensation arrangements, e.g., P4P models, as discussed further in Chapter 3. For example, if a service line's staff does not meet certain quality and/or cost benchmarks established by management, it may impact their potential bonus payment. It is important to note that, for models utilizing compensation-based financial incentives, it is essential, at least initially, to structure the incentives given when benchmarks are exceeded as bonuses, and not tie those incentives to the level of base salary. The use of such positive incentives, in contrast to negative incentives, may prevent the creation of a resentful and uncooperative environment between the service line staff and the health system's management.[12] For this reason, service line ACOs may require extra focus on physician/staff buy-in and culture transition.

Key Term	Definition
ACO Culture	An environment that emphasizes the importance of collaboration and quality as a means of lowering costs.

TRANSITION CHALLENGES

Irrespective of what structure a specific ACO adopts, each ACO should endeavor to achieve a similar goal, i.e., the coordination of patient services across the continuum of care to improve quality and lower expenditures. Even though most ACOs will likely have had provided some level of integrated care prior to their identifying as an ACO, some will have to transition at least a portion of their structures and/or procedures to strategically align with the ACO model and culture. According to the American Medical Group Association (AMGA), prior to the release of the MSSP Final Rule, more than 100 of its member groups had already achieved some level of integration and, therefore, were poised to become ACOs.[13] For these groups, the transition to a fully operational ACO, however extensive that transition might be, will at a minimum require the following attributes:

- Physician engagement
- Physician-driven management
- Adoption of best practices
- A focus on value to purchasers
- A focus on population health

Key Concept	Definition	Citation
ACO Goal	The coordination of patient care to improve quality and decrease expenditures.	*Accountable Care Organizations (ACO)*. Centers for Medicare & Medicaid Services, 2012. Online at: https://www.cms.gov/Medicare/Medicare-Fee-for-Service-Payment/ACO/index.html?redirect =/ACO/ (Accessed 5/30/12).

Distinct collaborations with peer organizations or consultants may ease the stress and learning curve pain associated with the transition to an ACO. Toward that end, Premier Healthcare Alliance (Premier)[14] initiated the Accountable Care Implementation Collaborative, a health system network designed to increase accountability by establishing partnerships with private payors to shift from volume-based payment models (i.e., FFS) to value-driven models.[15] The various transitional concerns that a developing ACO may encounter are addressed through the responsibilities of the workgroups established for Premier's collaborative, as illustrated in Exhibit 4.1.

Regardless of which structural or transitional model an ACO chooses to implement, the basic aspects of value-based purchasing will apply to all reimbursement models utilized by ACOs. As discussed in Chapter 3, value-based purchasing utilizes financial incentives that vary based on the proportion of risk that is shared between the ACO and the contracted payor.

OPERATIONAL CHALLENGES

Key Concept	Definition	Citation
Incentives	The ACO contract between the health plan and the service line ACO uses reimbursement models to incentivize service line staff to lower costs and increase quality. The health system may incentivize better outcomes and costs with various salary modes.	*Healthcare Innovation: How Plans and Providers Are Driving Change, Improving Care and Achieving Value in a Post Reform World.* Craig E. Samitt, paper presented at Cutting Costs and Raising Quality in Healthcare through Accountable Care Organizations, Chicago,: Active Communications International, September 16, 2011.

Imperative for the success of any ACO model are the inclusion and implementation of the following:

1. A method for establishing cost reduction targets and quality goals
2. Systems to monitor and measure data to determine financial incentives
3. The methods by which payors distribute achieved financial incentives to an ACO, and, subsequently, how the ACO distributes those incentives to participating entities and/or individuals

ACOs can be given financial incentives through two means: (1) shared savings (bonus) payments or (2) value-based reimbursement models. The models chosen for the offered incentives also will vary for both federal ACOs and commercial ACOs, as will the distribution of risk associated with each model. The varying amount of risk to which providers are exposed under different reimbursement models is illustrated in Figure 4.6.

The ACO model is only feasible if the level of risk an ACO acquires is offset by the probability of the ACO increasing its margins. This concept is expressed in the calculation below:

Operational Model of an ACO + Increased Efficiencies =

Ability to Manage Risk and Increase Margins[17]

Key Concept	Definition
Operational Model	The means of distributing financial incentives to an ACO is the main operational model an ACO must develop.

In coordination with a chosen model of financial incentives, ACOs must consider the means by which they plan to reduce patient expenditures. The expenditures associated with each patient are dependent on the type of value-based purchasing model implemented, e.g., under FFS models with

EXHIBIT 4.1
Accountable Care Implementation Collaborative Workgroups and Responsibilities

Workgroup	Responsibilities
People-Centered Foundation	• Define ideal experience and partner with community in the design of total care • Engage patients regarding their health and healthcare resources • Measure, monitor, and improve care experience and community health
Health Home	• Optimize primary care services, including population management and referral systems used by health homes • Manage primary care's involvement in other care settings (e.g., hospitals and nursing homes) • Develop systems for care coordination • Develop measurement and improvement systems for health home
High-Value Networks	• Develop a high-value delivery system for specialist, outpatient, inpatient, and all other care providers • Work with health homes to coordinate across continuum of care • Drive improvements in performance measures of success for overall ACO • Improve cost for facility and specialist services
Population Health Data Management	• Manage flow and analysis of clinical, financial, and health data across ACO • Develop HIT capability that leverages existing investments • Identify and develop business models that enable HIT
Payor Partnerships	• Develop model contract language and operating capabilities to align providers and payors • Facilitate data exchange, contractual terms, and operational processes with payor-partners • Develop aligned reimbursement methodologies for intra-ACO services (e.g., bundled payment arrangements) that could be administered by payor-partner
ACO Leadership	• Oversee all aspects of ACO, providing centralized management, strategic planning, and contract administration functions • Align compensation incentives with goals of ACO • Centralize medical management
Legal	• Provide legal guidance for ACO contracts • Evaluate and analyze ACO legal structures • Appropriately manage interactions across and between ACO members • Monitor ACO regulatory and legislative environment
Public Policy and Communications	• Develop and align policy from participant learning to promote ACOs in Medicare, Medicaid, and commercial market • Facilitate communication and knowledge transfer among participants
Measures Development	• Create measures to evaluate ACOs ability to reduce costs across the care continuum • Create measures to optimize quality of care across all ACO providers • Create measures to optimize population satisfaction with ACO • Develop measures to assess population health

Source: Premier Accountable Care Collaboratives—Driving to a People-Centered Health System. Premier Inc., 2011. Online at: https://www.premierinc.com/quality-safety/tools-services/ACO/ACO_WhitePaper_011410.pdf (Accessed 10/23/2012); Driving Population Health through Accountable Care Organizations. Susan DeVore and R. Wesley Champion, *Health Affairs*, vol. 30, no. 1, January 2011, p. 46.

shared savings bonus payments are tied to lowering payor expenditures, while those reimbursement models that share risk tie lower expenditures to overall margins. However, either model will be associated with lowering the cost of providing medical care. To lower expenditures, providers may seek to lower the amount of medical care provided by administering fewer tests, procedures, and visits or by utilizing cheaper medical care, i.e., less invasive procedures, less costly procedures, or the increased use of preventive care. For those ACOs reimbursed under FFS models, lowering patient expenditures may result in a conflict, and not insignificant concern, related to choosing between the guaranteed revenue achievable from the volume-based reimbursement FFS model and the potential for shared savings payments tied to lower costs. This dichotomy, between procedure

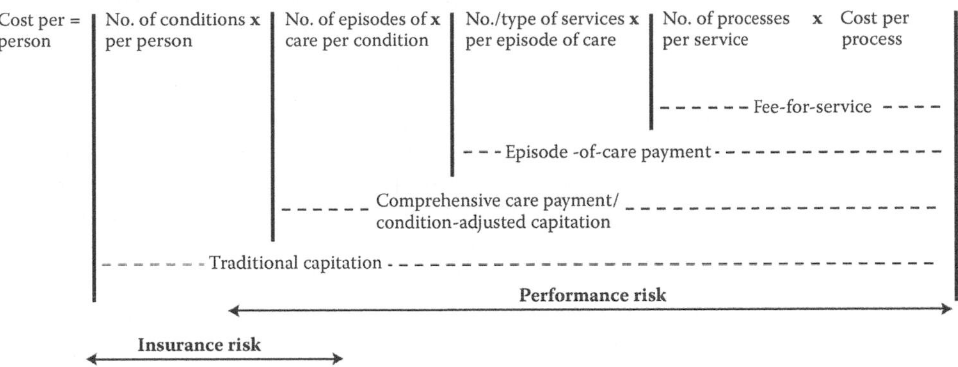

FIGURE 4.6 Provider risk spectrum for various reimbursement models. (Adapted from Endnote 16. With permission.)

volume and incentives for lowering cost, may influence the type of reimbursement model selected by the ACO and its contracted payor, and may highlight the significant difference between the operations of federal ACOs, which is restricted to FFS reimbursement, and commercial ACOs, which have the option to choose between FFS and other reimbursement models.

Key Concept	Definition	Citation
ACO Success	The ACO model is only feasible if the level of risk an ACO acquires is offset by the probability of the ACO increasing its margins.	*Managing Cost in an ACO Environment.* Brad Buxton, National Accountable Care Organization Congress: Los Angeles, November 1, 2011, p. 8.

Federal ACOs

Federal ACOs are reimbursed under a traditional FFS model, which still focuses on the volume of services provided rather than the value of services provided. As federal ACOs have no choice as to what reimbursement model they must accept, they will likely be focused on finding a compromise between volume-based FFS incentives and value-based shared savings incentives in order to maximize the potential financial rewards from shared savings payments.

While FFS reimbursement places little to no risk on the provider, federal ACOs must still manage risk through their shared savings payments. The one-sided distribution model allows federal ACOs to avoid risk (i.e., no shared losses) during their initial three-year contract in exchange for a smaller percentage of shared savings.[18] The two-sided risk model offsets the additional risk of possible shared losses by allowing the ACO to partake in a greater percentage of shared savings.[19] (The one-sided and two-sided models for shared savings payment disbursement are explained in detail in Chapter 2.)

ACOs under a one-sided risk model will be required at the end of the initial three-year contract period with CMS to transition to the two-sided model, and to assume the added risk of potential shared losses.[20] Although the prospect of not initially incurring the risk of shared losses may appeal to many potential ACOs, ACOs with larger beneficiary populations may achieve greater potential margins under the two-sided risk model, because the higher shared savings achievable under that model is more likely to offset the economic burdens of initial capital investment and ongoing operational costs. (A discussion of the financial feasibility of ACOs is provided in Chapter 7).

On December 19, 2011, the Center for Medicare and Medicaid Innovation (CMI) and CMS selected 32 interested healthcare entities to forgo traditional MSSP participation and branch into alternative reimbursement and shared savings models under the Pioneer ACO program.[21] The Pioneer ACO program is designed to offer higher risks and higher rewards than traditional federal ACOs can achieve under the limitations of the MSSP. Operationally, Pioneer ACOs are distinct in that, after the first two years of its contract term, Pioneer ACOs are given the option to transition from a volume-based FFS reimbursement model to a population-based payment model that incentivizes the value of services provided. The population-based payment model resembles, in some aspects, a capitated reimbursement structure, in that ACOs receive a prospective per-beneficiary monthly payment, i.e., per beneficiary per month (PBPM),[22] distinct from the per member per month (PMPM) payment under capitation, which applies to all patients covered by a health plan, in contrast to the PBPM, which applies only to those patients assigned by CMS as ACO beneficiaries. CMS has proposed several models of partial and full transition to the population-based model, discussed further in Chapter 2. The operational flexibility allotted to Pioneer ACOs is similar to the reimbursement models seen within the commercial ACO market.

Commercial ACOs

As discussed above, commercial ACOs contract with private payors and utilize a variety of value-based purchasing arrangements that each share differing amounts of risk between the ACO and the payor. Some commercial ACOs will emulate the federal MSSP, opting for a base FFS reimbursement model, accompanied by a shared savings arrangement. Other commercial ACOs may opt for reimbursement models that incentivize the value of services, ranging from pay-for-performance models to full capitation.[23] The risk associated with several of these reimbursement models is illustrated in Figure 4.6. Each type of reimbursement model is further described in Chapter 3.

There are no restrictions, for either federal ACOs or commercial ACOs, as to the number of payors with whom an ACO may enter into an ACO contract. Accordingly an ACO may operate in both federal ACO and commercial ACO markets. The flexibility of this multimarket scenario allows ACOs to take full advantage of the federal policy changes benefiting and supporting ACO development, while maximizing potential value-based financial incentives. Those ACOs that operate under multiple ACO contracts may be best served by choosing one operational model that is able to conform to each contract entered into, to lessen the complexity and ease the implementation of administrative and quality reporting requirements.

Factoid 4.2

The closest related ACO structures between the commercial and federal markets are the traditional federal ACO and a commercial health system ACO with an external payor.

Factoid 4.3

In the circumstance that compensation levels are used as a means of incentivizing physicians, it may be important to allow staff to receive extra salary when benchmarks are exceeded, so as to provide positive incentives and not create a distant and uncooperative environment between the staff and the health system. (Source: *Healthcare Innovation: How Plans and Providers Are Driving Change, Improving Care and Achieving Value in a Post Reform World.* Craig E. Samitt, paper presented at Cutting Costs and Raising Quality in Healthcare through Accountable Care Organizations, Chicago: Active Communications International, September 16, 2011.

COMPETITIVE MARKETPLACE CHALLENGES

Newly formed ACOs will have to overcome competitive obstacles stemming from both non-ACO providers and other ACOs. The geographic dispersion of existing ACOs suggests that geographic proximity to an existing ACO is correlated to new ACO development, i.e., ACOs tends to cluster around each other.[24] The increasing number of ACOs, as well as their tendency to emerge in the same market service areas, may heighten the need for ACOs to enter the competitive market in a carefully considered, strategic manner. The specific strategies and techniques by which an ACO addresses the competitive and other challenges within its market service environment may be, in part, dependent on the structural rules that govern it as an organization.

Federal ACOs

Under the MSSP, Medicare beneficiaries are given the freedom to seek care from a competing provider or leave an ACO entirely. This mobility may have negative consequences on potential shared savings payments available to ACOs in two possible circumstances:

1. Beneficiary migration could result in a significant change in the prospectively anticipated per-beneficiary benchmark for patient expenditures upon which ACO shared savings payments are based.
2. If poor quality of care is received by beneficiaries from providers outside the ACO, it might affect the ACO's quality metrics and consequently lower the ACO's shared savings payment, as well as expose the ACO to the risk of probation or termination.

These situations present extra incentives for a federal ACO to pursue strategies and techniques that lead to a high level of patient satisfaction in order to maintain patients within the ACO.

The MSSP's limits on ACO advertising complicate an ACO's patient-retention capabilities. While the Final Rule expanded ACO independence in advertising by eliminating the requirement that CMS must approve all marketing to beneficiaries, the Rule still allows CMS to disapprove of marketing material. The Final Rule requires that ACO advertising comply with the following guidelines:

1. Use CMS templates when available.
2. Do not be discriminatory.
3. Comply with the provision against beneficiary inducements.
4. Do not be materially inaccurate or misleading.[25]

As these guidelines are open to interpretation, federal ACOs should adopt competitive strategies and techniques when developing and implementing their marketing materials that provide maximum beneficiary loyalty and minimum attrition to competing providers, measure the comparable effectiveness of various types of advertising, and comply with regulatory guidelines in a manner that withstands scrutiny and CMS disapproval.

Commercial ACOs

Commercial ACOs are generally large health systems that are already established in the market, facilitating entry or expansion as compared to ACOs without such similar strengths. Without the marketing restrictions that limit federal ACOs, commercial ACOs will likely utilize competitive market strategies comparable to those used by any other integrated system, including Web sites, social media, press releases, billboards, and community outreach events. Commercial ACOs with internal payors may need strategic marketing to be less intense, because those beneficiaries covered by the internal health plan have little choice but to participate in the ACO. Instead these entities will strategically focus on internal marketing to promote culture shifts and provider acceptance.

In general, ACOs that successfully lower costs and increase quality, regardless of participation in the federal or commercial markets, have the benefit of touting their evidence-based quality reporting measures as a means to solicit and persuade patients to choose their ACO for the full spectrum of medical care needs, and retain them in the future.

Factoid 4.4

ACOs that successfully lower costs and increase quality, regardless of participation in the federal or commercial markets, should use their evidence-based quality reporting measures to persuade patients to choose their ACO for medical care.

CHAPTER SUMMARY

The range in possible interactions between ACO participants may lead to a wide variance in structural, transitional, operational, and competitive models utilized in ACO development and implementation. Structural decisions may be influenced by applicable regulations, capital resources, and market locations. While federal ACOs and commercial ACOs may have comparable provider relationships, CMS limits participation in the MSSP to a specific list of eligible entities. Commercial ACOs, not subject to CMS limitation, have significantly more flexibility in the structuring and development of the contractual arrangements that define them. Commercial ACOs with internal payor systems have the further autonomy to integrate as a single ACO organization, with no specific ACO contract, which provides additional flexibility and the potential for expanded financial benefits to both the ACO providers and the internal payor.

Provider buy-in, best practice adoption, financial feasibility, and patient population decisions are all important considerations for ACO transition models. For operational models, ACO participants must formulate a plan to reduce patient expenditures in order to maximize financial incentives based on the distinct or ACO contract(s), which each ACO enters into. Operational models also will need to address new interactions by the various ACO participants for the coordination of both clinical and administrative resources relied upon throughout the continuum of care to be provided to ACO beneficiaries, as well as the measurement of the performance of those resources, both on an individual and collective basis.

As the number of ACOs grows, there will invariably be increased competition for market share between ACOs and non-ACO providers. Successful ACOs will inevitably be those that determine a strategic and effective means of marketing to those patients whose care, as an ACO beneficiary, most influences the ACO's potential for achieving, with an acceptable risk profile, their shared savings payment or other financial incentives. Federal ACOs face additional challenges related to developing and implementing these competitive market strategies and tactics requisite to achieving and sustaining success in their market service areas (MSAs), as they are operating under restrictive provisions of the MSSP.

ACO models that operate in both the federal ACO and commercial ACO markets, with several ACO contracts between a variety of private payors and CMS, may prove to be the most feasible, both operationally and financially. These multimarket ACOs may benefit from both the structural flexibility of commercial ACOs and the regulatory safeguards and waivers available to federal ACOs, while also expanding the number of patient populations for which they may receive financial incentives.

Ultimately, a healthcare provider's selection of the appropriate model for the development, implementation, and operation of an ACO is a function of carefully considering the structural, operational, and reimbursement features that will best address the organization's: (1) potential for financial rewards; (2) operational capabilities, competitive posture, and adoptive capacity of its resources; (3) market; (4) capital formation capacity; and (5) appetite for and ability to manage risk, in a manner that will most effectively advance the mission, objectives, and overall strategic direction of the organization.

ENDNOTES

1. *The Leap to Accountable Care Organizations*. Jim Molpus, HealthLeaders Media Intelligence, HcPro, April 2011, p. 13.
2. *Pioneer Accountable Care Organization Model: General Fact Sheet*. Center for Medicare and Medicaid Services, December 19, 2011
3. *HHS Announces 89 New Accountable Care Organizations*. Health and Human Services, July 9, 2012. Online at: http://www.hhs.gov/news/press/2012pres/07/20120709a.html (Accessed 10/23/2012).
4. *2012 Healthcare Benchmarks: Accountable Care Organizations*, 2nd ed. Healthcare Information Network: Sea Grit, NJ, 2012, p. 7.
5. Within the survey, "sponsored" refers to the legal organization that directed the creation of the ACO. *Growth and Dispersion of Accountable Care Organizations: June 2012 Update*. David Muhlestein, et al., 2012, Salt Lake City, UT: Leavitt Partners, LLC., p. 9.
6. Ibid., pp. 6, 9.
7. Ibid., pp. 12, 13.
8. Medicare Program; Medicare Shared Savings Program: Accountable Care Organizations. *Federal Register* vol. 76, no. 212 (November 2, 2011), p. 67813.
9. The partial exclusivity requirement of the Final Rule is described in more detail in Chapter 2: Federal ACOs; Medicare Program; Medicare Shared Savings Program: Accountable Care Organizations, p. 67867.
10. Medicare Program; Medicare Shared Savings Program: Accountable Care Organizations, p. 67853.
11. Healthcare Innovation: How Plans and Providers Are Driving Change, Improving Care and Achieving Value in a Post Reform World. Craig E. Samitt, paper presented at *Cutting Costs and Raising Quality in Healthcare through Accountable Care Organizations*. Chicago: Active Communications International, September 16, 2011.
12. Ibid.
13. The Accountable Care Oarganization: Whatever Its Growing Pains, the Concept Is Too Vitally Important to Fail. Francis J Crosson, *Health Affairs*, vol. 30, no. 7, July 11, 2011, p. 1252.
14. The Premier Healthcare Alliance is a company that connects groups of providers and suppliers (currently over 2,715 hospital systems and integrated delivery systems, 56,000 nonacute healthcare facilities, 34,000 physician offices, and 800 suppliers) to reduce costs and improve care. *Is Premier Right For You?* Premier Inc., 2012. Online at: https://www.premierinc.com/wps/portal/premierinc/public/jointhealliance/whoitbenefits/!ut/p/b1/04_Sj9CPykssy0xPLMnMz0vMAfGjzOJNzQzMnJwMHQ3cvQwsDDxDzP1MnX18DS1MTIEKIoEKDHAARwN8-g18zaH68SggYL-XflRmUq5eeXKunoGepbmBhYWhkampoaGBibGlfrh-FH77TaEK8LjfzyM_N1W_IDc0ojI4IB0AH5syvA!!/dl4/d5/L2dBISEvZ0FBIS9nQSEh/ (Accessed 10/23/2012).
15. Driving Population Health through Accountable Care Organizations. Susan DeVore and R. Wesley Champion, *Health Affairs*, vol. 30, no. 1, January 2011, p. 41.
16. From Volume to Value: Better Ways to Pay for Health Care. Harold D. Miller, *Health Affairs*, vol. 28, no. 5, September/October 2009, p. 1419.
17. *Managing Cost in an ACO Environment*. Brad Buxton, National Accountable Care Organization Congress: Los Angeles, November 1, 2011, p. 8.
18. Medicare Program; Medicare Shared Savings Program: Accountable Care Organizations, pp. 67985–67986.
19. Ibid., pp. 67986–67987.
20. Ibid., p. 67985.
21. *Pioneer Accountable Care Organization Model: General Fact Sheet*. Centers for Medicare and Medicaid Services: Washington, D.C., December 19, 2011.
22. Ibid.

23. The Journey to Becoming an Accountable Care Organization (ACO). Namc J. Ham, MedVentive Inc., paper presented at *Cutting Costs and Raising Quality in Healthcare through Accountable Care Organizations*. Chicago: Active Communications International, September 15, 2011, p. 27; *HFMA's Value Project: Phase 2: Defining and Delivering Value.* Healthcare Financial Management Association: Westchester, IL, June 2012, p. 9.
24. *Growth and Dispersion of Accountable Care Organizations*. David Muhlstein, et al., Leavitt Partners, November 28, 2011. Online at: http://leavittpartnersblog.com/2011/11/growth-and-dispersion-of-accountable-care-organizations/ (Accessed 1/27/2012), p. 6.
25. Medicare Program; Medicare Shared Savings Program: Accountable Care Organizations, pp. 67947–67948.

Acronyms

Acronym	Definition
CMS	Centers for Medicare and Medicaid Services
MSSP	Medicare Shared Savings Program
GPO	Group Purchasing Organizations
PCP	Primary Care Providers
TIN	Tax Identification Number
FFS	Fee-For-Service
P4P	Pay-For-Performance
AMGA	American Medical Group Association
CMI	Center for Medicare and Medicaid Innovation
PBPM	Per Beneficiary Per Month
PMPM	Per Member Per Month

5 Impact of ACOs on the Healthcare Industry

Addressing Industry Concern

The introduction and evolution of ACOs has generated a significant amount of public reaction, and industry providers and payors have expressed concerns regarding how these emerging organizations may potentially impact the healthcare industry, contemplating both positive and negative consequences. In considering the value metrics of ACOs, the Four Pillars of Healthcare Industry Value, i.e., regulatory, reimbursement, competition, and technology, can be utilized as a construct to address and examine each stakeholder's anticipations and apprehensions, within the context of the current and prospective healthcare environment.

Key Concept	Definition	Citation
Four Pillars of Healthcare Industry Value	The four elements of the health care industry: reimbursement, regulatory, competition, and technology.	Health Capital Consultants

REGULATORY CONCERNS

The regulatory issues surrounding ACO development, implementation, and operation could impact the manner by which ACOs are established and adopted, as well as how ACO participants, and non-ACO providers, act within the competitive healthcare environment. The complex and integrated structure of ACOs might trigger regulatory scrutiny (which may act to restrict some types and levels of collaboration) on both federal and state levels, including:

1. Antikickback statutes
2. Prohibitions against physician self-referral (e.g., the Stark Law)
3. Civil monetary penalty laws
4. Corporate practice of medicine prohibitions
5. Antitrust laws

The increased scrutiny regarding fraud and abuse enforcement in healthcare arrangements has led to a complicated industry environment of opposing government policies, which both encourage an increase in the coordination of care and integration across health entities while, at the same time, discouraging it because providers are reluctant to innovate due to their rising concerns regarding avoiding scenarios that may suggest noncompliance with applicable law.

Impact on Providers

Antikickback Laws

Both federal and state antikickback laws have the potential to impact the formation and operation of ACOs. The Federal Antikickback Statute (AKS) is a criminal law that prohibits the acceptance of monetary incentives for referring health services paid for, in whole or part, by a federal healthcare program.[1] A violation of the AKS is considered a felony, punishable by either up to five years in prison, criminal fines up to $25,000, or both.[2] The AKS is designed to prevent physician payment for referrals that may occur under the pretext of another type of financial or management arrangement. The integration contracts between ACO participants and ACO provider/suppliers, especially in the commercial ACO market where an ACO is not required to be a single legal entity, creates financial relationships between participants, e.g., shared savings disbursement contracts, making a sound understanding of potential AKS violations, and how to avoid them, a requirement for all ACO participants.

The AKS contains a number of safe harbor exceptions, which could shield ACO participants from possible violations. Safe harbors set forth the criteria that, if met, identify an arrangement as compliant with the AKS, even if it would otherwise have been suspect. These safe harbors are intended to allow physicians to engage in certain business practices without the concern of prompting fraud and abuse allegations.[3] One safe harbor, particularly applicable to ACOs, is the direct employment of physicians by a hospital.[4] The majority of ACOs have a hospital-based core, which will likely contain an employed physician staff infrastructure that could shield ACO providers from AKS violations under the direct employment relationship safe harbor.

However, direct employment may not be a viable option for all ACOs, or for all physicians within an ACO. ACO participants should be aware that there are currently no explicit safe harbors for many of the financial arrangements between providers that may be present within an ACO, e.g.: (1) gain-sharing, an arrangement by which an ACO provides financial incentives for physicians meeting quality and efficiency criteria; or (2) bundled payments, an arrangement by which insurers provide a single payment for hospital and physician services that are typically linked to a single episode of care. These and other potential ACO financial arrangements were discussed further in Chapter 3 and Chapter 4.

Key Term	Definition	Citation
Safe Harbors	Exceptions to federal fraud and abuse laws that identify criteria that must be met to shield an arrangement from liability.	*Federal Anti-Kickback Law and Regulatory Safe Harbors*. Office of Inspector General (November 1999).

Under §3022 of the ACA (Patient Protection and Affordable Care Act, 2010), the secretary of Health and Human Services (HHS) has the authority to waive compliance with the AKS, "as may be necessary" to facilitate the use of any payment model for ACOs that the secretary determines may improve ACO quality and efficiency.[5] The MSSP Final Rule published by the Center for Medicare/Medicaid Services (CMS) defines and implements these waivers.

It is important to note that there is no preemption provision under the federal AKS, meaning that states are able to formulate their own antikickback legislation that may differ from the federal regulation. Many states have established their own antikickback laws, meaning that ACOs, and ACO participants, should review any state laws and regulations applicable to their market service area(s) in order to ensure compliance with state laws.

Stark Law

Key Term	Definition	Citation
Stark Law	The physician self-referral law that prohibits referrals to an organization of which that physician or that physician's family has a financial relationship.	*Stark Law: Civil Monetary Penalties*. vol. 42 U.S.C. 1320a–1327a (1989).

Some models for structuring the integration between physicians and healthcare entities, which is the basis for forming a successful ACO, may present challenges to avoid violating the federal physician self-referral law, known as the Stark Law. The Stark Law differs from the AKS in several key ways:

1. Stark Law violations are punishable by civil penalties, whereas AKS violations are considered criminal offenses.
2. While both laws prohibit specific physician referrals, the Stark Law prohibits referrals to an entity with which the referring physician has a financial relationship, while the AKS prohibits the acceptance of remuneration in exchange for referrals.
3. While the Stark Law is only applicable to referrals of Medicare and Medicaid patients, the AKS is applicable to patients under any federal program.[6]

Factoid 5.1

Stark Law prohibits physicians from referring Medicare patients for designated health services to an entity that the physician or an immediate family member of the physician has a financial relationship. (Source: *Financial Relationships between Physicians and Entities Furnishing Designated Health Services.* Vol. 42 CFR Section 411.351 (October 10, 2010).)

Key Term	Definition	Citation
Designated Health Services	Enumerated services that physicians are prohibited to provide under the Stark Law. Includes (1) clinical laboratory services; (2) physical therapy, occupational therapy, and outpatient speech-language pathology services; (3) radiology and certain other imaging services; (4) radiation therapy services and supplies; (5) durable medical equipment and supplies; (6) parental and enteral nutrients, equipment, and supplies; (7) prosthetics, orthotics, and prosthetic devices and supplies; (8) home health services; (9) outpatient prescription drugs; and (10) inpatient and outpatient hospital services.	*Financial Relationships between Physicians and Entities Furnishing Designated Health Services,* vol. 42 CFR Section 411.351 (October 10, 2010).

The Stark Law prohibits physicians from referring Medicare and Medicaid patients for designated health services (DHS) to an entity where the physician, or an immediate family member of the physician, has a financial relationship, which may include[7] (1) any direct or indirect ownership or any investment interest or compensation arrangement between a hospital and an entity providing DHS, e.g., a physician practice group. The DHS enumerated in the Stark Law include:

- Clinical laboratory services
- Physical therapy, occupational therapy, and outpatient speech-language pathology services
- Radiology and certain other imaging services
- Radiation therapy services and supplies
- Durable medical equipment and supplies
- Parental and enteral nutrients, equipment, and supplies
- Prosthetics, orthotics, and prosthetic devices and supplies
- Home health services
- Outpatient prescription drugs
- Inpatient and outpatient hospital services[8]

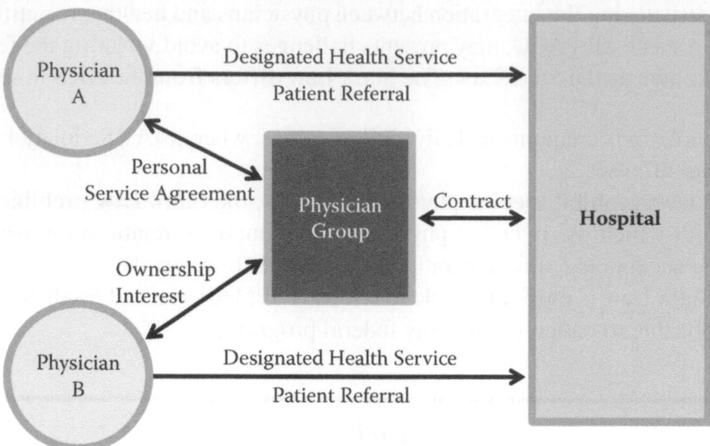

FIGURE 5.1 Direct/indirect Stark Law compensation exception.

Sanctions for violating the Stark Law vary depending on whether the physician had knowledge of the violation. If the physician who is being accused of noncompliance acted in good faith and without knowledge, he or she may simply be denied the Medicare reimbursement for the noncompliant claim. The penalties for knowingly (or a scenario where a referring physician should have had reason to know) violating Stark Law are more severe, e.g., a civil monetary penalty of up to $15,000 per item or service billed plus twice the amount claimed may be imposed.[9]

Similar to the AKS safe harbors, there are certain scenarios that are excluded from sanctions under the Stark Law, known as *exceptions*. Exceptions include those arrangements where there is little risk of abuse and that encourage integration among physicians.[10] The most common exceptions to Stark Law include: (1) an ownership/investment interest exceptions,[11] (2) a service exception,[12] and (3) a direct or indirect compensation arrangement exception.[13] A visual representation of the direct and indirect compensation exception required to avoid liability is illustrated in Figure 5.1.

In Figure 5.1, Physicians A and B are members of a Physician Group and are both making patient referrals to the hospital for DHS. Physician A has an indirect compensation agreement with the hospital, whereby the Physician Group acts as a barrier between Physician A and the hospital. In contrast, Physician B has an ownership interest in the Physician Group, which means that Physician B "stands in the shoes" of the Physician Group and has a direct compensation agreement with the Hospital.[14] In conjunction with the Medicare Shared Savings Program (MSSP), CMS established certain waivers to Stark Law and AKS, further protecting federal ACOs from potential allegations of fraud. These waivers are discussed below.

Factoid 5.2

Included in the compliance waiver is the circumvention of Stark Law's financial relationship restrictions. Under the waiver, "any financial relationship between or among the ACO, its ACO participants, and its ACO providers/suppliers that implicates the Physician Self-Referral Law" are waived. To be eligible for any of the waivers, the arrangements must be "reasonably related to the purpose of the Shared Savings Program." (Source: *Medicare Program; Final Waivers in Connection with the Shared Savings Program.* Vol. 76 Fed. Reg. Page 68001 (November 2, 2011).)

The waivers established to promote the success of federal ACOs are not applicable in the commercial ACO market, further subjecting commercial ACOs to possible noncompliance with the Stark Law. Commercial ACOs may have a higher potential of violating the Stark Law than their federal counterparts. While federal ACOs have to be a single, fully integrated legal entity, commercial ACOs have more flexibility in how they elect to structure their organizations. As a result, when determining the structure of the commercial ACO, participants are required to be proactive in avoiding those provider relationships that may be suspect.

Similar to the AKS, a majority of states also have their own legislative prohibitions against physician self-referrals that ACOs must be aware of, in order to maintain compliance. Of note, if an ACO is suspected of a violation of either the AKS or Stark Law, it also may be subject to legal action under the False Claims Act (FCA), a federal law that creates civil liability for any person who "... knowingly presents, or causes to be presented, a false or fraudulent claim for payment or approval. ..."[15] The FCA also enforces liability when a provider should have known, i.e., reckless disregard and deliberate ignorance, that a claim was fraudulent.[16] Violations under the Stark Law and AKS leave providers vulnerable to *qui tam* actions, where another individual can "turn them in" and the Draconian liabilities of treble damages are based on the amount of "damage" the government sustains, i.e., the total amount of claims submitted.[17]

Civil Monetary Penalties

Key Term	Definition	Citation
Civil Monetary Penalties Law	Some guidelines regarding civil monetary penalties have been codified into this federal law, which specifically prohibits, among other things, payments by hospitals to physicians in return for reducing or limiting care.	*Stark Law: Civil Monetary Penalties: Payments to Induce Reduction or Limitation of Services.* vol. 42 U.S.C. 1320a-7a(b) (1989).

Civil monetary penalties (CMP), as authorized through §1128(a) of the Social Security Act,[18] are a method by which the secretary of HHS may assess financial penalties for various types of illegal conduct, e.g., violating the federal AKS or Stark law.[19] Several guidelines regarding civil monetary penalties have been codified into a Civil Monetary Penalties Law (CMPL).[20] The CMPL specifically prohibits payments by hospitals to physicians in return for reducing or limiting care.[21] ACO participants have expressed concern that the potential cost-management techniques[22] utilized by ACOs, as well as the value-based reimbursement models possible for commercial ACOs, e.g., capitation, might be perceived as incentivizing ACO physicians to underutilize services and/or direct higher cost patients away from the ACO, in violation of the CMPL. However, ACO participants have the expectation as derived from certain elements of the preparticipation and participation waivers, discussed below, that they should be able to avoid allegations of CMPL violations of underutilization and inappropriate utilization by ensuring that their organization's structure is aimed at improving efficiency and controlling cost rather than merely cutting costs.[23]

CMS Waivers

Key Concept	Definition	Citation
Waivers	ACOs participating in the MSSP are eligible for five waivers established by HHS, including the interim final rule has five waivers: (1) an ACO preparticipation waiver, (2) an ACO participation waiver, (3) a shared savings distributions waiver, (4) a compliance with the Physician Self-Referral Law waiver, and (5) a patient incentive waiver. CMS issued an interim final rule detailing these waivers.	Medicare Program; Final Waivers in Connection with the Shared Savings Program. *Federal Register.* vol. 76, no. 212 (November 2, 2011). p. 67993.

The physician relationships that exist within a federal ACO participating in the MSSP may not be subject to some of the restrictions mandated under the Federal Antikickback Statute (AKS), the Federal Stark Law, or the Civil Monetary Penalties Law (CMPL), due to certain waivers established by HHS. In conjunction with the MSSP Final Rule, CMS issued on November 2, 2011, an Interim

Final Rule detailing five waivers to support the compliance of valid business arrangements under the AKS, Stark Law, and CMPL, including:

1. An ACO preparticipation waiver
2. An ACO participation waiver
3. A shared savings distributions waiver
4. A compliance with the physician self-referral law waiver
5. A patient incentive waiver[24]

The preparticipation waiver is designed "… to protect *bona fide* ACO investment, start-up, operating, and other arrangements that carry out the Shared Savings Program" [emphasis added].[25] Preparticipation and participation waivers were created with the expectation that "… risks of fraud and abuse, such as overutilization, inappropriate utilization, and underutilization, will be mitigated … by the Shared Savings Program design."[26] These two waivers are designed to transition seamlessly from preparticipation to participation, and the time duration for which each specific waiver is available to ACOs is limited. Preparticipation waivers begin one year preceding the ACO application due date for entities that are pursuing ACO status in good faith, and ends at either: (1) the date when an ACO is accepted into the MSSP and the ACO contract begins, or (2) the date the ACO's application is denied.[27] For accepted ACOs, the participation waiver automatically begins at the onset of the ACO contract.[28] While preparticipation and participation waivers protect an ACO during its development, the shared savings distribution waiver allows for the successful operation of an ACO.

The shared savings distribution waiver allows an ACO to distribute its earned shared savings payment among its ACO participants, ACO providers/suppliers, and ACO professionals in a manner that may otherwise violate the AKS, Stark Law, or CMPL. Under this waiver, even distributions to physicians outside of the ACO are allowed, if they are considered compensation for activities reasonably related to the purposes of the MSSP.[29] Of note is that if CMS determines that distributions are knowingly made in a manner that would "… induce [a] physician to reduce or limit medically necessary items or services to patients …," those arrangements would not qualify for the waiver.[30]

The compliance waiver acts as a catchall for self-referral financial relationships, circumventing Stark Law violations for many ACO financial relationships. Under the waiver, "… any financial relationship between or among the ACO, its ACO participants, and its ACO providers/suppliers that implicates the Physician Self-Referral Law" are waived, provided that (1) the ACO has entered into, and is in good standing with, its participation agreement; (2) the financial relationship is "reasonably related" to the purposes of the MSSP; and (3) the financial relationship falls under one of the currently available Physician Self-Referral (aka Stark Law) exceptions.[31] Where appropriate, the compliance waiver also may shield ACOs from potential AKS and CMPL violations related to self-referral arrangements.

The patient incentive waiver is designed to promote preventive care and patient engagement in care management programs. Without the waiver, arrangements such as providing beneficiaries with free or below-fair market value items and services to incentivize the utilization of services provided at an ACO may violate the AKS or the CMPL prohibition of beneficiary inducements. Of note is that the patient incentive waiver does not apply to manufacturers or vendors; however, the waiver does apply to any items or services a provider received at a discounted rate from a manufacturer or vendor.[32]

It is important that providers understand that, to be eligible for any of the waivers, the targeted arrangement must be "… reasonably related to the purposes of the Shared Savings Program."[33] As with previous safe harbors, exceptions, and waivers issued by CMS over the past several decades, the exact interpretation of these safe harbors, exceptions, and waivers will only be established following the actual experiences of ACOs, with a variety of structures, relationships, agreements, and MSSP distribution scenarios operating in a market.

Antitrust Violations

Key Term	Definition	Citation
Sherman Antitrust Act	Prohibits monopolies, contracts, combinations, and conspiracies that unreasonably restrain trade. Antitrust liability is analyzed using two standards: (1) per se illegality and (2) the rule of reason.	*Dictionary of Health Insurance and Managed Care*. David E. Marcinko, Springer Publishing, New York, 2006, p. 265.

Antitrust laws are designed to prevent monopolies and encourage competition in the marketplace. The Sherman Antitrust Act prohibits monopolies (monopolization, attempted monopolization, and conspiracies to monopolize), contracts, combinations, and, conspiracies that unreasonably restrain trade.[34] The Clayton Act prohibits: (1) price discrimination, (2) tying and exclusive dealing arrangements, and (3) mergers and joint ventures that could create a monopoly.[35] Authorized under the Federal Trade Commission Act, the Federal Trade Commission (FTC) has authority to bring actions against anticompetitive practices.[36] Antitrust liability is determined by analyzing business arrangements by one of two standards: (1) per se illegality and (2) the rule of reason. Per se illegality is a strict standard, meaning that the act is illegal on its face, e.g., price fixing. Alternatively, the rule of reason is a flexible standard that utilizes a comparative approach when evaluating a merger by analyzing the anticompetitive effects as compared to any procompetitive efficiencies, e.g., market dominance approaching a monopoly or concerted refusal to deal (group boycott).[37]

With the formation of a successful ACO, the collaboration among independent providers, who may have previously been considered competitors, may be perceived as creating a scenario for potential antitrust violations.[38] Requisite ACO activities, e.g., the negotiation of fees between independent providers participating in the ACO, might be perceived as price fixing.[39] Additionally, providers excluded from participating in an ACO may bring antitrust challenges against that ACO.

The Federal Trade Commission and the Department of Justice (FTC-DOJ) issued a final policy statement regarding antitrust issues and federal ACOs on October 28, 2011.[40] Within that policy statement, the FTC-DOJ set forth guidelines for antitrust "safety zones" available to all partially integrated federal ACO collaborations—but not mergers—of "… otherwise independent providers and provider groups that are eligible and intend, or have been approved, to participate in the [MSSP]."[41] Under the ACO antitrust guidelines, ACOs formed through the merger of two or more organizations will be evaluated under the FTC's Horizontal Merger Guidelines, which detail the agencies' policies and procedures regarding any merger and acquisition involving actual or potential competitors under federal antitrust laws.[42] Of note, while the FTC-DOJ final policy statement does not directly apply to commercial ACOs, the two agencies did include in the statement that the lower "rule of reason" standard for liability should be applied to arrangements where a federal ACO negotiates with a commercial ACO in order to meet patient care needs and improve the delivery of healthcare.[43]

Key Concept	Definition	Citation
Horizontal Integration	Financial integration that requires collaboration among rivals.	*Dictionary of Health Insurance and Managed Care*. Edward Marcinko, Springer Publishing, New York, 2006, p. 144.

Under the FTC-DOJ final policy statement, in order to determine the risk of potential anticompetitive effects from partially integrated federal ACO collaborations, an analysis of an ACO's share of services in its primary service area (PSA) must be conducted.[44] An ACO's market share is calculated through the Medicare Specialty codes (including outpatient and inpatient services) billed within the organization's PSA, defined in the final policy statement as "… the lowest number of postal zip codes from which the [ACO participant] draws at least 75 percent of its [patients]."[45]

Under the proposed policy statement, published on April 19, 2011, the FTC-DOJ had set three levels of potential risk based on the calculated market share: (1) no risk, (2) optional risk, and (3) high

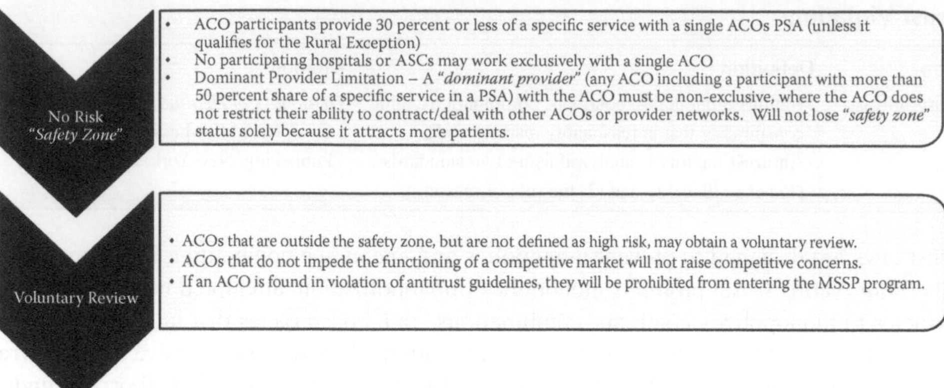

No Risk
"Safety Zone"
• ACO participants provide 30 percent or less of a specific service with a single ACOs PSA (unless it qualifies for the Rural Exception)
• No participating hospitals or ASCs may work exclusively with a single ACO
• Dominant Provider Limitation – A "dominant provider" (any ACO including a participant with more than 50 percent share of a specific service in a PSA) with the ACO must be non-exclusive, where the ACO does not restrict their ability to contract/deal with other ACOs or provider networks. Will not lose "safety zone" status solely because it attracts more patients.
Voluntary Review
• ACOs that are outside the safety zone, but are not defined as high risk, may obtain a voluntary review.
• ACOs that do not impede the functioning of a competitive market will not raise competitive concerns.
• If an ACO is found in violation of antitrust guidelines, they will be prohibited from entering the MSSP program.

Steps to Calculating an ACO Participants PSA Share

1. Identify all services provided by at least two ACO participants
2. Identify the PSA (*"lowest number of postal zip codes from which the participant draws at least 75 percent of its patients"*) for each participant providing the common service
3. For each common services, compare ACOs PSA share of the ACO participant

To be in the "*safety zone,*" the "*30 percent threshold must be met in each relevant PSA for each common service*"

FIGURE 5.2 Levels of antitrust risk for federal ACOs. (From Reference 49.)

risk, which level of risk determines what actions must be taken by the ACO and the FTC-DOJ to maintain compliance. ACOs with a high level of risk were to be subject to mandatory review if any service offered reached the 50% market share threshold for either a common service or the primary service area (PSA).[46] However, due to concerns regarding overly burdensome administrative requirement,[47] the mandatory review provision was not included within the final policy statement, and instead ACOs with questionable market power were offered a voluntary review. An illustrative depiction of the levels of risk ultimately established by the FTC-DOJ is diagrammed in Figure 5.2.[48]

Key Concept	Definition	Citation
Vertical Integration	Financial integration that requires collaboration among the various providers along a continuum of care.	*Dictionary of Health Insurance and Managed Care*. Edward Marcinko, Springer Publishing, New York, 2006, p. 293.

While the mandatory review provision is absent in the final policy statement, the FTC-DOJ did retain the dominate participant limitation, whereby any ACO participant who controls over 50 percent of any service within the PSA that no other participant provides, must be nonexclusive to the ACO for the ACO to remain within a safety zone.[50] The final policy statement states that any ACO that has a market presence outside of a safety zone is not assumed to be in violation of antitrust laws, However, ACOs in that circumstance may apply for a voluntary 90 day review to ensure compliance.[51] To remain compliant, the FTC identified four suspect categories of conduct that ACOs should avoid including:

1. Inhibiting commercial payors from directing patients toward certain providers
2. Tying the sale of services from the ACO to a commercial payor's purchase of services outside the ACO
3. Creating exclusive contracts with nonprimary care providers (e.g., specialists, hospitals, ASCs)
4. Inhibiting commercial payors from distributing provider cost, quality, efficiency, and performance information to enrollees.[52] Despite overall support, some concerns have been raised regarding the expansion to the FTC's traditional enforcement role to include oversight of provider participation in a Federal program.

Critics of the final statement on antitrust enforcement have been weary of the rigid phrasing of safe harbor pronouncements tied to vague language of suspect categories. In addition, provider advocate groups, e.g., the American Medical Association (AMA) and the American Hospital Association (AHA), have criticized the lack of an appeals process, especially given that other federal agencies, with similar control over participation eligibility are required under the Administrative Procedure Act[53] to provide minimum due process standards, including an appeals mechanism.[54]

An ACO may act to limit the suspicion of an antitrust violation by presenting itself as a single entity (given that these fully integrated organizations are not subject to the addition scrutiny rendered under the FTC-DOJ final policy statement, but only through traditional antitrust guidelines) through both: (1) financial integration, which requires that ACO participants share substantial financial risk through payment arrangements; and (2) clinical integration, expressed through a unified management structure.[55] Two types of integration exist: horizontal integration and vertical integration. Horizontal integration requires collaboration among rivals and may be more likely to result in increased prices for healthcare services and the development of an anticompetitive market.[56] In contrast, vertical integration requires collaboration among the ACO participating providers along a patient's continuum of care, which, as the central purpose of an ACO, may lessen antitrust scrutiny. Even though fully integrated ACOs are not specifically addressed as subject to antitrust scrutiny in the FTC-DOJ final policy statement, these organizations may still come under review through the traditional FTC processes.[57]

Corporate Practice of Medicine Laws

Key Term	Definition	Citation
Corporate Practice of Medicine (CPOM) prohibitions	These prohibitions, which exist in several states, bar a business corporation from practicing medicine or employing a doctor for the purposes of practicing medicine.	*Corporate Practice of Medicine Doctrine 50 State Survey Summary.* Mary Michal, et al., the Hospice and Palliative Care Practice Group of Reinhart Boerner Van Deuren, September 2006, p. 2.

The Corporate Practice of Medicine (CPOM) laws prohibit business corporations from engaging in the practice of medicine and employing doctors for the purpose of practicing medicine.[58] The CPOM laws are regulated on a state level, so any exceptions to the laws are unique to each state's specific CPOM legislation. However, there are two exceptions common to most states that allow for the standard practice of medicine by hospitals and physicians. Under these exceptions: (1) hospitals may employ doctors to practice medicine, so long as the hospital is a licensed entity; and (2) doctors may practice through a professional corporation, though generally all shareholders must also be licensed physicians.[59]

Each of the 50 states and the District of Columbia has a collection of statutory legislation dealing with topics affecting the CPOM.[60] However, the constraints of each regulation vary significantly by state.[61] ACOs operating in states with more restrictive CPOM regulations may experience obstructions for ACO participation, based on the specific state's legislation. For example, several states, i.e., California, Colorado, Illinois, Iowa, New York, New Jersey, and Texas, prohibit hospital employment of physicians for the provision of out-patient services, which could significantly constrain the structure of ACOs,[62] particularly given the opportunity for cost containment offered through these arrangements (discussed below).

Another hurdle for ACO development created by CPOM laws, e.g., the Texas Medical Practice Act, prohibits a physician's professional income from being divided on a percentage basis among nonphysicians, unless that nonphysician is an independent contractor.[63] Texas courts have raised concerns, most notably in *Flynn Brothers v. First Medical Associates*, with independent contractor agreements, holding that these types of agreements may not be utilized solely to circumvent the law if, in actuality, an employer–employee relationship exists between the parties.[64] Flynn Brothers, and similar case law, may be of particular importance for Commercial ACOs, where independent contractor agreements offer a relatively lower commitment method of integration.

Factoid 5.3

There is a concern regarding CMP laws that ACOs could start to underuse needed or effective care and steer sicker, higher-cost patients away from hospitals with gain-sharing programs. ACOs should ensure that their structure is aimed at improving efficiency and controlling cost rather than including incentives to underprovide care. (Source: *Physician-Hospital Clinical Integration: Navigating the Complexities*. Webinar presented by Strattford, October 10, 2010; *5 Key Regulatory Concerns for ACOs*. Lindsey Dunn, Becker's Hospital Review (September 14, 2010).)

The CPOM doctrine has been lauded by supporters as a means of maintaining the integrity of medical decisions made by physicians, because it removes any potential influences that a nonmedical entity, acting as an employer, might have on its physician employees.[65] Opponents of CPOM legislation maintain that such prohibitions merely act as barriers to the creation of alternative healthcare systems that may resolve current issues, e.g., the shortage of rural physicians.[66] Stakeholders concerned with the potential negative impact of CPOM laws on ACO formation have suggested that the least complicated solution for ACO arrangements, aside from the repeal of austere CPOM laws, would be the creation of exceptions, waivers, or safe harbors from the enforcement of CPOM laws through state regulatory edicts.[67]

Federal Tax Liability

Another concern for ACOs is how the creation of a new entity, through the integration of many existing organizations, may impact an ACO's tax status, because ACOs require the financial integration of participating providers, which may include both not-for-profit tax-exempt entities, as well as for-profit taxable entities.[68] Unaffiliated entities may attempt clarification by seeking an advanced Internal Revenue Service (IRS) ruling as to whether ACO participation would affect their tax status.[69]

In 2011, the IRS issued Notice 2011-20 regarding its anticipated treatment of any income received through the MSSP by a tax-exempt ACO participant.[70] According to this notice, the IRS intends to consider income resulting from MSSP participation to be within the permissible bounds of the tax-exempt arrangement, so long as the organization satisfies certain requirements, including that any and all contracts and transactions the entity in question enters into be at fair market value.[71] The IRS notice appears to present a favorable stance toward federal ACOs, suggesting that the basic operation of an ACO may satisfy the not-for-profit entities charitable purpose by "lessening of the burdens of the government."[72] However, the notice was not as lenient when considering tax-exempt issues related to commercial ACOs, stating that ACO activities, in and of themselves, are not charitable.[73]

State Insurance Law

State insurance departments have raised concerns regarding whether ACOs are defined as a risk-bearing entity, which are regulated under state insurance law.[74] If state agencies conclude that ACOs are risk-bearing entities under applicable state law, the ACO will be required to register with the state in accordance with that state's insurance law.[75] Whether these concerns come to fruition is contingent on the action of state insurance agencies and their eventual opinion regarding whether an ACO agreement between payors and providers manifests an assumption of risk subject to insurance regulation.

States also have adopted managed care or insurance regulations that impose burdensome requirements on healthcare providers that contract directly with self-insured employee benefit health plans, e.g., Employee Retirement Income Security Act of 1974 (ERISA) plans,[76] on a risk-bearing basis, in order to ensure protection for patient coverage from providers who are at risk of going out of business. ACOs that enter into applicable payor contracts may be subject to these state requirements, e.g.:

> … minimum capital requirements of $2,500,000 or more to ensure solvency; a required fidelity bond of $1,000,000 or more; approval of all marketing materials, provider contracts, forms, and rates; required disclosures to enrollees; requirements regarding types of care provided and how much care can be rationed; and exposure to examinations of the ACO's affairs at least once every five years.[77]

Excessive capital reserve requirements, marketing restrictions, operational rules, disclosure audits, and other regulatory burdens imposed through state law may limit the number of smaller ACOs that are financially able to meet those applicable state mandates.[78] The burdens of ACO regulation also fall on the payor that is party to an ACO contract, especially when the payor and the ACO are controlled by the same overall organization, e.g., a health system with an internal payor (described in Chapter 4).

Impact on Payors

While ACOs generally receive financial incentives through a form of value-based purchasing (VBP) agreement, the specific model will vary depending on whether the ACO is operating within the commercial ACO or federal ACO market, as well as for each specific ACO contract, reflecting the varying amounts of risk the payor and the ACO are willing to accept. Separate and aside from the consideration of shared savings bonus payments, payor reimbursement for ACO services will likely involve the same level of oversight and government scrutiny as any other traditional healthcare entity.

Some ACOs may choose to incorporate a VBP component to their physician compensation arrangements, e.g., pay for performance (P4P) schemes. As with any transaction, ACOs should ensure that all compensation arrangements comply with the regulatory standards of fair market value and commercial reasonableness.

Fair Market Value

Key Concept	Definition	Citation
Fair Market Value	The policy, under current law, that physicians must be compensated at fair market value for the services they provide.	*Financial Relationships between Physicians and Entities Furnishing Designated Health Services*, vol. 42 CFR Section 411.357 (October 10, 2010).

Under current federal law, any provider compensation arrangement must be at fair market value (FMV),[79] i.e., the most probable price that the subject interest should bring if exposed for sale on the open market. This standard of value assumes an anticipated hypothetical transaction in which the buyer and seller are each acting prudently with a reasonable equivalence of knowledge, and where the price is not affected by any undue stimulus or coercion.[80]

The calculation of FMV may be complicated if the ACO has recently implemented a VBP model, because historical data may not be representative of the current compensation arrangement. Establishing that compensation arrangements are within the range of FMV and are commercially reasonable[81] is requisite for ACO compliance with antikickback, Stark, and IRS regulations,[82] as well as for forecasting the expenses associated with an ACO necessary for the valuation of any enterprises, assets, or services.[83]

Commercial Reasonableness

Key Concept	Definition	Citation
Commercial Reasonableness	An agreement between a healthcare organization and physician should be "commercially reasonable," such that the agreement "appears to be a sensible, prudent business agreement, from the perspective of the particular parties involved, even in the absence of any potential referrals." CMS noted in 2004 that this standard introduced an "unwarranted subjective element" into the test for commercial reasonableness, and redefined the standard as follows: "If the arrangement would make commercial sense if entered into by a reasonable entity of similar type and size and a reasonable physician (or family member or group practice) of similar scope and specialty, even if there were no potential DHS referrals."	Medicare Program; Physicians' Referrals to Health Care Entities with Which They Have Financial Relationships (Phase II). *Federal Register* vol. 69, no. 59 (March 26, 2004), p. 16093.

Another regulation that must be surmounted, which is similar to FMV standards, is that an agreement between a healthcare organization and a physician must be commercially reasonable, based on the tasks, duties, responsibilities, and accountabilities (TDRA) required under the physician's specific job description. Initially, in 1998, the Centers for Medicare and Medicaid Services (CMS) stated that they would find any business arrangement to be commercially reasonable that "... appears to be a sensible, prudent business agreement, from the perspective of the particular parties involved, even in the absence of any potential referrals."[84] However, in 2004, CMS noted that this description introduced an "unwarranted subjective element" into the test for commercial reasonableness, and redefined the standard as follows:

> ... if the arrangement would make commercial sense if entered into by a reasonable entity of similar type and size and a reasonable physician (or family member or group practice) of similar scope and specialty, even if there were no potential DHS referrals.[85]

ACOs should be wary of arrangements in which physician compensation is a proportion of the revenues generated from physician responsibilities defined in the physician's specific employment agreement, and evaluate these payments as to their commercial reasonableness.[86] This is particularly the case in the commercial ACO market where provider compensation arrangements are more likely to be utilized as a means to achieve the aims of the ACO, i.e., utilizing financial incentives for quality and cost outcomes. In general, any agreement that displays a vastly disproportionate compensation to revenue ratio will likely be considered commercially unreasonable. In *United States v. Campbell*, an agreement between a medical school and a physician was found to not be commercially reasonable based on the physician's lack of adequate qualifications for the position, which qualifications were primarily academic in nature. The Court in Campbell held that an employment agreement's individual components must be perceived as commercially reasonable when considered independently as well as when considered as a whole.[87] ACOs may present complications in the analysis of commercial reasonableness, as many of the job descriptions utilized for governance and management would have been recently established and, therefore, specific TDRAs may still be uncertain. The total compensation that an ACO participant receives, including incentive payments in relation to the quality and cost metrics that an individual physician achieves, as with shared savings bonus payments, also may need to be considered during the analysis of commercial reasonableness.

The ACA and the Supreme Court

In March of 2012, the Supreme Court of the United States (SCOTUS) began reviewing whether the individual mandate of the ACA, which requires that individuals either purchase insurance or pay a penalty, exceeded Congress's authority under the Commerce Clause of the U.S. Constitution.[88] SCOTUS also considered whether Congress unconstitutionally coerced states to participate in the ACA provision that would expand eligibility for the Medicaid program in 2014.[89] For each provision, SCOTUS had to determine whether the section was severable, placing the constitutionality of the entire law into question.[90]

On June 28, 2012, SCOTUS released its highly anticipated ruling, upholding most of the ACA in a five to four vote.[91] Although SCOTUS found that the individual mandate provision was a tax (originally thought by commentators to cause the issue to not yet be ripe for review), SCOTUS upheld the matter under a narrow interpretation of the federal taxing authority.[92] SCOTUS also upheld the constitutionality of the Medicaid expansion provision, i.e., expanding eligibility for Medicaid to 133% of the poverty guidelines in 2014 with federal funding provided for newly eligible beneficiaries. However, the Court changed the provision to make state participation voluntary.

With the provisions of the ACA set to proceed as planned, with the exception of the Medicaid expansion state mandate, ACO stakeholders are anticipating both the positive and negative impacts that the law may have on patient throughput and revenue, e.g., hospitals will likely have less bad debt from unpaid hospital bills due to the vast increase of insured patients in 2014 under the individual mandate,[93] and payors will have to remain compliant with the recently implemented medical loss ratio[94] that may lessen their margins.[95]

While the development of ACOs would have likely continued in the commercial ACO market regardless of the outcome of the SCOTUS decision, the upholding of the law securely maintains the trajectory, with limited variation, of federal ACO implementation and growth, upon which providers, investors, or payors considering or currently participating in ACO development can rely.

REIMBURSEMENT CONCERNS

While shared savings payments under the MSSP incentivize ACOs to improve quality and decrease cost, providers have noted that the fee-for-service (FFS) reimbursement model that is utilized in the federal ACO market may provide, in contrast to desired goals, disincentives for quality improvement and affordability, instead incentivizing the volume of services provided.[96] ACOs seeking to transition away from FFS reimbursement may consider utilizing their non-Medicare payors to provide added value to the ACO through financial incentives applicable to an ACO's mission and goals, e.g., lowering costs and improving quality.[97]

Each reimbursement model presents varying amounts of risk shared between the provider and payor in an ACO contract (discussed in Chapter 4), which present differing concerns regarding either: (1) low quality of care incentives (experienced under capitation, where the provider receives a single payment per patient and may be incentivized to not provide necessary services in order to retain more of the payment), or (2) high cost of care incentives (experienced under FFS where the provider receives a payment per service rendered and may be incentivized to increase the volume of services to receive more payments). These two opposing ends of the risk spectrum must find a balance within an ACO contract for an ACO to succeed. Concerns regarding the reimbursement of ACOs focus on the management of the risk, described above, which influence the ability of an ACO to achieve financial incentives for quality and cost achievements.

Impact on Providers

An ACO may form as the outcome of some level of integration between existing healthcare enterprises, e.g., physician group practices or networks of practices, partnerships between hospitals and physicians, or hospital–physician employee models. The eventual integration structure chosen for an ACO may likely impact the type of reimbursement/compensation model utilized for both the ACO entity and individual ACO participants.

Hospitals

There is an apparent correlation of the number of beneficiaries that are assigned to an ACO by CMS, or under a specific commercial ACO contract, with the probability of ACO success.[98] The number of assigned beneficiaries has both a direct and an indirect impact on the ability of an ACO to achieve sufficient incentive payments to offset the cost of development, implementation, and operation. As a direct impact, a large number of beneficiaries result in each individual patient being less statistically significant in regards to those health outcomes and expenditures that are tied to incentive payments. A larger pool of beneficiaries allows an ACO to accommodate outlier patients, i.e., those patients who have higher than average healthcare costs, typically due to low health status or a chronic disease. Indirectly, a large number of beneficiaries suggest that the ACO is a larger organization that is likely to have more access to capital, resources, providers, and management staff, than a smaller organization. The size of large health systems, e.g., Advocate Health Partners, provides flexibility for operating in both the federal ACO and commercial ACO markets, due, in part, to the ability of the ACO to overcome traditional FFS incentives (discussed above), and to handle risk under various reimbursement models.[99]

Large Health Systems

Large health systems have greater access to capital resources and a diverse set of providers, e.g., specialists and primary care providers, which may be beneficial when forming an ACO. Larger institutions that are able to cross-fund their ACOs from internal equity and external debt may have a more probable chance for success.[100]

In addition, health systems that are already vertically integrated may experience a smoother transition into an ACO than less integrated organizations. For example, several large health systems, including the Mayo Clinic, Geisinger Health System, Kaiser Permanente, and the Cleveland Clinic, have been operating as de facto ACOs even prior to the development of the term ACO.[101] The ability of these, and similar[102] large health systems, to deliver integrated patient care was a driver of, and illustration for, the ACO model that Congress envisioned when drafting the MSSP.[103]

Despite positive indications that large health systems could benefit from ACO development, it is still unclear whether these ACOs will be able to accumulate the necessary savings to offset the amount of capital investment requisite for ACO development, implementation, and operation. For example, one method through which the Mayo Clinic provides comprehensive treatment to its patients is through the utilization of the most innovative and effective treatments available, which are often the most expensive.[104] New technologies and treatment methods often suffer from low reimbursement rates under the inpatient and outpatient prospective payments systems (IPPS and OPPS) used by Medicare, which is a consideration that is not generally included in evaluations of potential ACO success.[105] While large health systems may easily satisfy increased quality requirements and effectively coordinate care, low reimbursement rates and high capital costs for technology may make lowering costs difficult, which may negatively impact shared savings payments or other incentive payments.

In contrast to the main barriers of ACO success for large health systems, e.g., the achievement of shared savings in a FFS, IPPS, OPPS reimbursement environment, the main barrier of ACO success for physician-owned hospitals may emanate from their struggle with limitations placed on their basic operations.

Factoid 5.4

In terms of forming ACOs, hospitals have two options: either (1) employ a sufficient number of primary care physicians to support the number of Medicare beneficiaries required, or (2) operate as a well-structured physician hospital organization (PHO) or independent practice association (IPA). (Source: ACOs Forging the Links. Ken Terry, *Hospitals & Health Networks Magazine,* vol. 85, no. 1 (January 2011), p. 20.)

Physician-Owned Hospitals

The ACA strictly limits the ability of physician-owned hospitals (POHs) to expand and develop by prohibiting the addition of new beds and surgical units, and prohibiting physicians from increasing their percentage of ownership in a hospital, which effectively eliminates the whole-hospital exception under Stark Law, and essentially prohibits the opening of new POHs after 2011.[106] Some commentators have suggested that the prohibition against POH expansion will damage the value of[107] or ultimately entirely eliminate this type of healthcare provider entity from the market.[108] However, those POHs that have grandfathered status[109] may still be able to form ACOs and provide care to a large enough beneficiary population to generate incentive payments through, but not limited to, direct employment arrangements with physicians or indirect contracts with physician groups.

Bolstering the number of providers participating in the coordination of patient care may maximize the potential financial incentives, which a POH ACO can achieve. However, if complying with reform legislation prevents POHs from expanding, i.e., the POH remains stagnant, these organizations may not be able to accommodate an increased provider or beneficiary population, and, therefore, may not be able to achieve sufficient financial incentives for an ACO to be financially feasible or to successfully compete with other ACOs in a market service area.

Without a sufficient number of beneficiaries and providers, POH ACOs also may face challenges identifying payors that are willing to contract and share risk with a stagnant entity. Further, payors that are willing to contract with a stagnant POH may not be willing to share a substantial amount of reimbursement risk, limiting the options for financial incentives to various capitated models, which the stagnant POH may not have the internal management infrastructure to accommodate. With limited ability to accommodate reimbursement risk, POH ACOs may be best suited for the MSSP, which utilizes FFS payments. However, issues of size may still limit the ACOs likelihood of achieving meaningful shared savings payments under the MSSP, given that POHs tend to be driven by specialists,[110] which will impact the number of beneficiaries assigned to the ACO under the MSSP.[111] (For more information on the assignment of beneficiaries under the MSSP, see Chapter 2, Federal ACOs.)

For Profit versus Not-for-Profit

As mentioned earlier, in 2011 the IRS issued a notice stating that when not-for-profit, tax-exempt hospitals opt to integrate with for-profit physician and/or specialty practices to form an ACO, each entity should be conscious of regulations attached to tax exemption, e.g., maintaining a charitable purpose.[112] Purely for-profit entities may benefit from the implementation of the individual mandate and the Medicaid expansion in those states that choose to participate, as a result of fewer bad-debt patients due to a larger insured patient base. However, those ACOs that are either purely not-for-profit, or a mix of for-profit and not-for-profit entities, may face challenges maintaining the requisite adherence to their charitable purpose, e.g., not-for-profit hospitals that previously satisfied the IRS community benefit or charitable purpose requirement by providing healthcare services to uninsured individuals, may have to find an alternative means of providing charitable care.

Factoid 5.5

Nonprofit, tax-exempt hospitals desiring to form ACOs will need to be conscious of regulations attached to tax exemption, such as maintaining a charitable purpose, when choosing to integrate with physician and specialty practices. (Source: 5 Key Regulatory Concerns for ACOs. Lindsey Dunn, *Becker's Hospital Review* (September 14, 2010).)

Insurer Operated Practices

Although insurance companies have previously encountered criticism and regulatory scrutiny for expanding their scope of services into clinical settings, they may, nonetheless, choose to become involved with ACOs in response to the potential increase in competition from health systems that both have the providers and are expanding their implementation of internal payor systems.[113] In addition, those insurers that are not planning to enter into the ACO market have expressed concern that the size, and resulting negotiating leverage, of some ACOs may force health plans to increase reimbursement rates.[114]

A recent trend that may benefit ACOs is the expansion of insurers into the management of retail clinics.[115] Although it is unlikely that a retail clinic could operate as an independent ACO, ACO participation by insurer-owned retail clinics, which offer their insurer owners a higher level of control over retail clinic expenses, may reduce the overall administrative and other overhead costs of the clinic. By lowering these costs, the insurer owners can maximize the profit margins of the insurer-operated retail clinic, while at the same time contributing to an ACO's achievement of expenditure reduction targets.[116]

Physician Practices

Physician practices may participate in an ACO through several means, including, but not limited to: (1) integration with other practices to form a large multispecialty group practice or physician hospital organization, (2) selling their practice to a hospital in exchange for a direct employment agreement, or (3) contracting with an existing ACO to provide services to ACO patients for a share of achieved financial incentives. Physician practices also may choose to independently form either a federal ACO or a commercial ACO (i.e., without partnering with a larger entity) in a manner similar to the federal ACO developed by Wellmed Medical Management, a physician-owned practice management company comprised of hundreds of family practice and internal medicine physicians across 35 clinics in Texas and Florida, serving over 5,000 beneficiaries.[117] Of note is that since eligibility within the MSSP is contingent on an entity being able to manage the primary care of at least 5,000 assigned beneficiaries,[118] smaller, independent physician practice ACOs may not be able to pursue federal ACO status, and may be limited to the commercial ACO market. However, even in the commercial ACO market, ACOs with small numbers of beneficiaries may still face challenges achieving sufficient financial incentives to offset initial capital investments.[119]

Factoid 5.6

Physician practices may choose to form ACOs without partnering with hospitals, and will likely need to be large enough to handle at least 5,000 beneficiaries and either have the requisite resources to handle all their care or contract hospital services out. (Source: ACOs can work with physicians in charge. Victoria Stagg Elliott, *American Medical News* (January 31, 2011). Online at: www.ama-assn.org/amednews/2011/01/31/bisa0131.htm (Accessed 2/7/11).)

If a physician practice chooses to integrate with, or be consumed by, a larger organization, the reimbursement options available to the practice increase significantly. Under the MSSP, providers are reimbursed according to a fee-for-service model; however, the compensation each physician receives may be contingent on any number of models, e.g., work relative value units (wRVU) productivity-based compensation, pay-for-performance, or other various scenarios for the distribution of financial incentives received by the ACO for the cost and quality achievements of the physician. A more extensive list of the types of compensation arrangements available is shown in Table 5.1

Further, the compensation model chosen may be utilized to incentivize certain provider types based on the strategic plans of the ACO, e.g., a greater focus on primary care.

TABLE 5.1
Compensation Plan Options Physician Employees

Compensation Plans	Examples
Base salary	Equal compensation paid to each physician
Productivity-Based Compensation[a]	
Compensation based on a per RVU method	$ per wRVU or $ per total RVU; must not include compensation for nonclinical services
Compensation based on gross charges	40% of gross charges
Compensation based on cash collections	75% of cash collections
Base Salary Plus Bonus	
Incentive bonus based on productivity levels	wRVU generation, patient visits, gross charges, collections
Incentive bonus based on quality and/or beneficial outcomes	Following predetermined methodologies statistically proven to provide beneficial outcomes
Incentive payments based on legally permissible gainsharing	Basing compensation on shared savings produced by lowering operating costs from period to period
Incentive payments based on attainment of organizational performance goals	Development of a Center of Excellence
Annual stipend	Typically for administrative, research, consulting, and/or academic services

Source: Reference 120. With permission.

[a] Most productivity compensation arrangements should include a "cap" on the compensation.

Primary versus Specialty Care

Under the MSSP, beneficiaries will be assigned to an ACO according to their total prospective usage of primary care services provided by any ACO professional.[121] Due to the reliance on this criteria for beneficiary assignment, as well as an overall increased emphasis on primary care in both the federal ACO and commercial ACO markets, an ACO's ability to successfully achieve financial incentives, through the health and cost outcomes associated with assigned beneficiaries, will likely be reliant on the number and quality of primary care providers (PCP) available to the ACO. Further, an ACO's reliance on PCPs also may impact the reimbursement model chosen for a particular ACO contract within the commercial ACO market.

Key Term	Definition	Citation
Patient-Centered Medical Homes (PCMH)	Approaches the delivery of health care services through coordinated, centralized patient care with an emphasis on the primary care physician as manager of the patient's treatment.	*Joint Principles of the Patient-Centered Medical Home*. American Academy of Family Physicians, American Academy of Pediatrics, American College of Physicians, and American Osteopathic Association, February 2007.

Within an ACO, PCPs may adopt a similar role to the gatekeeper function that was provided by PCPs in the health maintenance organizations (HMOs) of the 1990s, which typically utilized a capitated payment model. This gatekeeper scenario may be most likely to occur when the ACO implements a patient-centered medical home (PCMH) model, which, as part of its operational structure, utilizes PCPs as the central figures accountable for a given patient's care. (A discussion of PCMHs is provided in Chapter 2, Federal ACOs.)

The MSSP Final Rule emphasizes increased access to cost-effective preventative care for assigned beneficiaries.[122] Following the publication of the MSSP Proposed Rule on April 7, 2011,[123] specialists voiced concerns that the increased use of preventative care, combined with a greater emphasis on cost-savings, would result in fewer referrals to specialists for tests and procedures. CMS addressed these concerns in the Final Rule by allowing specialists to join more than one ACO, thereby increasing their exposure to potential referrals.[124] Further, CMS expanded the method for the assignment of beneficiaries so that, under the Final Rule, assignment is determined by both those beneficiaries that use a PCP associated with an ACO and beneficiaries that see a specialist associated with an ACO as their PCP.[125] Specifically, under the Final Rule, specialists who provide all of the primary care services for a particular patient, such as a specialist in a rural area who is the only accessible physician, will be treated as a PCP for the purposes of ACO beneficiary assignment by CMS.[126] A full discussion of the MSSP beneficiary assignment methodology is provided in Chapter 2.

Specialists also have expressed concern that PCPs may be motivated to limit referrals for expensive procedures and special tests in order to meet cost-cutting objectives, thereby directly impacting specialist revenues. Participation by specialists in developing clinical guidelines for an ACO's operation may ease this concern by allowing specialists to influence the care prescribed by the referring PCP. A panel of radiologists argued that specialists should be involved in the development of clinical guidelines for ACOs.[127] Similarly, the American Academy of Orthopaedic Surgeons (AAOS) is promoting the participation of surgeons in the creation of ACO clinical guidelines for:

1. Defining the criteria use for referrals to specialties
2. Creating specifications for diagnostic and therapeutic interventions
3. Establishing quality metrics
4. Implementing methods to improve communications between specialty providers and PCPs[128]

Some specialty practices, where the specialist provides the majority of the patient's care once a diagnosis has been made, e.g., oncology,[129] may be large enough to form their own independent ACOs, e.g., the commercial ACO formed between Texas Oncology, a 345 oncologist, single-specialty practice with 135 sites of service around Texas and Southeastern Oklahoma,[130] and commercial payor, Aetna.[131] It is important to note that the MSSP requirement that federal ACOs must be able to offer primary care services for 5,000 beneficiaries, may limit the ability for specialty practices, which do not typically have participating PCPs, to quality for the MSSP, resulting in these practices being better served by pursuing commercial ACO status. However, some commentators have noted that the 5,000 beneficiaries required under the MSSP could potentially be cancer patients, thereby allowing larger oncology practices, with at least 5,000 patients, to participate in the federal ACO market.[132] Despite some curiosity and debate among oncologists regarding participation in the MSSP,[133] to date, there are no Federal ACOs that solely consist of oncology practices.

Key Term	Definition	Citation
ACO Professionals	Any provider of healthcare services within an ACO.	Medicare Program; Medicare Shared Savings Program: Accountable Care Organizations. *Federal Register*, vol. 76, no. 212, November 2, 2011, p. 67974.

Other concerns raised by specialists relate to the representation of particular specialties in the MSSP, e.g., psychiatric specialists have expressed frustration regarding the lack of representation of mental healthcare services in the 33 quality measures set forth in the MSSP Final Rule. According to the American Psychological Association (APA), only 2 of the 33 quality measures would be relevant to psychiatrists, i.e., depression screening and tobacco use and cessation.[134] The APA commented that the lack of quality measures related to psychiatry diminishes "... the incentive and ability of a psychiatrist to participate in an ACO."[135] In response to these concerns, CMS acknowledged that more quality measures should be put in place concerning mental health and substance abuse.[136] However, to date no action has been taken by CMS to augment the quality metrics examined for federal ACO financial incentives.

Although the emphasis of the ACA seems to be on primary care, the overall goal of an ACO is not limited to only providing primary care; rather, the objective is to emphasize better overall healthcare for patients. The development and operation of successful ACOs is intended to further this goal of better overall health for all. Therefore, the collaboration of primary care physicians and specialists in seeking to effectively coordinate care to provide the highest quality of services to their patients is a prerequisite to ACO success.

Ambulatory Surgery Centers and Other Outpatient Providers

Ambulatory surgery centers (ASC) offer significant opportunities for ACOs to lower costs, provide a convenient site of service, and create a true partnership with medical staff,[137] particularly specialists and surgeons, who have historically had closer ties to ASCs than hospitals.[138] While the secretary of HHS has the right to expand the list of entities eligible for the independent formation of federal ACOs, ASCs are not currently listed as independently eligible entities under the MSSP.[139] Further, for federal ACOs, under which the ACO must be a single legal entity in order to include an ASC in the shared governance and shared savings distributions, the central federal ACO[140] must utilize a different governance structure, e.g., an ownership interest in the ASC.[141] Alternatively, the ACO also may form a third party contract with an ASC, which sets forth a mechanism for shared savings disbursement, independent of the MSSP,[142] more similar to a commercial ACO, whereby distinct entities may simply contract with each other to coordinate care.

Factoid 5.7

More than ever, hospital managers need to know their market and their hospitals inefficiencies to start making investments in areas with greater patient volumes and margins in addition to community-based services where high-quality care can be offered at lower cost. (Source: Hospitals That Don't Move on ACOs Risk Losing MD Referrals. *ACO Business News,* vol. 1, no. 1, November 2010, p. 8.)

The integration of ASC patient information with the data records of the ACO may present challenges, particularly for those ACOs that do not operate as a single entity (i.e., federal ACOs utilizing third-party contracts or commercial ACOs), and will likely require the implementation of potentially costly interoperable electronic health record (EHR) systems. Because ASCs are not included in the Health Information Technology for Economic and Clinical Health Act (HITECH) regulation that determines the requirements for "meaningful use"[143] subsidies,[144] ASCs will have to pay for any requisite interoperable EHR systems or system improvements required for their participation with the ACO EHR without the financial assistance of federal grants.

Despite the possible investment burdens related to health information technology (HIT), ASCs may benefit from participation in either a federal ACO or a commercial ACO. As ACO providers evaluate ways to decrease hospital costs, they may opt to refer surgical outpatient services to an ASC, given that ASCs are associated with lower costs for providing care,[145] thereby increasing the volume of procedures performed at the ASC as well as the resulting revenue.[146]

Ancillary Providers and Allied Health Providers

Allied health professionals and ancillary care providers, e.g., physical therapists, chiropractors, pharmacists, podiatrists, optometrists, and dentists, are not included in the narrow definition of an

ACO professional specified in the MSSP Final Rule (see Chapter 2, Federal ACOs) and, therefore, may face challenges in participating in any shared savings disbursements. However, these professionals, from the first publication of the MSSP, have been advocating for their inclusion in the definition of an ACO professional under the MSSP. The American Physical Therapy Association (APTA) has stated that by allowing physical therapists to be ACO professionals within the MSSP, it would help reduce those healthcare costs associated with the administration of costly diagnostic tests for certain patient conditions, e.g., back pain.[147] Likewise, the American Chiropractic Association (ACA), in its response to CMS's request for information regarding the Proposed Rule, stated that incorporating chiropractors into regular patient care could dramatically decrease patient hospitalizations, thereby reducing healthcare costs within an ACO.[148] Additionally, a 2010 study by the National Community Pharmacists Association (NCPA) found that including pharmacists in patient-care teams, such as those involved in an ACO, would likely improve healthcare quality.[149]

Allied health professionals and ancillary care providers may still be included in the operations of a federal ACO, due to the MSSP's lack of specificity concerning what services or providers may participate in shared savings disbursements through third-party agreements with an ACO. In addition, while the MSSP limits the level of participation of ancillary providers and allied health providers, commercial ACOs have no such limitations and, therefore, may present another option for these providers to participate in the ACO market. Despite the possibility for some level of participation in the ACO market by allied health professionals, physicians have traditionally resisted the attempts of these providers to increase their scope of practice, which may ultimately limit the extent of their potential involvement in ACOs.[150]

Impact on Payors

The alignment of incentives necessary for the collaboration between providers and payors involved in an ACO is based on the mutual benefit of reducing costs. Similar to those issues of concern expressed by providers as to the impact on reimbursement yield and margins of capital spending to improve quality and reduce costs are the challenges and concerns anticipated by payors.

Private Insurance

Even before the publication of the MSSP Final Rule in November of 2011, private payors had begun participating in the commercial ACO market.[151] For example, as of October 2011, "[a]t least eight private health insurance plans [had] entered into ACO contracts with providers using a 'shared risk' payment model … mak[ing] providers eligible for bonuses if they keep costs below a certain threshold but assess[ing] financial penalties against them if they exceed spending targets."[152] Michael O'Neil, a senior vice president at Health Spring, Inc., a 340,000 member private insurance company[153] that is currently participating in several commercial ACO contracts[154] as well as an insurer operated ACO,[155] stated, in November 2010, that "… the risk at this time is that [an ACO] stops in the middle and doesn't create enough real change to realign the delivery system. If we go only part way, there could be backpedaling or abandonment of this shift."[156]

Concerns regarding antitrust scrutiny have never risen among private payors not participating in commercial ACO contracts. Commentators noted that the mandatory review suggested in the 2011 FTC-DOJ proposed policy statement on antitrust enforcement (discussed above) was designed to guide the creation of federal ACOs that are large enough to meet the healthcare delivery needs of their patients, but also small enough so as not to monopolize the private insurance market.[157] Of note is that the FTC-DOJ final policy statement removed the mandatory review provision, related to an ACO's, or an ACO participant's control of specific services in their primary service area (PSA).[158] This action may heighten concerns regarding competition from ACOs among private payors who are not afforded the same regulatory protections as federal ACOs in their ability to gain competitive leverage through market saturation.

Individually and Employer Purchased Insurance

Provider apprehension regarding the ability of patients to seek healthcare services outside of the ACO network is likewise a concern for participating private payors.[159] In response to these concerns, payors may offer reduced premiums to encourage beneficiaries to seek care within those ACOs with whom the private payor has contracted.[160] These incentives are similar to the in-network incentives utilized by traditional managed care plans, under which patients can receive care from in-network providers at a discount, as compared to the higher out-of-pocket costs incurred by patients when care is received from out-of-network providers.[161]

Some employers have expressed concerns regarding a possible domino effect resulting from provider consolidation resulting from the formation of ACOs, whereby the increased market leverage of these ACOs may result in higher prices for private sector purchasers, which in turn may cause insurance companies to raise the cost of group employer sponsored insurance plans.[162] In contrast, other employers perceive ACOs as a means of reducing healthcare costs, thereby making the provision of health benefits to employees more affordable,[163] which has been a significant concern for small business owners, as healthcare premiums have continued to rise over the past decade.[164] If ACOs are successful in promoting preventive services, patient population health may improve, translating into lower treatment and premium costs, as well as decreasing employee absences contributing to productivity benefits for employers.[165]

A 2011 survey by AON Hewitt found that 65% of the 674 responding U.S. employers were "interested" in utilizing an ACO for providing employee health benefits.[166] Noteworthy is that the survey results indicated that the "quality of care delivered" to employees was of equal importance to employers (82% of respondents) as was the "ability to manage the total cost of care" (81% of respondents). Additionally, the 2011 survey also indicated that employers preferred to receive information regarding ACO participation from insurance brokers or consultants (75%), in contrast to government agencies (24%), medical groups (18%), or hospitals (11%).[167]

Provider Operated Payors

Provider operated payors, e.g., a health plan with an internal payor (see Chapter 4), have both the complications and rewards associated with the payor and provider parties to an ACO contract. The historical impact of organizations similar to Kaiser Permanente, which operates the Kaiser Foundation Health Plan, may offer guidance as to the likely impact of provider operated payors on the continued development of both federal ACOs and commercial ACOs. A 2010 commentary on Kaiser's impact on the development of the ACO market noted:

> Some thought leaders consider vertical integration with an insurance provider to be core to the success of this ACO, since cost reductions achieved by the Permanente Medical Group are directly reflected in lower premiums to the insurer (the Kaiser Foundation Health Plan), in turn attracting more enrollees.[168]

However, it is unclear whether newly formed ACOs will successfully achieve vertical integration that large provider operated payors, similar to that of Kaiser, which may impact their potential to achieve the requisite cost reductions to be eligible for financial incentives.

State-Run Exchanges

Key Term	Definition	Citation
Health Insurance Exchange	"Public markets" for health insurance plans available within a state.	*Explaining Health Care Reform: What Are Health Insurance Exchanges?* Kaiser Family Foundation, May 2009.

The ACA mandates that states establish health insurance exchanges (HIEs) by 2014, including an online component that allows consumers to compare available plans.[169] Under the ACA, states have the option to: (1) develop their own HIE, (2) develop an HIE in conjunction with the federal government, or (3) have a federally developed HIE imposed on them.[170] As of October 2, 2012, 10 states and the District of Columbia have enacted legislation for the formation of an HIE, while 9 states have formally stated that they will not create an HIE.[171]

Currently, it is unclear in what manner ACOs will participate in the HIEs, e.g., either directly (an option only available to insurer operated Commercial ACOs[172]), or indirectly, through those payors with whom the ACO has established an ACO contract. Although the impact of ACOs on HIEs, and vice versa, will not be fully determined until some time after their implementation in 2014,[173] one benefit of HIEs to private payors is that they may be able to enhance their attractiveness to those ACO providers with which they have an ACO contract in place because of their potential influence directing patients through HIE provider panels.

Government Insurance

From a health policy perspective, the ultimate goal of ACO implementation is to: (1) lower healthcare costs, (2) improve quality of care, and (3) improve access to care.[174] As suggested by the outcomes from the Physician Group Practice (PGP) Demonstration, which operated from 2005 to 2010, ACOs may be able to lower Medicare costs by millions of dollars over the next decade.[175] A discussion of the PGP demonstration, and the outcomes achieved by participating providers, is provided in Chapter 1.

Medicare

ACOs are expected to lower Medicare costs by reducing both hospital readmission rates and the overutilization of healthcare services. During the first few years of ACO implementation, savings may be minimal compared to the current proportion of the federal budget dedicated to the overall Medicare program, i.e., $528 billion in 2013.[176] Nevertheless, should the long-term goals of ACOs be achieved, Medicare expenditures will likely be reduced, with estimates by the Congressional Budget Office (CBO) projecting approximately $4.9 billion in Medicare savings through 2019,[177] an amount representing less than 1% of total Medicare spending.[178]

Medicaid/CHIP

While the MSSP only applies to the Medicare program,[179] the Pediatric Accountable Care Organization Demonstration Project (PACO)[180] authorized states to apply to the secretary of HHS to participate in a four-year Medicaid ACO pilot for pediatric beneficiaries, beginning on January 1, 2012. As with the MSSP, the PACO program of each state is be required to meet the quality goals established by HHS and the state in which the PACO operates, as well as achieve the minimal levels of savings established by the state for services covered under the Children's Health Insurance Program (CHIP) and Medicaid, in order to receive incentive payments from the federal government.[181] If ACOs are fully incorporated into the Medicaid program, not just for pediatric services, there is the potential for these organizations to alleviate some of the budgetary constraints that many states experienced as a result of the Great Recession. (For more information on those Medicaid ACOs currently being developed, implemented, and operated on a state level, see Chapter 2, Federal ACOs.)

Impact on Beneficiaries

Key Term	Definition	Citation
Pediatric Accountable Care Organization Demonstration Project (PACO)	Federal ACO program involving pediatric medical providers.	Patient Protection and Affordable Care Act of 2010: Sec. 2706 Pediatric Accountable Care Organization Demonstration Project. HR 3590, Congress, March 28, 2010.

While ACOs are currently one of the most publicized topics in healthcare reform debate related to cost control, little discussion has been generated regarding how they will affect patients. Concern has been voiced within the healthcare community that ACOs may be just another form of gatekeeping medicine that may lead to a patient backlash, similar to the backlash that occurred in the 1990s resulting from the public's perception that HMO providers were more concerned with achieving financial margins than with providing quality care to their patients. However, these critics have noted that a potential public backlash may be avoided through the use of transparency initiatives and patient incentives.[182]

As previously discussed, patients assigned to an ACO are not restricted from seeking healthcare services from providers outside of the ACO; however, the ACO to which they are assigned will remain accountable for the health outcomes of that patient, regardless of the quality of care delivered by a provider outside of the ACO. Therefore, many ACOs and their contracted payors may choose to incentivize patients to seek healthcare services from an ACO provider, e.g., by lowering co-payments for staying within the ACO, or by raising out-of-pocket costs for services provided by physicians outside of the ACO,[183] similar to a preferred provider organization (PPO).[184] While there is currently no regulatory requirement related to lowering the cost of care experienced by ACO beneficiaries (discussed further in Chapter 8, Considerations of Value for the Positive Externalities of ACOs), patients may experience some cost benefit (in addition to any enhanced quality benefits) as a result of the use of lower premiums as an incentive for beneficiaries to continue to choose providers participating in the given ACO to which the beneficiary is assigned.

COMPETITION CONCERNS

Potential barriers to the operational success of newly formed ACOs include competition that providers and payors to an ACO contract will likely face from both other ACOs and non-ACO providers in keeping patients within the ACO to which they are assigned to ensure quality standards and maintain established value metrics. There is also a potential barrier that may rise from the antitrust enforcement activities of the FTC-DOJ. Despite removing the initial requirement subjecting "high risk" ACOs to a mandatory review process,[185] the FTC-DOJ final policy statement left intact strict compliance requirements related to a Federal ACO's PSA (discussed above).[186]

Impact on Providers

Provider integration, and the resulting increased size of an ACO, may allow the ACO to exert a greater amount of leverage on participating physicians to act in accordance with established policies and protocols related to achieving those cost and quality metrics for which an ACO is accountable. Increased provider consolidation, and the resulting reduction in marketplace competition, also may allow for large commercial ACOs to assert more control over pricing and, ultimately, physician reimbursement in the commercial insurance market. Further, as the use of hospitals by referring physicians may be reduced as physician group practices form their own ACOs, hospitals may need to adjust for the potential loss of referrals or consider joining the ACO market.[187]

Porter's Five Forces of Competition

Key Concept	Definition	Citation
Porter's Five Forces of Competition	Competitive strategy devised by Harvard's Michael D. Porter. Includes (1) potential entrants, (2) supplies, (3) buyers, (4) the threat of substitutes, (5) rivalry amongst existing competitors.	*Competitive Strategy: Techniques for Analyzing Industries and Competitors.* Michael E. Porter, New York: The Free Press, 1980, pp. 7–10.

Michael D. Porter, of Harvard Business School, developed a model regarding "competitive strategy" in the 1980s as a framework for analyzing the attractiveness of a market to new entrants.[188] Porter's approach creates "... a framework for understanding the five fundamental forces of competition in

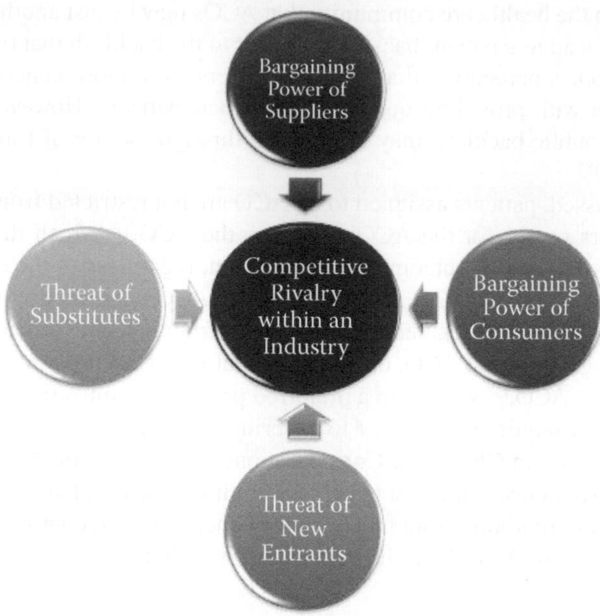

FIGURE 5.3 Porter's five forces.

an industry,"[189] and may serve as a basis for projecting how ACOs may effectively compete within the healthcare industry. A visual depiction of Porter's five fundamental forces of competition is illustrated in Figure 5.3.

The first force in Porter's analysis, The Impact of Potential Entrants, posits that the ease with which an enterprise enters the market is proportional to the threat this entity presents for existing market participants, i.e., more competitive entities will have an easier time entering a market than less competitive entities. Whether the new entrant is successful in entering and operating in a given market depends on how that entity is affected by typical barriers to success,[190] several of which may be applicable to prospective ACOs, as shown in Table 5.2.

Porter's second force in the competitive analysis, The Impact of Suppliers, describes how suppliers may exert power on industry participants by changing the price and quality of the goods or services they provide.[191] In the context of an ACO, this force encompasses the power that third party ACO suppliers have in determining the price, quality, and quantity of healthcare services provided by an ACO, through the price and quality of the goods supplied to the ACO by the ACO supplier under a third-party, shared savings distribution contract. A discussion of the method by which an ACO contracts with an ACO supplier is provided in Chapter 2, Federal ACOs, and Chapter 4. Hypothetical Models for the Development and Operation of ACOs.

Porter's third force, The Impact of Buyers, evaluates the capability of buyers of healthcare services (e.g., commercial and governmental payors and private pay patients) to control prices by bargaining and encouraging price competition.[192] This force contemplates the question: How much bargaining power do payors have regarding the healthcare services provided under an ACO model? For the third part of the competitive analysis, it may be useful to consider the following:

1. The volume of the healthcare services purchased by a buyer group: Large insurance companies choosing specific ACOs to refer all of their members gives the insurance company a type of concentrated buyer group power, i.e., strength in numbers.
2. Resources purchased that consume a higher percentage of a payors overall costs: The services provided by the ACO that are a large proportion of the costs incurred by a participating

TABLE 5.2
Potential Barriers for Prospective ACOs

Type of Barrier[1]	Potential Impact for ACOs
Economies of Scale	Larger ACOs have the capacity to treat more patients at less cost due to the potential for increased shared savings (see Chapter 7, Financial Feasibility Analysis for ACO Investments). However, these larger ACOs also face greater external competition from nonaffiliated hospitals as a result of their increased market presence.
Product Differentiation	This barrier encompasses patient preference for current providers and facilities. Emerging ACOs may have to incur significant expenditures in order to recruit new patients and overcome existing patient preferences. Conversely, ACOs with a previously established patient base from the participating providers, may benefit from these existing patient populations.
Capital Requirements	This barrier will likely be significant in restricting the creation of smaller ACOs, because a large capital investment will likely be required to form an ACO, and may or may not provide a return on the investment. The Center for Medicare and Medicaid Innovation (CMI) attempted to minimize this financial risk through the Advanced Payment Model *(*see Chapter 2: Federal ACOs*)*, through which eligible ACOs could receive shared savings payments upfront in order to mitigate initial capital expenditures.
Switching Costs	Electronic health records (EHR) and other health information technology (HIT) systems are a one-time cost that will likely be necessary for successful ACO implementation in order to monitor and record requisite patient outcomes and benchmarks.
Cost Disadvantages Independent of Scale	Experience, facility locations, and intangible assets are all advantages for established providers/payor entities planning to enter the ACO market.
Government Policy	While some perceive government policy as the catalyst for the ACO movement, other regulatory policies (e.g., antitrust and fraud and abuse regulations) may present a barrier to the success of ACOs in the marketplace.

Source: Adapted from *Competitive Strategy: Techniques for Analyzing Industries and Competitors*. Michael E. Porter, New York: The Free Press, 1980, pp 7–14.

payor, due to high patient volumes, may cause the payor to be more sensitive to price and, therefore, more willing to seek alternative purchasing options from alternative providers.

3. The personal characteristics of payors: The competitive trends and knowledge of payors may likely impact their bargaining power, and may be assessed through the following questions:
   a. Does the payor have reasonable access to alternative providers?
   b. Does the payor face any "switching costs"?
   c. Does the payor offer high cost insurance, e.g., high levels of coverage with many amenities, or low cost insurance, e.g., catastrophe insurance?
   d. Is the payor likely to enter into the provider marketplace, e.g., an insurer operated ACO?
   e. How well is the payor informed regarding the ACO marketplace?[193]

Porter's fourth force, regarding the Threat of Substitutes requires an analysis of what services in the market may act as substitutes for the services an ACO provides.[194] To a degree, ACOs provide a threat of substitute to the current healthcare marketplace; however, as costs continue to rise, the industry may move to a national health plan and risk pool (foreshadowed by the individual mandate is the ACA) and a single governmental payor (foreshadowed by the collaboration contracts seen within ACOs), as it has in many other developed countries. If a U.S. national health plan should be established, which many feel is inevitable, ACOs would have served merely as an interim phase, a transitional stepping-stone on the path to this new market substitute.

Finally, Porter's fifth force, The Impact of Rivalry among Existing Competitors, contemplates the type of competition among existing providers in a marketplace, e.g., hospitals and physician practices.[195] For ACOs operating in a given marketplace, substitutes might include any other competing ACO, as well as non-ACO providers, which a patient may consider utilizing for the delivery of healthcare services, e.g., physicians, midlevel providers, allied health providers, and alternative medicine providers. Specific examples of competitive concerns among various health industry stakeholders are discussed below.

Competitive Challenges for Hospitals and Physician Practices

Hospitals may face the potential for a reduction in their physician referral base as multipractice physician groups that may have different hospital affiliation integrate with one another to form ACOs.[196] A hospital may attempt to recoup this potential loss in patient referrals by aligning with physician practices and other outpatient centers, e.g., ASCs, to coordinate care, either through third party ACO contracts or some other integration effort, e.g., joint venture agreement or affiliation.[197]

Initial capital costs required to establish an ACO may provide larger ACOs with a competitive edge in the healthcare market, and may lead to their affiliation with smaller physician groups and solo practices seeking to participate in an ACO.[198] (See Chapter 6, Capital Finance Considerations for the Development and Operation of ACOs and Chapter 7, Financial Feasibility Analysis for ACO Investments.) Roland Goertz, former president of the American Academy of Family Physicians (AAFP), commented in 2010 that in lieu of conceding market and governance power to hospitals, physician practices should integrate care within their own ACOs to leverage capital and maintain leadership positions.[199]

Some small physician practices have considered forming independent practice associations (IPAs) whereby physicians affiliate with one another and contract as a larger group to provide healthcare services as a preliminary step toward ACO formation.[200] While IPAs are not a new integration strategy, they have been formed by some physicians as a way to gain more traction alongside hospitals in anticipation of a growing competitive ACO market.[201]

Physician hospital organizations (PHOs), which are a legal collaboration between a hospital and its physician staff, also may provide physicians with a means by which they can participate in the ACO market by overcoming traditional hospital medical staff structures and emphasizing the *value* of services provided, rather than the *volume* of services provided.[202] While PHOs first emerged in the 1990s,[203] several key characteristics differentiate the current PHO integration model from its predecessors, including greater transparency, more robust organizational structures and physician leadership, and a more equitable division of risks and rewards between participating physicians and the hospital.[204] PHOs have been viewed as a "pre-ACO model" that allows physicians to begin the process of integration necessary for eventual ACO formation.[205] PHOs transitioning to an ACO have considered collaborating with interested IPAs (which may be more likely to form independent ACOs), to further expand competitively into the ACO market.206

Although the start-up costs and capital requirements of ACO formation[207] may preclude most solo physician practitioners and small group practices from independently establishing an ACO, physician participation is critical to an ACO's development. Accordingly, the ultimate success of hospital-based ACOs will depend on their ability to effectively align, not only with primary care providers, but also with physicians of all specialties and subspecialties, in order to achieve adequate physician support ("buy-in") for ACO activities and maintain patient referral sources across the continuum of care.

Competitive Challenges for Insurer Operated ACOs

In addition to healthcare enterprises forming ACOs, insurer-operated ACOs also are being established, e.g., Cigna, United Healthcare, and Humana have announced their intention to form their own ACOs in the commercial ACO market.[208] In addition to their primary function as payors, these insurance companies contend that they have the potential to operate a successful ACO because of their ability to effectively and efficiently collect the patient data required to demonstrate that cost and quality targets were achieved.[209] The acceptance of insurer-operated ACOs by patients, however, may pose a challenge, as some patients may view ACOs as HMOs in disguise.[210] Within the context of the enormous patient resistance to the gatekeeper model of the 1990s, this concern may be greater when the ACO is operated by an insurer that is perceived to be more likely to impose greater restrictions on patient access to care.

Impact on Payors

ACO reimbursement models will vary significantly across different ACO contracts. Under the MSSP, CMS will continue to use a FFS model for federal ACO reimbursement, while private payors may operate under a variety of payment mechanisms, e.g., episode-based payments, partial capitation, full capitation, or global payments.[211] Regardless of whether or not the ACO model gains widespread acceptance in the U.S. healthcare delivery system, CMS and other insurers are nevertheless continuing to shift from traditional pay-for-volume reimbursement models (e.g., FFS) to pay-for-value models (e.g., episodes of care and bundled payments) that are often utilized in the commercial ACO market, and that incentivize lower readmission rates, better quality care, and population health management. Many of the commercial ACO contracts being established are designed with current federal programs in mind, e.g., the Medicare Value-Based Purchasing Program, in order to minimize the administrative burden associated with possibly conflicting incentives.[212] The strategies and tactics utilized by ACOs to lower costs and improve quality under pay-for-volume and pay-for-value reimbursement models are discussed in Chapter 4, Hypothetical Models for the Development and Operation of ACOs.

Competitive Aspects of Insurers versus Providers

While the continuation of an existing FFS model may ease the initial burden on providers transitioning to an ACO,[213] commercial ACOs are unlikely to retain the FFS model going forward, as they attempt to establish methods to reduce costs and maximize margins. Among the different types of reimbursement models, global payments may be the most favorable to payors, because this model reimburses providers with a single payment for the coverage of an entire population, placing a majority of the risk for lowering costs on the ACO.[214] Other reimbursement models include those that attempt to balance the risk between providers and payors, e.g., partial capitation, which allows for some cost-sharing and, therefore, less risk to the ACO.[215]

Although a global payment model may be perceived as too risky for some ACOs,[216] several payors have successfully implemented this reimbursement model, e.g., WellPoint, Inc., an Anthem Blue Cross subsidiary in California, employed global capitation in its five-year ACO pilot program. Similarly, Blue Cross Blue Shield of Massachusetts (BCBSMA) has been offering an "alternative quality contract" since 2009, which utilizes global payments in conjunction with quality incentives.[217] These and other examples of commercial ACO reimbursement models are discussed in Chapter 3, Commercial ACOs.

TECHNOLOGY CONCERNS

Health information technology (HIT) is associated with improving "... the health of individuals and the performance of providers, yielding improved quality, cost savings, and greater engagement by patients in their own healthcare,"[218] with the goal of reducing and eventually eliminating the limited information transfer capabilities of nonnetworked providers.[219] Successful ACOs not only require the presence of HIT, but also a "... sophisticated technology infrastructure to facilitate [their] objectives of improving quality and reducing cost."[220]

Impact on Providers

Of the 179 hospitals and health systems interviewed by HealthLeaders Media in August 2011, 70% ranked technology as one of the top three drivers affecting increases in their healthcare costs.[221] While an investment in technology represents one of the largest costs for healthcare organizations transitioning to an ACO, HIT also provides an opportunity for cost containment through increased operational efficiency and the ultimate reduction of long-term costs.[222]

Key Term	Definition	Citation
Health Information Technology (HIT)	Associated with improving "the health of individuals and the performance of providers, yielding improved quality, cost savings, and greater engagement by patients in their own health care.	The Benefits of Health Information Technology: A Review of the Recent Literature Shows Predominantly Positive Results. Melinda Beeuwkes Buntin, *Health Affairs,* vol. 30, no. 3, (March 2011), p. 464.

Electronic Health Records

Electronic Health Records (EHRs) are likely to have a significant impact on the success of an ACO. As defined by the Health Information Management Systems Society (HIMSS):

> The EHR is a longitudinal electronic record of patient health information generated by one or more encounters in any care delivery setting. Included in this information are patient demographics, progress notes, problems, medications, vital signs, past medical history, immunizations, laboratory data, and radiology reports. The EHR automates and streamlines the clinicians' workflow. The EHR has the ability to generate a complete record of a clinical patient encounter, as well as supporting other care-related activities directly or indirectly via interface, including evidence-based decision support, quality management, and outcomes reporting.[223]

EHR interoperability among ACO participants is critical to ensure that an ACO receives the full benefit of HIT utilization. Health Information Exchanges (HIEs) and Health Information Organizations (HIOs) were first publically promoted in April 2004 by President Bush,[224] to aid in the alignment of EHR systems. An HIE promotes "[t]he electronic movement of health-related information among organizations according to nationally recognized standards," while an HIO "… oversees and governs …" the development implementation and operation of an HIE.[225] As explained by HIMSS:

Key Term	Definition	Citation
Electronic Health Records (EHR)	A longitudinal collection of electron health information about individual patients and populations.	Gunter, T. D. and Terry, N. P. 2005. The Emergence of National Electronic Health Record Architectures in the United States and Australia: Models, Costs, and Questions. In *Journal of Medical Internet Research.* Online at: http://www.ncbi.nlm.nih.gov/pmc/articles/PMC1550638/Published online March 14 2005. Viewed 5/24/12

> [HIEs] are being developed as the infrastructure for data sharing between providers and to support access to the complete patient record across providers in many geographic regions of the country. HIEs will ultimately provide the vehicle for data sharing among provider practices and health systems through the Nationwide Health Information Network (NwHIN). HIMSS has been actively engaged with the development of HIEs and provides a wide range of tools and informational resources for professionals interested in HIE. … Development of health information exchange capability is a key component

in supporting providers achieving meaningful use requirements through use of interoperable electronic health records and other required software applications required to support achievement of meaningful use.[226]

Key Term	Definition	Citation
Health Information Exchange	The infrastructure for data sharing between providers and to support access to the complete patient record across providers in many geographic regions of the country.	Health Information Management Services Web site (HIMSS): http://www.himss.org/asp/topics_focusdynamic.asp?faid = 419

HIEs will likely help ACOs improve quality, while reducing costs, by ensuring that the EHR systems maintained by each ACO participant are properly exchanging data within the ACO's network, with minimal communication errors. A selection of broad technology categories that may be utilized for the successful development, implementation, and operation of ACOs are shown in Exhibit 5.1.

Factoid 5.8

Organizations wishing to participate in an ACO must participate in an HIE to help ensure proper communication and data exchange between participants. (Source: *Accountable Care Organizations-Health Information Technology (HIT.* Gerry Hinkley, Pillsbury Winthrop Shaw Pittman LLP, March 31–April 2, 2011. Online at: http://www.pillsburylaw.com/siteFiles/Events/ACOHealthInformationTechnologyHIT.pdf (Accessed July 6, 2011).)

The primary barriers to technological implementation cited by providers include the significant costs of implementing, or updating, an EHR system,[227] and the uncertainty of obtaining a return on the initial investment (ROI) related to the EHR system.[228] However, the federal government, through the HITECH act (discussed above), has attempted to alleviate these concerns by providing financial incentives for proper EHR implementation and utilization.[229] Through the use of grants and low interest loans,[230] these incentives may offset a portion of the significant capital costs associated with EHR investments and implementation.[231]

Key Term	Definition	Citation
Health Information Technology for Economic and Clinical Health (HITECH) Act	Federal legislation that provides financial incentives for proper EHR implementation and utilization.	*HITECH Programs.* U.S. Department of Health and Human Services, January 27, 2011. Online at: http://healthit.hhs.gov/portal/server.pt?e (Accessed July 7, 2011).

In addition to the significant capital requirements associated with HIT, another obstacle often faced when implementing an EHR system is physician resistance to change.[232] This resistance may be alleviated by educating physicians on the effectiveness of EHR and communicating with other providers on how to meet accountability benchmarks for cost and quality to achieve shared savings payments.[233] However, providers also have expressed concerns regarding the time and resources required for their organization to adopt and train providers on EHR systems.[234] In response, supporters of HIT utilization have noted that the implementation of these systems is a "vehicle, not a destination" for quality improvement, where improvement may lead to further benefits for providers.[235]

EXHIBIT 5.1
Technologies Utilized by ACOs

ACO Objective	Technology Enabler	How It Works	Benefits
Achieve Information continuity	Standards-based information exchange	Create comprehensive long-term patient care records	Instantly coordinated care records utilizing set standards
Facilitate care coordination and transition	Enabling interoperability technology can integrate with any application	HIE incorporates all data sets and utilizes interoperability standards to create a composite view of patient	Timely publishing of most recent data allows for timely remedial action in case of gaps in care
Support best practices, redesign care processes	Interoperable EMR/HIS applications	Interdisciplinary providers collaborate to develop and spread evidence-based guidelines and standard care processes	Promote accountability and track quality of care
Reduce waste, improve operational efficiency, manage risk	Business Intelligence	Leverage clinical, financial, and operational metrics to determine areas of waste or inefficiency	Promote accountability and reduce costs
Combine entities to form one legal entity	ACO management technology	Supports governance and management of the new care-delivery model (clinical and administrative care) to ensure clear accountability	Manage caregivers to plan, budget, and evaluate performance
Increase patient safety and enhance patient care	Clinical Decision Support functionality	Automatic health maintenance and best practice alerts, and other decision support tools	Enhance patient safety, increase quality, reduce costs, and satisfy late-stage meaningful use requirements
Engage patients	Integration with personal health record technologies (PHRs, patient portals, etc.)	Enable patients' access to their health information, and communicate with clinicians	Increased patient adherence with treatment protocols, better outcomes and increased patient engagement and satisfaction
Improve quality care outcomes	Standardized data sets that allow for analytics and reporting to support quality and outcomes metrics across the continuum of care	Aggregation and standardization of clinical and administrative data	Performance-based compensation system strategically aligned with improving outcome goals
Manage diseases	Alerts and reminders, population analysis	Population management	Achieve federal health outcomes goals

Although HIT systems often reduce common errors, the complexities of many of these systems may lead to new types of errors. Providers have expressed concerns that they may become too reliant on the assumed accuracy of EHR systems, which may result in errors if a system malfunctions or contains a flawed program design.[236] In addition, EHR systems do not always account for variations in workflow, e.g., staffing requirements, resource utilization and decision-making strategies, which are particularly important to the ability of an ACO to coordinate care among providers.[237]

Factoid 5.9

Capital requirements, such as HIT and resources required for ACO considerations and implementation, will undoubtedly serve as a limitation for some providers who wish to be involved as ACO. (Source: *Medicare Physician Payment: Care Coordination Programs Used in Demonstration Show Promise, But Wider Use of Payment Approach May Be Limited.* United States Government Accountability Office (February 2008) pp. 34–35.

Impact on Payors

The requirement of HIT for ACOs provides an advantage to payors, in that many payors already possess the requisite "… information technology infrastructure, data analysis, and actuarial capabilities …" to facilitate the effective and efficient operations of an ACO.[238] A further advantage of HIT for payors relates to their significant concern as to how to incentivize an ACO, with whom they have contracted, to lower the cost of care provided. While many private payors have opted to use their market leverage to incentivize providers to lower costs, other payors have offered providers incentives to implement interoperable EHR systems and use reported analytics to improve cost and quality outcomes.[239] (For more information on the type of support provided by private payors for ACO implementation of HIT, see Chapter 3.)

CHAPTER SUMMARY

The Four Pillars of Healthcare Industry Value, i.e., regulatory, reimbursement, competition, and technology, provide a conceptual framework for determining the value to be attributed to the enterprises, assets, and services operating within the healthcare delivery system as well as evaluating the impact of ACOs on the healthcare industry.

Healthcare enterprises and providers considering the development of either a federal ACO or a commercial ACO must be in compliance with those regulations applicable to ACOs, including:

1. Federal and state antikickback statutes
2. The Stark Law and state laws against physician self-referral
3. The False Claims Act
4. Civil Monetary Penalty laws
5. Corporate Practice of Medicine laws
6. Antitrust laws
7. IRS 501(c)(3) tax exempt status requirements

These regulations may posit a greater concern in the commercial ACO market, since CMS, FTC, DOJ, and IRS have all published either regulations or guidelines presenting waivers or safe harbors to promote the compliant operation of federal ACOs. ACOs also must meet applicable FMV and commercial reasonableness thresholds when structuring transactions and negotiating the contracts for ACO relationships.

Differing reimbursement structures may have varying levels of impact on the furtherance of the overall goals of ACOs, i.e., to lower costs and improve quality. While MSSP payments incentivize ACOs to improve quality and decrease cost, traditional FFS reimbursement models used for federal ACOs place greater emphasis on the volume of care provided. Particularly in the commercial ACO market, payors are shifting from pay-for-volume reimbursement models to pay-for-value models, which focus on lower readmission rates, better quality care, and population health management, all under the aegis of evidence-based medicine. Reimbursement concerns affecting payors in both the private and public sectors, including: (1) private insurers, (2) Medicare and Medicaid, and (3) small and large employer insurance plans, typically relate to the cost containment abilities of ACOs and the potential market power of ACOs.

An analysis of ACOs through Porter's Five Forces of Competition, i.e., (1) potential entrants, (2) suppliers, (3) buyers, (4) substitutes, and (5) rivalry among existing competitors, serves as a framework for how ACOs may compete within the healthcare marketplace. For example, small physician practices may be forced out of the ACO market as a result of the increased market leverage associated with consolidated healthcare entities. Additionally, the MSSP limits the ability of providers who perform primary care services from practicing outside of a single ACO, a restriction that is more applicable to PCPs than specialist providers. While the possibility for some level of participation in the ACO market by allied health professionals and ancillary service providers exists, the extent of this participation may be hindered by both the absence of these providers in the MSSP definition of an ACO professional and physician resistance to allowing providers to increase their scope of practice.

Factoid 5.10

The decrease in primary care providers is a current issue that is expected to worsen over time. (Source: Addressing the Primary Care Physician Shortage in an Evolving Medical Workforce. Shaheen E. Lakin and Cyndi Laird, *International Archives of Medicine,* vol. 2, no. 14 (May 5, 2009), p. 2.)

Technological tools, which increase clinical integration and efficiencies, may indirectly impact ACO development through their beneficial effects related to lowering cost and improving quality of care. The development and implementation of HIT will be imperative to the success of ACOs, due to the significant reporting requirements for establishing cost and quality benchmarking metrics.

Ultimately, concerns related to the impact of ACOs on the healthcare industry will revolve around the national fascination with ACOs promise of lowering healthcare costs and improving quality of care. With the June 28, 2012 SCOTUS decision, and reelection of President Obama on November 6, 2012, it is likely that the ACA will survive and continue to foster the development of ACOs. Given that the nature and structure of both federal ACOs and commercial ACOs will ultimately evolve as they continue to be defined (as data related to historical performance and efficacy becomes available), the question persists as to whether ACOs will provide a sustainable solution to the nation's rising healthcare spending and quality of care issues, or whether this new model of emerging healthcare organization will follow the ascendency and ultimate demise of the previous managed care models of the 1990s.

ENDNOTES

1. Federal Anti-kickback Statute, 42 U.S.C. 1320a-7b (2009).
2. Ibid.
3. *Fact Sheet: Federal Anti-Kickback Law and Regulatory Safe Harbors*. Office of Inspector General, November 1999. Online at: https://oig.hhs.gov/fraud/docs/safeharborregulations/safefs.htm (Accessed 5/25/12).
4. Anti-kickback Statute, 42 U.S.C. 1320a-7b (b)(3)(B), (2009).
5. Medicare Program; Final Waivers in Connection with the Shared Savings Program. *Federal Register*. vol. 76. no. 212, November 2, 2011, p. 67994.
6. Federal Anti-kickback Statute" 42 U.S.C. 1320a-7b (2009); Limitations on Certain Physician Referrals, vol. 43 U.S.C. 1395nn(g) (2010).

6. Limitations on Certain Physician Referrals, 1395nn(a).
7. Ibid., 1395nn(h)(6).
8. Ibid., 1395nn(g)(3); *Stark II Phase II Final Regulations*. Robert G. Homchick, et al., American Health Lawyers Association, Member Briefing, May 2004, p. 16.
9. *Health Law*. Barry R. Furrow, et al, St. Paul, MN: West Group, 2001, p. 997.
10. Limitations on Certain Physician Referrals, 1395nn(c).
11. Ibid., 1395nn(b), 1395(e)(3).
12. Ibid., 1395nn(e)(2)–(3).
13. *CMS Clarifies Stark "Stand in the Shoes" Provision*. Daniel H. Melvin, Eric B. Gordan, and Joan Polacheck, *Health Lawyers Weekly*, vol. VII, no. 29, July 24, 2009. Online at: http://www.mwe.com/index.cfm/fuseaction/publications.nldetail/object_id/47c655d8-9f02-42e2-b620-fabfb93ba956.cfm (Accessed 11/17/11).
14. False Claims Act, 31 U.S.C. 3729(a) (2011).
15. *Conducting a Compliance Review of Hospital–Physician Financial Arrangements*. Dennis S. Diaz, Davis Wright Tremaine, LLP., pp. 14–15.
16. False Claims Act..
17. §1128(a) of the Social Security Act is codified as "Civil Monetary Penalties," 42 U.S.C. 1320a-7a (2010).
18. *Civil Monetary Penalties and Affirmative Exclusions*. Office of Inspector General, Online at: http://oig.hhs.gov/fraud/ enforcement/cmp/index.asp (Accessed 5/22/12).
19. Civil Monetary Penalties, 42 U.S.C. 1320a-7a (2010).
20. Civil Monetary Penalties: Payments to Induce Reduction or Limitation of Services, 42 U.S.C. 1320a-7b (1989).
21. The hypothetical means by which an ACO may attempt to manage costs are discussed in Chapter 4: Hypothetical Models for the Development and Operation of ACOs.
22. Medicare Program; Final Waivers in Connection with the Shared Savings Program, pp. 67993–94.
23. Ibid., p. 67993.
24. Ibid., p. 68002.
25. Ibid., p. 68003.
26. Note: If there was a qualified arrangement, as defined by the Final Rule, in place prior to denial of an entity's ACO application, the preparticipation end date may be extended by six months. Further, if an ACO fails to submit an ACO application, it may obtain a waiver extension at the discretion of the HHS secretary; Medicare Program; Final Waivers in Connection With the Shared Savings Program, p. 68000.
27. Ibid., p. 68001.
28. Ibid., pp. 68001, 68006.
29. Ibid., p. 68001.
30. Ibid.; Current exceptions to the Physician Self-Referral Law are set forth in General Exceptions to the Referral Prohibition Related to Both Ownership/Investment and Compensation, 42 CFR § 411.355–411.357 (2010).
31. Medicare Program; Final Waivers in Connection with the Shared Savings Program, p. 68007.
32. Ibid., p. 68000.
33. Monopolies and Combinations in Restraint of Trade, 15 U.S.C.A. §1-7 (2012).
34. Ibid., §12–19.
35. Federal Trade Commission; Promotion of Export Trade and Prevention of Unfair Methods of Competition, 15 U.S.C.A. §41–58 (2012).
36. *Physician–Hospital Clinical Integration: Navigating the Complexities*. Ashley McKinney Fischer, et al., Strafford Webinar, October 14, 2010, p. 9.
37. Health Law Provision Raises Antitrust Concerns. Robert Pear, *The New York Times* (February 8, 2011).
38. Accountable Care Organizations: Promise of Better Outcomes at Restrained Costs; Can They Meet Their Challenges? C. Frederick Geilfuss and Renate M. Gray, *BNA's Health Law Reporter*, vol. 19, no. 956 (July 8, 2010), p. 4.
39. Statement of Antitrust Enforcement Policy Regarding Accountable Care Organizations Participating in the Medicare Shared Savings Program. *Federal Register* vol. 76, no. 209 (October 28, 2011), pp. 67026–67032.
40. Ibid., pp. 67026, 67027.
41. Ibid., p. 67027; *Horizontal Merger Guidelines*. U.S. Department of Justice and the Federal Trade Commission, August 19, 2010. Online at: http://www.justice.gov/atr/public/guidelines/hmg-2010.pdf (Accessed 6/5/2012).
42. Ibid., p. 67028.

43. Ibid., pp. 67028, 67031.
44. Ibid., p. 67028, citing Medicare Program: Physicians' Referrals to Health Care Entities with Which They Have Financial Relationships (Phase II). *Federal Register*, vol. 69, no. 59 (March 26, 2004), p. 16094, which further specifies that: "The final rule looks to the relocation of the recruited physician's medical practice, rather than the physician's residence. A physician will be deemed to have relocated to the hospital's geographic area (defined as the lowest number of contiguous postal zip codes from which the hospital draws at least 75% of its inpatients) if: (i) The physician has relocated the site of his or her practice a minimum of 25 miles; or (ii) at least 75% of the physician's revenues from services provided by the physician to patients (including services to hospital inpatients) are derived from services provided to new patients."
45. Proposed Statement of Antitrust Enforcement Policy Regarding Accountable Care Organizations Participating in the Medicare Shared Savings Program. *Federal Register* vol. 76, no. 75 (April 19, 2011), p. 21987.
46. Antitrust Markets and ACOs. David A. Argue and John M. Gale, Competition Policy International, *CPI Antitrust Chronicle*, May 2011, pp. 6–7.
47. Statement of Antitrust Enforcement Policy Regarding Accountable Care Organizations Participating in the Medicare Shared Savings Program, pp. 67028–67030.
48. Ibid.
49. Ibid., p. 67029.
50. Ibid., p. 67030.
51. Ibid., pp. 67029–67030.
52. Administrative Procedure Act, Pub. L. 79-404 (June 11, 1946).
53. The FTC-DOJ Antitrust Enforcement Policy for ACOs in the Aftermath of Public Comment. Robert W. McCann, Bureau of National Affairs, *Health Law Reporter*, vol. 20, no. 925, June 16, 2011, p. 3.
54. Herding Cats? What Health Care Reform Means for Hospital–Physician Alignment and Clinical Integration. Daniel H. Melvin and Chris Jedrey, McDermott, Will & Emery (October 13, 2010), p. 38.
55. Barak Richman: ACOs Should Not Involve Collaboration of Rivals. Sandra Yin, Fierce Healthcare (February 11, 2011). Online at: www.fiercehealthcare.com/node/53407/print (Accessed 2/16/11).
56. Statement of Antitrust Enforcement Policy Regarding Accountable Care Organizations Participating in the Medicare Shared Savings Program, p. 67027.
57. *Corporate Practice of Medicine Doctrine 50 State Survey Summary*. Mary Michal, et al., The Hospice and Palliative Care Practice Group of Reinhart Boerner Van Deuren, September 2006, p. 2.
58. Ibid.
59. *Corporate Practice of Medicine*. Thomson Reuters/West, 50 State Statutory Surveys, October 2011.
60. *Corporate Practice of Medicine Doctrine 50 State Survey Summary*.
61. *Implementing Accountable Care Organizations*. Stephen Shortell, et al., Advancing National Health Reform, Berkeley Law, Berkeley Center on Health, Economic & Family Security, May 2010, p. 11.
62. *Accountable Care Organizations versus Texas' Corporate Practice of Medicine Doctrine*. Craig A. Conway, Health Law Perspectives, University of Houston Law Center, October 2010, p. 4.
63. Ibid.
64. Ibid., p. 3.
65. Ibid.
66. Ibid., p. 4.
67. Accountable Care Organizations: Promise of Better Outcomes at Restrained Costs; Can They Meet Their Challenges.
68. Antitrust Worries May Be Addressed By "Safe Harbors" Coming from FTC. *ACO Business News*, vol. 1, no. 1, p. 4.
69. *Notice Regarding Participation in the MSSP through an ACO: Notice 2011-20*. Internal Revenue Service, 2011-16 I.R.B., April 18, 2011, p. 652.
70. Ibid., p. 655.
71. Ibid., p. 653.
72. Ibid., p. 655; *Tax-Exempt Hospitals and Accountable Care Organizations*. McDermott Will & Emery, April 27, 2011. Online at: http://www.mwe.com/publications/uniEntity.aspx?xpST=PublicationDetail&pub=6511&PublicationTypes=d9093adb-e95d-4f19-819a-f0bb5170ab6d (Accessed 4/6/2012).
73. Antitrust Worries May Be Addressed by "Safe Harbors: Coming from FTC. *ACO Business News*, vol. 1, no. 1, p. 4.
74. *Transforming Health Care through Accountable Care Organizations: A Critical Assessment*. Foley & Lardner, LLP, 2010. Online at: http://www.foley.com/files/tbl_s31Publications/FileUpload137/7574/ACO_White_Paper.pdf (Accessed 1/30/12), p. 53.

75. Ibid.
76. Ibid., p. 54.
78. Ibid.
79. Limitations on Certain Physician Referrals, 1395nn(e)(2)-(3).
80. *Valuing a Business: The Analysis and Appraisal of Closely Held Companies*, 5th ed. Shannon Pratt, New York: McGraw-Hill, 2008, p. 42.
81. Healthcare Valuation: The Financial Appraisal of Enterprises, Assets, and Services in the Era of Reform. Robert James Cimasi, Hoboken, NJ: John Wiley & Sons, Inc., 2013.
82. Program Integrity; Medicare and State Health Care Programs; Permissive Exclusions, 42 CFR 1001.952(d)(5) (2009).
83. *A Valuation Model for the Formation of ACOs*. American Health Lawyers Association, 2011. Online at: http://www.healthlawyers.org/News/Health%20Lawyers%20Weekly/Pages/ACOArticle.aspx (Accessed 1/30/12).
84. Medicare and Medicaid Programs; Physicians' Referrals to Health Care Entities with Which They Have Financial Relationships: Proposed Rule, *Federal Register* vol. 69, no. 6 (January 9, 1998), p. 1700.
85. Medicare Program; Physicians' Referrals to Health Care Entities with Which They Have Financial Relationships (Phase II). *Federal Register* vol. 69, no. 59 (March 26, 2004), p. 16093.
86. Setting Doctor Compensation Is Both Art and Science. John R. Boettiger & Jennifer H. Smith, *Healthcare Finance News*, July 2007. Online at: http://www.healthcarefinancenews.com/news/setting-doctor-compensation-both-art-and-science (Accessed 1/18/2012).
87. Commercial Reasonableness: The New Target. David B. Pursell, *Journal of Health Care Compliance,* vol. 13, no. 2, March/April 2011, p. 60; *United States v. Campbell*, 2011 U.S. Dist. LEXIS 1207, 22 (January 4, 2011).
88. Showdown Gets a Head Start. Rich Daly and Jessica Zigmond, *Modern Healthcare*, March 26, 2012; Patient Protection and Affordable Care Act, Sec. 2201, Pub. Law 111-148, 124 STAT 244 (March 23, 2010); *National Federation of Independent Business v. Sebelius*; *Department of Health and Human Services v. Florida*: Syllabus" Nos. 11-393, 11-398, and, 11-400, Slip Opinion, 567 U.S. (June 28, 2012), pp. 1–2.
89. Supreme Court Review of the Health Care Reform Law. Gregory D. Curfman, Brendan S. Abel, Renee M. Landers, *New England Journal of Medicine*, March 15, 2012, p. 978; *National Federation of Independent Business v. Sebelius, Department of Health and Human Services v. Florida et al.*; Florida: Opinion of ROBERTS, C. J., Nos. 11-393, 11-398 and, 11-400, Slip Opinion, 567 U.S. _ (June 28, 2012), pp. 1–2.
90. *National Federation of Independent Business v. Sebelius; Department of Health and Human Services v. Florida*, pp. 32–44.
91. Ibid.
92. Ibid.
93. Moody's: Supreme Court Decision on Healthcare Law Has Three Likely Outcomes. Dean Diaz, Moody's Investors Service, Inc., June 6, 2012. Online at: http://www.moodys.com/research/Moodys-Supreme-Court-decision-on-healthcare-law-has-three-likely-PR_247736 (Accessed 11/3/2012).
94. The final rule for the Medical Loss Ratio (MLR) requires insurance companies to spend 80% of insurance premiums on medical care and healthcare quality improvement in the individual and small group markets, and 85% of premiums on these components in the large group markets, exclusive of administrative costs. If an insurance company does not abide by the MLR, they must provide financial rebate to their members. Minimum Medical Loss Ratio, 45 C.F.R. §158.210 (2011); Medical Loss Ratio Requirements under the Patient Protection and Affordable Care Act, *Federal Register,* vol. 76, no. 235, (December 2, 2011), pp. 76574–76594.
95. The Bomb Buried in Obamacare Explodes Today—Hallelujah! Rick Ungar, *Forbes*, June 28, 2012. Online at: http://www.forbes.com/sites/rickungar/2011/12/02/the-bomb-buried-in-obamacare-explodes-today-halleluja/ (Accessed 7/5/ 2012).
96. The Design and Application of Shared Savings Programs: Lessons from Early Adopters. Joel S. Weissman, et al., *Health Affairs*, vol. 31, no. 9, September 2012, p. 1960.
97. Investors Not Likely to Provide ACO Funding Under Proposed Rule, Venture Capitalist Says. Sara Hansard, Bureau of National Affairs, *Health Law Reporter*, vol. 20, no. 1026, 2011.
98. An analysis of beneficiary size as related to ACO financial feasibility is provided in Chapter 7: Financial Feasibility Analysis for ACO Investments.
99. *Getting to There from Here: Evolving to ACOs through Clinical Integration Programs: Including the Advocate Health Care Example as Presented by Lee B. Sacks, M.D.* James J. Pizzo and Mark E. Grube, Kaufman, Hall & Associates, Inc., 2011, p. 9, 17, 18.

100. Investors Not Likely to Provide ACO Funding under Proposed Rule, Venture Capitalist Says.
101. Quality over Quantity. Bryn Nelson, *The Hospitalist* (December 2009). Online at: www.the-hospitalist.org/details/article/477391/quality_over_quantity.html, (Accessed 2/28/11).
102. Specifically those large health systems that participated in the Physician Group Practice Demonstration Project (PGP), discussed at length in Chapter 1: Background and the Path to ACOs.
103. Accountable Care Organizations (Chap. 2), in *Report to Congress: Improving Incentives in the Medicare Program.* Medicare Payment Advisory Commission, June 2009, pp. 39, 40.
104. *Will Mayo Clinic Save Money as an ACO*? Christopher Snowbeck and Don McCanne, Physicians for a National Health Program (February 8, 2011). Online at: www.pnhp.org/print/news/2011/february/will-mayo-clinic-save-money-as-an-aco (Accessed 2/28/11).
105. Experience with Medicare's New Technology Add-On Payment Program. Alexandra T. Clydem, et al., *Health Affairs*, vol. 27, no. 6, November 2008, p. 1640.
106. Patient Protection and Affordable Care Act, Sec. 6001, Pub. Law 111-148, 124 STAT 684-689 (March 23, 2010), as amended by Health Care and Education Reconciliation Act, Sec. 1106 Pub. Law 111-152, 124 STAT 1049-1050 (March 30, 2010).
107. The Valuation of Physician-Owned Hospitals in a Changing Reimbursement and Regulatory Environment. Robert James Cimasi, *The PHA Pulse*, Winter 2007/2008, pp. 13–16.
108. Physicians Post-PPACA: Not Going Bust At the Healthcare Buffet (Part 1 of 2). David W. Hilgers and Sidney Welch, *Physician News Digest*, March 15, 2012. Online at: http://www.physiciansnews.com/2012/03/15/physicians-post-ppaca-not-going-bust-at-the-healthcare-buffet-part-1-of-2/ (Accessed 11/3/2012).
109. POHs in operation, or in the process of expansion, prior to March 23, 2010, may continue their operations under the whole hospital exception; however, the circumstances under which they may expand is significantly limited to when the POH: (1) is located in a county with a population growth rate of at least 150% the state's population growth over the last five years; (2) has a Medicaid inpatient admission percentage of at least the average of all hospitals in the county; (3) is located in a state with below-national-average bed capacity; or (4) has a bed occupancy rate greater than the state average. Further, any expansion is subject to an application process through HHS. Patient Protection and Affordable Care Act, Sec. 6001, Pub. Law 111-148, 124 STAT 684-689 (March 23, 2010), as amended by Health Care and Education Reconciliation Act, Sec. 1106, Pub. Law 111-152, 124 STAT 1049-1050 (March 30, 2010).
110. Market Consolidation Seen as Threat to Doc-Owned Hospitals. Andis Robexnieks, *Modern Healthcare*, September 20, 2012. Online at: http://www.modernhealthcare.com/article/20120920/NEWS/309209951/market-consolidation-seen-as-threat-to-doc-owned-hospitals (Accessed 10/1/2012).
111. Medicare Program: Medicare Shared Savings Program: Accountable Care Organizations. *Federal Register.* vol. 76, no. 212 (November 2, 2011). p. 67851.
112. *Notice Regarding Participation in the MSSP through an ACO: Notice 2011-20*. Internal Revenue Service, 2011-16 I.R.B., April 18, 2011, p. 652.
113. The Accountable Care Organizations: Whatever Its Growing Pains, The Concept Is Too Vitally Important to Fail. Francis J. Crosson, *Health Affairs*, vol. 30, no. 7, July 2011, p. 1252.
114. Ibid.
115. Retail Clinics are those outpatient walk-in facilities located in grocery stores and department stores that provide simple care that emphasizes patient convince. An example of an insurer that operates retail clinics is the Bravo Health Advance Care Center, operated by Bravo Health, a private Medicare plan; Health Insurers Opening Their Own Clinics to Trim Costs. Christopher Weaver, *Kaiser Health News*, May 4, 2011. Online at: http://www.kaiserhealthnews.org/Stories/2011/May/04/Insurers-Turn-To-Clinics-For-Cost-Control.aspx (Accessed 5/31/2011).
116. Ibid.
117. Case Study of a Primary Care-Based Accountable Care System Approach to Medical Home Transformation. Robert L. Phillips, *Journal of Ambulatory Care Management*, vol. 34, no. 1, 2011, p. 67; *ACOs Can Work with Physicians in Charge*. Victoria Stagg Elliott, *American Medical News* (January 31, 2011). Online at: www.ama-assn.org/amednews/2011/01/31/bisa0131.htm, (Accessed 2/7/11); WellMed Facts. WellMed Medical Group, 2012. Online at: https://www.wellmedmedicalgroup.com/corporate/about-the-company/wellmed-facts/ (Accessed 10/24/2012).
118. Medicare Program: Medicare Shared Savings Program: Accountable Care Organizations, p. 67807.
119. See the feasibility discussion provided in Chapter 7, Financial Feasibility Analysis for ACO Investments.
120. *Fair Market Value: Analysis and Tools to Comply with Stark and Anti-Kickback Rules*. Robert A. Wade, and Marcie Rose Levine, Audio Conference, HC Pro, Inc., (March 19, 2008).

121. Medicare Program: Medicare Shared Savings Program: Accountable Care Organizations, p. 67983.
122. Ibid., p. 67880.
123. Medicare Program; Medicare Shared Savings Program: Accountable Care Organizations: Proposed Rule, *Federal Register*, vol. 76, no. 76, April 7, 2011.
124. Medicare Program: Medicare Shared Savings Program: Accountable Care Organizations, p. 67811.
125. Ibid., pp. 67855–56, 67983.
126. Ibid; *Role of Specialists in the Medicare Shared Savings Program (MSSP) Establishing Accountable Care Organizations (ACOs).* Hart Health Strategies, October 20, 2011. Online at: http://www.gastro.org/advocacy-regulation/regulatory-issues/accountable-care-organizations/AGA_ACO_Specialist_Role_102611.pdf (Accessed November 12, 2011).
127. What Is the Role of the Radiologist in Holding Down Health Care Cost Growth? Howard P. Forman, et al., *American Journal of Roentgenology*, vol. 197, no. 4. October, 2011, p. 919.
128. Specialists Have a Role in Medicare Shared Savings Programs. Toya M. Sledd, American Academy of Orthopaedic Surgeons, *AAOS Now*, July 2011. Online at: http://www.aaos.org/news/aaosnow/jul11/advocacy1.asp (Accessed January 16, 2012).
129. Once a person is diagnosed with cancer, much of their care revolves around cancer treatments. U.S. Oncology May Go National with Private-Sector ACO. Jennifer Horspool, *ACO Business News,* vol. 2, no. 1, January, 2011, p. 3.
130. About Texas Oncology. *Texas Oncology*, 2012. Online at: http://www.texasoncology.com/about-txo.aspx (Accessed 11/3/2012).
131. U.S. Oncology May Go National with Private-Sector ACO.
132. Ibid.
133. ACO Rule Leaves Oncologists Wondering How to Proceed. Lola Butcher, *Oncology Times*, vol. 34, no. 3, February 10, 2012, pp. 18–19; U.S. Oncology May Go National with Private-Sector ACO.
134. *Detailed Analysis of Accountable Care Organizations (ACO) Final Rule*. Julie Clements, Deputy Director for Regulatory Affairs, and Nick Meyers, Director of Government Relations, to Board of Trustees, APA Assembly, Council on Advocacy and Government Relations, APA Members, October 26, 2011. Online at: http://psych.org/MainMenu/AdvocacyGovernmentRelations/GovernmentRelations/Memo-ACO-Final-Rule.aspx?FT=.pdf (Accessed on January 16, 2012), pp. 2–3.
135. Ibid., p. 2.
136. More Quality Measures to Be Added to ACO Rule. Mark Moran, *Psychiatric News*, vol. 46, no. 24, p. 4a, December 16, 2011. Online at: http://psychnews.psychiatryonline.org/newsArticle.aspx?articleid=181066, (Accessed January 16, 2011).
137. *ASCs for ACOs: Is There an Advantage*? Shay Pratt, The Advisory Board, November 2, 2012. Online at: http://www.advisory.com/Research/Marketing-and-Planning-Leadership-Council/Service-Line-Transformation/2012/08/ASCs-for-ACOs-Is-there-an-advantage (Accessed 11/10/2012).
138. Accountable Care Organizations: Physician Participation Required. Howard F. Hahn and Torri A. Criger, American Health Lawyers Association, *AHLA Connections*, January 2011, p. 24.
139. Medicare Program: Medicare Shared Savings Program: Accountable Care Organizations, p. 67812.
140. The central Federal ACO entity includes those providers that are directly included within the ACO contract with CMS and do not participate in shared savings through third-party contracts with the ACO. An illustration of these interactions is provided in Chapter 4, Hypothetical Models for the Development and Operation of ACOs.
141. Can a Hospital Benefit from Partnering with Physicians? Allan Fine and Brandon Frazier, *Healthcare Financial Management*, vol. 65, no. 5, May 2011, pp. 70, 74; Accountable Care Organizations: Physician Participation Required. Howard F. Hahn and Torri A. Criger, American Health Lawyers Association, *AHLA Connections*, January 2011, pp. 24, 28; ASCs for ACOs: Is There an Advantage? Shay Pratt, *The Advisory Board*, November 2, 2012. Online at: http://www.advisory.com/Research/Marketing-and-Planning-Leadership-Council/Service-Line-Transformation/2012/08/ASCs-for-ACOs-Is-there-an-advantage (Accessed 11/10/2012).
142. See Chapter 4, Hypothetical Models for the Development and Operation of ACOs.
143. The Health Information Technology for Economic and Clinical Health Act (HITECH), part of the American Recovery and Reinvestment Act of 2009, requires Medicare providers to obtain “meaningful use” of EHR by the end of 2014 to avoid reimbursement penalties, and provides both financial incentives and programmatic support to overcome obstacles that have previously kept providers from adopting some form of an electronic record system. American Recovery and Reinvestment Act, Pub. Law 111-5, 123 Stat. 467-68 (February 17, 2009).

144. *Electronic Health Record (EHR) Incentive Program FAQs*. Centers for Medicare and Medicaid Services, February 2012. Online at: https://www.cms.gov/Regulations-and-Guidance/Legislation/EHRIncentivePrograms/downloads/FAQsRemediatedandRevised.pdf (Accessed 10/12/2012).
145. Letter from Ambulatory Surgery Center Association to Donald M. Berick, RE: CMS-1345-P; Request for Comments, Medicare Shared Savings Program, Accountable Care Organizations Proposed Rule, June 3, 2011.
146. Can a Hospital Benefit from Partnering with Physicians?, pp. 71, 73, 76.
147. Letter from APTA to CMS Regarding CMS's Request for Information Regarding ACOs. R. Scott Ward, American Physical Therapy Association to Donald Berwick, Centers for Medicare and Medicaid Services, December 3, 2010, p. 4.
148. Letter from ACA to CMS, Re: Medicare Program; Request for Information Regarding Accountable Care Organizations and the Medicare Shared Savings Program. Rick McMichael, American Chiropractic Association, November 29, 2010.
149. U.S. Pharmacists' Effect as Team Members on Patient Care: Systematic Review and Meta-Analyses. Marie A. Chisholm-Burns, et al., *Medical Care*, vol. 48, no. 10, October 2010, p. 923; Integrating Pharmacists into Accountable Care Organizations and Coordinated Care. National Community Pharmacists Association, *The Dose*, December 7, 2010. Online at: http://ncpanet.wordpress.com/2010/12/07/integrating-pharmacists-into-accountable-care-organizations-acos-and-coordinated-care/#more-627 (Accessed 12/9/10).
150. Scope of Practice Expansion Fuel Legal Battles. Amy Lynn Sorrel, *American Medical News,* March, 9, 2009. Online at: http://www.ama-assn.org/amednews/2009/03/09/prl20309.htm (Accessed 6/7/2012).
151. Insurers Work with Providers On Crucial ACO Components. *ACO Business News*, vol. 1, no. 1, November 2010, p. 5.
152. Next Steps for ACOs. *Health Affairs*, Health Policy Brief, January 31, 2012, p. 2.
153. In January 2012, Health Spring was acquired by Cigna, and now operates as a subsidiary of Cigna. *Cigna Completes Acquisition of HealthSpring*. Health Spring, Inc., Press Release, January 31, 2012. Online at: http://phx.corporate-ir.net/phoenix.zhtml?c=226354&p=irol-newsArticle&ID=1654641&highlight=cigna (Accessed 11/7/2012); Health Spring Deal Shows Commercial Appeal of ACOs. Bill McConnell, *The Deal Magazine*, November 4, 2011. Online at: http://decisionresourcesgroup.com/News-and-Events/In-The-News/HLI-Paula-Wade-TheDeal-com-110411 (Accessed 11/7/2012).
154. Health Spring, Inc. is one of the largest Medicare advantage plans in the nation. Based in Nashville, TN, Health Spring operates plans in Alabama, Delaware, Florida, Georgia, Illinois, Maryland, Mississippi, New Jersey, Pennsylvania, Tennessee, Texas, Washington, D.C., and West Virginia, as well as a national stand-alone prescription drug plan. *About Health Spring*. Health Spring, Inc., April 3, 2012. Online at: http://www.healthspring.com/About (Accessed 11/7/2012); Health Spring Deal Shows Commercial Appeal of ACOs.
155. Bravo Health, discussed above, is a Health Spring company. About Us. *Bravo Health*. Online at: http://www.bravohealth.com/AboutUs (Accessed 11/7/2012).
156. Insurers Work with Providers on Crucial ACO Components.
157. Proposed Statement of Antitrust Enforcement Policy Regarding Accountable Care Organizations Participating in the Medicare Shared Savings Program. *Federal Register* vol. 76, no. 75 (April 19, 2011), p. 21897; Next Steps for ACOs. *Health Affairs*, Health Policy Brief, January 31, 2012, p. 5.
158. Statement of Antitrust Enforcement Policy Regarding Accountable Care Organizations Participating in the Medicare Shared Savings Program. *Federal Register* vol. 76, no. 209 (October 28, 2011), p. 67026.
159. *Accountable Care Organizations in Medicare and the Private Sector: A Status Update*. Robert A. Berenson and Rachel A. Burton, The Robert Wood Johnson Foundation and The Urban Institute (November 2011). Online at: http://www.rwjf.org/files/research/73470.5470.aco.report.pdf (Accessed 1/16/12), pp. 3, 4.
160. Ibid., p. 3.
161. *Essentials of Managed Health Care*, 6th ed. Peter R. Kongstvedt, Burlington, MA: Jones and Bartlett Learning, LLC, 2013, p. 28.
162. Letter from PBGH to CMS Regarding ACOs. David Lansky, president and CEO of Pacific Business Group on Health, to Donald M. Berwick, Administrator of Centers for Medicare and Medicaid Services, February 14, 2011; Large Employers Air Doubts about ACOs. Rebecca Vesely, *Healthcare Business News*, February 15, 2011. Online at: http://www.modernhealthcare.com/article/20110215/NEWS/302159958 (Accessed 1/19/12).
163. *2011 Employer-Driven Accountable Care Organizations Survey Report: What They Are and What They Can Do for Your Organization*. Aon Hewitt and Polakoff Boland, 2011, p. 6.

164. Cost Containment Measures under Healthcare Reform. Small Business Majority, December 2, 2011. Online at: http://smallbusinessmajority.org/policy/docs/SBM_Small_Biz_Cost_Containment_120211.pdf (Accessed 1/20/12); Lower Premiums, Stronger Businesses: How Health Insurance Reform Will Bring Down Costs for Small Businesses. Meena Seshamani, HHS Web Communications and New Media Division. Online at: http://healthreform.gov/reports/smallbusiness2/smallbusiness2.pdf (Accessed 6/7/2012), p. 1.
165. Investing in Prevention Improves Productivity and Reduces Employer Costs. Centers For Disease Control. Online at: http://www.cdc.gov/policy/resources/Investingin_ReducesEmployerCosts.pdf (Accessed 10/31/2012).
166. *2011 Employer-Driven Accountable Care Organizations Survey Report*, pp. 3, 8.
167. Ibid., p. 4.
168. *Accountable Care Organizations in California: Lessons for the National Debate on Delivery System Reform*. James C. Robinson and Emma L. Dolan, Integrated Healthcare Association for Website Content, 2010. Online at: http://www.iha.org/pdfs_documents/home/ACO_whitepaper_final.pdf (Accessed 5/26/11), p. 15.
169. Patient Protection and Affordable Care Act, Sec. 2201, Pub. Law 111-148, 124 STAT 173, 175 (March 23, 2010).
170. Patient Protection and Affordable Care Act; Establishment of Exchanges and Qualified Health Plans; Exchanges Standards for Employers; Final Rule and Interim Final Rule. *Federal Register*, vol. 77, no. 59, March 27, 2012, pp. 18315, 18316.
171. *State Actions to Address Health Insurance Exchanges*. National Conference of State Legislatures, October 2012. Online at: http://www.ncsl.org/issues-research/health/state-actions-to-implement-the-health-benefit-exch.aspx (Accessed 11/11/2012).
172. The HIEs are only a means for determining the possible health plans available to individuals and small employers within the insurance market; therefore, only insurance companies will be listed on a state's HIE comparative Web page. Federal ACOs and traditional Commercial ACOs are entities, and, to date, have not been considered insurers, and will not be included in HIEs. For a more detailed description of each type of ACO, see Chapter 4: Hypothetical Models for the Development and Operation of ACOs.
173. Under the ACA, states must establish their HIE no later than January 1, 2014; Patient Protection and Affordable Care Act, Sec. 2201, Pub. Law 111-148, 124 STAT 173 (March 23, 2010).
174. Medicare Program: Medicare Shared Savings Program: Accountable Care Organizations. *Federal Register*, vol. 76, no. 212 (November 2, 2011), p. 67804.
175. *Physician Group Practice Demonstration Succeeds in Improving Quality and Reducing Costs*. Centers for Medicare and Medicaid, Press Release, August 8, 2011. Online at: http://www.cms.gov/Medicare/Demonstration-Projects/DemoProjectsEvalRpts/downloads/PGP_PR.pdf (Accessed 11/10/2012).
176. *The President's Budget for Fiscal Year 2013*: Department of Health and Human Services. The White House, Office of Management and Budget, Washington, D.C.: U.S. Government Printing Office, 2012, p. 114.
177. Letter from CBO to the U.S. House of Representatives Regarding Direct Financial Impact of the Reconciliation Act of 2010. Douglas W. Elmendorf, Congressional Budget Office, to Nancy Pelosi, U.S. House of Representatives, March 20, 2010, Table 5, p. 4.
178. FAQ on ACOs: Accountable Care Organizations, Explained. Jenny Gold, *Kaiser Health News*, January 13, 2011. Online at: http://www.kaiserhealthnews.org/stories/2011/january/13/aco-accountable-care-organization-faq.aspx (Accessed 1/17/12).
179. Patient Protection and Affordable Care Act, Sec. 3022, Pub. Law 111-148, 124 STAT 395 (March 23, 2010).
180. Ibid. 325–326.
181. Ibid.
182. The Missing Ingredient in Accountable Care. Pauline W. Chen, *The New York Times* (January 27, 2011). Online at: nytimes.com//2011/01/27/health/views/27chen.html?_r=1
183. Patient's Role in Accountable Care Organizations. Anna D. Sinaiko and Meredith B. Rosenthal, *New England Journal of Medicine*, vol. 363, no. 27, December 30, 2010, p. 2583–2584; The Missing Ingredient in Accountable Care.
184. A PPO is a managed care plan that allows members to choose from an array of participating health-care providers that have contracted with the health plan to provide services at a discount. *Essentials of Managed Health Care*, 6th ed. Peter R. Kongstvedt, Burlington, MA: Jones and Bartlett Learning, LLC, 2013, p. 28.

185. *Federal Trade Commission, Department of Justice Issue Final Statement of Antitrust Policy Enforcement Regarding Accountable Care Organizations.* Federal Trade Commission, News Release (October 20, 2011). Online at: http://www.ftc.gov/opa/2011/10/aco.shtm (Accessed 1/17/2012).
186. Statement of Antitrust Enforcement Policy Regarding Accountable Care Organizations Participating in the Medicare Shared Savings Program. *Federal Register* vol. 76, no. 209 (October 28, 2011).
187. Hospitals That Don't Move on ACOs Risk Losing MD Referrals. *ACO Business News*, vol. 1, no. 1, November 2010, pp. 7–8.
188. *Competitive Strategy: Techniques for Analyzing Industries and Competitors.* Michael E. Porter, New York: The Free Press, 1980, pp. xvii–xix.
189. Ibid., p. 1.
190. Ibid., p. 7.
191. Ibid., p. 27
192. Ibid., p. 24.
193. Ibid., pp. 24–26.
194. Ibid., pp. 4, 23.
195. Ibid., p. 17.
196. Hospitals That Don't Move on ACOs Risk Losing MD Referrals, pp. 7 –8.
197. Ibid.
198. Small Medical Groups Face Decisions in Affiliation, Infrastructure Set-Up for ACOs. *ACO Business News*, vol. 1, no. 2, December 2010, p. 1.
199. Ibid., pp. 1–2.
200. Accountable Care Organizations. Mark Merlis, *Health Affairs*, Health Policy Brief, July 27, 2010 (updated August 13, 2010), pp. 2, 4; Small Medical Groups Face Decisions in Affiliation, Infrastructure Set-Up for ACOs, p. 2.
201. Small Medical Groups Face Decisions in Affiliation, Infrastructure Set-Up for ACOs, p. 2.
202. A Model for Integrating Independent Physicians into Accountable Care Organizations. Mark C. Shields, Pankaj H. Patel, Martin Manning, and Lee Sacks, *Health Affairs*, vol. 30, no. 1, January 2011, p. 169.
203. Some were derisionally referred to as *Physician Hostage Organizations.*
204. New PHOs Are Being Structured as Stepping Stones to ACOs. *ACO Business News*, vol. 1, no. 2, December 2010, p. 6.
205. Ibid., p. 8.
206. PHO Prepares Detroit System for ACD Certification. Tiffany Jones, *ACO Business News,* vol. 1, no. 2, December 2010, p. 7.
207. For a discussion on the capital requirements of ACOs, see Chapter 6: Capital Considerations for the Development and Operation of ACOs.
208. FAQs on ACOs: Accountable Care Organizations, Explained. Jenny Gold, *Kaiser Health News,* October 21, 2011. Online at: http://www.kaiserhealthnews.org/stories/2011/january/13/aco-accountable-care-organization-faq.aspx (Accessed 1/17/12).
209. Ibid.
210. Ibid.
211. *Accountable Care Organizations: Can They Rein in Health Care Spending for States*? Robin N. Richardson to American Academy of Family Physicians Washington, DC: AAFP, June 9, 2010, pp. 4–5.
212. *Building ACOs and Outcomes Based Contracting in the Commercial Market: Provider and Payor Perspectives.* THINC (Taconic Health Information Network and Community), Fishkill, NY, October 2011, p. 6.
213. *Accountable Care Organizations: Can They Rein in Health Care Spending for States*?, p. 4.
214. Global Cap Dominates Some Private Sector Payment Models; Others Seek Partial Cap. *ACO Business News*, vol. 1, no. 1, November 2010, p. 1.
215. Ibid.
216. Ibid., p. 3.
217. Ibid., pp. 1–2.
218. The Benefits of Health Information Technology: A Review of the Recent Literature Shows Predominantly Positive Results. Melinda Beeuwkes Buntin, *Health Affairs*, vol. 30, no. 3, (March 2011), p. 464.
219. Paying for Electronic Health Records (EHRs). *MdBuyline*, vol. 3, no. 1, (January 2010), p. 1.
220. *Technology Fundamentals for Realizing ACO Success.* MEDICITY, Salt Lake City, UT, September 2010. Online at: http://www.himss.org/content/files/Medicity_ACO_Whitepaper.pdf (Accessed June 30, 2011), p. 3.

221. The Next Phase of Cost Control: Buzz Survey. Philip Betbeze, *Healthleaders Media Impact Analysis*, January 2012, pp. 4, 7.
222. Ibid., p. 12.
223. *EHR*. Health Information Management Systems Society, 2012. Online at: http://himss.org/asp/topics_ehr.asp (Accessed 5/21/2012).
224. On April 27, 2004 President Bush issued an executive order for the widespread adoption of interoperable EHRs and resulting in the creation of the Office of the National Coordinator for Health Information Technology, which facilitates regional HIO development. Executive Order 13335 of April 27, 2004: Incentives for the Use of Health Information Technology and Establishing the Position of the National Health Information Technology Coordinator. *Federal Register*, vol. 69, no. 84, April 30, 2004, p. 24059–24061; *About ONC*. Office of the National Coordinator for Health Information Technology, May 21, 2012. Online at: http://healthit.hhs.gov/portal/server.pt/community/healthit_hhs_gov__onc/1200 (Accessed 11/8/2012).
225. *Defining Key Health Information Technology Terms*. The National Alliance for Health Information Technology, Report to the Office of the National Coordinator for Health Information Technology, Department of Health and Human Services, April 28, 2008, p. 6.
226. *Health Information Exchange*. Health Information Management Systems Society, 2012. Online at: http://www.himss.org/asp/topics_focusdynamic.asp?faid=419 (Accessed 5/21/2012).
226. Paying for Electronic Health Records (EHRs).
227. Running the Numbers on an EHR: Applying Cost-Benefit Analysis in EHR Adoption. Tiankai Wang and Sue Biederman, *Journal of AHIMA*, vol. 81, no. 8 (August 2010), p. 32.
228. American Recovery and Reinvestment Act, Pub. Law 111-5, 123 Stat. 467-68 (February 17, 2009).
229. Paying for Electronic Health Records (EHRs).
230. Running the Numbers on an HER.
231. Working Group 6: The Role of Technology to Enhance Clinical and Education Efficiency. Steven E. Niessen, et al., *Journal of American College of Cardiology*, vol. 44, no. 2 (2004), p. 258.
232. How the Center for Medicare and Medicaid Innovation Should Test Accountable Care Organizations. Stephen M. Shortell, et al., *Health Affairs*, vol. 29, no. 7, (July 2010), p. 1296–1297.
233. Paying for Electronic Health Records (EHRs), pp. 3, 4.
234. Health Information Technology Is a Vehicle, Not a Destination: A Conversation with David J. Brailer. Arnold Mildtein, *Health Affairs*, vol. 26, no. 2 (2007), pp. w236, w238.
235. *Health Information Technology: Benefits and Problems*. Devon M. Herrick, et al., National Center for Policy Analysis, Dallas, TX. Report No. 327 (April 2010), pp. 13–14.
236. Ibid., p. 15.
337. *Everything You Need to Know about Accountable Care Organizations: In Plain English*. American Academy of Family Physicians, TransforMed. Online at: http://www.transformed.com/pdf/ACO_FAQ.pdf (Accessed 11/4/2012).
238. Private Payor Movement to Accountable Reimbursement Model. Mark Kuntz, *Executive Insight*, October 24, 2012. Online at: http://healthcare-executive-insight.advanceweb.com/Features/Articles/Private-Payor-Movement-to-Accountable-Reimbursement-Model.aspx (Accessed 11/8/2012).

Acronyms

Acronym	Definition
AAFP	American Academy of Family Physicians
AAOS	Academy of Orthopaedic Surgeons
ACA	American Chiropractic Association
AHA	American Hospital Association
AKS	Federal Anti-Kickback Statute
AMA	American Medical Association
APA	American Psychological Association
APTA	American Physical Therapy Association
AQC	Alternative Quality Contract
ARRA	American Recovery and Reinvestment Act

continued

Acronym	Definition
ASC	Ambulatory Surgery Centers
BCBSMA	Blue Cross Blue Shield of Massachusetts
CBO	Congressional Budget Office
CHIP	Children's Health Insurance Program
CMP	Civil Monetary Penalties
CMPL	Civil Monetary Penalties Law
CMS	Centers for Medicare and Medicaid
CPOM	Corporate Practice of Medicine
DHS	Designated Health Services
DOJ	Department of Justice
ERISA	Employee Retirement Income Security Act
FCA	False Claims Act
FFS	Fee For Service
FMV	Fair Market Value
FTC	Federal Trade Commission
HER	Electronic Health Record
HHS	U.S. Department of Health and Human Services
HIE	health insurance exchanges
HIMSS	Health Information Management Systems Society
HIO	Health Information Organizations
HIT	Health Information Technology
HITECH	Health Information Technology for Economic and Clinical Health Act
HMO	Health Maintenance Organizations
IPA	Independent Practice Associations
IPPS	Inpatient Prospective Payments System
IRS	Internal Revenue Service
MSA	Market Service Area
MSSP	Medicare Shared Savings Program
NCPA	National Community Pharmacists Association
NeHIN	Nationwide Health Information Network
OIG	Office of Inspector General
OPPS	Outpatient Prospective Payments System
P4P	Pay For Performance
PACO	Pediatric Accountable Care Organization Demonstration Project
PCMH	Patient-Centered Medical Home
PCP	Primary Care Provider
PGP	Physician Group Practice Demonstration
PHO	Physician Hospital Organizations
PHR	Personal Health Record
POH	Physician-Owned Hospitals
PPO	Preferred Provider Organization
PSA	Primary Service Area
ROI	Return on Investment
SCOTUS	Supreme Court of the United States
TDRA	Tasks, Duties, Responsibilities, and Accountabilities
TIN	Tax Identification Number
VBP	Value-Based Purchasing
wRVU	Work Relative Value Units

6 Capital Finance Considerations for the Development and Operation of ACOs

BACKGROUND

In considering ACO formation, prospective participants must devise a financial plan that will provide adequate funding for the initial capital investment related to the organization's ongoing working capital and operational costs. Until an ACO is self-sustaining, capital from the initial investments will finance the new organization, which will require significant investment in information technology and administrative systems, an expansion of human resources, and the ability to cover the risk of financial loss as well as capital needs for other ACO purposes. An organization seeking to operate an ACO should investigate whether their ACO has adequate capitalization to execute their business plan.[1]

Key Concept	Definition	Citation
Cash Management	Business methodology used to determine how: Healthcare entitles self-insure professional liability risks to offset the current medical malpractice insurance crisis; nonprofit healthcare entities must replace plants and equipment with cash or debt, not by issuing investor owned equity funds; hospital bonds and pension must be funded; hospital donations, gifts, and endowment funds must be managed.	*Dictionary of Health Economics and Finance.* David Edward Marcinko and Hope Rachel Hetico, New York, Springer Publishing Co., 2007, p. 64.

The opportunities as well as the recent constraints and limitations of an ACO's available funding sources (discussed below in more detail in light of the recent downturn and financial disruption) should be assessed and understood in selecting a strategy that best reflects the local healthcare market. This strategy also should be secure and reliable enough to avoid capital shortfalls that may later hinder an ACO's implementation and expansion. The funding of ongoing ACO costs will require a strategy that generates sufficient income to cover operational expenses and capital costs by increasing efficiency and maximizing reimbursement revenue, as well as covering shared savings incentives.

Key Concept	Definition	Citation
Investment	The process of adding to or replenishing capital stock. The purchase of an asset in anticipation of its rise in value.	*Dictionary of Health Economics and Finance.* David Edward Marcinko and Hope Rachel Hetico, New York, Springer Publishing Co., 2007, p. 201.

As the healthcare industry transitions from a volume-driven payment system toward an outcome-centered, value-based reimbursement system, developing a sustainable financial model is imperative and will require complicated, in-depth analyses of the challenges and opportunities necessary to support an ACO investment. Healthcare organizations typically rely on three sources of funding. Financing can be achieved through debt, equity, or internally generated surpluses from revenue. This financing includes various forms of capital from short-term financing, taxable long-term financing, and tax-exempt bond financing to private and public equity markets. Choosing the optimal combination of each of the sources of capital depends upon the size and makeup of the organization and what types of financing are required as well as the tax posture of the entity.

Factoid 6.1

Publicly traded equity markets allow healthcare organizations to access large sums of capital based upon the fluctuating value of their equity. (Source: *Healthcare Capital Finance: In Good and Challenging Times*. David A. Lips, Washington, D.C.: American Health Lawyers Association, 2009, p. 8.)

Different capital financing options are available to healthcare entities depending on whether the organization is a for-profit or a non-profit entity. For example, publicly traded equity markets allow for-profit healthcare organizations to access large sums of capital based on the fluctuating value of their equity,[2] either through an initial public offering (IPO) or by a secondary equity offering (SEO) for companies already traded in public markets. The capital accumulated through sales of equity may be used by the company to finance future growth opportunities (i.e., ACO development) or to repay existing debt.

Key Concept	Definition	Citation
Finance	The study, sources, timing, and channels of private or public funds, and the authority to raise and distribute those funds. The study of economic markets.	*Dictionary of Health Economics and Finance*. David Edward Marcinko and Hope Rachel Hetico, New York, Springer Publishing Co., 2007, p. 146.

Throughout the healthcare industry's history, financing has come from various sources, including "philanthropic donations, public grants, tax-subsidized operating surpluses, and investments from nonprofit organizations based in other industries."[3] Both for-profit and nonprofit healthcare organizations seek capital financing from these various sources, although each entity displays unique financing characteristics that reflect their respective missions. For example, nonprofit entities rely more heavily on philanthropy, donations, government grants or tax breaks, and traditional debt.[4] For-profit healthcare entities, in contrast, tend to rely on a combination of "equity capital and debt" as financing sources. However, due to regulatory limitations, nonprofit healthcare organizations are ineligible to participate in public equity markets.[5] Rather, these entities typically raise capital by (1) tax-exempt bonds to finance their operations, strategic initiative, and other capital-related needs; (2) rely on charitable donations from both individuals and organizations as an alternative method of financing; and (3) leverage significant flows of cash deposits into favorable financing terms from lender institutions both on an interim basis or a more permanent lending relationship. In addition, both for-profit and nonprofit organizations may enter private capital markets through venture capital investors and buyout funds, as well as private REITs (real estate investments trusts) and conduit lending structures, which allow organizations to access equity capital without subjecting the entity to overly burdensome regulations and the reporting requirements of the public equity market.

History of Healthcare Financing

Capital finance is an integral component of a healthcare organization's long-term financial sustainability. Traditionally, solo practitioners and small-to-medium physician group practices secured financing for their professional practices through local commercial lenders using their practice's cash deposits as leverage and pledging their accounts receivable and furniture and equipment as collateral, often supplemented by personal guarantees as recourse to the lender.[6] As the healthcare industry has evolved, so have the sources of capital for small-to-medium medical providers, as well as for large healthcare organizations, including asset-based lending (e.g., AR (accounts receivable) financing) and cash flow lending based on historical performance and the borrower's demonstrated ability to repay.

In addition to the underwriting concerns of capital providers, healthcare lenders are influenced by three additional areas:

1. Low margins and high costs of healthcare services
2. Persistent policy and "regulatory uncertainty" of the healthcare industry
3. Caution regarding the ultimate outcome of healthcare reform

Customarily, 50% of a healthcare organization's assets have been financed with equity, the remainder being financed by debt. However, this ratio differs among the various types of healthcare delivery entities (i.e., hospitals, outpatient clinics, ambulatory providers, skilled nursing facilities, long-term care facilities, etc.).[7]

Contemporary healthcare organizations have a multitude of borrowing options, including bond financing, commercial lending, mezzanine lending, equity, sale-leaseback, and seller "take back" financing.[8] It is likely that private ACOs will utilize similar financing, while some federal ACOs will take advantage of CMS's cost sharing initiatives detailed in the Final Rule and perhaps the flow of funds timing of the CMS Advanced Payments Initiative (as described in Chapter 2).[9]

The Financial Crisis: 2007–2009

Healthcare entities do not operate in a vacuum and their access to capital is affected by trends in the broader economy and capital markets. The capital markets utilized by healthcare entities also do not operate in a vacuum. Wide ranging factors impacting the world economy can reverberate through markets and affect the functioning of capital markets in every industry. The interconnectedness of worldwide financial markets warrants a review of the recent history of global market turmoil in order to better understand its impacts on the healthcare industry.

To determine the roots of the Great Recession,[10] it is necessary to understand the historical developments in international finance as well as the financial innovations and political motivations that predated the housing boom and subsequent economic decline. The roots of the recent financial turmoil in the United States, and throughout the world, can be traced back to the housing bubble in the U.S. domestic real estate market during the early and mid-2000s. The increased demand for housing was driven by many factors; perhaps the most important driver was the extended period of historically low interest rates in the United States during the late 1990s and early-to-mid-2000s. The housing bubble was the product of this earlier credit bubble, as cheap and easy access to loanable funds increased demand for housing, which in turn pushed housing prices higher. The effects of the resulting economic downturn reverberated throughout the economy, including the healthcare industry manifested by a dramatic retraction in the availability of capital and the newly imposed strict lending conditions on those credits that were granted.

Key Term	Definition	Citation
International Monetary Fund (IMF)	An organization of 188 countries with the stated goal of ensuring the stability of the international monetary system—the system of exchange rates and international payments that enables countries to transact with one another.	*About the IMF*. International Monetary Fund. Online at: http://www.imf.org/external/np/exr/facts/glance.htm (Accessed 5/24/12).

The credit bubble of the late 1990s and early 2000s arose, in large part, out of greater access to loanable funds caused by the foreign currency crises, terrorist attacks, and dubious financial market innovations. The Asian financial crisis (1997–1998) saw the collapse of several Asian currencies. A speculative attack on the currency of Thailand (the baht) resulted in the revaluation of that currency, which had previously been pegged to the U.S. dollar. This revaluation rippled throughout the Asian markets as wary international investors reevaluated their exposure in this region. This crisis eventually led to an International Monetary Fund (IMF) intervention to stabilize several currencies. The fallout from this retreat within the Asian markets was a flight to quality as anxious investors, looking to protect their assets, shifted the allocation of their capital to less risky assets, particularly the U.S. government debt. Additionally, Asian governments, attempting to assuage concerns surrounding their domestic currencies, began accumulating U.S. debt instruments to back their currency and stem the outflow of international capital. The cumulative effect of these concurrent events led to an excess demand for U.S. debt instruments that drove up bond prices and constricted yields, thereby lowering domestic U.S. interest rates.

Key Term	Definition	Citation
Federal Reserve Bank	The central bank of the United States that provides the nation with a safer, more flexible, and more stable monetary and financial system.	*The Federal Reserve System: Purposes and Functions*. The Board of Governors of the Federal Reserve System. June, 2005.

Even after the Asian crises had subsided, Asian demand for U.S. debt remained high (and remains high today). Due to a variety of cultural and psychological factors, Asian countries have historically had higher saving rates than their western counterparts. The Asian savings glut continued to put downward pressure on U.S. interest rates throughout the decade of the 2000s.

In responding to the terrorist attacks of 9/11, the monetary policy of the Federal Reserve Bank contributed to the low interest rates already prevalent in the United States. Equity markets were shaken by the terrorist attacks, as investor fears about subsequent attacks and the general uncertainty related to U.S. foreign policy acted to depress capital markets worldwide. The Federal Reserve reacted swiftly by increasing the money supply available through open market purchases of U.S. federal government debt, increasing the amount of loanable funds available in debt markets and decreasing interest rates to help reassure markets. This, in turn, spurred aggregate demand by lowering the borrowing costs for consumers and providing easy access to capital for business investment. The Federal Reserve Bank pursued this policy of low interest rates until 2004.

During this time, Asian demand for U.S. debt continued to rise and the Federal Reserve Bank actively pursued expansionary monetary policy. Financial institutions also began to create innovative financial instruments that provided access to new sources of funds within the debt markets, most notably Collateralized Debt Obligations (CDOs). CDOs are created through the structuring of multiple debt obligations into a single security, which is tailored to meet the investing needs of various financial market participants. The basic theory underlying the creation of a CDO is that, by properly diversifying the underlying debt instruments, the exposure to default risk from each underlying security can be mitigated.

Key Term	Definition	Citation
Collateralized Debt Obligation (CDO)	A way of packaging credit risk. Several classes of securities (known as tranches) are created from a portfolio of bonds and there are rules for determining how the cost of defaults are allocated to classes.	*Options, Futures, and other Derivatives*, 8th ed. John C. Hull, Boston: Pearson, 2012, p. 794.

One particular class of CDOs, called Mortgage Backed Securities (MBSs), played a critical role in the Great Recession. As the name suggests, MBSs are bundles of residential or commercial mortgages, which are packaged together and sold off to investors. Due to the geographic diversity, the risks perceived by investors in these securities were lower than the perceived risk of a typical debt security. This fact, coupled with the ability of the security to be compiled with certain portions of the underlying mortgages (e.g., interest-only franchises), which allowed the MBS to be tailored to meet specific investor's needs, created a high demand for these products. Commercial and investment banks, seeking new mortgages for their MBS product, quickly depleted the available stock of existing home mortgages and began to aggressively increase demand for newly created mortgages. In turn, the pass-through model began to shift the risk of default from the mortgage lender to an abstracted third-party investor.

Key Term	Definition	Citation
Mortgage-Backed Securities (MBS)	A security that entitles the owner to a share in the cash flows realized from a pool of mortgages.	*Options, Futures, and Other Derivatives*, 8th ed. John C. Hull, Boston: Pearson, 2012, p. 804.

This novel source of mortgage financing impacted the mortgage market by providing access to new sources of capital (i.e., MBS investors) and helping to maintain lower interest rates. However, even offering low interest rates was not sufficient to satisfy Wall Street's demand for mortgage assets. In an attempt to fulfill this excess demand, lenders began to relax standards (entering into the so-called *subprime* loans) to increase the throughput of mortgage assets to the MBS market. Several agency issues evolved around the ability of loan originators to sell off the mortgage default risk in the MBS market. This issue was exacerbated further by the difficulty felt by market participants in assessing the true risks encompassed in an investment in a MBS.

Investors in the MBS market continued to perceive these securities as low risk, even after the standards for qualifying for a mortgage were lowered, due to the diversification benefit of the bundled mortgages underlying them. The investors believed that by bundling them, even though the individual mortgages were of subprime quality, their exposure to the credit risk of a specific mortgage would be lessened. This holds true only to the extent that defaults in the underlying mortgages are uncorrelated. Historically, U.S. real estate market returns had shown that housing defaults were generally uncorrelated, particularly when spread across geographic regions, reinforcing the notion held by many investors that MBSs were low risk investments. This perception fueled increased demand by commercial banks, investment banks, pension funds, and other institutional investors for MBSs, spreading the exposure to these assets throughout the economy.

Key Term	Definition	Citation
Subprime Loan	A type of loan that is offered at a rate above prime to individuals who do not qualify for prime rate loans. Usually, subprime borrowers are often turned away from traditional lenders because of their low credit ratings or other factors that suggest that they have a reasonable chance of defaulting on the debt repayment.	*Financial Institutions Management.* Anthony Saunders and Marcia Million Cornett, Boston: 2006, p. 149.

At the meeting of the Federal Open Market Committee of the Federal Reserve Bank in June 2004, it was decided that the target federal funds rate (a key rate in determining other interest rates in the economy, including mortgage rates) would be increased from 1 to 1.25%. The committee justified its decision by citing recent improvements in the labor market and the recent upturn in inflation. The Federal Reserve continued increasing the targeted federal funds rate by a 0.25% at a time during their quarterly meetings for the next three years. These increases placed upward pressure on all U.S. interest rates, including mortgage rates. Over that time, the target federal funds rate increased from 1% in June of 2004 to 5.25% in August of 2007.

Key Term	Definition	Citation
Federal Open Market Committee	A major component of the federal reserve system. The FOMC oversees open market operations, which is the main tool used by the Federal Reserve to influence overall monetary and credit conditions.	*The Federal Reserve System: Purposes and Functions.* The Board of Governors of the Federal Reserve System. June, 2005, p. 3.

A significant portion of the mortgages underlying the subprime MBSs were adjustable rate mortgages (ARMs), mortgages whose rates periodically reset based upon the prevailing interest rates on the contractually agreed upon reset date. The Federal Reserve's policy of ratcheting the target federal funds rate up over the 2004–2007 period resulted in a significant increase in the interest expense related to these mortgages. The resetting of the adjustable mortgage rates set off a cascade of defaults. These defaults were widespread and not geographically contained. MBSs, whose low perceived risk (and consequently high rating) was based upon the assumption that a diversified mortgage portfolio would reduce the investors' exposure to default risks, suddenly became much riskier. As the true extent of the risks borne by these assets became evident, investors began selling off MBSs. This panicked sell-off and uncertainty related to MBSs' risks eventually froze the market for MBSs.

Key Term	Definition	Citation
Federal Funds Rate	The rate at which depository institutions trade balances at the Federal Reserve.	*The Federal Reserve System: Purposes and Functions.* The Board of Governors of the Federal Reserve System. June, 2005. p. 3.

The absence of market prices for MBSs, and uncertainty about the extent of the exposure of a single share in an MBS to the emerging default risks of subprime mortgages, made the valuation of institutions, which held MBSs, difficult to assess, thereby spreading the panic beyond the MBS market. Questions regarding corporate exposure to MBS risk led to questions about the creditworthiness of organizations. Large financial institutions with significant positions in MBSs began to hoard capital as reserves to offset potential losses on their MBS portfolios, which prevented access to liquidity throughout capital markets. A spike in the perceived counterparty risk related to firms' holding of MBSs led to the cessation of the functioning, even for historically successful, highly profitable, and risk averse corporations, of the ultrashort term corporate paper market (loans for 30 days or less) in the fall of 2007. The corporate paper market was largely taken over by the Federal Reserve Bank in an effort to support otherwise healthy corporations that, in the absence of short-term financing, were at risk of insolvency.

The uncertainty and corresponding alarm over the perception of previously unrecognized risk quickly spread throughout equity markets, driving share prices down. Corporations responding to the impending recession began reducing output and laying off workers, thereby reducing aggregate demand and leading to further output reductions and layoffs, which resulted in a general decline in the gross domestic product (GDP) for the United States. This sequence of events led to what has been characterized as the Great Recession, manifested by sluggish growth in both output and employment.

Key Term	Definition	Citation
Adjustable Mortgage Rate	A mortgage whose interest rate adjusts with movements in an underlying market index interest rate. Attributed as a partial cause of the recent housing market collapse that began in 2006.	*Financial Institutions Management.* Anthony Saunders and Marcia Million Cornett, Boston: 2006, p. 293.

Key Term	Definition	Citation
Gross Domestic Product (GDP)	The total value of all goods and services produced domestically by a nation during a year. It is equivalent to gross national product minus net investment income from foreign nations.	*Merriam Webster's Collegiate Dictionary.* Merriam Webster, 1999, p. 514.

The healthcare industry, in general, was not directly involved in the housing crisis that precipitated the financial downturn of the past few years. However, the interconnectedness of financial markets has led to a spillover of the negative impacts of the recession into the healthcare market. The steep decline and slow recovery of the labor markets is one of the far-reaching impacts of the recession. During the prerecession period (2002–2007), the average monthly unemployment rate was 5.3%.[11] Immediately prior to the recession, in June 2007, the U.S. unemployment rate was 4.6%.[12] In contrast, the postrecession period has seen an average monthly unemployment rate of 9.2%, with its peak of 10.0% occurring in October of 2009 and a recent rate of 7.8%.[13] These downcast employment statistics have had a direct impact on investors' perception of risk for healthcare entities.

Reduced employment due to the fallout from the recent financial crisis has either reduced the level of coverage for many Americans or completely eliminated their access to health insurance. In 2010, the Joint Economic Committee of the U.S. Congress published a report headlined, *Health Care Coverage at Record Low,* stating that in 2010, 55.3% of the population was covered by employment-based insurance, down from 65.1% in 2000[14] and that a significant portion of the reported decline was attributable to the recent recession.[15] Reduced employment due to the fallout from the recent financial crisis has either reduced the level of coverage for many Americans or completely eliminated their access to health insurance. The reduction in employment-based insured individuals has the dual effect on healthcare entities of (1) reducing demand for healthcare services due to greater out of pocket expenses for individuals, and (2) increasing the proportion of the population that is uninsured (a fact that presents a greater financial risk to healthcare providers).

In addition to the recent financial turmoil's impact of reduced access to health insurance (and, thereby, healthcare), there also has been a reduction in income for many households leading to diminished demand for healthcare services. As reported by the U.S. Bureau of Labor Statistics, the level of underemployed workers, defined as involuntary part-time workers, was 4.2 million in the October–November period of 2007 and had increased to 8.9 million by the October–November period of 2009, a 112% increase.[16] Traditionally, part-time workers have limited access to healthcare benefits and reduced income.[17] The sensitivity of healthcare expenditures can be quantified by using the Income Elasticity of Demand, a measure of the responsiveness of the demand for healthcare services to changes in income. The income elasticity metric represents the expected percent change, based on historical trends, in quantity demanded of healthcare services resulting from a 1% increase in income. As such, positive income elasticity indicates demand for healthcare services move in tandem with income. Reductions in income, consequently, should result in reduced quantities demanded. These goods are typically referred to by economists as *normal goods.* A 2002 Rand Corporation article reported estimates of the elasticity of demand for healthcare services to be between 0.5 and 0.8, implying that healthcare services can be considered a normal good.[18] Accordingly, the decreasing income of many individuals due to the increased level of underemployment should be expected, as a "normal good," to impact the healthcare market by undermining demand for healthcare services.

Key Concept	Definition	Citation
Utilization	Use of services. Utilization is commonly examined in terms of patterns or rates of use of a single service or a type of service, such as hospital care, physician visits, or prescription drugs. Measurement of utilization of all medical services in combination is usually done in terms of dollar expenditures. Use is expressed in rates per unit of population at risk for a given period, such as the number of admissions to the hospital per 1,000 persons aged older than 65 per year or the number of visits to a physician per person per year for an annual physical.	*Dictionary of Health Insurance and Managed Care.* David Edward Marcinko and Hope Rachel Hetico, New York, Springer Publishing Co., 2006, p. 292.

The increased perception of risk from potential investors leads to increased capital costs for healthcare enterprises. In some sectors of the healthcare industry, risk adverse investors, both equity and debt, demand greater recompense to offset the added risk assumed by investment in the healthcare industry in light of the recent uncertainty related to healthcare reform and the availability of funding for healthcare services. Increased capital expenses restrict the number of capital investment projects, including ACOs, which can be considered financially feasible. In this investment environment, potential investors require sound financial planning and analysis prior to investment in an ACO.

In addition to enhanced risk perceptions of potential investors, healthcare entities may find financing through traditional bank lending and bond markets constrained as well. As a result of the financial crisis, investors *flight to quality*, defined as their tendency to shift capital allocations to less risky assets (i.e., from equity to bonds) during periods of financial distress, has depressed interest rates. Investors have been adjusting their portfolios by increasing their bond holdings and reducing their equity holdings. This rebalancing of portfolios has increased the supply of loanable funds and held borrowing costs low. Federal Reserve oversight and international banking standards have led many banks to increase their holdings of reserves and trim their portfolio of riskier loan assets. In addition, to hedge against default risks, many banks have increased the burden of loan covenants on new debt, thereby increasing the implicit borrowing costs through draconian lending policies with strict capital reserve and cash flow requirements, even while maintaining lower explicit interest costs. A January 2009 study by the American Hospital Association (AHA) found that 53% of responding hospitals considered the unavailability of "usual sources of capital" as a very important factor in their decision to postpone capital projects.[19] The report also stated that 73% of respondents indicated that access to capital from "banks [and] financial services companies" was at least somewhat harder to obtain, with 33% characterizing it as significantly harder or that they have no access.[20] Similar trends were noted in the market for taxable and nontaxable bonds.

The above trends highlight the complicated nature of assessing the potential value of an ACO investment in today's healthcare market. In addition to the more narrow firm-level considerations, broader macroeconomic events may dramatically impact demand expectations and capital access. Any analysis of the value metrics of ACOs should be tempered by a consideration of general economic trends and an understanding of the impacts of seemingly unrelated economic events that can be transmitted to the healthcare industry through interconnected financial capital markets. The success or failure of many ACO projects may rely on the ability of a healthcare entity's management to appropriately assess and mitigate these risks.

Healthcare Financing Issues

Narrow profit margins and high costs often make traditional lenders reluctant to enter the arena of healthcare financing. This is an issue of particular concern because hospitals and other healthcare entities are more reliant on credit than most industries. Capital expenditures play an increasingly important role in hospitals' sustainability, as both facilities and equipment are necessary to provide increasingly capital-intensive, technologically driven medical care for sufficient numbers of patients and their treating physicians to make an ACO a viable investment. The unique financial needs of healthcare organizations require lenders that understand the intricacies of healthcare capital expenditures. Financial institutions comprised of former healthcare industry managers who understand a healthcare organization's functions and needs are integral to a healthcare enterprise in choosing a financing partner. In addition to capital, these lenders also may provide management capital and impetus toward enhancing efficiency and cost-cutting initiatives for healthcare borrowers.[21]

Key Term	Definition	Citation
Capital Expenditures	The cash outflows that a firm incurs to acquire long-lived assets, both tangible (e.g., buildings, equipment, furniture, and fixtures) and intangible (e.g., computer software, patents, work product).	*Financial Accounting: A Valuation Emphasis.* John S. Hughes, Frances L. Ayres, and Robert E. Hoskin, Hoboken, NJ: 2005, pp. 274, 536.

OVERVIEW OF CAPITAL CONCEPTS

Many healthcare enterprises currently seeking ACO status are large, integrated health systems, where the cost of technology, if not already in place, is likely to be the most significant capital requirement in their development as an ACO.[22] An outcome-centered payment system requires the development of a sustainable financial plan. It will require complicated, in-depth analysis of the challenges of capital and operating costs, as well as a realistic assessment of the opportunity for significant financial benefit that might be associated with ACO investment. These requirements can serve as the basis for an argument to successfully win over investors and allow for the accumulation of the capital necessary to develop an ACO.

Key Term	Definition	Citation
Integrated Health System	A managed care system in the United States that includes a hospital organization that provides acute patient care, a multispecialty medical care delivery system, the capability of contracting for any other needed services, and a payor. Services are provided to enrollees of the health plan.	*Dictionary of Health Insurance and Managed Care.* David Marcinko, New York: Springer Publishing Group, 2006, p. 161.

Capital Investment for ACO Development

The development of an ACO will initially require significant levels of capital investment to establish the necessary infrastructure for ACO success. These investments, as described below, include:

- Network development and management
- Care coordination, quality improvement, and utilization management
- Clinical information systems
- Data analytics

Network Development and Management

A portion of an organization's startup costs will have to be dedicated to network development and management for ACO creation, which is likely to be between CMS's $1.7 million estimate and the AHA's $12 million figure.[23] Initial capital requirements associated with ACO network development and management will be significant compared to continued operational expenses. Capital for network development will likely be focused toward fostering relationships between ACO participants and merging their various, divergent goals.[24] Additional capital requirements may include coordination with associated ACO participants in order to provide the full spectrum of healthcare in lieu of developing these services within the organization.

Care Coordination, Quality Improvement, and Utilization Management

Activities requiring capital for ACO development include coordinating care, improving quality, and managing healthcare utilization rates among patients. Though the amount of capital needed for the installation, adoption, and training associated with electronic health record (EHR) implementation will likely be significant, a functioning EHR system is necessary for an ACO to achieve its care coordination, quality improvement, and utilization management goals.[25] One major source of data about the development of workable ACOs is "The Work Ahead" study, a case study of four organizations conducted by the AHA. In this study, one of the four healthcare systems studied utilized a combination of hospitalists and discharge managers in its hospital to deliver coordinated care and reduce hospital readmissions. The facility noted that the capital requirements for this program range from $160,000 to $250,000 annually, with more capital likely to be allocated for the first year.[26]

Key Term	Definition	Citation
Electronic Health Record (EHR)	A longitudinal collection of electronic health information about individual patients and populations.	Gunter, T. D. and Terry, N. P. 2005. The Emergence of National Electronic Health Record Architectures in the United States and Australia: Models, Costs and Questions. *Journal of Medical Internet Research.* Online at: http://www.ncbi.nlm.nih.gov/pmc/articles/PMC1550638/Published (Accessed 5/24/12).

Improved quality of care generally coincides with increased participation and collaboration between providers/suppliers and their beneficiaries. This increased collaboration generally corresponds with increased capital requirements for existing health systems not designed for this increased collaboration. For example, management programs for chronic conditions and medications were utilized in the AHA's *The Work Ahead* case study to deliver improved quality care to patients and beneficiaries. The capital required for human resources, hardware, software, and infrastructure to run and support such programs will likely be significant, as the vast majority of healthcare organizations are not designed for long-term and involved disease management.[27]

Clinical Information Systems

Key Concept	Definition	Citation
Clinical Information System	A computer network system that supports patient care; relating exclusively to the information regarding the care of a patient, rather than administrative data, this hospital-based information system is designed to collect and organize data.	*Dictionary of Health Information Technology and Security.* David Edward Marcinko and Hope Rachel Hetico, New York, Springer Publishing Co., 2007, p. 54.

Capital requirements for clinical information systems will likely be significant, as EHR implementation is expected to account for a vast majority of this cost. CMS required EHR utilization in the Proposed Rule, but relaxed the constraint in the Final Rule. The Proposed Rule indicated that half of the "ACO's primary care physicians" must be "meaningful EHR users" to "continue participation in the Shared Savings Program." However, the Final Rule loosened the requirement, classifying EHR use as only one of the quality measures used to calculate potential shared savings.[28] Despite this relaxed requirement, it is still likely that significant initial capital allocation for EHR implementation will be required for the development of a clinical information system designed to efficiently and effectively meet the aims of the ACO network. Although not required, CMS noted that ACOs that possess an enriched understanding and use of EHR and IT (Information Technology) systems "will likely find it easier to be successful under the Shared Savings Program."[29] According to data from *The Work Ahead*, one subject of the study incurred capital development expenditures of approximately $2.5 million to adopt a health information exchange (HIE), a system to translate various EHRs into a single format for sharing records across different EHR systems.[30]

Key Term	Definition	Citation
Health Information Exchange	"Public markets" for health insurance plans available within a state.	*Explaining Health Care Reform: What Are Health Insurance Exchanges?* Kaiser Family Foundation, May 2009.

Data Analytics

CMS's ACO quality measures require data collection and analysis for reporting progress on outcomes and claims within the ACO. In addition to capital for EHRs and other clinical information systems, it is likely the ACO will require capital to be allocated for separate data analytics systems designed to track and monitor necessary data regarding quality measures for reporting.[31] However, the costs associated with data analytics will be significantly less than those associated with EHR development. For example, one of the four private ACOs analyzed in the AHA's *The Work Ahead*, had developmental costs for data analysis software of $40,000, while the annual operating costs were $1,800 per physician (approximately $100,000).[32] As these figures demonstrate, the initial capital investment involved in ACOs may be high, but the annual operating costs may be even higher.

Expenses Related to Ongoing ACO Operation

In addition to the capital required for the initial ACO formation (the startup costs), there also will be costs associated with its ongoing operation. Operating costs for an ACO include network development and management, quality improvements, utilization management, clinical information systems, and data analytics.

Network Development and Management

Network management for an ACO can include a variety of services and infrastructures that must be maintained in order to keep the organization functional. To assure the development of successful networks, ACOs must incur several expenses related to:

1. Providing management and staff
2. Leveraging the health system's management resources
3. Engaging legal and consulting support
4. Developing financial and management information support systems
5. Recruiting/acquiring primary care professionals
6. Developing and managing relationships with specialists
7. Developing and managing relationships with postacute care networks
8. Developing contracting capabilities
9. Compensating physician leaders[33]

Operational expenses for management and staff development will likely be small, at first, and grow accordingly with the long-term sustainability plans and size of the ACO. One healthcare organization started with a 6-member management team, ultimately expanding to 22 members (1 staff member for every 41 physicians).[34] Such growth is emblematic of the necessity of effective communication between the management and the working entities in the ACO.

According to the same study, which observed both the initial and the ongoing costs for ACO development, a small hospital (approximately 200 beds) and a large hospital (approximately 1,200 beds) have a wide range of ongoing annual costs. Annual costs for the aforementioned categories for a small hospital are roughly $2.9 million a year, whereas a large hospital may require roughly $5.7 million a year.[35]

Factoid 6.2

Operational expenses for management and staff development will likely be small, at first, and grow accordingly with the long-term sustainability plans and size of the ACO. One healthcare organization started with a 6-member management team, ultimately expanding to 22 members (1 staff member for every 41 physicians). Such growth is emblematic of the necessity of effective communication between the management and the working entities in the ACO. (Source: *The Work Ahead: Activities and Costs to Develop an Accountable Care Organization*. American Hospital Association, April 2011, p. 4.)

Care Coordination, Quality Improvement, and Utilization Management

Care coordination, quality improvement, and utilization management are important for maintaining an ACO from a clinical standpoint. As with network development and management, in order to achieve ongoing success in three aspects of ACO operations, an organization may experience expenses associated with the following:

- Disease registries
- Care coordination and discharge follow-up
- Specialty-specific disease management
- Hospitalists
- Integration of inpatient and ambulatory approaches in service lines
- Patient education and support
- Medication management
- Achieving designation as a patient-centered medical home[36]

According to the AHA, the associated ongoing cost for care coordination, quality improvement, and utilization management for a small hospital was approximately $1.5 million annually, while the associated total ongoing cost for a large hospital was approximately $3.9 million annually.[37]

Factoid 6.3

Annual costs for the aforementioned categories for a small hospital are roughly $2.9 million a year, whereas a large hospital may require roughly $5.7 million a year. Source: *The Work Ahead: Activities and Costs to Develop an Accountable Care Organization*. American Hospital Association, April 2011, p. 2.)

Clinical Information Systems

An ACO also must maintain clinical information systems in order to function properly. These systems include "electronic health record[s] (EHR[s]), intra-system EHR interoperability, and linking to a health information exchange (HIE)."[38] Without these IT tools, an ACO would not be able to coherently maintain all of the patient information being constantly created and exchanged, or be able to keep up with the organization's day-to-day management needs.

Similar to the costs associated with ongoing care coordination, data show that the ongoing cost to a small hospital to maintain these IT systems is approximately $1.5 million a year, while for a large hospital, the cost grows to approximately $3.9 million a year.[39]

Data Analytics

Data analytics is the term given to the nonclinical data management of a healthcare entity. Technology to collect and analyze data under the ACO model will likely play an increased role as hospitals seek to analyze new forms of information to target potential cost savings and track quality measures for reporting. Like clinical data, nonclinical data are important to the upkeep of a properly maintained ACO. The activities associated with this category include: analysis of care patterns, quality reporting costs, and other activities and costs.[40] It has been estimated that meaningful information from data analytics will only be available from an ACO operation after approximately four years of data mining.[41] The gap between the implementation of data analysis software and the production of meaningful information for managerial decision making will require ACO organizations to leverage operational costs until the technology is able to produce valuable results. AHA's recent estimate of ongoing costs associated with data analytics for small healthcare systems is approximately $385,000 per year, with approximately 20% of these costs linked to tracking quality reporting measures. For larger healthcare entities, the AHA estimates overall costs at $650,000 annually, with approximately 15% of these costs linked to tracking CMS quality reporting measures.[42] However, this estimate is likely to be high, as CMS decreased the number of quality reporting measures from 65 to 33 in the Final Rule.[43]

COST OF CAPITAL AND CAPITAL STRUCTURE

Capital Structure Decisions

Key Term	Definition	Citation
Capital Structure	The mix of the various debt and equity capital maintained by a firm. Also called *financial structure*. The composition of a corporation's securities used to finance its investment activities; the relative proportions of short-term debt, long-term debt, and owners' equity.	*Corporate Finance*, 4th ed. Ross, Westerfield, Jaffe, and Roberts, Ontario, Canada, McGraw-Hill Ryerson, 2005, p. 939.

A healthcare organization's capital structure is sensitive to market conditions and its short- and long-term goals for expansion in a changing healthcare environment. An organization's capital structure decision is how it plans to finance daily operations as well as how it plans to finance growth within the organization. Capital structure is generally comprised of both short- and long-term debt, and common and preferred stocks/equities. It should only be finalized once the organization's goals are clearly defined, and when the timeline for financing its needs is known. Organizations seek the optimal ratio between debt and equity financing by which to derive the maximum benefit for stakeholders of the organization, e.g., the community (which benefits from a tax-exempt organization), or the shareholders in an investor-owned organization.[44]

Key Term	Definition	Citation
Debt	Loan agreement that is a liability on the firm. An obligation to repay a specified amount at a particular time.	*Corporate Finance,* 4th ed. Ross, Westerfield, Jaffe, and Roberts, Ontario, Canada, McGraw-Hill Ryerson, 2005, p. 941.

TABLE 6.1
Historical Debt-to-Equity Ratio for Publically Traded Hospitals

Year	Year Debt to Total Capitalization (%)	Debt to Total Capitalization Trailing Five Year Average (%)	Debt to Market Value of Equity (%)	Debt to Market Value of Equity Trailing Five Year Average (%)
2001	15.09%	21.82%	17.77%	27.90%
2002	13.14%	15.52%	15.40%	19.27%
2003	16.40%	17.49%	19.78%	21.95%
2004	19.57%	30.94%	24.32%	44.79%
2005	14.44%	28.21%	16.88%	39.30%
2006	21.27%	27.12%	27.02%	37.21%
2007	22.69%	27.71%	29.36%	38.34%
2008	53.17%	36.79%	117.65%	59.02%
2009	62.47%	41.52%	176.26%	71.21%
2010	43.51%	44.86%	77.04%	81.35%
2011	64.04%	58.46%	179.28%	142.19%

Source: Endnote 47. With permission.

Key Term	Definition	Citation
Equity	Ownership interest of common and preferred shareholders in a corporation. Also, total assets minus total liabilities, or net worth.	*Corporate Finance,* 4th ed. Ross, Westerfield, Jaffe, and Roberts, Ontario, Canada, McGraw-Hill Ryerson, 2005, p. 943.

The theory of capital structure is often viewed as "a unique mix of debt and equity that minimizes the overall cost of financing assets."[45] Historically, the capital structure ratios of nonprofit health entities were relatively consistent, while for-profit healthcare organizations' ratios tended to reflect sensitivity to market conditions.[46] Debt-to-equity ratio trends for publicly traded hospitals are seen in Table 6.1.

The above information also is displayed graphically in Figure 6.1.

It is of note that the debt-to-equity ratio tends to differ between for-profit and nonprofit hospitals due to varying access to equity markets.[49] There is recent evidence that the depressed hospital capital structure in 2009–2010 recovered as hospitals were able to access different sources of capital to improve weak capital structures encountered during the Great Recession.[50] This improvement suggests a pattern that may represent a widening in the access to capital for healthcare entities looking to develop ACOs.

CAPITAL ALLOCATION

Overview of Capital Budgeting

Investment in a new project, such as an ACO, may be financed either internally or externally, referring to the source of funds used for the investment. In furthering the investment decision, capital budgeting is "the process of selecting long-lived assets, projects, and programs according to financial criteria."[51] Internally financed projects are funded from the reserves or cash flows of the organization, i.e., cash flows that would otherwise be available for distribution to the organization's investors (owners within for-profit enterprises or the community within nonprofit enterprises). Therefore, reinvestment of current earnings is a form of equity financing. Owing to the fact that it

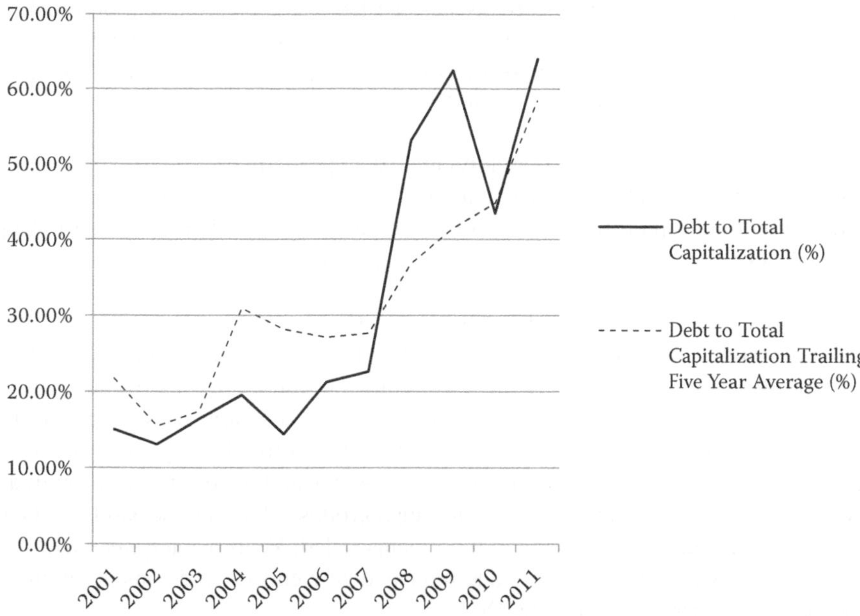

FIGURE 6.1 Historical debt to total capitalization in the healthcare industry. (From Endnote 48.)

is the fiduciary responsibility of the healthcare entity's management to only reinvest in projects that are expected to return at least the equity holders' required rate of return, the cost of equity for an internally financed project would be equal to the investors' required rate of return. Alternatively, externally financed projects derive their funding from sources outside the organization, which can be either debt or equity.

Healthcare entities utilize debt financing to meet the extended goals, and sustain the continued viability of the organization. Long-term debt financing for healthcare organizations represents any debt that is repaid over a period of time that extends beyond a single year and can be drawn from various sources. These sources of long-term debt for healthcare organizations include "private and municipal bond markets [...] loans, capital leases, mortgage, or real estate financing, participation in real estate investment trusts, taxable bonds, notes, [...] certificates of participation, and tax-exempt bonds."[52]

However, the financial composition of long-term debt between nonprofit and for-profit healthcare entities often differs. Historically, nonprofit health systems have relied on "[p]ublic issues of long-term, tax-exempt debt," which "remain the largest source of low-cost capital financing for most nonprofit hospitals and health systems."[53] A recent examination of nonprofit hospital systems throughout the nation found that approximately 95% of the long-term debt of hospitals and health systems in the nation is comprised of tax-exempt debt.[54] For-profit systems typically carry significantly higher percentages of long-term debt compared to nonprofit organizations. In addition, long-term debt financing increases correspondingly with the size of the healthcare system.[55]

Factoid 6.4

Historically, nonprofit health systems have relied on "[p]ublic issues of long-term, tax-exempt debt" that "remain the largest source of low-cost capital financing for most nonprofit hospitals and health systems." (Source: An Examination of Contemporary Financing Practices and the Global Financial Crisis on Nonprofit Multi-Hospital Health Systems. Louis J. Stewart and Pamela C. Smith, *Journal of Health Care Finance*, vol. 37, no. 3, 2011, p. 3.)

Because large health systems and hospitals may be best situated to transition quickly into an ACO model, it is likely that long-term debt financing between these existing healthcare organizations and an ACO will share significant similarities in composition and source. Long-term debt financing challenges unique to ACOs may include:

- The variable creditworthiness of the individual ACO participants.
- Division of contributions between participants to repay long-term debts.
- How the individual capital needs of ACO participants can be adequately met through an umbrella ACO organization with disparate participating provider entities.

Smaller entities that wish to form ACOs but have insufficient operational cash flow to fund ACO capital needs might alternatively seek equity financing through select venture capital sources. However, utilizing venture capital may present difficulties because ACOs have not proved to be a financially viable investment even at the threshold level of venture capital risk expectations. In the 1990s, healthcare organizations attempted to form preferred provider organizations (PPOs) and point-of-service plans (POSs), structures that resemble ACOs and were formed through a surge of mergers and acquisitions among hospitals and physician groups.[56] Despite the assets of the hospitals and various sources of funding, a majority of these plans failed. Venture capitalists will most likely recall this recent history between investors and managed care entities and consider it an additional risk when deciding whether to invest in ACOs.

Key Term	Definition	Citation
Venture Capital	Early stage financing of young companies seeking to grow rapidly.	*Corporate Finance,* 4th ed. Ross, Westerfield, Jaffe, and Roberts, Ontario, Canada, McGraw-Hill Ryerson, 2005, p. 955.

ACOs may have a challenge in proving the attractiveness of their investment prior to any meaningful capital being invested by venture capitalists. Despite challenges, it is of note that the venture capital firm Kleiner Perkins Caufield & Byers, an early investor in brand names, such as Amazon.com, AOL, and Google, has already invested $61 million in the St. Louis-based Essence Group Holdings Corp., a company that assists healthcare organizations in forming ACOs.[57] The overall cost of capital for a prospective capital project is a combination of the cost of the debt financing component, as well as the cost of the equity financing component (alternatively referred to as the weighted average cost of capital—WACC) reflecting the influence of investor expectation from each form of financing. The WACC represents the overall financing cost of the project, and, when it is in excess of the expected overall return on investment, the project will fail to generate value for the organization, i.e., the highest and best use of the capital employed in the project might be to invest in an alternative project with a higher expected overall return.

Key Term	Definition	Citation
Weighted Average Cost of Capital (WACC)	The average cost of capital on the firm's existing projects and activities. The weighted average cost of capital for the firm is calculated by weighting the cost of each source of funds by its proportion of the total market value of the firm. It is calculated on a before- and after-tax basis.	*Corporate Finance*, 4th ed. Ross, Westerfield, Jaffe, and Roberts, Ontario, Canada, McGraw-Hill Ryerson, 2005, p. 955.

As the healthcare industry changes, with a greater focus being placed on meaningful use, accountable care, and outpatient services, the issues of attaining capital have grown in importance for many healthcare entities. Many providers have begun looking beyond traditional sources of capital to alternative forms of long-term financing, e.g., asset specific financing. As the economy recovers from the effects of the Great Recession, sources of capital are expanding for healthcare entities in need of capital resources. However, these organizations must be willing to explore a wider array of options than in the past as well as to efficiently and accurately assess the risk associated with each option.[58]

CHAPTER SUMMARY

Before an organization begins to develop and operate an ACO, it is important that the organization decides how to address demanding capital requirements. A viable financial model should be created through consideration of available financing options including debt financing, equity financing, and internally generated capital. The effect of the Great Recession on the healthcare industry, coupled with low profits and high costs, as well as uncertainty regarding the outcome of healthcare reform, has diminished much of the capital available to healthcare organizations. These same factors may present barriers to capital acquisition for successful ACO development.

In order to develop and maintain requisite levels of capital to overcome the current economic environment, developing ACOs will have to address capital considerations in unique ways, dependent in part on their size and status. Further, the capital structure of ACOs will differ between for-profit and nonprofit entities due to strict regulatory guidelines limiting nonprofit organizations from participating in public equity markets. Similarly, different investment options will be feasible for large entities versus small entities.

Although ACOs have not, as of yet, proved to provide significant, or even positive, returns for investors, they have begun to attract the interest of some venture capitalists. Regardless of where investment funds originate, the development of capital is vital to the implementation and continued operation of ACOs, and it is important for developing organizations to understand the financial needs required by such an undertaking.

ENDNOTES

1. The Accountable Care Organization: Whatever Its Growing Pains, the Concept Is Too Vitally Important to Fail. Francis J Crosson, *Health Affairs*, vol. 30, no. 7, July 11, 2011, p. 1252.
2. *Healthcare Capital Finance in Good and Challenging Times*. David A. Lips, Washington, D.C.: American Health Lawyers Association, 2009, p. 8.
3. Capital Finance and Ownership Conversions in Health Care. James C. Robinson, *Health Affairs*, vol. 19, no. 1, 2000, p. 57.
4. Conversion of HMOs and Hospitals: What's at Stake? Bradford H. Gray, *Health Affairs*, vol. 16, no. 2, 1997, p. 31.
5. An Examination of Contemporary Financing Practices and the Global Financial Crisis on Nonprofit Multi-Hospital Health Systems. Louis J. Stewart and Pamela C. Smith, *Journal of Health Care Finance*, vol. 37, no. 3, 2011, p. 1.
6. How to Choose the Right Capitalization Option. Jim Vaughan and Joan Wise, *Healthcare Financial Management,* vol. 50, no. 12, December 1996, p. 72.
7. *Essentials of Health Care Finance*. William O. Cleverly, Gaithersburg, MD: Aspen Publishers, Inc., 1997, p. 370.
8. Financing Issues for Healthcare Providers and Companies. Deborah Gordon and Lisa Lenderman, Seyfarth Shaw, LLP and MidCap Financial, LLC, paper presented at the American Health Lawyers Association Annual Meeting: Boston, June 27, 2011.
9. Medicare Program; Medicare Shared Savings Program: Accountable Care Organizations. *Federal Register* vol. 76, no. 212 (November 2, 2011), p. 67835.
10. The Great Recession and Government Failure. Gary S. Becker, *The Wall Street Journal*, September 2, 2011. Online at: http://online.wsj.com/article/SB10001424053111904199404576536930606933332.html (Accessed 4/26/2012).
11. *Labor Force Statistics from the Current Populations Survey: Original Data Value. Bureau of Labor Statistics*, U.S. Department of Labor, June 20, 2012. Online at: http://data.bls.gov/timeseries/LNS14000000 (Accessed 6/20/12).

12. Ibid.
13. Ibid.
14. *Health Care Coverage at Record Low*. U.S. Congress Joint Economic Committee, Fact Sheet: Health Insurance Coverage in 2010 (September 13, 2011), p.2, Online at: http://www.jec.senate.gov/public/?a=Files.Serve&File_id=d35dc4dc-9762-4a91-94b5-eb83a2a17772 (Accessed 6/20/12).
15. Ibid.
16. The Nation's Underemployed in the "Great Recession" of 2007–09. Andrew Sum and Ishwar Khatiwada, *Monthly Labor Review*, November 2010, p. 4.
17. Ibid.
18. *The Elasticity of Demand for Health Care: A Review of the Literature and Its Application to the Military Health System*. Jeanne S. Ringel, et al., to Office of the Secretary of Defense, Washington, D.C., RAND Health & National Defense Research Institute, 2005, p. 27–28.
19. *Report on the Capital Crisis: Impact on Hospitals*. American Hospital Association, Chicago: January 2009, p. 5.
20. Ibid., p. 8.
21. *Looking Outside: Using External Capital Sources to Overcome Budget Constraints*. Dan Morse, GE Healthcare Financial Services. Online at: http://www.gehealthcarefinance.com/includes/OurSolutions/montgomery.pdf (Accessed January 5, 2012).
22. *Accountable Care Organizations: 10 Things You Need to Know about Accountable Care*. Eleanor Burton and Virginia Traweek, Institute for Health Technology Transformation, 2011, pp. 25–26.
23. Ibid., pp. 24–25.
24. *The Work Ahead: Activities and Costs to Develop an Accountable Care Organization*. American Hospital Association, April 2011.
25. *The Importance of Health Information Technology for Accountable Care Organizations*. Amy K. Fehn, American Bar Association, June 1, 2011, p. 1.
26. *The Work Ahead*, p. 8.
27. Ibid., p. 7.
28. Medicare Program; Medicare Shared Savings Program: Accountable Care Organizations and Medicare Program: Waiver Designs in Connection with the Medicare Shared Savings Program and the Innovation Center; Proposed Rule and Notice. *Federal Register*, vol. 76, no. 67 (April 7, 2011), pp. 19599–19600; Medicare Program; Medicare Shared Savings Program: Accountable Care Organizations. *Federal Register* vol. 76, no. 212 (November 2, 2011), p. 67902.
29. Medicare Program; Medicare Shared Savings Program: Accountable Care Organizations, p. 67902.
30. *The Work Ahead*, p. 10.
31. Ibid., p. 2.
32. Ibid., p. 10.
33. Ibid., p. 2.
34. Ibid., p. 4.
35. Ibid., p. 2.
36. Ibid.
37. Ibid.
38. Ibid.
39. Ibid.
40. Ibid.
41. *Getting Ready for Accountable Care Organizations*. Joseph Goedert, Health Data Management, April 1, 2011. Online at: http://www.healthdatamanagement.com/issues/19_4/getting-ready-for-accountable-care-organizations-42230-1.html?zkPrintable=1&nopagination=1 (Accessed 1/13/2012).
42. *The Work Ahead*, p. 2.
43. Medicare Program; Medicare Shared Savings Program: Accountable Care Organizations, p. 67891.
44. *The Handbook of Financing Growth*. Kenneth H. Marks, Larry E. Robbins, Gonzalo Fernández, and John P. Funkhouser, Hoboken, NJ: John Wiley & Sons, pp. 22–23.
45. Capital Structure Strategy in Health Care Systems. John R.C. Wheeler, Dean G. Smith, Howard L. Rivenson, and Kristin L. Reiter, *Journal of Health Care Finance*, vol. 26, no. 4, 2000, p. 43.
46. Ibid., p. 47.
47. *Ibbotson SBBI: 2012 Valuation Yearbook— Median data for SIC code 806: Hospitals*. Chicago: Morningstar, Inc., 2001–2011. Historical Data accessed at http://ccrc.morningstar.com/IndSearch.aspx# (Accessed 4/25/2012).
48. Ibid

49. Capital Structure Strategy in Health Care Systems, p. 43.
50. 8 Strategies for Hospital Borrowers in 2011. James W. Blake, Eric A. Jordahl, and Andrew J. Majka, *Healthcare Financial Management*, vol. 65, no. 4, April 2000, p. 74.
51. *Financial Management in Health Care Organizations*. Robert A. McLean, Albany, NY: Delmar Publishers, 2003, p. 192.
52. *Healthcare Capital Finance in Good and Challenging Times*, p. 7.
53. An Examination of Contemporary Financing Practices and the Global Financial Crisis on Nonprofit Multi-Hospital Health Systems, p. 3.
54. Ibid., p. 5.
55. Patterns of Financing for the Largest Hospital Systems in the United States. William O. Cleverley and Jane Baserman, *Journal of Healthcare Management*, vol. 50, no. 6, November 2005, p. 362.
56. The Health Care Reforms of the 1990s: Failure or Ultimate Triumph. Robert F. Rich and Kelly M. Merrick, Selected Works, May 2009. Online at: http://works.bepress.com/cgi/viewcontent.cgi?article=1000&context=robert_rich (Accessed 1/5/12).
57. Leading Venture Capitalists Place a Bet on ACOs. Christopher Weaver, *Kaiser Health News*, July 20, 2011. Online at: http://capsules.kaiserhealthnews.org/index.php/2011/07/leading-venture-capitalists-place-a-bet-on-acos/ (Accessed 1/18/12).
58. *Hospital Financing Options for the Future*. Healthcare Financial Management Association, Educational Report, August 2012, pp. 2, 8.

Acronyms

Acronym	Definition
AHA	American Hospital Association
ARM	Adjustable Rate Mortgage
CDO	Collateralized Debt Obligations
EHR	Electronic Health Record
GDP	Gross Domestic Product
HIE	Health Information Exchange
IMF	International Monetary Fund
IPO	Initial Public Offering
MBS	Mortgage Backed Securities
POS	Point-of-Service Plan
PPO	Preferred Provider Organization
SEO	Secondary Equity Offering
WACC	Weighted Average Cost of Capital

7 Financial Feasibility Analysis for ACO Investments

As discussed in Chapter 1, there is a growing imperative for implementing models of healthcare delivery in the United States, which maximizes beneficial outcomes per dollar of expenditure through managed competition, and ACOs are one of the latest innovations to address that growing challenge by means of technological and procedural advances. However, as with all new technologies, there is the corresponding demand for capital investment, often stated by the adage "No Bucks, No Buck Rogers."[1] To increase the probability of success in ACO formation, prospective participants should closely examine all aspects of the investment. As additional information becomes available regarding the operating performance and capital requirements of ACO formations, the nature of the preinvestment analysis should trend toward being less of a forecast based on hypothetical assumptions and more an empirically grounded benchmarking to normative industry data.

CASE STUDIES: REAL INVESTMENTS OF CAPITAL

As described in Chapter 6, there are four areas in which developing ACO enterprises will initially invest their capital: (1) network development and management; (2) care coordination, quality improvement, and utilization management; (3) clinical information systems; and (4) data analytics. In a study conducted by the American Hospital Association (AHA), entitled *The Work Ahead: Activities and Costs to Develop an Accountable Care Organization*, each enterprise studied made an initial front-end investment in staff and organization to coordinate ACO activities.[2] This initial investment provided the ACOs with their management leaders, including:

1. Chief executive officer
2. Medical director
3. Chief financial officer

These leaders were given certain responsibilities, including:

1. Communicating with (and finding gaps in) the physician network
2. Developing organizational strategies
3. Developing the ACO's approach to providing the full continuum of care[3]

Of the studied entities, ACOs organized by health systems heavily relied on health system management to meet these responsibilities.[4] Physicians performing management roles also were compensated for participation in such activities as governance meetings.[5] In addition to investments in leadership, the ACOs studied made a variety of other initial investment decisions. Integral to the concept of an ACO is the ability to provide a wide variety of services. Consequently, common investments included acquiring and developing a variety of:

1. Primary care physicians
2. Nurse practitioners
3. Physician assistants
4. A network of specialty providers[6]

Startup costs also included ongoing legal costs, ranging from $24,000 per year to $55,000,[7] and additional nonlegal consulting services involving physician integration and organizational development strategies, and actuarial and financial analyses.[8]

Of the ACOs studied, all were aggressively pursuing disease management strategies. Those ACOs participating in the study also invested in care coordination, quality improvement, and utilization management, mainly through disease registries as well as specialty-specific disease management.[9]

Another key element in the newly formed ACOs in the AHA study was the employment of hospitalists, hospital-based general physicians, with an annual salary ranging from $160,000 to $250,000.[10] The examined ACOs also invested heavily in the focus on patient education and support programs, including diabetes patient educational centers and emergency medicine resources for the uninsured.[11]

An important source of potential efficiency and cost gains may be the ACOs focus on the implementation of healthcare information technology. The consolidation of financial information among the member entities of an ACO requires a common practice management system, which early on represented a key capital investment among the ACOs participating in the AHA study.[12] In order to meet their clinical information system needs, newly formed ACOs also invested heavily in electronic health records with installation costs, software licenses, hardware, paper records conversion, and office staff costs amounting to between $40,000 and $75,000 per physician.[13]

Factoid 7.1

In order to meet their clinical information system needs, newly formed ACOs invested heavily in electronic health records with installation costs amounting to between $40,000 and $75,000 per physician, which included software licenses, hardware, paper records conversion, and office staff costs. (Source: *The Work Ahead: Activities and Costs to Develop an Accountable Care Organization.* American Hospital Association (April 2011), p. 9.)

Electronic health record (EHR) systems also typically include data repositories or warehouses, which are necessary for storing and accessing transactional data useful for analyzing insurance claims and data from non-EHR-using physicians.[14] In addition to the initial installation and setup costs for the EHR systems, additional costs were incurred as well to provide system interoperability.[15] These costs, though typically minimal (in the range of $15,000), were immensely important, because they allowed physicians to share clinical and claims data in a meaningful way.[16]

Among the ACOs included in the AHA study, analysis and reporting of patient care and quality data required in the formation of an ACO led to significant capital investment in information systems capable of collecting and analyzing this type of group data. The staff of each of these ACOs integrated and analyzed data from a variety of sources utilizing software, which cost the observed ACOs approximately $40,000 for initial installation and approximately $100,000 a year for maintenance.[17]

Overall, total startup costs for the observed ACOs ranged from $5 to $12 million with ongoing annual costs ranging from $6 to $14 million.[18] The studied ACO's incurred significant expenses related to analyzing patient records and tracking key measurements to meet quality reporting requirements, which also necessitated additional data warehousing and a substantial staff investment.[19] Accordingly, as ACOs increase in size, both capital and operational costs in support of data analytics programs are likely to grow as well.

THE INVESTMENT DECISION

Whether or not an enterprise is in the healthcare industry, the general tenet guiding the decision to accept or reject an investment should be to only undertake projects that seek to maximize the expected value of the enterprise to its owners. Additionally, managers should consider investments in the context of the enterprise's overall missions and goals as well as its ethical standards. An investment may improve the financial position of the enterprise, but if it detracts from the enterprise's mission goals or violates the ethical standards of the enterprise, then, from the perspective of the owners, the value of the enterprise (inclusive of nonfinancial or nonmonetary considerations) may be diminished. The ultimate decision to accept or reject an investment should be oriented toward this guiding principle. The analysis below describes a set of value metrics that are available to assist managers in determining whether investing in an ACO will add to or detract from a healthcare enterprise's financial value; however, making this decision remains the responsibility of each individual enterprise's management team, which must seek to determine the extent to which an ACO conforms or diverges from the overall vision of the specific enterprise. Another way in which to express this management task is that each enterprise needs to make a determination as to the "need, fit, and risk" of attributes of the investment to the enterprise pursuing ACO development.

The process of evaluating capital budget projects should begin with an analysis of the project and any enterprise-specific issues. In the case of an ACO, the investing enterprise should consider the impact that participation in an ACO may have on the enterprise's wider financial goals prior to an analysis of the financial implications of the investment. Healthcare enterprise leaders considering investing in an ACO should review the sources of revenue within the ACO model and their enterprise's ability to leverage its institutional expertise and access the necessary capital to initiate an ACO and incur initial losses.

Revenue generation in the ACO model is derived from shared cost reductions. Healthcare entities capable of reducing patient costs to payors will share in a portion of those cost reductions. For example, under the federal ACO model, a healthcare entity that reduces patient costs for CMS (Centers for Medicare and Medicaid Services) will receive, depending on the specific model chosen, between 50% and 60% of the cost reduction. In the absence of the cost reduction sharing model, CMS (or a private payor in the commercial market) would reap 100% of the benefit from cost reductions and participating healthcare entities would have no incentive to reduce healthcare costs. Managers of healthcare enterprises contemplating investment in an ACO should carefully assess the realistic and probable ability of their enterprise to achieve those required cost reduction benchmarks as the basis of obtaining the MSSP (Medicare Shared Savings Program) shared payments. The expected cost reductions will be utilized as inputs into any quantitative evaluation of the financial merits of the ACO investment and may have a significant impact on the resulting value metric and the final investment decision.

Key Term	Definition	Citation
Opportunity Cost	Most valuable alternative that is given up. The rate of return used in NPV computation is an opportunity interest rate.	*Corporate Finance,* 4th ed. Ross, Westerfield, Jaffe, and Roberts, Ontario, Canada: McGraw-Hill Ryerson, 2005, p. 949.

In addition to considering whether or not achieving the cost sharing revenue is possible, managers of enterprises contemplating investment in an ACO also should consider the significant expertise or depth required to effectuate those cost reductions. If the enterprise's leadership lacks the expertise to adequately manage the transition process, further unanticipated expenses may be incurred as the enterprise improves its institutional knowledge base, and those expenses may be significant and material to the investment decision. The analysis of these expenses should include both explicit expenses (e.g., consulting contracts or the hiring of additional employees) and implicit expenses (e.g., the opportunity cost of the time spent improving the enterprise's current staff's stock of human capital through education and training). The anticipated revenue received from the investment in an ACO should be compared with total expenses when making the decision to accept or reject investment in an ACO.

Key Concept	Definition	Citation
Time Value of Money	Price or value put on time. Time value of money reflects the opportunity cost of investing at a risk-free rate. The certainty of having a given sum of money today is worth more than the certainty of having an equal sum at a later date because money can be put to profitable use during the intervening time.	*Corporate Finance,* 4th ed. Ross, Westerfield, Jaffe, and Roberts, Ontario, Canada: McGraw-Hill Ryerson, 2005, p. 954.

Healthcare enterprise's leaders also should consider whether the current fiscal status of their enterprise will even allow for the anticipated significant initial capital investment in an ACO. Before embarking on an in-depth analysis of the possible impacts of ACO investment, it would be prudent to first determine if the enterprise has a reasonable probability of obtaining access to adequate capital. A review of the enterprise's debt policy, along with their current level of debt, as well as the enterprise's debt capacity, may be warranted. In addition, managers of the enterprise also may review the enterprise's access to equity through either internal sources (e.g., the current cash flow of the entity) or from external sources (e.g., private equity, venture capital, or publicly traded equity markets). Access to sufficient capital is a binding constraint on investment in an ACO regardless of the results of a financial analysis.

Before initiating an in-depth financial analysis of the investment in an ACO, managers should consider the probability of achieving cost sharing revenue, the expenses related to acquiring the necessary expertise to realize any possible revenue from cost sharing, and the enterprise's access to capital markets. Largely, these considerations will be specific to each enterprise contemplating investment in an ACO. Once a healthcare entity has overcome these initial threshold concerns, then further robust and in-depth analysis of the ACO investment opportunity is warranted. For the purposes of this chapter, it will be assumed that (1) the healthcare entity is capable of achieving the maximum cost sharing revenue allowed under the MSSP, (2) that the anticipated costs reflect all relevant costs included in the ACO investment, and (3) that the healthcare entity has adequate access to the necessary capital.

VALUE METRICS

The definition of the term *value metrics* derives from several disciplines and is commonly used throughout academic, professional, and commercial endeavors. For example, mathematical processes typically refer to value metrics as a means of defining trigonometric functions in comparison to a norm.[20] In the field of logistics and workflow process analyses, value metrics are referred to as a method to measure the ability of these disciplines to impact the execution of the planning, derived from their activities, on the "value" of the enterprise under which they operate.[21] Additionally, actuarial disciplines define value metrics as a method of capturing relevant capital risk considering a variety of financial impacts to determine value.[22]

In the case of healthcare, and ACOs specifically, the meaning of the term value metrics also applies to an expanded perspective as to the term value, as described by HFMA (the Healthcare Financial Management Association), in its 2011 report, *Defining and Delivering Value*, to wit:

> As in any industry, value in healthcare is defined through the relationship of two factors: the quality of care and the price paid for it.
>
> Based on these findings, HFMA recommends the following guidelines for the development and use of *value metrics*: [emphasis added]
>
> - Work to replace process metrics with patient-centered functional outcomes.
> - Align value metrics with the "triple aim" of improving care for individuals, improving the health of populations, and reducing the per capita costs of healthcare.

- Focus on a limited set of metrics to drive performance.
- Use payment incentives and penalties selectively, emphasizing performance on metrics that have been proven or that stakeholders agree are most likely to drive desirable quality or cost outcomes.
- Report provider-specific performance to end users in a way that is understandable and actionable. [23]

These concepts related to the term *value metrics* are further explicated upon in the consideration of the term *value* as the function of the measurement of the relationship between the cost of capital formation/investment aspects of developing an ACO and the returns to that investment in the form of both financial returns and nonmonetary benefits.

Various methodologies are available to analyze the expected value added by a prospective capital investment. The calculation of each of these value metrics may be useful in assisting managers of healthcare enterprises as they decide whether to invest in an ACO. Among the metrics available to analysts, the most commonly utilized include:

- The payback period and the discounted payback period methods
- The Accounting Rate of Return method
- The Net Present Value Method
- The Internal Rate of Return Method

Each of these methods has its strengths and weaknesses, and the merits and drawbacks of each method should be carefully considered for every investment project before selecting a method to utilize in the investment analysis.

Factoid 7.2

Various methodologies are available to analyze the expected value added by a prospective capital investment. Among the metrics available to analysts, the most commonly utilized include the payback period and the discounted payback period methods, the Accounting Rate of Return method, the Net Present Value Method, and the Internal Rate of Return Method. (Source: Health Capital Consultants, St. Louis, MO.)

As discussed in the introduction to this book, the value metrics of the healthcare delivery system are shaped by four elements, i.e., the four pillars of healthcare valuation: (1) regulatory, (2) reimbursement, (3) competition, and (4) technology. These elements serve as a framework for analyzing the viability, efficiency, efficacy, and productivity of healthcare enterprises. The metrics described in this chapter will assist an enterprise's management in determining the impact of ACO development on the overall value of the enterprise. The types of analyses described below provide a numerical measure of the expected magnitude of the probable change in value to be derived from ACO development, as well as clear principles upon which an enterprise's management can base their investment decisions, including their consideration of the requirements for capital formation, financial feasibility, and economic returns.

Cash Flow Analysis

The calculation of the various metrics first requires an analysis of the expected economic benefit that will accrue to the stakeholders in the ACO project. The analysis in this section calculates the potential profitability within the federal ACO market for ACOs of varying size. For the purpose of this analysis, a small ACO is defined as providing services for only 5,000 Medicare beneficiaries, the minimum number of beneficiaries required for participation in the MSSP. A medium ACO provides services to 20,000 beneficiaries and a large ACO provides services to 80,000 beneficiaries. In addition, under the initial three-year contract, federal ACOs have the option to choose a one-sided model (low reward, low risk) or a two-sided model (higher reward, higher risk) for shared savings payments. The following analysis considers both options.

Key Concept	Definition	Citation
Cash Flow	Cash generated by the firm and paid to creditors and shareholders. It can be classified as (1) cash flow from operations, (2) cash flow from changes in fixed assets, and (3) cash flow from changes in net working capital.	*Corporate Finance,* 4th ed. Ross, Westerfield, Jaffe, and Roberts, Ontario, Canada: McGraw-Hill Ryerson, 2005, p. 939.

Please note that, under the MSSP, ACOs may only achieve shared savings when Medicare beneficiary costs are determined to be below a calculated benchmark and in excess of an indicated minimum savings rate (MSR). An anticipated benchmark and MSR for ACOs of various sizes is illustrated in Table 7.1,

Federal ACOs are capped at the amount of shared savings they may receive. The cap for the one-sided models is 10% of the calculated benchmark, and the cap for the two-sided models is 15%. Under the best case scenario, an ACO that has met all quality goals (so as not to have their shared savings decreased) would achieve enough cost reductions to receive the maximum shared savings, equal to their cap. An illustration of the maximum amount of shared savings that an ACO could expect to achieve under the MSSP is shown in Table 7.2.

Factoid 7.3

Federal ACOs are capped at the amount of shared savings they may receive. The cap for the one-sided models is 10% of the calculated benchmark, and the cap for the two-sided models is 15%. (Source: Medicare Program; Medicare Shared Savings Program: Accountable Care Organizations. *Federal Registry* vol. 76, no. 212, §425.602-6, November 2, 2011, pp. 67986–67987.

TABLE 7.1
General Federal ACO Information for Shared Savings and Losses

	Small ACOs	Medium ACOs	Large ACOs
General ACO Information			
Number of Medicare Beneficiaries	5,000	20,000	80,000
Average Per Capita Cost	$8,000	$8,000	$8,000
Benchmark (i.e., Predicted Beneficiary Expenditures)	$40,000,000	$160,000,000	$640,000,000
One-Sided			
Minimum Savings Rate (MSR)	3.9%	2.5%	2.0%
Minimum Amount of Cost Reduction Required to Experience Shared Saving	$1,560,000	$4,000,000	$12,800,000
Two-Sided			
Minimum Savings Rate (MSR)	2.0%	2.0%	2.0%
Minimum Amount of Cost Reduction Required to Experience Shared Saving	$800,000	$3,200,000	$12,800,000

Source: Endnote 24.

TABLE 7.2
Maximum Shared Savings

	Small ACOs	Medium ACOs	Large ACOs
Total Savings Payment Cap (i.e., Maximum Shared Savings an ACO May Achieve)			
10% for One-Sided ACO	$4,000,000	$16,000,000	$64,000,000
15% for Two-Sided ACO	$6,000,000	$24,000,000	$96,000,000

Source: Endnote 25.

TABLE 7.3
Range of Cost Reduction Resulting in Shared Savings (in millions)

	Small ACOs		Medium ACOs		Large ACOs	
	Minimum	Maximum	Minimum	Maximum	Minimum	Maximum
Range of Cost Reduction to Achieve Shared Savings ($)						
One-Sided	1.6	8.0	4.0	32.0	12.8	128.0
Two-Sided	0.8	10.0	3.2	40.0	12.8	160.0

Source: Endnote 26.

From the first dollar above the calculated benchmark, any cost reductions above the minimum savings rate (MSR) up to the cap will result in shared savings. The range of cost reduction from the benchmark that would result in shared savings for each ACO size classification and shared savings disbursement option is displayed in Table 7.3

As indicated in Table 7.3, the two-sided model for shared savings distribution establishes a much greater financial incentive than the alternative one-sided model. In exchange for a higher percentage of their cost reductions being applied to shared savings (i.e., 60% for ACOs with a two-sided model as compared to 50% for ACOs with one-sided model), ACOs choosing the two-sided model are exposed to the added risk of potential shared losses as well. A visual representation of the shared savings and losses possible within both the one-sided and two-sided disbursement models is shown in Figure 7.1.

Similar to the threshold requirements for shared savings, ACOs must exceed their calculated cost benchmark by at least 2% before they are liable for any shared losses (see Figure 7.1). In addition to the 2% threshold, the MSSP sets a cap on the portion of shared losses that an ACO may be responsible to pay. To limit the exposure to downside risk for new ACOs, the MSSP gradually increases the shared losses cap, allowing for greater possible losses to the ACO based on the contract year. This gradual cap increase is designed to encourage participation in the two-sided model. The greatest amount of shared losses an ACO may be liable for under the MSSP, for each ACO size classification over the three-year contract term, is illustrated in Table 7.4.

The worst case scenario for any ACO occurs when the enterprise exceeds its calculated benchmark by a sufficient amount to be liable for the applicable capped shared losses amount. Once the 2% buffer is reached, an ACO will be liable for a portion of shared losses from the first dollar over the benchmark up to the designated cap for the given year. The range of expenditures over the benchmark that would result in shared losses for each ACO size classification, and for each year of the contract term, is displayed in Table 7.5.

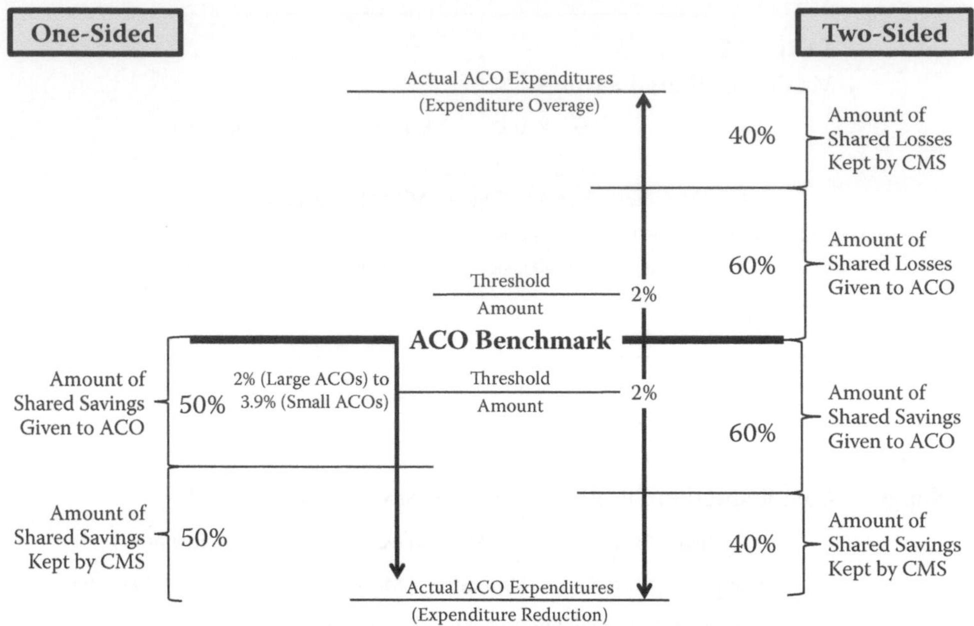

FIGURE 7.1 One-sided and two-sided distribution models for federal ACOs. (Endnote 27.)

TABLE 7.4
Maximum Shared Losses

	Small ACOs	Medium ACOs	Large ACOs
Total Losses Payment Cap (i.e., Maximum Amount for Which an ACO May Be Liable)			
Year 1: (5% cap)	$2,000,000	$8,000,000	$32,000,000
Year 2 (7.5% cap)	$3,000,000	$12,000,000	$48,000,000
Year 3: (10% cap)	$4,000,000	$16,000,000	$64,000,000

Source: Endnote 28.

Under the one-sided and two-sided models, ACOs are responsible for the supplementary startup costs and operational expenses related to the ACO. Although the Final MSSP Rule removed the healthcare information technology (HIT) requirements (i.e., electronic health record systems) for ACO status, there is a consensus among healthcare providers that, without HIT, an ACO will be unable to generate the necessary quality and cost reports, which may result in reductions in their expected shared savings payments.

To justify the significant expense associated with ACO development and operation, a potential ACO investor should consider whether the anticipated annual shared savings will offset the required ACO-related capital expenditures. Given the cap on shared savings, some ACOs (primarily small ACOs) may not be able to accumulate the necessary financial benefit to offset the ACO related costs. The annual expected cash flow for ACOs of each size may be estimated by assuming a "best case" scenario in which an ACO achieves the maximum shared savings, and, therefore, the maximum expected future cash flows (i.e., the expected cost savings less the expected operational

TABLE 7.5
Range of Cost Overage Resulting in Shared Losses (in millions)

	Small ACOs		Medium ACOs		Large ACOs	
	Minimum	Maximum	Minimum	Maximum	Minimum	Maximum
	Range of Cost Overage Resulting in Shared Losses ($)					
One-Sided	No Risk					
Two-Sided: Year 1	0.8	3.3	3.2	13.3	12.8	53.3
Two-Sided: Year 2	0.8	5.0	3.2	20.0	12.8	80.0
Two-Sided: Year 3	0.1	6.7	3.2	26.7	12.8	106.7

Source: Endnote 29.

costs of the ACO) over the initial three-year contract term, and considering the necessary initial startup investment.

The cash flow analysis, as seen in Table 7.6 and Table 7.7, first requires that a forecast be made of the potential revenue to be generated by an ACO; in this case, the "best case scenario" revenue generated by the anticipated shared savings under the chosen distribution model (Table 7.6 and Table 7.7, row 5) was utilized. Next, the ACO's anticipated operating costs were allocated between fixed costs (those that do not vary with the number of beneficiaries) and variable costs (those that vary with the number of beneficiaries). Fixed costs (Table 7.6 and Table 7.7, rows 7 through 10) remain constant across all ACOs regardless of the number of beneficiaries served by the ACO.[30] Variable costs (Table 7.6 and Table 7.7, rows 13 through 45), in contrast, increase as the number of beneficiaries increase. For the purposes of this analysis, it was assumed that variable costs would increase by a fixed amount per additional beneficiary. Net income for the ACO was then calculated by subtracting total costs (Exhibit 7.1 and Exhibit 7.2, line 46) from the anticipated "best case scenario" revenue. It was further assumed that the ACO would continue to achieve the "best case scenario" revenue for the entire initial three-year term of the ACO agreement and that the operating costs of the ACO would remain constant. Therefore, expected future cash flows from the ACO for years two and three were equal to the initial year's cash flow.

The Cash Flow analysis for ACOs of various sizes, under a two-sided shared savings disbursement model is shown in Exhibit 7.1.

The Cash Flow analysis for ACOs of various sizes under a one-sided shared savings disbursement model is shown in Exhibit 7.2.

Feasibility Analysis

A basic feasibility analysis can be performed utilizing the results in Exhibits 7.1 and 7.2. A federal ACO, utilizing the assumptions above, under the two-sided model, may require somewhere between 5,000 and 15,000 Medicare beneficiaries before being expected to generate positive cash flows (i.e., cash flows in excess of operating expenses). Further, under the one-sided model, a federal ACO, under the best case scenario assumption, may achieve a positive cash flow with somewhere between 25,000 and 35,000 Medicare beneficiaries.

Generation of positive cash flow is a necessary, but not sufficient, condition for the investment in the ACO project to have a positive impact on the overall value of the enterprise. As was stated above, the goal of a healthcare enterprise's management should be to maximize the value of the enterprise to its stakeholders (e.g., investors/owners or beneficiaries in the community served). Anticipation in consideration of only a positive cash flow from an investment project alone lacks sufficiency for determining the success of a project because the anticipated gains should be weighed

TABLE 7.6
Payback Periods for ACOs of Various Sizes: Two-Sided Model

	Small ACOs		Medium ACOs				Large ACOs		
Number of Medicare Beneficiaries	5,000	15,000	25,000	35,000	45,000	55,000	65,000	75,000	80,000
Expected Annual Net Cash Flow	($300,000)	$2,039,625	$7,032,083	$14,677,375	$24,975,500	$37,926,458	$53,530,250	$71,786,875	$81,910,000
Required Initial Investment	$5,315,000	$6,206,333	$7,097,667	$7,989,000	$8,880,333	$9,771,667	$10,663,000	$11,554,333	$12,000,000
Payback Period (Years)	**N/A**	**3.04**	**1.01**	**0.54**	**0.36**	**0.26**	**0.20**	**0.16**	**0.15**

TABLE 7.7
Payback Periods for ACOs of Various Sizes: One-Sided Model

	Small ACOs		Medium ACOs				Large ACOs		
Number of Medicare Beneficiaries	5,000	15,000	25,000	35,000	45,000	55,000	65,000	75,000	80,000
Expected Annual Net Cash Flow	**($2,300,000)**	**($3,960,375)**	**($2,967,917)**	$677,375	$6,975,500	$15,926,458	$27,530,250	$41,786,875	$49,910,000
Required Initial Investment	$5,315,000	$6,206,333	$7,097,667	$7,989,000	$8,880,333	$9,771,667	$10,663,000	$11,554,333	$12,000,000
Payback Period (Years)	**N/A**	**N/A**	**N/A**	**11.79**	**1.27**	**0.61**	**0.39**	**0.28**	**0.24**

EXHIBIT 7.1
Anticipated Annual Cash Flow for a Federal ACO, Based upon the Number of Medicare Beneficiaries Served: Two-Sided Model

		Small ACOs		Medium ACOs				Large ACOs			
1	Number of Medicare Beneficiaries	5,000	15,000	25,000	35,000	45,000	55,000	65,000	74,000	75,000	80,000
2	Average Cost per Patient (1)	$8,000	$8,000	$8,000	$8,000	$8,000	$8,000	$8,000	$8,000	$8,000	$8,000
3	Total Costs (2)	$40,000,000	$120,000,000	$200,000,000	$280,000,000	$360,000,000	$440,000,000	$520,000,000	$592,000,000	$600,000,000	$640,000,000
4	Maximum Cost Sharing Percentage (3)	15.00%	15.00%								
5	Maximum Cost Sharing Revenue (4)	$6,000,000	$18,000,000	$30,000,000	$42,000,000	$54,000,000	$66,000,000	$78,000,000	$88,800,000	$90,000,000	$96,000,000
6	**Fixed Costs (5)**										
7	Engaging legal and consulting support	$125,000	$125,000	$125,000	$125,000	$125,000	$125,000	$125,000	$125,000	$125,000	$125,000
8	Developing contracting capabilities	$150,000	$150,000	$150,000	$150,000	$150,000	$150,000	$150,000	$150,000	$150,000	$150,000
9	Patient education and support	$100,000	$100,000	$100,000	$100,000	$100,000	$100,000	$100,000	$100,000	$100,000	$100,000
10	Other activities and costs	$100,000	$100,000	$100,000	$100,000	$100,000	$100,000	$100,000	$100,000	$100,000	$100,000
11	**Total Fixed Costs**	$475,000	$475,000	$475,000	$475,000	$475,000	$475,000	$475,000	$475,000	$475,000	$475,000
12	**Variable Costs (6)**										
13	Providing ACO Management and Staff	$1,450,000	$3,850,000	$5,583,333	$6,650,000	$7,050,000	$6,783,333	$5,850,000	$4,440,000	$4,250,000	$3,200,000
14	*Per Patient*	*$290*	*$257*	*$223*	*$190*	*$157*	*$123*	*$90*	*$60*	*$57*	*$40*
15	Leveraging the health system's management resources	$200,000	$526,250	$754,167	$883,750	$915,000	$847,917	$682,500	$449,550	$418,750	$250,000
16	*Per Patient*	*$40*	*$35*	*$30*	*$25*	*$20*	*$15*	*$11*	*$6*	*$6*	*$3*
17	Developing financial and management information support systems	$80,000	$212,000	$306,667	$364,000	$384,000	$366,667	$312,000	$230,880	$220,000	$160,000

continued

EXHIBIT 7.1 (continued)

Anticipated Annual Cash Flow for a Federal ACO, Based upon the Number of Medicare Beneficiaries Served: Two-Sided Model

		Small ACOs		Medium ACOs				Large ACOs			
18	*Per Patient*	*$16*	*$14*	*$12*	*$10*	*$9*	*$7*	*$5*	*$3*	*$3*	*$2*
19	Recruiting/acquiring primary care professionals, right-sizing practices $800,000	$2,120,000	$3,066,667	$3,640,000	$3,840,000	$3,666,667	$3,120,000	$2,308,800	$2,200,000	$1,600,000	
20	*Per Patient*	*$160*	*$141*	*$123*	*$104*	*$85*	*$67*	*$48*	*$31*	*$29*	*$20*
21	Compensating physician leaders	$75,000	$199,750	$290,833	$348,250	$372,000	$362,083	$318,500	$250,490	$241,250	$190,000
22	*Per Patient*	*$15*	*$13*	*$12*	*$10*	*$8*	*$7*	*$5*	*$3*	*$3*	*$2*
23	Hospitalists	$160,000	$424,000	$613,333	$728,000	$768,000	$733,333	$624,000	$461,760	$440,000	$320,000
24	*Per Patient*	*$32*	*$28*	*$25*	*$21*	*$17*	*$13*	*$10*	*$6*	*$6*	*$4*
25	Electronic health record (EHR)	$1,200,000	$3,207,500	$4,691,667	$5,652,500	$6,090,000	$6,004,167	$5,395,000	$4,399,300	$4,262,500	$3,500,000
26	*Per Patient*	*$240*	*$214*	*$188*	*$162*	*$135*	*$109*	*$83*	*$59*	*$57*	*$44*
27	Disease registries	$10,000	$26,500	$38,333	$45,500	$48,000	$45,833	$39,000	$28,860	$27,500	$20,000
28	*Per Patient*	*$2*	*$2*	*$2*	*$1*	*$1*	*$1*	*$1*	*$0*	*$0*	*$0*
29	Care coordination and discharge follow-up $1,000,000	$2,675,000	$3,916,667	$4,725,000	$5,100,000	$5,041,667	$4,550,000	$3,737,000	$3,625,000	$3,000,000	
30	*Per Patient*	*$200*	*$178*	*$157*	*$135*	*$113*	*$92*	*$70*	*$51*	*$48*	*$38*
31	Specialty-specific disease management	$150,000	$397,500	$575,000	$682,500	$720,000	$687,500	$585,000	$432,900	$412,500	$300,000
32	*Per Patient*	*$30*	*$27*	*$23*	*$20*	*$16*	*$12*	*$9*	*$6*	*$5*	*$4*
33	Medication management	$100,000	$262,500	$375,000	$437,500	$450,000	$412,500	$325,000	$203,500	$187,500	$100,000
34	*Per Patient*	*$20*	*$18*	*$15*	*$13*	*$10*	*$8*	*$5*	*$3*	*$3*	*$1*
35	Achieving designation as a patient-centered medical home	$15,000	$39,625	$57,083	$67,375	$70,500	$66,458	$55,250	$39,035	$36,875	$25,000

36 *Per Patient*	*$3*	*$3*	*$2*	*$2*	*$2*	*$1*	*$1*	*$1*	*$0*	*$0*
37 Intrasystem EHR interoperability (hospitals, medical practices, other)	$200,000	$525,000	$750,000	$875,000	$900,000	$825,000	$650,000	$407,000	$375,000	$200,000
38 *Per Patient*	*$40*	*$35*	*$30*	*$25*	*$20*	*$15*	*$10*	*$6*	*$5*	*$3*
39 Linking to a health information exchange (HIE)	$100,000	$265,000	$383,333	$455,000	$480,000	$458,333	$390,000	$288,600	$275,000	$200,000
40 *Per Patient*	*$20*	*$18*	*$15*	*$13*	*$11*	*$8*	*$6*	*$4*	*$4*	*$3*
41 Analysis of care patterns	$210,000	$557,250	$807,500	$960,750	$1,017,000	$976,250	$838,500	$631,590	$603,750	$450,000
42 *Per Patient*	*$42*	*$37*	*$32*	*$27*	*$23*	*$18*	*$13*	*$9*	*$8*	*$6*
43 Quality reporting costs	$75,000	$197,500	$283,333	$332,500	$345,000	$320,833	$260,000	$173,900	$162,500	$100,000
44 *Per Patient*	*$15*	*$13*	*$11*	*$9*	*$8*	*$6*	*$4*	*$2*	*$2*	*$1*
45 Total Variable Costs	**$5,825,000**	**$15,485,375**	**$22,492,917**	**$26,847,625**	**$28,549,500**	**$27,598,542**	**$23,994,750**	**$18,483,165**	**$17,738,125**	**$13,615,000**
46 **Total Costs (7)**	$6,300,000	$15,960,375	$22,967,917	$27,322,625	$29,024,500	$28,073,542	$24,469,750	$18,958,165	$18,213,125	$14,090,000
47 **Net Income (8)**	**($300,000)**	**$2,039,625**	**$7,032,083**	**$14,677,375**	**$24,975,500**	**$37,926,458**	**$53,530,250**	**$69,841,835**	**$71,786,875**	**$81,910,000**

Source: Endnote 31.

Notes:

1 See Table 7.1, Line 3 above.

2 Equals the number of Medicare patients (Line 1) times the average cost per patient (Line 2).

3 Equals the maximum allowable portion of costs savings available for cost sharing. Source: Medicare Program; Medicare Shared Savings Program: Accountable Care Organizations. *Federal Register*, vol. 76, no. 212 (November 2, 2011), p. 67987.

4 Equals total costs (Line 3) times the maximum cost sharing percentage (Line 4).

5 Fixed costs are defined as costs that do not vary with the number of patients.

6 Variable costs are defined as costs that increase with the number of patients.

7 Equals the sum of Total Fixed Costs (Line 11) and Total Variable Costs (Line 45).

8 Equals Maximum Cost Sharing Revenue (Line 5) less Total Costs (Line 46).

EXHIBIT 7.2
Net Present Value Calculations: One-Sided ACO

		Small ACOs		Medium ACOs				Large ACOs			
1	Number of Medicare Beneficiaries	5,000	15,000	25,000	35,000	45,000	55,000	65,000	75,000	80,000	1
2	Average Cost per Patient (1)	$8,000	$8,000	$8,000	$8,000	$8,000	$8,000	$8,000	$8,000	$8,000	2
3	Total Costs (2)	$40,000,000	$120,000,000	$200,000,000	$280,000,000	$360,000,000	$440,000,000	$520,000,000	$600,000,000	$640,000,000	3
4	Maximum Cost Sharing Percentage (3)	10.00%	10.00%	10.00%	10.00%	10.00%	10.00%	10.00%	10.00%	10.00%	4
5	Maximum Cost Sharing Revenue (4)	$4,000,000	$12,000,000	$20,000,000	$28,000,000	$36,000,000	$44,000,000	$52,000,000	$60,000,000	$64,000,000	5
6	**Fixed Costs (5)**										**6**
7	Engaging legal and consulting support	$125,000	$125,000	$125,000	$125,000	$125,000	$125,000	$125,000	$125,000	$125,000	7
8	Developing contracting capabilities	$150,000	$150,000	$150,000	$150,000	$150,000	$150,000	$150,000	$150,000	$150,000	8
9	Patient education and support	$100,000	$100,000	$100,000	$100,000	$100,000	$100,000	$100,000	$100,000	$100,000	9
10	Other activities and costs	$100,000	$100,000	$100,000	$100,000	$100,000	$100,000	$100,000	$100,000	$100,000	10
11	**Total Fixed Costs**	**$475,000**	**$475,000**	**$475,000**	**$475,000**	**$475,000**	**$475,000**	**$475,000**	**$475,000**	**$475,000**	**11**
12	**Variable Costs (6)**	**12**									
13	Providing ACO Manage and Staff	$1,450,000	$3,850,000	$5,583,333	$6,650,000	$7,050,000	$6,783,333	$5,850,000	$4,250,000	$3,200,000	13
14	Per Patient	$290	$257	$223	$190	$157	$123	$90	$57	$40	14
15	Leveraging the entity's management resources	$200,000	$526,250	$754,167	$883,750	$915,000	$847,917	$682,500	$418,750	$250,000	15
16	Per Patient	$40	$35	$30	$25	$20	$15	$10	$6	$3	16
17	Developing financial and management support systems	$80,000	$212,000	$306,667	$364,000	$384,000	$366,667	$312,000	$220,000	$160,000	17
18	Per Patient	$16	$14	$12	$10	$9	$7	$5	$3	$2	18
19	Recruiting/acquiring PCPs	$800,000	$2,120,000	$3,066,667	$3,640,000	$3,840,000	$3,666,667	$3,120,000	$2,200,000	$1,600,000	19
20	Per Patient	$160	$141	$123	$104	$85	$67	$48	$29	$20	20
21	Compensating physician leaders	$75,000	$199,750	$290,833	$348,250	$372,000	$362,083	$318,500	$241,250	$190,000	21
22	Per Patient	$15	$13	$12	$10	$8	$7	$5	$3	$2	22

23	Hospitalists	$160,000	$424,000	$613,333	$728,000	$768,000	$733,333	$624,000	$440,000	$320,000	23
24	Per Patient	$32	$28	$25	$21	$17	$13	$10	$6	$4	24
25	Electronic health record (EHR)	$1,200,000	$3,207,500	$4,691,667	$5,652,500	$6,090,000	$6,004,167	$5,395,000	$4,262,500	$3,500,000	25
26	Per Patient	$240	$214	$188	$161	$135	$109	$83	$57	$44	26
27	Disease registries	$10,000	$26,500	$38,333	$45,500	$48,000	$45,833	$39,000	$27,500	$20,000	27
28	Per Patient	$2	$2	$2	$1	$1	$1	$1	$0	$0	28
29	Care coord. and discharge follow-up	$1,000,000	$2,675,000	$3,916,667	$4,725,000	$5,100,000	$5,041,667	$4,550,000	$3,625,000	$3,000,000	29
30	Per Patient	$200	$178	$157	$135	$113	$92	$70	$48	$38	30
31	Specialty specific disease management	$150,000	$397,500	$575,000	$682,500	$720,000	$687,500	$585,000	$412,500	$300,000	31
32	Per Patient	$30	$26	$23	$19	$16	$12	$9	$5	$4	32
33	Medication management	$100,000	$262,500	$375,000	$437,500	$450,000	$412,500	$325,000	$187,500	$100,000	33
34	Per Patient	$20	$18	$15	$13	$10	$8	$5	$3	$1	34
35	Achieving designation as a PCMH	$15,000	$39,625	$57,083	$67,375	$70,500	$66,458	$55,250	$36,875	$25,000	35
36	Per Patient	$3	$3	$2	$2	$2	$1	$1	$0	$0	36
37	Intra-system EHR interoperability	$200,000	$525,000	$750,000	$875,000	$900,000	$825,000	$650,000	$375,000	$200,000	37
38	Per Patient	$40	$35	$30	$25	$20	$15	$10	$5	$3	38
39	Linking to a HIE	$100,000	$265,000	$383,333	$455,000	$480,000	$458,333	$390,000	$275,000	$200,000	39
40	Per Patient	$20	$18	$15	$13	$11	$8	$6	$4	$3	40
41	Analysis of care patterns	$210,000	$557,250	$807,500	$960,750	$1,017,000	$976,250	$838,500	$603,750	$450,000	41
42	Per Patient	$42	$37	$32	$27	$23	$18	$13	$8	$6	42
43	Quality reporting costs	$75,000	$197,500	$283,333	$332,500	$345,000	$320,833	$260,000	$162,500	$100,000	43
44	Per Patient	$15	$13	$11	$9	$8	$6	$4	$2	$1	44
45	**Total Variable Costs**	**$5,825,000**	**$15,485,375**	**$22,492,917**	**$26,847,625**	**$28,549,500**	**$27,598,542**	**$23,994,750**	**$17,738,125**	**$13,615,000**	**45**
46	**Total Costs (7)**	**$6,300,000**	**$15,960,375**	**$22,967,917**	**$27,322,625**	**$29,024,500**	**$28,073,542**	**$24,469,750**	**$18,213,125**	**$14,090,000**	**46**
47	**Net Income (8)**	**($2,300,000)**	**($3,960,375)**	**($2,967,917)**	**$677,375**	**$6,975,500**	**$15,926,458**	**$27,530,250**	**$41,786,875**	**$49,910,000**	**47**
48	Start Up Costs (9)	$5,315,000	$6,206,333	$7,097,667	$7,989,000	$8,880,333	$9,771,667	$10,663,000	$11,554,333	$12,000,000	48

continued

EXHIBIT 7.2 (continued)
Net Present Value Calculations: One-Sided ACO

		Small ACOs		Medium ACOs				Large ACOs			
49	Required Rate of Return (10)	14.73%	10.17%	7.67%	7.23%	6.79%	6.35%	6.13%	6.13%	6.13%	49
50	Present Value of Future Revenue Sharing (11)	($5,274,686)	($9,819,811)	($7,695,005)	$1,770,316	$18,377,252	$42,298,722	$73,413,659	$111,431,149	$133,092,715	50
51	**Net Present Value of ACO Investment (12)**	**($10,589,686)**	**($16,026,145)**	**($14,792,671)**	**($6,218,684)**	**$9,496,919**	**$32,527,055**	**$62,750,659**	**$99,876,816**	**$121,092,715**	**51**

Notes:
1 See Table 7.1, Line 3 above.
2 Equals the number of Medicare patients (Line 1) times the average cost per patient (Line 2).
3 Equals the maximum allowable portion of costs savings available for cost sharing.
4 Equals total costs (Line 3) times the maximum cost sharing percentage (Line 4).
5 Fixed costs are defined as costs that do not vary with the number of patients.
6 Variable costs are defined as costs that increase with the number of patients.
7 Equals the sum of Total Fixed Costs (Line 11) and Total Variable Costs (Line 45).
8 Equals Maximum Cost Sharing Revenue (Line 5) less Total Costs (Line 46).
9 Represent the initial investment required to initiate the ACO.
10 Required rate of return was calculated as the weighted average cost of capital for the hospital industry. See calculations in Tables 7.8 and 7.9, below.
11 Equals Net Income (Line 47) times the Income Multiple (Line 50).
12 Equals the Present Value of the Future Revenue Sharing (Line 50) less the Start Up Costs (Line 48).

against the initial investment outlay. An investment may be capable of generating a positive cash flow without ever accumulating enough expected benefit to offset the startup investment costs. From a strictly financial perspective, an investment project that fails to generate positive net cash flow will never be able to accrue enough net economic benefit to the project stakeholders to offset the initial investment.

It is possible, though, that certain indirect benefits may accrue to the stakeholders in the ACO. If these benefits are sufficient in magnitude to compensate the stakeholders, either monetarily or nonmonetarily, for their initial investment and the ongoing losses experienced by the operation of the ACO, then the investment may make rational sense. These possible positive externalities will be discussed in Chapter 8. The discussion and calculation the various value metrics, noted above, based on the assumed cash flow analyses are illustrated in Table 7.6 and Table 7.7.

Payback Period and Discounted Payback Period Methods

For an investment, such as an ACO, the simplest value metric to calculate is the Payback Period Method. The Payback Period Method calculates the "expected number of years required to recover the original investment."[33] The intuition underlying this methodology is that an investment with a protracted payback period would be undesirable to an investor due to the delay in the return on and return of their investment capital. In the particular instance of the ACO investment analyzed here, the initial term of the federal ACO contract with CMS is three years. If the payback period for the ACO investment exceeds this three-year boundary, then the likelihood of receiving the return on or even the return of the invested capital would be contingent upon continuing to contract with CMS. Due to the uncertainty related to the future prospect of renegotiating the federal ACO contract, investors would prefer that the investment payback period be less than the initial three-year term. The results of the payback period analysis for ACOs of various sizes are seen in Table 7.6.

Key Term	Definition	Citation
Payback Period	An investment decision rule that states that all investment projects with payback periods equal to or less than a particular cutoff period are accepted, and all of those that pay off in more than the particular cutoff period are rejected. The payback period is the number of years required for a firm to recover its initial investment required by a project from the cash flow it generates.	*Corporate Finance,* 4th ed. Ross, Westerfield, Jaffe, and Roberts, Ontario, Canada: McGraw-Hill Ryerson, 2005, p. 949.

The payback period analysis shows that for small ACOs, the expected time required to pay back the initial investment will exceed the initial three-year term of the ACO contract, but as the ACO's size increases, the required payback period reduces dramatically, down to less than two months (0.15 years) for ACOs with 80,000 Medicare beneficiaries. The results of the payback period analysis for ACOs of various sizes under the one-sided model are seen in Table 7.7.

Key Term	Definition	Citation
Discounted Payback Period Method	An investment decision rule in which the cash flows are discounted at an interest rate and the payback rule is applied on these discounted cash flows.	*Corporate Finance,* 4th ed. Ross, Westerfield, Jaffe, and Roberts, Ontario, Canada: McGraw-Hill Ryerson, 2005, p. 942.

The payback period analysis for the one-sided ACO model again shows a strong preference for larger ACOs, with only the larger ACOs of 45,000 beneficiaries and above being capable of paying back the initial investment within the three-year contract time frame.

Concerns have been raised regarding the payback period method, particularly the failure of this analysis to consider the timing of the cash flows. The payback period method gives equal weight to cash flows regardless of the time period within which they are recognized. Typical investors would require compensation for the delay in accessing their invested capital. The longer the delay, the greater the amount of compensation that will be required. Due to the uncertainty related to future events, rational investors will only postpone current consumption (i.e., through investing) if they reasonably expect to have an opportunity for increased consumption in the future. This time, value of money[34] reflects the cost of obtaining the necessary capital required for the ACO investment in the form of payments to the debt and equity holders. The lack of consideration of the present value of the cash flows utilized in the payback period analysis creates a tendency to underestimate the true (i.e., in present value terms) payback period.

This present value shortcoming can be addressed by utilizing a modified method, i.e., the discounted payback period method. As the name implies, the discounted payback period method converts each cash flow into its present value equivalent by discounting at an appropriate risk-adjusted rate.[35] The payback period is then calculated utilizing these cash flows adjusted to present value. The results of the discounted payback period method are set forth in Table 7.8 and Table 7.9.

As derived from the payback period analysis, the larger the ACO, the shorter the payback period. This is again evident in the results of the discounted payback period method for both the one-sided and two-sided ACO models.

AARR Method

An alternative metric for measuring the value impact of a capital budgeting project is the average accounting rate of return (AARR) method, which is calculated by dividing the average net income for the project by the initial investment cost. This provides a measure of the annual return on the investment as expressed in accounting measures.

For the illustrative example of the ACO investment, the net income for the project is anticipated to be the same for all three years of the analysis. Then, averaging the net income for the three years will result in the net income from a single year (i.e., 50% of the maximum cost reductions for the one-sided model and 60% of the maximum cost reductions for the two-sided model). The AARR is then expressed as the average expected net cash flow as a percent of the initial investment. The results of the AARR method for ACOs of various sizes are shown in Table 7.10 and Table 7.11.

The indicated results from utilizing the AARR method agrees with the payback period methods, in that it confirms the suggestion that smaller ACOs will have difficulty adding value to their enterprises. This agreement between methods is not surprising because both metrics rely on the same cash flow analysis. It is notable that the larger ACOs, with the quick payback periods, have a significantly greater AARR.

While the AARR method provides insight to the analysis regarding the relative return of a project in accounting terms, its main drawback is that, by utilizing the average net income amount, it fails to consider the timing of the net income. The net income in the most recent period is given equal weight as the net income in more remote periods, in opposition to standard financial and economic theory, which posits that, all things being equal, investors will prefer receiving cash flows sooner rather than later, and that any delay in receipt of expected and anticipated benefit comes at a cost.

Net Present Value

Another useful metric for evaluating a projected likelihood of success, defined as a project that increases the overall enterprise's value, is the net present value (NPV). The NPV of an investment project is the discounted value of the differences over time between monetary costs and benefits in each period.[36] For healthcare enterprises seeking to determine whether to form an ACO, the NPV analysis provides a financial investment basis for determining whether to accept the decision to

TABLE 7.8
Discounted Payback Period Method: Two-Sided ACO Model

	Small ACOs		Medium ACOs				Large ACOs		
Number of Medicare Beneficiaries	5,000	15,000	25,000	35,000	45,000	55,000	65,000	75,000	80,000
Average Expected Net Cash Flow	($300,000)	$2,039,625	$7,032,083	$14,677,375	$24,975,500	$37,926,458	$53,530,250	$71,786,875	$81,910,000
Required Rate of Return	14.73%	10.17%	7.67%	7.23%	6.79%	6.35%	6.13%	6.13%	6.13%
Discounted Cash Flow Year 1	($261,475)	$1,851,377	$6,531,415	$13,688,201	$23,388,057	$35,662,481	$50,438,942	$67,641,269	$77,179,795
Discounted Cash Flow Year 2	($227,897)	$1,680,504	$6,066,393	$12,765,691	$21,901,512	$33,533,650	$47,526,153	$63,735,066	$72,722,755
Discounted Cash Flow Year 3	($198,631)	$1,525,401	$5,634,480	$11,905,354	$20,509,451	$31,531,896	$44,781,575	$60,054,443	$68,523,102
Total Discounted Cash Flow Years 1–3	($688,002)	$5,057,282	$18,232,289	$38,359,246	$65,799,019	$100,728,027	$142,746,670	$191,430,778	$218,425,652
Discounted Payback Period	**N/A**	**N/A**	**1.09**	**0.58**	**0.38**	**0.27**	**0.21**	**0.17**	**0.16**
Startup Costs	$5,315,000	$6,206,333	$7,097,667	$7,989,000	$8,880,333	$9,771,667	$10,663,000	$11,554,333	$12,000,000

TABLE 7.9
Discounted Payback Period Method: One-Sided ACO Model

	Small ACOs		Medium ACOs				Large ACOs		
Number of Medicare Beneficiaries	5,000	15,000	25,000	35,000	45,000	55,000	65,000	75,000	80,000
Average Expected Net Cash Flow	($2,300,000)	($3,960,375)	($2,967,917)	$677,375	$6,975,500	$15,926,458	$27,530,250	$41,786,875	$49,910,000
Required Rate of Return	14.73%	10.17%	7.67%	7.23%	6.79%	6.35%	6.13%	6.13%	6.13%
Discounted Cash Flow Year 1	($2,004,640)	($3,594,851)	($2,756,608)	$631,724	$6,532,137	$14,975,746	$25,940,411	$39,373,733	$47,027,757
Discounted Cash Flow Year 2	($1,747,209)	($3,263,063)	($2,560,344)	$589,149	$6,116,954	$14,081,786	$24,442,383	$37,099,947	$44,311,960
Discounted Cash Flow Year 3	($1,522,837)	($2,961,897)	($2,378,053)	$549,444	$5,728,161	$13,241,190	$23,030,865	$34,957,469	$41,752,998
Total Discounted Cash Flow Years 1–3	($5,274,686)	($9,819,811)	($7,695,005)	$1,770,316	$18,377,252	$42,298,722	$73,413,659	$111,431,149,	$133,092,715
Discounted Payback Period	**N/A**	**N/A**	**N/A**	**12.65**	**1.36**	**0.65**	**0.41**	**0.29**	**0.26**
Startup Costs	$5,315,000	$6,206,333	$7,097,667	$7,989,000	$8,880,333	$9,771,667	$10,663,000	$11,554,333	$12,000,000

TABLE 7.10
Average Accounting Rate of Return (AARR): Two-Sided ACO Model

		Small ACOs		Medium ACOs				Large ACOs			
1	Number of Medicare Beneficiaries	5,000	15,000	25,000	35,000	45,000	55,000	65,000	75,000	80,000	1
2	Average Expected Net Cash Flow	($300,000)	$2,039,625	$7,032,083	$14,677,375	$24,975,500	$37,926,458	$53,530,250	$71,786,875	$81,910,000	2
3	Startup Costs	$5,315,000	$6,206,333	$7,097,667	$7,989,000	$8,880,333	$9,771,667	$10,663,000	$11,554,333	$12,000,000	3
4	Accounting Rate of Return	–5.64%	32.86%	99.08%	183.72%	281.25%	388.13%	502.02%	621.30%	682.58%	4

TABLE 7.11
Average Accounting Rate of Return (AARR): One-Sided ACO Model

	Small ACOs		Medium ACOs				Large ACOs		
Number of Medicare Beneficiaries	5,000	15,000	25,000	35,000	45,000	55,000	65,000	75,000	80,000
Average Expected Net Cash Flow	($2,300,000)	($3,960,375)	($2,967,917)	$677,375	$6,975,500	$15,926,458	$27,530,250	$41,786,875	$49,910,000
Startup Costs	$5,315,000	$6,206,333	$7,097,667	$7,989,000	$8,880,333	$9,771,667	$10,663,000	$11,554,333	$12,000,000
Accounting Rate of Return	–43.27%	–63.81%	–41.82%	8.48%	78.55%	162.99%	258.18%	361.66%	415.92%

form an ACO or reject it. Healthcare enterprises may employ a NPV analysis to evaluate an ACO's potential impact on the enterprise's financial profile, as well as on its needs for total available capital and allocation decisions related to utilization of existing capital.[37] These healthcare enterprises should seek to determine whether the additions to net cash flow generated from the formation of the ACO over the lifetime of the ACO will be greater than the initial startup and maintenance costs of the project after consideration of the enterprise's cost of capital, as well as the probability of obtaining both a return on and a return of investment capital. For many enterprises contemplating ACO formation, a NPV analysis may indicate a probability that the expected return is not sufficient and, thus, the venture is too risky to undertake.

Key Term	Definition	Citation
The Net Present Value Method	The present value of future cash returns, discounted at the appropriate market interest rate, minus the present value of the cost of the investment.	*Corporate Finance,* 4th ed. Ross, Westerfield, Jaffe, and Roberts, Ontario, Canada: McGraw-Hill Ryerson, 2005, p. 948.

The cash flows calculated in Table 7.6 and Table 7.7 were discounted using a calculated WACC (weighted average cost of capital), adjusted for the size of each ACO,[38] to arrive at its present value equivalent.[39] The resulting sum of the present value equivalent cash flows represents the value of the expected future economic benefit of ownership of the ACO, as of the present date.

The NPV of the investment in the ACO was then calculated as the sum of the present value equivalent cash flows less the ACO startup costs (Exhibit 7.3 and Exhibit 7.4, line 2). The NPV analysis for ACOs of various sizes, under a two-sided shared savings disbursement model, is illustrated in Exhibit 7.3.

The NPV analysis for ACOs of various sizes, under a one-sided shared savings disbursement model, is illustrated in Exhibit 7.4.

Unlike the previous methods discussed above, the NPV analysis considers not only the expected future economic benefit, but, through the present value adjustment, the timing of those expected future cash flows as well. Recall that the discounted payback period method also considers the timing of the expected cash flows of an ACO investment, but its insistence on selecting projects with the shortest payback period creates a preference for shorter term, more liquid investments at the expense of longer term, less liquid investments with greater value potential. The NPV analysis avoids this myopic tendency by determining the present value equivalent of all future cash flows. As a result, using an NPV analysis may prevent an enterprise from disregarding a long-term project with greater potential value, a potentially likely occurrence when using the discounted payback period method.

Internal Rate of Return

Closely related to the NPV method is the internal rate of return (IRR) method. The IRR method attempts to determine a "hurdle" rate, i.e., the minimum accepted rate of return for a project for the proposed investment. Based on the anticipated future economic benefits that will accrue to the stakeholders in the ACO (see Table 7.6 and Table 7.7), the IRR represents the required rate of return that would render the NPV of the project equal to zero.[40] In other words, the IRR represents the maximum rate (in percentage terms) at which the project's investors, both debt and equity, could be compensated for the project to leave the value of the enterprise unchanged. The IRR is useful for comparison to the project's cost of capital. A cost of capital in excess of the IRR indicates that the project would fail to generate sufficient net economic benefit to offset its expected operational and capital costs and would be an inefficient use of the available capital. An IRR, which exceeds a project's cost of capital, on the other hand, indicates that the project would likely improve the value

EXHIBIT 7.3

Net Present Value Calculations for ACOs of Various Size Classifications: Two-Sided Model

		Small ACOs		Medium ACOs				Large ACOs			
1	Number of Medicare Beneficiaries	5,000	15,000	25,000	35,000	45,000	55,000	65,000	75,000	80,000	1
2	Average Cost per Patient (1)	$8,000	$8,000	$8,000	$8,000	$8,000	$8,000	$8,000	$8,000	$8,000	2
3	Total Costs (2)	$40,000,000	$120,000,000	$200,000,000	$280,000,000	$360,000,000	$440,000,000	$520,000,000	$600,000,000	$640,000,000	3
4	Maximum Cost Sharing Percentage (3)	15.00%	15.00%	15.00%	15.00%	15.00%	15.00%	15.00%	15.00%	15.00%	4
5	Maximum Cost Sharing Revenue (4)	$6,000,000	$18,000,000	$30,000,000	$42,000,000	$54,000,000	$66,000,000	$78,000,000	$90,000,000	$96,000,000	5
6	**Fixed Costs (5)**										**6**
7	Engaging legal and consulting support	$125,000	$125,000	$125,000	$125,000	$125,000	$125,000	$125,000	$125,000	$125,000	7
8	Developing contracting capabilities	$150,000	$150,000	$150,000	$150,000	$150,000	$150,000	$150,000	$150,000	$150,000	8
9	Patient education and support	$100,000	$100,000	$100,000	$100,000	$100,000	$100,000	$100,000	$100,000	$100,000	9
10	Other activities and costs	$100,000	$100,000	$100,000	$100,000	$100,000	$100,000	$100,000	$100,000	$100,000	10
11	**Total Fixed Costs**	**$475,000**	**$475,000**	**$475,000**	**$475,000**	**$475,000**	**$475,000**	**$475,000**	**$475,000**	**$475,000**	**11**
12	**Variable Costs (6)**	**12**									
13	Providing ACO Manage and Staff	$1,450,000	$3,850,000	$5,583,333	$6,650,000	$7,050,000	$6,783,333	$5,850,000	$4,250,000	$3,200,000	13
14	Per Patient	$290	$257	$223	$190	$157	$123	$90	$57	$40	14
15	Leveraging the entity's management resources	$200,000	$526,250	$754,167	$883,750	$915,000	$847,917	$682,500	$418,750	$250,000	15
16	Per Patient	$40	$35	$30	$25	$20	$15	$10	$6	$3	16
17	Developing financial and management support systems	$80,000	$212,000	$306,667	$364,000	$384,000	$366,667	$312,000	$220,000	$160,000	17
18	Per Patient	$16	$14	$12	$10	$9	$7	$5	$3	$2	18
19	Recruiting/acquiring PCPs	$800,000	$2,120,000	$3,066,667	$3,640,000	$3,840,000	$3,666,667	$3,120,000	$2,200,000	$1,600,000	19
20	Per Patient	$160	$141	$123	$104	$85	$67	$48	$29	$20	20
21	Compensating physician leaders	$75,000	$199,750	$290,833	$348,250	$372,000	$362,083	$318,500	$241,250	$190,000	21

22	Per Patient	$15	$13	$12	$10	$8	$7	$5	$3	$2	22
23	Hospitalists	$160,000	$424,000	$613,333	$728,000	$768,000	$733,333	$624,000	$440,000	$320,000	23
24	Per Patient	$32	$28	$25	$21	$17	$13	$10	$6	$4	24
25	Electronic health record (EHR)	$1,200,000	$3,207,500	$4,691,667	$5,652,500	$6,090,000	$6,004,167	$5,395,000	$4,262,500	$3,500,000	25
26	Per Patient	$240	$214	$188	$161	$135	$109	$83	$57	$44	26
27	Disease registries	$10,000	$26,500	$38,333	$45,500	$48,000	$45,833	$39,000	$27,500	$20,000	27
28	Per Patient	$2	$2	$2	$1	$1	$1	$1	$0	$0	28
29	Care coord. and discharge follow-up	$1,000,000	$2,675,000	$3,916,667	$4,725,000	$5,100,000	$5,041,667	$4,550,000	$3,625,000	$3,000,000	29
30	Per Patient	$200	$178	$157	$135	$113	$92	$70	$48	$38	30
31	Specialty-specific disease management	$150,000	$397,500	$575,000	$682,500	$720,000	$687,500	$585,000	$412,500	$300,000	31
32	Per Patient	$30	$26	$23	$19	$16	$12	$9	$5	$4	32
33	Medication management	$100,000	$262,500	$375,000	$437,500	$450,000	$412,500	$325,000	$187,500	$100,000	33
34	Per Patient	$20	$18	$15	$13	$10	$8	$5	$3	$1	34
35	Achieving designation as a PCMH	$15,000	$39,625	$57,083	$67,375	$70,500	$66,458	$55,250	$36,875	$25,000	35
36	Per Patient	$3	$3	$2	$2	$2	$1	$1	$0	$0	36
37	Intra-system EHR interoperability	$200,000	$525,000	$750,000	$875,000	$900,000	$825,000	$650,000	$375,000	$200,000	37
38	Per Patient	$40	$35	$30	$25	$20	$15	$10	$5	$3	38
39	Linking to a HIE	$100,000	$265,000	$383,333	$455,000	$480,000	$458,333	$390,000	$275,000	$200,000	39
40	Per Patient	$20	$18	$15	$13	$11	$8	$6	$4	$3	40
41	Analysis of care patterns	$210,000	$557,250	$807,500	$960,750	$1,017,000	$976,250	$838,500	$603,750	$450,000	41
42	Per Patient	$42	$37	$32	$27	$23	$18	$13	$8	$6	42
43	Quality reporting costs	$75,000	$197,500	$283,333	$332,500	$345,000	$320,833	$260,000	$162,500	$100,000	43
44	Per Patient	$15	$13	$11	$9	$8	$6	$4	$2	$1	44
45	**Total Variable Costs**	**$5,825,000**	**$15,485,375**	**$22,492,917**	**$26,847,625**	**$28,549,500**	**$27,598,542**	**$23,994,750**	**$17,738,125**	**$13,615,000**	**45**
46	**Total Costs (7)**	**$6,300,000**	**$15,960,375**	**$22,967,917**	**$27,322,625**	**$29,024,500**	**$28,073,542**	**$24,469,750**	**$18,213,125**	**$14,090,000**	**46**

continued

EXHIBIT 7.3 (continued)
Net Present Value Calculations for ACOs of Various Size Classifications: Two-Sided Model

		Small ACOs		Medium ACOs				Large ACOs			
47	Net Income (8)	($300,000)	$2,039,625	$7,032,083	$14,677,375	$24,975,500	$37,926,458	$53,530,250	$71,786,875	$81,910,000	47
48	Start Up Costs (9)	$5,315,000	$6,206,333	$7,097,667	$7,989,000	$8,880,333	$9,771,667	$10,663,000	$11,554,333	$12,000,000	48
49	Required Rate of Return (10)	14.73%	10.17%	7.67%	7.23%	6.79%	6.35%	6.13%	6.13%	6.13%	49
50	Present Value of Future Revenue Sharing (11)	($688,002)	$5,057,282	$18,232,289	$38,359,246	$65,799,019	$100,728,027	$142,746,670	$191,430,778	$218,425,652	50
51	**Net Present Value of ACO Investment (12)**	**($6,003,002)**	**($1,149,052)**	**$11,134,622**	**$30,370,246**	**$56,918,686**	**$90,956,360**	**$132,083,670**	**$179,876,444**	**$206,425,652**	**51**

Notes:

1 See Table 7.1, Line 3 above.
2 Equals the number of Medicare patients (Line 1) times the average cost per patient (Line 2).
3 Equals the maximum allowable portion of costs savings available for cost sharing.
4 Equals total costs (Line 3) times the maximum cost sharing percentage (Line 4).
5 Fixed costs are defined as costs that do not vary with the number of patients.
6 Variable costs are defined as costs that increase with the number of patients.
7 Equals the sum of Total Fixed Costs (Line 11) and Total Variable Costs (Line 45).
8 Equals Maximum Cost Sharing Revenue (Line 5) less Total Costs (Line 45).
9 Represent the initial investment required to initiate the ACO.
10 Required rate of return was calculated as the weighted average cost of capital for the hospital industry. Utilizing a cost of equity based upon a build up method considering a risk free rate plus several premia for equity risk, industry risk, size risk and project specific risk. Cost of debt was estimated as the Baa corporate bond rate as of 4/2/2012, as reported by the Federal Reserve Bank. The industry average debt to total capitalizaton, as reported in the 2012, based on 2011 data, Ibbotson Cost of Capital Yearbook, was utilized as a proxy for the expected capital structure of the project.
11 Equals Net Income (Line 47) times the Income Multiple (Line 50).
12 Equals the Present Value of the Future Revenue Sharing (Line 50) less the Start Up Costs (Line 1).

EXHIBIT 7.4

Net Present Value Calculations for ACOs of Various Size Classifications: One-Sided Model

		Small ACOs		Medium ACOs				Large ACOs			
1	Number of Medicare Beneficiaries	5,000	15,000	25,000	35,000	45,000	55,000	65,000	75,000	80,000	1
2	Average Cost per Patient (1)	$8,000	$8,000	$8,000	$8,000	$8,000	$8,000	$8,000	$8,000	$8,000	2
3	Total Costs (2)	$40,000,000	$120,000,000	$200,000,000	$280,000,000	$360,000,000	$440,000,000	$520,000,000	$600,000,000	$640,000,000	3
4	Maximum Cost Sharing Percentage (3)	10.00%	10.00%	10.00%	10.00%	10.00%	10.00%	10.00%	10.00%	10.00%	4
5	Maximum Cost Sharing Revenue (4)	$4,000,000	$12,000,000	$20,000,000	$28,000,000	$36,000,000	$44,000,000	$52,000,000	$60,000,000	$64,000,000	5
6	**Fixed Costs (5)**										**6**
7	Engaging legal and consulting support	$125,000	$125,000	$125,000	$125,000	$125,000	$125,000	$125,000	$125,000	$125,000	7
8	Developing contracting capabilities	$150,000	$150,000	$150,000	$150,000	$150,000	$150,000	$150,000	$150,000	$150,000	8
9	Patient education and support	$100,000	$100,000	$100,000	$100,000	$100,000	$100,000	$100,000	$100,000	$100,000	9
10	Other activities and costs	$100,000	$100,000	$100,000	$100,000	$100,000	$100,000	$100,000	$100,000	$100,000	10
11	**Total Fixed Costs**	**$475,000**	**$475,000**	**$475,000**	**$475,000**	**$475,000**	**$475,000**	**$475,000**	**$475,000**	**$475,000**	**11**
12	**Variable Costs (6)**										**12**
13	Providing ACO Manage and Staff	$1,450,000	$3,850,000	$5,583,333	$6,650,000	$7,050,000	$6,783,333	$5,850,000	$4,250,000	$3,200,000	13
14	Per Patient	$290	$257	$223	$190	$157	$123	$90	$57	$40	14
15	Leveraging the entity's management resources	$200,000	$526,250	$754,167	$883,750	$915,000	$847,917	$682,500	$418,750	$250,000	15
16	Per Patient	$40	$35	$30	$25	$20	$15	$10	$6	$3	16
17	Developing financial and management support systems	$80,000	$212,000	$306,667	$364,000	$384,000	$366,667	$312,000	$220,000	$160,000	17
18	Per Patient	$16	$14	$12	$10	$9	$7	$5	$3	$2	18
19	Recruiting/acquiring PCPs	$800,000	$2,120,000	$3,066,667	$3,640,000	$3,840,000	$3,666,667	$3,120,000	$2,200,000	$1,600,000	19
20	Per Patient	$160	$141	$123	$104	$85	$67	$48	$29	$20	20
21	Compensating physician leaders	$75,000	$199,750	$290,833	$348,250	$372,000	$362,083	$318,500	$241,250	$190,000	21

continued

EXHIBIT 7.4 (continued)

Net Present Value Calculations for ACOs of Various Size Classifications: One-Sided Model

		Small ACOs		Medium ACOs				Large ACOs			
22	Per Patient	$15	$13	$12	$10	$8	$7	$5	$3	$2	22
23	Hospitalists	$160,000	$424,000	$613,333	$728,000	$768,000	$733,333	$624,000	$440,000	$320,000	23
24	Per Patient	$32	$28	$25	$21	$17	$13	$10	$6	$4	24
25	Electronic health record (EHR)	$1,200,000	$3,207,500	$4,691,667	$5,652,500	$6,090,000	$6,004,167	$5,395,000	$4,262,500	$3,500,000	25
26	Per Patient	$240	$214	$188	$161	$135	$109	$83	$57	$44	26
27	Disease registries	$10,000	$26,500	$38,333	$45,500	$48,000	$45,833	$39,000	$27,500	$20,000	27
28	Per Patient	$2	$2	$2	$1	$1	$1	$1	$0	$0	28
29	Care coord. and discharge follow-up	$1,000,000	$2,675,000	$3,916,667	$4,725,000	$5,100,000	$5,041,667	$4,550,000	$3,625,000	$3,000,000	29
30	Per Patient	$200	$178	$157	$135	$113	$92	$70	$48	$38	30
31	Specialty-specific disease management	$150,000	$397,500	$575,000	$682,500	$720,000	$687,500	$585,000	$412,500	$300,000	31
32	Per Patient	$30	$26	$23	$19	$16	$12	$9	$5	$4	32
33	Medication management	$100,000	$262,500	$375,000	$437,500	$450,000	$412,500	$325,000	$187,500	$100,000	33
34	Per Patient	$20	$18	$15	$13	$10	$8	$5	$3	$1	34
35	Achieving designation as a PCMH	$15,000	$39,625	$57,083	$67,375	$70,500	$66,458	$55,250	$36,875	$25,000	35
36	Per Patient	$3	$3	$2	$2	$2	$1	$1	$0	$0	36
37	Intra-system EHR interoperability	$200,000	$525,000	$750,000	$875,000	$900,000	$825,000	$650,000	$375,000	$200,000	37
38	Per Patient	$40	$35	$30	$25	$20	$15	$10	$5	$3	38
39	Linking to a HIE	$100,000	$265,000	$383,333	$455,000	$480,000	$458,333	$390,000	$275,000	$200,000	39
40	Per Patient	$20	$18	$15	$13	$11	$8	$6	$4	$3	40
41	Analysis of care patterns	$210,000	$557,250	$807,500	$960,750	$1,017,000	$976,250	$838,500	$603,750	$450,000	41
42	Per Patient	$42	$37	$32	$27	$23	$18	$13	$8	$6	42
43	Quality reporting costs	$75,000	$197,500	$283,333	$332,500	$345,000	$320,833	$260,000	$162,500	$100,000	43
44	Per Patient	$15	$13	$11	$9	$8	$6	$4	$2	$1	44
45	**Total Variable Costs**	**$5,825,000**	**$15,485,375**	**$22,492,917**	**$26,847,625**	**$28,549,500**	**$27,598,542**	**$23,994,750**	**$17,738,125**	**$13,615,000**	**45**

46	**Total Costs (7)**	**$6,300,000**	**$15,960,375**	**$22,967,917**	**$27,322,625**	**$29,024,500**	**$28,073,542**	**$24,469,750**	**$18,213,125**	**$14,090,000**	**46**
47	**Net Income (8)**	**($2,300,000)**	**($3,960,375)**	**($2,967,917)**	**$677,375**	**$6,975,500**	**$15,926,458**	**$27,530,250**	**$41,786,875**	**$49,910,000**	**47**
48	Start Up Costs (9)	$5,315,000	$6,206,333	$7,097,667	$7,989,000	$8,880,333	$9,771,667	$10,663,000	$11,554,333	$12,000,000	48
49	Required Rate of Return (10)	14.73%	10.17%	7.67%	7.23%	6.79%	6.35%	6.13%	6.13%	6.13%	49
50	Present Value of Future Revenue Sharing (11)	($5,274,686)	($9,819,811)	($7,695,005)	$1,770,316	$18,377,252	$42,298,722	$73,413,659	$111,431,149	$133,092,715	50
51	**Net Present Value of ACO Investment (12)**	**($10,589,686)**	**($16,026,145)**	**($14,792,671)**	**($6,218,684)**	**$9,496,919**	**$32,527,055**	**$62,750,659**	**$99,876,816**	**$121,092,715**	**51**

Notes:

1 See Table 7.1, Line 3 above

2 Equals the number of Medicare patients (Line 1) times the average cost per patient (Line 2).

3 Equals the maximum allowable portion of costs savings available for cost sharing.

4 Equals total costs (Line 3) times the maximum cost sharing percentage (Line 4).

5 Fixed costs are defined as costs that do not vary with the number of patients.

6 Variable costs are defined as costs that increase with the number of patients.

7 Equals the sum of Total Fixed Costs (Line 11) and Total Variable Costs (Line 45).

8 Equals Maximum Cost Sharing Revenue (Line 5) less Total Costs (Line 46).

9 Represent the initial investment required to initiate the ACO.

10 Required rate of return was calculated as the weighted average cost of capital for the hospital industry. Utilizing a cost of equity based upon a build up method considering a risk free rate plus several premia for equity risk, industry risk, size risk, and project specific risk. Cost of debt was estimated as the Baa corporate bond rate as of 4/2/2012, as reported by the Federal Reserve Bank. The industry average debt to total capitalizaton, as reported in 2012, based on 2011 data, Ibbotson Cost of Capital Yearbook, was utilized as a proxy for the expected capital structure of the project.

11 Equals Net Income (Line 47) times the Income Multiple (Line 50).

12 Equals the Present Value of the Future Revenue Sharing (Line 50) less the Start Up Costs (Line 48).

of the enterprise. There exists a strong relationship between NPV and IRR: A project with a positive NPV will, by necessity, have an IRR that exceeds the project's cost of capital, so long as the rate of discount applied in the NPV analysis equals the project's cost of capital. An important limitation of the IRR method is that it is possible for two projects to have identical IRRs but different NPVs, depending on the timing and magnitude of the expected cash flows and the size of the initial investment. In this type of situation, the IRR would provide no guidance in the selection between two projects. However, for the purposes of determining the feasibility of the ACO investment, the IRR and the NPV will be indistinguishable in their policy recommendations.

Key Term	Definition	Citation
Internal Rate of Return Method	A discount rate at which the net present value of an investment is zero. The IRR is a method of evaluating capital expenditure proposals.	*Dictionary of Health Insurance and Managed Care.* David E. Marcinko, Springer Publishing, New York, 2006, p. 161.

The IRR analysis for ACOs of various sizes, under a two-sided shared savings disbursement model, is shown in Table 7.12.

The IRR analysis for ACOs of various sizes, under a one-sided shared savings disbursement model, is shown in Table 7.13.

It should be noted that, in the above analysis, it is not possible to calculate a meaningful IRR in the absence of positive cash flows (cash flows sufficient to offset the initial required investment within the initial three-year ACO contract term). As a result, Table 7.12 and Table 7.13 do not include calculated IRRs for the smaller ACOs.

Further Feasibility Analysis

The above analysis was performed under the assumption that the ACO would be capable of achieving the maximum cost reduction shared revenue under the one- and two-sided disbursement models. Utilizing the NPV approach, as presented above, it also is possible to determine the minimum amount of cost reductions an enterprise would be required to achieve, over the initial three-year term of the ACO contract, to avoid a negative value impact for the overall enterprise (i.e., a negative NPV). Similar to the logic underlying the IRR, the anticipated level of cost reductions could be adjusted to the point that a zero NPV is produced. This level of cost reduction would represent a benchmark that healthcare entities considering ACO investment would have to exceed to anticipate a positive value impact to the ACO investment. The percent cost reductions necessary to achieve a zero net present value for an ACO investment under the "best case scenario" assumptions are presented in Figure 7.2.

Key Concept	Definition	Citation
Break-Even Analysis	Analysis of the level of sales at which a project would make zero profit.	*Corporate Finance,* 4th ed. Ross, Westerfield, Jaffe, and Roberts, Ontario, Canada: McGraw-Hill Ryerson, 2005, p. 938.

Enterprises considering investment in an ACO should assess whether the necessary cost reductions are attainable, given the number of beneficiaries they serve. This analysis confirms the conclusions of earlier evaluations, which indicate that larger ACOs have a higher likelihood of success. This scale advantage can be primarily attributed to the ability of large ACOs to apply modest per beneficiary cost savings across a large number of beneficiaries.

TABLE 7.12
Internal Rate of Return Calculations for ACOs of Various Size Classifications: Two-Sided Model

	Small ACOs		Medium ACOs				Large ACOs		
Number of Medicare Beneficiaries	5,000	15,000	25,000	35,000	45,000	55,000	65,000	75,000	80,000
Average Expected Net Cash Flow	($300,000)	$2,039,625	$7,032,083	$14,677,375	$24,975,500	$37,926,458	$53,530,250	$71,786,875	$81,910,000
Startup Costs	$5,315,000	$6,206,333	$7,097,667	$7,989,000	$8,880,333	$9,771,667	$10,663,000	$11,554,333	$12,000,000
Internal Rate of Return			**82.88%**	**174.88%**	**275.95%**	**384.72%**	**499.69%**	**619.63%**	**681.15%**
Sum of the Discounted Net Cash Flows			$7,097,719	$7,988,942	$8,880,403	$9,771,636	$10,663,019	$11,554,355	$12,000,023
Net Present Value			$0	$0	$0	$0	$0	$0	$0

TABLE 7.13
Internal Rate of Return Calculations for ACOs of Various Size Classifications: One-Sided Model

	Small ACOs		Medium ACOs				Large ACOs		
Number of Medicare Beneficiaries	5,000	15,000	25,000	35,000	45,000	55,000	65,000	75,000	80,000
Average Expected Net Cash Flow	($2,300,000)	($3,960,375)	($2,967,917)	$677,375	$6,975,500	$15,926,458	$27,530,250	$41,786,875	$49,910,000
Startup Costs	$5,315,000	$6,206,333	$7,097,667	$7,989,000	$8,880,333	$9,771,667	$10,663,000	$11,554,333	$12,000,000
Internal Rate of Return					**59.01%**	**152.91%**	**252.28%**	**357.89%**	**412.83%**
Sum of the Discounted Net Cash Flows					$8,880,301	$9,771,726	$10,662,966	$11,554,278	$12,000,083
Net Present Value					$0	$0	$0	$0	$0

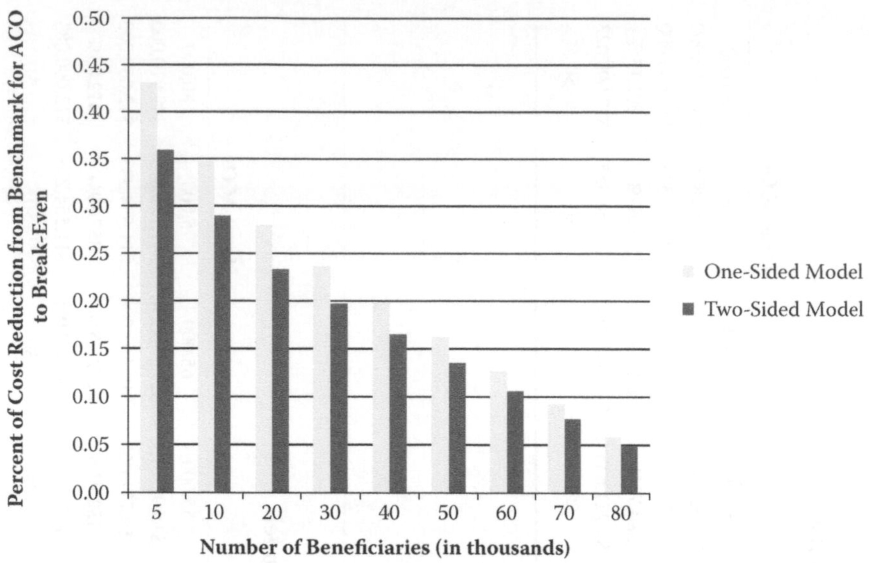

FIGURE 7.2 Break-even analysis for ACOs of various sizes.

CHAPTER SUMMARY

Developing ACO enterprises requires initial investments of capital in the areas of (1) network development and management; (2) care coordination, quality improvement, and utilization management; (3) clinical information systems; and (4) data analytics.

Those considering an investment in an ACO must seek to determine whether this investment will maximize the expected value of the enterprise to its stakeholders, i.e., investors/owners or beneficiaries in the community served, which includes consideration of both monetary and nonmonetary benefits and costs. Before undertaking an in-depth financial analysis of investment in an ACO, healthcare entities should carefully consider the economic and enterprisal impacts of the investment. Several metrics exist to assist the management of a healthcare enterprise in determining the financial feasibility of an ACO investment, including:

- Payback and discounted payback methods
- The average accounting rate of return (AARR)
- The net present value (NPV) method
- The internal rate of return (IRR) method

Generation of positive cash flow is a requisite, but not entirely sufficient, condition for the expectation of future value attributed to investment in an ACO project. An investment project that fails to generate positive net cash flow will not accumulate sufficient net economic benefit to offset the initial investment, although it is possible that indirect benefits may accrue to the stakeholders in the ACO.

The payback period method is one of the simplest methods to calculate value metrics for an investment such as an ACO. This method calculates the "expected number of years required to recover the original investment."[41] However, it does not consider the present value of the cash flows utilized in the analysis and, as a result, will tend to underestimate the true payback period. The discounted payback period method addresses this present value shortcoming by converting each cash flow into its present value equivalent by discounting at an appropriate risk-adjusted rate.[42]

An alternative metric for measuring the value impact of a capital budgeting project is the average accounting rate of return (AARR) method, which is calculated by dividing the average net income for the project by the initial investment cost.

Another useful metric for evaluating a projected likelihood of increasing the overall enterprise's value is the net present value (NPV) method, defined as the discounted value of the differences over time between monetary costs and benefits in each period.[43]

Similar to the NPV, the internal rate of return (IRR) method attempts to determine the rate of return that would render the NPV of the project equal to zero.[44] The IRR represents the maximum rate (in percentage) at which the project's investors could be compensated for the project to leave the value of the enterprise unchanged.

An analysis using these methods indicates that larger ACOs have a higher probability of success, most likely due to the effect of an economy of scale in that they can apply modest per beneficiary cost savings across a larger beneficiary population.

ENDNOTES

1. *The Right Stuff*. Tom Wolfe and Philip Kaufman, 1983 motion picture; based on *The Right Stuff*. Tom Wolfe, New York: Picador, 1979.
2. *The Work Ahead: Activities and Costs to Develop an Accountable Care Organization*. American Hospital Association, Chicago, (April 2011), p. 4.
3. Ibid.
4. Ibid., p. 5.
5. Ibid., p. 7.
6. Ibid., p. 6.
7. Ibid., p. 5.
8. Ibid.
9. Ibid., p. 7.
10. Ibid., p. 8.
11. Ibid.
12. Ibid., p. 6.
13. Ibid., p. 9.
14. Ibid., p. 10.
15. Ibid., p. 9.
16. Ibid.
17. Ibid., p. 10.
18. Ibid., pp. 13, 16.
19. Ibid., p. 10.
20. On the Plane Geometry with Generalized Absolute Value Metric. A. Bayar, et al., in *Mathematical Problems in Engineering*. New York: Hindawi Publishing, 2008, pp. 1, 4.
21. *PEM: A Framework Enabling Continual Optimization of Workflow Process Executions Based upon Business Value Metrics*. Melissa J. Buco, et al., paper presented at the 2005 IEEE International Conference on Services Computing (SCC'05), Orlando, FL, July 2005, p. 2.
22. Defining Risk Appetite. Sim Segal, *Journal of Risk Management*, July 2006, p. 19.
23. *Defining and Delivering Value*. Healthcare Financial Management Association, Westchester, IL, June 2012, p. 1.
24. Medicare Program; Medicare Shared Savings Program: Accountable Care Organizations. *Federal Register* vol. 76, no. 212, (November 2, 2011), pp. 67986–67987; Table 16: Per Enrollee Expenditures and Average Annual Percent Change in Medicare Spending and in Private Health Insurance Premiums, Calendar Years 1969–2010. In *National Health Expenditures Tables, Centers for Medicare and Medicaid Services, 2011*. Online at: https://www.cms.gov/Research-Statistics-Data-and-Systems/Statistics-Trends-and-Reports/NationalHealthExpendData/Downloads/tables.pdf (Accessed 4/19/2012).
25. Medicare Program; Medicare Shared Savings Program: Accountable Care Organizations, pp. 67986–67987.

26. Ibid.
27. Ibid.
28. Ibid.
29. Ibid.
30. Please note, due to the short time frame of this analysis (three years) and the uncertainty related to future adjustments to the cost benchmarks utilized to determine the cost sharing revenue, ACO cost projections do not include an adjustment for anticipated inflation.
31. Medicare Program; Medicare Shared Savings Program: Accountable Care Organizations, p. 67987; *The Work Ahead: Activities and Costs to Develop an Accountable Care Organization*, pp. 11–16.
32. Ibid.; Ibid.
33. *Essentials of Managerial Finance*, 9th ed. J. Fred Weston and Eugene F. Brigham, 1990, Chicago: The Dryden Press, p. 564.
34. *Dictionary of Health Economics and Finance*. David Edward Marcinko and Hope Rachel Hetico, New York: Springer Publishing, 2007, p. 359.
35. *Corporate Finance*, 4th ed. Ross, Westerfield, Jaffe, and Roberts, Ontario, Canada: McGraw-Hill Ryerson, 2005, p. 942.
36. *The Dictionary of Health Economics*, 2nd ed. Anthony J. Culyer, Northampton, MA: Edward Elgar Publishing Limited, 2010, p. 347.
37. Capital Planning for Clinical Integrations. Daniel M. Grauman, et al., *Healthcare Financial Management Association Journal,* vol. 65, no. 4 (April 2011 reprinted), p. 5.
38. See Table 7.7, The anticipated annual cash flow for a federal ACO, based on the number of Medicare beneficiaries served: One-sided model; Endnote 10.
39. It should be noted that the WACC utilized in this analysis is based on industry norms, as reported in the Ibbotson *2011 Cost of Capital Yearbook* and the Ibbotson *SBBI 2012 Valuation Yearbook.* As such, the WACC calculated above may not be reflective of the actual cost of capital for a specific investor in an ACO, and significant changes to the utilized WACC may materially alter the results of the NPV analysis.
40. *Dictionary of Health Insurance and Managed Care*. David Marcinko, New York: Springer Publishing Group, 2006, p. 161.
41. *Essentials of Managerial Finance*.
42. *Corporate Finance*.
43. *The Dictionary of Health Economics*.
44. *Dictionary of Health Insurance and Managed Care*.

Acronyms

Acronym	Definition
AARR	Average Accounting Rate of Return
ACO	Accountable Care Organization
CMS	Centers for Medicare and Medicaid Services
HIT	Healthcare Information Technology
IRR	Internal Rate of Return
MSR	Minimum Savings Rate
MSSP	Medicare Shared Savings Program
NPV	Net Present Value

8 Considerations of Value for the Positive Externalities of ACOs

Healthcare industry stakeholders have consistently disagreed over the relative costs and potential benefits of ACOs. Notwithstanding this uncertainty, there is growing support for the position that the ACO concept has value, if not the current proposed structures for ACOs and their implementation and operation. Outside of the potential of financial return to investors from ACO development (as discussed in the previous chapter), an ACO also is likely to have nondirect investment-related beneficial effects for third parties. These external benefits received by third parties are known as *positive externalities,* which occur when a third party has a legitimate interest in a particular outcome.[1] For the purposes of this chapter, the outcome addressed is the successful development and implementation of ACOs, by which value may accrue to third parties including patients, employers, and the broader U.S. population (SOCIETY); health systems, hospitals, and physicians (PROVIDERS); and managed care organizations, commercial insurers, and Medicare (PAYORS). Each of these third parties may benefit from ACOs, in which benefits may be differentiated between monetary and nonmonetary.

Key Term	Definition	Citation
Positive externalities	Positive effects or benefits on third parties (e.g., society, providers, or payors).	*Health Care Economics,* 6th ed. Paul J. Feldstein, Clifton Park, NY: Thomson Delmar Learning, 2005, p. 424.

DEFINING VALUE

> Desires and interests are, as we have seen, themselves causal conditions of results. As such, they are potential means and have to be appraised as well. ... There is an indefinite number of proverbial sayings, which, in effect, set forth the necessity of not treating desires and interests as final in their first appearance but of treating them as means—that is, of appraising them and forming objects or ends-in-view on the ground of what consequences they will tend to produce in practice. ... They are summed up in the old saying, *Respice finem,* a saying which marks the difference between simply having end-in-view for which any desires suffices, and looking, examining, to make sure that the consequences that will actually result are such as will be actually prized and valued when they occur.[2]
>
> **John Dewey**
> *Theory of Valuation, 1939*

All value is the expectation of future benefit.[3] In the healthcare industry, this expectation of future benefit, on an economic basis, can be measured as "health outcomes achieved per dollar spent."[4] A visual depiction of the measurement of the expectation of future economic benefit in the healthcare industry is illustrated in Figure 8.1.

Key Concept	Definition	Citation
Value	The expectation of future economic benefit. In the healthcare industry, this is measured by "health outcomes achieved per dollar spent."	What Is Value in Health Care? Michael E. Porter, *The New England Journal of Medicine,* December 23, 2010. Online at: http://www.nejm.org/doi/full/10.1056/NEJMp1011024 (Accessed 11/22/11).

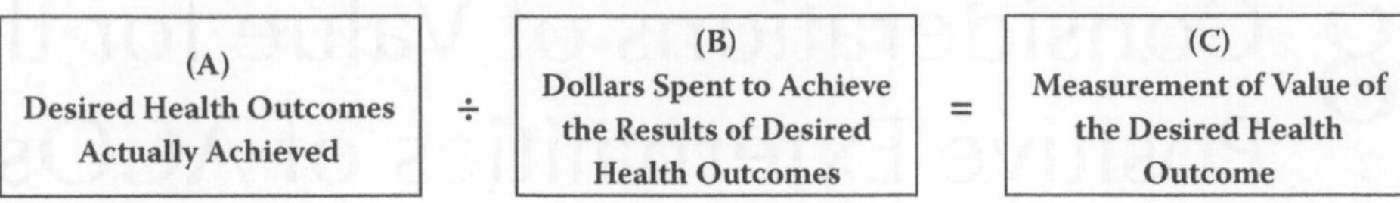

FIGURE 8.1 Measurement of the expectation of value in healthcare.

The equation in Figure 8.1 represents a means by which the value of the externalities associated with ACO development can be measured. Health outcomes may refer to a variety of healthcare activities specifying the type of benefit (or value) an ACO can include. The equation also may be utilized to track changing trends in value for various healthcare activities. For example, consider the benefit to be derived from the desired outcome of lowering the prevalence of a chronic disease for a specified patient population within an ACO:

$$(A_1 \div B_1) - (A_2 \div B_2) = C$$

A_1 = Chronic Disease Rate in Year 1 of ACO Development
B_1 = Dollars Spent in Year 1 Resulting in the Disease Rate
A_2 = Chronic Disease Rate in Year 2 of ACO Development
B_2 = Dollars Spent in Year 2 Resulting in the Disease Rate
C = Change in Value

Over time, the calculated change in value (which may be monetary or nonmonetary benefits) could be used to draw conclusions as to the trends in the value offered by ACO development for population health, as indicated by the chosen chronic disease.

Key Term	Definition	Citation
Benchmark	Derived from similar processes or services in an industry, competitors, or internal organization in order to set a level of care as a goal to be attained.	Glossary of Terms Commonly Used in Health Care. *AcademyHealth,* 2004 edition, Agency for Healthcare Research and Quality, U.S. Dept. of HHS.

Within this example, the initial measure of value acts as an internal benchmark against which a specific ACO's success or failure going forward can be measured. Value measurement also can be compared to external benchmarks to assess an ACO's positive externalities against a population (e.g., regional, state, national) or a competitor.[5] These external benchmarks allow population health outcomes, and their values, to be considered within a larger scope. In both the federal and commercial ACO markets, payors have distinguished which outcomes are monitored, which may impact the broad health outcomes that will be used to define overall ACO value.

Within the federal ACO market, the Centers for Medicare and Medicaid Services (CMS) have chosen three overall measures of ACO value. These values mimic the three-part aim of healthcare reform legislation,[6] and also are echoed in the Medicare Shared Savings Program (MSSP) legislation: "(1) better care for individuals. (2) better health for populations. and (3) lower growth in [Medicare] expenditures."[7] Many commercial ACOs have followed their federal counterparts, adopting a parallel three-pronged approach to defining value. For example, Premier ACO Collaboratives[8] define the value that may be attained through ACO development to include: (1) "population health status," (2) "the patient's care experience," and (3) "total cost of care."[9] Northwest Metro Alliance,[10] a collaboration of physicians, hospitals, and clinics, indicated a similar approach, stating that its ACO "focused on achieving the 'Triple Aim' of healthcare" and defined the triple aim as "high quality care, exceptional patient experience, and affordability."[11]

Key Concept	Definition	Citation
Three-part aim of healthcare reform legislation	(1) Better care for individuals, (2) better health for populations, and (3) lower growth in Medicare expenditures.	Medicare Program; Medicare Shared Savings Program: Accountable Care Organizations, Final Rule, *Federal Register,* vol. 76, no. 112 (November 2, 2011), p. 67803.

Each prong of the three-part aim can be appropriated into smaller scopes of value (i.e., based on specific health outcomes) depending on how an ACO chooses to quantify value. An ACO may measure the value of better care for individuals by tracking health quality outcomes for each of the 33 quality metrics required by CMS per dollar spent to actually achieve them. The benefit of ACO development on population health may be assessed by noting changes in any combination of health outcomes, including:

- Admissions rates per dollar spent
- Health literacy rates per dollar spent
- Obesity rates per dollar spent

Key Concept	Definition
Nonmonetary value	Value as measured by quality or outcome improvements.

Similarly, monetary data can be sorted to track:

- Administrative cost reductions per dollar spent
- Clinical cost reductions per dollar spent
- Federal spending reductions per dollar spent

Key Concept	Definition
Monetary value	Value usually observed in the form of cost reductions or lower overall expenditures.

Whether operating under a federal or a commercial contract, an ACO's overall achievement of specific outcomes, tracked and reported, will provide evidence of the creation of value (i.e., future economic benefit within the U.S. healthcare delivery system) in the form of improved outcomes per dollar spent. Remember that, in addition to examining the impact of the value of ACOs from the perspective of variations in scope, the benefit of an ACO also can be differentiated between monetary and nonmonetary gains. Each benefited third party (i.e., SOCIETY, PROVIDERS, and PAYORS) has the potential to experience both types of benefit.

VALUE TO SOCIETY

Key Concept	Definition
Value to society	The interest held based on the perceived future benefits that will be contributed to society as a whole.

The interest(s) held by SOCIETY in the development and implementation of ACOs represents a positive social externality. The value that an ACO conveys to SOCIETY can be described as the perceived future benefits that ACOs will contribute to the U.S. patient population, or a subpopulation. Especially important when identifying and establishing the scope of a positive externality within a large external group is the appropriate selection of defined measures of comparison, e.g., benchmarking health outcomes against industry norms and historical trends that must be in place in order to quantify the value added by ACOs. Benchmarks for patient populations, before and after ACO development, on both a regional and/or national level, are useful in determining the existence of statistically significant evidence of improved population health outcomes, which can be used as an indication of whether an ACO has truly added societal value.

Monetary Value

The monetary societal value received from ACOs will likely be observed in the form of cost reductions. Efficiencies achieved by ACOs and the effects of coordinated care may benefit society in the form of:

1. Cost reductions for patient populations[12]
2. Cost reductions for the community that an ACO serves
3. Lower overall healthcare expenditures as a percentage of gross domestic product (GDP)
4. Slowing of the current national growth of healthcare expenditures

Cost of Healthcare

As referenced in Chapter 1, (1) the cost of healthcare in the United States has been increasing at a dramatic rate and is currently nearing 18% of U.S. GDP (gross domestic product), (2) there is a growing national sentiment that current health outcomes achieved are not commensurate with each dollar spent,[13] and (3) recent increases in spending have not been accompanied by improvements in outcomes.[14] Within the current healthcare environment, if value is regarded as outcomes achieved per dollar spent, then the value of healthcare to society has clearly been perceived as decreasing.[15] ACOs are being implemented in both the public and private healthcare sectors (in part) to respond to societal demands that the value of healthcare, in terms of a cost-benefit relationship, be improved. As the largest single purchaser of healthcare in the United States, accounting for 23% of personal health expenditures in 2009, Medicare spending has been a particular target for limiting growth in healthcare spending.[16]

Factoids 8.1

The cost of healthcare in the Unites States has been increasing at a dramatic rate and is currently nearing 20% of U.S. GDP. (Source: Why Not the Best? Results from a National Scorecard on U.S. Health System Performance. *The Commonwealth Fund,* September 2006. Online at: http://www.commonwealthfund.org/~/media/Files/Publications/In%20the%20Literature/2006/Sep/U%20S%20%20Health%20System%20Performance%20%20A%20National%20Scorecard/951_Commission_why_not_the_best%20pdf.pdf (Accessed 2/1/12).)

CMS has estimated that the MSSP alone could generate $940 million in federal healthcare expenditure reductions.[17] Lower costs for the Medicare program may have a significant effect on the growth of overall healthcare expenditures because spending for the Medicare program is projected to expand dramatically over the next 25 years, due to demographic changes (e.g., the admittance of an aging baby boomer population into Medicare eligibility). This estimated increase in spending may be constrained through ACO development by allowing the Medicare program to more efficiently manage the current and anticipated surge of aging Medicare participants. While ACOs may provide monetary value for governmental payors, it is unclear whether smaller populations will experience similar positive externalities.

Factoid 8.2

Medicare is the largest single purchaser of healthcare in the United States, accounting for 23% of personal health expenditures in 2009. (Source: *A Data Book: Health Care Spending and the Medicare Program*. Medicare Payment Advisory Commission, June 2010, p. 5.)

Key Concept	Definition	Citation
Negative externalities	Negative effects or costs for third parties (e.g., society, providers, or payors).	*Health Care Economics*, 6th ed. Paul J. Feldstein, Clifton Park, NY: Thomson Delmar Learning, 2005, p. 424.

While ACOs offer the potential for positive externalities that indicate societal value, ACOs may also create negative externalities, whereby a third party has a disinterest in the development of an ACO,[18] e.g., when development would lead to an incurred cost for the third party. Even though ACOs incentivize lowering patient expenditures by providers, it has yet to be seen whether these cost reductions trickle down to lower expenses for patients or the community served by an ACO.[19] Lacking any mandate for the distribution of shared payments to patients, the monetary societal value for patients will necessarily be dependent on the altruism of providers and/or insurers to apply these shared payments in lowering the costs borne by patients, an event that providers and insurers have not traditionally been inclined to do. If patient costs remain stagnant, patients will not share in the benefits of ACO development, and may be indifferent toward ACOs. However, if patients experience price inflation as a result of increased provider market leverage, ACO development would result in a negative externality to the patient. This may become a realized concern, as historically, lower costs for businesses, resulting from greater size and market leverage, have resulted in higher costs for consumers.[20] If patients do not experience cost savings from ACOs, a large component of ACOs societal value will not be achieved.

Productivity Measures

A significant contributor to the monetary value employers receive from their employees is based on levels of productivity, i.e., the amount of work product an employee produces in a given amount of time. While variations exist between the levels of productivity achieved by individual employees, lost productivity time is greatly impacted by the incidence of illness within an employed population. Lost work due to illness results in approximately $225.8 billion in losses per year for employers ($1,685 per employee per year).[21] Across industries, as the prevalence of chronic diseases increases, health-related loss of productivity also is likely to climb.[22] ACOs aim to improve quality outcomes and lower beneficiary expenditures, each of which may have a positive impact on population health (see below). If employee populations succumb to lower rates of illness resulting in fewer health-based losses in productivity, employers will receive a significant benefit from ACO development. Additionally, greater efficiency in healthcare delivery models, e.g., healthcare information technology (HIT) and improved process management, should result in maximizing productivity rates among healthcare employees, adding monetary societal value.[23]

Nonmonetary Value

An ACO's nonmonetary societal value is characterized by the coordination of care leading to improved quality outcomes and greater access to care, two of the three aims of healthcare reform, and of ACOs. ACOs aim to create value, as measured by quality outcome improvements, through regulation of quality reporting and changes in reimbursement policy. Societal value, as measured by increased population access to care, may be most significantly affected by an ACO's ability to provide access to high quality preventative, primary, and specialist services to all patients across the continuum of care.

Quality of Care

Whether governed under the MSSP, or under private contracts between providers and payors, an ACO must assess the quality of care its beneficiaries receive using a defined set of quality metrics and benchmarks in order to qualify for incentive payments. The MSSP mandates that federal ACOs measure and report on 33 quality outcomes, (see Chapter 2, section MSSP Final Rule). Regulated by CMS, these health outcomes are standardized across all ACOs participating in the MSSP, making them easier to compare.[24] In addition to measures of health outcomes, both patients and providers, under the MSSP, will be required by CMS to survey patients to generate patient satisfaction data. Satisfaction surveys aim to address patient perceptions regarding access to providers and communication with physicians. These patient perception quality metrics are a portion of the MSSP-mandated quality measures.[25]

Key Term	Definition	Citation
National Committee for Quality Assurance (NCQA)	Founded in 1979 to accredit and coordinate quality assurance programs in managed care organizations.	Glossary of Terms Commonly Used in Health Care. *AcademyHealth,* 2004 edition, Agency for Healthcare Research and Quality, U.S. Dept. HHS.

Although commercial ACOs could potentially have extreme variation of quality measures among individually agreed upon contracts, the private market may choose, at least initially, to simply utilize standardized measures recently made available for public reporting. The National Committee for Quality Assurance (NCQA) Accountable Care Accreditation program (see Chapter 3, section Quality and Other Reporting Requirements), which governs all ACOs, has set standards for quality metrics that are used to determine whether an ACO attains accreditation. These standards may establish some systematic quality outcome metrics to be measured and reported by ACOs within both federal and commercial markets. Despite potential inconsistencies, various transparency initiatives within the healthcare industry (e.g., the hospital value-based purchasing program) may require all ACOs to submit comparable regional and national public reporting data.[26]

The commercial market follows similar publication guidelines. The Cleveland Clinic's Department of Quality reports the aggregated quality outcomes data to four public reporting programs that, in turn, publish quality reports, including the Joint Commission Performance Measurement Initiative, the CMS Hospital Compare Web site, the Ohio Department of Health, and the Cleveland Clinic Quality Performance Report.[27] Increased transparency through publication may provide a more accurate assessment of the societal value of ACOs. Quality metrics also may be influenced and fostered by emerging trends in reimbursement within the commercial ACO market.

Under the MSSP, ACOs will be reimbursed under a traditional fee-for-service (FFS) model, and shared savings payments will be used to incentivize quality improvements. FFS models traditionally incentivize volume of patients treated, in contrast to the value of care (i.e., quality of care per dollar spent) given to patients. In addition to possible shared savings payments based on expenditure reductions, private payors are experimenting with alternative reimbursement structures that emphasize value-based purchasing that shift a portion of the financial risk from the insurer to the provider. The various forms of risk-sharing reimbursement models are detailed in Chapter 5. While shared risk models are still in their infancy in the healthcare industry, they have their roots in shared savings programs like those associated with ACOs, and have the potential to significantly influence positive quality value outcomes.[28] Quality is the primary nonmonetary societal focus of ACOs, but other nonmonetary externalities, such as access to care, may also impact societal value.

Access to Care

Although ACOs are not directly linked to the current initiatives attempting to increase healthcare access (i.e., expanding Medicaid coverage or increasing the number of insured), they may have a significant effect on participating patients' access to primary care, preventative care, and specialist referrals as a function of their focus on coordinating patient care. Studies presenting data on the number of individuals nationwide, and in various regions of the United States, who receive insufficient care, could provide a means of assessing the value (i.e., increased access per dollar spent) of ACO development for distinct types of care. Additionally, as ACOs become more efficient, it is anticipated that providers may be able to manage larger patient volumes, consequently expanding access to care.

When assessing value, selection of appropriate benchmark statistics is imperative. Measurements indicating low access to care due to lack of insurance within a population would be an ill-fitted benchmark for ACO value assessments. ACO development will likely have little influence on the level of insurance coverage in the United States; therefore, improvements in access resulting from a greater number of insured may skew quantifications of ACO value. Choosing appropriate benchmarks is a concern for any type of value being examined.

Even successful ACOs have the potential to generate negative externalities concerning societal access to healthcare, e.g., limiting access to care. Current ACO development suggests that ACOs tend to cluster in similar geographic areas.[29] ACO governing boards should be watchful for potential negative impacts on low-income populations, which traditionally lack access to care, because ACO development may not occur in these areas, exacerbating health disparity issues in underserved areas. Further, ACOs may reinforce disparities by funneling patients from specific ethnic groups into one ACO, and targeting patients with historically high health statuses, to maximize financial incentives.[30] The perception of the level of societal value ACO development can provide, in regards to public health population needs, may be influenced by the ACO's impact on these vulnerable populations.

VALUE TO PROVIDERS

Key Concept	Definition
Value to providers	Interest in the form of potential return on investment, bonus payments, and indirect monetary benefits from efficiency improvements and nonmonetary benefits, such as increased autonomy and increased access to resources.

In considering the benefits, PROVIDERS may have diverse viewpoints on the perception of value. Some may be investors or owners, focusing on financial feasibility analyses similar to those provided by Chapter 7, while others may be ACO participants who may have an interest in the outcomes of ACO development and the possible monetary and nonmonetary positive externalities. While the benefits providers may receive from ACO development are discussed in the following sections, a specific breakdown by type of provider is shown in Table 8.1 and Table 8.2.[31]

MONETARY VALUE

ACO entities receive monetary value from ACO development from returns on ACO investments resulting from shared savings payments or improved efficiencies. ACOs may opt to disburse shared savings in excess of capital needs to ACO providers in the form of financial bonuses, thereby also disbursing the monetary value. Providers do not need to be directly employed by the ACOs to receive a portion of shared savings, nor do they need to be physicians, but it can include a variety of types and levels of employees.[32] The ACO governing board has the discretion to determine which

TABLE 8.1
Value to Professional Providers

		Professionals			
		Physicians	**Allied Health Professionals**	**Midlevel Providers**	**Technologists**
Federal	Economic	• Increased income based on health outcomes of assigned patients • Flexibility to participate in multiple ACOs, as long as physician complies with exclusivity guidelines[b]	• Potential increased income based on monetary measures[a] • Ability to participate in provider panels	• Potential increased income based on quality care measures[a] • Flexibility to participate in multiple ACOs, as long as midlevel provider complies with exclusivity guidelines[b]	• Importance of EHR adoption to success in quality measures direct impact on incentive based reimbursement
	Noneconomic	• Enhanced management and individualized treatment of chronic diseases in special populations • Efficient preappointment protocols to streamline appointments and expand face-to-face interaction with patient	• Care and disease management centered on individual patient needs involving family members • ACO participants required to have "*meaningful participation*" in ACO governing body	• Potentially higher patient volume and utilization if incorporated into participating ACO model • ACO participants required to have "*meaningful participation*" in ACO governing body	• Significant role in managing patient data systems to meet triple aims of ACO model • More lenient criteria for implementing EHRs into smaller ACO models • Increased usage of EHRs in ACOs
Commercial	Economic	• Compensation reflects individual contribution to quality care • Increased income based on incentive based quality measurements	• Compensation reflects individual contribution to quality care • Ability to participate in provider panels	• Increased compensation for quality care and health outcomes	• Integral component in efficient, cost-saving care across various divided components of the ACO model
	Noneconomic	• Improved quality of care through collaboration with supporting organizations	• Increased recognition and authority to impact patient management	• Increased recognition and authority to impact patient management	• Support clinical staff in efficient use of data systems for efficient care, and increased continuity of care • Increased usage of EHRs in ACOs

[a] Contingent on physician's decision to distribute potential reimbursement based on quality measures.
[b] Participating in multiple ACOs must comply with CMS's exclusivity guidelines pertaining to use of tax identification numbers (TINs) outlined in the final ACO rule.

TABLE 8.2
Value to Institutional Providers

		Institutions			
		Hospitals	**Practices**	**Long-Term Care**	**Home Health**
Federal	Economic	• Decreased financial risk in pursuing ACO model • Financial reimbursement based on quality measures • Increased revenue based on high quality scores	• Less financial risk in implementing potential ACO framework • Potential for expanded revenue through incentive-based quality measure payments • Increased revenue based on high quality scores	• Continuity of care and collaboration with primary providers decreases costs of care by increasing efficiency	• Continuity of care and collaboration with primary providers decreases costs of care by increasing efficiency
	Noneconomic	• Improved health outcomes on recorded quality measures • Individualized care and attention for chronic diseases in special populations	• Better health outcomes for patients, and increased care efficiency • Structural flexibility in individual composition of ACO model	• Better health outcomes based on strengthened relationships with local hospitals, participating in federal ACOs, and continuity of care through shared information	• Improved patient health outcomes by joining an eligible ACO model • Better continuity of care between inpatient and outpatient facilities
Commercial	Economic	• Cost savings through collaboration, efficiency, and partnerships • Reduce administrative waste and inefficiencies to cut expenses	• Incorporation into larger system through acquisition • Potential for increased overall revenue and profits when drawing resources from affiliated system	• Efficient use of existing information from long-term care in the event of acute inpatient episode, lowering costs	• Fewer errors and test duplication leads to overall cost savings
	Noneconomic	• Better overall health outcomes for patients participating in the ACO collaborative model	• Increased utilization of network resources and capital	• Better health outcomes through more involved disease management techniques (i.e., health coaches, etc.)	• Follow-up care involving patient family members to better health outcomes through accountability • Knowledge of difficulties transitioning from inpatient care to unique home health needs

providers will be included in shared savings distributions. Some commercial ACOs also provide direct monetary value to participating providers in the form of value-based reimbursement models and physician compensation arrangements, which are more common in ACOs with an internal payor.

ACOs that achieve shared savings, either in the commercial or the federal market, also likely will experience greater financial returns from the increased efficiency of their practice (e.g., lower administrative costs, more efficient physician time management, and fewer billing mistakes).[33] Providers also may experience enhanced utility in the form of access to a larger market share because ACO development is often associated with mergers, joint ventures, and other methods of market consolidation. As physicians and hospitals in a community join together under the umbrella of an ACO, referrals will likely stay within that collaboration of caregivers.[34] The positive externalities associated with consolidation may be nonmonetary as well.

NONMONETARY VALUE

ACO development is a driver of continued hospital acquisition of employed physicians. Nonmonetary value for ACO participants is largely characterized by those benefits that may arise from a hospital–physician relationship as well as the level of participation in governance and increased access to expand provider and patient network by the ACO model.

Style of Practice

From a physician perspective, hospital employment provides value through decreased financial risk and more desirable work-life balance.[35] This change in the style of practice aligns with recent demographic shifts related to age and gender. Mimicking national population trends, the physician population is aging and diversifying. A greater percentage of physicians are over 55 years of age, and the number of female physicians is increasing.[36] These changing demographics influence providers' perceptions of value. Whereas in the past, providers generally valued profits over personal time, today's providers are prioritizing a more flexible work-life balance. In addition to work-life balance improvements, ACOs may provide greater practice efficiencies by providing access to advanced levels of technology.

Key Term	Definition
Best Practices	Providers can use ACO comparative analyses to evaluate strengths and weaknesses of practices in order to develop best practices, which lead to greater efficiencies.

Access to sophisticated technology allows physicians to access information on outcomes, a benchmark as well as an ability to evaluate their services in greater depth than previous paper and pencil processes. Particularly within the commercial market, where value-based reimbursement models impact physician compensation, financial incentives provide physicians with a motivation to lower individual expenditures resulting in direct monetary value to providers participating in an ACO. Improvements in the ability of providers to gather data for evidence-based medicine also may lead to better development of best practices based on the strengths and weaknesses that become apparent from a comparative outcome analyses. Greater efficiencies gained from best practices could result in both monetary (i.e., lower administrative costs and fewer billing errors) and nonmonetary (i.e., better patient outcomes leading to improved reputation and lessened stress resulting from inefficient practice behaviors) value for physicians. Some commercial ACOs provide their participating providers with outcome reports to facilitate the use of evidence-based strategic planning. Within Cigna's Collaborative Accountable Care program, each participating provider practice receives an annual report, which assesses the provider's performance in the areas of patient access, care coordination, adherence to evidence-based medicine, prescribing practices, and value-based referrals.[37] Provider awareness of ACO efficiencies is of particular importance to give ACOs an emphasis on physician leadership and involvement.

Autonomy

ACOs may allow physicians to maintain a greater degree of autonomy than was the case in past managed care models, where physicians traditionally relinquished practice autonomy in exchange for the benefits of hospital employment.[38] The typical ACO depends on the independent decision making of providers by allowing physicians to direct care for their patients and encouraging all participants to contribute to ACO management. The MSSP specifically mandates that "the ACO must provide for meaningful participation in the composition and control of the ACO's governing body for the ACO participants."[39]

ACOs in both commercial and federal markets may need to embrace the necessity of physician leadership and set up guidelines to ensure physician autonomy. The Joint Principles for Accountable Care Organizations include a provision on autonomy, stating that, "[t]he Accountable Care Organization should demonstrate strong leadership from among physicians and other healthcare professionals … in its administrative structure, policy development, and decision-making processes; clinical integration in the provision of care. …"[40] Buy-in to the ACO governance principals for every physician provider participating may significantly influence the potential value offered by ACO development. Even those physician providers who are not directly involved in governance may benefit from the expanded and closer network created through the integration of providers from ACO development.

Access to Expanding Social Networks

Social capital can be broadly defined as: "… access to and use of resources embedded in social networks."[41] Value from social capital can be quantified by viewing the returns from investments in social relations. ACOs function as a large network of providers. Clinical and administrative integration may facilitate a flow of information that offers providers insight into new opportunities and efficiencies.[42] Providers may experience both monetary and nonmonetary value when they utilize sociostructural resources to obtain better outcomes.[43]

Although some critics have claimed that social capital is not quantifiable, others have viewed the value of networks as a comparative study of what a participant may be able to achieve in one network as opposed to another.[44] Despite concerns regarding quantification, several effective techniques do exist for measuring the strength of a network (e.g., saturation surveys) based on network resources, contact statuses, and an individual's strength of connection to the network.[45]

VALUE TO PAYORS

Key Concept	Definition
Value to payors	Primarily monetary benefits including the value of increased profits from shared savings and lower reimbursement expenditures.

PAYOR interest in ACO development will likely be primarily monetary, i.e., the value of increased profits from shared savings and lower reimbursement expenditures. Nonmonetary value may be indirect, with ACOs affecting payors' market power within the healthcare industry.

Monetary Value

Contracting between ACOs and payors allows for both parties to benefit from shared savings. A portion of the benefit realized from patient expenditure reductions achieved by an ACO will be kept by the associated payor. Ultimately, as ACOs gain efficiency and their benchmark for anticipated patient expenditures is reduced, it is expected that payors may be able to lower their reimbursement payments to the ACO. Within the federal ACO market, where CMS is the payor that contracts with an ACO, improved ACO patient outcomes may create additional monetary value for CMS, over and above CMS's portion of the shared savings, by leading to fewer administrative complications regarding billing and readmissions. Private payors with similar claims and readmission issues also may experience similar value. Payors that expand into the healthcare service industry may sustain additional value, discussed above in the section on value to providers, including potential return on investment, efficiencies, and productivity gains.

Nonmonetary Value

The aligned incentives of pursuing shared saving from the development of ACOs creates an incentive for establishing a more cooperative lens by providers viewing payors, who have traditionally been perceived as more interested in their own monetary gains than patient health, or provider feasibility.[46] In addition to being on the forefront of a restructuring of the healthcare delivery system, ACOs have provided payors with an outlet to expand into clinical services, offering them more control and greater market leverage. While the value of reputation is difficult to benchmark and, therefore, difficult to quantify, overall trends may indicate the value of improved benefit to payor reputation over time.

Value is contingent on the ACO model's long-term success or failure and its ability to translate success into monetary benefits (i.e., shared savings payments) or savings directly to society, providers, and payors. The existence of these external benefits may provide the impetus to invest in ACOs, even in the absence of immediate, direct monetary benefits.

CHAPTER SUMMARY

All market decisions have the potential to affect parties outside of the immediate participants. These effects are known as externalities, and can be either positive or negative. The implementation of ACOs is likely to result in externalities for many third parties, including PROVIDERS, PAYORS, and SOCIETY. Whether these third parties experience positive externalities or negative externalities depends on whether they experience an increase in value or an increase in cost.

Many of the expected outcomes of ACO implementation are positive externalities. It is likely that the healthcare industry will experience value, as measured by "health outcomes achieved per dollar spent." Changes in this measurement of value may provide a way to analyze trends in the value to third parties correlated to ACOs development. Reporting requirements for federal ACOs established by CMS use such value metrics to analyze *individual care*, *population health,* and *reductions in expenditure growth.* These three value metrics have been mirrored by commercial ACOs in order to better understand improvements in outcomes per dollar spent. It is important to understand that the positive externalities potentially being created by ACOs are not limited to monetary value (i.e., added cash flows from shared savings, effects on the cost of healthcare, effects on the percentage of GDP (gross domestic product) spent on healthcare, and effects on productivity). Nonmonetary value may be associated with improvements to the quality of care, increases in access to care, greater physician autonomy than typically provided in employment arrangements, styles of practice more aligned with modern lifestyle consideration, and expanded social networks.

Not all externalities are positive, and ACOs may produce some negative impacts. It is possible that ACOs may not reduce costs for patients if the savings generated does not trickle down past providers. While stagnant costs for healthcare services represent a neutral impact, increases in costs for patients would be a negative externality. Understanding which situations may result in negative externalities allows policy makers and providers to appropriately avoid such circumstance, thereby increasing the overall value attribute to ACO development. Measurement of outcomes data, in addition to every area of ACO development, may benefit from a consultant's expert opinion, which is addressed in Chapter 9.

ENDNOTES

1. *Health Care Economics*, 6th ed. Paul J. Feldstein, Clifton Park, NY: Thomson Delmar Learning, 2005, p. 424.
2. *Theory of Valuation*. John Dewey, The University of Chicago Press, Chicago, 1966, p. 32–33.
3. *Valuing a Business: The Analysis and Appraisal of Closely Held Companies*, 4th ed. Shannon P. Pratt, Robert F. Reilly, and Robert P. Schweihs, New York: McGraw Hill, 2001, p. 40.
4. What is Value in Health Care? Michael E. Porter, *The New England Journal of Medicine*, vol. 363, no. 36, December 23, 2010, p. 2477.
5. *Benchmarking in Healthcare*, 2nd ed. Maria R. Aviles (ed.) Oakbrook Terrace, IL: Joint Commission Resources, 2012, pp. 1–4.
6. Patient Protection and Affordable Care Act, Public Law 111-148, (March 23, 2010).
7. Medicare Program; Medicare Shared Savings Program: Accountable Care Organizations, Final Rule, *Federal Register*, vol. 76, No. 212 (November 2, 2011), p. 67803.
8. Located in South Carolina, Premier ACO Collaborative is an alliance of hospitals and other healthcare facilities including 24 health systems and 80 hospitals. Hospitals That Don't Move on ACOs Risk Losing MD Referrals. *ACO Business News*, vol. 1, no. 1, November 2010, p. 7.
9. *Premier ACO Collaboratives—Driving to a Patient-Centered Health System*. Premier, Inc., May 20, 2010. Online at: http://www.premierinc.com/about/news/10-may/aco-white-paper.pdf (Accessed 11/17/11), p. 4.
10. Located in Minnesota, Northwest Metro Alliance is an alliance between an IPA (Health Partners Medical Group) and a group of Health Facilities (Allina Hospitals and Clinics) and is self-described as a "learning lab for an Accountable Care Organization." *HealthPartners and Allina Hospitals and Clinics: Northwest Metro Alliance*. HealthPartners. Online at: http://www.healthpartners.com/ucm/groups/public/@hp/@public/documents/documents/cntrb_008919.pdf (Accessed 11/17/2011).
11. Ibid.
12. A Decade of Health Care Cost Growth Has Wiped Out Real Income Gains for an Average U.S. Family. David I. Auerbach and Arthur L. Kellermann, *Health Affairs*, vol. 30, no. 9, 2011, p. 1634.
13. *Why Not the Best? Results from a National Scorecard on U.S. Health System Performance*. The Commonwealth Fund, New York, September 2006, Online at: http://www.commonwealthfund.org/~/media/Files/Publications/In%20the%20Literature/2006/Sep/U%20S%20%20Health%20System%20Performance%20%20A%20National%20Scorecard/951_Commission_why_not_the_best%20pdf.pdf (Accessed 2/1/12).
14. *Valuing Health Care: Improving Productivity and Quality*. Kauffman Task Force on Cost-Effective Health Care Innovation, Kansas City, MO: Kauffman Foundation, April 2012, p. 3.
15. Is American Health Care Uniquely Inefficient? Alan M. Garber and Jonathan Skinner, *Journal of Economic Perspective,* vol. 22, no. 4 (September 2008), p. 37.
16. *A Data Book: Health Care Spending and the Medicare Program*. Medicare Payment Advisory Commission, June 2011, p. 5.
17. Next Steps for ACOs: Will This New Approach to Health Care Delivery Live Up to the Dual Promises of Reducing Costs and Improving Quality of Care. Robert A. Berenson and Rachel A. Burton, *Health Affairs*, January 31, 2012, p. 4.
18. *Health Care Economics*.
19. Health Care Industry Urged to Move on Accountable Care Organizations Now. Sara Hansard, *BNA's Health Law Reporter*, vol. 19, no. 933 (July 8, 2010).
20. *Accountable Care Organizations in Medicare and the Private Sector: A Status Update*. Robert A. Berenson and Rachel A. Burton, Robert Wood Johnson Foundation and Urban Institute, November 2011, pp. 8–9.
21. Lost Productive Work Time Costs from Health Conditions in the United States: Results from the American Productivity Audit. Walter F. Stewart, et al., *The Journal of Occupational and Environmental Medicine*, vol. 45, no. 12, December 2003, pp. 1239, 1241.

22. *Health and Productivity among U.S. Workers*. Karen Davis, et al., The Commonwealth Fund, Issue Brief, August 2005, p. 2.
23. *Valuing Health Care: Improving Productivity and Quality*, p. 58.
24. Medicare Program; Medicare Shared Savings Program: Accountable Care Organizations, Final Rule, pp. 67888–67890.
25. Ibid., p. 67891.
26. Medicare Program; Hospital Inpatient Value-Based Purchasing Program. *Federal Register*, vol. 76, no. 88, May 6, 2011, p. 26490.
27. *Heart and Vascular Institute: 2010 Outcomes*. Cleveland Clinic, 2010. Online at: http://my.clevelandclinic.org/Documents/outcomes/2010/oucomes-hvi-2010.pdf (Accessed 11/23/11).
28. *Promising Payment Reform: Risk-Sharing with Accountable Care Organizations*. Suzane F. Delbanco, The Commonwealth Fund, July 2011. Online at: http://www.commonwealthfund.org/~/media/Files/Publications/Fund%20Report/2011/Jul/1530Delbancopromisingpaymentreformrisksharing%202.pdf (Accessed 11/17/11), pp. vi–vii, 29.
29. *Growth and Dispersion of Accountable Care Organizations*. David Muhlestein, et al., Leavitt Partners, November 2011. Online at: http://pages.optify.net/aco-whitepaper (Accessed 3/22/2012), p. 6.
30. Accountable Care Organizations and Health Care Disparities. Craig Evan Pollack and Katrina Armstrong, *Journal of the American Medical Association*, vol. 305, no. 16, April 27, 2011, p. 1706; Hospitals' Geographic Expansion in Quest of Well-Insured Patients: Will the Outcome Be Better Care, More Cost, or Both? Emily R. Carrier, Marisa Dowling, and Robert A. Berenson, *Health Affairs*, vol. 31, no. 4, April 2012, p. 827.
31. Accountable Care Organizations, Explained. Jenny Gold, *Kaiser Health News*, Also on National Public Radio, January 18, 2011. Online at: http://www.npr.org/2011/04/01/132937232/accountable-care-organizations-explained (Accessed July 1, 2011); The Model of the Future? Avery Johnson, *The Wall Street Journal*, March 28,2011. Online at: http://online.wsj.com/article/SB10001424052748703300904576178213570447994.html (Accessed 5/14/2011); *ACO Case Study New West Physicians—Denver, Colorado*. Dean C. Coddington and Keith D. Moore, to American Hospital Association, Washington, D.C.: January, 2011, p. 4; Medicare Program; Medicare Shared Savings Program: Accountable Care Organizations, p. 67969; *Joint Principles for Accountable Care Organizations*. American Academy of Family Physicians, Press Release November 19, 2010. Online at: http://www.aafp.org/online/en/home/media/releases/2010b/aco-jointprinciples.html (Accessed 12/10/2010); *Medicare Physician Group Practice Demonstration: Physicians Groups Continue to Improve Quality and Generate Savings under Medicare Physician Pay-for-Performance Demonstration*. Centers for Medicare & Medicaid Services, July 2011. Online at: https://www.cms.gov/DemoProjectsEvalRpts/downloads/PGP_Fact_Sheet.pdf (Accessed 6/22/2011); Case Study of a Primary Care-Based Accountable Care System Approach to Medical Home Transformation. Robert L. Phillips, et al., *Journal of Ambulatory Care Management* vol. 34, no. 1, 2011, p. 69; Want Higher ACO Payments? Get Higher Quality Scores. Joseph Goedert, *Health Data Management Breaking News,* October 27, 2011. Online at: http://www.healthdatamanagement.com/news/aco-accountable-care-shared-savings-43503-1.html (Accessed 11/15/2011); *HHS Announces New Incentives for Providers to Work Together through Accountable Care Organizations When Caring for People with Medicare*. U.S. Department of Health and Human Services, News Release (October 20, 2011). Online at: http://www.hhs.gov/news/press/2011pres/10/20111020a.html (Accessed 11/18/2011); *Home Care Experts Weigh in on Accountable Care Organizations*. Tracy Body, et al., Nurse.com, November 7, 2011. Online at: http://news.nurse.com/article/20111107/NY01/111070060 (Accessed 11/18/2011); CMS Attempts to Reignite Interest in ACOs: Commentary on the Final Medicare Shared Savings Program Regulations. Thomas E. Bartrum, et al., *American Health Lawyers Association Connections*, vol. 15, no. 11, p. 23. Online at: http://www.healthlawyers.org/News/Connections/Documents/2011/November2011/Feature2_November2011.pdf (Accessed 11/18/2011).
32. Medicare Program; Medicare Shared Savings Program: Accountable Care Organizations. *Federal Register* vol. 76, no. 67, November 2, 2011, p. 67976.
33. *From Acquisition to Integration: Transforming a Hospital into an ACO*. John T. Fink and Sean Hartzel, Healthcare Financial Management Association, November 2010. Online at: http://hfma.org/templates/print.aspx?id=22988 (Accessed 3/12/2012), p. 3.
34. Referral and Consultation Communication between Primary Care and Specialists Physicians: Finding Common Ground. Ann O'Malley and James Reschovsky, *Archives of Internal Medicine*, vol. 171, no. 1, January 10, 2011, p. 64.
35. *The New Era for Hospital–Physician Alignment*. Healthcare Financial Management Association, Westchester, IL, January 2011, p. 2.

36. *Physician Characteristics and Distribution in the US: 2011 Edition*. American Medical Association, American Medical Association Press, 2011, p. 8.; *Physician Characteristics and Distribution in the US: 2012 Edition*. American Medical Association, American Medical Association Press, 2012, p. 8.
37. Collaborative Accountable Care: CIGNA's Approach to Accountable Care Organizations. CIGNA, Bloomfield, CT, April, 2011. Online at: http://newsroom.cigna.com/images/9022/media_gallery/knowledge_center/CollaborativeCare_WhitePaper_2011.pdf (Accessed 11/22/11) p. 5.
38. What's the Difference between an ACO and Managed Care? *Healthcare Economist*, August 23, 2011. Online at: http://healthcare-economist.com/2011/08/22/whats-the-difference-between-an-aco-and-managed-care/ (Accessed 2/1/12).
39. Medicare Program; Medicare Shared Savings Program: Accountable Care Organizations, Final Rule, p. 67976.
40. *Joint Principles for Accountable Care Organizations*. American Academy of Family Physicians, et al., November 17, 2010. Online at: http://www.acponline.org/advocacy/where_we_stand/other_issues/aco-principles-2010.pdf (Accessed 11/23/11).
41. *Building a Network Theory of Social Capital*. Nan Lin, Social Capital, Hawthorne, NY: Walter de Gruyter, Inc., 2001, p. 5.
42. Ibid., pp. 6–7.
43. *Foundations of Social Theory*. James S. Coleman, Cambridge, MA: Harvard University Press, 1990.
44. *Structural Holes: The Social Structure of Competition*. Ronald S. Burt, Cambridge, MA: Harvard University Press, 1992, p. 12.
45. *Building a Network Theory of Social Capital*, pp. 14–16.
46. *Explanation of Benefits*. Ian Morrison, Hospitals and Health Networks, September 2, 2008. Online at: http://www.hhnmag.com/hhnmag_app/jsp/articledisplay.jsp?dcrpath=HHNMAG/Article/data/09SEP2008/080902HHN_Online_Morrison&domain=HHNMAG (accessed 3/29/2012).

Acronyms

Acronym	Definition
CMS	Centers for Medicare and Medicaid Services
FFS	Fee-For-Service
GDP	Gross Domestic Product
HIT	Healthcare Information Technology
MSSP	Medicare Shared Savings Program
NCQA	National Committee for Quality Assurance

9 The Role of the Healthcare Consultant

OVERVIEW

Rapidly changing regulations, reimbursement issues, competitive forces, and technological advancements characterize healthcare delivery as an industry sector that continuously evolves in a tumultuous environment. The scope of this volatility has periodically crescendoed, in the post WWII era, to a level that manifests a paradigm shift requiring significant restructuring of the very foundation of the enterprises and institutions that comprise the U.S. healthcare delivery system. To respond to these changes, healthcare providers have typically sought the advice and counsel of industry thought leaders with particular expertise and command of the knowledge base related to specific aspects of this changing environment. The healthcare consulting field has grown exponentially over the past 50 years, and despite the recent downturn in the economy, it earned revenues of approximately \$34.1 billion in 2008, with revenues expected to grow with a compounded annual growth rate of 5.3% through 2012.[1]

Factoid 9.1

Most new governmental initiatives create a surge of consulting opportunities. (Source: ACOs Spell Gold Rush for Health Care Consultants. Bara Vaida, Kaiser Health News, April 2, 2011. Online at: http://www.kaiserhealthnews.org/Stories/2011/April/03/aco-consultant-gold-rush.aspx?p = 1 (Accessed 4/7/2011).

The scope of healthcare consulting services related to assisting healthcare entities include navigating complex industry challenges across each of the Four Pillars of the Healthcare Industry:

1. Rapidly changing regulatory edicts and increased enforcement activities
2. Continual stress on reimbursement yields for providers
3. Increasing competitive challenges and peril
4. Costs associated with technological advancements

The increased diversity in the range and more robust scope of services that consultants provide has been met by professionals and industry thought leaders who have entered the consulting arena from a wide array of professional backgrounds, including finance and economics, information systems/information technology, process management, accounting, law, insurance and actuarial, health administration, medicine, nursing, public health, and academics.

Within this dynamic milieu, the emergence of ACOs has led to anticipation, excitement, concern, and often outright confusion for both healthcare providers and their consultants. Consultants have noted that while most new governmental initiatives in healthcare create a surge of consulting opportunities, ACOs also are accompanied by a proliferation of new healthcare delivery options beyond what was previously available,[2] and, as such, provide a wealth of expanded opportunity for consulting engagements.

While healthcare consulting requires specialized healthcare industry knowledge in consideration of the unique clinical nature and societal good of the services that healthcare clients provide, it should be noted that healthcare entities are commercial business enterprises as well, and subject to many of the same market forces as nonhealthcare industries, with similar needs for consulting methods and processes found in those commercial enterprises. This chapter will discuss the need for various consulting services that may arise from the development, implementation, and ongoing management of ACOs, as well as the nature of those engagements and the types of consultants that typically provide those services.

ECONOMIC AND FINANCIAL CONSULTING SERVICES RELEVANT TO ACOS

While there are several types of consulting services that may be useful to healthcare enterprises and providers considering participation in an ACO, the modalities for categorizing the provision of those services may be characterized into two general classifications, i.e., episodic consulting services and continuity consulting services.

Episodic (as well as extended episodic) are those services provided in response to a specially defined, finite need for a determinate engagement typically more external and independent from the actions of internal management. In contrast, continuity (or annuity) services are rendered on an ongoing basis and are often more entwined with the internal activities of management. Typically, the nature and scope of the required service determines the modality of the consulting activity. For example, a certified audit, often referred to as attestation services, requires the independence of an episodic consulting engagement, while the ongoing preparation of financial statements and tax returns often requires the services provided by a continuity (annuity) engagement.

Key Term	Definition
Attestation Services	A certified audit.

Key Term	Definition	Citation
Independence	Being free from the influence or control of another.	Independent. In *Black's Law Dictionary,* 9th ed. Bryan A. Garner, ed. St. Paul, MN: West, 2009, p. 838.

Key Term	Definition
Annuity Services	Continuity services provided on an annual basis.

Key Term	Definition
Episodic Consulting Services	Services provided on a discrete engagement basis, wherein each project has separate deliverables and timetables, and often a different engagement agreement detailing the terms of each.

The great divide between episodic consulting services and continuity consulting services is based on the nature of the services to be provided and the level of independence[3] required of any conclusion or opinion rendered specific to the engagement. Many episodic consulting services require the consultant to render his/her independent observations, findings, conclusions, and opinions as a central deliverable of the engagement. As these conclusions and opinions are often relied upon by investors, lenders, and other stakeholders who have a legal expectation as to the fiduciary nature of the ACO's relationship with them, the consultant's work product must be rendered with the requisite level of independence so as to avoid any implication or inference that there may have been any other consideration (e.g., the prospect of future employment of the consultant for continuity services) influencing the consultant's independent judgment. Like Caesar's wife, the consultant's actions, work process, and relationship with the client, and ultimate opinion, "must be above suspicion."

Key Term	Definition
Continuity Consulting Services	Services provided on an ongoing basis.

Episodic Services

Episodic healthcare consulting services, i.e., those provided on a discrete engagement basis, will have separate deliverables and timetables, and (often) a different engagement agreement detailing the terms of each episodic project. Episodic consulting services that are particularly important for the development, implementation, and operation of an ACO, include:

1. *Capital formation advisory services*, e.g., determining: (a) the amounts of capital; and (b) the appropriate mix of the types and sources of capital (debt and equity) available to, and required for, the initial development and sustained operation of the ACO. A more detailed discussion of basic capital financing for healthcare entities and the specific sources of capital available is provided in Chapter 6.
2. *Feasibility analysis*, including forecasting the predicted return on investment and the likelihood that the probable margins of the operation of the ACO will offset the initial capital required for its development. A more detailed discussion of feasibility analysis for varying sizes of ACOs is provided in Chapter 7.
3. *Value Metrics analysis* for each potential ACO, stakeholders must know the probability that the ACO will be viable, which can only be determined through a thorough understanding of those measures of value (both monetary and nonmonetary) that the ACO is attempting to achieve. A more detailed discussion of monetary and nonmonetary value is set forth I Chapter 8.
4. *Transaction planning and intermediary services* to assist with: mergers and acquisitions, transfer, lease, or other contracting for ACO participants, providers/suppliers, or ACO professionals in the formation and structuring of an ACO.
5. *Valuation (financial appraisal)* of specific enterprises, assets, and services involved in the transactions in the formation and structuring of an ACO.
6. *Legal services* for the development of organizational and governance structure and preparation of documents for memorializing the deal.
7. *Consulting assistance* with provider credentialing, accreditation, certification and licensure, including tracking and determination of primary care provider status and beneficiary assignment.
8. *Consulting assistance* with the calculation, allocation, and documentation of ACO shared savings for their distribution across providers.
9. *Turnaround/management restructuring services.*
10. *Strategic planning services*, i.e., marketing, feasibility, and service line analysis.
11. *Litigation support services.*

Continuity Services

Consulting services that are typically provided on an ongoing basis are commonly referred to as *continuity services*. There are several types of continuity services, including:

1. Financial statement preparation services
2. Assistance with revenue cycle: coding, billing, and claims resolution process

3. Cost management: supply side and cost center analysis and performance improvement services
4. Information systems/information technology project implementation or hardware or software upgrades
5. Operational management *services* for both the coordination and maintenance of the informatics requisite for quality and cost reporting metrics in documenting an ACO's achievement of required benchmarks and achievement of targets for shared saving payments
6. Corporate compliance and risk management audit services for monitoring a wide variety of legal and regulatory issues on a consistent basis: important for ACOs as with most other healthcare provider organizations

---

Factoid 9.2

Healthcare consultants also may assist ACOs beyond the development and implementation of compliance programs with continuous services, such as risk assessments, training programs, policy and procedure manuals, and auditing support. (Source: *Healthcare Management: Corporate Compliance.* The Rehmann Group, Saginaw, MI.)

Some continuity services are provided on a particular reoccurring timeframe, typically annual, and are known as *annuity services*. Annuity services can generate a long-term relationship between the healthcare consultant and the healthcare entity. Services that are typically provided on an annual basis include:

1. *Financial audit and attestation services*: Important for ACOs as with most other healthcare provider organizations, these annual audits review the financial condition and solvency status, as well as the historical performance of the ACO, identifying and commenting on items such as financial profitability as well as operational efficiencies of revenue cycle elements: coding, billing, and claims resolution process.
2. *Tax filing services*: For federal, state, and local taxes, including provider taxes in certain markets.

Key Concept	Definition	Citation
Financial Statement Preparation	Consultants compile information given from management without analysis and, therefore, cannot certify the accuracy of the documents. Solely to present information.	*Statements on Standards for Accounting and Review Services.* The American Institute of Certified Public Accountants, December 1978. Online at: http://www.aicpa.org/download/members/div/auditstd/AR-00100.PDF (Accessed 3/18/2010); *Responsibilities and Functions of the Independent Auditor.* The American Institute of Certified Public Accountants, November 1972. Online at: https://www.aicpa.org/download/members/div/auditstd/AU-00110.PDF (Accessed 3/18/2010).

Key Concept	Definition	Citation
Financial Statement Audits	Consultant examines all documents thoroughly and determines whether the entity does or does not comply with GAAP in all material respects, financial position, results of operations, and cash flows. Typically done as an annuity service.	*Statements on Standards for Accounting and Review Services.* The American Institute of Certified Public Accountants, December 1978. Online at: http://www.aicpa.org/download/members/div/auditstd/AR-00100.PDF (Accessed 3/18/2010); *Responsibilities and Functions of the Independent Auditor.* The American Institute of Certified Public Accountants, November 1972. Online at: https://www.aicpa.org/download/members/div/auditstd/AU-00110.PDF (Accessed 3/18/2010).

Key Term	Definition
Value Metrics Services	Services that consider the potential value of an ACO investment in the current healthcare marketplace.

Many of these services can be offered on either an episodic or continuity basis, simply by changing the scope of the engagement. For example, financial auditing can be provided for a specific time and instance, or annually, in response to the reporting needs of an entity, such as tax filing periods.

Factoid 9.3

Consultants often provide a wide array of IT services to ACOs, including assistance in the transition to EHRs (electronic health records), the implementation of information tracking and security systems for purposes of data reporting, assistance with the maintenance of the ACO's data network, and the development of the ACO's Web site or other marketing tools. (Source: *iMBA Healthcare Information Technology*. Medical Business Advisors, Inc., Norcross, GA. Online at: http://www.medicalbusinessadvisors.com/services-information.asp (Accessed 11/3/2009).

A listing of consulting services and an illustrative classification of their modality (i.e., episodic or continuity services) is shown in Table 9.1.

While many of the consulting activities discussed above and depicted in Table 9.1 may be useful, or even essential, to an ACO and its stakeholders, perhaps the most important may be value metrics, financial feasibility, and valuation (financial appraisal) consulting services related to the formation of an ACO in order to avoid the conundrum of "getting all dressed up with nowhere to go."

Value Metric Services

Key Term	Definition	Citation
Revenue Cycle	All administrative and clinical functions that contribute to the capture, management, and collection of patient service revenue.	*Revenue Cycle Education Improvement Strategies*. Colleen Malmgren, Fairview Health Services http://www.mnhima.org/2009annual/doclibrary/Revenue-Cycle-ManagementStrategies.pdf (Accessed 5/24/12).

As indicated in Chapter 7, the definition of the term *value metrics* is derived from several disciplines and is commonly used throughout academic, professional, and commercial endeavors. As applied to ACOs, the term *value* may be considered as the function of the measurement of the relationship between the cost of capital formation/investment aspects of developing an ACO, and the returns to that investment, in the form of both financial returns and nonmonetary benefits.

The general tenet guiding the decision to accept or reject an investment should be to undertake only those investment projects that seek to maximize the expected value of the enterprise to its owners. Even if an investment may improve the financial position of the enterprise, if it detracts from the enterprise's mission or goals or is contrary to the ethical standards of the enterprise, the value of the enterprise (inclusive of nonfinancial or nonmonetary considerations) may be diminished. Additionally, any analysis of the value metrics that may be attributed to an ACO should be tempered by a consideration of general economic trends, and an understanding of the impacts of seemingly unrelated economic events that can be transmitted to the healthcare industry through interconnected financial capital markets. The success or failure of many ACO projects may rely upon the ability of a healthcare entity's management to appropriately assess and mitigate these risks.

TABLE 9.1
Categorization of Healthcare Consulting Services

Areas of Consulting Services	Description	Type	Modality
Accounting and Tax-Related Services	Assist with financial statement auditing processes and tax filings	Bookkeeping and Financial Accounting	Continuity
		Financial Statement Preparation Auditing and Assurance Services	Continuity
		Tax Services	Annuity
		Management/Cost Accounting	Continuity
Revenue Cycle Services	Assist in navigating reimbursement and regulatory parameters to properly code and charge for services rendered, and then to obtain payment through the claims resolution and collection process.	Coding and Charting	Annuity/Episodic
		Billing and Claims Resolution	Continuity
		Reimbursement Yield Enhancement	Episodic
Regulatory Related Services	Assist healthcare professionals in remaining compliant with strict regulatory restrictions, in addition to aiding in the acquisition and maintenance of accreditations, certifications, and licensing.	Corporate Compliance Audit	Episodic
		Risk Management	Episodic
		Provider Accreditation, Certification, Licensing	Episodic
		Certificate-of-Need	
Structure and Governance and Organizational Structure Consulting	Assist with practice start-up activities (e.g., staffing and marketing) as well as the development of a practice mission to ensure staff buy-in.	Practice Start-Up Services	Episodic
		Organizational Development Services	Episodic
		Physician Compensation and Income Distribution	Episodic

Operational Management Consulting	Consult on basic business and practice management, as well as implementation and management of HIT.	Supply-Side/Purchasing Consulting	Episodic
		Insurance Consulting	Episodic
		Practice Operational Management Services	Continuity
		Information Systems/Information Technology Services	Episodic
		Facilities Assessment	Episodic
		Operational Throughput	Episodic
		Turnaround/Management Restructuring Services	Episodic
Transition Planning	Assist with physician successorship, retirement planning, and valuation of an enterprise, asset, or service.	Financial/Investment Planning and Retirement Services	Annuity/Episodic
		Successorship/Exit Planning	Episodic
		Valuation Services	Episodic
		Intermediary Services	Episodic
Strategic Planning and Business Development	Assist with strategic planning activities in an effort to maintain profitable business structures in the midst of constantly changing regulatory and reimbursement environments.	Marketing Analysis	Episodic
		Feasibility Analysis	Episodic
		Service Line Analysis	Episodic
Litigation Support	Consult with legal counsel during litigation engagements by providing healthcare consulting services or expert witness testimony.	Expert Witness	Episodic
		Non-Testimonial Support	Annuity/Episodic

The above mentioned considerations highlight the complexities related to appropriately assessing the potential value of an ACO investment in the current healthcare marketplace. Revenue generation in the ACO model is derived from shared cost reductions. Healthcare entities capable of reducing patient costs to payors will share in a portion of those cost reductions. To justify the significant expense associated with ACO development and operation, a potential ACO investor should consider whether the anticipated annual shared savings will offset the required ACO-related capital expenditures. Given the cap on shared savings, some ACOs (primarily small ACOs) may not be able to accumulate the necessary financial benefit to offset the ACO-related costs. It is possible, however, that certain indirect benefits may accrue to the stakeholders in the ACO. If these benefits are sufficient in magnitude to compensate the various stakeholders, either monetarily or nonmonetarily, for their initial investment and any financial operating losses experienced by the ACO, then the investment may make rational sense (see Chapter 8).

Financial Feasibility Services

Key Term	Definition
Financial Feasibility Services	Services that either develop, or evaluate, a sustainable financial model that will provide adequate funding for the initial capital investment related to the ACO, as well as the ongoing working capital and operational costs required of the ACO going forward.

Capital expenditures play an increasingly important role in the financial sustainability of a healthcare enterprise, as both facilities and equipment are necessary to provide increasingly capital-intensive, technologically driven medical care for sufficient numbers of patients, and their treating physicians, to make an ACO a viable investment. As the healthcare industry transitions from a volume-driven payment system toward an outcome-centered, value-based reimbursement system, the development of a sustainable financial model that will provide adequate funding for the initial capital investment related to the ACO will be required, as well as the determination of ongoing working capital and operational costs required of the ACO going forward.

Before initiating an in-depth financial analysis of the investment in an ACO, managers should consider the probability of achieving cost sharing revenue, the expenses related to acquiring the necessary expertise to realize any possible revenue from cost sharing, and the enterprise's access to capital markets. In the event that the results of a feasibility analysis indicate that there may be inefficiencies associated with the ACO's revenue cycle, clients may want to seek the advice of a healthcare consultant who has experience with the particular healthcare revenue cycle at issue, including, but not limited to:

- Coding and charting procedures
- Charge capture
- Reimbursement policies
- Billing procedures
- Claim resolution methods
- Shared savings distribution plans

Factoid 9.4

Consultants with experience in coding, strategic design, billing, charting, quality enhancement strategies, and reimbursement models may find all of these skills useful to a developing ACO. (Source: *Charge Master Consulting.* T. T. Mitchell Consulting, Inc., Syracuse, NY. Online at: http://www.ttmitchellconsulting.com/chargemaster.html (Accessed 1/8/10).)

To increase the probability of a successful ACO formation, prospective participants should closely examine all aspects of the investment, as the worst case scenario for any ACO occurs when the enterprise exceeds their calculated benchmark by a sufficient amount to be liable for the applicable capped shared losses amount. As described in Chapter 6, there are four areas in which developing ACO enterprises will initially invest their capital: (1) network development and management; (2) care coordination, quality improvement, and utilization management; (3) clinical information systems; and (4) data analytics.

As additional information becomes available regarding the operating performance and capital requirements of ACO formations, the nature of the preinvestment analysis should trend toward being less of a forecast based on hypothetical assumptions and more of an empirically grounded benchmarking to normative industry data. Several metrics exist to assist the management of a healthcare enterprise in determining the financial feasibility of an ACO investment, including: (1) payback and discounted payback methods, (2) the average accounting rate of return, (3) the net present value (NPV) method, and (4) the internal rate of return (IRR) method (see Chapter 7 for a detailed discussion of these metrics).

Valuation (Financial Appraisal) Services: Establishing Fair Market Value and Commercial Reasonableness

Legal advisory services provided by competent healthcare legal counsel, who are experienced with the healthcare transactional marketplace, should address the strict regulatory requirements applicable to the transactions, contracts, and complex relationships likely to be encountered by an ACO, e.g., Anti-kickback, False Claims Act, Stark Law, Fraud and Abuse, Antitrust, and Tax Exempt Status ACO. Ongoing changes in the structure, operation, and financing of many healthcare provider enterprises, assets, and services, like ACOs, will likely result in an even greater amount of regulatory scrutiny from such regulatory bodies as Office of Inspector General (OIG), the Internal Revenue Service (IRS), the Department of Justice (DOJ), and the Federal Trade Commission (FTC). In many situations, ACO stakeholders, typically through the offices of their legal counsel, will seek the services of certified valuation professionals to ensure that any underlying transactions of healthcare enterprises' assets or services related to the development of the ACO (e.g., joint venture, merger, acquisition, contacting) meet applicable standards as to the regulatory thresholds fair market value (FMV) and commercial reasonableness (CR). Most likely, the valuation consulting assignment that most often may be requested by the ACO's legal counsel will be one related to the preparation and development of a certified opinion related to the FMV and CR connected to the transactional activities as may be involved in the integration, affiliation, acquisition, and divestiture of the various provider enterprises and interests participating in an ACO.

Key Term	Definition
Fair Market Value	The most probable price that the subject interest should bring if exposed for sale on the open market.

Key Term	Definition	Citation
Commercial Reasonableness	An arrangement that makes commercial sense, "if entered into by a reasonable entity of similar type and size and a reasonable physician (or family member or group practice) of similar scope and specialty, even if there were no potential DHS referrals."	Medicare Program; Physicians' Referrals to Health Care Entities with Which They Have Financial Relationships (Phase II). *Federal Register* vol. 69, no. 59 (March 26, 2004), p. 16093.

A certified opinion, prepared in compliance with professional standards by an independent, credentialed valuation professional and supported by adequate documentation that each of the proposed elements of the transaction are both at FMV and CR, will significantly enhance the likelihood of the ACO establishing a risk adverse, defensible position that the ACO is in compliance in the event that it faces regulatory scrutiny. In developing a certified opinion of FMV and CR, certain financial analyses may be required, including, e.g., the development of:

1. Financial projections and pro forma reports
2. Forecasts, budgets, and provider income/shared savings distribution plans
3. Economic and demographic analyses and trend reports
4. Patient utilization demand forecasts
5. Reimbursement yield and payor mix reports

Key Concept	Definition
Certified Opinion	An opinion of value prepared in compliance with professional standards by an independent credentialed valuation professional and supported by adequate documentation that each of the proposed elements of the transaction are both at FMV and CR.

Additionally, healthcare legal counsel will need to collaborate with appropriate tax counsel to ensure that the ACO meets the mandates required for maintaining its 501(c)(3) tax exempt status in the event that tax-exempt enterprises, e.g., tax-exempt hospital or health system, are parties to the ACO. A further discussion on this is found in Chapter 5.

Key Term	Definition	Citation
501(c)(3) organization	An organization that is exempt from taxation. Such organizations may be a corporation, community chest, fund, or foundation, and operate exclusively for nonprofit purposes (e.g., religious, charitable, scientific, testing for public safety, literary, or educational purposes. No private party gains any profit from the organization's net earnings, and no substantial part of its activities attempt to influence any political campaign on behalf of (or in opposition to) any candidate for public office.	Cornell Law Web site. Online at: http://www.law.cornell.edu/uscode/text/26/501 (Accessed 5/24/12).

Factoid 9.5

The ACA (Patient Protection and Affordable Care Act, 2010) also introduced several new requirements for 501(c)(3) organizations, including the community needs assessment and §501(r), for which consultants may offer guidance. (Source: *Services.* Healthcare Management Consultants, Chicago. Online at: http://www.healthcaremgmt.com/tax.html (Accessed 7/28/2009).)

SELECTING AND WORKING WITH CONSULTANTS

While clients often rely on professional designations and academic credentials in making a determination that their selected consultant possesses the requisite skills to produce the desired deliverable for the client's particular needs, these designations and credentials should not be the only selection criteria. ACO stakeholders should adhere to a disciplined process for soliciting specified consulting services for a well-defined set of consulting needs from firms that have the set of skills and professional standing to render those specific services, regardless of which niche services a particular consultant may offer when guiding the ACO through the various stages of development, implementation, and ongoing management.

Key Concept	Definition
Deliverables of an Engagement	Those observations, findings, conclusions, and opinions of the consultant, as well as specific items, e.g., financial proforma, requested by the client and listed in the engagement agreement.

Consultant Skills and the Body of Knowledge

With an expanding universe of information available on almost every imaginable topic related to healthcare delivery to previously unknown levels of intricacy, specificity, and complexity, it may be said that:

> It's clear that the growth of all human knowledge,
> The core essential of our learning potential,
> Has been not arithmetic, nor even geometric,
> Its expansion has truly been exponential.
> And with the world bloated from data infusion,
> Even simple tasks demand specialists to complete,
> And the ensuing confusion, begs the inescapable conclusion,
> That general knowledge is, alone, quite obsolete.
> It can't be fixed with native intelligence,
> This lack of specialized, industry perceptions.
> It's the futility of seeking the answers,
> When one can't truly even posit the questions.

Cimasi

It has increasingly become the role of the consultant to traverse this expansive ocean of complex information, in order to accurately identify, classify, and appropriately store the correct information needed for client engagements, then timely and efficiently retrieve this information, so as to communicate the pertinent data in a precise, focused, intelligent, and comprehensible manner that serves the specific needs of the client project.

Factoid 9.6

Better, Faster, Cheaper. (Source: From the consultants view, the project may be completed better and faster, but then it's not cheaper; faster and cheaper, but then it's not better; and, finally, better and cheaper, but then it's not faster.)

Accordingly, it is essential that ACOs select consultants for their projects who exhibit a command of the requisite body of knowledge and can demonstrate by their experience that they have mastered the technical skills, as well as the organizational and strategic capabilities required to complete each of the deliverables within the stated scope of the engagement, regardless of the consultant's stated areas of expertise, educational background, or professional credentials.

Key Term	Definition	Citation
Federal Rule of Evidence 702 (i.e. Daubert Rule')	State testimony must adhere to the following: (1) be based on sufficient facts or data, (2) be the product of reliable principles and methods, and (3) the consultant has applied the principles and methods reliably to the facts of the case.	*Daubert v. Merrell Dow Pharms,* Inc. 509 U.S. 579 (1993); Federal Rules of Evidence, Rule 702 (Dec. 1, 2006).

Clients expect that the professional consultants they engage should not only possess (or be able to timely and cost-effectively research and obtain) the requisite body of knowledge, but that the information accrued and reported be characterized as value-added in its quality, efficacy, and reliability. This concept is seen throughout the various disciplines of expertise and, especially, in light of the new gatekeeper role required of judges under the *Daubert v. Merrell Dow Pharmaceuticals* case precedent and subsequent case law,[4] consultants understand, more than ever, that they cannot support their independent conclusions and opinions simply by means of an *ipse dixit* (it is, because I say it is) type of argument.

As a result, consultants and analysts, in every discipline, must thoroughly understand the types, sources, and validity of the research and empirical data they rely upon, as well as the basic applications of these data in accordance with accepted methodology as set forth in the canon of authoritative literature and professional standards in their area of expertise. The consequences of not complying with contemporary expectations and requirements for robust research, rigorous analytical discipline, and competent acuity may not only damage their ACO clients with bad advice, but also may constitute grounds for being excluded from testifying as an expert in court or agency hearings in the event of a dispute or regulatory enforcement action involving their ACO client, and lead to legal liability for consultants, particularly those providing advice in the financial sector, e.g., certified valuators and appraisers.[5]

While it's accepted that the collection and application of efficacious research and accurate empirical data are required as part of the consultant's task in applying the scientific method throughout the development of a replicable and supportable set of observations and finding, as well as the reporting of independent conclusions and opinions to ACOs, the rigors and expense of implementing this process manifests a consistent tension between the needs and demands of clients and their projects and the limited resources clients are willing (or able) to make available for their completion.

An old adage in the consulting profession is that from the three available qualities by which a consulting engagement may be completed, i.e., better—faster—cheaper, the client may select only two, at least from the consultant's point of view. In that vein, the project may be completed better and faster, but then it's not cheaper; faster and cheaper, but then it's not better; and, finally, better and cheaper, but then it's not faster.

Of course, from the client's perspective, all three qualities are required from a consultant for each project. In addressing the fee negotiations accompanying the selection of a consultant, ACO stakeholders, as informed clients, should be mindful that professional consultants should always approach this conundrum in consideration of the Daubert Standard, i.e., with adequate fees that reflect the cost of sufficient staffing and time to apply both the requisite research and accepted analytical methodologies in developing their observations and findings, reaching supportable conclusions, and rendering their opinions and advice.

Organizational and Strategic Capabilities

Clients should expect that the consulting professionals they hire will approach each engagement strategically, which requires specialized knowledge of the overall healthcare industry, a sound understanding of ACOs and other emerging healthcare organizations as well as an appreciation of general business principles. A determination as to whether a chosen consultant's abilities were acquired from research, schooling, or experience is imperative when entering into a consulting engagement.

Key Concept	Definition	Citation
Organizational Development	Development of mission and vision and ensuring staff acceptance of these principles.	*Organizational Development: An Overview.* Organizational Development Consulting & Training. Online at: http://www.orgdct.com/overview.htm (Accessed 11/25/2009).

Consulting engagements for healthcare enterprises should focus on the economic conditions and events that result from several factors, including (1) changing delivery system relationships driven by new technologies and clinical treatment advances, (2) aging patient demographics, (3) changing payor and reimbursement scenarios, (4) increasing regulatory and competitive pressures, and (5) other factors specific to the healthcare industry. Not only is a detailed knowledge regarding ACOs important, but consultants also must be able to organize work processes to focus on the information and analysis that fits the needs of the client.

The Consulting Process

The success of any undertaking or enterprise involves a process of first parsing the project into a number of individual tasks and activities that must be completed for the deliverables to be achieved. The definition of these tasks and activities rely on a process of obtaining a number of specific inputs, from clients and others, as to the nature, scope, and objectives of the project. These inputs then serve as the basis for allocating these discrete tasks and activities into manageable, comprehensible, and actionable groups (often referred to as *phases*) that inform the engagement of the consultant as well as the structure and direction of the project.

Key Concept	Definition
The Phases of a Consulting Engagement	(1) Request for proposal, (2) proposal, (3) engagement agreement, (4) data gathering and research, (5) analytical process, (6) technical tools, and (7) reporting of deliverables.

An illustration of the typical phases of a consulting engagement is illustrated in Figure 9.1.

Data Gathering & Research

Clients should expect that, for any given ACO engagement, the selected consultant will need to be provided access to the necessary data to complete the assignment, which information is obtained through both specific research and general research.

Specific research consists of gathering information from the subject healthcare organizations, including: financial, business, operational, staffing, and other information. Further, for specific research, the consultant will need to be provided internal information from the subject enterprise.

General research relies on information that is available through published governmental and nongovernmental public sources, as well as proprietary private ones, and includes information related the healthcare market:

- Regional, state, and national economic conditions
- Competitor analysis from various types of healthcare facilities
- Insurance options and payor relations
- Benchmarking statistics
- Reimbursement trends
- Specialty or industry trends
- Supplier trends
- Many other relevant topics

In addition to gathering research, a consultant must be able to analyze the research obtained before providing cost-effective and timely observations, findings, conclusions, and opinions that are relevant and supportive to the client.

There are three general types of research that may be considered in ACO consulting engagements, i.e., (1) primary research, (2) secondary research, and (3) tertiary research. Primary research,

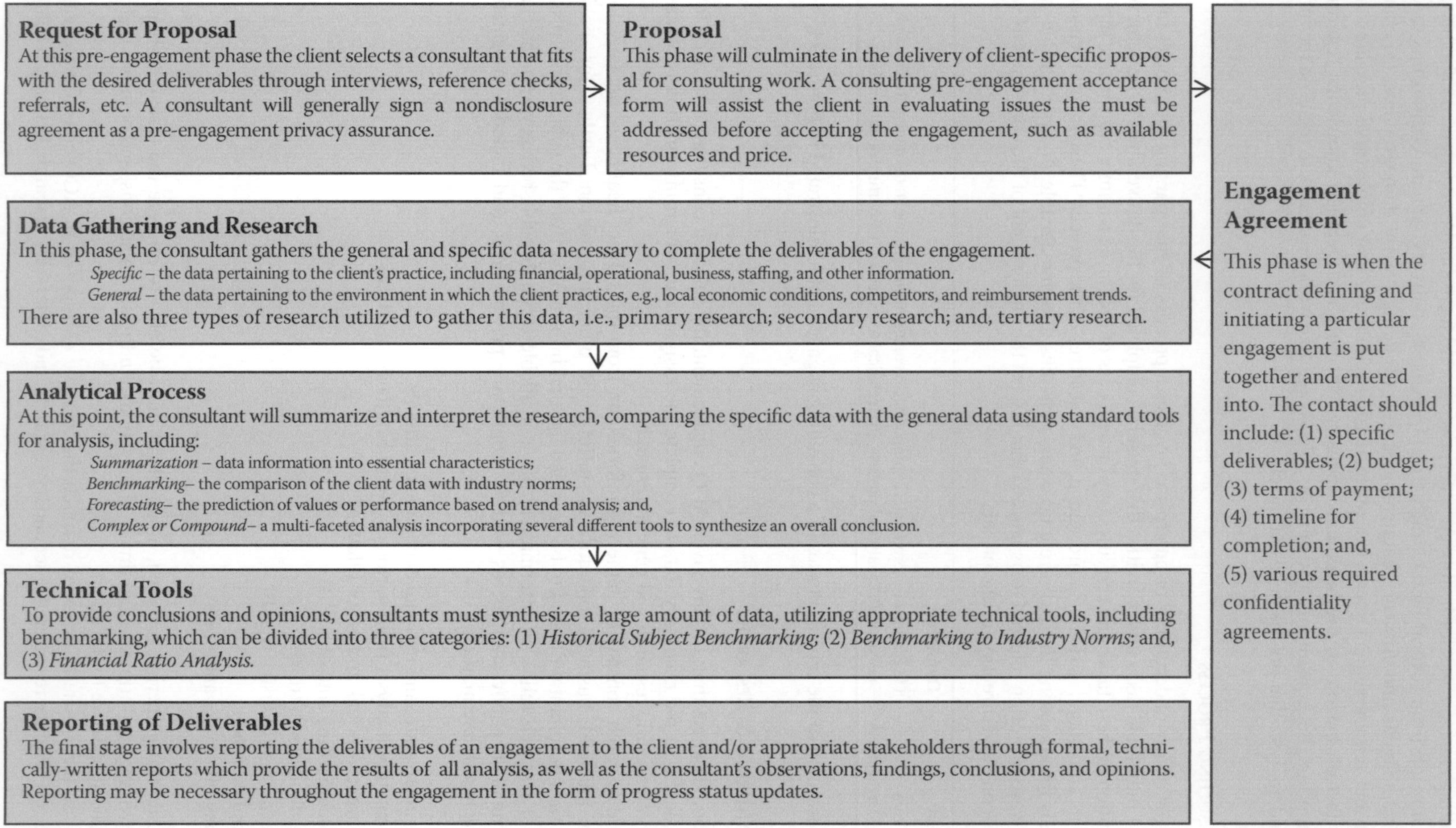

Request for Proposal
At this pre-engagement phase the client selects a consultant that fits with the desired deliverables through interviews, reference checks, referrals, etc. A consultant will generally sign a nondisclosure agreement as a pre-engagement privacy assurance.

Proposal
This phase will culminate in the delivery of client-specific proposal for consulting work. A consulting pre-engagement acceptance form will assist the client in evaluating issues the must be addressed before accepting the engagement, such as available resources and price.

Engagement Agreement
This phase is when the contract defining and initiating a particular engagement is put together and entered into. The contact should include: (1) specific deliverables; (2) budget; (3) terms of payment; (4) timeline for completion; and, (5) various required confidentiality agreements.

Data Gathering and Research
In this phase, the consultant gathers the general and specific data necessary to complete the deliverables of the engagement.

Specific – the data pertaining to the client's practice, including financial, operational, business, staffing, and other information.

General – the data pertaining to the environment in which the client practices, e.g., local economic conditions, competitors, and reimbursement trends.

There are also three types of research utilized to gather this data, i.e., primary research; secondary research; and, tertiary research.

Analytical Process
At this point, the consultant will summarize and interpret the research, comparing the specific data with the general data using standard tools for analysis, including:

Summarization – data information into essential characteristics;
Benchmarking– the comparison of the client data with industry norms;
Forecasting– the prediction of values or performance based on trend analysis; and,
Complex or Compound– a multi-faceted analysis incorporating several different tools to synthesize an overall conclusion.

Technical Tools
To provide conclusions and opinions, consultants must synthesize a large amount of data, utilizing appropriate technical tools, including benchmarking, which can be divided into three categories: (1) *Historical Subject Benchmarking;* (2) *Benchmarking to Industry Norms*; and, (3) *Financial Ratio Analysis.*

Reporting of Deliverables
The final stage involves reporting the deliverables of an engagement to the client and/or appropriate stakeholders through formal, technically-written reports which provide the results of all analysis, as well as the consultant's observations, findings, conclusions, and opinions. Reporting may be necessary throughout the engagement in the form of progress status updates.

FIGURE 9.1 Phases of a consulting engagement.

also known as *original research* or *empirical data*, includes the collection of industry data, e.g., questionnaires, market research, observations, which are then synthesized into a conclusion or description of findings. Secondary research utilizes the primary research done by others, e.g., studies, reports, surveys, and analyzes the content for a thorough understanding of the environment and market for a particular area. Tertiary research, also known a *meta-analysis* (or *meta-study*), is a distilled collection of secondary sources that provide an analysis of the synthesis of others' primary research.

The empirical data of primary research, as well as the analytical observations, findings, conclusions, and opinions derived from secondary research, are the raw materials that provide the foundation for consulting engagements, and comprise an integral component of the ultimate observations, findings, and conclusions reported to clients. The accuracy and efficacy, of course, is limited to the quality of the underlying research and empirical data utilized, as well as the acumen and sagacity of the consultant.

The Consulting Analytical Process

The process of consulting analysis involves summarizing and interpreting the information gathered and synthesizing the specific research and general research obtained, often by means of comparison of one to the other. This analysis can range from providing simple summaries of the compiled research to a more in-depth and complex econometric analysis. There are various analytical tools for analysis that consultants utilize, including:

1. ***Summarization***: Includes tables, matrices, abstracts, etc. that are designed to allow for the distillation of a body of information into one or more of its essential characteristics. These tools provide clients with an overview or comparison of information.
2. ***Benchmarking:*** Refers to the comparison of specific research data on the subject with industry norms, and may include a simple variance analysis on a single characteristic, such as a patient outcome metric related to "readmission within 30 days of discharge." Benchmarking analysis also may involve numerous variables, with comparisons both to internal and external data, and may be incorporated within another, larger analysis.
3. ***Forecasting***: Generally involves trend analysis and produces a prediction of future values or financial performance, e.g., financial pro formas, budgets, demand analysis, and space or staffing forecasts.
4. ***Complex or Compound Analysis***: A multifaceted analysis that may incorporate several different tools to synthesize an overall conclusion. A large proportion of consulting analysis falls into this category. An example of several ACO engagement deliverables that would require a complex or compound analysis is listed below:
    a. *Payor source evaluation*, e.g., an analysis of the resources, methods, and historical performance of payors participating in ACO contracts and shared savings distribution.
    b. *Information systems assessment,* e.g., an analysis of the technical and capital cost HIT needs specific to achieving reporting and quality metrics.
    c. *Risk assessment/feasibility analysis*, e.g., the probability that income from an ACO arrangement will offset initial and operation capital requirements.

While the process of obtaining the requisite data and research provides consultants with an adequate grasp of the body of knowledge applicable to a particular ACO consulting engagement, it is the efficacy of the consultant's subsequent application of generally accepted analytical methods to that data that determines the successful outcome of the assignment. Accordingly, ACOs need to engage a consultant that not only has the organizational and strategic capabilities to harness his/her acquired body of knowledge, but also the technical skills to utilize the various analytical tools required to meet the deliverables required of a particular project.

Technical Tools

The technical tools that consultants need to employ to provide clients with the conclusions and opinions that are deliverable under a particular engagement involve the synthesis of a substantial amount of data that may be pertinent to the client project, as well as the appropriate analysis, calculations, and considerations of the various types and forms of that data following its synthesis. Among these technical tools is the benchmarking process, which may be divided into three categories:

1. *Historical Subject Benchmarking*: Compares the current or most recently reported performance to past performance, a process involving the adjustment and comparison of historical data with current data. This method compares "like with like," thereby facilitating the examination of the Subject Entity's historical performance over a period of time; identification of changes in performance within the Subject Entity as well as anomalies, e.g., extraordinary and nonrecurring events; and the prediction of future performance over time.
2. *Benchmarking to Industry Norms*: Compares internal Subject Entity specific data to survey data from other entities within the same industry sector and subsector for the purpose of identifying its relative strengths, weaknesses, and related measures of risk.
3. *Financial Ratio Analysis*: Compares measurements of internal ratios to generally established industry norms expressed as ranges of positive or negative trends for that industry sector. Ratios are typically calculated as measurements of various financial and operational characteristics that illustrate the financial status of the Subject Entity.

Industry benchmarking data may be obtained from several publicly available sources, e.g., trade and professional associations; federal and state government agency reports and studies; foundations and think tanks; local chambers of commerce, business leagues, economic development councils; and for-profit research organizations.

Reporting of Consulting Engagement Deliverables

While clients and their selected consultants typically work in a collaborative and iterative manner, ultimately it is the consultant's responsibility to fulfill the deliverables of a specific engagement. In assisting with the development, implementation, and ongoing operations of an ACO, an effective consultant must articulate often complex ideas and concepts to the client within his/her area of expertise and the needs of the particular engagement. Accordingly, in addition to expertly developing the observations, findings, conclusions, and opinions derived from the analyses performed in the engagement, the consultant must be an expert as well in communicating them to ACO leadership. This must be done in the periodic presentation of progress status updates, as well as in a final report that is delivered, often in the format of a formal written report to the client. As explained by Lee Iacocca, past CEO of Chrysler, "You can have brilliant ideas, but if you can't get them across, your ideas won't get you anywhere."

CHAPTER SUMMARY

The emergence of ACOs has created a multitude of opportunities for episodic and continuity consulting services, perhaps the most important of which may be those value metrics and financial feasibility consulting services related to ACO formation. Additionally, valuation (financial appraisal) services that involve obtaining a certified opinion of value (prepared in compliance with regulatory edicts and professional standards related to the Fair Market Value and commercial reasonableness) will likely be required for those transactional events that are required for the formation of the ACO. In the event that those types of economic and financial consulting services are needed, a certified valuation professional, working with legal counsel, will likely be best suited to perform the requisite consulting services in an efficient and effective manner that will withstand regulatory scrutiny. Selecting the appropriate healthcare consultant will require that the specific healthcare provider (e.g., hospitals or physician groups) considering ACO participation identify the type and scope of consulting service they are seeking, and establish both the specific deliverables and an appropriate budget to achieve those objectives considered important for the project.

ENDNOTES

1. *Consulting Industry Overview*. Plunkett Research, Ltd, Plunkett's Consulting Industry Almanac 2009. Online at: http://www.plunkettresearch.com/Industries/Consulting/ConsultingStatistics/tabid/177/Default.aspx (Accessed 1/4/09); Healthcare *Consulting Marketplace 2009–2012: Opportunities in Life Sciences, Provider, Payer, and Government Markets; Research Summary*. Kelly Matthews and Derek Smith, Kennedy Consulting Research & Advisory, BNA Subsidiaries, Inc., Peterborough, NH, 2009, p. 2.
2. ACOs Spell Gold Rush for Health Care Consultants. Bara Vaida, *Kaiser Health News*, April 2, 2011. Online at: http://www.kaiserhealthnews.org/Stories/2011/April/03/aco-consultant-gold-rush.aspx?p=1 (Accessed 4/7/2011).
3. Legally, the term *independent* means being free from the influence or control of another. "Independent" in *Black's Law Dictionary*, 9th ed. Bryan A. Garner (ed.), St. Paul, MN: West, 2009, p. 838.
4. The Daubert Standard for the admissibility of expert witness testimony is flushed out between three U.S. Supreme Court cases, commonly referred to as the Daubert trilogy, i.e., *Daubert v. Merrell Dow Pharmaceuticals, General Electric Co. v. Joiner,* and *Kumho Tire Co. v. Carmichael. Daubert v. Merrell Dow Pharmaceuticals, Inc.*, 509 U.S. 579 (1993); *General Electric Co. v. Joiner*, 522 U.S. 136 (1997); *Kumho Tire Co. v. Carmichael*, 526 U.S. 137 (1999).
5. *IRS New Rules: Pension Protection Act and Beyond*. Robert James Cimasi, et al., Business Valuation Resources (BVR) and Institute of Business Appraisers (IBA). BVR Teleconference. March 18, 2009.

Acronyms

Acronym	Definition
NPV	Net Present Value
IRR	Internal Rate of Return
OIG	Office of Inspector General
IRS	Internal Revenue Service
DOJ	Department of Justice
FTC	Federal Trade Commission
FMV	Fair Market Value
CR	Commercial Reasonableness

Conclusion

In the face of systematic growth in healthcare costs and public disquiet regarding quality of care, the movement toward coordinated care, enhanced quality and outcomes, and cost containment will occur whether or not ACOs gain widespread acceptance over the course of the Medicare Shared Savings Program (MSSP). New regulations for Medicare reimbursement and quality reporting have already gone into effect, which principally add a value-based purchasing component to basic reimbursement mechanisms and may be essential to ensure the future sustainability and viability of healthcare delivery in an uncertain economic environment.

President Harry Truman once said, "*The only thing new in this world is the history that you don't know.*" Despite the current publicity and enthusiasm surrounding the emerging Affordable Care Organizations (ACO) models, the ideals of cost savings are not new and may create feelings of déjà vu for those familiar with the proliferation of managed care in the 1990s, which mirrored a similar anticipation. As we know now, these aspirations for change from managed care plans gradually gave way to resentment toward providers and insurance companies. Recall that, at the height of the managed care backlash, 72% of Americans believed that cost savings mainly benefited insurance companies and employers, with little trickle-down benefit to the individual.[1]

Similar sentiments being applied to ACOs may be possible, given the public's changed perception of managed care plans. Commentary on the managed care backlash notes that "experience in other industries suggests [i.e., airlines and banking] *that Americans have limits on how far they will allow marketplace decisions to put them at individual risk.*"[2] To mitigate that risk and to avoid backlash issues similar to those seen in the 1990s, U.S. Department of Health and Human Services (HHS) designed the MSSP for mass appeal among providers,[3] detailing distinct pathways for organizations further along the ACO pipeline as well as for those who are considering their initial foray into the development of an ACO.

Unlike health maintenance organizations (HMOs), which were run by insurance companies, ACOs are designed to allow healthcare professionals to maintain responsibilities for decision making, have voluntary participation, and are not permitted to use aggressive methods to control costs, such as preauthorization and closed provider networks that were seen within HMOs.[4] Regardless of whether ACOs meet expectations, they will push forward the concepts of accountability, tangible outcomes, and lower costs.

Success of federal ACOs under the MSSP and commercial ventures under similar models will likely depend on (1) the size of the initial investment as compared to shared savings achieved within the first three years of operation; (2) actual amount of initial capital investments toward research, development, IT management, and personnel; and (3) ability of organizations to plan capital investments of ACO magnitude without confirmed future savings payments. Healthcare enterprises with mature ACO-like infrastructures (i.e., similar to that of the PGP (physician group practice) demonstration participants, Mayo Clinic, Kaiser Permanente, etc.) will likely experience success at a greater rate than piecemeal organizations haphazardly constructed without weighing the potential benefits and substantial risk that accompanies ACO formation.

To succeed, ACOs will need what managed care lacked: payor support, cooperation between physicians and hospitals, up-front financial resources, and time for integration, but perhaps, most importantly, public acceptance.[5] The success of healthcare delivery is after all a human activity, the assessment of which John Dewey once wrote:

> In the field of human activities, there are at present an immense number of facts of desires and purposes existing in rather complete isolation from one another. But there are no hypotheses of the same empirical order which are capable of relating them to one another so that the resulting propositions will serve

> as methodic controls of the formation of future desires and purposes, and thereby, of new valuations. The material is ample. But the means for bringing its constituents into such connections that fruit is borne are lacking.[6]

In the end, these requirements for the success of ACOs may be best considered within the context of three timeless proverbs:

> Whereof what's past is prologue.
>
> **William Shakespeare**
> *The Tempest*

ACOs are the most recent phase of a managed competition; they have no definition apart from the lessons of the history of managed care. The experiments of managed care were the necessary steps that provide the foundation for today's ACOs. From prepaid group plans developed by Blue Cross and Blue Shield and through HMOs, the PGP demonstration, the work of Elliott Fischer, physician alignment, the ACA, and, ultimately, the MSSP, there has been a continuum of progress toward ACOs. Most major changes to public policy in America have followed this course of gradual evolution, from suffrage to civil rights. True and lasting change comes as a result of a succession of steps taken in an incremental and iterative manner, not as a simple lightning stroke, especially when dealing with issues as complex and on the scale of the U.S. healthcare system.

> The child is father to the man.
>
> **William Wordsworth**
> *The Rainbow*

ACOs have the potential to outshine those previous models of accountable care (i.e., managed care) from which they evolved. The coordination and redesign of the patient care practice and the reliance on evidence-based medicine will likely create a receptive environment to achieve the quality and cost objectives sought by healthcare policy leaders. The current focus on benchmarks, information technology, reporting, and establishing mutually agreed upon metrics hold the potential for building and leading the foundation for achieving specified quality objectives and lead to beneficial, and confirmed, outcomes.

> For every time there is a season.
>
> **Ecclesiastes**

One clear distinction between ACOs and the 1990's experiments in managed care may be the current environment in which ACOs have emerged. The increased turmoil regarding continued threats to physician reimbursement under the sustainable growth rate; the increasing political storm surrounding the slow pace of economic recovery from the 2008 *Great Recession*[7] within the accompanying clamor for deficit reduction; the pressure to reduce Medicare spending; and the rising insurance premium costs for small businesses and families provide fertile ground for healthcare policy reform. While the demographic trends were clear even during previous phases of managed competition, in the early 1980s and 1990s, the country had yet to feel the full impact of the aging U.S. population. Twenty years later, the U.S. population is significantly older, with a higher incidence and prevalence of chronic disease. The current path of U.S. healthcare delivery has caused some to speculate as to the existence of a demographic time bomb ultimately ending in a form of healthcare Armageddon. In response to such dramatic concerns, ACOs may have an opportunity to succeed and survive, due to the impetus for change.

ENDNOTES

1. Understanding the Managed Care Backlash. Robert J. Blendon et al., *Health Affairs*, vol. 17, no. 4, July/August: 88, 1998.
2. Ibid., p. 91.
3. *Administration Releases Proposed Rules for Medicare Accountable Care Organizations*. Ceci Connolly et al., McKinsey Center for U.S. Health System Reform, April 1, 2011, p. 2.
4. Ibid.
5. The Accountable Care Organization: Whatever Its Growing Pains, The Concept Is Too Vitally Important to Fail. Francis J. Crosson, *Health Affairs*, vol. 30, no. 7, July 2011: 1254.
6. *Theory of Valuation*. John Dewey, The University of Chicago Press, Chicago, 1966, p. 61.
7. The Great Recession and Government Failure. Gary S. Becker, The Wall Street Journal, September 2, 2011. Online at: http://online.wsj.com/article/SB10001424053111904199404576536930606933332.html (Accessed 4/26/2012).

Epilogue

On June 28, 2012, the Supreme Court of the United States (SCOTUS) upheld 5 to 4, the constitutionality of the Affordable Care Act (ACA) and/or several of its provisions. The highly anticipated decision stunned industry leaders and commentators by supporting SCOTUS's decision through the federal taxing authority.[1] The significance of this decision will reach every area of healthcare as the changes mandated under the ACA go into effect as planned. The provisions of the ACA, and the Congressional power codified through the SCOTUS opinion may make the move toward national risk pools all the more inevitable to accommodate future demands. Given the background of the delivery of healthcare services in other societies, some type of national health insurance may likely be the ultimate conclusion to many of the current issues within the U.S. healthcare industry. In that vein, Affordable Care Organization (ACOs) may well be a necessary step on the path to a *National Single Payor Insurance* model.

The future drivers of healthcare delivery are the same as those occurring today: exponential growth of Medicare enrollees, increasing complexity and associated costs of technology; the personalization of medicine, and the fiscal burnout due to slow economic growth, high unemployment, and record federal deficit and debt. The first baby boomers enrolled in Medicare in 2010. As the rest of the cohort follows, the impact on the Medicare program will be significant, with an estimated 92.8 million people enrolled in Medicare by 2050.[2] The increased demand for healthcare services caused by this demographic time bomb will likely strain not only budgets, but the already limited physician supply. Today, Medicare spending accounts for 15% of the federal budget and is expected to grow at an average annual rate per capita of 3.5% between 2010 and 2019.[3] This situation is further complicated as initiatives to limit healthcare spending need to be accomplished within significant political pressure not to damage the present level of patient care or place undue financial burdens on the elderly.[4] On its current trajectory, the Medicare program may well become unsustainable, making the Medicare policy debate a main driver of healthcare reform.[5]

Despite current legislative efforts to manage and control the rising cost of healthcare, continued technological advancements will likely force costs upwards. Correlations between the cost of medical services and the quality improvements resulting from technology advancements may further exacerbate health disparities based on income and class, which runs contrary to the current aims of healthcare reform. In addition to cost, technology also will drive the approach and possibilities available during the provision of care and services as the personalization of medicine (e.g., genomics) continues to develop.

Knowledge concerning the future drivers of healthcare should affect future strategies and organizational design. Several of the many initiatives set into motion under the healthcare reform legislation will no doubt push forward the ideals set forth within the healthcare reform's triple aim (i.e., access, quality, and cost). As the healthcare industry moves forward, policy makers and healthcare administrators should keep in mind that simply lowering the cost of healthcare does not necessarily increase access, nor do increases in quality necessarily require parallel increases in cost.

How the healthcare industry will address future challenges is still uncertain; however, the question as to whether ACOs are a logical step toward Alain Enthoven's (American economist and professor at Stanford Graduate School of Business) concept of managed competition is a dynamic and volatile topic, involving the economic concerns of almost every stakeholder, each with constituencies, advocacy groups, and lobbyists. Each of these stakeholders currently operates under a pretense of commercial competitive markets at a time when a majority of those markets are dominated by a single payor, and the consolidation of hospitals and physician providers continues at a rapid pace.

Ultimately, the economic survival of all U.S. healthcare delivery may need to be framed within universal and centralized risk pool, and some version of a single payor system. This transformation will demand the further codification of treatment protocols derived from evidence-based medicine, as well as the, heretofore, illusive quality metrics expectable to both providers and payors as the basis for *value-based reimbursement.* The ensuing disruption of healthcare delivery from the current free market model to universal coverage, by any measure a dramatic change to the healthcare delivery system, will not happen overnight, no matter how dire the economic and social situation. However, inevitably change will come, because *any economic system that remains static dies.*

Substantive change in U.S. healthcare delivery will be, by necessity, an iterative process, likely with several phases of political bloodletting. Today, ACOs present a relevant step forward, creating *value-based reimbursement synergies* between high-quality and beneficial outcomes in pursuit of lower overall costs. However, ACOs are not likely to be the light at the end of the tunnel because, even if they succeed, more changes will be required. While the path forward is not yet apparent and there is still significant uncertainty as to whether another alternative exists, our current trajectory is unsustainable. Finding the solution is not a matter of a lack of money or a paucity of ideas, but rather the existence of a public and political will for change. Whether one views it as a blessing or a curse, it is undeniable that, "*we live in interesting times.*"[6]

ENDNOTES

1. *National Federation of Independent Business v. Sebelius*, Certiorari to the United States Court of Appeals for the Eleventh Circuit, S.C. Slip Opinion No. 11-393, June 28, 2011.
2. Medicare Spending and Financing. Kaiser Family Foundation, Fact Sheet, September 2011. Online at: http://www.kff.org/medicare/upload/7305-06.pdf (Accessed 1/1/2012).
3. Ibid.
4. Ibid.
5. The Wyden-Ryan Proposal—A Foundation for Realistic Medicare Reform. Joseph R. Antos, *New England Journal of Medicine*, vol. 366, no. 10, March 8, 2012: 879.
6. Day of Affirmation Address. Robert F. Kennedy, given to the University of Cape Town, South Africa, June 6, 1966. Online at: http://www.jfklibrary.org/Research/Ready-Reference/RFK-Speeches/Day-of-Affirmation-Address-news-release-text-version.aspx (Accessed 6/17/2012).

Bibliography

REGULATORY

4 Reasons to Wait on ACOs. Philip Betbeze. HealthLeaders Media. Online at: http://www.healthleadersmedia.com/print/LED-274402/4-Reasons-to-Wait-on-ACOs (accessed 12/27/2011).

4 Steps to Get Out of ACO Limbo. Molly Gamble ASC Communications, Chicago, 2011.

5 Challenges for Co-Ops. Margaret D. Tocknell, HealthLeaders Media, September 7, 2011. Online at: http://www.healthleadersmedia.com/page-2/HEP-270610/5-Challenges-for-COOPs (accessed 10/13/2011).

6 Target Markets for Accountable Care Partnerships. J. F. Damore and B. Gray, HealthLeaders Media, July 14, 2011. Online at: http://www.healthleadersmedia.com/print/PHY-268582/6-Target-Marketsfor-Accountable (accessed 7/21/2011).

10 ACO Blunders You Can Avoid. Marget D. Tocknell, HealthLeaders Media, August 17, 2011. Online at: http://www.healthleadersmedia.com/print/HEP-269879/10-ACO-BlundersYou-Can-Avoid (accessed 08/18/2011).

10 Key Planning Elements for Launching an ACO. *ACO Business News*, Atlantic Information Services, Inc., vol. 1, no. 1, November 2010.

10 Potential Blunders by Providers in ACOs. Molly Gamble, Becker's Hospital Review, August 10, 2011.

10 Ways CMS's Value-Based Purchasing Proposal Is Flawed. Cheryl Clark, HealthLeaders Media. Online at: http://www.healthleadersmedia.com/print/QUA-263564/10-WaysCMSs-ValueBased-Purchasing.

15 U.S.C. § 80a-8: Registration of investment companies.

21st-Century Health Care: The Case for Integrated Delivery System. Francis J. Crosson, *The New England Journal of Medicine*, vol. 361, no. 14, October 1, 2009.

27 States Debate ACO-Related Bills, But Just 10 Enact Laws. Judy P. Tursman, *ACO Business News*, Atlantic Information Services, Inc., vol. 2, no. 8, August 2011.

42 CFR 412, et al. Medicare and Medicaid Programs; Electronic Health Record Incentive Program; Proposed Rule. *Federal Register* 73 Fed. Reg. 23685–23698.

42 CFR 1001 Federal Health Care Programs: Fraud and Abuse; Statutory Exception to the Anti-Kickback Statute for Shared Risk Arrangements; Final Rule. vol. 64, no. 223, November 19, 1999.

42 U.S.C. 1320a-7b: Civil Monetary Penalties. 42 U.S.C. 1320a-7a (2010).

42 United States Code Section 1320a-7b: Criminal Penalties for Acts Involving Federal Health Care Programs, May 20, 2009. Online at: http://www.law.cornell.edu/uscode/42/usc_sec_42_00001320— -a007b,html (accessed 5/3/2011).

45 C.F.R 425: Medicare Program; Medicare Shared Savings Program: Accountable Care Organization.

2011 State Legislation: Accountable Care Organizations. Robin Richardson, March 2011. Online at: http://www.aafp.org/online/etc/medialib/aafp_org/documents/policy/state/statehealthpolicy/acoleg.Par.0001.File.tmp/ACO%20State%20Legislation%202011.pdf (accessed 2/28/2011).

2012 Benchmarks in Patient Registry Use for Accountable Care. Healthcare Intelligence Network (HIN), January 2012.

AAFP Statement: AAFP Commends CMS for Improving Medicare ACO Final Rule, Announcing the Advance Payment Model. Glen Stream. October 21, 2011. Online at: http://www.aafp.org/online/en/home/media/releases/2011newsreleases-statements/acofinal-rule.html (accessed 11/14/2011).

About GAO. U.S. Government Accountability Office. Online at: http://www.gao.gov/about/index.html (accessed 5/25/2012).

About HHS. U.S. Department of Health & Human Services. Online at: http://www.hhs.gov/about/ (accessed 5/25/2012).

About the Health Care Report Card Compendium. Agency for Healthcare Research and Quality. Online at: https://www.talkingquality.ahrq.gov/content/reportcard/about.aspx (accessed 05/25/2012).

About the Joint Commission. Online at: http://www.jointcommission.org/about_us/about_the_joint_commission_main.aspx (accessed 1/19/2012).

Accelerated Development Learning Sessions. Online at: http://innovations.cms.gov/areas-offocus/seamless-and-coordinated-care-models/acolearningsession/ (accessed 7/15/2011).

Accountable Care: The Journey Begins. Keith D. Moore and Dean C. Coddington. Online at: http://www.hfma.org/Templates/Print.aspx?id=22068 (accessed 7/7/2011).

Accountable Care at Academic Medical Centers: Lessons from Johns Hopkins. Scott A. Berkowitz and Edward D. Miller, *The New England Journal of Medicine*, vol. 1, no. 12, February 2, 2011. Online at: http://www.nejm.org/doi/full/10.1056/NEJMp1100076 (accessed 2/4/2011).

Accountable Care Collaborative. 2011. Online at: http://www.colorado.gov/cs/Satellite/HCPF/HCPF/1233759745246 (accessed 02/28/2011).

Accountable Care Organization Provisions in the Patient Protection and Affordable Care Act. Emma Dolan, Integrated Healthcare Association, May 1, 2010 (accessed 6/9/2010).

Accountable Care Organization: Quality and Efficiency Metrics. Gail M. Amundson, Quality Quest for Health, November 2, 2011.

Accountable Care Organization: Accelerated Development Learning Program. Online at: https://acoregister.rti.org/ (accessed 7/15/2011).

Accountable Care Organization 2012 Program Analysis: Quality Performance Standards Narrative Measure Specifications—Final Report, December 12, 2011.

Accountable Care Organization (ACO) Principals. 2010. Online at: http://www.hida.org/AM/Template.cfm?Section=Home&TEMPLATE=/CM/ContentDisplay.cfm&CONTENTID=14410 (accessed 3/15/2012).

Accountable Care Organization (ACO) Regulations: First Look. David Harlow, April 03 2011. Online at: http://healthblawg.typepad.com/healthblawg/2011/04/accountable-careorganization-aco-regulations-first-look.html (accessed 04/15/11).

Accountable Care Organization Pilot Will Help Improve Quality and Lower Costs. Monarch HealthCare, May 25, 2010. Online at: http://www.marketwire.com/pressrelease/Monarch-HealthCare-Partners-Anthem-Blue-Cross-Chosen-Innovative-National1265703.htm (accessed 2/28/2011).

Accountable Care Organization Proposed Regulations: Resources. March 31, 2011. Online at: http://www.kaiserhealthnews.org/Stories/2011/March/31/ACO-Documents-In-TheNews.aspx (accessed 2/13/2012).

Accountable Care Organization Prototypes: Winners and Losers? Harris Meyer. *Health Affairs*, vol. 30, no. 7, July 2011.

Accountable Care Organization Provisions of Health Care Reform. Robert W. Lundy and Paul A. Deeringer, California Hospital Association, May 2010.

Accountable Care Organizations: Physician/Hospital Integration. Bill Aseltyne, Paul DeMuro, Laura Jacobs, Paul Katz, and Daniel Meron. *American Bar Association Health Law* Section, vol. 21, no. 6, August 2009.

Accountable Care Organizations: Proposed Regulations Finally Released. J. P. Rich, David L. Klatsky, and Peter Boland. Strafford Publications, Inc., April 27, 2011. Online at: http://www.straffordpub.com/products/accountable-care-organizationsproposed-regulations-finally-released-2011-04-27 (accessed 4/7/2011).

Accountable Care Organizations: Reality or Just a Passing Fancy? Max Reiboldt, Coker Group Newsletter, vol. 10, no. 10, December 2010. Online at: http://cokergroup.com/files/newsletters/CokerConnection_Newsletter_Volume_10_Number_10,_December_2010.pdf (accessed 1/20/2011).

Accountable Care Organizations: The Proposal and the Basics. Adrienne Dresevic and Carey F. Kalmowitz The Association for Medical Imaging Management (AHRA), May 2011. Online at: http://link.ahraonline.org/2011/05/01/accountable-care-organizations-the-proposaland-the-basics (accessed 5/4/2011).

Accountable Care Organizations: A Physician-Centric Model. Excellentia Advisory Group, St. Peters, MO, February 10, 2011.

Accountable Care Organizations: CMS Hosting Special Conference Call, McDermot, Will, and Emery, June 24, 2010.

Accountable Care Organizations: AHA Research Synthesis Report. American Hospital Association (AHA), June 2010. Online at: http://www.hret.org/accountable/resources/ACOSynthesis-Report.pdf (accessed 5/2011).

Accountable Care Organizations: What, How and Are They the Future? Teresa Koenig. The Camden Group, Chicago, September 15, 2011.

Accountable Care Organizations: Comments on ACO Rule Say More Flexibility Needed for Broad-Based Participation. *Health Lawyers Weekly*, vol. 19, no. 23, June 10, 2011. Online at: http://www.healthlawyers.org/News/Health%20Lawyers%20Weekly/Pages/2011/June%202011/June%2010%202011/CommentsOnACORuleSayMoreFlexibilityNeededForBroadBasedParticipation.aspx (accessed 6/10/2011).

Accountable Care Organizations: Principles. American Medical Group Association (AMGA), May 28, 2010. Online at: http://www.amga.org/AboutAMGA/ACO/principles_aco.asp (accessed July 27, 2010).

Accountable Care Organizations: Physician Perspective. David W. Hilgers and Amy K. Fehn, American Bar Association (ABA), March 8, 2012.

Accountable Care Organizations: Analysis of Proposed ACO Regulations. Erica Brode, Cliff Sarkin, and Sara Watson. Insure the Uninsured Project. April 2011.

Accountable Care Organizations: Legal Challenges in Care Transformation. Fredrick C. Geilfuss, Foley and Lardner LLP, Chicago, September 15, 2011.

Accountable Care Organizations: Executive Briefing for Health Care Decision Makers. Faegre Baker Daniel, LLP, Denver, January 29, 2010. Online at: http://www.faegrebd.com/10896 (accessed 2/20/2012).

Accountable Care Organizations: Structures and Legal Issues. C. F. Geilfuss, Foley and Lardner LLP, Chicago, October 12–14, 2011.

Accountable Care Organizations: The End of Innovation in Medicine. Scott Gottlieb, American Enterprise Institute for Public Policy Research, February 2011.

Accountable Care Organizations: "Facts and Fiction." Mathew J. Levy, Michael J. Schoppmann, and Stacy L. Marder, Kern Augustine Conroy & Schoppmann, P.C., Garden City, NY.

Accountable Care Organizations: What Is an ACO? Online at: http://www.ncqa.org/tabid/1312/Default.aspx.

Accountable Care Organizations: Part 1. Debajyoti Pati, May 31 2011. Online at: http://www.healthcaredesignmagazine.com/article/accountable-care-organizations-part-1 (accessed 11/15/11).

Accountable Care Organizations. Strategic Health Care, Plante Moran and Squire, Sanders & Dempsey LLP, Cleveland, April 8, 2011.

Accountable Care Organizations: Preparing for the Changing Landscape. Elliot S. Fisher and James W. Squires. Online at: http://www.mpho.org/resource/d/54071/ElliottFisherKeynoteAddress9.22.11PRISM.pdf (accessed 4/4/2012).

Accountable Care Organizations. Peter A, Pavarini, American Health Lawyers Association. *AHLA Connections*. February 2012.

Accountable Care Organizations (ACO). Centers for Medicare & Medicaid Services. Online at: http://www.cms.gov/Medicare/Medicare-Fee-for-Service-Payment/ACO/index.html (accessed 5/30/2012).

Accountable Care Organizations (ACO) Draft 2011 Criteria: Overview. National Committee for Quality Assurance (NCQA), October 19, 2011.

Accountable Care Organizations (ACO's) and Revisiting Managed Care. Mike Magee, Health Commentary, 2011. Online at: http://healthcommentary.org/?page_id=4103 (accessed 4/18/2011).

Accountable Care Organizations after Healthcare Reform: Structuring ACOs That Avoid Violations of Antitrust, Fraud, Patient Privacy, and Stark Laws. Strafford Webinar, July 7, 2010.

Accountable Care Organizations and Payment Reform: Setting a Course for Success. Marc Bard, Michael Nugent Navigant Consulting, Inc., 2011. Online at: http://www.navigant.com/~/media/site/downloads/healthcare/acctcarewhitepaperbrochure_ us_hc.ashx (accessed March 5, 2012).

Accountable Care Organizations and the CMD Proposed Rule for the Medicare Shared Savings Program. Cerner, 04/13/2011. Online at: http://www.cerner.com/ACOs_and_CMD_proposed_Rule/?langType=1033 (accessed 4/18/2011).

Accountable Care Organizations at Academic Medical Centers. John A. Kastor, Massachusetts Medical Society, February 2, 2011. Online at: http://www.nejm.org/doi/full/10.1056/NEJMp1013221? (accessed 2/3/2011).

Accountable Care Organizations for the Commercially Insured Population: From HMO to PPO? James Robinson, Berkeley Center for Health Technology. Online at http://www.ehcca.com/presentation/aco-congress2/1.3_1.pdf (accessed March 13, 2012).

Accountable Care Organizations Give Capitation Surprise Encore: Many see ACOs as the model for reform, but if provider groups dole out payment, then what roles will health plans play? Frank Diamond. *Managed Care Magazine*, MediMedia USA, September 2009. Online at: http://www.managedcaremag.com/archives/0909/0909.accountablecare.html (accessed 4/25/2011).

Accountable Care Organizations Hold Promise, But Will They Achieve Cost and Quality Targets. Peter Boland, Phil Polakoff, and Ted Schwab, Managed Care Magazine, MediMedia, USA, Online at http://www.managedcaremag.com/archives/1010.ACOs.html (accessed March 13, 2012). October 2010.

Accountable Care Organizations in California: Lessons for the National Debate on Delivery System Reform. James C. Robinson and Emma L. Dolan, 2010.

Accountable Care Organizations in Medicare and the Private Sector: A Status Update. Robert A. Berenson and Rachel A. Burton, November 2011. Online at: http://www.urban.org/publications/412438.html (accessed 11/16/11).

Accountable Care Organizations Revisited: Physician Issues under the New Regulations and Guidance. American Health Lawyers Association (AHLA), Webinar, November 16, 2011.

Accountable Care Organizations II: Questions and More Questions. Mark S. Hedberg, ABA Health eSource, July 22, 2010. Online at: http://www.americanbar.org/newsletter/publications/aba_health_esource_home/Volume6_ SE2_hedberg.html (accessed 7/18/2011).

Achieving Breakthrough Chronic Disease Outcomes: A Key to ACO Success. Bob Matthews, MediSync, PriMed Physicians, Tinley Park, IL, September 16, 2011.

ACO Advance Payment Applications Due March 30. March 14, 2012. Online at: http://www.amaassn.orWamalpub/amawire12012-march-14/2012-mar... (accessed 3/20/2012).

ACO Case Study: New West Physicians: Denver, Colorado. Keith D. Moore and Dean C. Coddington, McManis Consulting, American Hospital Association (AHA), January 2011. Online at: www.aha.org/aha/content/2011/pdf/aco-case-new-west-physicians.pdf (accessed 5/13/2011).

ACO Case Study: Catholic Medical Partners: Buffalo, New York. Keith D. Moore and Dean C. Coddington, American Hospital Association (AHA), January 2011. Online at: http://www.aha.org/aha/content/2011/pdf/aco-case-Catholic-med-partners.pdf (accessed 5/13/2011).

ACO Concerns Elicit Enticements from CMS' Berwick. Cheryl Clark, May 18, 2011. Online at: http://www.healthleadersmedia.com/page-1/LED-266312/ACO-Concerns-Elicit-Enticements-from-CMS-Berwick (accessed 5/18/2011).

ACO Final Rules Released. HealthLeaders Media Staff, October 20, 2011. Online at: http://www.healthleadersmedia.comprint/HEP-27333/ACO-Final-Rule (accessed 10/20/2011).

ACO Hurdles, Risks, Could Dampen Provider Enthusiasm. John Commins, HealthLeaders Media, May 11, 2011. Online at: http://www.healthleadersmedia.com/content/PHY266033/ACO-Hurdles-Risks-Could-Dampen-Provider-Enthusiasm (accessed 6/16/2011).

ACO Legal Issues Update. Robert Homchick, Jill Gordon, and Douglas C. Ross, presented at 2nd National ACO Conference, November 2, 2011.

ACO Model, The: The Benefits and Consequences of an Integrated System. Martin Hickey, Navigant Corporate Research Group, Inc., Chicago.

ACO Payments: Risk, Reward, and Reviewing Your Healthcare Partners. Keith L. Martin Physicians Practice, April 31, 3011.

ACO Proposed Rule, The: A [Skeptical] View from 'The Street. Sheryl R. Skolnick, April 6 2011. Online at: http://acowatch.wordpress.com/2011/04/06/the-aco-proposed-rule-a-viewfrom-the-street/ (accessed 04/15/11).

ACO Proposed Rules Spotlight Physician–Hospital Alignment. John Commins, HealthLeaders Media, April 5, 2011. Online at: http://www.healthleadersmedia.com/print/LED-264521/ACO-Proposed-Rules-SpotlightPhysicianHospital-Alignment (accessed 4/8/2011).

ACO Regs Are Seen as Not Leading Patients to Migrate; PCP is Crucial. *ACO Business News*, Atlantic Information Services, Inc., vol. 2, no. 6, Atlantic Information Services, Inc., June 2011.

ACO Regulations, The: Some Answers, More Questions. John K. Iglehart, Massachusetts Medical Society, April 13, 2011. Online at: http://www.nejm.org/doi/full/10.1056/NEJMp1103603?viewType=Print&viewClass=Print (accessed 4/16/2011).

ACO Regulations Announced. *National Association of Managed Care Physicians (NAMCP) Journal*, vol. 8, no. 6, HMP Communications, LLC, June 2011.

ACO Rule Finalized for Medicare Shared Saving Program. Monica Hogan, *Medtech Insights*, vol. 13, no. 9, October 1, 2011.

ACO Rule Leaves Oncologists Wondering How to Proceed. Lola Butcher, *Oncology Times,* vol. 34, no. 3, February 10, 2012.

ACO Rules, The: Striking the Balance between Participation and Transformative Potential. Meredith B. Rosenthal, David M. Cutler, and Judith Feder, *The New England Journal of Medicine*, 2011.

ACO Rules Receive Guarded, Mixed Reviews. John Commins, HealthLeaders Media, April 4, 2011. Online at: http://www.healthleadersmedia.com/print/LED-264455/ACO-Rules-Recieve-Guarded-Mixed-Reviews (accessed 4/8/2011).

ACO Strategy and Organizational Structure. Daniel T. Roble and Lorry Spitzer, Ropes & Gray, Boston, November 16, 2010.

ACO Update: Pioneer ACO Program Participants. G. Garrison, Medical Distribution Solutions, Inc., October 20, 2011. Online at: http://blog.jhconline.com/aco-update-pioneer-acoprogram-participants.htm (accessed 11/16/11).

ACOs: What's Important in the Proposed Rules? Steve Beck and Gail Brandt, Fredrikson & Byron, Webinar, Minneapolis, May 11, 2011.

ACOs: The Final Rule and New Opportunities. John M. Kirsner, Paul Lee, Marian Lowe, and Peter A. Pavarini, Squire, Sanders & Dempsey LLP, Cleveland, November 3, 2011.

ACOs: Understanding Them from a Physician's Perspective. Randy Cook, AmpliPHY Physician Services, Greenbranch Publishing Inc., Phoenix, MD, January 11, 2012.

ACOs: How Do You Get There from Here? Lee A. Jarousse, Siemens Medical Solutions Hospitals & Health Networks (H&HN), March 1, 2011. Online at: http://www.hhnmag.com/hhnmag_app/jsp/articledisplay.jsp?dcrpath=HHNMAG/Article/data/03MAR2011/0311HHN_FEA_gatefold&domain=HHNMAG (accessed 5/18/2011).

ACOs: Balancing Antitrust Concerns against Efficiencies. Annette M. Boyle, Advanstar Communication Inc., November 16, 2011. Online at: http://www.modernmedicine.com/modernmedicine/Modern+Medicine+Now/ACOsBalancing-antitrust-concerns-against-efficien/ArticleStandard/Article/detail/749004 (accessed 11/18/11).

ACOs: Stuck in the Wrong Conversation? Gordon Mountford, HCPRO, June 10, 2011. Online at: http://www.healthleadersmedia.com/content/TEC-267226/ACOs-Stuck-in-the-WrongConversation.html## (accessed 11/22/2011).

ACOs: Creating the Medical Home. Daniel Casciato, October 13, 2011. Online at: http://www.medicalofficeloday.corrVcontenl.asp?article=5332&utm_soUf. (accessed 10/13/2011).

ACOs: Applying 20th Century Laws to 21st Century Ideas. Henry C. Fader, Pepper Hamilton LLP, December 13, 2010. Online at: http://www.pepperlaw.com/publications_update.aspx?ArticleKey=1957 (accessed 8/2/2011).

ACOs: IRS Notice Leaves Many Questions. John R. Holdenried, Baird Holm Law Firm, Omaha, AHLA Connections, August 2011.

ACOs: Will High Start Up Costs and Downside Risk Limit Interest in This Health Care Reform Darling? Kelly Leahy, Squire, Sanders & Dempsey LLP, Cleveland, April 21, 2011. Online at: http://www.accountablecareforum.com/payment-methodologies/acos-will-high-start-upcosts-and-downside-risk-limit-interest-in-this-health-care-reform-darling/ (accessed 05/12/2011).

ACOs: Analysis Shows Potential Savings, Losses for Groups That Want to Form ACOs. Nathaniel Weixel, Bureau of National Affairs, Inc. (BNA), April 27, 2011. Online at: http://healthlawrc.bna.com/hlrc/4225/split_display.adp?fedfid+20690361&vname+hcenotallissues&fn=20690361&jd=a0c77n2p4q9&split=0 (accessed 04/27/2011).

ACOs and the Enforcement of Fraud, Abuse, and Antitrust Laws. Robert F. Leibenluft, Massachusetts Medical Society, December 22, 2010. Online at: http://healthpolicyandreform.nejm.org/?p=13453 (accessed 12/23/2010).

ACOs Are Obama-Speak for HMOs. Sally C. Pipes, March 1, 2011. Online at: http://www.forbes.com/2011/02/28/obamacare-aco-hmo-opinions-sally-pipes.html (accessed 3/2/2011).

ACOs beyond Medicare. Victoria Boyarsky, Howard Kahn, David Mirkin, and Rob Parke, Milliman, Seattle, April 2011. Online at: http://publications.milliman.com/publications/healthreform/pdfs/acos-beyondmedicare.pdf.

ACOs Can Pay Off with Time, Pilot Project Indicates. Annette M. Boyle, August 24, 2011. Online at: http://license.icopyright.net/user/viewFreeUse.act?fuid=MTQxNDk4NDc= (accessed 10/13/2011).

ACOs Fit within Fraud Exceptions; Industry Wants Certainty of Waivers. *ACO Business News*, Atlantic Information Services, Inc., vol. 2, no. 3, March 2011.

ACOs Get Broad Waivers from the Fraud & Abuse Laws. McDermott, Will & Emery, November 10, 2011. Online at: http://www.mwe.com/info/news/wp1111a.pdf (accessed 11/18/2011).

ACOs May Find the Long Arm of State Law Extends to Them. *ACO Business News*, Atlantic Information Services, Inc., vol. 2, no. 1, January 2011.

ACOs Must Meet Eight Criteria. *ACO Business News*, Atlantic Information Services, Inc., vol. 1, no. 11, November 2010.

ACOs, or Else: Are ACOs a Strategic Imperative for Providers? Paul A. Deeringer. Health Law Resource Center, Bureau of National Affairs, Inc. (BNA), May 5, 2011. Online at: http://healthlawrc.bna.com/hlrc/display/batch_print_display.adp (accessed 6/16/2011).

ACOs See No Shortage of State Laws Governing Them. *ACO Business News*, Atlantic Information Services, Inc., vol. 2, no.1, January 2011.

ACOs Waste Millions of Dollars Chasing Unconstitutional ObamaCare, According to Health Plan Expert. Wayne Iverson, Association of American Physicians and Surgeons, April 25, 2011. Online at: http://www.aapsonline.org/newsoftheday/001547 (accessed 4/28/2011).

ACOs Widen Marketing's Scope. Anna Webster, Health Leaders Media. July 20, 2011. Online at: http://www.healthleadersmedia.com/print/MAR-268809/ACOs-Widen-Marketings-Scope (accessed 07/21/2011).

Additional Information about Accountable Care Organizations. April 6, 2011. Online at: http://www.wallerlaw.com/articles/2011/04/06/additional-information-about-accountablecare-organizations.175341 (accessed 07/18/2011).

Administration Releases Proposed Rules for Medicare Accountable Care Organizations. Ceci Connolly, McKinsey Center for U.S. Health System Reform, April 1, 2011.

Advance Payment. Online at: http://innovations.cms.gov/areas-of-focus/seamless-and-coordinatedcare-models/advance-payment/ (accessed 7/15/2011).

Advance Payment Accountable Care Organization (ACO) Model. Center for Medicare & Medicaid Innovation, April 10, 2012. Online at: http://innovations.cms.gov/Files/factsheet/Advance-Payment-Model-ACO-Fact-Sheet.pdf (accessed 4/25/2012).

Advance Payment Model. Online at: http://innovations.cms.gov/areas-of-focus/seamless-andcoordinated-care-models/advance-payment/ (accessed 2/8/2012).

Advance Payment Solicitation. Centers for Medicare & Medicaid Innovation. Online at: http://innovations.cms.gov/documents/paymentcare/APACO_Solicitation_10_20_11_Compliant1.pdf (accessed 3/2/2012).

Advanced Practice Registered Nurses: Crucial Full Partners in ACOs and Beyond. Mary J. Schumann, Project Hope, May 13, 2011. Online at: http://healthaffairs.org/blog/2011/05/13/advanced-practice-registered-nurses-crucial-fullpartners-in-acos-and-beyond/ (accessed 5/15/2011).

Advancing Health Care Equity through Improved Data Collection. Joel S. Weissmann and Romana Hasnain-Wynia. *New England Journal of Medicine*, vol. 364, no. 24, Massachusetts Medical Society, June 16, 2011.

Advancing Public Reporting through A New "Aggregator" to Standardize Data Collection on Providers' Cost and Quality. Harold S. Luft. vol. 3, no. 3, March 2012. Online at: http://content.healthalfuirs.orgfcontentl31/3/619.full (accessed 3/20/2012).

Aetna, Banner Partner on ACO. Bernie Monegain, November 21, 2011. Online at: http//www.healthcareitnews.com/print/3802 (accessed 11/28/2011).

Affordable Care Act Gives Providers New Options to Better Coordinate Health Care. May 17, 2011. Online at: http://www.healthcare.gov/news/factsheets/accountablecare05172011a.html (accessed 6/6/2011).

Affordable Care Act Helps 32 Health Systems Improve Care for Patients, Saving Up to $1.1 Billion: Leading Healthcare Providers Will Be Pioneer Accountable Care Organizations. U.S. Department of Health & Human Services, December, 2011. Online at: http://www.hhs.gov/news/press/2011pres/12/20111219a.html (accessed 12/27/11).

Affordable Care Act Initiative to Lower Costs, Help Doctors and Hospitals Coordinate Care. U.S. Department of Health & Human Services. Online at: http://www.hhs.gov/news/press/2011pres/08/20110823a.html (accessed 10/24/2011).

Agencies Release Rules, Policies for Shared Savings Program. Nathaniel Weixel, Bureau of National Affairs, Inc. (BNA), October 20, 2011. Online at: www.healthlawrc.bna.com (accessed 10/20/2011).

AHA Comments on ACOs, Innovation Center at CMS Forum. November 23, 2010. Online at: http://www.ahanews.com/...app/jsp/display.jsp?dcrpath=AHANEWS/AHANewsNowArticle/data/ann_112310_forum&domain=AHANEWS (accessed 11/29/2010).

AHA Participates in FTC Workshop on ACO Antitrust Issues. May 9, 2011. Online at: http://www.ahanews.com/ahanews_app/jsp/display.jsp?dcrpath=AHANEWS/AHANewsNowArticle/data/ann_050911_ACO&domain=AHANEWS (accessed June 16, 2011).

AHIP: Plans Can Assist Providers with Data to Improve Care in ACOs. *ACO Business News*, Atlantic Information Services, Inc., vol. 2, no. 8, August 2011.

AHIP Statement on ACO Regulations, Karen Ignagni, America's Health Insurance Plans, October 20, 2011. Online at: http://www.ahip.org/News/Press-Room/2011/AHIP-Statementon-ACO-Regulations.aspx (accessed 11/11/2011).

AMA: Final ACO Rule Offers Promise to Improve Care Delivery. Peter W. Carmel, October 20, 2011. Online at: http://www.ama-assn.org/ama/pub/news/news/final-aco-rule.page (accessed 11/14/2011).

AMA Adopts Policy on Accountable Care Organizations. Emily P. Walker, MedPage Today, LLC. November 12, 2010. Online at: http://www.medpagetoday.com/PracticeManagement/PracticeManagement/23326 (accessed 11/15/2010).

American Recovery and Reinvestment Act of 2009, The: Public Law 111-5, Pub. Law 111-5, February 17, 2009.

AMGA Raises Red Flag on "Burdensome" ACO Rules. John Commins, May 13, 2011, Online at: http://www.healthleadersmedia.com/print/LED-266149/AMGA-Raises-Red-Flag-on-Burde (accessed 7/8/2011).

Analysis: ACOs Could Have the Medicare Muscle to Transform Health System. Michael L. Millenson, *Kaiser Health News*, Henry J. Kaiser Family Foundation, May 2, 2012.

Anti-Kickback Statute: Criminal Penalties for Acts Involving Federal Health Care Programs. 42 U.S.C. § 1320a–7b.

Antitrust: Analysis of DOJ/FTC Proposed Policy on Accountable Care Organizations. Robert E. Bloch and Scott P. Perlman, May 12, 2011.

Antitrust, Antifraud Barriers to Entry for Accountable Care Organizations. Jeffery R. Ruggiero, and Kirk Ogrowsky, Bureau of National Affairs, Inc. (BNA), December 1, 2010. Online at: http://healthlawrc.bna.com/hlrc/display/alpha.adp?mode=topics&letter=A&frag_id=19606594&item=2BB88AF970D049BA2C0DE60C642CB7DE&prod=hlin (accessed 4/21/2011).

Antitrust Considerations in ACO Formation. Ashley M. Fischer, Webinar, McDermott, Will, & Emery, Chicago, March 1, 2011.

Antitrust Markets and ACOs. David A. Argue and John M. Gale, *CPI Antitrust Chronicle*, Competition Policy International, Inc. May 1, 2011.

Antitrust Proposed Antitrust Guidance for Accountable Care Organizations from the Federal Trade Commission and Department of Justice. Douglas Ross, BNA Insights. April 28, 2011. Online at: http://healthlawrc.bna.com/hlrc/display/batch_Print_Display_adp (accessed 4/28/2011).

Antitrust Worries May Be Addressed By "Safe Harbors" Coming from FTC. *ACO Business News*, Atlantic Information Services, Inc., vol. 1, no. 1, November 2011.

APHA Annual Meeting Highlights Lifelong Wellness. Charlotte Tucker, *The Nation's Health*, May/June 2012.

AR Section 60: Framework for Performing and Reporting Compilation and Review Engagements. Statements on Standards for Accounting and Review Services, December 2009. Online at: http://www.aicpa.org/Research/Standards/CompilationReview/DownloadableDocuments/AR-00060.pdf (accessed 1/4/2012).

AR Section 100: Compilation and Review of Financial Statements.

Are Accountable Care Organizations in Your Vocabulary? Henry C. Fader, Pepper Hamilton LLP, Philadephia, April 15, 2010.XOnline at: http://www.pepperlaw.com/publications_update.aspx?ArticleKey=1757 (accessed 8/2/2011).

Are ACOs a Financial Suicide Pact? Doug Perednia, April 1, 2011. Online at: http://roadtohellth.com/2011/04/are-acos-a-financial-suicide-pact/ (accessed 04/15/11).

Assessing an ACO Prototype: Medicare's Physician Group Practice Demonstration. John K. Iglehart, *New England Journal of Medicine*, vol. 364, no. 3, Massachusetts Medical Society, December 22, 2010. Online at: http://www.nejm.org/doi/pdf/10.1056/NEJMp1013896 (accessed 12/23/2010).

Attorneys Debate How to Best Protect ACOs from Running Afoul of Antitrust Law. Sarah Barr, Bureau of National Affairs, Inc. (BNA), January 27, 2011. Online at: http://news.bna.com/hlln/HLLNWB/split_display.adp?fedfid19137312&vname=hlrnotallissues&fn=19137315&jd=a0c6d2h9h4&split=0 (accessed 1/26/2011).

AU Section 110: Responsibilities and Functions of the Independent Auditor. AICPA Code of Professional Conduct, November 1972. Online at: http://www.aicpa.org/Research/Standards/AuditAttest/DownloadableDocuments/AU00110.pdf (accessed 1/4/2012).

Aurora Health Balks at ACOs under Proposed Rules. John Commins, May 18, 2011. Online at: http://www.healthleadersmedia.com/print/LED-266311/Aurora-Health-Balks-at-ACOs-Under-Proposed-Rules (accessed 5/20/2011).

Banner Health Offered Pioneer ACO Status: Phoenix System Has Until Mid-November to Accept CMS Contract. The Advisory Board Company, November 4, 2011. Online at: http://www.advisory.com/Daily-Briefing/2011/11/04/Banner-Health-offered-Pioneer-ACO-statu (Accessed 11/16/11).

Barak Richman: ACOs Should Not Involve Collaboration of Rivals. Barak Richman, February 11, 2011. Online at: http://www.fiercehealthcare.com/story/barak-richman-acos-shouldnot-involve-collaboration-rivals/2011-02-11 (accessed 2/16/2011).

Being Chosen for MSSP Pilot Is "Wonderful, Terrifying," CEO Says. Julia Strange, *ACO Business News*, Atlantic Information Services, Inc., vol. 3, no. 5, Atlantic Information Service, Inc., May 2012.

Better to Best: Value-Driving Elements of the Patient Centered Medical Home and Accountable Care Organizations. Health2 Resources, Vienna, VA, March 2011.

Black's Law Dictionary: Definitions of Terms and Phrases of American and English Jurisprudence, Ancient and Modern. Henry C. Black, St. Paul, MN: West Publishing, 1990.

Blueprint for ACO Success: Clinical, Quality & Compliance Considerations for an Accountable Care Organization. Jeffery R. Ruggiero and Mark Shields, Healthcare Intelligence Network, Sea Girt, N, HFMA Annual Meeting, Las Vegas, NV, 2012.

Brave New World: The Effects of Health Reform Legislation on Hospitals, Ingenix, Eden Prairie, MN.

Broken Covenant in U.S. Healthcare, The. Michael G. Cassatly and William H. Bergquist, *Journal of Medical Practice Management*, vol. 27, no. 3.

Budget of the U.S. Government—Fiscal Year 2013: Executive Summary and Appendix. Office of Management and Budget. Online at: budget.gov.

Build-Up, The: High Hopes for ACOs. Online at: http://www.hfma.org/Templates/Print.aspx?id=27788 (accessed 7/7/2011).

Building a Medical Neighborhood for the Medical Home. Elliott S. Fisher, *The New England Journal of Medicine*, vol. 359, no. 12, September 18, 2008.

Building a Successful Community-Based ACO, Second Annual ACO Congress: Los Angeles. Ann Boynton, Juan Davila, Steve McDermott, and John Wray. CalPERS, Blue Shield of California, Hill Physicians Medical Group, November 2, 2011.

Building Blocks of ACOs, The: The Challenges. Jennifer Dennard, Porter Research, November 23, 2010. Online at: http://www.porterresearch.com/Resource_Center/Blog_News/Industry_News/2010/November/The_Building_Blocks_of_ACOs.html (accessed 12/22/2010).

Call Yourself an ACO? Prove It. Cheryl Clark, HealthLeaders Media. Online at http://www.Healthleadersmedia.com/page-1/LED-273369/Call-Yourself-an-ACO-Prove-It (accessed March 23, 2012). November 16, 2011.

Can Accountable Care Organizations Improve the Value of Health Care by Solving the Cost and Quality Quandaries? Timely Analysis of Immediate Health Policy Issues. Kelly J. Devers and Robert A. Berenson, October 2009. Online at: http://www.rwjf.org/files/research/acosummaryfinal.pdf (accessed 1/1/2012).

Can Participation in an ACO Cause a Nonprofit Hospital's Bonds to Become Taxable? Alexander B, Buchanan, *Accountable Care News*, Health Policy Publishing LLC, April 2012.

Capital Analysis Self-Tutorial. GE Healthcare Financial Services General Electric Company, 2011. Online at: www.gehealthcare.com/inen/services/financial/education/hfs_khtrain_menu.html (accessed 7/6/2011).

Care Coordination Experiments Deliver Hope, But Doubt Remains. Haydn Bush, February 28, 2011. Online at: http://hhndailynews.blogspot.com/2011/02/care-coordinationexperiments-deliver.html (accessed 10/13/11).

Carilion Clinic Conversion Enters New Phase, Will Pilot New Payment Structure for Private Insurance and Medicare. Carilion Clinic, July, 21, 2009. Online at: http://www.carilionclinic.org/Carilion/Brookings-Carilion+news+release (accessed February 28, 2011).

Cash for Care: Annual Medicare Payment Reg Focuses on Quality. Maureen McKinney, *Modern Healthcare*, April 30, 2012.

Catching Up with…: Margaret E. O'Kane. *Accountable Care News*, vol. 3, no. 2, Health Policy Publishing LLC. February 2012.

Catching Up With…: Elliott S. Fisher. *Accountable Care News,* vol. 3, no. 6, Health Policy Publishing LLC, June 2012.

Catching Up with Douglas A. Hastings. Douglas A. Hastings, *Accountable Care News*, vol. 3, no. 5, Health Policy Publishing LLC, May 2012.

Cautious Path Forward on Accountable Care Organizations, Barak D. Richman and Kevin A. Schulman, vol. 305, no. 6, American Medical Association (AMA), February 9, 2011.

Center for Medicare and Medicaid Innovation (CMMI) Initiatives. 2011. Online at: https://www.aamc.org/initiatives/reform/demosandpilots/214880/cmmiinitiatives.html (accessed 7/15/11).

Chasing Unicorns: The Future of ACOs. Ian Morrison. *H&HN Weekly*, January 3, 2011.

CIGNA and Medical Clinic of North Texas Launch "Patient-Centered Medical Home" Project Program to Provide Better Care Coordination. CIGNA, September 1, 2009. Online at: http://newsroom.CIGNA.com/KnowledgeCenter/ACO (accessed 11/16/2011).

Civil Monetary Penalties and Affirmative Exclusions. Office of Inspector General, Department of Health and Human Services, Washington, D.C.

Clinical Integration: The Key to Real Reform. *TrendWatch*, February 2010.

Closing the Quality Gap. April 2011. Online at: http://www.ahrq.gov/clinic/tp/gappcmhtp.htm (accessed 5/9/2011).

CMS ACO Regulations Part 2: A Deep Dive into the Revised Regulations. Bruce M. Fried and Mara McDermott, November 1, 2011. ACO Congress.

CMS Announces ACA Bundled Payment Demonstration. *AHANewsNow*, American Hospital Association. Online at: http://www.ahanews.com/ (accessed 10/24/2011).

CMS Announces ACO "Pioneer" Program and Advanced Payment Initiative. Kaiser Family Foundation, May 17, 2011. Online at: http://healthreform.kff.org/Scan/2011/May/CMSAnnounces-ACO-Pioneer-Program-and-Advanced-Payment-Initiative.aspx (accessed 7/15/2011).

CMS Announces First-Round MSSP ACO Picks. Lauren Gaffney and Daniel Kuninsky, American Health Lawyers Association (AHLA), April 11, 2012. Online at: www. healthlawyers.org/Members/PracticeGroups/TaskForces/ACO/alerts/Pages/CMSAnnouncesFirst-RoundMSSPACOPicks.aspx (accessed 1/25/2013).

CMS Asks Physicians for Input on ACOs. *ACO Business News*, Atlantic Information Services, Inc., vol. 1, no. 2, December 2010.

CMS Attempts to Reignite Interest in ACOs: Commentary on the Final Medicare Shared Savings Program Regulations. Thomas E. Bartrum, Baker Donelson Bearman Caldwell & Berkowitz PC, November 2011. Online at: http://www.healthlawyers.org/News/Connections/Documents/2011/November2011/Feature2_November2011.pdf (accessed November 18, 2011).

CMS Clarifies Key ACO Eligibility Requirements. Mintz Levin, Stephanie D. Willis, and Christi Braun, March 20, 2012. Online at: http://www.jdsupra.com/post/documentViewer.aspx?fid=d1862fe4-0fb0-476b-bd50bd13db6a46ce (accessed 3/23/2012).

CMS Clarifies Stark "Stand in the Shoes" Provision. Deniel H. Melvin, McDermott, Will, & Emery. vol. VII, no. 29, July 24, 2009.

CMS Faces Divisions within the Agency on ACO Rules: Enormous Distance Remains. *ACO Business News*, Atlantic Information Services, Inc., vol. 1, no. 1, November 2010.

CMS Finally Proposes to Waive Certain Fraud and Abuse Laws for ACOs. Gary. J McRay and Nicole E. Stratton, Foster Swift Collins & Smith, Lansing, MI, April 8, 2011.

CMS, IRS, Antitrust Agencies Issue Proposals for ACOs under ACA Shared Savings Program. Nathaniel Weixel, Peyton M. Sturges, Brian Broderick, and Diane Freda, Health Law Resource Center Bureau of National Affairs, Inc. (BNA), April 7, 2011. Online at: http://healthlawrc.bna.com/hlrc/display/batch_print_display.adp (accessed 6/16/2011).

CMS Issues Highly Anticipated ACO Proposed Rules. Larry Goldberg, Bureau of National Affairs, Inc. (BNA), May 8, 2011. Online at: http://healthlawrc.bna.com/hlrc/display/story_list.adp?mode=ins&frag_id=20367488&prod=hlin (accessed 4/21/2011).

CMS Issues Proposed Rule on Accountable Care Organizations. vol. 19, no. 13, April 1, 2011. Online at: http://www.healthlawyers.org/Health%20Lawyers%20Weekly/Pages/2011/April%202011/April%2001%202011/CMSIssuesProposedRuleOnAccountableCareOrganizations.aspx (accessed 4/1/2011).

CMS Launches Pioneer ACO Program: Other Initiatives to Encourage Participation. Nathaniel Weixel, Bureau of National Affairs, Inc. 20 HLR 748. May 19, 2011. Online at: http://healthlawrc.bna.com/hlrc/display/batch_print_display.adp (accessed 5/18/2011).

CMS Makes Major Changes to ACO Rule in Bid to Increase Provider Participation. Rachana Dixit, Inside Washington Publishers, October 20, 2011. Online at: insidehealthpolicy.com (accessed 10/20/2011).

CMS Medicare Chief Blum Says ACO Regulations to Be Released before November 1. Healthcare Update News Service, October 18, 2011.

CMS Official Cites Concerns That ACO Bar "Too High" But Solicits More Industry Input. Sara Hansard, Bureau of National Affairs, Inc., 20 HLR 749, May 19, 2011.

CMS Officials Say ACOs Must Be Serious about Change: Rule Expected Mid-January. Bureau of National Affairs, Inc., vol. 19, no. 1698, December 9, 2010.

CMS Proposed Rule on Medicare Shared Savings Program: Accountable Care Organizations HFMA Summary of CMS Fact Sheets and Other CMS Documents. March 31, 2011.

CMS Releases Proposed Regulations Regarding Formation of Accountable Care Organizations. Emily J. Cook and David L. Klatsky, McDermott, Will, & Emery, April 8, 2011. http://www.mwe.com/index.cfm/fuseaction/publications.nldetail/object_id/3bf8ec047a4d (accessed 4/17/2011).

CMS's PGP Demo Yields $31 Million in Year Four Savings. *ACO Business News*, Atlantic Information Services, Inc., vol. 2, no. 1, January 2011.

CMS Seeks Input Mainly on ACO Structure, But Market Power Issues Remain a Concern. *ACO Business News*, Atlantic Information Services, Inc., vol. 1, no. 2, Atlantic Information Service, Inc., December 2010. Online at: http://aishealth.com/archive/nabn1210-02.

CMS Sends Proposed ACO Rule to OMB for Review, Release Expected Soon. vol. 20, no. 286, Bureau of National Affairs, Inc. (BNA).

CMS Spotlights Physician-Friendly Changes in Final ACO Rule. Charles Fiegl, *American Medical News*, October 20, 2011. Online at: http://www.amaassn.org/amednews/2011/10/17/gvsf1020.htm (accessed 11/14/2011).

Colorado Puts 60,000 Patients into Regional Medicaid ACO Plans. *ACO Business News*, Atlantic Information Services, Inc., vol. 1, no. 2, December 2010.

Commercial ACO Program. Aldo De La Torre, *Anthem Health*, November 2, 2011.

Commercial Reasonableness: The New Target. David Pursell, *The Journal of Health Care Compliance*, vol. 13, no. 2, March/April 2011.

Committee on the Costs of Medical Care, The: 25 Years of Progress. I. S. Falk, *American Journal of Public Health*, vol. 48, no. 8.

Committee on the Costs of Medical Care Reports, *The American Journal of Nursing Center for Medicare and Medicaid Innovation*, vol. 32, no. 12, December 1932.

Comprehensive Primary Care Initative. Online at: http://www.innovations.cms.gov/initiatives/cpci/ (accessed 1/4/2012).

Comprehensive Primary Care Initiative. Center for Medicare and Medicaid Innovation. Online at: http://www.innovations.cms.gov/initiatives/Comprehensive-Primary-CareInitiative/index.html.

Conducting a Compliance Review of Hospital–Physician Financial Arrangements. Dennis S. Diaz, Davis Wright Tremaine LLP, Los Angeles, CA.

Congratulations … and Now the Real Work on ACOs Begins. Steven Lieberman, Health Affairs Blog, April 12, 2012.

Consolidated Appropriations Act, Pub. Law 106-554 114 Stat. 2763.

Consultant: Give Physicians "Value Proposition" to Invest in an ACO. *ACO Business News*, Atlantic Information Services, Inc., vol. 2, no. 3, March 2011.

Consumer–Purchaser Disclosure Project Brief Analysis of Medicare Shared Savings (ACO) Proposed Rules: Revised April 12, 2011.

Controlling Healthcare Spending—The Massachusetts Experiment. Zirui Song and Bruce E. Landon, *The New England Journal of Medicine*, Massachusetts Medical Society, April 26, 2012.

Controversial Draft Medicare ACO Regulations, The: Analysis, Comments and Recommended Action. Gary S. Davis, McDermott, Will, & Emery, Chicago.

Corporate Practice: State by State Listing of Relevant Statutes, Cases, and Opinions. American Academy of Emergency Medicine. Online at: http:\\www.aaem.org/corporatepractice/states.php (accessed 2/4/2010).

Corporate Practice of Medicine Doctrine 50 State Survey Summary. Mary H. Michal, Meg S. Pekarske, and Matthew K. McManus, Reinhart Boerner Van Deuren S.C., September 2006.

Cost Survey for Primary Care Practices. Medical Group Management Association (MGMA). USA: Medical Group Management Association (MGMA).

Creating Accountable Care Organizations in Massachusetts. Harold D. Miller, Massachusetts Payment Reform, Second in a Series, Massachusetts Hospital Association, November 2009.

Creating High-Performance Care Organizations: AMGA National Summit on ACOs: Where Are We Now? Where Are We Going?. September 29–October 1, 2010.

Credentialing Challenges for ACOs: Framing the Issues. Rick Sheff, AHLS, June 28, 2011.

Daubert v. Merrell Dow Pharmaceuticals, 509 U.S. 579 (1993), 6/28/1993.

Daubert v. Merrell Dow Pharmaceuticals, Inc., 113 Supreme Court Reporter (509 U.S. 578).

Day of Affirmation Address. John F. Kenendy. Online at: http://www.jfklibrary.org/Research/Ready-Reference/RFK-Speeches/Day-ofAffirmation-Address-news-release-text-version.aspx#.

Dealing with Antitrust Fallout from Health Care Reform. Ankur Kapoor and Dan Vitelli, Bureau of National Affairs, Inc. (BNA), December 9, 2010 (accessed 12/16/2010).

Deep Dive into Accountable Care, A: What You Need to Know about the Latest Healthcare Movement. Navigant Consulting, Inc., Winter 2011. Online at: http://media.navigantconsulting.com/emarketing/Documents/Healthcare/NAV2-1796211-FNL-1.pdf (accessed 4/25/2011).

Degrees of Accountability: Everyone's Looking to Gain an Edge in the Upcoming Regs Governing ACOs. Melanie Evans, Crain Communications Inc., December 20, 2010. Online at: https://home.modernhealthcare.com/clickshare/authenticateUserSubscription.do?CSProduct=modernhealthcaresub&CSAuthReq=1:373412740846482:AID%7CIDAID=20101220/MAGAZINE/101219958%7CID=:634900344574B51A890E64CBB6C14B78&AID=20101220/MAGAZINE/101219958&title=Degrees%20of%20accountability&ID=&CSTargetURL=http://www.modernhealthcare.com/apps/pbcs.dll/login?AssignSessionID=373412740846482&AID=20101220/MAGAZINE/101219958 (accessed 1/2/2011).

Deja Vu All Over Again. Nathan S. Kaufman. FutureScan 2012, Society for Healthcare Strategy and Market Development.

Despite Notable No-Shows, Pioneer Largely Attracts Applicants that CMS Expected. *ACO Business News*, Atlantic Information Services, Inc., vol. 2, no. 10, October 2011.

Do You Know the Fair Market Value of Quality? Jen Johnson, Healthcare Financial Management, 63.10, October 2009.

Doctor's Duty to the State, The. John B. Roberts, American Medical Association (AMA), 1908.

Dodging an ACO Chilling Effect: Regulators Ease Up on Provider Collusion Warnings. Joe Carlson, October 31, 2011.

DOJ, FTC Inform Congress That Expedited ACO Review Is Coming. *ACO Business News*, Atlantic Information Services, Inc., vol. 2, no. 1, January 2011.

DOJ Official Says ACO Guidelines Will Help to Avoid Antitrust Violations. Sarah Barr, Bureau of National Affairs, Inc., vol. 19, no. 1691, December 9, 2010. Online at: http://healthlawrc.bna.com/hlrc/display/batch_print_display.adp (accessed February 17, 2012).

Downside Risk in Practice. Javier Estrada, vol. 18, no. 1, 2006.

Economists Caution: ACOs May Not End Wasteful Health Spending. Jordan Rau, August 30, 2011. Online at: http://capsules.kaiserhealthnews.org/index.php/2011/08/economistscaution-no-free-lunch-for-u-s-health-care/ (accessed 11/15/11).

Editor's Corner: ACOs: Lessons from Weld. Michael S Dukakis, *Accountable Care News*, vol. 3, no. 6, Health Policy Publishing LLC.

Eight Things Hospital CEOs Should Know about ACO Regulations. David E. Kopans, May 5, 2011.

Employer Interest in ACOs Rises Notably, But Provider Consolidation Is a Concern. *ACO Business News*, Atlantic Information Services, Inc., vol. 2, no. 11, November 2011.

Engineering the Care Delivery/Management Team across the Continuum. Josh Bennet and Denise B. Prince, Premier, Inc., November 3, 2011.

Enhancing Care Management with a Palliative Care Partnership. Brian Michaelsen, Heritage Provider Network. Online at: http://www.ehcca.com/presentations/acocongress2/michaelson_pc3.pdf (accessed 3/13/2012).

Episode-Based Payments: Charting a Course for Health Care Payment Reform. Hoangmai H. Pham, Paul B. Ginsburg, Timothy K. Lake, and Myles M. Maxfield, No. 1 National Institute for Health Care Reform, January 2010. Online at: http://www.nihcr.org/EpisodeBasedPayments.html.

Essence of Accountable Care, The. Rita E. Numerof and Stephen E. Rothenberg, Health Forum, March 10, 2011. Online at: http://www.hhnmag.com/hhnmag/HHNDaily/HHNDailyDisplay.dhtml?id=7670002189 (accessed 3/21/2011).

Establishes Medicaid Accountable Care Organization Demonstration Project in DHS: Fiscal Analysis. N.J. S. Bill No. 2443, March 28, 2011. Online at: http://www.njleg.state.nj.us/2010/Bills/S2500/2443_E1.HTM (accessed 11/8/2011).

Evaluation of the Costs and Benefits of Household Energy and Health Interventions at Global and Regional Levels: Summary. Guy Hutton, Eva Rehfuess, Fabrizio Tediosi, and Svenja Weiss, 2006.

Evolution of Care Delivery: Accountable Care Organizations and Preparing for Implementation. Colin B. Konschak and Joanne Bohn, DIVURGENT. Online at: http://divurgent.com/images/ACOWhitePaperFINAL.pdf (accessed 4/27/2011).

Evolve and Integrate a New Imperative for Ambulatory Care: Developing a Fully Integrated Ambulatory Care System Is a Critical Strategy for Ensuring Success under Healthcare Reform. Tracy K. Johnson and Suzanne Borgos, Healthcare Financial Management, April 2012.

Evolving to an ACO (2011: May 26): Better Patient Outcomes and Lower Expenditures. Tom Deas, Healthcare Financial Management Association (HFMA), webinar sponsored by Sandlot.

Exclusive Survey: Most Primary Care Physicians Expect to Join an ACO. Morgan Lewis, Jr., Advanstar Communication Inc. December 21, 2011. Online at: http://www.modernmedicine.com/modernmedicine/Modern+Medicine+Now/Exclusivesurvey-Most-primary-care-physiciansexpe/ArticleStandard/Article/detail/753570?contextCategoryId=48598 (accessed 12/27/2011).

Exclusivity: Antitrust Concerns for ACOs. Rashi Mittal, Mintz, Levin, Cohn, Ferris, et al., August 2011. Online at: http://www.americanbar.org/...sletter/publications/aba_health_esource_home/aba_health_law_esource_1108_aco_mittal.html (accessed 1/17/2012).

Exemption from Tax on Corporations, Certain Trusts, etc. 26 U.S.C. § 501 *Federal Register*.

Experiments with ACOs Successful in Private Sector. Joanne Wojcik, Business Insurance, April 17, 2011. Online at: http://www.businessinsurance.com/article/20110417/ISSUE01/304179979# (accessed 4/4/2012).

Experts Predict CMS Will Use Prospective Patient Attribution Methodology in Regs. Eric Cahow, *ACO Business News*, Atlantic Information Services, Inc., vol. 2, no. 1, January 2011.

Fact Sheet: Medicare FQHC Advanced Primary Care Practice Demonstration. October 24, 2011. Online at: http://www.cms.gov/apps/media/press/factsheet.asp?Counter=4137&intNumPerPage=10&checkDate=&checkKey=&srchType=1&numDays=3500&srchOpt=0&srchData=&keywordType=All&chkNewsType=6&intPage=&showAll=&pYear=&year=&desc=&cboOrder=date (accessed 5/31/12).

Facts about Hospital Accreditation. The Joint Commission. Online at: http://www.jointcommission.org/assets/1/18/Hospital_Accreditation_1_31_11.pdf (accessed 06/01/2012).

False Claim Act: 31 USC 3729-3733, 2011. 31 USC 3729-3733 (2011).

FAQs about Qualified Domestic Relations Orders. U.S. Department of Labor, December 16, 2009. Online at: http://www.dol.gov/ebsa/faqs/faq_qdro.html (accessed 05/25/2012).

Federal Agencies Address Legal Issues Regarding Accountable Care Organizations. 42 CFR 400.202. March 31, 2011. Online at: http://www.google.com/url?sa=t&rct=j&q=&esrc=s&source=web&cd=2&ved=0CD0QFjAB&url=http%3A%2F%2Fwww.asahq.org%2F~%2Fmedia%2FFor%2520Members%2FAdvocacy%2FASA%2520in%2520Washington%2FACOs%2FACO%2520Fact%2520Sheet%2520Legal%2520Issues%252003%252031%25202011.ashx&ei=LZ9jT9KhEan9sQKdl92bCw&usg=AFQjCNHnFQXr3JwAzSB33OtQoP3elHjrNQ&sig2=vtoFo6emkR2rkRYsqDkRdQ (accessed 3/16/2012).

Federal Agencies Move to Address Antitrust, Fraud and Abuse Concerns for ACOs. vol. 9, no. 13, American Health Lawyers Association (AHLA), April 1, 2011. Online at: http://healthlawyers.org/News/Health%20Lawyers%20Weekly/Pages/2011/April%202011/April%2001%202011/FederalAgenciesMoveToAddressAntitrust,FraudAndAbuseConcernsForACOs.aspx (accessed 4/1/2011).

Federal Agencies Release Proposed Rules for Accountable Care Organizations. Steven F. Banghart, Ungaretti & Harris. Online at: http://www.uhlaw.com/publications/detail.aspx?pub=512 (accessed March 5, 2012).

Federal Anti-Kickback Law and Regulatory Safe Harbors. Department of Health and Human Services. Online at: http://oig.hhs.gov/fraud/docs/safeharborregulations/safefs.htm (accessed 05/21/12).

Federal Plan Would Streamline Medicare. Kelly Kennedy, April 1, 2011. Online at: http://www.usatoday.com/news/washington/2011-04-01AccountableCare01_ST_N.htm?csp=34news (accessed 4/1/2011).

Federal Trade Commission, Department of Justice Issue Final Statement of Antitrust Policy Enforcement Regarding Accountable Care: Guidance Will Help Health Care Providers from Procompetitive ACOs and Protect Health Care Consumers from Higher Prices and Lower Quality Care. U.S. Federal Trade Commission. Online at: http://www.ftc.gov/opa/2011/100/aco.shtm (accessed 5/25/2012).

Federal Trade Commission, Department of Justice Issue Final Statement of Antitrust Policy Enforcement Regarding Accountable Care Organizations. Federal Trade Commission, October 20, 2011. Online at: http://www.ftc.gov/opa/2011/10/aco.shtm (accessed 1/17/2012).

Final ACO Regulations: Will Medicare ACOs Now "Work" and Attract Greater Industry Interest? Atlantic Information Service, Inc., November 15, 2011, webinar.

Final ACO Rule Offers Promise to Improve Care Delivery. Peter W. Carmel, American Medical Association (AMA), October 20, 2011. Online at: http://www.amaassn.org/ama/pub/news/news/final-aco-rule.page (accessed 11/14/2011).

Final ACO Rules Released: Significant Changes Seen. Melanie Evans, HealthLeaders Media, October 20, 2011.

Final CMS MSSP Regulations Are Expected This Month. *ACO Business News*, Atlantic Information Services, Inc., vol. 2, no. 10, October 2011.

Final MSSP Rule Will Encourage Variety in ACOs, May Attract the Inexperienced. *ACO Business News*, Atlantic Information Services, Inc., vol. 2, no. 11, November 2011.

Final Rule: Changes to Whole Hospital and Rural Provider Exceptions to the Physician Self-Referral Prohibition and Related Changes to Provider Agreement Regulations. vol. 75, no. 226, November 24, 2010.

Finance's Team and Reform Planning for 2011. Mike Nugent, Navigant Healthcare Financial Management Association (HFMA), Chicago, December 14, 2010.

Financial Implications of ACOs for Providers, The. James Reynolds and Daniel Roble, vol.65, no. 10, October 2011. Online at: http://www.hfma.org/Templates/InteriorMaster.aspx?id=29091 (accessed 11/15/2011).

Financing Issues for Healthcare Providers and Companies. AHLA Annual Meeting, Deborah Gordon, June 27, 2011.

Five Participants "Should Be Enough" to Test Advance Payment Model. Leslie Champlin, *ACO Business News*, Atlantic Information Services, Inc., vol. 3, no. 5, May 2012.

Florida, et al. v. United States Department of Health and Human Services, et al. Writ of Certiotari, Motion No. 11-400, November 14, 2011.

Flow of Funds and Credit Risk Issues for ACOs. Anne P. Ogilby and John O. Chelsey, Ropes and Gray, LLP, January 13, 2010, webinar.

Forget MSSP, You've Already Started a Commercial ACO. Karen Minich-Pourshadi, March 5, 2012. Online at: http://www.healthleadersmedia.com/printiFIN-277334/Forget-MSS... (accessed 3/20/2012).

Forging the Way: ACOs Taking Hold Despite Loose Definitions, with Different Methods—and Varying Results. Melanie Evans, Modern Healthcare. August 29, 2011.

Fraud and Abuse: Back Atop List of Top 10 Health Law Priorities. Bloomberg BNA Bureau of National Affairs, Inc. (BNA), January 10, 2011. Online at: http://www.bna.com/fraudabuse-back-pr5073 (accessed 1/17/2012).

Fraud and Abuse Waivers under the Medicare Shared Savings Program. Robert G. Homchick, Davis Wright Tremaine LLP, San Francisco. Online at: http://www.ehcca.com/presentations/acocongress2/1.5_2_h1.pdf (accessed 3/13/2012).

Frequently Asked Questions: Hospital Value-Based Purchasing Program. Centers for Medicare & Medicaid Services (CMS), March 9, 2012. Online at: http://www.cms.gov/Medicare/Quality-Initiatives-Patient-AssessmentInstruments/hospital-value-based-purchasing/Downloads/FY-2013-Program-Frequently-Asked-Questions-about-Hospital-VBP-3-9-12.pdf (accessed 4/25/2012).

Frequently Asked Questions (FAQs): About CMS's 2011 Accountable Care Organization Accelerated Development Learning Sessions. Centers for Medicare & Medicaid Innovation. Online at: https:llacoregister.rti.org/index.cfm?fuseaction=dspfaq (accessed 12/9/2011).

FTC Announces Public Workshop on Antitrust and Accountable Care Organizations. Mitchell J. Katz and Jessica Hoke, Federal Trade Commission, May 2, 2011. Online at: http://www.ftc.gov/opa/2011/05/acoworkshop.shtm (accessed 05/02/11).

FTC-DOJ Antitrust Enforcement Policy for ACOs in the Aftermath of Public Comment, The. Robert W. McCann, Health Law Resource Center Bureau of National Affairs, Inc. (BNA), June 16, 2011. Online at: http://healthlawrc.bna.com/hlrc/display/batch_print_display.adp (accessed 6/16/2011).

FTC, DOJ Get Favorable Industry Reviews on ACO Antitrust Policy. *ACO Business News*, Atlantic Information Services, Inc., vol. 2, no. 5, May 2011.

FTC, DOJ Open ACO Antitrust Guidelines to Public Comment. John Commins, Atlantic Information Services, Inc., HealthLeaders Media, April 1, 2011. Online at: http://www.healthleadersmedia.com/print/LED-264430/FTC-DOJ-Open-ACO-Antitrust-Guidelines-to-Public-Comment (accessed 4/1/2011).

FTC to Develop Safe Harbors and Expedited Review Process. Ashley M. Fischer, McDermott, Will & Emery, Chicago, October 6, 2010. Online at: http://www.mwe.com/index.cfm/fuseaction/publications.nldetail/object_id/c271228291ec-40ab-9270-a970cb0ba847.cfm (accessed 10/14/2010).

GAO: Stakeholders Differ on Adequacy of Provider Antitrust Guidance. *AHA News Now*, April 17, 2012.

Geisinger Medical Center Quality Report: Summary of Quality Information. Online at: http://www.qualitycheck.org/qualityreport.aspx?hcoid=6048# (accessed 1/19/12).

Geisinger's Multi-ACO Efforts May Not Be Easily Replicated. *ACO Business News*, Atlantic Information Services, Inc., vol. 2, no. 4, April 1, 2011.

General Electric Company v. Joiner: 118 Supreme Court Reporter (522 U.S. 135). 522 U.S. 136, L.Ed.2d 508 (1997).

Getting Ready for ACOs. Joseph Goedert, *Health Data Management*—Source Media, Inc., vol. 19, no. 4, April 1, 2011. Online at: http://www.healthdatamanagement.com/issues/19_4/getting-ready-for-accountable-careorganizations-42230-1.html (accessed 5/2011).

Getting to There from Here: Evolving to ACOs through Clinical Integration Programs. James J. Pizzo and Mark E. Grube, KaufmanHall, Skokie, IL.

Getting Up to Speed: Execs Detail IT Needs, Investments Required to Support an ACO. Melanie Evans, *Modern Healthcare*, February 20, 2012.

Getting Up to Speed on the Financial Crisis: A One-Weekend-Reader's Guide. Gary Gorton and Andrew Metrick, *Journal of Economic Literature*, vol. 50, no. 1, 2012.

Giving Providers a Head Start with ACOs. Gary Baldwin, HealthData Management. Online at: http://www.healthdatamanagement.com/news/HIMSS12-Anthem-ACO-44032-1.html (accessed March 5, 2011).

Global Cap Dominates Some Private-Sector Payment Models: Others Seek Partial Cap. *ACO Business News*, Atlantic Information Services, Inc., vol. 1, no. 1, November 2010. Online at: http://aishealth.com/archive/nabn1110-02.

Gold Rush Is On, The. Marian C. Jennings. FutureScan 2012, Society for Healthcare Strategy and Market Development.

Good Start on ACO Model. Rebecca Vesely, *Modern Healthcare*, April 11, 2011.

Great Expectations: The Obama Administration and Health Care Reform. Jonathan Oberlander, *The New England Journal of Medicine*, vol. 360, no. 4, October 10, 2007.

Group Health Cooperative of Seattle, Washington, Takes on Leadership Role. September 1, 2010. Online at: http://www.hca.wa.gov/press_release/quality-outcome-targeted-in-new-health-care0.html (accessed 02/28/2011).

Groups Seek Chronic Disease Management under an "Accountable Care" Framework. *ACO Business News*, Atlantic Information Services, Inc., vol. 2, no. 4, April 2011.

Growing an ACO: Easier Said Than Done. Jason Roberson, American College of Healthcare Executives (ACHE), *Healthcare Executives*, vol. 36, no. 5, September/October 2010.

Guidelines for Conducting Cost-Benefit Analysis of Household Energy and Health Interventions. Guy Hutton and Eva Rehfuess, 2006.

H.R. 6111 Section 204: Medicare Medical Home Demonstration Project (Tax Relief and Health Care Act of 2006).

Handbook of Financing Growth: Strategies and Capital Structure. Kenneth H. Marks, Larry E. Robbins, Gonzalo Fernandez, and John P. Funkhouser, Hoboken, NJ: John Wiley & Sons.

Headquarters by State for Entities That Sponsor ACOs. *ACO Business News*, Atlantic Information Services, Inc.,vol. 3, no. 2, February 2012.

Health Care and Education Reconciliation Act of 2010. Public Law 111-152. PL 111-152, 123 Stat. 1029 (March 30, 2010). 2011.

Health Care Antitrust Law Alert: The FTC and DOJ Release Accountable Care Organization Antitrust Policy Statement. Jan P. Levine and Robin P. Summer, Pepper Hamilton LLP, Philadelphia, April 5, 2011. Online at: http://www.pepperlaw.com/publications_update.aspx?ArticleKey=2067 (accessed 40641).

Health Care Organizations Participating in CMS Pioneer ACO Model. *ACO Business News*, Atlantic Information Services, Inc.,vol. 3, no. 1, January 2012.

Health Care Reform. Deloitte Center for Health Solutions Deloitte Development LLC., April 4, 2011. Online at: http://www.deloitte.com/view/en_US/us/Insights/Browse-by-ContentType/Newsletters/health-care-reform-memo/e738ddadc712f210VgnVCM3000001c56f00aRCRD.htm (accessed 4/15/2011).

Health Care Spending, Quality, and Outcomes: More Isn't Always Better. Elliot S. Fisher, David Goodman, Jonathan Skinner, and Kristen Bronner, February 27, 2009. The Dartmouth Institute for Health Policy and Clinical Practice.

Health Information Technology: Initial Set of Standards, Implementation Specifications, and Certification Criteria for Electronic Health Record Technology: Final Rule. Department of Health and Human Services, vol. 45, no. 170, July 28, 2010.

Health Law: Cases, Materials and Problems, 3rd ed. Barry R. Furrow, Thomas L. Greaney, Sandra H. Johnson, Timothy S. Jost, and Robert L. Schwartz, Eagan, MN: West Group Publishers, 1997.

Health Law Provision Raises Antitrust Concerns. Robert Pear, *The New York Times*. February 9, 2011. Online at: http://www.nytimes.com/2011/02/09/health/policy/09health.html?_r=1 (accessed 2/8/2011).

Health Law Section Files Comments on ACO Regulations. Proposed by CMS. ABA. Online at: http://www.americanbar.org/groups/health_law/news_announcements/aba_health_law_sec... (accessed 7/29/2011).

Health Providers Wary about New Plan for Medicare ACOs Released by CMS. Health Law Resource Center Bureau of National Affairs, Inc. (BNA), April 7, 2011. Online at: http://healthlawrc.bna.com/hlrc/display/batch_print_display.adp (accessed 06/16/2011).

Health Reform: Accountable Care Organizations—The Real Thing This Time? New America Foundation, July 21, 2009. Online at: http://health.newamerica.net/blogposts/2009/health_reform_accountable_care_organizations_the_real_thing_this_time-17277 (accessed 4/4/2011).

Health Reform: The Legal Fight Moves to the Next Level. Timothy Jost, Project Hope, May 10, 2011. Online at: http://healthaffairs.org/blog/2011/05/10/health-reform-the-legal-fight-moves-to-the-next-level/ (accessed 5/15/2011).

Health System Reform: Health Providers Wary about New Plan for Medicare ACOs Released by CMS. Ralph Lindeman, Bureau of National Affairs, Inc. (BNA),April 7, 2011. Online at: http://healthlawrc.bna.com/hlrc/batch_print_display.adp?searchid=14183921 (accessed 4/11/2011).

Healthcare Capital Finance in Good and Challenging Times. David A. Lips, American Health Lawyers Association, 2009.

The Healthcare Executive's Guide to ACO Strategy. Coker Group Health Leaders Media. Online at: http://www.hcmarketplace.com/Prod.cfm?id=9464&s=EB110320A&e_topic=WS_HLM2.

Healthcare Leaders Prep for the ACO Model. Philip Betbeze, HealthLeaders Media, September 14, 2010. Online at: http://www.healthleadersmedia.com/print/MAG256430/Healthcare-Leaders-Prep-for-the-ACO-Model (accessed 3/7/2012).

Healthcare Management: Corporate Compliance. The Rehman Group, July 28, 2009. Online at: http://www.rehmann.com/pdfs/SellSheets/hc_compliance.pdf.

Healthcare Marketing in Transition: Practical Answers to Pressing Questions, 1st ed. Terrence J. Rynne, New York: McGraw Hill, January 1995.

Healthcare Reform: The Law and its Implications: Toward Accountable Care: How Healthcare Reform Will Shape Provider Integration. Peter A. Pavarini, American Health Lawyers Association (AHLA), May 12, 2010. Online at: http://www.healthlawyers.org/Events/Programs/Materials/Documents/HCR10/pavarini.pdf.

HealthPartners and Allina Hospitals and Clinics: Northwest Metro Alliance. HealthPartners, Allina Hospitals and Clinics HealthPartners. Online at: http://www.healthpartners.com/ucm/groups/public/@hp/@public/documents/documents/cn trb_008919.pdf (accessed 11/17/2011).

Herding Cats: What Health Care Means for Hospital–Physician Alignment and Clinical Integration. David Melvin and Chris Jedrey, McDermott, Will, & Emery, Bureau of National Affairs, Inc. (BNA), October 13, 2010.

HHI's Episode-of-Care Total Joint Replacement Model Development. Horizon Healthcare Innovations, *ACO Business News*, Atlantic Information Services, Inc., April 2012.

HHS Announces New Incentives for Providers to Work Together through Accountable Care Organizations When Caring for People with Medicare: New Tools to Help Doctors and Other Health Care Providers Improve Quality of Care. Department of Health and Human Services, October 20, 2011. Online at: http://www.hhs.gov/news/press/2011pres/10/20111020a.html (accessed 11/18/2011).

HHS Names Pioneer ACOs. Jessica Zigmond and Richard Daly, Modern Healthcare Crain Communications, Inc., December, 2011. Online at: http://www.modernhealthcare.com/article/20111219/NEWS/312199905 (accessed 2/9/2012).

HHS Releases Final ACO Rule. Richard E. Ward, Reward Health Sciences, Inc., October 20, 2011. Online at: http://rewardhealth.com/archives/1769 (accessed 01/20/2012).

HHS Unveils ACO Rules Proposal. John Commins, HealthLeaders Media, March 31, 2011. Online at: http://www.healthleadersmedia.com/print/LED-264373/HHS-Unveils-ACO-Rules-Proposal (accessed 4/1/2011).

High Performance Accountable Care: Physician Group Practice Demonstration Evaluation Report. Stuart Guterman, Stephen Schoenbaum, Karen Davis, Cathy Schoen, and Anne-Marie J. Audet, The Commonwealth Fund, Washington, D.C., April 1, 2011.

History and Principles of Managed Competition, The. Alain C. Enthoven, *Health Affairs*, vol. 12, no. 1, 1993.

HITECH and Funding Opportunities. Online at: http://www.healthit.hhs.gov/portal/server.pt/community/healthit_hhs_gov__hitech_and_funding_opportunities/131 (accessed 7/7/2011).

Horizontal Merger Guidelines. U.S. Department of Justice, Federal Trade Commission, August 19, 2010. Online at: www.justice.gov/atr/public/guidelines/hmg-2010.pdf.

Hospital Budgets on the Rise as Purchasing Patterns Shift, Survey Finds. Monica Hogan. *The RPM Report*, March 2012.

Hospital Systems May Lead ACOs, But Plans Could Help Define Them. *ACO Business News*, Atlantic Information Services, Inc., Atlantic Information Services, vol. 2, no. 6, June 2011.

Hospital, Your Care Coordinator The: Some Centers Now Take Charge of Keeping People Healthy and at Home. Catherine Arnst, July 26, 2010. Online at: http://health.usnews.com/health-news/best-hospitals/articles/2010/07/26/the-hospitalyour-care-coordinator (accessed August 4, 2010).

Hospitals and Care Systems of the Future. American Hospital Association, Washington, D. C., September 2011. Online at: www.aha.org/content/11/hospital-care-systems-of-future-2010.pdf.

Hospitals at a Crossroads: Achieving Success in an Era of ACOs. *Aegis Health Group*, vol. 2, no. 2, Aegis Group. 2011.

Hospitals, Docs Are Assuming Leadership in Majority of ACO Governance Structures. *ACO Business News*, Atlantic Information Services, Inc., vol. 3, no. 3, March 2012.

Hospitals' Geographic Expansion in Quest of Well-Insured Patient: Will the Outcome Be Better Care, More Cost, or Both? Emily R. Carrier, Marisa Dowling, and Berenson A. Robert, *Health Affairs*, April 2012.

Hospitals Grapple with How Much Control They Give Docs, Observer Says. *ACO Business News*, Atlantic Information Services, Inc., vol. 3, no. 3, March 2012.

Hospitals, Health Systems Give Mixed Reviews on CMS's Draft ACO Regulations. *ACO Business News*, Atlantic Information Services, Inc., vol. 2, no. 5, May 1, 2011.

How CMS's Final Regulations for Accountable Care Organizations Fall Flat. John S. Hoff, The Heritage Foundation, no. 2647, January 30, 2012. Online at: http://thf_media.s3.amazonaws.com/2012/pdf/bg2647.pdf (accessed 4/25/2012).

How Do We Develop ACOs That Are Designed to Bring Hospitals and Physicians Closer Together While at the Same Time Abide by Laws Designed to Separate Them? John Wyand, Squire, Sanders & Dempsey LLP, Cleveland, May 5, 2011. Online at: http://www.accountablecareforum.com/regulatory-compliancelegal-waivers/how-do-wedevelop-acos-that-are-designed-to-bring-hospitals-and-physicians-closer-together-whileat/ (accessed 05/12/2011).

How Fast Will ACOs Spread? Karen M, Cheung, no. 2546, November 4, 2011. Online at: http://www.fiercehealthcare.com/print/node/63949 (accessed 12/27/2011).

How Intermountain Trimmed Health Care Costs through Robust Quality Improvement Efforts. Brent C. James, and Lucy A. Savitz, *Health Affairs*, June 2011. Online at: http://content.healthaffairs.org/content/early/2011/05/17/hlthaff.2011.0358.full.html (accessed 5/21/2011).

How One Practice Made EMR Improve Workflow, Patient Care and Revenue. Advisory Publications, *Cardiology Practice Advisor*, May 2001.

How the Center for Medicare and Medicaid Innovation Should Test Accountable Care Organizations. Stephen M. Shortell, Lawerence P. Casalino, Elliot S. Fishe,. Project Hope, *Health Affaires*, vol. 29, no. 7, July 2010. Online at: http://content.healthaffairs.org/content/29/7/1293.abstract.

How to Abstract: Primers on Key Selected Topics. vol. 13, no. 3, May/June 2010. Online at: http://www.mcareol.com/mcolfree/framepublication.html (accessed 3/13/2012).

How to Create Accountable Care Organizations. Harold D. Miller, 2009, online at www.health.state.mn.us/healthreform/announce/Miller100518.pdf.

How to Develop an Effective Accountable Care Organization. Abe Levy, Aric Sharp, and Scott Hayworth, Hospitals & Health Networks (H&HN), April 7, 2011. Online at: http://www.hhnmag.com/hhnmag/HHNDaily/HHNDailyDisplay.dhtml?id=6470003245 (accessed 4/11/2011).

How to Make Comparative Effectiveness Work. Wendy Everett, Project Hope, *Health Affairs*, May 10, 2011. Online at: http://healthaffairs.org/blog/2011/05/10/how-to-make-comparative-effectivenesswork/ (accessed 5/15/2011).

I. S. Falk, the Committee on the Costs of Medical Care, and the Drive for National Health Insurance, Milton I. Roemer, vol. 75, no. 8, 1985.

Identifying Legal and Strategic Challenges of Accountable Care. Douglas Hastings, Healthcare Financial Management, 2011, June 65(6).

Imaging Groups Balk at Blue Cross $300B Savings Plan. *HealthImaging*, October 6, 2011. Online at: http://www.healthimaging.com/index.php?option=com_articles&view=article&id=29847:imaging-groups-balk-at-blue-cross-300b-savings-plan (accessed 10/06/11).

Impact of Accountable Care Organizations on EP Services Remains Undefined. Online at: http://www.hrsonline.org/Policy/CodingReimbursement/aco_rule_summary.cfm (accessed 11/15/2011).

Impact of the Economy and Healthcare Reform on Capital Facility Programs and What Lies Ahead, The. John E. Kemper, KLMK Group, January 2011.

Implementation of Recovery Auditing at the Centers for Medicare and Medicaid Services: FY 2010, Report to Congress as Required by Section 6411 of Affordable Care Act. Centers for Medicare & Medicaid Services, Baltimore, MD.

Implementing Accountable Care Organizations. Stephen M. Shortell, Lawrence P. Casalino, and Elliott S. Fisher, Berkeley Law, University of California Press, Berkeley, CA, May 2010. http://www.law.berkeley.edu/files/chefs/Implementing_ACOs_May_2010.pdf.

Implementing Health Care Reform: An Interview with HHS Secretary Kathleen Sebelius. Massachusetts Medical Society, January 5, 2011. Online at: http://healthpolicyandreform.nejm.org/?p=13542 (accessed 1/5/2011).

Implementing Qualifications Criteria and Technical Assistance from Accountable Care organizations. Stephen Shortell and Lawrence P. Casalino, *The Journal of the American Medical Association*, vol. 303, no. 17, 2010.

Implications of the Medicare Shared Savings Program Regulations for Health Care Providers, The: Progress on the Road to Accountable Care? Doug Hastings, Brad Benton, and Steven Hester, Bureau of National Affairs, Inc. (BNA), April 8, 2011.

In ACO's Shadows, Bundled Payment Takes Off. Haydn Bush. September 19, 2011. Online at: http://www.hhmag.com/hhmag/HHNDaily/HHNDailyDisplay.dhtml?id (accessed 10/13/2011).

In an ACO, Who's Accountable? Philip Betbeze, HealthLeaders Media, April 14, 2011. Online at: http://www.healthleadersmedia.com/page-2/MAG-264787/In-an-ACO-Whos-Accountable (accessed 4/28/2011).

In Their Own Words: ACOs Should Have a Health Plan Perspective. *ACO Business News*, Atlantic Information Services, Inc., vol. 2, no. 11, November 2011.

In Their Own Words: Industry Can't Rely on "Status Quo." *ACO Business News*, Atlantic Information Services, Inc., vol. 3, no. 3, March 2012.

Incentives for the Use of Health Information Technology and Establishing the Position of the National Health Information Technology Coordinator: Executive Order 13335 of April 27, 2004. *Federal Register,* vol. 69, no. 84, April, 30, 2004.

Industry Comments Show Some Consensus in Provider Oposition to Key Components of CMS's Proposal for the Medicare Shared Savings Program. R. B. Rawlings and Scott P. Downing, August 2011. Online at: http://www.americanbar.org/newsletter/publications/aba_health_esource_home/aba_health_law_esource_1108_aco_rawlings.html (accessed 10/20/11).

Industry Insiders Clarify MSSP Participation in Multiple ACOs. *ACO Business News*, Atlantic Information Services, Inc., vol. 3, no. 1, January 1, 2011.

Industry News. *Accountable Care News*, vol. 3, no. 5, Health Policy Publishing, LLC, May 2012.

Industry News. *Accountable Care News,* vol. 3, no. 6, Health Policy Publishing, LLC, June 2012.

Industry Tells CMS Transparency, Equity Are Needed on ACO Reg. *ACO Business News*, Atlantic Information Services, Inc., vol. 2, no. 1, January 2011.

Innovations in ACO Development Massachusetts Alternative Quality Contact. Barbara Spivak.

Insights and Implications of CMS ACO Final Rule: Health Alert. Hogan Lovells, October 27, 2011. Online at: http://ehoganlovells.com/ve/7131j9190W7761JiY/VT=1%20 (accessed 11/18/2011).

Insurer Sees Medicaid ACOs as Partner, Not Threat. *ACO Business News*, Atlantic Information Services, Inc., vol. 2, no. 2, February 2011.

Insurers Find MSSP ACO Applicants Want Their Help in IT, Compliance, Marketing. *ACO Business News*, Atlantic Information Services, Inc., vol. 3, no. 2, February 2012.

Insurers Health Care Providers at Odds on Rules for Accountable Care Organizations. Jordan Rau. January 9, 2011. Online at: http://www.washingtonpost.com/wp-dyn/content/article/2011/01/09/AR2011010903401.html (accessed 1/23/2011).

Insurers Work with Providers on Crucial ACO Components. *ACO Business News*, Atlantic Information Services, Inc., vol. 1, no. 1, November 2011.

Integrated Delivery Systems: Perspectives from the Government Agencies. Susan De Santi, Gail Kursh, Ruth Madrigal, Terri Postma, and Vicki Robinson. Online at: www.healthlawyers.org/Events/Programs/Materials/Document/AM11/robinson_etal_slides.pdf (accessed 1/27/2012).

Integrating Pharmacists into Accountable Care Organizations (ACOs) and Coordinated Care. December 7, 2010. Online at: http://ncpanet.wordpress.com/2010/12/07/integratingpharmacists-into-accountable-care-organizations-acos-and-coordinated-care (accessed 12/9/2010).

Intel-GE Care Innovations Guide: Using Virtual Care Coordination to Foster Health, Independent Living. GE Company, Intel-GE Care Innovations, 2011.

Involve the Right Professionals. Jason H. Sussman, A Guide to Financial Strategies for Hospitals.

IPAs, PHOs Need Eight Critical Factors to Create Successful ACOs, Observer Says Casalino. *ACO Business News*, Atlantic Information Services, Inc., vol. 3, no. 5, Atlantic Information Service, Inc., May 2012.

IRS Appraiser Penalties: Pension Protection Act and Beyond. Robert J. Cimasi, William S. Forsberg, Michael A. Gregory, and Howard A. Lewis, BVR.

Is an ACO for You: PCPs Will Be at the Core of the Medicare Organizations, But Make Sure Joining One Will Be Worth Your Time. Morgan Lewis, *Medical Economics*, vol. 89, no. 4, February 25, 2012.

Is There a Statistician in the House? CMS Implements Its Predictive Modeling Program. Allyson J. Labban, Smith Moore Leatherwood, LLC, Atlanta, July 2011.

IT Groups Fret That Patients Will Opt Out of Data Sharing in Difficult-to-Meet Regs. *ACO Business News*, Atlantic Information Services, Inc., vol. 2, no. 6, June 2011.

It's a New Day and New Mindset, with New Solutions for Success. David Graser, McKesson Corporation. 2011.

Joint Negotiations: Integration, ACOs and Antitrust. Christine L. White, June 28, 2011, online at www.healthlawyers.org/Events/Programs/Materials/Documents/AM11/white_slides.pdf.

Joint Principles for Accountable Care Organizations. American Academy of Family Physicians, November 19, 2010. Online at: http://www.acponline.org/advocacy/where_we_stand/other_issues/aco-principles2010.pdf (accessed 6/3/2011; 11/23/11).

Journey to Becoming an Accountable Care Organization (ACO), The. Nancy J. Ham, MedVentive, Inc., Waltham, MA, 2011.

Kaiser Permanente HealthConnect Electronic Health Record. Kaiser Permanente, 2012. Online at: http://xnet.kp.org/newscenter/aboutkp/healthconnect/index.html (accessed 2/15/2012).

Key ACO Principles. Mark McClellan. Online at: http://www.ehcca.com/presentations/acocongress1/mcclellan_1_1.pdf (accessed 3/2/2012).

Key Findings from HSC's 2010 Site Visits: Health Care Markets Weather Economic Downturn, Brace for Health Reform. Laurie E. Felland, Joy M. Grossman, and Ha T. Tu, Center for Studying Health System Change, Washington, D.C., May 2011.

Key Uncertainties of the Proposed ACO Rule: A Polsinelli Shughart Update. Polsinelli Shughart PC. Health Care Law e-Alert Polsinelli Shughart PC, April 2011. Online at: http://www.polsinelli.com/publications/healthcare/upd0411-2hc.htm (accessed 4/28/2011).

Keys to Success: Effective ACOs Depend on Management: Studies. Rebecca Vesely, Crain Communications Inc., April 18, 2011.

Labor Force Statistics from the Current Populations Survey: Original Data Value. Bureau of Labor Statistics, U.S. Department of Labor. Online at: http://data.bls.gov/timeseries/LNS14000000.

Lack of Consensus on Adequacy of Antitrust Guidance for Provider Collaboration, GAO Says. American Health Lawyers Association (AHLA), April 20, 2012 (accessed 4/23/2012).

Large Healthcare Purchaser Takes Risky Leap into ACOs. Janice Simmons, HealthLeaders Media, April 8, 2010. Online at: http://www.healthleadersmedia.com/content/QUA-249275/Large-Healthcare-Purchaser-Takes-Risky-Leap-Into-ACOs (accessed 8/16/2010).

Largest Medicare ACO Impact May Come in Southern California. Walter Kopp, *Accountable Care News*, Health Policy Publishing LLC, vol. 3, no. 3, March 2012.

Latest Medicare Projections Renew Alarm on Long-Term Sustainability. Doug Trapp, *American Medical News*, April 14, 2008. Online at: http://www.ama-assn.org/amednews/2008/04/14/gvl10414.htm (accessed 01/01/2012).

Launching Accountable Care Organizations: The Proposed Rule for the Medicare Shared Savings Program. Donald M. Berwick, Massachusetts Medical Society, March 31, 2011. http://healthpolicyandreform.nejm.org/?p=14106 (accessed 4/1/2011).

Leading Change in Health Care: Building a Viable System for Today and Tomorrow. Ian Morrison, Health Forum, Inc., Chicago, 2011.

Leap to Accountable Care Organizations, The. Jim Molpus, HCPro, April 2011.

Learning from Failure in Health Care Reform. Jonathan Oberlander, *The New England Journal of Medicine*, 357, October 25, 2007.

Lessons from the Field: Making Accountable Care Organizations Real. Timothy K. Lake, Kate A. Stewart, and Paul B. Ginsburg, Center for Studying Health System Change, January 2011. Online at: http://www.nihcr.org/Accountable-Care-Organizations.html (accessed 1/2011).

Letter from AAFP to CMS: Regarding CMS Request for Information on Potential Regulations for Accountable Care Organization and the Medicare Shared Savings Model (CMS-1345-NC). Lori Heim, December 3, 2010.

Letter from ACA Regarding CMS Request for Information Regarding ACOs. Rick McMichael, November 29, 2010.

Letter from ACA to CMS Re: Medicare Program; Request for Information Regarding Accountable Care Organizations and the Medicare Shared Savings Program. Rick McMichael, November 29, 2010. Online at: http://theintegratorblog.com/index.php?option=com_content&task=view&id=719&Itemid... (accessed 1/28/2012).

Letter from AHA to CMS: RE: ACOs. Linda E Fishman, November 17, 2010 (accessed 11/17/2010).

Letter from AHA to CMS: Re: Medicare Program; Request for Information Regarding Accountable Care Organizations and the Medicare Shared Savings Program. Linda E. Fishman, December 3, 2010.

Letter from AHA to CMS: Regarding Study on ACOs. Linda Fishman, May 13, 2011.

Letter from AHA to CMS: Regarding Advanced Payment Initiative, Linda E. Fishman, June 17, 2011.

Letter from AHA to CMS: Re: Medicare Program; Medicare Shared Savings Program; Accountable Care Organizations. Rick Pollack, American Hospital Association, June 1, 2011.

Letter from AHIP to CMS: Regarding CMS-1345-NC Medicare Program; Request for Information Regarding Accountable Care Organizations and the Medicare Shared Savings Program. Carmella Bocchino, December 3, 2010.

Letter from AHIP to CMS: RE CMS-1345-P; Proposed Rule Regarding Medicare Program; Medicare Shared Savings Program: Accountable Care Organizations. Carmella Bocchino, America's Health Insurance Plans (AHIP), June 6, 2011.

Letter from AMA Regarding CMS Request for Information Regarding ACOs. Michael D. Maves, December 2, 2010.

Letter from AMA to CMI, CMS: Regarding Advanced Payment Initiative. Michael D. Maves, June 16, 2011.

Letter from Ambulatory Surgery Center Association (ASC) to CMS: RE: CMS-1345-P; Request for Comments, Medicare Shared Savings Program, Accountable Care Organizations. David Shapiro, June 3, 2011.

Letter from American Telemedicine Association to CMS: Reference: File code CMS-1345P. April 25, 2011.

Letter from AMGA to CMS: Re: CMS-1345-NC, Request for Information Regarding Accountable Care Organizations. Donald W. Fisher, December 3, 2010.

Letter from AMGA to CMS: Re: Medicare Shared Savings Program: Accountable Care Organizations. Donald W. Fisher, American Medical Group Association (AMGA), May 11, 2011. Online at: http://www.amga.org/advocacy/MGAC/Letters/05112011.pdf (accessed 5/26/2011).

Letter from APA Deputy Director for Regulatory Affairs and Director of Government Relations to APA Board of Trustees, Assembly, Council on Advocacy and Government Relations, Members: Detailed Analysis of Accountable Care Organizations (ACO) Final Rule. Julie Clements and Nick Meyers, October 26, 2011. Online at: http://www.psych.org/MainMenu/AdvocacyGovernmentRelations/GovernmentRelations/Memo-ACO-Final-Rule.aspx?FT=.pdf (accessed 11/17/11).

Letter from APTA to CMS: Subject: File Code CMS-1345-NC (Accountable Care Organizations). R. Scott Ward, December 3, 2010.

Letter from CBO to Nancy Pelosi: Re: CBO Estimate of Reconciliation Act of 2010. Douglas W. Elmendorf.

Letter from Dave and Alex. Dave Zito and Alex Hunter, Navigant Consulting, Inc., Winter 2011.

Letter from HFMA to CMS: Re File Code: CMS-1345-P. Richard L Clarke, June 3, 2011.

Letter from Hill Physicians to CMS: Regarding CMS Request for Information Regarding ACOs. Bruce Bob and Steve McDermott. Hill Physicians Medical Group, Inc., December 3, 2010.

Letter from MedPAC to CMS: RE: File code CMS-1345-NC. Glenn M. Hackbarth, November 22, 2010.

Letter from MedPac to CMS: Re File Code CMS-1345-P. Glenn M. Hackbarth, June 6, 2011.

Letter from MGMA to CMS: Re CMS-1345-P Medicare Shared Savings Program: Accountable Care Organizations. William F. Jessee, June 1, 2011.

Letter from NCQA to CMS. Margaret O'Kane, June 6, 2011.

Letter from PGP Demonstration Program to CMS.

Letter from Physician Group Practice (PGP) Demonstration Multi-Speciality Groups to CMS: Regarding NPRM for ACOs. Nicholas Wolter, May 12, 2011.

Letter from Senators to FTC and DOJ Regarding Antitrust Guidance for ACOs, Michael F. Bennet, February 11, 2011.

Letter from U.S. Senators to the DOJ and FTC (cc: CMS): Regarding Antitrust Guidance on ACOs. Mark Udall, February 11, 2011.

Letter from United States Senate to HHS. Tom Coburn, May 24, 2011.

Letter to CMS from AHA. Linda E. Fishman, May 13, 2011.

Letter to Congressional Requesters from James C. Cosgrove: Re: Federal Antitrust Policy: Stakeholders' Perspectives Differed on the Adequacy of Guidance for Collaboration among Health Care Providers. James C. Cosgrove, U.S. Government Accountability Office.

Limitation on Certain Physician Referrals. 42 U.S.C. § 1395nn, *Federal Register.*

Limitations on Certain Physician Referrals. U.S. Congress, 42 U.S.C. 1395nn. 2010.

Looking behind the Curtain at Structures and Capabilities of ACOs. Sharon Cheng, Squire, Sanders & Dempsey LLP, May 11, 2011. Online at: http://www.accountablecareforum.com (accessed 5/11/2011).

Lost in Translation: Como se Dice, Patient Protection and Affordable Care Act? James O. Breen, *The New England Journal of Medicine*, vol. 366, no. 22.

Lost to Follow-Up: The Public Health Goals of Accountable Care. Neil S. Calman, Diane Hauser, and Dave A. Chokshi, Archives of Internal Medicine. Online at: http://archinte.jamanetwork.com/article.aspx?volume=172&issue=7&page=584 (Accessed 5/3/2012).

Maine: Study Primary Care Medical Practice. National Academy for State Health Policy. Online at: http://www.nashp.org/med-home-states/maine.

Making Good on ACOs' Promises: The Final Rule for the Medicare Shared Savings Program. Donald M. Berwick, vol. 365, no. 9, November 10, 2011.

Managed Care Backlash, The: Did Consumers Vote with Their Feet. Susan M. Marquis, Jeannette A. Rogowski, and Jose J. Escaree, *Inquiry*, 41, Winter 2004/2005.

Mass. Plan, Health System Begin Medicaid-Focused ACO. *ACO Business News*. vol. 1, no. 2, December 2010.

Massachusetts Health Reform Experiment, The: An Update. Alice A. Coombs, vol. 2, no. 3, Health Policy Publishing, LLC, March 2011.

Massachusetts Plan, Health System Begin Medicaid-Focused ACO. *ACO Business News*, Atlantic Information Services, Inc., vol. 1, no. 2, December 2010.

Massachusetts Weighs Bill to Enable Formation, Track Trends of ACOs. *ACO Business News*, Atlantic Information Services, Inc., vol. 2, no. 8, August 2011.

Mayo Clinic, Other Premier Medical Groups Call Obama Plan on Healthcare Quality Unworkable. Ricardo Alonso-Zaldivar,*Washington Post*, May 11, 2011. Online at: http://www.washingtonpost.com/business/mayo-clinic-other-premier-medical-groupscall-obama-plan-on-health-care-quality-unworkable/2011/05/11/AFE0IZrG_story.html (accessed 5/20/2011).

MDs Cite Payment, Governance, Other Worries on Draft MSSP Reg. *ACO Business News*, Atlantic Information Services, Inc., vol. 2, no. 4, April 2011.

Meaningful Use of Health Information Technology: From Public Policy to Changing Care. Paul Tang, *Healthcare Trends and Implications*, Futurescan, Society for Healthcare Strategy and Marketing Development..

Medicaid Accountable Care: Accountable Care Organizations, Medicaid, and Medicaid Health Plans. John Pourciau, Sellers Dorsey Medicaid Health Plans of America.

Medicaid Accountable Care Organization Demonstration Project. Robert Wood Johnson Foundation, Princeton, N, June 27, 2010. Online at: http://www.healthreformgps.org/resources/medicaidaccountable-care-organization-demonstration-project/ (accessed 2/7/2011).

Medicaid Accountable Care Organizations: Opportunities for State Cost Control. Derek Delia and Louise B. Russell, March 14, 2011. Online at: http://healthcarecostmonitor.thehastingscenter.org/louiserussell/medicaid-accountablecare-organizations-opportunities-for-state-cost-control/ (accessed 11/7/2011).

Medical Group and Hospital: A Model for Clinical Integration. Richard Afable and Alan Puzarne, Online at: http://www.ehcca.com/presentations/acocongress2/3.2_2.pdf (accessed 3/2/2012).

Medical Homes and Accountable Care Organizations: If We Build It, Will They Come? June 28–30, 2009. Online at: http://www.academyhealth.org/files/publications/RschInsightMedHomes.pdf.

Medical Loss Ratio Requirements under the Patient Protection and Affordable Care Act. *Federal Register*, vol. 76, no. 235.

Medicare "Accountable Care Organizations:" Shared Savings Program—New Section 1899 of Title XVIII: Preliminary Questions and Answers. Online at: http://www.aanp.org/NR/rdonlyres/D0A6E8A2-8800-4C45-9642-62E33FE98BCF/4835/ACOQAMedicare.pdf (accessed 3/16/2012).

Medicare ACOs: Details from the Fraud and Abuse Perspective. Kathleen McDermott, Michael W. Paddock, and Mark Bonanno, American Health Lawyers Association (AHLA), Washington, D.C., May 24, 2011.

Medicare ACOs Will Have to Address Patient Primary, Security. *ACO Business News*, Atlantic Information Services, Inc., Atlantic Informatoin Services, Inc., vol. 2, no. 12, December 2011.

Medicare Demonstrations: Details for Medicare Medical Home Demonstration. August 31, 2011. Online at: http://www.cms.gov/DemoProjectsEvalRpts/MD/itemdetail.asp?itemID=CMS1199247 (accessed 1/4/2012).

Medicare Enrollment: National Trends 1966–2010. Online at: https://www.cms.gov/MedicareEnRpts/Downloads/HI2010.pdf (accessed 1/1/2012).

Medicare Federally Qualified Health Center: Advanced Primary Care Practice Demonstration. October 24, 2011.

Medicare Improvements for Patients and Providers Act of 2008: Section 133 Expanding Access to Primary Care Services. January 3, 2008.

Medicare Physician Group Practice Demonstration: Physicians Groups Continue to Improve Quality and Generate Savings under Medicare Physician Pay-for-Performance Demonstration. July, 2011. Online at: https://www.cms.gov/DemoProjectsEvalRpts/downloads/PGP_Fact_Sheet.pdf (accessed 11/21/2011).

Medicare Physician Group Practice Demonstration, The: Lessons Learned on Improving Quality and Efficiency in Health Care. Michael Trisolini, Jyoti Aggarwal, Musetta Leung, Gregory Pope, and John Kautter, vol. 9 (Jan.). The Commonwealth Fund, February 2008.

Medicare Physician Payment: Care Coordination Programs Used in Demonstration Show Promise, But Wider Use of Payment Approach May Be Limited. February 2008, online at www.gao.gov/products/GAO-08-65..

Medicare Program: Physicians' Referrals to Health Care Entities with Which They Have Financial Relationships (Phase II). Michael D. Maves, vol. 69, no. 59, June 24, 2004.

Medicare Program: Medicare Shared Savings Program; Accountable Care Organizations: Final Rule. vol. 76, no. 212, 76 F.R. 212 (2011), November 2, 2011.

Medicare Program: Request for Information Regarding Accountable Care Organizations and the Medicare Shared Savings Program. vol. 75, no. 221, November 17, 2010.

Medicare Program: Hospital Inpatient Value-Based Purchasing Program. 42 C.F.R. 422, 480.

Medicare Program: Solicitation for Proposals for the Physician Group Practice Demonstration. FR 67 no. 188.

Medicare Program; Advanced Payment Model. CMS-5505-N,. October 20, 2011.

Medicare Program; Final Waivers in Connection with the Shared Savings Program. *Federal Register*, vol. 76, no. 212, November 2, 2011.

Medicare Program; Medicare Shared Saving Program: Accountable Care Organizations and Medicare Program: Waiver Designs in Connection with the Medicare Shared Savings Program and the Innovation Center; Proposed Rule and Notice. vol. 76, no. 67, April 7, 2011.

Medicare Program; Physicians' Referrals to Health Care Entities with Which They Have Financial Relationships (Phase II). vol. 69, no. 59, March 26, 2004.

Medicare's Accountable Care Organization Regulations: How Will Medicare Beneficiaries Who Reside in Medically Underserved Communities Fare? Sara Rosenbaum and Peter Shin, Policy Research Brief #23, RCHN Community Health Foundation, April 20, 2011. Online at: http://www.gwumc.edu/sphhs/departments/healthpolicy/dhp_publications/pub_uploads/dhpPublication_6EFAAA15-5056-9D20-3DBE579D20C06F05.pdf (accessed 5/1/2011).

Medicare Shared Savings Program: Accountable Care Organizations (ACO) Final Rule. Hart Health Strategies. Online at: http://www.hrsonline.org/Policy/CodingReimbursement/upload/ACOFinalRuleSummary.pdf (accessed November 15, 2011).

Medicare Shared Savings Program: A New Proposal To Foster Better, Patient-Centered Care. Department of Health & Human Services, Centers for Medicare & Medicaid Services, March 31, 2011.

Medicare Shared Savings Program: Application Process and Overview of the Advance Payment Model Application. Kelly Hall, Centers for Medicare & Medicaid Services.

Medicare Shared Savings Program Accountable Care Organizations, The: The Proposed Rule. American Hospital Association (AHA), April 26, 2011. Online at: http://www.aha.org/aha/advisory/2011/110426-regulatory-adv.pdf (accessed 5/2011).

Medicare Shared Savings Program ACOs Starting April 1, 2012. *ACO Business News*, Atlantic Information Services, Inc., vol. 3, no. 5, Atlantic Information Service, Inc., May 2012.

Medicare Touts Success of Demonstrations That Paved the Way for ACOs. Jane Norman, The Commonwealth Fund, August 8, 2011. Online at: http://www.commonwealthfund.org/Newsletters/Washington-Health-Policy-in-Review/2011/Aug/August-15-2011/Medicare-Touts-Success-of-Demonstrations.aspx (accessed 4/4/2012).

Medicare Woos Skeptics: Medicare ACO Options Added after Criticism. Charles Fiegl, vol. 54, no. 11, June 6, 2011. Online at: http://www.ama-assn.org/amednews/2011/05/30/gv110520.htm.

MedPAC Makes Recommendations to CMS on ACOs. Gary S. Davis, Ashley M. Fischer, Christopher M. Jedrey, Webb Millsaps, and J. P. Rich, McDermott, Will, & Emery, Chicago, December 7, 2010.

Meet the Demands of Health Care Reform with Lower Costs and New Value. Accenture, Chicago. Online at: http://www.accenture.com/SiteCollectionDocuments/PDF/Accenture_Meet_the_Demands_of_Health_Care_Reform_with_Lower_Costs_and_New_Value.pdf (accessed 3/2/2012).

Meeting Fraud and Abuse Challenges in the Brave New World of Health Reform: What's in Store for ACOs? Carrie Valiant, Bureau of National Affairs, Inc. (BNA), December 15, 2010. Online at: http://healthlawrc.bna.com/hlrc/display/alpha.adp?mode=topics&letter=A&frag_id=19628211&item=2BB88AF970D049BA2C0DE60C642CB7DE&prod=hlin (accessed 4/21/2011).

Meeting the Challenges of Building ACOs: Ropes and Gray's Expertise and Experience. Ropes and Gray LLP, Boston, 2010.

MGMA Members Discuss Proposed ACO Rule. Casey Crotty, July 2011, MGMA Connexion, vol. 11, no. 6.

Minn. Blues Plan, Fairview Health Retool Incentives in ACO Model. James McManus and Mary Edwards, vol. 3, no. 4, April 2012.

Minutes of the Federal Open Market Committee. Washington, D.C.: The Federal Reserve Board, June 30, 2004. Online at: http://www.federalreserve.gov/fomc/minutes/20040630.htm.

Model for Integrating Independent Physicians into Accountable Care Organizations, A. Mark C. Shields, Pankaj H. Patel, Martin Manning, and Lee Sacks, *Health Affairs*, vol. 30, no. 1, January 2011. Online at: http://content.healthaffairs.org/content/30/1/161.full.html (accessed 1/17/2011).

Model of the Future, The?: The Health-Care Law Promoted Accountable-Care-Organizations. But It's Hard to Know What They Are. Avery Johnson, *The Wall Street Journal,* March 28, 2011. Online at: http://online.wsj.com/article/SB10001424052748703300904576178213570447994.html (accessed 5/14/2011).

Monopolies and Combinations in Restraint of Trade. 15 U.S.C §12-27. October 15, 1914.

More Quality Measures to Be Added to ACO Rule. Mark Moran, *PsychNews*, vol. 46, no. 24, December 16, 2011. Online at: http://psychnews.psychiatryonline.org/newsArticle.aspx?articleid=181066 (accessed 1/16/2011).

More Than 1 Million Medicare Beneficiaries Enrolled in Health Law Savings Program. Julian Pecquet, The Hill, April 10, 2012.

Most Doctors Headed for Penalty over Medicare Quality Reporting. Charles Fiegl, *American Medical News*, vol. 55, no. 11, American Medical Association.

Most Hit Quality Targets, But Not Cost Goals. Mary Ellen Schneider, *Cardiology News,* August 1, 2007. Online at: http://www.ecardiologynews.com/index.php?id=8736&type=98&tx_ttnews%5Btt_news%5D=86058&cHash=da03e20e36 (accessed 4/4/2012).

Movin' on without You: Getting Ready for ACO Implementation without Word from Antitrust Regulators. Max Reynolds, Bureau of National Affairs, Inc. (BNA), March 24, 2011. Online at: http://healthlawrc.bna.com/hlrc/4237/split_display.adp?fedfid=20121856&vname=hlrnotallissues&wsn=495268000&searchid=14282844&doctypeid=8&type=oadate4news&mode=doc&split=0&scm=4237&pg=0 (accessed 3/28/2011).

MSSP Antitrust Policy Has Industry Concerned about Monopolies. *ACO Business News*, Atlantic Information Services, Inc., vol. 2, no. 11, November 2011.

MSSP Offers Legal Protections Not Found in Private Sector. *ACO Business News*, Atlantic Information Services, Inc., vol. 3, no. 1, January 2012.

MSSP Participants Should Know Their "Hurdle Rate," Health Observer Contends. *ACO Business News*, Atlantic Information Services, Inc., vol. 3, no. 3, March 2012.

MSSP's Initial 27 Applicants Draw Cautious Optimism, Show Variety of Approaches. Johnson Fried Barrett, *ACO Business News*, Atlantic Information Services, Inc., vol. 3, no. 5, Atlantic Information Service, Inc., May 2012.

N.J. Coalitions Work toward Medicaid ACOs in Bid to Fix Fragmented Delivery of Care. *ACO Business News*, Atlantic Information Services, Inc., vol. 2, no. 2, February 2011.

Nation's Underemployed in the Great Recession of 2007-09, The. Andrew Sum and Ishwar Khatiwada, *Monthly Labor Review*, vol. 133, no. 11, U.S. Department of Labor. Online at: http://www.bls.gov/opub/mlr/2010/11/art1full.pdf.

National Accountable Care Organization Congress: Private Sector Partnerships Setting the Bar for Reform. Karen Ignagni, November 2, 2011.

National Federation of Independent Business, et al., *Petitioners v. Kathleen Sebelius, Secretary of Health and Human Services, et al. Department of Health and Human Services, et al., v. Florida et al. Florida, et al., Petitioners v. Department of Health and Human Services et al.:* On Writs of Certiorari to the United States Court of Appeals for the Eleventh Circuit. [FINAL RULING]. Supreme Court of the United States. *Natl. Federation of Independent Business v. Sebelius*, Nos. 11-393, 11-398 and, 11-400, 2012 BL 160004, 53 EBC 1513 (U.S. June 28, 2012). Supreme Court of the United States. Online at: http://www2.bloomberglaw.com/public/document/Natl_Federation_of_Independent_Business_v_Sebelius_No_Nos_11393_1 (accessed 7/23/12).

National Federation of Independent Business, Kaj Ahlburg, and Mary Brown v. Kathleen Sebelius, et al.: Writ of Certiotari, Motion No. 11-393. Writ of Certiotari, Motion No. 11-393, November 14, 2011.

A National Strategy to Put Accountable Care into Practice. Mark McClellan, Lewis McKethanm, Julie L. Lewis, Joachinm Roski, and Elliott S Fisher, Project HOPE, *Health Affairs*, vol. 29, no. 5, May 1, 2010.

NCQA Accountable Care Organization Accreditation. 2011. Online at: http://www.ncqa.org/LinkClick.aspx?fileticket=Mv2IW8SCCvI%3D&tabid=1312 (accessed 1/27/12).

NCQA ACO Performance Measures. *ACO Business News*, Atlantic Information Services, Inc., vol. 2, no. 12, December 2011.

NCQA Makes a Bid to Manage ACO Accreditation Process. *ACO Business News*, Atlantic Information Services, Inc., vol. 1, no. 2, December 2010.

NCQA Plans to Issue One Set of Standards That Fits All Categories of ACO Applicants. *ACO Business News*, Atlantic Information Services, Inc., vol. 2, no. 9, September 2011.

NCQA's Final ACO Standards in July May Have Later Impact on Medicare. *ACO Business News*, Atlantic Information Services, Inc., vol. 2, no. 6, June 2011.

NCQA Share ACO Accreditation Standards. Molly Gamble, ASC Communications, November 15, 2011.

NCQA Unveils Draft ACO Criteria, Seeks Public Comment on Measures. *ACO Business News*, Atlantic Information Services, Inc., vol. 1, no. 1, November 2010.

NEJM: Shift from "patient" to "consumer" undermines medicine. *HealthImaging*, October 13, 2011. Online at: http://www.cardiovascularbusiness.com/index.php?option=com_articles&view=article&id=29931 (accessed 10/13/11).

NEJM Report of ACO Financial Model Fails to Include Risk of Delayed Start on Transformation. Richard E. Ward, Reward Health Sciences, Inc., March 30, 2011. Online at: http://rewardhealth.com/?s=NEJM+report+of+aco+financial+model+fails+to+include (accessed 01/13/2012).

New Accountable Care Organization Pilot Program. Chesire Medical Center, 42 CFR 410.74, July 15, 2010. Online at: http://www.chesiremed.com/index.php?option=com_content&task=view&id=840&Itemid=345 (accessed 2/28/2011).

New ACO Regulations: Discover the Opportunities and Pitfalls Ahead. Erik Johnson and Mark Hedberg, Atlantic Information Service, Inc., May 5, 2011.

New ACO Rules Outline Gains and Risks for Doctors, Hospitals. Jordan Rau, Phil Galewitz, and Bara Vaida, The Henry J. Kaiser Family Foundation, March 31, 2011. http://www.kaiserhealthnews.org/Stories/2011/March/31/ACO-rules.aspx?p=1 (accessed 4/1/2011).

New "ACO-Type" Demo Offers Opportunities for Primary Care. *ACO Business News*, Atlantic Information Services, Inc., vol. 2, no. 11, November 2011.

New CMMI Pilot Seeks to Align with ACOs in Private Sector, Medicaid, Even MA Plans. *ACO Business News*, Atlantic Information Services, Inc., vol. 2, no. 6, June 2011.

New Economics of Accountable Healthcare and Legal Implications for Providers. Peter A. Pavarini, vol. 19, no. 19, May 9, 2011.

New Fraud and Abuse Paradigm for ACOs, A: Blurring the Distinction between Providers and Payers. Robert Belfort, Bureau of National Affairs, Inc. (BNA), March 23, 2011. Online at: http://healthlawrc.bna.com/hlrc/display/alpha.adp?mode=topics&letter=A&frag_id=20209813&item=2BB88AF970D049BA2C0DE60C642CB7DE&prod=hlin (accessed April 21, 2011).

New Healthcare Delivery Models under the PPACA: Where Does Home Health Fit? Robert W. Markette, Benesch Attorneys at Law, AudioEducator. August 4, 2011.

New Jersey: New Jersey Medicaid Accountable Care Organization. National Academy for State Health Policy. Online at: http://www.nashp.org/aco/new-jersey.

New Jersey Physician-Driven Model Seeks Whole-Person Patient Care. *ACO Business News*, Atlantic Information Services, Inc., vol. 2, no. 3, March 2011.

New Laws in Texas Could Make It "Less Cumbersome" to Form ACOs. *ACO Business News*, Atlantic Information Services, Inc., vol. 2, no. 7, July 2011.

The New Patient Experience Imperative. Gienna Shaw, HealthLeaders Media.

New Payment and Delivery Models under Health Reform Require New Relationships between Physicians and Hospitals. Janice A. Anderson and Heidi Shaw, Bureau of National Affairs, Inc. (BNA), November 18, 2010. Online at: http://news.bna.com/hlln/display/batch_print_display.adp?serarchid=13466061 (accessed 11/18/2010).

New PHOs Are Being Structured as Stepping Stones to ACOs. *ACO Business News*, Atlantic Information Services, Inc., vol. 1, no. 2, December 2010.

A New Quality Compass: Hospital Boards' Increased Role under the Affordable Care Act. Elisabeth Belmont, Claire C. Haltom, Douglas A. Hastings, Robert G. Homchick, and Lewis Morris, vol. 30, no. 7, July, 2011.

The New Role of Hospitalists: Keeping Patients Out of the Hospital. Cynthia Litt and Eugene Kim, Cedars–Sinai, Los Angeles.

News Briefs. *ACO Business News*, Atlantic Information Services, Inc., vol. 2, No. 12, December 2011.

News Briefs. *ACO Business News*. Atlantic Information Services, Inc., vol. 2, no. 2, February 2011.

News Briefs. *ACO Business News*, Atlantic Information Services, Inc., vol. 2, no. 1, January 2011.

News Briefs. *ACO Business News*, Atlantic Information Services, Inc., vol. 2, no. 3, March 2011.

News Briefs. *ACO Business News*, Atlantic Information Services, Inc., vol. 2, no. 7, July 2011.

News Briefs. *ACO Business News*, Atlantic Information Services, Inc., vol. 2, no. 5, May 2011.

News Briefs. *ACO Business News*, Atlantic Information Services, Inc., vol. 2, no. 11, November 2011.

News Briefs. *ACO Business News*, Atlantic Information Services, Inc., vol. 3, no. 2, February 2012.

News Briefs. *ACO Business News*, Atlantic Information Services, Inc., vol. 3, no. 3, March 2012.

News Briefs. *ACO Business News*, Atlantic Information Services, Inc., vol. 2, no. 6, June 2011.

News Briefs. *ACO Business News*, Atlantic Information Services, Inc., vol. 2, no. 9, September 2011.

News Briefs. *ACO Business News*, Atlantic Information Services, Inc., vol. 1, no. 1, November 2010.

News Briefs. *ACO Business News*, Atlantic Information Services, Inc., vol. 2, no. 4, April 2011.

News Briefs. *ACO Business News*, Atlantic Information Services, Inc., vol. 3, no. 1, January 2012.

News Briefs. *ACO Business News*, Atlantic Information Services, Inc., vol. 2, no. 10, October 2011.

News Briefs. *ACO Business News*, Atlantic Information Services, Inc., vol. 1, no. 2, December 2010.

News Briefs. *ACO Business News*, Atlantic Information Services, Inc., vol. 3, no. 4, April 2012.

News Briefs. *ACO Business News*, Atlantic Information Services, Inc., vol. 3, no. 5, Washington, DC, May 2012.

News Release November 18, 2011: New NCQA Accreditation Program Identifies ACOs That Are Most Likely to Succeed. National Committee for Quality Assurance (NCQA), November 18, 2011. Online at: http://www.ncqa.org/tabid/1450/Default.aspx.

Next Steps for ACOs: Will This New Approach to Health Care Delivery Live Up to the Dual Promises of Reducing Costs and Improving Quality of Care. January 31, 2012. Health Policy Brief, Health Affairs.

Norton Focuses on Changes Needed Anyway in ACO Effort. *ACO Business News*, Atlantic Information Services, Inc., vol. 2, no. 10, October 2011.

Not Ready for Takeoff? May 17, 2011. Online at: http://modernhealthcare.comarticle/20110517/BLAGS01/305179983/?template=print (accessed 7/7/2011).

Obamacare Can Live Even If the Mandate Dies. Peter Coy and Ralph Lindeman, *Bloomberg BusinessWeek,* April 9–15, 2012.

Office of the National Coordinator for Health Information Technology (ONC), The. Online at: http://healthit.hhs.gov/portal/server.pt/community/healthit_hhs_gov_onc/1200 (accessed 11/8/12).

OIG Official Says Fraud, Abuse Law Waivers Likely to Be Applied Consistently to All ACOs. Health Law Resource Center Bureau of National Affairs, Inc. (BNA), May 5, 2011. Online at: http://healthlawrc.bna.com/hlrc/display/batch_print_display.adp (accessed 6/16/2011).

On the Road to Better Value: State Roles in Promoting Accountable Care Organizations. Kitty Purington, Anne Gauthier, Shivani Patel, and Christina Miller, The Commonwealth Fund, February 2011. Online at: http://www.commonwealthfund.org/~/media/Files/Publications/Fund%20Report/2011/Feb/On%20the%20Road%20to%20Better%20Value/1479_Purington_on_the_road_to_better_value_ACOs_FINAL.pdf (accessed 5/2011).

On Their Terms: Providers Take Own Directions with ACOs. Vince Galloro, *Modern Healthcare*, August 15, 2011.

Onerous Regulations Put ACOs on Ropes: Health Insurers Can Be Doing More to Come Up with Creative Way to Pay Providers and Organize Care. Frank Diamond, Managed Care, June 2011.

Operationalizing Stark: From Complexity to Reality: Life after October 2009 Changes to "Under Arrangements" and "Per-Click/Percentage" Ann DesRuisseaux, Craig Holden, and Donald H. Romano, March 24, 2009.

Opposition to Draft ACO Regulations Spells Trouble for Federal Programs. *ACO Business News*, Atlantic Information Services, Inc., vol. 2, no. 7, July 2011.

Oregon Gears Up to Establish "Coordinated Care Organizations." *ACO Business News*, Atlantic Information Services, Inc., vol. 2, no. 12. December 2011.

Oregon Launches Medicaid CCOs, Plans to Incorporate Dual Eligibles. *ACO Business News*, Atlantic Information Services, Inc., vol. 3, no. 10, Atlantic Information Services, Inc.

Organizing an ACO: Proposed Rules Governing the Medicare Shared Savings Program. Mark S. Hedberg, Hunton and Williams LLP, Richmond, VA, May 5, 2011.

Organizing the U.S. Health Care Delivery System for High Performance. Anthony Shih, Karen Davis, Stephen Schoenbaum, et al., The Commonwealth Fund, Washington, D.C.

OSF Healthcare, Rockford Health Call Off Merger with FTC block. Karen Cheung, FierceHealthcare. Online at: http://www.fiercehealthcare.com/story/osf-healthcare-rockford-healthcall-merger-ftc-block/2012-04-13 (accessed 05/20/2012).

Out of Camelot, Knights in White Coats Lose Way. Sandeep Jauhar, New York Times, online at: www.nytimes.com/2011/02/01/health/01essay.html?_r=0, January 31,2011 (accessed 2/2/2011).

Outdated Regulations Are Barriers to Provider Alignment, AHA Says. *ACO Business News*, Atlantic Information Services, Inc., vol. 2, no. 3, March 2012.

Outline of Health Care Overhaul Legislation. March 2010. Online at: http://www.aoa.org/Documents/HCR-Outline.pdf (accessed January 28, 2011).

Overview: What Is an ACO? February 7, 2012. Online at: https:/Iwww.cms.gov/ACOI (accessed 3/20/2012).

Overview of the Administration's ACO Policy: Opportunities and Challenges, An. Sara Rosenbaum, vol. 19, no. 20, Bureau of National Affairs, Inc. (BNA), May 16, 2011.

Overweight and Out of Shape: ACO Regs Need a Major Makeover By Ron Klar. Project Hope. April 7, 2011. http://healthaffairs.org/blog/2011/04/07/overweight-and-out-ofshape-aco-regs-need-a-major-makeover/print/ (accessed 4/25/2011).

Parent Organizations of MA Plans May Apply for ACO Pioneer Pilot. *ACO Business News*, Atlantic Information Services, Inc., vol. 2, no. 7, July 2011.

Part 1 of Critique of Milliman's Whitepaper on Non-Medicare ACOs: Misinterpreting the Milliman "Well Managed" Actuarial Model? Richard E. Ward, Reward Health Sciences, Inc., May 5, 2011. Online at: http://rewardhealth.com/archives/679 (accessed 07/07/2011).

Part 2 of Critique of Milliman's Whitepaper on Non-Medicare ACOs: Overly Optimistic about Inpatient Use Management, Alarmingly Pessimistic about Primary Care Process Transformation. Richard E. Ward, Reward Health Sciences, Inc., May 8, 2011. Online at: http://rewardhealth.com/archives/682 (accessed 07/07/2011).

Patient Protection and Affordable Care Act: Public Law 111-148, Pub. Law 111-148, 124 Stat. 119 (2010), March 23, 2010.

Patient Protection and Affordable Care Act; Establishment of Exchanges and Qualified Health Plans; Exchange Standards for Employers: Final Rule, Interim Final Rule. *Federal Register*, vol. 77, no. 59, 77 FR 59 (March 27, 2012).

Patients May Present ACO Concerns of Their Own, Official Says. Rich Daly, Crain Communications Inc., May 2, 2011. Online at: http://www.modernhealthcare.com/article/20110502/NEWS/305029918/0%26template=emailart (accessed 5/1/2011).

Pay-For-Performance. American Academy of Family Physicians. Online at: http://www.aafp.org/online/en/home/policy/policies/p/payforperformance.html (accessed 5/25/2012).

Pediatric ACO Program in Reform Law Is Delayed by Lack of Funding. *ACO Business News*, Atlantic Information Services, Inc., vol. 2, no. 9, September 2011.

PHO Prepares Detroit System for ACO Certification. *ACO Business News*, Atlantic Information Services, Inc., vol. 1, no. 2, December 2010.

Physician Alignment Biggest Obstacle to ACOs. Pamela L. Dolan, *Journal of the American Medical Association* (JAMA), vol. 54, no. 15, August 8, 2011.

Physician Alignment in an Era of Change. Joe Cantlupe, HealthLeaders Media, September 14, 2010.

Physician Group Practice Demonstration: First Evaluation Report. Michael O. Leavitt, Report to Congress, 2006. Online at: https://www.cms.gov/reports/downloads/Leavitt1.pdf (accessed 3/28/2012).

Physician Group Practice Demonstration Succeeds in Improving Quality and Reducing Costs: All Participating Practices to Continue in 2-Year PGP Transition Demonstration. August 8, 2011. Online at: https://www.cms.gov/DemoProjectsEvalRpts/downloads/PGP_PR.pdf (accessed 3/29/2012).

Physician Groups Issue Principles for ACO Structure, Payment. November 23, 2010. Online at: http://www.ahanews.com/...sp/display.jsp?dcrpath=AHANEWS/AHANewsNowArticle/data/ann_112310_physicians&domain=AHANEWS (accessed 11/29/2010).

Physician–Hospital Integration in the Era of Health Reform. Mary Witt and Laura Jacobs, The Camden Group, Los Angeles, December, 2010.

Physician-Owned Hospitals: Endangered Species? Chris Silva, June 28 2010. Online at: http://www.ama-assn.org/amednews/2010/06/28/gvsa0628.htm (accessed 08/04/11).

Picking Up the Scent: Wave of Practice Acquisitions by Hospitals Has Antitrust Regulators on Notice. Joe Carlson, Modern Healthcare, Online at: http://www.modernhealthcare.com/article/20120609/MAGAZINE/306099971 (accessed 06/13/12).

Pioneer Accountable Care Organization (ACO) Model Program: Frequently Asked Questions—Addendum. July 13, 2011.

Pioneer Accountable Care Organization Beneficiary Alignment and Financial Reconciliation Specifications. Henry Bachofer, Gregory Pope, John Kautter, and Cordon Newhart, July 14, 2011. Online at: http://associationdatabase.com/aws/SHC/asset_manager/get_file/35748/072211_pioneer_aco_specs.pdf (accessed March 2, 2012).

Pioneer Accountable Care Organization Model: General Fact Sheet. December 19, 2011. Online at: http://www.innovations.cms.gov/documents/pdf/PioneerACOGenerall_Fact_SheetFINAL_12_19_11.pdf (accessed 3/2/2012).

Pioneer ACO Alignment and Financial Reconciliation Methods. Center for Medicare & Medicaid Innovation, 7.1, November 21, 2011.

Pioneer ACO Application. Online at: http://innovations.cms.gov/area-of-focus/seamless-and-coordinated-care-models/pioneer-aco-application (accessed 7/15/2011).

Pioneer ACO Model. Online at: http://innovations.cms.gov/areas-of-focus/seamless-and-coordinatedcare-models/pioneer-aco/ (accessed 6/16/2011).

Pioneer ACO Model, The. Healthcare Financial Management Association HFMA. Online at: http://www.hfma.org/PioneerACOModel/ (accessed 11/26/2011).

Pioneer ACO Model Offers Participants Flexibility. Margaret D. Tocknell, HealthLeaders Media, December 20, 2011.

Pioneer ACO Special Open Door Forum Conference Call: Transcript. Barbara Cebuhar, June 7, 2011. Online at: htpp://downloads.com.gov/media/audio/060711PioneerACO.mp3.

Pioneer Begins a New Phase in Industry Redesign. John Toussaint, Accountable Care News, vol. 3, no. 3, March 2012.

Plans Broad Patient View, Expertise with Risk Could Drive Future ACO Development. *ACO Business News*, Atlantic Information Services, Inc., vol. 2, no. 10, October 2011.

Policy Challenges in Modern Health Care: Entrepreneurial Challenges to Integrated Health Care, 1st ed. James C. Robinson, Rutgers University Press, New Brunswick, NJ, April 8, 2005.

Potential Impact of the New Accountable Care Organization Regulations on the Pharmaceutical and Medical Device Industries, The. Skadden LLP, New York, April 26, 2011.

Preconference I: CMS ACO Regulations, Part 2: A Deep Dive into the Revised Regulations. SNR Denton, Washington, D.C., November 1, 2011.

Preliminary Data from ACO Models Show Improving Quality; Some Question Results. DeMarco Siler Coffina and Mark Slitt. *ACO Business News*, Atlantic Information Services, Inc., vol. 2, no. 4, April 2012.

Premier Comments on ACO Rules: Health Data Management—Source Media, Inc., April 1, 2011. Online at: http://www.healthdatamanagement.com/news/rule-shared-savings-accountablecare-organizations-premier-comments-42226-1.html (accessed 4/1/2011).

Premier Offers Its Members a Blueprint for Building ACOs. *ACO Business News*, Atlantic Information Services, Inc., vol. 1, no. 1, November 2010.

Presenting Your Story to the Capital Markets. Lee A. Runy, Hospitals & Health Networks (H&HN), June 2008. Online at: http://www.hhnmag.com/hhnmag_app/jsp/articledisplay.jsp?dcrpath=HHNMAG/Article/data/06JUN2008/0806HHN_FEA_Gatefold&domain=HHNMAG (accessed 06/28/11).

Primary Care, Medical Homes Are Significant in ACO Development. *ACO Business News*, Atlantic Information Services, Inc., vol. 2, no. 4, April 2011.

Primary Care Update: Light at the End of the Tunnel? John K. Iglehart, *The New England Journal of Medicine*, vol. 366, no. 23.

Privacy and Security of ACOs, The: Improving Patient Care While Complying with HIPAA. Adam H. Greene and Helen E. Ovsepyan, *AHLA Connections*, vol. 16, no. 5.

Private Payers May Diverge from Medicare in Forming ACOs Amid Consolidation Issues. *ACO Business News*, Atlantic Information Services, Inc., vol. 2, no. 5, May 1, 2011.

Prognosis Is Unclear for Delivery Reforms Following Debt Panel's Failure. *ACO Business News*, Atlantic Information Services, Inc., vol. 2, no. 12, December 2011.

Program Identifies Accountable Care Organizations Likely to Succeed. Ron Rajecki, November 30 2011. Online at: http://www.modernmedicine.com/modernmedicine/article/articleDetail.jsp?id=750757 (accessed 12/07/11).

Promote Broad Adoption of the Patient Centered Medical Home: Through Creation and Funding of an Innovation Center and Other New Programs under H.R. 3590.

Proposed Accountable Care Organization Antitrust Guidance, The: A First Look. Joe Miller, Project Hope, April 14, 2011. Online at: http://healthaffairs.org/blog/2011/04/14/theproposed-accountable-care-organization-antitrust-guidance-a-first-look/ (accessed 4/16/2011).

Proposed Antitrust Policy May Make It Hard for Providers to Join ACOs. *ACO Business News*, Atlantic Information Services, Inc., vol. 2, no. 7, July 2011.

Proposed CMS Regulation Kills ACOs Softly. Steven Lieberman, Project Hope, April 6, 2011. Online at: http://healthaffairs.org/blog/2011/04/06/proposed-cms-regulation-kills-acossoftly/print (accessed 4/25/2011).

Proposed Rule versus Final Rule for Accountable Care Organizations (ACOs) in the Medicare Shared Savings Program: Major Changes. *ACO Business News*, Atlantic Information Services, Inc., vol. 2, no.11, November 2011.

Proposed Statement of Antitrust Enforcement Policy Regarding Accountable Care Organizations Participating in the Medicare Shared Savings Program. vol. 76, no. 75, 76 F.R. 75 (2011), April 19, 2011.

Proposed Waivers of the Fraud & Abuse Laws for ACOs, The: Have OIG and CMS Gone Far Enough? Daniel H. Melvin and Webb Millsaps, McDermot, Will & Emery, Chicago, May 3, 2011.

Provider Groups Support ACO Concept, Oppose Implementation Regulations. June 8, 2011. Online at: http://www.mcknights.com/provider-groups-support-aco-concept-opposeimplementation-regulations/printarticle/204758/ (accessed 07/07/2011).

Providers Cheer ACO Final Rule: Reactions to the Revised Cut. Karen Cheung-Larivee. October 21, 2011. Online at: www.fiercehealthcare.com/story/providers-cheer-aco-final-rule-reactions-revised-cut/2011-10.21.

Public Coverage Programs: Solving the Enrollment Dilemma. Alain C. Enthoven, May 9 2011. Online at: http://healthaffairs.org/blog/2011/05/09/public-coverage-programs-solving-theenrollment-dilemma/ (accessed 05/16/2011).

The Public, Managed Care, and Consumer Protections. *Kaiser Health News*, January 2006.

Public Reporting of Health Care Quality: Principles for Moving Forward. David Lansky, Health Affairs Blog, April 9, 2012.

Purpose over Pay. Stephanie Sloan and Rod Fralicx, Hospitals & Health Networks (H&HN).

Q&A: Methodist Health CEO on an ACO Alternative. Margaret D. Tocknell, HealthLeaders Media, June 1, 2011. Online at: http://www.healthleadersmedia.com/page-2/TEC266802/QA-Methodist-Health-CEO-on-an-ACO-Alternative (accessed 06/30/2011).

Q&A with Former Medicare and Medicaid Chief Donald Berwick: Be Willing to Embrace Change. Teddi D. Johnson, *The Nation's Health*, May/June 2012.

Quality Frameworks for PPACA. *ACO Business News*, Atlantic Information Services, Inc., vol. 2, no. 5.

Quality Matters in Focus: Building Accountable Care Organizations That Improve Quality and Lower Costs—A View from the Field. Sarah Klein, June/July 2010. Online at: http://www.commonwealthfund.org/Newsletters/Quality-Matters/2010/June-July2010/In-Focus.aspx (accessed 1/20/2012).

Quality Measures and Performance Standards. Centers for Medicare and Medicaid Services. Online at: https://www.cms.gov/Medicare/Medicare-Fee-for-Service-Payment/sharedsavingsprogram/Quality_Measures_Standards.html (accessed 05/22/12).

Quality Measures Continue to Matter for Physicians in the Accountable Care Organization Era. Ann Bittinger, American Health Lawyers Association (AHLA), Washington, D.C. Online at: http://www.healthlawyers.org/Events/Programs/Materials/Documents/AM11/bittinger.pdf (accessed 3/7/2012).

Questions and Answers about ACOs. February 17, 2012. Online at: http://www.kaiserhealthnews.orgfdaily-reports/20 12/februaryl1 7/aco (accessed 3/20/2012).

Quick Definitions for National Health Expenditure Accounts (NHEA) Categories. Online at: https://www.cms.gov/NationalHealthExpendData/downloads/quickref.pdf (accessed 03/12/12).

Reduced ICU Infections Are Indicator That Advocate ACO Model Is Working. *ACO Business News*, Atlantic Information Services, Inc., vol. 2, no. 2, February 2011.

Reform's Impact: Staff and Service Cuts Expected. Philip Betbeze. Optum HealthLeaders Media, December 2011.

Reforming Healthcare Reform in the 112th Congress, Joseph R. Antos, vol. 364, Massachusetts Medical Society, January 6, 2011. Online at: http://www.nejm.org/doi/full/10.1056/NEJMp1012299 (accessed 1/5/2011).

Reforming the Health Care System: The Universal Dilemma. Uwe E. Reinhardt, *American Journal of Law & Medicine*, 1993.

Report to Congress: Improving the Medicare Quality Improvement Organization Program—Response to the Institute of Medicine Study. Michael O Leavitt. Online at: https://www.cms.gov/QualityImprovementOrgs/downloads/QIO_Improvement_RTC_fnl.p df.

Report to the Congress: Regional Variation in Medicare Service Use. January 2011, Medicare Payment Advisory Commission.

Report to the Congress: Improving Incentives in the Medicare Program. June 2009, Medicare Payment Advisory Commission.

Requirements for a Determination That a Facility or an Organization Has Provider-Based Status. 42 CFR 413.65, October 1, 2005.

A Review of the Evidence on Hospital Cost-Shifting. Christina Zimmerman, vol. 14, no. 3, Robert Wood Johnson Foundation, Princeton, NJ, May 2011.

Rhode Island's Novel Experiment to Rebuild Primary Care from the Insurance Side. Christopher F, Koller, Troyen A. Brennan, and Michael H. Bailit, *Project Hope*, vol. 29, no. 5, May 2010. Online at: http://content.healthaffairs.org/content/29/5/941.abstract (accessed 4/17/2011).

Rising Healthcare Costs May Be Impervious to Courts, Regulators. Philip Betbeze, HealthLeaders Media, July 1, 2011. Online at: http://www.healthleadersmedia.com/print/LED268129/Rising-Healthcare-Costs-May-be-Impervious-to-Courts-Regulators (accessed 7/1/2011).

Role of Pharmaceuticals in Achieving ACO Success: Developing a Framework. Robert W. Dubois, Marv Feldman, and Julie Sanderson-Austin, Premier, Inc., Charlotte, NC.

Role of Pharmacy in Medicare, Commercial ACOs Remain Unclear. *ACO Business News*, Atlantic Information Services, Inc., vol. 2, no. 2, February 2012.

Role of Specialists in the Medicare Shared Savings Program (MSSP) Establishing Accountable Care Organizations (ACOs). Hart Health Strategies, October 20, 2011. Online at: http://www.gastro.org/advocacy-regulation/regulatory-issues/accountable-care-organizations/AGA_ACO_Specialist_Role_102611.pdf (accessed November 12, 2011).

Roles of Patient-Centered Medical Homes and Accountable Care Organizations in Coordinating Patient Care, The. David Meyers, Debbie Peikes, Janice Genevro, Greg Peterson, Erin F. Taylor, et al., December 2010.

Ropes & Gray Analysis of CMS Proposed ACO Rule and Related Agency Issuances. Ropes and Gray LLP, Boston, April 7, 2011.

Roundtable: Building a Business Case for Quality Healthcare. Jim Molpus, Francois De Brantes, Maureen Spivak, Daniel Varga, and Thomas Bartrum, July 2006.

Rules Aim to Reshape Medical Practices. Avery Johnson, April 1, 2011. Online at: http://online.wsj.com/article/SB10001424052748704530204576235153525838820.html (accessed 4/1/2011).

RWJF Recommends Adjustments to Proposed ACO Rule. Jeff Byers, Robert Wood Johnon Foundation, June 13, 2011. Online at: http://www.cmio.net/index.php?option=com_articles&article=28227 (accessed 6/16/2011).

Sample Healthcare Representations and Warranties in Financing Transactions. Deborah Gordon and Lisa Lenderman. Online at: http://www.healthlawyers.org/events/programs/materials/documents/am11/gordon_lender man.pdf (accessed 03/13/12).

Section Eight: Medicare Spending, *Medicare Chartbook, 4th ed*., 2010, Kaiser Family Foundation.

Selected Interest Rates (Weekly)—H.15. April 9, 2012. Online at: http://www.federalreserve.gov/releases/H15/20120409/ (accessed 4/26/2012).

Selected Participants in the Pioneer ACO Model. *Modern Healthcare*, December 19, 2011. Online at: http://www.modernhealthcare.com/assets/pdf/CH768931219.DOC.

Selected State Medicaid Payment Initiatives Related to Accountable Care. *ACO Business News*, Atlantic Information Services, Inc., vol. 2, no. 10, October 2011.

Services: Tax Services. Healthcare Management Consultants, July 28, 2009. Online at: http://www.healthcaremgmt.com/tax.html (accessed 7/28/2009).

Setting Up a Practical Accountable Care Organization: The Goal Must Always Be to Provide Patients with Better Care at Lower Costs. K. J. Lee, June 25, 2011.

Several Windows of Opportunity Close, But Options Remain. Tanya K. Hahn. Online at: http://www.hfma.org/Publications/Newsletters/Strategic-Financial-Planning/Archives/2011/Spring/Several-Windows-of-Opportunity-Close,-but-Options-Remain/ (accessed 04/15/11).

Shared Savings Program Application: Steps to the Shared Saving Program Application Process. Centers for Medicare & Medicaid Services. Online at www.cms.gov.

Shared Savings Program for Accountable Care Organizations: A Bridge to Nowhere? Robert A. Berenson, *The American Journal of Managed Care*, vol. 16, no. 10, October 2010.

Shifting Health Care Landscape, The: Lessons from the Clinton Era. Jeff Selberg, Project Hope, May 13, 2011. Online at: http://healthaffairs.org/blog/2011/05/15/the-shifting-healthcare-landscape-lessons-from-the-clinton-era/ (accessed 5/13/2011).

Skepticism Greets Medicare ACO Shared Savings Program: The Proposed Rule for Accountable Care Organizations Allows Physicians to Share Quality Rewards, But Some Experts Question How Many Will Buy into the Program. Charles Fiegl, April 18, 2011. Online at: http://www.ama-assn.org/amednews/m/2011/18/g110418.htm (accessed 4/20/2011).

Slower Growth in Medicare Spending: Is This the New Normal? Chapin White and Paul B. Ginsburg, *The New England Journal of Medicine*, vol. 366, no. 12, March 22, 2012.

Social Security Act: Shared Savings Program. 42.U.S.C. 1395jjj Sec 1899.

Special Report: ACOs and Imaging. Brendon Nafziger, DotMed.com, Inc., October 21, 2010. Online at: http://www.dotmed.com/news/story/14573?p_begin=0 (Accessed 1/31/11).

Specialists Have a Role in Medicare Shared Savings Programs. Toya M. Sledd, American Academy of Orthopaedic Surgeons American Academy of Orthopaedic Surgeons (AAOS).

Specialty Docs Have Concerns Over Role in Medicare ACOs. *ACO Business News*, Atlantic Information Services, Inc., vol. 2, no. 5, May 1, 2011.

Spending Scarce Resources on the Wrong Capital Budget Requests: Not In My Hospital!. ECRI Institute, 2010.

Spotting a Unicorn: ACOs Inch Closer to Reality. Dan Diamond, California Healthline, September 29, 2010. Online at: http://www.californiahealthline.org/road-to-reform/2010/spotting-a-unicorn-acos-inch-closer-to-reality.aspx (accessed 07/08/2011).

Stakeholders' Perspectives Differed on the Adequacy of Guidance for Collaboration among Health Care Providers. James C. Cosgrove, U.S. Government Accountability Office. Online at www.gao.gove/products/GAO-12-291R. http://www.gao.gov/products/GAO-12-291R.

Stakeholders Urge Greater Flexibility, Inclusion of Small Practices in ACO Rules. Nathaniel Weixel. Online at: http://news.bna.comlhllnldisplaylbatch rint_display.adp (accessed 12/16/2010).

Stalking the ACO Unicorn: What the Proposed Regulations for Accountable Care Organizations (ACOs) Mean. PricewaterhouseCoopers LLP, April 2011. Online at: http://pwchealth.com/cgi-local/hregister.cgi?link=reg/stalking-the-aco-unicorn.pdf (accessed 4/24/2011).

Standards and Guidelines for the Accreditation of Accountable Care Organizations. National Committee for Quality Assurance (NCQA), Washington, D.C.

Standards Set for Joint Ventures to Improve Health Care. Robert Pear, March 31, 2011, New York Times.

Stark Regulations. 42 CFR part 411, October 1, 2010.

State Accountable Care Activity Map. National Academy for State Health Policy. Online at: http://nashp.org/state=accountable-care-activity-map.

State Actions to Implement the Health Benefit Exchange. Online art: http://www.ncsl.org/issues-research/health/state-actions-to-implement-the-health-benefit-exch.aspx (accessed 11/12/2012).

State Employee Health Commission. Maine Revised Statutes Title 5 Sec. 285-A.

State of New Jersey Senate, No. 2443: Legislative Fiscal Estimate, March 28, 2011. Online at: http://www.njleg.state.nj.us/2010/Bills/S2500/2443_E1.PDF (accessed 11/8/2011).

State of New Jersey Senate, No. 2443, December 6, 2010. Online at: http://www.njleg.state.nj.us/2010/Bills/S2500/2443_I1.PDF (accessed 11/7/2011).

Statement of Antitrust Enforcement Policy Regarding Accountable Care Organizations Participating in the Medicare Shared Savings Program: Final Policy Statement. vol. 76, no. 209, 76 FR 209, October 28, 2011.

Statement of the American Medical Association to the Federal Trade Commission, the Centers for Medicare & Medicaid Services and the Office of Inspector General of the Department of Health and Human Services: Medicare Program. Workshop regarding Accountable Care Organizations, and implications regarding antitrust, physician self-referral, anti-kickback, and civil monetary penalty laws, September 27, 2010.

Statements on Standards for Accounting and Review Services. December 1978. Online at: http://www.aicpa.org/download/members/div/auditstd/AR-00100.PDF (accessed 3/18/2010).

Strategic Alignment Is Best Path for Payors/Providers of ACOs. *ACO Business News*, Atlantic Information Services, Inc., vol. 2, no. 5, May 2011.

Structural Changes: Build a healthcare delivery model that works for your practice. Marc D. Halley.

Summary of Proposed Rule Provision for Accountable Care Organizations under the Medicare Shared Savings Program. March 31, 2011. Online at: http://www.kaiserhealthnews.org/~/media/Files/2011/CMS%20ACO%20Fact%20Sheet%20%20Summary%20Proposed%20Rule%20110331.pdf (accessed 6/6/2011).

Super Committee Gets Scores of Recommendations, ACO Reg on Deck. Inside Washington Publishers, October 17, 2011. Online at: http://insidehealthpolicy.com.Inside-Health-General/Health-Reform-Inside (accessed 10/17/2011).

Supplementary Medical Insurance Benefits for the Aged and Disabled. LexisNexis Publishing, Dayton, OH.

Supreme Court Decision on Healthcare Law Has Three Likely Outcomes. Moody's Investor Service. Online at: http://www.moodys.com/research/UShealthcareThree-Likely-Outcomes-of-the-Supreme-Courts-Pending-Decision-PBC_142544.

Supreme Court Review of the Health Care Reform Law. Gregory D. Curfman, Brendan S. Abel, and Renee M. Landers, *The New England Journal of Medicine*.

Survey: Hospital Hiring-Spree of Docs to See Upswing. HealthImaging, October 12, 2011. Online at: http://www.healthimaging.com/index.php?option=com_articles&article=29918 (accessed 10/12/11).

Survey: Forming an ACO Ultimately Is a People Problem. Brenda L. Mooney, June 29, 2011, Medical Economics.

Survey: Health Execs, Payors Wary of ACOs. Mary Stevens, June 28, 2011. Online at: http://www.cmio.net/index.php?option=com_articles&article=28495 (accessed 03/13/2012).

Tax-Exempt Hospitals and Accountable Care Organizations. McDermott, Will & Emery, Chicago, April 27, 2011. Online at: http://www.mwe.com/index.cfm/fuseaction/publications.nldetail/object_id/d87595a50e4a-4cb3-a03d-19b45825fbca.cfm (accessed 4/28/2011).

Tax-Exempt Hospitals May Be Able to Form ACOs, Keep Their Status. *ACO Business News*, Atlantic Information Services, Inc., vol. 2, no. 7, July 2011.

Tax Relief and Health Care Act of 2006. H.R. 6111. 2006.

Tax Relief and Health Care Act of 2006. Pub. L. 109-432.

Taxpayers Laughing At, Not with, Obama's Accountable Care Organizations: Once Again, the Democrats' Health Care Law Proves to Be a Joke. Tevi Troy, April 12, 2011. Online at: http://www.weeklystandard.com/blogs/taxpayers-laughing-not-obamas-accountable-careorganizations_557318.html (accessed 4/15/11).

Testing ACOs: Medicare Seeks Trial Run with Physician Group. Melanie Evans, April 11, 2011, *Modern Healthcare*.

Texas ACO That Has Improved Mortality Rates on MA Patients Will Keep Its Model. *ACO Business News*, Atlantic Information Services, Inc., vol. 2, no. 7, July 2011.

Though Appreciated, ACO Final Rules Produce Little Change in Leaders' Intentions. Philip Betbeze, Health Leaders Media. 2011.

Thought Leader's Corner: How Do You Assess the Legacy of Don Berwick's Tenure at CMS on Health Care Policy and Implementation? Peter Boland, Debra L. Ness, and Wes Champion, vol. 3, no. 2, Health Policy Publishing LLC, February 2012.

Thought Leader's Corner. Bruce Perkins, Kim Looney, Charles S. Wright, Joseph Miller, Mindy Hatton, et al., *Accountable Care News*, Health Policy Publishing LLC, April 2012.

Thoughts on Reform: When ACOs, Vectors, and Spin Collide. Michael Silver, June 16, 2011, HealthLeaders Media.

Three Steps to an Effective Practice Budget: By Tracking Your Expenses and Comparing Them To Benchmarks, You Can Create A Practice Budget That's Useful and Easy to Maintain. Keith Borglum, January 2004.

Title I Food Stamp Provisions: Public Law 105-33. U.S. Government. 111 STAT 251 Government Printing Office.

To Be an ACO, or Not to Be. Karen Minich-Pourshadi, HealthLeaders Media, April 4, 2011. Online at: http://www.healthleadersmedia.com/content/FIN-264501/To-Be-An-ACO-Or-Not-To-Be.html (accessed 4/4/2011).

To Err Is Human: Building a Safer Health System. Committee on Quality of Healthcare in America, Washington, D.C.: National Academy Press.

Top 12 Healthcare Buzzwords for 2012. Cheryl Clark, December 27, 2011. Online at: http://www.healthleadersmedia.com/content/QUA-274645/Top-12-HealthcareBuzzwords-for-2012.html (accessed 12/27/11).

Top Healthcare Reform Issues for Managed Care No One Is Thinking about. Paper presented at the 2011 Annual Meeting of American Health Lawyers Association, Stephanie Kanwit, Manatt, Phelps, & Phillips LLP, June 29, 2011.

Toward Accountable Care: How Healthcare Reform Will Shape Provider Integration. Bernadette M. Broccolo, McDermott, Will, & Emery, Chicago, July 21, 2011.

Transformation of America's Hospitals, The: Economics Drives a New Business Model. Kenneth Kaufman and Mark E. Grube, Futurescan 2012: Healthcare Trends and Implications 2012–2017.

Transforming Health Care through Accountable Care Organizations: A Critical Assessment. Foley and Lardner LLP, 2010. Online at: http://www.foley.com/files/tbl_s31Publications/FileUpload137/7574/ACO_White_Paper.pdf (accessed 1/30/12).

Transparency Reports and Reporting of Physician Ownership or Investment Interests: Applicable Group Purchasing Organization. U.S. Congress. 42 U.S.C. § 1320a-7h(e)(1).

Two Medicare ACO Programs, The: Medicare Shared Savings and Pioneer—Risk/Actuarial Differences. Bruce Pyenson, Kathryn Fitch, Kosuke Iwasaki, and Michele Berrios, Milliman, July 8, 2011.

TX Bills of Interest as of April 19, 2011. America's Health Insurance Plans (AHIP), April 19, 2011.

U.S. Health Care Costs. Eric Kimbuende, Usha Ranji, Janet Lundy, and Alina Salganicoff, March 1, 2010. Online at: http://www.kaiseredu.org/Issue-Modules/US-Health-CareCosts/Background-Brief.aspx (accessed 6/30/2011).

UNC Health Care System & BlueCross BlueShield of North Carolina Model Medical Practice: A Blueprint for Successful Collaboration. Jeffery Ruggiero, Asim Varma, Ted Lotchin, Ron Smith, and Kenin FitzGerald, Arnold and Porter LLP, Washington, D.C.

Unchecked Provider Clout in California Foreshadows Challenges to Health Reform. Robert A. Berenson, Paul B. Ginsburg, and Nicole Kemper, vol. 29, no. 4, April 2010, *Health Affairs*.

Under Construction, under Fire: Physician Groups Urge CMS to Make Changes to Proposed ACO Model. Annette M. Boyle, June 25, 2011, *Medical Economics*.

Understanding Health Care Financial Management: Text, Cases, and Models, 2nd ed. Louis C. Gapenski, Association of University Programs in Health Administration (AUPHA) Press/Health Administration Press.

United States v. Campbell. WestLaw 2011 WL 43013, 2011 U.S. Dist. LEXIS 1207, January 4, 2011.

University Medical Center ACO Eyes Private Plans for the Future. *ACO Business News*, Atlantic Information Services, Inc., vol. 2, no. 11, November 2011.

Utah Wants to Use ACOs to Control Medicaid Spending. Doug Trapp American Medical Association (AMA), July 8, 2011. Online at: http://www.ama-assn.org/amednews/2011/07/04/gvse0708.htm (accessed 11/08/2011).

Va. Health System Works on ACO, But Concedes Gaps in Its Expertise. *ACO Business News*, Atlantic Information Services, Inc., vol. 2, no. 4, April 1, 2011.

Valuation Model for the Formation of ACOs, A. 2011. Online at: http://www.healthlawyers.org/News/Health%20 Lawyers%20Weekly/Pages/ACOArticle.aspx (accessed 1/30/2012).

Valuing a Business: The Analysis and Appraisal of Closely Held Companies, 5th ed. Shannon P. Pratt and Alina V. Niculita, New York: McGraw Hill.

Vermont Accountable Care Organization Pilot, The: A Community Health System to Control Total Medical Costs and Improve Population Health. Jim Hester, Julie Lewis, and Aaron McKethan, The Commonwealth Fund, May 2012.

Vertical Integration and Organizational Networks in Health Care. James C. Robinson and Lawrence P. Casalino, *Health Affairs*, vol. 15, no. 1, Project HOPE (accessed 1-30-12).

Viability of ACOs: Reasonable Rules and Wise Use of HCIT. Joe Bormel, June 25, 2011. Online at: http://www.healthcare-informatics.com/blogs/joe/viability-acos-reasonable-rulesand-wise-use-hcit (accessed 1/6/2012).

Weighing the Benefits and the Risks of ACOs. Chad Mulvany. Online at: http://www.hfma.org/Templates/Print.aspx?id=22672 (accessed 7/7/2011).

What Can We Learn from the Managed Care Backlash of the 1990s? Can We Avoid an ACO Backlash? Richard E. Ward, Reward Health Sciences, Inc., September 10, 2011. Online at: http://rewardhealth.com/archives/1392.

What Health Reform Means for Medicine. Thomas Saving, May 12, 2011. Online at: http://healthaffairs.org/blog/2011/05/12/what-health-reform-means-for-medicare/ (accessed 05/16/11).

What Providers Need to Know: Accountable Care Organizations: Fact Sheet. March 31, 2011. Online at: http://www.cms.gov/MLNProducts/downloads/ACO_Providers_Factsheet_ICN907406.pdf (accessed 3/16/2012).

What's the Difference between an ACO and Managed Care? *Healthcare Economist*, August 23, 2011. Online at: http://healthcare-economist.com/2011/08/22/whats-the-differencebetween-an-aco-and-managed-care/ (accessed 2/1/12).

What Shared Savings Program Final Rule Means for CI Programs. Sarah O'Hara, The Advisory Board Company, October 28, 2011. Online at: http://www.advisory.com/Research/Health-Care-Advisory-Board/Blogs/NetworkAdvantage/2011/10/What-the-shared-savings-program-final-rule-means-for-CI-programs (accessed 11/14/2011).

What We're Doing. Online at: http://innovations.cms.gov/initiatives/ (accessed 1/4/2012).

Whatever ACA's Legal Outcome, ACOs Will Survive Medicare. *ACO Business News*, Atlantic Information Services, Inc., vol. 2, no. 1, January 2012.

Who Should Own the Medical Home? 2011. Online at: http://www.cardiovascularbusiness.com/index.php?view=article&id=296 (accessed October 13, 2011).

Who, What, When and How of ACOs, The: A Polsinelli Shughart Update. Polsinelli Shughart PC, 2011.

Why Risk-Based Contracts Are Worthwhile. Karen Minish-Pourshadi, HealthLeaders Media, October 8, 2012.

Will Mayo Clinic Save Money as an ACO? Christopher Snowbeck, February 5, 2011. Online at: http://www.pnhp.org/print/news/2011/february/will-mayo-clinic-save-money-as-an-aco.

Will the FTC Kill ACOS and Clinical Integration? Mark Reiboldt, *Washington Report, GreenBranch,* vol. 27, no. 4, January/February 2012.

Work Ahead, The: Activities and Costs to Develop an Accountable Care Organization. Keith D. Moore and Dean C. Coddington, American Hospital Association (AHA), April 2011. Online at: http://www.aha.org/aha/content/2011/pdf/aco-white-paper-cost-dev-aco.pdf (accessed 5//13/2011).

Workshop Examines Effects of Waiver Authority on Development of ACOs. J. P. Rich and Webb Millsaps, McDermott, Will & Emery, Chicago, October 11, 2010. Online at: http://www.mwe.com/index.cfm/fuseaction/publications.nldetail/object_id/27c34c4882c5-4f46-8acf-77a1cea77d31.cfm (accessed 10/14/2010).

Workshop Regarding Accountable Care Organizations, and Implications Regarding Antitrust, Physician Self-Referral, Anti-Kickback, and Civil Monetary Penalty (CMP). Centers for Medicare & Medicaid Services (CMS), Washington, D.C., October 5, 2010.

Wyden-Ryan Proposal, The: A Foundation for Realistic Medicare Reform. Joseph R. Antos, *New England Journal of Medicine*, vol. 366, no. 10. Online at: http://www.nejm.org/doi/pdf/10.1056/NEJMp1200446 (accessed 6/18/2012).

Your Move: Hospitals Are Predicting, Adapting to Change. Gienna Shaw, HealthLeaders Media, October 13, 2010. Online at: http://www.healthleadersmedia.com/print/MAG-257349/Your-Move-Hospitals-are-Predicting-Adapting-to-Change (accessed 11/17/2010).

REIMBURSEMENT

2% Solution, The: Health Systems Prepare for Coming Medicare Cuts. *Modern Healthcare*, May 5, 2012.

4 Unpleasant Predictions for 2012. Karen Minich-Pourshadi, October 17, 2011. Online at: http://www.healthleadersmedia.com/print/FIN-272195/4-Unpleasant-Pred... (accessed 10/17/2011).

2011 Employer-Driven Accountable Care Organizations Survey Report: What They Are and What They Can Do for Your Organization. AON Hewitt, Polakoff Boland Aon Hewitt.

About Minnesota Health Action Group. Minnesota Health Action Group. 2012. Online at: http://mnhealthactiongroup.org/about/ (accessed 10/22/12).

About HealthSpring. Online at: http://www.healthspring.com/About (accessed 11/7/12).

About Medpac. Online at: http://medpac.gov/about.cfm (accessed 5/25/2012).

About the Blue Cross and Blue Shield Association. Blue Cross Blue Shield Association, 2011. Online at: http://www.bcbs.com/about-the-association/ (accessed 12/27/2011).

About Us. Bravo Health. Online at: http://www.bravohealth.com/AboutUs (accessed 11/7/12).

Accountability and the Revenue Cycle. John Glaser, October 11, 2011. Online at: http://www.hhnmag.com/hhnmag/HHNDaily/HHNDailyDisplay.dhtml?id... (accessed 10/13/2011).

Accountable Care: A Culture and Payment Change. Michele Madison, June 22, 2011. Online at: http://blogs.ajc.com/health-flock/2011/06/22/accountable-care-a-culture-and-payment-change/ (accessed 7/7/2011).

Accountable Care Organization and PPACA after November 2, 2010. Catherine Woods, *Healthcare Reform Magazine*, December 6, 2010. Online at: http://www.healthcarereformmagazine.com/article/accountable-care-organizations0.html (accessed 04/21/2011).

Accountable Care Organizations. David Glass and Jeff Stensland, Medicare Payment Advisory Commission (MedPAC), July 9, 2008.

Accountable Care Organizations: A Roadmap for Success (Guidance on First Steps), 1st ed. Bruce Flareau, Joanne Bohn, and Colin Konschak, Virginia Beach, VA: Convurgent Publishing, LLC.

Accountable Care Organizations: Will They Deliver? Marsha Gold, Mathematica Policy Research, Inc., January 2010.

Accountable Care Organizations: Accountable for What, to Whom, and How? Elliott S. Fischer and Stephen M. Shortell, *Journal of the American Medical Association*, vol. 304, no. 15, October 20, 2010.

Accountable Care Organizations: Analysis and Implications. Powers Pyles Sutter & Verville PC, Washington, D.C., April 13, 2011.

Accountable Care Organizations: Payor-ACO Payment Issues. J. P. Rich, McDermott, Will & Emery, Chicago, March 29, 2011. Online at: http://www.mwe.com/info/aco/aco0311c.pdf (accessed 4/6/2012).

Accountable Care Organizations: Proposed Regulations Finally Released: Accountable Care Provider Reimbursement Strategies. Peter J. Rich, David L. Klatsky, and Peter Boland, Polakoff Boland Strafford Publications Inc., Berkeley, CA.

Accountable Care Organizations versus Accountable Care: Is There a Difference? Alice G. Gosfield, *Journal of the National Comprehensive Cancer Network*, June 2011.

Accountable Care Strategies: Lessons from the Premier Health Care Alliance's Accountable Care Collaborative. Amanda J. Forster, Blair G. Childs, Joseph F. Damore, Susan D. DeVore, and Eugene A Kroch.

Accountable for Value. Richard R. Clarke. Online at: http://www.hfma.org/Templates/Print.aspx?id=27064 (accessed 07/07/11).

Accountable Care Organizations: Where Are We? Jay Christiansen, Faegre Baker Daniels, Minneapolis, MN.

Achieving Accountable and Affordable Care: Key Health Policy Choices to Move the Health Care System Forward. Judy Feder and David Cutler, Center for American Progress, Washington, D.C., December 2012.

ACO Fairy Tale Faces a Rumpelstiltskin Moment: Guest Opinion. Michael L. Millenson, Henry J. Kaiser Family Foundation, April 19, 2011. Online at: http://www.kaiserhealthnews.org/Columns/2011/April/041811millenson.aspx (accessed 4/19/2011).

ACO Final Rule: 10 Healthcare Leaders Sound Off. October 25, 2011. Online at: http://www.healthleadersmedia.com/page-1/LED-272477/ACO-Final-Rule-10Healthcare-Leaders-Sound-Off (accessed 1/27/12).

ACO HMO Enrollment as a Percentage of Total Insured Californians, 2008. *ACO Business News*, Atlantic Information Services, Inc., vol. 2, no. 9, September 2011.

ACO Is the Hottest Three-Letter Word in Health Care. Jenny Gold, Henry J. Kaiser Family Foundation, January 13, 2011. Online at: http://www.kaiserhealthnews.org/Stories/2011/January/13/ACO-accountable-care-organization-FAQ.aspx (accessed 1/23/2011).

ACO or Not, Fairview Builds Shared Savings into All Payer Contracts. Philip Betbeze, HealthLeaders Media, May 23, 2011. Online at: http://www.healthleadersmedia.com/print/HEP-266457/ACO-or-Not-Fairview-Builds-Shared-Savings-into-All-Payer-Contracts (accessed 5/23/2011).

ACO Partnerships Deliver Fewer Hospital Days, Readmissions, Says Study. Emily Mullin, Dorland Health.

ACO Stakeholders at Conference Call for Transparency, Patient Input, Innovation. *ACO Business News*, Atlantic Information Services, Inc., vol. 2, no. 7, July 2011.

ACO Study Identifies Opportunities for Action. Miles Snowden, Corporate Research Group, May 31, 2012.

ACO Team, The: Payers and Providers Need to Play Together To Make Accountable Care Organizations Successful. David Ruppert, Hospitals & Health Networks (H&HN), September 29, 2011. Online at: http://www.hhnmag.com/hhnmag/HHNDaily/HHNDailyDisplay.dhtml?id=8680009864 (accessed 10/13/11).

ACO Transformation Will Heighten Health Plans' Role as the Clinical Analytics Exchange. Gantry Group, January 30, 2012.

ACO Wake-Up Call, The: A Hospital Confronts Payment Reform with a Physician Joint Venture.Stephen G. Morrissette, *Trustee Magazine*, April 2012. Online at: http://www.trusteemag.com/trusteemag/dhtml/article-display.dhtml?dcrpath=TRUSTEEMAG/Article/data/04APR2012/1204TRU_FEA_ACO&domain=TRUSTEEMAG (accessed 4/20/2012).

ACOs: Small & Rural Hospitals. April 29, 2011. Online at: http://www.aha.org/aha/advocacy/annual-meeting/ (accessed 4/29/2011), American Hospital Association.

ACOs: Trick or Treat? Matthew Weinstock, Hospitals & Health Networks (H&HN), October 13, 2011. Online at: http://www.hhnmag.com/hhnmag/HHNDaily/HHNDailyDisplay.dhtml?id=7160005138 (accessed 10/13/2011).

ACOs and the Future of Health Care. Ron Wince, Hospitals & Health Networks (H&HN), July 26, 2011. Online at: http://www.hhnmag.com/hhnmag/HHNDaily/HHNDailyDisplay.dhtml?id=5510004361 (accessed 07/29/2011).

ACOs, Co-ops and Other Options: A "How-to" Manual for Physicians Navigating a Post-Health Reform World. Stephen M. Fatum and Robert M. Martin, American Medical Association (AMA), 2011.

ACOs May Better Coordinate Care among Providers, Insurers. CMIO. Online at: http://www.cmio.net/index.php?option=com_articles&view=article&id=29268 (accessed 10/13/11).

ACOs Promise, Not Panacea. Donald M. Berwick, *JAMA*, September 12, 2012, vol. 308, no. 10.

Additional Input Regarding Accountable Care Organizations (ACOs) and the Medicare Shared Savings Program: Letter to Donald M. Berwick (CMS) from David Lansky (PBGH). David Lansky, Pacific Business Group on Health (PGBH).

Advanced Payment Model to Lure Critical Access Hospitals, Rural Providers. Karen M. Cheung, *FierceHealthcare,* October 21, 2011.

Alternatives to ACOs: Value-Based Reimbursement Models: Financial, Strategic, and Operational Implications. Paper presented: ECG Management Consultants, Inc. Cutting Costs and Raising Quality in Healthcare through Accountable Care Organizations, ACO Summit: Chicago, September 15, 2011.

AMA Asks Medicare to Start Paying Doctors for Care Coordination. Cheryl Clark, October 11 2011. Online at: http://www.healthleadersmedia.com/content/PHY-271922/AMAAsks-Medicare-to-Start-Paying-Doctors-for-Care-Coordination.html (accessed 10/13/11).

Auction Rate Securities. U.S. Securities and Exchange Commission. Online at: http://www.sec.gov/investors/ars.htm (accessed 5/25/2012).

Becoming Accountable: Opportunities and Obstacles for ACOs by Harold S Luft. October 6, 2010. http://healthpolicyandreform.nejm.org/?p=12750 (accessed 04/14/2011).

Becoming Accountable. Philip L. Ronning, Healthcare Financial Management Association (HFMA), November 2010.

Beginner's Guide to Selecting an EHR, A: A Step-By-Step Guide to Help You Select and Purchase an EHR That Is Right for Your Practice. Welch Allyn, Skaneateles, NY.

Benefit Designs Wrapped Around ACOs Are Still Rare but Growing. *ACO Business News*, Atlantic Information Services, Inc., vol. 2, no. 10, Atlantic Information Services, Inc.

Better Care and the Bottom Line. Joe Cantlupe, HealthLeaders Media, June 1, 2011.

Beyond ACOs: Value-Based Purchasing and Other Accountable Care Delivery Options. Bloomberg BNA, Drinker Biddle & Reath LLP, Philadelphia.

Beyond the "R Word"? Medicine's New Frugality. Gregg M. Bloche. *The New England Journal of Medicine*, Massachusetts Medical Society, May 3, 2012.

Blue Cross Blue Shield of Massachusetts: The Alternative QUALITY Contract. Blue Cross Blue Shield of Massachusetts, Blue Cross and Blue Shield Association, May 2010.

Blues a History of the Blue Cross and Blue Shield System, The. Robert Cunningham and Robert M. Cunningham, DeKalb, IL: Northern Illinois University.

Bomb Buried in Obamacare Explodes Today: Hallelujah, The! Rick Ungar, *Forbes.*

Bridging Employed Physician Compensation Plans into a New World of ACOs. Ron Vance, Navigant Consulting, Inc., Chicago, Winter 2011.

Building a Bridge from Fragmentation to Accountability: The Prometheus Payment Model. Francois de Brantes, Meredith B. Rosenthal, and Michael Painter, vol. 361, no. 11, September 10, 2009.

Building Blocks of ACOs, The: The Benefits. Jennifer Dennard, Porter Research, October 21, 2010. Online at: http://www.porterresearch.com/Resource_Center/Blog_News/Industry_News/2010/October/ACO_Feature_Part_1.html (accessed 12/22/2010).

Bundled Payment a Stepping-Stone for ACOs? I Don't Buy It. Rob Lazerow, The Advising Board Company.

Bundled Payment Pilots Should Seek Predictable Episodes of Care. Lutes,, Carl Rathjen, *ACO Business News*, Atlantic Information Services, Inc., vol. 2, no. 4, April 2012.

Bundled Payments. American Medical Association, December, 2011. Online at: http://www.ama-assn.org/ama/pub/physician-resources/practice-management-center/claims-revenuecycle/managed-care-contracting/evaluating-payment-options/bundled-payments.page? (accessed 10/30/12).

Bundled Payments for Care Improvement Initiative. Centers for Medicare & Medicaid Services.

Buoyed by Outpatient Growth: Despite Hurdles, For-Profits Report Revenue Gains. Beth Kutscher, *Modern Healthcare.*

Buying, Selling & Merging a Medical Practice: Proven Valuation and Negotiation Strategies. Kenneth M. Hekman, Burr Ridge, IL: Irwin/McGraw-Hill Professional Publishing.

Can the Medical Home Survive Long-Term? Karen Minich-Pourshadi, August 8, 2011. Online at: http://www.healthleadersmedia.com/print/FIN-269505/Can-the-Medical... (accessed 10/13/2011).

Capitation, Salary, Fee-for-Service and Mixed Systems of Payment: Effects on the Behavior of Primary Care Physicians (Review). T. Gosden, F. Forland, I. S. Kristiansen, M. Sutton, B. Leese, et al., The Cochrane Library, January, 2012.

Case Studies from Private-Sector ACOs: What Works and Why? Atlantic Information Services, Inc.

Charge Master Consulting. T. T. Mitchell Consulting, January 2010. Online at: http://www.ttmitchellconsulting.com/chargemaster.html.

Cigna-MCNT ACO Arrangement Posts Big Quality, Financial Gains. *ACO Business News*, Atlantic Information Services, Inc., vol. 2, no. 10, October 2011.

Cigna Plans Aggressive Expansion for ACO-Like Program. Margaret D. Tocknel, HealthLeaders Media, August 9, 2012.

CIGNA's Approach to Accountable Care Organizations, A White Paper: The KNH Interview. Joanne Silberner, Henry J. Kaiser Family Foundation, July 25, 2011. Online at: http://www.kaiserhealthnews.org/Stories/2011/July/25/halvorson-Q-and-A-kaiserpermanente-accountable-care-organizations.aspx (accessed 11/15/11).

CMS Bundled-Payment Program Seeks to Remove Cooperation Barriers. *ACO Business News*, Atlantic Information Services, Inc., vol. 2, no. 9, September 2011.

CMS Final Rule Implements $850 Million Hospital Value-Based Purchasing Program. Nathaniel Weixel, Health Law Resource Center Bureau of National Affairs, Inc. (BNA), May 5, 2011. Online at: http://healthlawrc.bna.com/hlrc/display/batch_print_display.adp (accessed 6/16/2011).

CMS Shared Savings Program: Key Issues and Financial Considerations. Paper presented at the ACO Congress, Los Angeles, November 1, 2011.

CO-OP Health Plans: More Competition, New Choices for Consumers and Small Businesses. Online at: http://www.healthcare.gov/news/factsheets/coops07182011a.html (accessed 8/7/2011).

Complete Capitation Handbook, The: How to Design and Implement At-Risk Contracts for Behavioral Healthcare. Michael A. Freeman. Tiburnon, CA: CentraLink Publications.

Controlling HealthCare Costs Another American Way: The Success of Kaiser Permanente, an Integrated American Health-Care Firm, Offers Lessons for Insurers and Hospitals at Home and Abroad. *The Economist Newspaper Ltd*, The Economist Group, April 29, 2010. Online at: http://www.economist.com/node/16009167 (accessed 11/17/11).

Cost Benefit Analysis. Online at: http://www.cdc.gov/owcd/EET/CBNfixed/TOC.html (accessed 7/8/2010).

Cost Containment: Overcoming Challenges. Philip Betbeze, HealthLeaders Media, November 2011. Online at: http://content.hcpro.com/pdf/content/273185.pdf (accessed 3/7/2012).

Cost Containment Measures under Healthcare Reform. Small Business Majority, December 2, 2011. Online at: http://smallbusinessmajority.org/policy/docs/SBM_Small_Biz_Cost_Containment_120211.pdf (accessed 1/20/12).

Creating Accountable Care Organizations: The Extended Hospital Medical Staff. Elliot S. Fisher, Douglas O. Staiger, Julie P.W. Bynum, and Daniel J. Gottlieb, vol. 26, No. 1, December 5, 2006.

Critical Access Hospital: Rural Health Fact Sheet Series. U.S. Department of Health and Human Services, Centers for Medicare & Medicaid Services, January 2012.

Critical Access Hospital Wants Support of Large System in Weighing MSSP Option. *ACO Business News*, Atlantic Information Services, Inc., vol. 2, no. 8, August 2011.

Decade of Health Care Cost Growth Has Wiped Out Real Income Gains for an Average U.S. Family, A. David I. Auerbach and Arthur L. Kellermann, vol. 30, no. 9, September 2011.

Design and Application of Shared Savings Programs, The: Lessons from Early Adopters. Joel S. Weissman, Michael Bailit, Meridith B. Rosenthal, and Guy D'Andrea, *Health Affairs*, vol. 31, No. 9.

Designing and Implementing Health Care Provider Payment Systems: How-To Manuals. John C. Langenbrunner, Cheryl Cashin, and Sheila O'Dougherty, The World Bank, USAID, Washington, D.C.

Early Results of a Marketwide ACO Initiative: The Alternative Quality Contract (AQC). Dana G. Safran, November 2, 2011.

Early Returns on Accountable Care, The: Newly Minted ACOs Grapple with Allocating Resources and Adjusting Operations to Put the Theory to Work. *Modern Healthcare.*

Economic Evaluation in Health: Saving Money or Improving? Dan Chisholm and David B. Evans, vol. 10, no. 3, 2007, *Journal of Medical Economics.*

Economics of Financing Medicare, The. Katherine Baicker and Michael E. Chernew. Online at: http://www.nejm.org/doi/pdf/10.1056/NEJMp1107671 (accessed July 29, 2011).

Elasticity of Demand for Health Care, The: A Review of the Literature and Its Application to the Military Health System. Jeanne S. Ringel, Susan D. Hosek, Ben A. Vollaard, and Sergej Mahnovski. Online at: http://www.rand.org/pubs/monograph_reports/2005/MR1355.pdf.

Electronic Health Record (EHR) Incentive Program FAQs. Online at: tps://www.cms.gov/Regulations.../FAQsRemediatedandRevised.pdf (accessed 10/25/2012).

Employers Look to ACOs to Increase Value, Keep Costs in Check. Chris Anderson, November 3, 2011. Online at: http://www.healthcareitnews.com/news/employers-look-acosincrease-value-keep-costs-check (accessed 1/19/12).

End of Fee-for-Service Medicine, The? Proposals for Payment Reform in Massachusetts. Robert Steinbrook, *The New England Journal of Medicine*, vol. 361, no. 11, September 10, 2010.

End of Health Insurance Companies, The. Ezekiel J. Emanuel and Jeffrey B. Liebman, January 30, 2012. Online at: http://opinionator.blogs.nytimes.com/2012/01/30/the-end-of-health-insurance-companies/ (accessed 3/30/2012).

Ensuring the Fiscal Sustainability of Health Care Reform. Michael E. Chernew, Lindsay Sabik, Amitabh Chandra, and Joseph P. Newhouse, *The New England Journal of Medicine*, Massachusetts Medical Society, January 7, 2010.

Episode-Based Performance Measurement and Payment: Making It a Reality. Peter S. Hussey, Melony E. Sorbero, Ateev Mehrotra, Hangsheng Liu, and Cheryl L. Damberg, vol. 28, no. 5, September/October 2009.

Essentials of Healthcare Finance, 7th ed. William O. Cleverley, Paula. H. Song, James O. Cleverley. Sudbury, MA: Jones & Bartlett Learning, 2011.

Essentials of Managed Health Care, 6th ed. Peter R. Kongstvedt, Beard Group, Chicago, 2012.

Everything You Need to Know about Accountable Care Organizations (in Plain English). Online at: www.transformed.com/pdf/ACO_FAQ.pdf (accessed 11/3/12).

Experience with Medicare's New Technology Add-On Payment Program. Alexandra T. Clyde, Lindsay Bockstedt, Jeffrey A. Farkas, and Christine Jackson, *Health Affairs*, vol. 27, no. 6, November/December 2008.

Experienced Providers Should Draw Payer Interest in CMS's "Pioneer" ACO Program. *ACO Business News*, Atlantic Information Services, Inc., vol. 2, no. 1, January 2012.

Explanation of Benefits. Ian Morrison, September 2, 2008. Online at: http://hhnmag.com/hhnmag_app/jsp/articledisplay.jsp?dcrpath=HHNMAG/Article/data/09SEP2008/080902HHN_Online_Morrison&domain=HHNMAG (accessed 3/29/2012).

Fair Market Value and Regulatory Considerations for the ACO Model. Kevin Cope, LarsonAllen LLP, Minneapolis, MN. Online at: http://www.larsonallen.com/EFFECT/Shared_Savings_and_Fair_Market_Value_in_the_ACO_Model.aspx (accessed 09/30/11).

FAQ: The CPC Initiative and Participation in Other CMS Initiatives. Online at: http://www.google.com/url?sa=t&rct=j&q=%22the%20cpc%20initiative%20and%20participation%20in%20other%20cms%20initiatives%22&source=web&cd=1&cad=rja&ved=0CDAQFjAA&url=http%3A%2F%2Fwww.innovations.cms.gov%2FFiles%2Fx%2FComprehensive-Primary-Care-Initiative-Frequently-AskedQuestions.pdf&ei=wwGYUNjQNeec2QWLuoDgAg&usg=AFQjCNEeaLDxCXSwZ2tkCEO2nfPZ1BTiTA (accessed 11/5/2012).

Finance Leaders Report. HealthLeaders Media Industry Survey, 2011.

Financial Management in Health Care Organizations. Robert A. McLean, New York: Delmar Publishers, Inc.

Financial Management of Hospitals and Healthcare Organizations, The, 3rd ed. Michael Nowicki, Health Administration Press, Chicago, 2004.

Financial Relationships between Physicians and Entities Furnishing Designated Health Services. vol. 42 CFR Section 411.351, 411.355–411.357, October 10, 2010.

Finding the Money: Creating a Cost Reduction Game Plan. Jonathan L. Lauer, The Healthcare Performance Alliance, Charlotte, NC, September 16, 2011.

For ACO Adoption Success, Leave Cost Out of It. Karen Minich-Pourshadi, HealthLeaders Media. Online at: http://www.healthleadersmedia.com/print/FIN-281394/for-acoadoption-success-leave-cost-out-of-it.htm.

From Volume to Value: Better Ways to Pay for Health Care. Harold D. Miller, *Health Affairs*, vol. 28, no. 5, September/October 2009.

Funds Targeted for Innovation Center. *ACO Business News*, Atlantic Information Services, Inc., vol. 2, no. 3, March 2011.

Future of ACOs & Payment Innovations. Ernie Schwefler, Anthem, Indianapolis, IN, November 2, 2011.

Gauging the Financial Impact of Physicians on Hospitals: Data on Physician Activity and Revenue within Hospitals Can Inform a Hospital's Strategy to Employ or Financially Integrate with Physicians. James Lifton, Healthcare Financial Management Association, Westchester, IL, April 2012.

Geographic Variation in Health Care Spending: Medicare Spending per Beneficiary, 2005. February 2008.

Getting Ready for Accountable Care Organizations. Joseph Goedert, Health Data Management, vol. 19, no. 4, Source Media, Inc., April 1, 2011. Online at: http://www.healthdatamanagement.com/issues/19_4/getting-ready-for-accountable-careorganizations-42230-1.html (accessed 5/2011).

Guide to Accountable Care Organizations, and Their Role in the Senate's Health Reform Bill, A. Jordan T. Cohen, March 11, 2010. Online at: http://www.healthreformwatch.com/2010/03/11/a-guide-to-accountable-careorganizations-and-their-role-in-the-senates-health-reform-bill/ (accessed 01/05/12).

Guide to Physician Performance—Based Reimbursement: Payoffs from Incentives, Clinical Integration & Data Sharing. Health Intelligence Network, May 2011.

Health and Productivity among U.S. Workers. Karen Davis, Sara R. Collins, Michelle M. Doty, Alice Ho, and Alyssa L. Holmgren, The Commonwealth Fund.

Health Care Coverage at Record Low: Fact Sheet: Health Insurance Coverage in 2010. U.S. Congress, September 13, 2011. Online at: http://www.jec.senate.gov/public/?a=Files.Serve&File_id=d35dc4dc-9762-4a91-94b5eb83a2a17772.

Health Reform and the Patient-Centered Medical Home: Policy Provisions and Expectations of the Patient Protection and Affordable Care Act. The Commonwealth Fund, October 2010. Online at: http://www.safetynetmedicalhome.org/safetynet/upload/SNMHI_PolicyBrief_Issue2.pdf.

Healthcare Innovation: How Plans and Providers Are Driving Change, Improving Care, and Achieving Value in a Post Reform World. Craig E. Samitt, September 16, 2011.

Healthcare Leaders React to Super Committee's Failure. Cheryl Clarke, November 23 2011. Online at: http://www.healthleadersmedia.com/content/LED-273610/Healthcare-LeadersReact-to-Super-Committees-Failure.html (accessed 11/28/11).

Healthcare Model for the 21st Century, A: Patient-Centered, Integrated Delivery Systems. Delos M. Cosgrove,. vol. 60, no. 3, The American Medical Group Association, March 2011. Online at: http://my.clevelandclinic.org/Documents/redefining-healthcare/amga-mar-2011.pdf (accessed 11/17/2011).

Healthcare Revenue Cycle Management: A TripleTree Industry Analysis. TripleTree, Minnapolis, MN, 2006.

Herzlinger Predicts ACOs, PCMHs Will Fail. Regina E. Herzlinger, Managed Care Magazine, MediMedia USA.

Hospital Employment of Docs May Not Drive Clinical Integration. *ACO Business News*, Atlantic Information Services, Inc., vol. 2, no. 3, March 2012.

Hospitals, IHNs Can Cut Teeth on ACOs by Covering Own Workers. *ACO Business News*, Atlantic Information Services, Inc., vol. 2, no. 10, Atlantic Information Services, Inc.

How Much Do Hospitals Cost Shift? A Review of the Evidence. Austin Frakt, vol. 89, no. 1, January 2011. Online at: http://onlinelibrary.wiley.com/doi/10.1111/j.14680009.2011.00621.x/full (accessed 4/25/11).

How Payment Reforms Can Help Achieve a High Performance Health System. Karen Davis, November 1, 2011.

How to Choose the Right Capitalization Option. Jim Vaughan and Joan Wise, *Healthcare Financial Management*, vol. 50, no. 12, December 1996.

IHI: Berwick on ACOs, Congress, Fraud. Cheryl Clark, December 7, 2011. Online at: http://www.healthleadersmedia.com/content/QUA-274038/IHI-Berwick-on-ACOsCongress-Fraud.html (accessed 12/07/11).

Implications for ACOs of Variations in Spending Growth. Michael J. McWilliams and Zirui Song, *The New England Journal of Medicine*, Massachusetts Medical Society, May 3, 2012.

Innovative Alternative Delivery and Payment Models: Private Sector Initiatives. *ACO Business News*, Atlantic Information Services, Inc., vol. 2, no. 7, July 2011.

Insurers, Healthcare Providers Spar over ACO Regulations. Lindsey Dunn, January 10, 2011. Online at: http://www.beckershospitalreview.com/hospital-physician-relationships/insurershealthcare-providers-spar-over-aco-regulations.html (accessed 01/21/11).

Introduction to Cost Accounting. Steven A. Finkler, in *Issues in Cost Accounting for Health Care Organizations*, New York: Aspen Publishers, 1994.

Investing in Prevention Improves Productivity and Reduces Employer Costs: Maximizing Prevention Benefits for American Business. William C. Weldon, Centers for Disease Control and Prevention, Atlanta, GA.

Key Design Elements of Shared-Savings Payment Arrangements. Michael Bailit and Christine Hughes, Bailit Health Purchasing, LLC, vol. 20, no. 1539, Commonwealth Fund, August, 2011. Online at: http://www.commonwealthfund.org/Publications/IssueBriefs/2011/Aug/Shared-Savings-Payment-Arrangements.aspx (accessed November 17, 2011).

Law of Economics of Pay for Performance, Bundled Payments and Shared Savings, The. Robert G. Homchick and Albert Hutzler, Davis Wright Tremaine LLP, HealthCare Appraisers, Inc.

Leading a Value-Based Culture. John Morrissey. Online at: http://www.trusteemag.com/trusteemap_app/jsp/articledisplay.jsp?dcrpath=TRUSTEEMAG (accessed 7/8/2011).

Lessons from Medicare's Demonstration Project on Disease Management, Care Coordination, and Value-Based Payment. Congressional Budget Office, January 2012.

Limitations of Rural Providers May Make Them Think Twice about MSSP Participation. *ACO Business News*, Atlantic Information Services, Inc., vol. 2, no. 4, April 2011.

The Long-Term Effect of Premier Pay for Performance on Patient Outcomes. Ashish K. Jha, Karen E. Joynt. John E. Orav, and Arnold M. Epstein, *The New England Journal of Medicine*, Massachusetts Medical Society, March 28, 2012. Online at: nejm.org (accessed 4/17/2012).

Maine General. Online at: http://www.mainegeneral.org/body.cfm?id=13 (accessed 11/17/2011).

Making the Best of Hospital Pay for Performance. Andrew Ryan and Jan Blustein, *The New England Journal of Medicine*, Massachusetts Medical Society, April 26, 2012.

Making the Value Proposition in Benefit Design. Health Care Financing & Organization, June 6, 2010. Online at: http://www.hcfo.org/publications/making-value-proposition-benefit-design (Accessed: 6/18/2010).

Managed Care Museum TimeLine: The History of Managed Care and More. Online at: http://www.managedcaremuseum.com/timeline.htm (accessed 4/25/2012).

Managing the Risks of Accountable Care. Max Reynolds, HFMA, July 2011. Online at: http://www.hfma.org/Templates/Print.aspx?id=27518 (accessed 9/14/2011).

Mass. Blues Unveils Favorable Findings on ACO-Type Model. *ACO Business News*, Atlantic Information Services, Inc., vol. 2, no. 4, April 2011.

Medical Care for the American People: The Final Report of the Committee on the Costs of Medical Care. The Committee on the Costs of Medical Care, The University of Chicago Press, October 31, 1932.

Medical Group Responses to Global Payment: Early Lessons from the "Alternative Quality Contract" in Massachusetts. Robert E. Mechanic, Palmira Santos, Bruce E. Landon, and Michael E. Chernew, vol. 30, no. 9, September 2011.

Medical Home For All, A? Physicians and Payers Transforming Primary Care. Jane DuBose, HealthLeaders-InterStudy HealthLeaders Media, Spring 2011.

Medical Practice Today: What Members Have to Say. Medical Group Management Association (MGMA), Englewood, CO, July 1, 2011.

Medicare ACOs: Not the Best Way to Start. Nathan Kaufman, Hospital & Health Networks (H&HN), Chicago.

Medicare Acute Care Episode Demonstration for Orthopedic and Cardiovascular Surgery. Centers for Medicare Medicaid Services (CMS), April 1, 2010. Online at: http://www.cms.gov/DemoProjectsEvalRpts/downloads/ACE_web_page.pdf (accessed 8/3/2010).

Medicare Physician Group Practices: Innovations in Quality and Efficiency. Michael Trisolini, Gregory Pope, John Kautter, and Jyoti Aggarwal, Commonwealth Fund, December 2006.

Minimum Medical Loss Ratio. 45 C.F.R. § 158.210 (2011).

Minnesota: Minnesota Health Care Delivery Systems Demonstration. National Academy for State Health Policy. Online at: http://www.nashp.org/aco/minnesota.

Minnesota and the Emerging ACO. George J. Isham, MetroDoctors, *The Journal of the Twin Cities Medical Society*.

Monarch Healthcare. Online at: http://www.monarchhealthcare.com/ (accessed 11/17/11).

More Than 40 Health Systems Join Premier Healthcare Alliance Accountable Care Organization Readiness Collaborative to Improve Community Health. Premier, Inc., August 12, 2010. Online at: http://www.premierinc.com/about/news/10-aug/aco081210.jsp (accessed 02/28/2011).

MTM Has Patchy Payment System: ACOs Ultimately May Shoulder Cost. *ACO Business News*, Atlantic Information Services, Inc., vol. 2, no. 10.

Multi-Track Financing: By Adopting a Diversified and Flexible Funding Approach, Healthcare Borrowers Can Position Themselves to Respond Rapidly to Changing Circumstances That Precipitate a Need to Shift Priorities among Available Financing Options. Steven W. Kennedy, Jr., John Randolph, and Anthony J. Taddey, Healthcare Financial Management, May 2012.

National Health Expenditures Aggregate, Per Capita Amounts, Percent Distribution, and Average Annual Percent Change: Selected Calendar Years 1960–2010. Online at: https://www.cms.gov/NationalHealthExpendData/downloads/tables.pdf (accessed 3/16/2012).

National Health Expenditures by Type of Service and Source of Funds: Calendar Years 1960–2009. Centers for Medicare & Medicaid Services (CMS). Online at: http://www.cms.hhs.gov/NationalHealthExpendData/(Historical; National Health Expenditures by type of service and source of funds, CY 1960-2009; file nhe2009.zip).

New Affordable Care Act Tools Offer Incentives for Providers to Work Together When Caring for People with Medicare. October 20, 2011. Online at: http://www.healthcare.gov/news/factsheets/2011/10/accountable-care10... (accessed 10/20/2011).

New American Compromise, The. Ian Morrison, *Hospitals and Health Networks*, vol. 61, no. 8, September 2008.

New CMMI Initiative May Appeal to Smaller Practices in Areas Where ACOs Pose Hurdles. Rachana Dixit, Inside Washington Publishers, October 12, 2011. Online at: www.insidehealthpolicy.com (accessed 10/12/2011).

New Healthcare Organizations Will Truly Manage Care. Richard Stefanacci, *Managed Care*, vol. 21, no. 5.

New Jersey to Launch Pilot Accountable Care Organization. August 26, 2009. Online at: http://www.rwjf.org/childhoodobesity/digest.jsp?id=21842.

New Wave of Hospital Consolidation, The: New Drivers, Players, and Models Define the Latest Wave of Consolidations Involving Hospitals. Lisa Goldstein, Healthcare Financial Management, April 2012.

Nuts and Bolts of ACO Financial and Operational Success: Calculating and Managing to Actuarial Utilization Targets. Kate Fitch, Catherine Murphy-Barron, and David Mirkin, Milliman & Robertson Inc., July 2011.

Opportunities and Challenges for Episode-Based Payment. *The New England Journal of Medicine* (accessed July 13, 2012).

Optimizing Health Care Delivery by Integrating Workplaces, Homes, and Communities: How Occupational and Environmental Medicine Can Serve as a Vital Connecting Link between Accountable Care Organizations and the Patient-Centered Medical Home. Robert K. McLellan, Bruce Sherman, Ronald R. Loeppke, Judith McKenzie, Kathryn L. Mueller, et al., *Journal of Occupational and Environmental Medicine*, vol. 54, no. 4, April 2012. Online at: http://journals.lww.com/joem/Fulltext/2012/04000/Optimizing_Health_Care_Delivery_by _Integrating.20.aspx.

Pathways to Quality Health Care: Rewarding Provider Performance: Aligning Incentives in Medicare. National Academy of Sciences.

Pay for Performance. December, 2011. Online at: http://www.ama-assn.org/ama/pub/physician-resources/practice-management-center/claims-revenue-cycle/managed-carecontracting/evaluating-payment-options/pay-for-performance.page? (accessed 12/29/2011).

Pay for Performance (P4P): AHRQ Resources. December, 2011. Online at: http://www.ahrq.gov/qual/pay4per.htm.

Paying for Care Episodes and Care Coordination. Karen Davis, *The New England Journal of Medicine*.

Paying Physicians by Capitation: Is the Past Now Prologue. Samuel H Zuekas and Joel W. Cohen, Project Hope, vol. 29, no. 9, September 2010.

Payment Change: 3 Ways to Set Your Course for Success. Michael E. Nugent, Healthcare Financial Management Association (HFMA), April 2010. Online at: http://www.hfma.org/WorkArea/linkit.aspx?LinkIdentifier=id&ItemID=19355 (accessed 4/27/2011).

Payment Expert Says Primary Care Physicians Should Drive ACOs: Q&A Discussion Highlights Opportunities, Pitfalls for Primary Care and ACOs. James Arvantes, October 5, 2011. Online at: http://www.aafp.org/online/en/home/publications/news/newsnow/practice-professional-issues/20111005millerqa.html (accessed 1/30/12).

Payment Reform: Current and Emerging Reimbursement Models. Paul N. Casale, Gregory S. Thomas, Linda D. Gillam, Jerry D. Kennett, Sandra Lewis, et al.

Payment Reform, Accountable Care, and Risk: Early Lessons for Providers. Michael E. Nugent, Healthcare Financial Management Association (HFMA). Online at: http://www.hfma.org/Templates/Print.aspx?id=22994 (accessed 07/07/2011).

Performance-Based Payment Incentives May Harm Nursing Conditions. February 9, 2011. Online at: http://www.surgistrategies.com/news/2011/02/performance-based-payment-incentives-may-harm-nur.aspx (accessed 2/10/2011).

Physician Alignment Poses Challenges for ACOs. John Commins, July 12 2011. Online at: http://www.healthleadersmedia.com/page-1/PHY-268447/Physician-Alignment-PosesChallenge-for-ACOs (accessed 10/08/12).

Physician, Hospital Groups Guarded on CMS Advance Payment ACO Initiative. Nathaniel Weixel, vol. 20, no. 987, Bureau of National Affairs, Inc. (BNA), June 30, 2011.

Physicians Post-PPACA: Not Going Bust at the Healthcare Buffet (Part 1 of 2). David W. Hilgers and Sidney S. Welch, *Physicians News Digest.* Online at: http://www.physiciansnews.com/2012/03/15/physicians-post-ppaca-not-going-bust-atthe-healthcare-buffet-part-1-of-2/ (accessed 11/3/12).

Physicians Seek Federal Funds to Finance EMRs. Alicia Ault, April 15, 2007, *Internal Medicine News.*

Physicians Will Lead ACOs Forward. *American Medical News*, vol. 55, No. 10.

Pioneer ACO Applicants Offer Proposals for Innovative Payment Methodologies. *ACO Business News*, Atlantic Information Services, Inc., vol. 2, no. 9, September 2011.

Pioneer ACO Deadline Extended. Margaret D. Tocknell, Health Leaders Media. June 10, 2011. Online at: http://www.healthleadersmedia.com/print/TEC-267205/Pioneer-ACO-Deadline-Extended (accessed 6/16/2011).

Pioneer ACO Model, The: Program Details and Implications for Participating Providers. Health Care Advisory Board.

Pioneer Model, The: CMS's Alternative Shared Savings Program for ACOs. Emily J. Cook and Lauren N. Hanley, McDermott, Will, & Emery, Chicago, May 23, 2011.

Plans Will Seek Out NCQA Standards on Accountable Care, Observers Predict. *ACO Business News*, Atlantic Information Services, Inc., vol. 2, no. 12, December 2011.

"Population-Based," Meet "Patient-Centered": Two Vaunted Ideas of Health Care, Experts Say, Should Be Perfectly Aligned. Timothy Kelley, *Managed Care*, May 2012.

Premier ACO Collaboratives: Driving to a Patient-Centered Health System. Premier, Inc., May 20, 2010. Online at: http://www.premierinc.com/about/news/10-may/aco-white-paper.pdf (accessed 11/17/2011).

Premier ACO Collaboratives. Kaiser Permanente. Online at: http://xnet.kp.org/newscenter/aboutkp/healthconnect/index.html (accessed 11/18/11).

Primary Care Financing Matters: A Roadmap for Reform. Arlene Ash, Randall Ellis, Andrea Kronman, and Allan Goroll, December 2010.

Private Payor Movement to Accountable Reimbursement Model. Matt Kuntz. Online at: http://healthcare-executive-insight.advanceweb.com/Features/Articles/Private-Payor-Movement-to-Accountable-Reimbursement-Model.aspx (accessed 11/8/12).

Promising Payment Reform Organizations: Risk-Sharing with Accountable Care. Suzanne F. Delbanco, Kristine Martin-Anderson, Catherine E. Major, Mary Beth Kiser, and Brynnan W. Toner, July 2011.

Proposed ACO Rules Attract Public Gripes. Cheryl Clark, June 9, 2011. Online at: http://www.healthleadersmedia.com/page-1/TEC-267158/Proposed-ACO-Rules-Attract-Public-Gripes (accessed 07/07/011).

Prospective or Retrospective Beneficiary Assignments to Calculate Eligibility for Shared Savings. Lisa Han.

Providers Favoring ACOs Charge Ahead. Karen M. Cheung, FierceHealthcare.

Providers Should Be Aware of MSSP Challenges, Observers Say. *ACO Business News*, Atlantic Information Services, Inc., vol. 2, no. 12, December 2011.

Rapidly Evolving Physician-Payment Policy: More Than the SGR. Paul B. Ginsburg, *The New England Journal of Medicine,* vol. 364, no. 2, Massachusetts Medical Society, January 13, 2011. Online at: http://www.nejm.org/doi/full/10.1056/NEJMhpr1004028 (accessed 4/18/2011).

Relationship between Physician Compensation Strategies and the Intensity of Care to Medicare Beneficiaries, The. Bruce E. Landon, James D. Reschovsky, James A. O'Malley, Hoangmai H. Pham, and Jack Hadley, Health Services Research Health Research and Educational Trust, December 2011.

Rewards and Their Risks. Joe Carlson, *Modern Healthcare*, April 30, 2012.

The Road to Fee-for-Value and Accountable Care Models. Optum, Inc. Online at: www.optum.com.

Rural Docs Question Benefits of Investing in Medicare ACOs. *ACO Business News*, Atlantic Information Services, Inc., vol. 2, no. 12, December 2011.

Sacramento Pilot Used "Basic Improvements" to Achieve Savings. *ACO Business News*, Atlantic Information Services, Inc., vol. 2, no. 4, April 2011.

Shared Risk Payment in Private-Sector ACOs: Four Approaches. *ACO Business News*, Atlantic Information Services, Inc., vol. 2, no. 4, April 2011.

Societal Perceptions of Physicians: Knights, Knaves or Pawns. Sachin H. Jain and Christine Cassel, vol. 304, no. 9, American Medical Association (AMA), September 1, 2010.

Spending Differences Associated with the Medicare Physician Group Practice Demonstration. Carrie H. Colla, David E. Wennberg, Ellen Meara, Daniel Gottlieb, Valerie A. Lewis, et al., *Journal of the American Medical Association*, American Medical Association. Online at: http://jama.jamanetwork.com/ (accessed 9/13/2012).

Study: No Strong Link between Funding Models, Primary Care Quality. Morgan Lewis, Jr., Advanstar Communication Inc., December 21, 2011. Online at: http://www.modernmedicine.com/modernmedicine/Modern+Medicine+Now/Study-No-strong-link-between-funding-models-primar/ArticleStandard/Article/detail/753574?contextCategoryId=40169&ref=25 (accessed 12/27/2011).

Study: Office-Based Primary Care Doctors Missing Out on Early ACOs. Morgan Lewis, Jr., December 14, 2011. Online at: http://www.modernmedicine.com/modernmedicine/Modern+Medicine+Now/StudyOffice-based-primary-care-doctors-missingout/ArticleStandard/Article/detail/752459?ref=25 (accessed 12/27/2011).

Test-Driving an ACO: Norton Healthcare, Humana Already Seeing Results in First Year of Pilot Project. Melanie Evans, September 5, 2011, *Modern Healthcare*.

Thumbs Down: ACO Plan Draws More Criticism from Top Execs. Melanie Evans, May 30, 2011, *Modern Healthcare*.

To Join or Not to Join an ACO. Doug Farrago. Online at: http://authenticmedicine.com/?p=390 (accessed 12/7/2011).

Top PCMH Challenge? Coordinating Care with Referral Docs. John Commins. July 21 2011. Online at: http://www.healthleadersmedia.com/page-1/PHY-268852/Top-PCMH-Challenge-Coordinating-Care-with-Referral-Docs (accessed 10/13/11).

Understanding Your Capital Options. Christopher T. Payne, May 2012, Healthcare Financial Management.

Using Individualized Guidelines to Optimize Cost and Quality for Accountable Care Organization. David Eddy.

Valuation Strategies: Compensation Agreements. March 2010.

Value-Based Insurance Design. February 11, 2011. Online at: http://healthcare-economist.com/2011/02/11/value-based-insurance-design/ (accessed 11/15/2011).

Value-Based Payment and Accountable Care: Are We Making Progress. *The Wall Street Journal*, Dow Jones & Company, Inc., October 12, 2011.

Value-Based Purchasing for Hospitals. Jordan M. VanLare, Jean Moody-Williams, and Patrick H. Conway, vol. 31, no. 1, January, 2012. Online at: http://content.healthaffairs.org/content/31/1/249.1.full.html (accessed 3/28/12).

Value Equation, The. Jeni Williams, Healthcare Financial Management Association (HFMA). Online at: http://www.hfma.org/Templates/Print.aspx?id=23573 (accessed 04/15/2011).

Value in Health Care: Current State and Future Directions. Healthcare Financial Management Association (HFMA), June 2011.

Valuing Health Care: Improving Productivity and Quality. Kauffman Task Force on Cost-Effective Health Care Innovation, Ewing Marion Kauffman Foundation, Kansas City, MO.

Variable Rate Demand Obligation (VRDO). Municipal Securities Rulemaking Board. Online at: http://msrb.org/msrb1/glossary/view_def.asp?vID=4310 (accessed 5/25/2012).

Wasting Money on Private Plans. Bill Davis, *Modern Healthcare*, April 9, 2012.

What Is the Role of the Radiologist in Holding Down Health Care Cost Growth? Howard P. Forman, Norman J. Beauchamp, Alan Kaye, David B. Larson, and Alexander Norbash, *American Journal of Roentgenology*, vol. 194, no. 4, October 2011. www.ajronline.org/content/197/4/919.full (accessed 11/3/12).

What Legal Drama? Administration, Providers Charge Ahead on ACA. Rich Daly, *Modern Healthcare*, April 9, 2012.

What's Your ACO Gripe? Haydn Bush, Health Forum, Inc., April 25, 2011. Online at: http://hhndailynews.blogspot.com/2011/04/whats-your-aco-gripe.html (accessed 4/26/2011).

Who's Driving Health Care's Transformation? Bill Santamour, *HHN Magazine*, April 2012.

Why Are ACOs Doomed for Failure. Thomas P. Weil, Medical Practice Management, Greenbranch Publishing LLC.

Will ACOs Reduce Health Care Costs?. *ACO Business News*, Atlantic Information Services, Inc., vol. 2, no. 6, June 2011.

Will the Baby Boom be a Boon to Hospitals? Don't Count On It. Jeff Goldsmith, in *Futurescan 2012: Healthcare Trends and Implications 2012–2017*, Chicago: Health Administration Press.

Will Your Data Support Value-Based Payment? Healthcare Financial Management Association, May 2012.

Wisconsin Systems Launch Accountable Care Network: And Begin Working with Prayers. Patricia A. Ruff, Healthcare Financial Management Association (HFMA). 2011. Online at: http://www.hfma.org/Templates/InteriorMaster.aspx?id=25787 (accessed 07/07/11).

Working Capital Management. Narender K. Jane and Darya Ganj, New Delhi: A.P.H. Publishing Corporation, 2004.

COMPETITION

2 Pitfalls of Physician-Hospital Alignment. Karen Minich-Pourshadi, HealthLeaders Media, April 16, 2012. Online at: http://www.healthleadersmedia.com/page-1/FIN-279002/2-Pitfalls-of-PhysicianHospital-Alignment (accessed 4/23/2012).

3 Strategic Alerts for Financial Leaders. Karen Minich-Pourshadi, HealthLeaders Media, May 14, 2012.

5 Reasons Why ACOs Could Fail. Cheryl Clark, January 7, 2011. Online at: http://www.healthleadersmedia.com/content/LED-261056/5-Reasons-Why-ACOs-Could-Fail## (accessed 1/17/2011).

5 Secrets to ACO Success. Margaret D. Tocknell, HealthLeaders Media, June 29, 2011. Online at: http://www.healthleadersmedia.com/print/HEP-267998/5-Secrets-to-ACO-Success (accessed 06/30/2011).

5 Things You Need to Understand about Looming Health Care Changes. Carey Goldberg, February 21, 2011. Online at: http://www.commonhealth.wbur.org/2011/02/aco-5-things/ (accessed 2/28/2011).

7 Critical Success Factors for ACOs. Michelle McNickle, *Healthcare IT News*. Online at: http://www.healthcareitnews.com/news/7-critical-success-factors-acos (accessed 06/08/12).

8 Strategies for Hospital Borrowers in 2011. James Blake, Eric A. Jordahl, and Andrew J Majka, *Healthcare Financial Management*, vol. 65, no. 4, April 2011.

9 Ways Better Data Can Drive Hospital Bundled Payment Initiatives. Bob Herman, iVantage Health Analytics.

10 "Facts" on Accountable Care Organizations. Gary Baldwin, Health Data Management Blogs. Online at: http://www.healthdatamanagement.com/blogs/health_care_technology_news_ACOs-42560-1.html (accessed October 13, 2011).

13 Hot ACO Buzzwords All Providers Should Know. Cheryl Clark, HealthLeaders Media, April 6, 2011. Online at: http://www.healthleadersmedia.com/print/LED-264581/13-HotACO-Buzzwords-All-Providers-Should-Know (accessed 4/11/2011).

2010 Medical Home Performance Benchmarks: Adoption, Utilization and Results. The Healthcare Intelligence Network, Sea Girt, NJ, 2010.

2010 Outcomes: Heart & Vascular Institute. Sydell and Arnold Miller Family Heart & Vascular Institute. Online at: http://my.clevelandclinic.org/Documents/heart/OutcomePDFs/2010/hvi-book-2011.pdf (accessed 11/22/2011).

2011 Benchmarks in Accountable Care Organizations: Metrics from Early ACO Adopters. Healthcare Intelligence Network (HIN), Sea Girt, NJ.

2012 Healthcare Benchmarks: Accountable Care Organizations. Healthcare Intelligence Network (HIN), Sea Girt, NJ.

About Metro Health. Metro Health. Online at: http://metrohealth.net/about-metro.

About the Quality & Patient Safety Institute. Cleveland Clinic, 2011. Online at: http://my.clevelandclinic.org/about-cleveland-clinic/quality-patient-safety/about-quality-safety-institute.aspx (accessed 1/19/2012).

ACCA: Creating a Service Line Agreement with Nonintegrated Groups. Kaitlyn Dmyterko, April 13, 2011. Online at: http://www.cardiovascularbusiness.com/index.php?option=com_articles&article=27257&publication=29&view=portals (accessed 4/16/2011).

ACCA: ACOs Demand Culture Change. Kaitlyn Dmyterko, April 20, 2011. Online at: http://www.cardiovascular-business.com/index.php?option=com_articles&view=article&id=27382&division=cvb (accessed 4/16/2011).

Accenture Provides The Christ Hospital a Prescription for High Performance by Helping It Achieve Independence. Accenture. Online at: http://www.accenture.com/SiteCollectionDocuments/PDF/Accenture_Health_Public_Servi ce_The_Christ_Hospital_Infrastructure.pdf (accessed 3/2/12).

Access to Capital: Implications for Hospital Consolidation. Daniel M. Grauman, John M. Harris, and Christine Martin, Healthcare Financial Management Association (HFMA), April 2010. Online at: www.hfma.org.

Accountable Care Collaboratives: The Drive to High-Value Healthcare. Premier, Inc., 2011. Online at: http://www.premierinc.com/quality-safety/tools-services/ACO/index.jsp (accessed 1/23/2011).

Accountable Care Directory 2012. MCOL Healthquest, 2012.

Accountable Care; Expected to Save Millions for Medicare. Phil Galewitz, Jordan Rau, and Bara Vaida, *Kaiser Health News*, The Henry J. Kaiser Family Foundation, March 21, 2011. Online at: http://www.mcclatchydc.com/2011/03/31/v-print/111354/accountable-careexpected-to-save.html (accessed 4/1/2011).

Accountable Care Organizations: A New Idea for Managing Medicare. Jane Cys, *American Medical News*, Aug. 31, 2009. Online at: http://www.ama-assn.org/amednews/2009/08/31/gvsa0831.htm (accessed 8/16/2010).

Accountable Care Organization, The: Whatever Its Growing Pains, the Concept Is Too Vitally Important to Fail. Francis J. Crosson, vol. 30, no. 7, July 1, 2011.

Accountable Care Organization, The: Not Ready for Prime Time. Jeff Goldsmith, August 17, 2009. Online at: http://healthaffairs.org/blog/2009/08/17/the-accountable-careorganization-not-ready-for-prime-time/ (accessed 1/5/12).

Accountable Care Organizations. Mark Merlis, *Health Affairs*, July 27, 2010 (updated August 13, 2010). Online at: http://www.healthaffairs.org/healthpolicybriefs/brief.php?brief_id=23.

Accountable Care Organizations: Promise of Better Outcomes at Restrained Costs; Can They Meet Their Challenges? C. F. Geilfuss and Renate M. Gray. Bureau of National Affairs, Inc. (BNA), June 30, 2010.

Accountable Care Organizations: Analysis and Implications. Powers Pyles Sutter & Verville PC, Washington, D.C., April 13, 2011 (accessed 4/25/2011).

Accountable Care Organizations: The Practical Reality. Douglas A. Hastings, Bureau of National Affairs, Inc. (BNA), June 2, 2010 (accessed 11/2010).

Accountable Care Organizations: The Fork in the Road. Thomas L. Greaney, Massachusetts Medical Society, December 22, 2010. Online at: http://healthpolicyandreform.nejm.org/?p=13451 (accessed 12/23/2010).

Accountable Care Organizations: Your Guide to Strategy, Design, and Implementation. Marc Bard and Mike Nugent, Chicago: Health Administration Press. 2011.

Accountable Care Organizations: Can They Rein in Health Care Spending for States? Robin N. Richardson, June 9, 2010.

Accountable Care Organizations: A Primer for Orthopaedic Surgeons, 1st ed., February 2011.

Accountable Care Organizations: Overview of HealthCare Partners—A Physician-Led Model. Robert Margolis, HealthCare Partners, November 2, 2011.

Accountable Care Organizations: The Next Phase. January 6, 2011. Online at: http://healthaffairs.org/press/2011_01_06_2.php (accessed 7/7/2011).

Accountable Care Organizations: What Is Required to Make Them Work? James L. Holly, March 10, 2011.

Accountable Care Organizations: Training Family Doctors. September 5, 2010. Online at: http://usafamilymedicine.wordpress.com/2010/09/05/accountable-care-organizations (accessed 10/10/2011).

Accountable Care Organizations: New Form of Integrated Delivery or Monopolist. Robert A. Berenson, The Urban Institute, December 3, 2010.

Accountable Care Organizations: An Opportunity to Transform Care. David Lansky, Health Affairs, April 22, 2011. Online at: http://healthaffairs.org/blog/2011/04/22/accountable-careorganizations-an-opportunity-to-transform-care/ (accessed 04/25/2011).

Accountable Care Organizations: A New Model for Sustainable Innovation. Deloitte Center for Health Solutions, Deloitte Development LLC, 2010.

Accountable Care Organizations: The Case for Flexible Partnerships between Health Plans and Providers. Jeff Goldsmith, vol. 30, no. 1, January 2011.

Accountable Care Organizations: Under the Health Reform Law, Medicare Will Be Able to Contract with These to Provide Care to Enrollees. What Are They and How Will They Work? Mark Merlis, *Health Affairs,* August 13, 2010. Online at: http://www.healthaffairs.org/healthpolicybriefs/brief.php?brief_id=23.

Accountable Care Organizations (ACOs): Implications for Ambulatory Surgery Centers. *Healthcents*, September 27, 2010 (accessed 1/25/2011).

Accountable Care Organizations (ACOs). CIGNA. Online at: http://newsroom.CIGNA.com/KnowledgeCenter/ACO (accessed 11/16/2011).

Accountable Care Organizations and Antitrust: Restructuring the Health Care Market. Richard M. Scheffler, Stephen M. Shortell, and Gail R. Wilensky, *Journal of the American Medical Association*, vol. 307, no. 14.

Accountable Care Organizations and Community Empowerment. Benjamin F. Springgate and Robert H. Brook, *JAMA*, vol. 305, no. 17, May 4, 2011.

Accountable Care Organizations and ESRD: The Time Has Come. Allen R. Nissenson, Franklin W. Maddux, Ruben L. Velez, Tracy J. Mayne, and Jess Parks, World Kidney Forum AJKD, 2012.

Accountable Care Organizations and Evolving Integrated Delivery Systems—the New Frontier in Compliance Challenges: ACOs Are a Call to Compliance Officers to Keep Stepping Up to the Next Evolution of Health Care. Paul R. DeMuro, *Journal of Health Care Compliance,* January 2010. Online at: http://find.galegroup.com/ezp.slu.edu (accessed 4/4/2011).

Accountable Care Organizations and Health Care Disparities. Chris E. Pollack and Katrina Armstrong, *Journal of the American Medical Association*, vol. 305, no. 16, April 27, 2011.

Accountable Care Organizations-Health Information Technology (HIT). Gerry Hinkley, Pillsbury Winthrop Shaw Pittman LLP, March 31–April 2, 2011.

Accountable Care Organizations in 2012: ACO Participation Doubles in 12 Months. Healthcare Intelligence Network. Online at: http://www.hin.com/library/registeraco12.html (accessed 06/21/12).

Achieving Accountability in a Large Geographically Diverse Multispecialty IPA. James Dougherty and Carole Black, The Medical Group of Ohio and OhioHealth Group, Valence Health.

An ACO: Lessons Learned from a Physician Practice Perspective. Todd Fowler and Craig Anderson, Holzer Clinic, September 15, 2011.

ACO Blueprints: Options in Accountability. Margaret Dick Tocknell, *Health Leaders*, May 2012.

ACO Case Study: Memorial Hermann: Houston, Texas. Keith D. Moore and Dean C. Coddington, American Hospital Association (AHA), January 2011. Online at: www.aha.org/aha/content/2011/pdf/aco-case-mem-hermann.pdf (accessed 5/13/2011).

ACO Case Study: Metro Health: Grand Rapids, Michigan. Keith D. Moore and Dean C. Coddington, American Hospital Association (AHA), January 2011. Online at: http://www.aha.org/aha/content/2011/pdf/aco-case-new-metro-health.pdf (accessed May 13, 2011).

ACO Congress Preconference Session: ACO Value-Based Risk Contracting. Polakoff Boland, November 1, 2011.

ACO Creation Driven by Commercial Market. Philip Betbeze, HealthLeaders Media, April 29, 2011. Online at: http://www.healthleadersmedia.com/content/LED-265538/ACOCreation-Driven-by-Commercial-Market.html (accessed 5/1/2011).

ACO Groups Outperform Rest of Network on Clinical Quality. Blue Cross Blue Shield of Massachusetts. *ACO Business News*, Atlantic Information Services, Inc., vol. 2, no. 4, April 2011.

ACO Handbook, The: A Guide to Accountable Care Organizations, 1st ed. Peter A. Pavarini,Washington, D.C.: American Health Lawyers Association (AHLA), 2012.

ACO Invitations: A Date Worth Debating. Tom Ealey, Medical Group Management Association (MGMA), October 2011.

ACO Model, The—A Three Year Financial Loss. Trent Haywood and Keith Kosel, March 23, 2011. Online at: http://healthpolicyandreform.nejm.org/?p=13937&query=TOC (accessed 3/23/11).

An ACO Overview. Toshiba America Medical Systems, Inc., 2011. Online at: http://medical.toshiba.com/promo/general/aco/downloads/ACO-CORP-Sales-Sheet2011.pdf.

An ACO Overview: What You Need to Know. Toshiba America Medical Systems, Inc., 2011. Online at: http://toshibainsight.com/2011/06/an-aco-overview-what-you-need-to-know/ (accessed 08/02/2011).

ACO Payments May Hinge More on Geography Than Quality. John Commins, HealthLeaders Media, May 2, 2012.

ACO Pioneers to Launch by Year's End? Karen M. Cheung, Fierce Markets, September 13, 2011. Online at: http://www.fiercehealthcare.com/story/aco-pioneers-launch-years-end/2011-0913 (accessed 11/16/2011).

ACO Planned in New York. Jaimy Lee, March 20, 2012. Online at: http://www.modernhealthcare.com/article/20120320INEWS/303209987/ (accessed 3/20/2012).

ACO Readiness Planning: A Strategic Overview for Provider Executives. Health Access Solutions, San Francisco, CA.

ACO Regulations Put Spotlight on 65 Indicators for Care Delivery. Bill Melville, The Institute for Healthcare Consumerism, 2011.

ACO Reinsurance Options. Kathryn A. Bowen, *Accountable Care News*, vol. 3, no. 2, Health Policy Publishing LLC, February 2012.

ACO's Can Accommodate Various Practice Sizes. Lois A. Bowers, *ModernMedicine*, October 19, 2012.

ACO's, Family Medical Homes, Shared Savings Programs, Collaborative Care: What Are They and How Do They Work? David Higlers. Brown McCarroll, LLP, Austin, TX, December 16, 2010.

ACO Special Report: The Right Medicine for Our Ailing Health System. Alan S. Gassman, June 25, 2011. Online at: http://www.modernmedicine.com/modernmedicine/article/articleDetail.jsp?id=728456 (accessed 3/16/12).

ACO Special Report: Under Construction, Under Fire. Annette M. Boyle, June 25, 2011. Online at: http://license.icopyright.net/user/viewFreeUse.act?fuid=MTM0MDQ3ODY%3D (accessed 6/30/2011).

ACO Start-Up Costs Higher Than Estimates: Saving Rate Should Be Revised, AHA Says. Sarah Barr and Nathaniel Weixel, Bureau of National Affairs, Inc., 20 HLR 750, May 19, 2011. Online at: http://healthlawrc.bna.com/hlrc/display/batch_print_display.adp (accessed May 26, 2011).

ACOs: Attorneys Crafting ACOs Cite Tax Treatment, Business Model Structures as Key Concerns. Diane Freda and Peyton M. Sturges, Bureau of National Affairs, Inc. (BNA), March 24, 2011. Online at: http://healthlawrc.bna.com/hlrc/4237/split_display.adp?fedfid=20121900&vname=hlrnotallissues&wsn=495241000&searchid=142826 (accessed 3/28/2011).

ACOs: Tailoring Your Own Solutions. HealthLeaders Media, December 27, 2010.

ACOs: The Alegent Experience. Navigant Consulting, Inc., Chicago, December 7, 2010.

ACOs: Making Sure We Learn from Experience. Elliot Fisher and Stephen Shortell. Online at: http://www.commonwealthfund.org/Blog/2012/Apr/ACOs-Making-Sure-We-Learnfrom-Experience.aspx.

ACOs and Supply Chain: Brace for Impact. Caroline Kolman, Navigant Consulting, Inc., Winter 2011.

ACOs Are Bursting Out All Over. Jenny Gold, The Henry J. Kaiser Family Foundation, December 1, 2011. Online at: capsules.kaiserhealthnews.org/index.php/2011/12/acos-are-bursting-out-all-over/?referrer=search (accessed 1/17/2012).

ACOs Can Help Enable Conversations on Overlooked Issue of End-of-Life Care. *ACO Business News*, Atlantic Information Services, Inc., vol. 2, no. 12, December 2011.

ACOs Can Work with Physicians in Charge: A Study Looks at the Effectiveness of a Primary Care-Led Accountable Care Organization. Victoria S. Elliott, American Medical Association (AMA), January 31, 2011. Online at: http://www.ama-assn.org/amednews/2011/01/31/bisa.htm (accessed 2/7/2011).

ACOs Cite Reduced Hospital Visits, Use of Nurses to Track Patients. Mark Slitt Sanderford Wong, *ACO Business News*, Atlantic Information Services, Inc., vol. 2, no. 4, April 2012.

ACOs: Driving Providers toward Quality vs. Quantity in Healthcare. David Nace, vol. 5, no. 2, McKesson Corporation, 2011.

ACOs Forging the Links. Ken Terry, Hospitals and Health Networks Health Forum, Inc., January 2011.

ACOs Generate High Interest, But Is Bar Set Too High? Philip Betbeze, HealthLeaders Media, April 22, 2011. Online at: http://www.healthleadersmedia.com/content/LED265258/ACOs-Generate-High-Interest-But-Is-Bar-Set-Too-High.html (accessed 4/28/2011).

ACOs Shine Spotlight on Physician Employment. Carrie Vaughan, HealthLeaders Media, May 10, 2011. Online at: http://www.healthleadersmedia.com/print/PHY-265935/ACOsShine-Spotlight-on-Physician-Employment (accessed 5/13/11).

ACOs Spell Gold Rush for Health Care Consultants. Bara Vaida, April 2, 2011. Online at: http://www.kaiserhealthnews.org/Stories/2011/April/03/aco-consultant-goldrush.aspx?p=1 (accessed 4/7/2011).

Adding Value? HTAs and Systematic Reviews of Health Economic Evidence. Michael Drummond, Rob Anderson, Louis Niessen, Ian Shemilt, and Luke Vale.

Addressing the Primary Care Physician Shortage in an Evolving Medical Workforce. Shaheen E. Lakhan and Cyndi Laird, vol. 2, no. 14, BioMed Central Ltd., May 5, 2009.

Administration Offers New Path for ACOs. Jenny Gold, The Henry J. Kaiser Family Foundation, May 17, 2011. Online at: http://www.kaiserhealthnews.org/Stories/2011/May/17/ACOinitiatives.aspx?p=1 (accessed 6/10/2011).

Adopt Patient-Centered Medical Home on the Way to an ACO. *ACO Business News*, Atlantic Information Services, Inc., vol. 2, no. 6.

Advocate Health Care, Blue Cross and Blue Shield of Illinois Sign Agreement Focusing on Improving Quality, Bending the Health Care Cost Curve. BlueCross BlueShield of Illinois. Online at: http://www.bcbsil.com/company_info/newsroom/news/advocate_announcement.html.

Advocate Makes Move toward ACO. *ACO Business News*, Atlantic Information Services, Inc., vol. 1, no. 1, November 2010.

Aetna Building National ACO Network. Margaret D. Tocknell, HealthLeaders Media. Online at: http://www.healthleadersmedia.com/print/HEP-280191/aetna-building-national-aconetwork.

Aetna Cites "True Partnership," Reduced Costs in ACO Model. Richard Scott, Dorland Health, April 4, 2011. Online at: http://www.dorlandhealth.com/clinical_care/trends/Aetna-CitesTrue-Partnership-Reduced-Costs-in-ACO-Model_1737.html (accessed 4/4/2011).

Aetna Expands Banner ACO Deal to Include More Technical Support. *ACO Business News*, Atlantic Information Services, Inc., vol. 2, no. 6.

Aetna Forms New ACOs: Unveils Outcomes on Medicare Models. *ACO Business News*, Atlantic Information Services, Inc., vol. 2, no. 1, January 2012.

Aetna Rolls Out Individual ACO-Based Plans in Roanoke. *ACO Business News*, Atlantic Information Services, Inc., vol. 2, no. 6.

Aetna's Unusual Medicare Plan Uses ACO-Style Approach: The Outcomes Have Been Promising for Some 20,000 Elderly People and the Insurer Wants to Replicate the Effort in Other Lines of Business. Frank Diamond, MediMedia USA, January 2011. http://www.managedcaremag.com/archives/1101/1101.planwatch.html (accessed 11/15/11).

After the Crisis: How Revenue Agencies Are Achieving High Performance. Accenture. Online at: http://www.accenture.com/SiteCollectionDocuments/PDF/Accenture_Institute_Health_Public_Service_Value_Revenue_After_the_Crisis_High_Performance.pdf (accessed 3/2/2012).

AJR: How to Stop Worrying and Love the ACO Model. Evan Godt, October 12, 2011. Online at: http://www.healthimaging.com/index.php?option=com_articles&view=article&id=29909:ajr-how-to-stop-worrying-and-love-the-aco-mode (accessed 10/12/2012).

Aligning the Accountable Care Community. Reggie Townsend, IL: Knowledge-Advantage, Inc., Gaithersburg, MD, September 16, 2011.

Alternative Approaches to Measuring Physician Resource Use: Medicare/Medicaid Research and Demonstration. David Knutson, Bryan Dowd, and Robert Kane, Craig Caplan Centers for Medicare & Medicaid Services (CMS), March 2010.

Analysis of Capital Spending and Capital Financing among Large U.S. Non-Profit Health Systems. Lewis J. Stewart, *Journal of Healthcare Finance*, vol. 38, no. 3.

Analytics for ACOs: Measuring the Depth before Diving in. Singletrack Analytics LLC, Marlton, NJ, 2011.

Analyzing Shifts in Economic Risks to Providers in Proposed Payment and Delivery System Reforms. Jeff Goldsmith, Project Hope, vol. 29, no. 7, July 2010. Online at: http://content.healthaffairs.org/cgi/content/full/29/7/1299 (accessed 11/16/2010).

Anthem Launches Two ACO Pilots, May Create Up to 12 in California. *ACO Business News*, Atlantic Information Services, Inc., vol. 2, no. 5, May 2011.

Antitrust Considerations in Implementing a Clinical Integration Program. Christi J. Braun, Bureau of National Affairs, Inc. (BNA), April 21, 2011 Online at: http://healthlawrc.bna.com/hlrc/4209/split_display.adp?fedfid=20130321&vname=hlreref2 &fcn=1&wsn=1&fn=20130321&split=0.

Applying for the Medicare Shared Savings Program: An Integrated Delivery System's Perspective. Jackie Gisch, *Accountable Care News*, vol. 2, no. 6, Health Policy Publishing LLC. June 2012.

Applying Lean Production in Healthcare Facilities. Jon M. Buggy and Jennifer Nelson, vol. 6, no. 5.

Are ACOs Unaffordable? Jeff Elliott, HealthLeaders Media, March 28, 2011. Online at: http://www.healthleadersmedia.com/print/FIN-264180/Are-ACOs-Unaffordable (accessed 3/28/2011).

Are You Ready for an ACO? Margaret D. Tocknell, HealthLeaders Media, June 5, 2012.

Are You Ready for Value-Driven Health Care? Online at: http://www.google.com/url?sa=t&rct=j&q=are%20you%20ready%20for%20value-driven%20health%20care%3F%20hfma&source=web&cd=1&ved=0CCQQFjAA&url=http%3A%2F%2Fwww.hfma.org%2FWorkArea%2Flinkit.aspx%3FLinkIdentifier%3Did%26ItemID%3D3198&ei=RnJiT8qYEpT_sQLVsKikDA&usg=AFQjCNHcxa4y83e3Mq2kpXTlEBHh5Lvl0Q&cad=rja (accessed 3/15/2012).

ASCs for ACOs: Is There an Advantage? Shay Pratt, The Advisory Board Company. Online at: http://www.advisory.com/Research/Marketing-and-Planning-LeadershipCouncil/Service-Line-Transformation/2012/08/ASCs-for-ACOs-Is-there-an-advantage (accessed 11/12/2012).

Assembling a Pioneer ACO from an IPA Chassis. Nancy Boerner, *CAPG Health*, vol. 6, no. 4.

Assessing ACO Interest. Margaret D. Tocknell, HealthLeaders, April 2012.

Assessing the Impact of the Medicare Shared Savings Program Proposed Rule on Accountable Care Organization Development: Further Observations at the Nexus of Policy, Business, and Law. Douglas Hastings, Bureau of National Affairs, Inc. (BNA), April 15, 2011. Online at: http://healthlawrc.bna.com/hlrc/display/story_list.adp?mode=ins&frag_id=20543003&prod=hlin (accessed 4/21/2011).

Assessment of Cost Trends and Price Differences for U.S. Hospitals. Margaret E. Guerin-Calvert and Guillermo Israilevich, Compass Lexecon, Chicago, March 2011.

Auction Rate Securities. Douglas Skarr, Sacramento, CA, August 2004.

Avoiding the Plunge: Looming Fiscal Deadlines Pose Challenges for Healthcare, Nation. David May, *Modern Healthcare*.

Baylor's Frederick Savelsbergh on Capital Financing Strategy. Frederick Savelsbergh. Online at: http://www.hfma.org/Templates/Print.aspx?id=22973 (accessed 04/27/11).

Behavioral Health Observers Urge ACO Developers to Target Holistic Health Care. *ACO Business News*, Atlantic Information Services, Inc., vol. 2, no. 3, March 2011.

Benchmarking in Health Care. 2nd ed., Joint Commission Resources, Oakbrook Terrace, IL, 2012.

Bending the Health Care Cost Curve: More Than Meets the Eye? Kenneth Kaufman, *Health Affairs* blog, April 13, 2012.

Best Health Care Results for Populations (A Three-Part Aim): Achieving the Optimal Balance of Good Health, Positive Patient Experience of Care, and Low Per Capita Cost for a Population.

Billings Clinic Enhances Quality of Care under Federal Demonstration Project. Billings Clinic, July 11, 2007. Online at: http://www.billingsclinic.com/body.cfm?id=568 (accessed 3/28/2012).

Blazing a Trail: Pioneer ACOs Test Strategies with Five Pay Options. Melanie Evans, *Modern Healthcare*, April 9, 2012.

Blue Shield, Blue Cross Reach Accord on Merger: 2 Medical Plans Agree on Merger. Max H. Seigel, March 12, 1974 (accessed 11/21/11).

Blue Cross Blue Shield of Massachusetts' Alternative Quality Contract System. Pershing Yoakley & Associates, Knoxville, TN.

Breaking Down Barriers to Creating Safety Net Accountable Care Organizations. Stephen M. Shortell, Ann M. Marciarille, Matt Chayt, and Sarah Weinberger, University of California, Berkeley Law, August 2011.

Bridge to Accountable Care Organizations, The: Analysis from HealthLeaders Media. Jim Molpus, HealthLeaders Media, January 2011. Online at: http://www.healthleadersmedia.com/breakthroughs/get-PDF.cfm?PDF=261719.pdf (accessed 1/2011).

Bridging Business & Healthcare: Healthcare Management Consultants for Dispute Resolution, Valuation & Clinical Compliance. Mark Browne, Pershing Yoakley & Associates, February 16, 2011. Online at: http://healthcareblog.pyapc.com/articles/accountablecare-organizations/ (accessed 4/17/2011).

Brief History of Managed Care, A. Online at: http://www.thci.org/downloads/briefhist.pdf (accessed 12/28/2011).

Broker Develops Liability Insurance: How ACO Operates Will Drive Need. Frank Castro, Hedberg Belfort. *ACO Business News*, Atlantic Information Services, Inc., vol. 2, no. 5, Atlantic Information Service, Inc., May 2012.

BSC Sets Precedent for Other ACO Models, Health Observers Say. *ACO Business News*, Atlantic Information Services, Inc., vol. 2, no. 4, April 2011.

Building a Culture of Collaboration from the Ground Up. June 27, 2011.

Building a Medical Home, Piece by Piece. Candace Stuart, 2011. Online at: http://www.cardiovascularbusiness.com/index.php?option=com_articles&view=article&id=29645:building-a-medical-home-piece-by-piece (accessed 10/13/11).

Building a Network Theory of Social Capital. Nan Lin, Social Capital, New York, 2001.

Building ACO Foundations: Lessons from Kaiser Permanente's Integrated Delivery Model. Jim Molpus, Health Leaders Media Rounds, May 30, 2012.

Building ACOs and Outcome Based Contracting in the Commercial Market: Provider and Payor Perspectives. THINC, Fishkill, NY, October 2011.

Building Blocks of ACOs, The: What Does the Future Hold? Jennifer Dennard, December 7, 2010. Online at: http://porterresearch.com/Resource_Center/Blog_News/Industry_News/2010/December/The_Building_Blocks_of_ACOs.html (accessed 12/22/2010).

Building Regulatory and Operational Flexibility into Accountable Care Organizations. Steven Leiberman and John Bertko, *Health Affairs*, vol. 30, no. 1, January 19, 2011.

Building the Path to Accountable Care. Elliott S. Fisher, Mark B. McClellan, and Dana G. Safran, *The New England Journal of Medicine*, vol. 365, no. 26, December 29, 2011.

Bundled Payments Show Long-Term Promise: Observer Says. *ACO Business News*, Atlantic Information Services, Inc., vol. 2, no. 1, January 2012.

Burned Out or Fired Up? Hospital Executives Face Unprecedented Pressures. Some Are Opting to End Their Careers, But Many Others Are Pumped Up and Eager to Lead Their Organizations into a New Era. Haydn Bush, *Hospitals and Health Networks Magazine*, April 2012.

BURTON: Accountability Care Organizations Need Good Data. Michelle Burton. Online at: http://www.ibj.com/article/print?articleld=33219 (accessed 3/20/2012).

California Blue Shield's "Three-Way" Risk Model Plans No Premium Hikes, More Expansions. *ACO Business News*, Atlantic Information Services, Inc., vol. 2, no. 4, April 2011.

Capital BC Says ACO Savings Stemmed from Waste Reduction. *ACO Business News*, Atlantic Information Services, Inc., vol. 2, no. 6.

Capital Budgeting in Hospital Management Using the Analytic Hierarchy Process. M. M. Tarimcilar and Shahriar Z. Zhaksari, *Socio-Economic Planning Services*, vol. 25, no. 1, Pergamon Press, 1991.

Capital Finance and Ownership Conversions in Health Care. James C. Robinson, *Health Affairs*, vol. 19, no. 1, 2000.

Capital Planning for Clinical Integration. Daniel Grauman, *Healthcare Financial Management*, vol. 65, no. 4, April 2011.

Capital Structure Strategy in Health Care Systems. John R. Wheeler, Dean G. Smith, Howard L. Rivenson, and Kristin L. Reiter, vol. 26, no. 4, Aspen Publishers, Inc., 2000.

Carving Out the Pharmacist's Role in the ACO. Joanne Kaldy, March 16, 2012. Online at: http://www.antibody-antibodies.com/pubmed.php?pmid=22421516 (accessed 4/04/2012).

Case Study Demonstrates Benefits of a Primary Care-Based Accountable Care Organization. Robert Graham Center, Washington, D.C., January 6, 2011.

Cash Management in Health Care Systems. Howard L. Rivenson, John R. Wheeler, Dean G. Smith, and Kristin L. Reiter, *Journal of Health Care Finance*, vol. 26, no. 4, Summer 2000.

Catching Up with…: Paul H. Keckley. *Accountable Care News,* vol. 2, no. 3, Health Policy Publishing LLC, March 2011.

Catching Up with…: Gail Wilensky. *Accountable Care News,* vol. 2, no. 11, Health Policy Publishing LLC, October 2011.

Catching Up with...: Jay Want, MD. *Accountable Care News,* vol. 3, no. 3, March, 2012.

Catching Up with...: Donald W. Fisher. *Accountable Care News*, Health Policy Publishing, LLC, April 2012.

Catholic Medical Partners. Catholic Medical Partners Independent Practice Association. Online at: http://www.chsbuffalo.org/ForPhysicians/CIPA.

Chairman Cox Announces End of Consolidation Supervised Entities Program. U.S. Securities and Exchange Commission, Washington, D.C., September 26, 2008.

Chasing Unicorns: The Future of ACOs. Ian Morrison, January 3, 2011. Online at: http://hhnmag.com/hhnmag_app/jsp/articledisplay/jsp?dcrpath=HHNMAG/Article/data/01JAN2011/010411HHN_Weekly_Morrison&domain=HHNMAG (accessed 3/29/2012).

CIGNA and Dartmouth-Hitchcock Launch "Patient-Centered Medical Home" Program to Provide Better Care Coordination. CIGNA, June 10, 2008. Online at: http://newsroom.CIGNA.com/KnowledgeCenter/ACO (accessed 11/16/2011).

CIGNA and Health Choice Launch Collaborative Accountable Care Program to Improve Health, Lower Costs. CIGNA, September 8, 2011. Online at: http://newsroom.CIGNA.com/KnowledgeCenter/ACO (accessed 11/16/2011).

CIGNA and Holston Medical Group (HMG) Launch Patient-Centered Medical Home Pilot Program for the Tri-Cities and Southwest Virginia Region. CIGNA. Online at: http://newsroom.CIGNA.com/KnowledgeCenter/ACO (accessed 11/16/2011).

CIGNA and ProHealth Physicians Create Enhanced Care Coordination Program. CIGNA, October 8, 2009. Online at: http://newsroom.CIGNA.com/KnowledgeCenter/ACO (accessed 11/16/2011).

CIGNA and St. John's Mercy Medical Group Launch Collaborative Accountable Care Pilot Program in St. Louis for Better Care Coordination. CIGNA. Online at: http://newsroom.CIGNA.com/KnowledgeCenter/ACO (accessed 11/16/2011).

CIGNA Completes Acquisition of HealthSpring: Cigna Expands Global Portfolio into Seniors and Medicare Segments. Online at: http://phx.corporate-ir.net/phoenix.zhtml?c=226354&p=irolnewsArticle_print&ID=1654641&highlight= (accessed 11/7/12).

CIGNA Medical Group Receives Highest Level of Recognition for Physician Group Medical Homes from National Committee for Quality Assurance. CIGNA, March 8, 2011. Online at: http://newsroom.CIGNA.com/KnowledgeCenter/ACO (accessed 11/16/0011).

Cigna: "Path Is Unchanged" Regardless of Supreme Court Ruling. Mark Slitt, *ACO Business News*, Atlantic Information Services, Inc., vol. 2, no. 5, Atlantic Information Service, Inc., May 2012.

CIGNA, Piedmont Physicians Launch ACO Pilot Program. Chris Anderson, MedTech Publishing Company LLC, September 9, 2010. Online at: http://www.healthcarefinancenews.com/print/19296 (accessed February 25, 2011).

CIGNA Will Expand to 30 ACOs by End of 2011, Begin Downside. *ACO Business News*, Atlantic Information Services, Inc., vol. 2, no. 5, May 1, 2011.

Clinical Integration: A Roadmap to Accountable Care, 2nd ed. Bruce Flareau, Virginia Beach, VA: Convurgent Publishing, LLC, 2011.

Clinical Transformation: Dramatic Changes as Physician Employment Grows. Accenture. Online at: http://www.accenture.com/SiteCollectionDocuments/PDF/Accenture_Clinical_Transforma tion.pdf (accessed 3/2/2012).

CMS Announces First-Round MSSP ACO Picks. Lauren Gaffney and Daniel Kuninsky, American Health Lawyers Association, April 11, 2012.

CMS Announces Three ACO Initiatives. Jessica Zigmond and Melanie Evans, *Modern Healthcare*, May 17, 2011. Online at: http://www.modernhealthcare.com/article/20110517/NEWS/305179972 (accessed 5/18/2011).

CMS Grants Providers $122M to Improve Care, Cut Costs. Cheryl Clark, Health Leaders Media. Online at: http://healthleadersmedia.com/print/FIN-279921/ (accessed 5/10/2012).

CMS Medicaid Shared Savings Programs—Accountable Care Organizations: Summary of Comments Submitted to the Centers for Medicare & Medicaid Services. Premier, Inc., Charlotte, NC, October 19, 2010.

CMS Selects 27 ACOs as First Participants in Medicare Shared Savings Program. American Health Lawyers Association (AHLA), April 13, 2012 (accessed 4/23/2012).

Co-Sponsored PPO-Based Plans Are Next for Aetna-Carilion ACO. *ACO Business News*, Atlantic Information Services, Inc., vol. 2, no. 10, October 2011.

Collaborating to Improve Care and Cut Costs. Joe Cantlupe, Intelligence HealthLeaders Media, June 2012. Online at: http://content.hcpro.com/pdf/content/280838.pdf.

Collaborative Accountable Care: CIGNA's Approach to Accountable Care Organizations: A White Paper. CIGNA, April 1, 2011. Online at: http://www.kaiserhealthnews.org/Stories/2011/July/25/halvorson-Q-and-A-kaiserpermanente-accountable-care-organizations.aspx (accessed 11/15/2011).

Commercial ACO Market Research Findings. MedeAnalytics, Emeryville, CA, February 21, 2011.

Commercial ACOs: A Recurring Theme with New Opportunities. June 15, 2011.

Commercial ACOs May Find Footing Where CMS Slips. Margaret D. Tocknell, HealthLeaders Media, August 31, 2011. Online at: http://www.healthleadersmedia.com/page-2/HEP270395/Commercial-ACOs-May-Find-Footing-Where-CMS-Slips## (accessed 10/13/2011).

Communication Failures: An Insidious Contributor to Medical Mishaps. Kathleen M. Sutcliffe, Elizabeth Lewton, and Marilynn M. Rosenthal, vol. 79, no. 2, February 2004.

Community Leader's Guide to Hospital Finance, A: Evaluating How a Hospital Gets and Spends Its Money. Sarah G. Lane, Elizabeth Longstreth, and Victoria Nixon, The Access Project, Washington, D.C., 2001.

Competing for the Future. Gary Hamel and C. K. Prahalad, Cambridge, MA: Harvard Business School Press.

Competitive Strategy: Techniques for Analyzing Industries and Competitors. Michael E. Porter, New York: The Free Press, 19.

Complex Health-Care Law Turns into Payday for Consultants. Bara Vaida, April 2, 2011. Online at: http://www.washingtonpost.com/national/complex-health-care-law-turns-into-payday-for-consultants/2011/04/01/AFPkQXQC_story.html (accessed 10/10/2011).

Comprehensive Primary Care Initiative, The. September 28, 2011. Online at: http://www.healthcare.gov/news/factsheets/2011/09/primary-care09282011a.html (accessed 10/17/11).

Constructing Accountable Care Organizations: Some Practical Observations at the Nexus of Policy, Business, and Law. Douglas A. Hastings, Bureau of National Affairs, Inc., vol. 19, no. 25, June 24, 2010.

Consumer-Driven Plans: Serious Impact on Practice Finances. Greenbranch Publishing Inc., Phoenix, MD, 2011.

Consumer Operated and Oriented Plans (CO-OPs): An Interim Assessment of Their Prospects: Timely Analysis of Immediate Health Policy Issues. Bradford H. Gray, August 2011.

Contracts Should Spell Out Everyone's Role in an ACO. Steven M. Harris, American Medical Association (AMA), May 9, 2011. Online at: http://www.ama-assn.org/amednews/2011/05/09/bicb0509.htm (accessed 11/18/2011).

Conversion of HMOs and Hospitals: What's at Stake. Bradford H. Gray, vol. 16, no. 2, 1997.

Coordinated ED, The. HealthLeaders Media, April 2011.

Coordinating Care in the Medical Neighborhood: Critical Components and Available Mechanisms. Erin F. Taylor, Timothy Lake, Jessica Nysenbaum, Greg Peterson, and David Meyers, AHRQ Publication, June 2011.

Corporate Finance, 4th ed. Stephen A. Ross, Randolph W. Westerfield, Jeffrey F. Jaffe, and Gordon S. Roberts, Toronto, Canada: McGraw-Hill Ryerson.

Corporate Social Responsibility (CSR) Trend, The. Barbara Louge and James Wallace, vol. 20, no. 1, Morgan Stanley, December 2008.

Cost of Capital 2001 Yearbook, Data through December 2001-2011: Statistics for Sic Code 806. Ibbotson Associates, Chicago, 20022012.

"Cost of Capital" and Total "Cost to Own," The. Shawn McBride, July 7, 2011. Online at: http://blogs.ajc.com/health-flock/2011/07/07/the-%E2%80%9Ccost-ofcapital%E2%80%9D-and-total-%E2%80%9Ccost-to-own%E2%80%9D/ (accessed 3/13/2012).

Cost of Caring, The: Drivers of Spending on Hospital Care. American Hospital Association (AHA), March 2011. Online at: http://www.aha.org/aha/trendwatch/2011/11mar-twcostofcaring.pdf (accessed 4/2011).

Cost of Confusion, The: Healthcare Reform and Value-Based Purchasing. Trent Haywood, *Healthcare Financial Management*, vol. 64, no. 10, October 2010.

Costs of Medical Care, The: A Summary of Investigations on the Economic Aspects of the Prevention and Care of Illness. I. S. Falk, C. Rufus Rorem, and Martha D. Ring, No. 27, The University of Chicago, 1927.

Could ACOs Appear on the Medicare Payment Horizon. Janice Simmons, April 13, 2009. Online at: http://www.healthleadersmedia.com/content/HEP-231332/Could-ACOs-Appear-on-the-Medicare-Payment-Horizon.html (accessed 04/14/09).

Could ACOs Reinforce Disparities among Patient Populations? Cheryl Clark, HealthLeaders Media, April 29, 2011. Online at: http://www.healthleadersmedia.com/content/LED265516/Could-ACOs-Reinforce-Disparities-Among-Patient-Populations.html (accessed 5/3/2011).

Creating an ACO Marketing Language. Tadd Pullin and Michael Barber, HealthLeaders Media, July 27, 2011.

Creating Shareholder Value: A Guide for Managers and Investors. Alfred Rappaport, (rev. ed.), New York: The Free Press, 1997.

Creating Shareholder Value: The New Standard for Business Performance. Alfred Rappaport, New York: MacMillan Publishing Company, 1986.

Crystal Run's ACO Puts Physicians in Driver's Seat. Margaret D. Tocknell, HealthLeaders Media, April 18, 2012.

Cultivating Physician-Hospital Alignment in the ACO Era. Max Reiboldt and James Canedy, HCPro, Danvers, MA, July 20, 2011.

Defining and Delivering Value. Healthcare Financial Management Association, June 2012.

Defining Healthcare Value. January 14, 2010. Online at: http://healthcare-economist.com/2010/01/14/defining-healthcare-value/ (accessed 11/15/2011).

Derivative Financial Instruments and Nonprofit Health Care Providers. Louis J. Stewart and Vincent Owhoso, Winter 2004.

Designing a Patient-Centered ACO. Michealle Gady. *Accountable Care News*, vol. 2, no. 4, Health Policy Publishing, LLC, April 2012.

Developing Healthcare Facilities for a Changing Environment: Healthcare Organizations Should Consider Financial Goals before Deciding on Real Estate Strategies. Fred Campobasso and Joe Kucharz.

Dictionary of Health Economics, 2nd ed. Anthony Culyer, Northhampton, MA: Edward Elgar Publishing Inc., 2005.

Dictionary of Health Economics and Finance. David E. Marchinko and Hope R. Hetico, New York: Springer Publishing Company, Inc., 2006.

Dictionary of Health Insurance and Managed Care. David E. Marchinko, New York: Springer Publishing Company, Inc., 2006.

Dividends and Dividend Policy. H. K. Baker, Hoboken, NJ: John Wiley & Sons, 2009.

Doctor-Owned Centers Spark Criticism, Scrutiny. Rob Stein, February 28, 2011. Online at: http://www.washingtonpost.com/wpdyn/content/article/2011/02/28/AR2011022805378_pf.html (accessed 2/18/2011).

Doctors on Deck: ACOs Led by Doctors Seek to Manage Costs, Quality and Hospital Relationships. Melanie Evans, *Modern Healthcare*, April 16, 2012.

Doing More with Less: Making the Most of Resources in a Lean World. Susan Birk, *Healthcare Executive*, May/June 2012.

Doing More with Less: Credit Implications of Hospital Transition Strategies in Era of Reform. Moody's Investors Service.

Doing Together What None of Us Can Do Alone. Minnesota Health Action Group. Online at: http://mnhealthactiongroup.org.

Driving Population Health through Accountable Care Organizations. Susan DeVore and R. W. Champion, Project Hope, vol. 30, no. 1, January 2011 (accessed 1/10/2011).

Drug, Device Makers Face Gains along with Risks in ACO Ventures. *ACO Business News*, Atlantic Information Services, Inc., vol. 2, no. 9, September 2011.

Early Lessons from a Shared Risk, Integrated Care Organization Serving a Commercial Population. Glenn Melnick and Lois Green. Online at: http://healthaffairs.org/blog/201/05/15/ (accessed 5/24/2012).

Early Lessons from Accountable Care Models in the Private Sector: Partnerships between Health Plans and Providers. Aparna Higgins, Kristin Stewart, Kristin Dawson, and Carmella Bocchino, *Health Affairs*, vol. 30, no. 9, September 2011.

Economic and Demographic Trends Signal an Impending Physician Shortage: A New Model of Workforce Projections, Based on Physician Supply and Utilization, Predicts an Impending Physician Shortage, Which the Nation Cannot Afford to Ignore. Richard A. Cooper, Thomas E. Getzen, Heather J. McKee, and Prakash Laud, Project Hope, January 1, 2002.

Economics of for-Profit and Not-for-Profit Hospitals, The. Uwe E. Reinhardt, *Health Affairs*, vol. 19, no. 6, 2000.

Effective Policy Governance, Oversight, and Management. Michael Rasmussen, Corporate Integrity LLC, Alexandria, VA, March 2012.

Empirical Evidence for Decreasing Returns to Scale in a Health Capital Model. Titus Galama, Patrick Hullegi, Erik Meijer, and Sarah M. Outcault, RAND Labor and Population.

Employers Say Calif. Managed Care Experience Drives ACO Activity. *ACO Business News*, Atlantic Information Services, Inc., vol. 2, no. 9, September 2011.

End of Us vs. Them, The. Philip Betbeze, *HealthLeaders*, April 2012.

Engaging Staff with Team-Based Performance Sharing. Healthcare Financial Management, May 2012.

Essential Guide to Accountable Care Organizations: Challenges, Risks and Opportunities of the ACO Model. Healthcare Intelligence Network (HIN), 2010.

Essential Meditative Skills Post Healthcare Reform: A Modified Mediation Model. June 29, 2011.

Essentials of Health Care Finance, 4th ed. William O. Cleverley, Paula H. Song, and James Cleverley, New York: Aspen Publishers.

Estimating Physicians' Work for a Resource-Based Relative-Value Scale. William C. Hsiao, Peter Braun, Douwe Ynterna, and Edmund Becker, *New England Journal of Medicine* (NEJM), September 29, 1988. Online at: http://www.nejm.org/doi/full/10.1056/NEJM198809293191305 (accessed 3/1/2011).

Ever-Changing Healthcare Landscape, The. *CAPG Health*, vol. 6, no. 4.

Examination of Contemporary Financing Practices and the Global Financial Crisis on Nonprofit Multi-Hospital Health Systems, An. Louis Stewart, *Journal of Health Care Finance*, vol. 37, no. 3, 2011.

Exempt Organizations: Tax-Exempt Hospitals Should Not Be Viewed as ACO Funding Source, Practitioner Warns. Diane Freda, Bureau of National Affairs, Inc. (BNA), April 28, 2011 (accessed 4/28/2011).

Exeter Health Resources Takes Leadership Role by Participating in New Hampshire's First Statewide Accountable Care Organization Pilot Program. Exeter Health Resources. Online at: http://www.corephysicians.org/news-and-health-library/core-news/accountable-care-organization/ (accessed 02/28/2011).

Expanding the ACO Concept to Encourage Innovation, Accountability and High Performance and the Value Health Plans Bring to Delivery System Transformation. America's Health Insurance Plans (AHIP), August 2010. Online at: http://www.ftc.gov/os/comments/aco/100927ahip-paper.pdf (accessed 11/2011).

Fear of ACO Commitment, The: It's All in the Details. Haydn Bush, July 27, 2011.

Federal Health Care Reform 2009: Start-Up Capital Costs for Health Care Co-ops and A Public Plan. October 30, 2009.

Federal Pediatric Demo Is Still in Flux: Ohio Shows Interest in ACO Model. *ACO Business News*, Atlantic Information Services, Inc., vol. 2, no. 2, February 2012.

Federal Reserve System Purposes & Functions, The, 9th ed. U.S. Federal Reserve System.

Federal Trade Commission: Promotion of Export Trade and Prevention of Unfair Methods of Competition. 15 U.S.C. 41-58.

Financial Incentives for Healthcare Professionals May Be Ineffective. Emily Mullin, Dorland Health. Online at: http://www.dorlandhealth.com/clinical_care/trends/2250.html (accessed 05/22/12).

Financial Institutions Management: A Risk Management Approach, 5th ed., New York: McGraw-Hill Irwin, 2011.

Financial Planning Model for Estimating Hospital Debt Capacity, A. David S. Hopkins, Dan Heath, and Peter Levin, *Public Health Reports*, vol. 97, no. 4, July–August 1982.

Florida Blue Launches Oncology ACO. Margaret D. Tocknell, HealthLeaders Media. Online at: http://www.healthleadersmedia.com/content/LED-280059/Florida-Blue-Launches-Oncology-ACO (accessed 5/14/2012).

Flurry of ACO Activity Spurs Growth of Consultants, Venders. *ACO Business News*, Atlantic Information Services, Inc., vol. 2, no. 10, October 2011.

Forgotten Players in ACO Development: Nursing Homes, The. Neville M. Bilimoria, Medical Practice Management, Greenbranch Publishing, Phoenix, MD, March/April 2012.

Form Follows Function: How to Build a Strong ACO. Thomas M. Priselac, Hospitals & Health Networks (H&HN), May 16, 2011. Online at: http://www.hhnmag.com/hhnmag/HHNDaily/HHNDailyDisplay.dhtml?id=8410007224 (accessed 5/18/11).

Forms of Value and Valuation: Theory and Applications. John W. Davis and Rem B. Edwards, New York: University Press of America, 1991.

Foundations of Social Theory. James S. Coleman, Cambridge, MA: The Belknap Press of Harvard University Press, 1990.

Four of Five Metropolitan Markets Lack Competition in Health Insurance, AMA Says. Sara Hansard, October 26, 2011. Online at: http://www.bna.com/four-five-metropolitan-n12884904016/ (accessed 1/17/12).

Four Pillars of Successful ACO Clinical Integration. Martin Graf and Milton J. Schachter, *Hospitals & Health Networks Daily*. Online at: http://www.hhnmag.com/hhnmag/HHNDaily/HHNDailyDisplay.dhtml?id=9880008411, April 19, 2012.

From Acquisition to Integration: Transforming a Hospital into an ACO. John N. Fink and Sean T. Hartzell, November 2010.

From Courtship to Marriage: Part I: Why Health Reform Is Driving Physicians and Hospitals Closer Together. PriceWaterhouseCoopers (PwC), 2010.

From Courtship to Marriage: Part II: How Physicians and Hospitals Are Creating Sustainable Relationships. PriceWaterhouseCoopers (PwC), April 2011.

From Volume to Value: The Transition to Accountable Care Organizations. Keith D. Moore and Dean C. Coddington, American Hospital Association (AHA), April 2011. Online at: http://www.aha.org/aha/content/2011/pdf/aco-white-paper-transition-to-aco.pdf (accessed May 13, 2011).

Future Shock: Are You Ready for New Payment Methods. David N. Gans, *MGMA Connexion*, May/June 2012.

Geisinger Chief Glenn Steele: Seizing Health Reform's Potential to Build a Superior System. Susan Dentzer, Project Hope, vol. 29, no. 6, June 1, 2010. Online at: http://content.healthaffairs.org/content/29/6/1200.full.html (accessed June 16, 2011).

Geisinger Health System: Successful Case Studies in Accountable Care. Kevin F. Brennan. Geisinger Health System, Danville, PA, October 1, 2010. http://www.ehcca.com/presentations/acocongress1/brennan_2.pdf (Accessed 11/17/11).

Geisinger Quality Measures. Geisinger Health System, Danville, PA. Online at: http://www.geisinger.org/quality/chooseHospital.html (accessed 1/19/12).

Get Ready for Healthcare Conglomerates. Philip Betbeze, HealthLeaders Media, April 14, 2011. Online at: http://www.healthleadersmedia.com/page-2/MAG-264923/Get-Ready-forHealthcare-Conglomerates (accessed 4/28/2011).

Getting from Volume to Value in Healthcare: Balancing Challenges & Opportunities. *Forbes Insights*, All scripts.

Getting to There from Here: Evolving to ACOs through Clinical Integration Programs. James J. Pizzo and Mark E. Grube, 2011.

Getting Up to Speed on the Financial Crisis: A One-Weekend-Reader's Guide. Gary Gorton and Andrew Metrick, *Journal of Economic Literature*, March 2012.

Golden Payoff for Effective Care Management, The. John Schmitt and Semite Mishra, *Navigant Pulse*, July 22, 2011.

Great Recession and Government Failure, The. Gary S. Becker, *Wall Street Journal*, September 2, 2011. Online at: http://online.wsj.com/article/SB10001424053111904199404576536930606933332.html (accessed 7/13/2012).

Group Practice Journal, vol. 60, no. 3, Alexandria, VA: American Medical Group Association (AMGA), March 2011.

Group Practices: Consider This about ACOs. Warren Skeat and Kenneth Larson, November 2011. Online at: http://www.pwc.com/us/en/health-industries/assets/pdf/medicalpractice-digest-november-2011.pdf.

Growth and Dispersion of Accountable Care Organizations. David Milstein, Andrew Crashaw, Tom Merrill, and Christian Pena, November 2011. Online at: http://leavittpartnersblog.com/2011/11/growth-and-dispersion-of-accountable-care-organizations/ (accessed 1/27/2012).

Guest Commentary: The Conundrum of Capitalizing ACOs. Ron Shinman, Fierce Health Finance, March 8 2011. Online at: http://www.fiercehealthfinance.com/story/guestcommentary-conundrum-capitalizing-acos/2011-03-08 (accessed 04/12/11).

Guide to Consulting Services for Emerging Healthcare Organizations, A. Robert J. Cimasi, Hoboken, NJ: John Wiley & Sons, 1999.

Guide to Financing Strategies for Hospitals, A: With Special Consideration for Smaller Hospitals. American Hospital Association (AHA), Washington, D.C., December 2010.

Head of Major HMO Sees Openings for Accountable Care Organization: The KHN Interview. Joanne Silberner, July 25 2011. Online at: http://www.kaiserhealthnews.org/Stories/2011/July/25/halvorson-Q-and-A-kaiserpermanente-accountable-care-organizations.aspx (accessed 11/21/11).

Health Care Economics, 5th & 6th eds. Paul J. Feldstein, New York: Delmar Publishers Inc., 2005.

Health Care Economics 101 and the Supreme Court. Jill Hurwitz, *Health Affairs* blog. Online at: http://healthaffairs.org/blog/2012/05/23/health-care-economics-101-and-the-supremecourt/print (accessed 05/27/2012).

Health Care Industry Urged to Move on Accountable Care Organizations Now. Sara Hansard, *BNA Health Care Daily*, 19 HLR 933.

Health Care Interests Push to Make ACOs Pay Off for Them. Phil Galewitz and Jenny Gold, Henry J. Kaiser Family Foundation, October 10, 2010. Online at: http://www.kaiserhealthnews.org/Stories/2010/October/11/health-care-interests-ACOs (accessed 10/18/2010).

Health Care Opinion Leaders' Views on Transparency and Pricing. Krista Tselikas, Karen Davis, and Stuart Guterman, The Commonwealth Fund, vol. 102.

Health Care Reforms of the 1990s, The: Failure or Ultimate Triumph. Robert F. Rich and Kelly M. Merrick, May 2009. Online at: http://works.bepress.com/cgi/viewcontent.cgi?article=1000&context=robert_rich (accessed 1/5/2012).

Health Care's New Rorschach Test: When You Look at ACOs, What Do You See? William Prentice, June 2011.

Health Care Spending in the United States and Selected OECD Countries. Henry J. Kaiser Family Foundation, April 28, 2011. Online at: http://www.kff.org/insurance/snapshot/OECD042111.cfm (accessed 5/1/2011).

Health Insurers Opening Their Own Clinics to Trim Costs. Christopher Weaver, *Kaiser Health News*, Kaiser Family Foundation.

Health Partners. Online at: http://www.healthpartners.com/public/about/ (accessed 11/17/11).

Health Plan Quality Improvement Strategy Reporting under the Affordable Care Act: Implementation Considerations. Emma Hood, David Lansky, Joachim Roski, and Lisa Simpson, The Commonwealth Fund, April 2012. Online at: http://www.commonwealthfund.org/~/media/Files/Publications/Fund%20 Report/2012/Apr/1592_Hoo_hlt_plan_qual_improve_strategy_report_v2.pdf (accessed 4/25/2012).

Health Plans Don't Always Play Hardball with Providers. Margaret D. Tocknell, HealthLeaders Media. Online at: http://healthleadersmedia.com/print/HEP-279928 (accessed 5/10/2012).

Healthcare Capital Projects: How to Avoid Common Problems. Darren Venues, Healthcare Financial Management Association (HFMA), April 1, 2011. Online at: http://www.hfma.org/Templates/InteriorMaster.aspx?id=25891 (accessed 4/27/11).

Healthcare Costs, Accountable Care Organizations, and Kaiser Permanente. March 28, 2011. Online at: http://letstalkbooksandpolitics.blogspot.com/2011/03/healthcare-costs-accountablecare.html (accessed 11/17/11).

Healthcare Performance Alliance, The. 2011. Online at: www.healthcareperformancealliance.com (accessed 9/21/2011).

Healthcare Reform Pits Physicians against Hospitals. Margaret D. Tocknell, April 21, 2011. Online at: http://www.healthleadersmedia.com/print/PHY-265202/Healthcare-Reform-PitsPhysicians-Against-Hospitals (accessed 4/21/2011).

Healthcare Solutions Lie in Patient Care. Ernie Vesta, vol. 2, no. 11, Health Policy Publishing, October 2011.

HealthPartners' Triple Aim Approach to Aligning Hospital, Payers, and Physicians. Healthcare Financial Management Association (HFMA), August 29, 2011. Online at: http://www.hfma.org/Templates/InteriorMaster.aspx?id=28534 (accessed 11/17/11).

HealthSpring Deal Shows Commercial Appeal of ACOs. Bill McConnell, The Deal Magazine. Online at: http://decisionresourcesgroup.com/News-and-Events/In-The-News/HLIPaula-Wade-TheDeal-com-110411 (accessed 11/7/12).

Henry Ford System Drives Ahead toward Development of an ACO. *ACO Business News*, Atlantic Information Services, Inc., vol. 2, no. 3, March 1, 2011.

HHS Announces 89 New Accountable Care Organizations. U.S. Department of Health & Human Services. Online at: http://www.hhs.gov/news/press/2012pres/07/20120709a.html (accessed 10/23/2012).

High Performing Healthcare Systems: Delivering Quality by Design. G. R Baker, Anu Macintosh-Murray, Christina Porcellato, et al., Exton, PA: Longwoods Publishing.

Home Care Experts Weigh in on Accountable Care Organizations. Tracey Boyd and Janice P. Lynch, Nurse.com, November 7, 2011. Online at: http://news.nurse.com/article/20111107/NY01/111070060 (accessed 11/18/2011).

Home Health Care's Role in ACOs. Stephen Tweed, Leading Home Health Services, Redford, MI, August 3, 2011.

Hospital Alliance Announces Launch of Accountable Care Organization Efforts. Nathaniel Weixel, May 27, 2010. Online at: http://news.bna.com/hlln/display/batch_print_display.asp.

Hospital CEOs Manage Staff Time, Inventory to Cut Costs. Del Jones, September 10, 2009. Online at: http://www.usatoday.com/money/industries/health/2009-09-09-saving-money-hospitals_N.htm (accessed 1/13/2012).

Hospital Executives Survey: U.S. News and Fidelity Investments Surveyed Executives at 1,852 Hospitals. Staff, *U.S. News*, July 18, 2011.

Hospital Insights: Capital Spending. Richard Pizzi, February 15, 2011. Online at: http://www.healthcarefinancenews.com/news/hospital-insights-capital-spending (accessed January 5, 2012).

Hospital Mergers and Acquisitions: Opportunities and Challenges. Karen Minich-Pourshadi, HealthLeaders Media, November 2010.

Hospital of the Future, The. Gienna Shaw, July 13, 2011. Online at: http://www.healthleadersmedia.com/page-1/MAG-268318/The-Hospital-of-the-Future (accessed 07/21/11).

Hospital Readiness for Population-Based Accountable Care. Health Research & Educational Trust, Current Progress in Hospital Participation.,April 2012.

Hospitals, Physicians Must Overcome Tensions: Each Can "Give Up Something." *ACO Business News*, Atlantic Information Services, Inc., vol. 2, no. 4, April 2011.

Hospitals Race to Employ Physicians: The Logic behind a Money-Losing Proposition. Robert Kocher and Nikhil Sahni, *The New England Journal of Medicine*, vol. 364, no. 19, May 12, 2011.

Hospitals Scrutinize ACOs. Margaret D. Tocknell, HealthLeaders, April 16, 2012.

Hospitals That Don't Move on ACOs Risk Losing MD Referrals. *ACO Business News*, Atlantic Information Services, Inc., vol. 1, no. 1, November 2010.

Hospitals Will Look to Health Plans for Support on ACO's Clinical Data. Gantry Group. *ACO Business News*, Atlantic Information Services, Inc., vol. 2, no. 3, March 2012.

How Can Nurses Be Best Utilized in ACOs? Mary J. Schumann, *Accountable Care News*, vol. 3, no. 2, Health Policy Publishing, February 2012.

How Hospitals Can Shape Sustainable Cost Control. Karen Minich-Pourshadi, HealthLeaders Media. Online at: http://www.healthleadersmedia.com/content/COM-281205/HowHospitals-Can-Shape-Sustainable-Cost-Control (accessed 06/13/12).

How Rivals Built an ACO. Margaret D. Tocknell, HealthLeaders Media, May 14, 2012.

How to Finance and Build Your ACO. David A. Lips, HealthLeaders Media, December 20, 2010. Online at: http://www.healthleadersmedia.com/print/LED-260798/How-to-Finance-andBuild-Your-ACO (accessed 1/5/2011).

How to Present the Business Case for Healthcare Quality to Employers. Sean Nicholson, Mark V. Pauly, Daniel Polsky, Catherine M. Baase, and Gary M. Billotti, November 2005.

How to Put Your Money Where Your Strategy Is. Stephen Hall, Dan Lovallo, and Reinier Musters, *McKinsey Quarterly*, March 2012.

If Accountable Care Organizations Are the Answer, Who Should Create Them? Victor R. Fuchs and Leonard D. Schaeffer, *Journal of the American Medical Association*, vol. 307, no. 21.

If You Build It, Will They Come? Designing Truly Patient-Centered Health Care. Christine Bechtel and Debra L. Ness, vol. 29, no. 5, May 2010.

Implementing Accountable Care Organizations: Ten Potential Mistakes and How to Learn from Them. Sara Singer and Stephen M Shortell, *Journal of the American Medical Association*, vol. 306, no. 7.

Implications of Proposed Rule on Accountable Care Organizations. Healthcare Financial Management Association (HFMA), Chicago, March, 2012.

Importance of Working Capital Management for Hospital Profitability: Evidence from Bond-Issuing, Not-for-Profit U.S. Hospitals, The. Simone Rauscher and John R Wheeler, 2011.

In Their Own Words: Lean ACOs Improve Outcomes, Lower Costs. *ACO Business News*, Atlantic Information Services, Inc., vol. 2, no. 2, February 2011.

In Their Own Words: Primary Care, Medical Homes Are Significant in ACO Development. *ACO Business News*, Atlantic Information Services, Inc., vol. 2, no. 4, April 1, 2011.

In Their Own Words: Building a "Sustainable ACO Community." *ACO Business News*, Atlantic Information Services, Inc., vol. 2, no. 8, August 2011.

In Their Own Words: Summa Health Sees $8.5 Million in Savings. *ACO Business News*, Atlantic Information Services, Inc., vol. 2, no. 5, May 2012.

Incremental Cost Estimates for the Patient-Centered Medical Home, The. Stephen Zuckerman, Katie Merrell, Robert Berenson, David Gans, William Underwood, et al., The Commonwealth Fund, October 2009.

Industry News: Genesis-Aetna Alliance May Preview ACO Deals to Come. *Accountable Care News,* vol. 2, no. 2, Health Policy Publishing, October 2011.

Industry News. *Accountable Care News,* vol. 3, no. 2, Health Policy Publishing, February 2012.

Innovation: Needed, But Not Rocket Science. Susan Dentzer, Project Hope, vol. 30, no. 3, March 1, 2011. Online at: http://content.healthaffairs.org/content/30/3/378.full.html (accessed 6/16/2011).

Insights into Developing Accountable Care Organizations: The Henry Ford Physician Network. Accenture. Online at: http://www.accenture.com/SiteCollectionDocuments/PDF/Accenture_Insights_into_Developing_Accountable_Care_Organizations.pdf (accessed 3/2/2012).

Integrated Delivery Network (IDN). Glen McDaniel, Gerson Lehrman Group, Inc., 2011. Online at: http://www.glgresearch.com/Dictionary/HC-Integrated-Delivery-Network(IDN).html (accessed 1/24/2012).

Integrated Health Care Delivery/ACOs. Paper presented at the Second National Accountable Care Organization Congress, AON Hewitt, November 1, 2011.

Integrated Rolling Forecasts: The Foundation for Sustainable Cost Reduction. Dean Sorensen, *Strategic Financial Planning Newsletter*, Summer 2012.

Integration Platforms to Streamline ACO Data Are Being Pursued by Tech Companies. Perez Johnson and Judimarie Thomas, *ACO Business News*, Atlantic Information Services, Inc., vol. 2, no. 4, April 2012.

Interest Will Shift from Medicare ACOs to Private Payors, Consultant Says. Leigh Page, May 18, 2011.

Intermountain Shares Strategies, Deflects ACO Comparisons. Haydn Bush, Hospitals & Health Networks (H&HN), April 4, 2011. Online at: http://www.hhnmag.com/hhnmag/HHNDaily/HHNDailyDisplay.dhtml?id=200005967 (accessed 4/11/2011).

Introduction to the Theory of Value, An: On the Lines of Menger, Wieser, and Bohm-Bawerk, 4th ed. William Smart, New York: MacMillan Publishing.

Investors Not Likely to Provide ACO Funding under Proposed Rule, Venture Capitalist Says. Sara Hansard, Bureau of National Affairs, Inc., vol. 20, no. 1026, BNA, Inc., 40731.

Is American Health Care Uniquely Inefficient. Alan M. Garber and Jonathan Skinner, *Journal of Economic Perspective*, vol. 22, no. 4.

Is Your Organization Ready to Become an Accountable Care Organization: Here Are 10 Questions to Ask. Douglas Hastings, vol. 19, no. 1, Bureau of National Affairs, Inc. (BNA), January 2010 (accessed 8/2010).

Issues in Cost Accounting for Health Care Organizations. Steven A. Finkler, New York: Aspen Publishers. Online at: www.healthcaremgmt.com/rpa.html (accessed 06/05/2012).

Joint Principles for Accountable Care Organizations Released by Organizations Representing More Than 350,000 Primary Care Physicians. November 19, 2010. Online at: http://www.aafp.org/online/en/home/media/releases/2010b/aco-jointprinciples.html (accessed 12/5/2010; 12/10/2010).

Joint Principles of the Patient-Centered Medical Home. February 2007. Online at: http://www.aafp.org/online/etc/medialib/aafp_org/documents/policy/fed/jointprinciplespcmh0207.Par.0001.File.dat/022107medicalhome.pdf (accessed 1/2/2012).

Kansas City Hospital System Seeks to Develop "Integrated Pediatric Network." *ACO Business News*, Atlantic Information Services, Inc., vol. 2, no. 2, February 2012.

Kicking Off ACOs: Improvements Already in the Works. Rick Gilfillan, Center for Medicare & Medicaid Innovations, April 10, 2012. Online at: http://www.healthcare.gov/blog/2012/04/kickingoffacos.html (accessed 4/25/2012).

Large Employer's Air Doubts about ACOs. Rebecca Vesely, February 15, 2011. Online at: http://www.modernhealthcare.com/article/20110215/NEWS/302159958 (accessed 1/19/12).

Larger, Busier Hospitals Witness Higher Readmission Rates: Studies. Emily Mullin, Dorland Health, New York, May 14, 2012.

Larger Plans Will Continue to Drive ACOs, as Providers Contend with Diverse Market. *ACO Business News*, Atlantic Information Services, Inc., vol. 2, no. 1, January 2012.

Leadership in Creating Accountable Care Organizations. Gerard F. Anderson, *Journal of Internal Medicine*, vol. 36, no. 11, May 10, 2011.

Leading Venture Capitalists Place a Bet on ACOs. Christopher Weaver, July 20, 2011. Online at: http://capsules.kaiserhealthnews.org/index.php/2011/07/leading-venture-capitalists-placea-bet-on-acos/ (accessed 1/18/2012).

Lessons from the Field: Making Accountable Care Organizations Real. Timothy K. Lake, Kate A. Stewart, and Paul B. Ginsberg, vol. 2, no. 3, Health Policy Publishing, March 2011.

Lessons from the Physician Group Practice Demonstration: A Sobering Reflection. Gail R. Wilensky, *The New England Journal of Medicine*, vol. 365, no. 18, November 3, 2011.

Lessons Learned: Transforming to a Value Care Organization While Tripling Capacity. Castulo de la Rocha, Martin Serota, and J. D. Serota, AltaMed Health Services Corp., Los Angeles, ACO Congress.

Liar's Poker: Rising through the Wreckage on Wall Street. Michael Lewis, New York: Penguin Group Inc., 2010.

Listening to the Senior Voice: A Seasoned Ear to Accountable Care. Torrance Hospital IPA Medical Group, November 1, 2011.

Local "Giants" Partnership to Transform Volume into Value in Landmark ACO Program. Blue Cross Blue Shield Association, Chicago, August 11, 2011.

Looking Outside: Using External Capital Sources to Overcome Budget Constraints. Dan Morse. Online at: http://www.gehealthcarefinance.com/includes/OurSolutions/montgomery.pdf (accessed 1/5/2012).

Lost Productive Work Time Costs from Health Conditions in the United States: Results from the American Productivity Audit. Walter F. Stewart, Judith A. Ricci, Elsbeth Chee, and David Morganstein, *Journal of Occupational and Environmental Medicine*, vol. 45, no. 12.

Lower Premiums, Stronger Businesses: How Health Insurance Reform Will Bring Down Costs for Small Businesses. Meena Seshamani, Healthreform.gov. Online at: http://healthreform.gov/reports/smallbusiness2/smallbusiness2.pdf (accessed 6/7/2012).

Making Care Coordination and Clinical Integration Pay Off: The Promises Coordinated Health Care Seem Obvious. Dean C. Coddington and Keith D. Moore, Business Intelligence Healthcare Financial Management, April 2012.

Manage Your Inventory and Save. Judy Capko, Physicians Practice, March 12, 2009. Online at: http://www.physicianspractice.com/display/article/1462168/162436] (accessed February 15, 2012).

Managed Competition Theory As a Basis for Health Care Reform. Catherine T. Dunlay and Peter A. Pavarini, *Akron Law Review*, 1993–1994.

Market Meld: DaVita's Deal with a Large Physician-Management Group Shows the Lines Are No Longer Clear in Healthcare. Jaimy Lee, *Modern Healthcare*, May 28, 2012.

Mass. Blues Signs Up Children's Hospital to Revised AQC Model. *ACO Business News*, Atlantic Information Services, Inc., vol. 2, no. 3, March 2012.

McClellan: ACOs Difficult But Possible. Karen M. Cheung, FierceHealthcare. Online at: http://www.fiercehealthcare.com/story/mcclellan-acos-difficult-possible/2011-06-27 (accessed 05/20/12).

MD Groups Move Forward with ACO Development Despite Risks. *ACO Business News*, Atlantic Information Services, Inc., vol. 1, no. 1, November 2010.

Meaningful Use of Health Information Technology: From Public Policy to Changing Care. Paul Tang, Healthcare Trends and Implications, Futurescan.

Medica Partners with Four Diverse ACOs on Unique Private Health Exchange Models. *ACO Business News*, Atlantic Information Services, Inc., vol. 2, no. 10, Atlantic Information Services, Inc.

Medical Group and Hospital Collaboration: ACO Congress. Sharp, November 1, 2011.

Medical Home: Transforming the Delivery of Healthcare. Anne Llewellyn, September 2, 2011. Online at: http://www.dorlandhealth.com/cip_weekly/Medical-Home-Transforming-theDelivery-of-Healthcare_1904.html (accessed 10/13/2011).

Medical Home Improvement Guide, vol. I: FAQs on Patient-Centered Care. Healthcare Intelligence Network (HIN).

Medicare Accountable Care Organizations. David Sayen, *CAPG Health*, vol. 6, no. 4.

Medicare ACO Proposed Rule, The: Legal Structure, Governance, and Regulatory Sections. Douglas Hastings, Project Hope, April 5, 2011. Online at: http://healthaffairs.org/blog/2011/04/05/the-medicare-aco-proposed-rule-legal-structuregovernance-and-regulatory-sections/ (accessed 4/25/2011).

Medicare ACOs: The Integration of Financial and Clinical Integration. Douglas Hastings, *Health Affairs* blog, April 11, 2012.

Medicare ACOs No Longer Mythical Creatures: The Proposed Medicare Shared Savings Rule Makes ACOs More Tangible for Providers, but Also Contains a Few Surprises. Chad Mulvany, Healthcare Financial Management Association, June 2011.

Medicare and Medicaid Programs; Physicians' Referrals to Health Care Entities with Which They Have Financial Relationships. *Federal Register*, vol. 63, no. 6, January 9, 1998.

Medicare Payment Models to Watch. Allison Brennan, *MGMA Connexion*, May/June 2012.

Medicare Physician Group Practice Demonstration Project Racks Up $38.7 Million in Savings. Chris Anderson, *Healthcare Finance News*, December 13, 2010. Online at: http://www.healthcarefinance-news.com/news/medicare-physician-group-practicedemonstration-project-racks-387-million-savings (accessed 4/4/2012).

Medicare Plan for Payments Irks Hospitals. Robert Pear, *The New York Times*. Online at: http://www.nytimes.com/2011/05/31/health/policy/31hospital.html?pagewanted=all (accessed 06/12/12).

Medicare Zero: A Comprehensive Analysis of the Impact of Health Reform and the Debt Deal on Medicare Funding of Hospitals and Strategies for Financial Survival. Ken Perez, MedeAnalytics, 2011.

MEDPAC Probes Effectiveness of Accountable Care Organizations. Jane Norman, Commonwealth Fund. Online at: http://www.commonwealthfund.org/Newsletters/Washington-Health-Policy-in-Review/2009/Apr/April-20-2009/MEDPAC-Probes-Effectiveness-of-Accountable-Care-Organizations.aspx (accessed 11/12/09).

Methods for the Economic Evaluation of Health Care Programmers, 3rd ed. Michael F. Drummond, Bernie J. O'Brien, Greg L. Stoddart, and George W. Torrance, New York: Oxford University Press, 2005.

MGMA/Faegre & Benson to Host Integrated Delivery System Round Table for Elite Health System Leaders. Surgistrategies, January 27, 2011. Online at: http://www.surgistrategies.com/news/2011/01/mgma-faegre-benson-to-host-integrateddelivery-sy.aspx (accessed 02/05/11).

MGMA Study Finds Many Practices Are Interested in Becoming a Patient-Centered Medical Home. July 19, 2011. Online at: http://www.mgma.com/print.aspx?id=1366853 (accessed 10/13/2011).

Miles to Go: Proposed ACO Regs Are Lacking on Clinical Integration, Increase Risks and Costs. Richard Umbdenstock, April 11, 2011. Online at: http://www.modernhealthcare.com/article/20110411/MAGAZINE/304119983# (accessed 8/1/2011).

Missing Ingredient in Accountable Care, The. Pauline W. Chen, January 27, 2011. Online at: http://www.nytimes.com/2011/01/27/health/views/27chen.html (accessed 2/14/2011).

Models of Collaboration. Aetna, 2011. Online at: http://www.aetnaacs.com/models-of-collaboration.html (accessed 1/25/2012).

Monopolies Threaten Health Care Cost Controls. Merrill Goozner, February 3, 2011. Online at: http://www.thefiscaltimes.com/Articles/2011/02/03/Monopolies-Threaten-Health-Care-Cost-Controls.aspx (accessed 3/2/2011).

Montefiore's Balanced Portfolio of Capital Investments. Joel Perlman. Online at: http://www.hfma.org/Templates/Print.aspx?id=25165 (accessed 4/15/2011).

More Pediatric ACOs Are Forming, but Challenges Loom with Narrower Focus. *ACO Business News*, Atlantic Information Services, Inc., vol. 2, no. 6.

More Physicians Calling the Shots in Latest Round of ACOs. Charles Fiegl, *American Medical News,* April 23, 2012.

N.J. Lawmakers Advance Bill on Rewards for Preventing, Controlling Illnesses among N.J. Poor. Susan K. Livio and Seth Augenstien, January 24, 2011. Online at: http://www.nj.com/news/index.ssf/2011/01/lawmakers_approve_bill_on_rewa.html (accessed 2/7/2011).

Navigating Health Care Reform: An Employer's Guide. UnitedHealthcare, 2011.

Navigating Today's Opportunities for Capital. Karen M. Sandrick, *Healthcare Financial Management*, vol. 62, no. 12, December 2008.

NCQA 2011 ACO Criteria and Implications for ACO Governance, The. Douglas A. Hastings, 19 HLR 1573, November 11, 2010.

New Accountable Care Organization Collaboratives Will Focus on Creating Healthier Communities. Premier, Inc., May 20, 2010. Online at: http://www.premierinc.com/about/news/10-may/aco052010.jsp (accessed 11/16/11).

New Healthcare, The: Do We Shop for Quality at Neimans or Filenes. Robin L. Nagele and Sidney Welch. Online at: http://www.healthlawyers.org/Events/Programs/Materials/Documents/AM11/nagele_welch.pdf.

New Power Players, The. Stephanie Sloan and Rod Fralicx, Hospitals & Health Networks (H&HN), June 16, 2011. Online at: http://www.hhnmag.com/hhnmag/HHNDaily/HHNDailyDisplay.dhtml?id=250009059 (accessed 6/16/2011).

New Skills Emerge for Leaders in Accountable Care. Richard Scott, Dorland Health, March 21, 2011. Online at: http://www.dorlandhealth.com/case_management/trends/New-SkillsEmerge-for-Leaders-in-Accountable-Care_1724.html (accessed 4/4/2011).

New State Laws Encourage ACO Formation. *ACO Business News*, Atlantic Information Services, Inc., vol. 2, no. 6.

New Study Finds the Start Up Costs of Establishing an ACO to be Significant. American Hospital Association, May 13, 2011. Online at: http://www.aha.org/presscenter/pressrel/2011/110513-pr-aco.shtml (accessed 1/16/2012).

Northern California ACO to Be a Model for National Efforts: J. K. Kraft, Aldo De La Torre, *Accountable Care News*, vol. 2, no. 11, Health Policy Publishing, October 2011.

Norton Healthcare and Humana Launch Accountable Care Organization in Louisville, KY: Program Intended to Increase Quality and Efficiency of Health Care. Norton Healthcare, 2010. Online at: http://www.nortonhealthcare.com/body.cfm?xyzpdqabc=0&id=1402&action=detail&ref=356 (accessed 11/30/2010).

Norton, Humana Commercial ACO Notches Cost Savings. Jim Mopus, HealthLeaders Media, August 8, 2011. Online at: http://www.healthleadersmedia.com/content/LED-269502/Norton-Humana-CommercialACO-Notches-Cost-Savings.html (accessed 10/13/2011).

Nurses, Care Coordinators Are Gaining Importance in ACOs. *ACO Business News*, Atlantic Information Services, Inc., vol. 2, no. 2, February 2012.

Nurturing e-Patients in the Medical Home and the ACO. Nancy B. Finn, *Accountable Care News,* vol. 2, no. 5.

OECD Health Data 2011: Frequently Requested Data. November 2011. Online at: http://www.oecd.org/document/16/0,3746,en_2649_37407_2085200_1_1_1_37407,00.htm l (accessed 1/4/2012).

On the Plane Geometry with Generalized Absolute Value Metric. A. Bayar, S. Ekmekci, and Z. Akca Hindawi.

Oncologists Drive toward Single-Specialty ACOs, But Other Specialists Hit the Brakes. *ACO Business News*, Atlantic Information Services, Inc., vol. 2, no. 1, January 2011.

Oncology Payment Model Requires Detailed Review before Move to ACO. *ACO Business News*, Atlantic Information Services, Inc., vol. 2, no. 6.

Oncology Poses Tough Issues for ACOs: Views on Solutions Differ. *ACO Business News*, Atlantic Information Services, Inc., vol. 2, no. 9, September 2011.

Options, Futures, and Other Derivatives, 7th ed. John C. Hull, Upper Saddle River, NJ: Prentice-Hall, Inc., 2008.

Outlier: ACOs Carry Some Gingrich DNA. March 17, 2012. Online at: http://www.modemhealthcare.comlarticle/20 120317/MAGAZINEI3 0... (accessed 3/20/2012).

Partners in Health: How Physicians and Hospitals Can Be Accountable Together. Stephen M. Shortell, Stuart Guterman, Francis J. Crosson, and Laura A. Tollen, The Kaiser Permanente Institute for Health Policy, September 27, 2010.

Patient-Centered Care Redistributes Responsibility. Betty A. Marton, Health Leaders Media. Online at: http://healthleadersmedia.com/print/PHY-279857 (accessed 5/10/2012).

Patient-Centered Medicine and ACOs: It's Not Just about Primary Care. James B. Rickert, *Accountable Care News*, Health Policy Publishing, vol. 2, no. 5.

Patients' Role in Accountable Care Organizations. Anna D. Sinaiko and Meredith B. Rosenthal, *The New England Journal of Medicine*, vol. 363, no. 27, Massachusetts Medical Society, November 10, 2010. Online at: http://healthpolicyandreform.nejm.org/?p=13018 (accessed 12/30/2010).

Patterns of Financing for the Largest Hospital Systems in the United States by William Cleverley; Jane Baserman. Vol. 50. No. 6. November/December 2005.

PEM: A Framework Enabling Continual Optimization of Workflow Process Executions Based upon Business Value Metrics. Melissa J. Buco, Rong N. Chang, Laura Z. Luan, Edward So. Chunqiang Tang, et al., New York: IBM.

Performance Improvement in Health Care: Seizing the Moment. David Blumenthal, *The New England Journal of Medicine*, vol. 366, no. 21.

Physician Characteristics and Distributions in the US: 2012 Edition. American Medical Association.

Physician Employment Trends Will Force Payers, Hospitals and Vendors to Revise Business Strategies, According to Accenture Survey. *Wall Street Journal*, June 13, 2011. Online at: http://online.wsj.com/article/PR-CO-20110613-902747.html#printMode (accessed 7/5/2011).

Physician Group Practice Demonstration: Evaluation Report. Kathleen Sebelius, Report to Congress, 2009.

Physician–Hospital Clinical Integration: Navigating the Complexities. Strafford Publications, Inc., July 21, 2011.

Physician Value Index, The: A Tool for Effective Physician Integration. Jay Reddy, Online at: http://www.hfma.org/Templates/Print.aspx?id=24919 (accessed 04/15/11).

Physicians, Health Systems Should Weigh Other Delivery Reforms in Building ACOs. *ACO Business News*, Atlantic Information Services, Inc., vol. 2, no. 2, February 2011.

Physicians Uncertain about Taking Part in ACOs. Victoria S. Elliott, December 5 2011. Online at: http://www.ama-assn.org/amednews/2011/12/05/bisb1205.htm (accessed 12/07/2011).

Physicians versus Hospitals as Leaders of Accountable Care Organizations. Robert Kocher and Nikhil Sahni, Massachusetts Medical Society, November 10, 2010. Online at: http://www.nejm.org/doi/full/10.1056/NEJMp1011712 (accessed 11/15/2010).

Pilot Programs and Demonstration Projects: The Patient Protection and Affordable Care Act (PPACA) and Health Care and Education Reconciliation Act of 2010. Premier, Inc. Online at: http://www.premierinc.com/about/advocacy/issues/10/healthcarereform/Pilots-Demos-Grants-PPACA.pdf (accessed 11/18/2011).

Pioneer ACOs to Ring in the New Year. Karen M. Cheung, FierceHealthcare. Online at: http://www.fiercehealthcare.com/story/pioneer-acos-ring-new-year/2011-12-22 (accessed 05/20/12).

Pioneer ACOs Won't Be Unveiled Until Nov. 18: 55-75 Applied. *ACO Business News*, Atlantic Information Services, Inc., vol. 2, no. 11, November 2011.

Pioneering Quality and Cost Improvements for Medicare Patients through Patient Engagement. Bart Asner, *Accountable Care News*, Health Policy Publishing, April 2012.

Positioning Specialty Services for ACOs. Philip Ronning, *Accountable Care News*, vol. 3, no. 2, Health Policy Publishing, February 2012.

Poster Boys Take a Pass on Pioneer ACO Program. Jenny Gold, Henry J. Kaiser Family Foundation, September 14, 2011. Online at: http://www.kaiserhealthnews.org/Stories/2011/September/14/ACO-Pioneers-Medicarehospitals.aspx (accessed 11/16/2011).

Practice Management: Roles for Specialty Societies and Vascular Surgeons in Accountable Care Organizations. Philip P. Goodney, Elliot S. Fisher, Richard P. Cambria, *Journal of Vascular Surgery*, vol. 55, March 2012.

Premier Accountable Care Collaboratives: Driving to a People-Centered Health System. Premier, Inc., 2011.

Price Trends in Single- and Multispecialty Physician Practices. Bradley T. Ewing, Kim Powell, and Mark A. Thompson, *Journal of Medical Practice Management,* vol. 27, no. 3, 2011.

Primary Care. American Academy of Family Physicians (AAFP), 2012. Online at: http://www.aafp.org/online/en/home/policy/policies/p/primarycare.html#Parsys0003 (accessed 1/24/2012).

Primary Care and Accountable Care: Two Essential Elements of Delivery-System Reform. Diane R. Rittenhouse, Stephen M. Shortell, and Elliott S. Fisher, vol. 361, no. 24, December 10, 2009. Online at: http://www.nejm.org/doi/pdf/10.1056/NEJMp0909327 (accessed 4/16/2012).

Primary Care and ACOs: From Medical Homes to Medical Neighborhoods. David Nace and Kevin Grumback, November 2, 2011.

Primary Care Shortage. Esme Cullen, Usha Ranji, and Alina Salganicoff, April 2011. Online at: http://www.kaiseredu.org/Issue-Modules/Primary-Care-Shortage/Background-Brief.aspx (accessed 7/5/2011).

Principles of Corporate Finance, 9th ed. Richard A. Brealey, Stewart C. Myers, and Franklin Allen, New York: McGraw Hill, 2008.

Private-Payer Innovation In Massachusetts: The "Alternative Quality Contract." Michael E. Chernew, Robert E. Mechanic, Bruce E. Landon, and Dana G. Safran, Project Hope, *Health Affairs*, vol. 30, no. 1, January 2011.

Private Payor Participation in Accountable Care Organization: Limitations, Risk, and Opportunities. Kimberly Gold, et al., vol. 9, no. 1, American Bar Association. Online at: http://www.americanbar.org.

Private Sector ACO Models Rooted in Rugged Individualism. Philip Betbeze, HealthLeaders Media, September 13, 2011. Online at: http://www.healthleadersmedia.com/print/MAG-270758/Private-Sector-ACO-Models-Rooted-in-Rugged-Individualism (accessed 3/7/2012).

Process Improvements Vital to Cost Containment. John Commins, HealthLeaders, May 2012. Online at: http://www.healthleadersmedia.com/content/FIN-281100/Process-Improvements-Vital-to-Cost-Containment.html.

Provider Creates LLC to Aid In Shared Savings Initiatives. Natalie Bentley, *ACO Business News*, Atlantic Information Services, Inc., vol. 2, no. 4, April 2012.

Provider Restructuring: Opportunities to Achieve High Performance. Accenture. Online at: http://www.accenture.com/SiteCollectionDocuments/PDF/Accenture_Innovation_Center_Health_Provider_Restructuring.pdf (accessed 3/2/2012).

Provider Seeks Early Accreditation from NCQA to Improve Upon Its ACO. *ACO Business News*, Atlantic Information Services, Inc., vol. 2, no. 2, February 2012.

Providing Accountability: Accountable Care Concepts for Providers. David K. Nace and Jeff Gartland, RelayHealth, 2011. Online at: http://www.relayhealth.com/resource-library/whitepapers/Providing-Accountability-Accountable-Care-Concepts-for-Providers.html (accessed March 2011).

Providing Accountable Care: Strategy and Structure: Payor Perspectives on Provider Realignment & ACOs. Joel L. Michaels, McDermott, Will & Emery, Chicago, March 15, 2011.

Providing Accountable Care: Strategy and Structure: Best Practices, Evidence Based Care, and the Evolution of Clinical Care in the ACO Era. Richard Lopez, March 1, 2011.

Providing Accountable Care: Strategy and Structure: Tax Planning for ACO Development and Operations. Douglas M. Mancino, McDermott, Will, & Emery, Chicago, March 1, 2011.

Physician Acquisition: What to Avoid after the Deal Is Complete. Mark Driscoll and Anthony, Healthcare Financial Management, April 2012.

Quality over Quantity: Accountable Care Organizations Link-Physician Payments to Hospital Outcomes. Bryn Nelson, Society of Hospital Medicine, December 2009. Online at: http://www.the-hospitalist.org/details/article/477391/Quality_over_Quanity.html (accessed 7/28/2010).

Recession Contributes to Slowest Annual Rate of Increase in Health Spending in Five Decades. Anne Martin, David Lassman, Lekha Whittle, and Aaron Catlin, vol. 30, no. 1, January 2011.

Referral and Consolation Communication between Primary Care and Specialists Physicians: Finding Common Ground. Ann S. O'Malley and James D Reschovsky, vol. 171, no. 1, American Medical Association (AMA), January 10, 2011 (accessed 1/24/2011).

Reforming Payments to Healthcare Providers: The Key to Slowing Healthcare Cost Growth While Improving Quality? Mark McClellan, vol. 25, no. 2, Spring 2011.

Report: Primary Care, Robust Report Power ACOs. April 15, 2011. Online at: http://www.cmio.net/index.php?option=com_articles&article=27274 (accessed 4/15/2011).

Report of the Committee on the Cost of Medical Care, The. W. H. Smith, February 1, 1933.

Report of the Committee on the Costs of Medical Care: Its Significance to the Medical Profession. Arthur C. Christie, vol. XXVIII, no. 5, 1933.

Report of the Committee on the Costs of Medical Care, The. *The Journal of the American Medical Association*, vol. 99, no. 24.

Report on the Capital Crisis: Impact on Hospitals. American Hospital Association (AHA), January 2009.

Responding to Healthcare Reform: A Strategy Guide for Healthcare Leaders. Daniel B. McLaughlin, American College of Healthcare Executives (ACHE).

Revenue Cycle Strategies for Accountable Care: An ACO Case Study with Healthcare Partners, a Pioneer ACO. Healthcare Informatics GE Healthcare, March 15, 2012.

Reviving Primary Care through the Medical Home Model. Anne Llewellyn, November 21, 2011. Online at: http://www.dorlandhealth.com/cip_weekly/1985.html (accessed 11/28/2011).

Risk, Uncertainty, and Profit. Frank H. Knight, Mineola, NY: Dover Publications, 2006.

Risks and Rewards of Variable-Rate Debt. Eric A. Jordahl, Healthcare Financial Management, May 2012.

Running the Numbers on ACO's: Cutting Costs and Raising Quality in Healthcare through Accountable Care Organizations. Daniel M. Graumanm DGA Partners, New York and Philadelphis, September 16, 2011.

RX Managers Contest Exclusion from ACO Reg: Payment Also Is an Issue. *ACO Business News*, Atlantic Information Services, Inc., vol. 2, no. 8, August 2011.

Scope of Practice Expansion Fuel Legal Battles. Amy L. Sorrel, American Medical News. Online at: http://www.ama-assn.org/amednews/2009/03/09/prl20309.htm (accessed 6/7/2012).

Scripps, Advocate, Mountain States Test Pioneer ACO Waters. Haydn Bush, Hospitals & Health Networks (H&HN), September 7, 2011. Online at: http://www.hhnmag.com/hhnmag/HHNDaily/HHNDailyDisplay.dhtml?id=2180001382 (accessed 11/16/11).

Scripps Announces ACO-Like Integrated Delivery Network. Cheryl Clark, HealthLeaders Media, June 13, 2011. Online at: http://www.healthleadersmedia.com/content/TEC267273/Scripps-Announces-ACOlike-Integrated-Delivery-Network (accessed 6/16/2011).

Self-Funded Plans Will Help Drive ACO Trend in 2012: Insiders Predict. *ACO Business News*, Atlantic Information Services, Inc., vol. 2, no. 1, January 2012.

Services: Retirement Plan Administration. Healthcare Management Consultants. Online at: http://www.healthcaremgmt.com/rpa.html (accessed 7/28/2009).

Setting Doctor Compensation Is Both Art and Science. John R. Boettiger and Jennifer H. Smith, July 2007. Online at: http://www.healthcarefinancenews.com/news/setting-doctor-compensation-both-art-and-science (accessed 1/18/2012).

Shared Services Centers Can Drive Significant Savings. Jim McDowell, Healthcare Financial Management Association, June 2011.

Sharp Healthcare Gains Volume via Employer's Tiered Network. Online at: http://www.hfma.org/Templates/Print.aspx?id=25239 (accessed 4/15/2011).

Six Strategic Variables in Predicting the Impact of Accountable Care. Mark Hiller, *Health Affairs* blog. Online at: http://healthaffairs.org/blog/2012/05/22/six-strategic-variables-inpredicting-the-impact-of-accountable-care/print (accessed 05/27/2012).

Small Medical Groups Face Decisions in Affiliation: Infrastructure Set Up for ACOs. *ACO Business News*, Atlantic Information Services, Inc., vol. 1, no. 2, December 2010.

So You Want to Be an ACO Data Analyst? 10 Steps to First Year Success. Bob Kelley, *Accountable Care News*, Health Policy Publishing, April 2012.

Social Transformation of American Medicine, The: The Rise of a Sovereign Profession and the Making of a Vast Industry. Paul Starr, New York: Basic Books, 1984.

Solving the ACO Conundrum. John M. Harris, Daniel M. Grauman, and Rashi Hemnani. Online at: http://www.hfma.org/Templates/Print.aspx?id=23532 (accessed 07/07/11).

Some of Those That Applied for Pioneer—and Some That Didn't. *ACO Business News*, Atlantic Information Services, Inc., vol. 2, no. 10, October 2011.

Squeezing the Funding You Need from Today's Capital Sources. Deborah C. Gordon, vol. 64, no. 4, April 1, 2010.

Stanford Presenteeism Scale: Health Status and Employee Productivity. Cheryl Koopman, Kenneth R. Pelletier, James F. Murray, Claire E. Sharda, Marc L. Berger, et al., *Journal of Occupational and Environmental Medicine*, vol. 44, no. 1.

Statement on Final ACO Rule. Rich Umbdenstock, October 20, 2011. Online at: http://www.aha.org/presscenter/pressrel/2011/111020-st-acorule.pdf (accessed 11/10/2011).

Stop-Loss Coverage for ACOs Is Not a Necessity, Observers Say. *ACO Business News*, Atlantic Information Services, Inc., vol. 2, no. 6, June 2011.

Strategic Options: It's Not ACO or Nothing. Mark DuBow, HealthLeaders Media, September 2, 2011. Online at: http://www.healthleadersmedia.com/content/LED-270490/Strategic-Options-Its-NotACO-or-Nothing.html (accessed 10/13/2011).

Structural Holes: The Social Structure of Competition. Ronald S. Burt, Cambridge, MA: Harvard University Press, 1995.

Successful Commercial ACOs: Early Adopters Answer Your Questions. HealthLeaders Media, March 22, 2012.

Successful Pilot Tests Clear the Way for July Debut of ACO Standards. National Committee for Quality Assurance (NCQA). Online at: http://www.ncqa.org/tabid/1330/Default.aspx.

Succession Planning and the Physician Practice: Is Your Practice Prepared? Jon-David Deeson, *Journal of Medical Practice Management*, vol. 22, no. 6, May/June 2007.

Superior Health Partners: A Quest for an ACO. Dave Graser, Marquette General Health System, Healthcare Information and Management Systems Society (HIMSS), May 10, 2011.

Swiss Experiment Shows Physicians, Consumers Want Significant Compensation to Embrace Coordinated Care. Peter Zweifel, Project Hope, *Health Affairs*, vol. 30, no. 3, March 2011.

Texas Retirees Get New Options for Health Care, Including ACOs. *ACO Business News*, Atlantic Information Services, Inc., vol. 2, no. 1, January 2011.

Theory of Valuation: Frontiers of Modern Financial Theory, vol. 1. Sudipto Bhattacharya and George M. Constantinides, Landham, MD: Rowan & Littlefield Publishing.

Theory of Valuation, 10th ed. John Dewey, New York: Dover Publications, 1958.

Theory of Value: An Axiomatic Analysis of Economic Equilibrium. Gerard Debreu, New Haven, CT: Yale University Press, 1972.

Thought Leader's Corner: What Are the Key Health Plan Opportunities and Risks as ACOs Unfold? Michael Rohwer, Christina Severin, and Bruce Perkins, *ACO Business News*, Atlantic Information Services, Inc., vol. 2, no. 3, Health Policy Publishing, March 2011.

Thought Leader's Corner: If You Were Designing the Pioneer Model, What Would Be the Ideal Balance of Risk and Reward? Phil Polakoff and Jay Want, *ACO Business News*, Atlantic Information Services, Inc., vol. 2, no. 11, Health Policy Publishing, October 2011.

Thought Leader's Corner, Doug Hastings, Wes Champion, Donald W Fisher, and William DeMarco, *Accountable Care News*, Health Policy Publishing, vol. 2, no. 5, May 2011.

Thought Leader's Corner: Dr. Terry McGeeney from TransforMED has said that patient engagement is the Achilles heel of the patient-centered medical home. What do you think the Achilles heel is for ACOs? Katherine A. Schneider, Jaan E. Sidorov, Ernie Vesta, Nicholas Bonvicino, Torsten Bernewitz, et al., *Accountable Care News*, Health Policy Publishing, vol. 2, no. 6, June 2011.

The Timeline for Accountable Care: The Rollout of the Payment and Delivery Reform Provisions in the Patient Protection and Affordable Care Act and the Implications for Accountable Care Organizations. Douglas A. Hastings, Bureau of National Affairs, Inc. (BNA), March 25, 2010 (accessed 7/2010).

Tips for Medical Practice Success in the Upcoming Accountable Care Era. Julian D. Bobbitt, *Journal of Medical Practice Managment*, vol. 27, no. 4, Greenbranch Publishing Inc., Phoenix, MD, January/February 2012.

Toolkit. The Brookings Institute, January 2011. Online at: https://xteam.brookings.edu/bdacoln/Documents/ACO%20Toolkit%20January%202011.pdf (accessed 11/17/2011).

Top Health Industry Issues of 2011. Warren Skea and Brett M Hickman. Online at: http://www.pwc.com/us/en/health-industries/publications/top-issue-03-aco.jhtml (accessed 06/16/11).

Total HMO Enrollment, July 2010. Kaiser State Health Facts. Online at: http://www.statehealthfacts.org/comparemaptable.jsp?cat=7&ind=348 (accessed 06/06/12).

Transforming Physician Practices to Patient-Centered Medical Homes: Lessons from the National Demonstration Project. Paul A. Nutting, Benjamin F. Crabtree, William L. Miller, Kurt C. Strange, and Elizabeth Stewart, Project Hope, vol. 30, no. 3, March 1, 2011. Online at: http://content.healthaffairs.org/content/30/3/439.full.html (accessed 6/16/2011).

Treatment Outcomes. Cleveland Clinic. Online at: http://my.clevelandclinic.org/about-cleveland-clinic/quality-patient-safety/treatment-outcomes.aspx (accessed 11/22/2011).

Trends in Asset Structure between Not-for-Profit and Investor-Owned Hospitals. Paula H. Song and Kristin L. Reiter, Thousand Oaks, Ca: SAGE Publications, November 11, 2010 (accessed 01/12/12).

Two Hundred Years of Hospital Costs and Mortality: MGH and Four Eras of Value in Medicine. Gregg S. Meyer, Akinluwa A. Demehin, Xiu Liu, and Duncan Neuhauser, *The New England Journal of Medicine*, vol. 366, no. 23.

U.S. Health System, The: Origins and Functions. Marshall W. Raffel, Hoboken, NJ: John Wiley & Sons, 2010.

Understanding the Managed Care Backlash. R. J. Blendon, M. Brodie, J. M. Benson, D. E. Altman, and L. Levitt, vol. 17, no. 4, July/August 1998.

United Is Buying Calif. Doctor Group Working with WellPoint on ACO. *ACO Business News*, Atlantic Information Services, Inc., vol. 2, no. 10, October 2011.

Unsettled State of the ACO, The. Margaret D. Tocknell, HealthLeaders Media, April 2012.

Unveiling the Unicorn: A Leader's Guide to ACO Preparation. Paul Aslin, *Journal of Healthcare Managment*, vol. 56, no. 4, July 2011.

US Oncology May Go National with Private-Sector ACO. Judy P. Tursman, *ACO Business News*, Atlantic Information Services, Inc., vol. 2, no. 1, January 18, 2011. Online at: http://w.aishealth.com/archive/nabn0111-06 (accessed 11/10/2011).

Valuation: Its Nature and Laws, Being an Introduction to the General Theory of Value. Wilbur M. Urban, New York: MacMillan Publishing Company, 1909.

Valuation Handbook: Valuation Techniques from Today's Top Practitioners, The. Thomas Rawley and Benton E. Gup, Hoboken, NJ: John Wiley & Sons, 2009.

Valuation Methods and Shareholder Value Creation. Pablo Fernandez, San Diego, CA: Academic Press, Inc., 2002.

Valuation of Hospitals & Medical Centers: Analyzing and Measuring Hospital Assets and Market Value, The. James J. Unland, Chicago: Probus Publishing Company, 1979.

Valuation of Physician-Owned Hospitals in a Changing Reimbursement and Regulatory Environment, The. Robert J. Cimasi, *The PHA Pulse*, Winter 2007/2008.

Valuation of Property, The: A Treatise on the Appraisal of Property for Different Legal Purposes, Vol. 1, James C. Bonbright, New York: McGraw Hill Company, 1937.

Value-Based Contracting and Accountable Care Organizations. United Healthcare, 2011.

Value-Based Contracts and Care Delivery: A Collaborative Approach. Peggy L. Naas, November 1, 2011.

Value Maps: Valuation Tools That Unlock Business Wealth. Warren D. Miller, Hoboken, NJ: John Wiley & Sons.

Variation Reduction: Engaging Physicians to Improve the Value Equation. Lawrence Shapiro, November 1 2011.

Venture Capital Invests in ACO Suppliers, Not ACOs Themselves. *ACO Business News*, Atlantic Information Services, Inc., vol. 1, no. 2, December 2010.

Vinson Ruling in Florida Seen as Unlikely to Have Major Impact on ACO Ventures. *ACO Business News*, Atlantic Information Services, Inc., vol. 2, no. 3, March 2011 (accessed 2/2011).

Virginia's Carilion Clinic and Aetna to Form an ACO. *Healthcare Finance News*. Online at: http://www.healthcarefinancenews.com/news/virginias-carilion-clinic-and-aetna-formaco (accessed 05/21/12).

Want Higher ACO Payments? Get Higher Quality Scores. Joseph Goedert, Health Data Management, October 27, 2011. Online at: http://www.healthdatamanagement.com/news/acoaccountable-care-shared-savings-43503-1.html (accessed 11/15/2011).

We Can Have It All: ACOs Can Be Driving Force in Health Systems Delivering Quality Care, Low Costs. Donald M. Berwick, *Modern Healthcare*, May 23, 2011.

Wellmark, Iowa Health System Buck Trend, Launch ACO to Operate in Some Rural Areas. *ACO Business News*, Atlantic Information Services, Inc., vol. 2, no. 6.

What Are ACO Start-Up Costs? Karen M. Cheung, Fierce Markets, October 26, 2011. Online at: http://www.fiercehealthcare.com/story/what-are-acos-start-costs/2011-10-26 (accessed 11/17/2011).

What Are the Issues in Undertaking Systematic Reviews Including Economic Evidence? June 6–9, 2010.

What Is Value in Health Care? Michael E. Porter, *The New England Journal of Medicine*, vol. 363, no. 26, Massachusetts Medical Society, December 23, 2010. Online at: http://www.nejm.org/doi/full/10.1056/NEJMp1011024 (accessed 11/22/11).

What's the Difference between ACOs and "AC-Like" Arrangements. Vince Kuraitis, *Accountable Care News*, Health Policy Publishing, vol. 2, no. 5.

Who's in the Driver's Seat? Matthew Weinstock, Hospital & Health Networks, vol. 85, no. 5.

Why Accountable Care Organizations Won't Deliver Better Health Care—and Market Innovation Will. Rita E. Numerof, April 18, 2011.

Why Are Insurers Buying Physician Groups? Ken Terry, Hospital & Health Networks. Online at: http://www.hhnmagcom, January 2012.

Why Not the Best? Results from a National Scorecard on U.S. Health System Performance. September 2006. Online at: http://www.commonwealthfund.org/~/media/Files/Publications/In%20the%20Literature/2 006/Sep/U%20S%20%20Health%20System%20Performance%20%20A%20National%20Scorecard/951_Commission_why_not_the_best%20pdf.pdf (accessed 2/1/2012).

Will Reform Mean More Competition for Patients? Haydn Bush, Hospitals & Health Networks (H&HN), October 12, 2011. Online at: http://www.hhnmag.com/hhnmag/HHNDaily/HHNDailyDisplay.dhtml?id=232000504 (accessed 10/13/11).

With ACOs, There's a Thin Line between Collaboration and Monopoly. Karen M. Cheung, FierceHealthcare. Online at: http://www.fiercehealthcare.com/node/693332/print (accessed 5/20/2012).

With Ark., ACOs Now Scarce, Future Systems Could Reverse Trend. *ACO Business News*, Atlantic Information Services, Inc., vol. 2, no. 2, February 2012.

Without a Roadmap: What Direction Will ACOs Travel? Sandra E. Quilty, vol. 7, no. 3, American Bar Association (ABA). November 2010. Online at: http://www.abanet.org/health/esource/Volume7/03/quilty.html (accessed 11/5/2010).

Would an ACO by Any Other Name Smell as Sweet? Lyda Phillips, HealthLeaders, Spring 2012.

Your (and Mayo's) Unending Quest to Transform Health Care. Bill Santamour, September 12, 2011. Online at: http://www.hhnmag.com/hhnmag/HHNDaily/HHNDailyDisplay.dhtml?id=9910003636 (accessed 10/13/11).

Your Mission, Should You Choose to Accept It … . J. L. Feder, Project Hope, *Health Affairs*, vol. 29, no. 11, November 1, 2010.

ZS Interview: How Incentives and Savvy Marketing Can Help Health-Care Providers Bridge the Revenue Gap. Angela B. Lee, ZS Associates, Evanston, IL, 2012.

TECHNOLOGY

2011 Capital Spend: EMR Dominates Budgets. Karen Minich-Pourshadi, HealthLeaders Media, March 2011.

About Texas Oncology. Online at: http://www.texasoncology.com/about-txo.aspx (accessed 11/3/12).

About Us. Online at: http://www.usoncology.com/network/AboutUs (accessed 11/3/12).

Accountability for the Provision of Care. 2011. Online at: http://www.himss.org/asp/topics_accountablecare.asp (accessed 3/9/2012).

Accountable Care (2011: July 12): How Health Information Exchange and Enterprise Analytics Enable the Next Generation Health System. Bruce Palsulich, Healthcare Informatics, Foster City, CA.

Accountable Care Organizations: Health IT's Critical Role. Bruce M. Fried, October 25, 2010. Online at: http://www.ihealthbeat.org/perspectives/2010/accountable-care-organizationshealth-its-critical-role.aspx (accessed 4/18/2011).

Accountable Care Organizations: A Framework for Evaluating Proposed Rules. Mark McClellan and Elliott Fisher, Project Hope, March 31, 2011. Online at: http://healthaffairs.org/blog/2011/03/31/accountable-care-organizations-a-framework-forevaluating-proposed-rules/ (accessed 4/15/2011).

Accountable Care Organizations: 10 Things You Need to Know about Accountable Care. Eleanor Burton and Virginia Traweeh, Institute for Health Technology Transformation, New York, 2011.

Accountable Care Organizations Could Dramatically Affect Radiology Practice. Steven Gerst, December 13, 2010. Online at: http://www.diagnosticimaging.com/practice-management/content/article/113619/1756594 (accessed 1/31/2011).

Accounting for Cyber Exposure. Kathryn A. Bowen, *Accountable Care News*, vol. 2, no. 6, Health Policy Publishing, LLC.

ACO Data Sharing Will Depend on Technology, a Little Faith. Gienna Shaw, HealthLeaders Media, April 5, 2011. Online at: http://www.healthleadersmedia.com/print/TEC264549/ACO-Data-Sharing-Will-Depend-on-Technology-a-Little-Faith (accessed 4/8/2011).

ACO-Focused HOT Firms Are a Major Venture Capital Target. *ACO Business News*, Atlantic Information Services, Inc., vol. 1, no. 11, November 2010.

ACO Management Depends on IT. Tom Enders, Jordan Battani, and Walt Zywiak, HealthLeaders Media, November 19, 2010. Online at: http://www.healthleadersmedia.com/print/LED259279/ACO-Management-Depends-on-IT (accessed 2/7/2011).

ACO Performance Measurement: Current and Future. Dolores Yanagihara, Integrated Healthcare Association, November 2, 2011.

ACO Readiness in 2011: Physician-Led Accountable Care Organizations Wave of the Future. Healthcare Intelligence Network, February 2011.

ACO Recruiting Turns to Non-Physicians. Joe Cantalupe. Online at: http://www.healthleadersmedia.com/print/PHY-286044/ACO-Recruiting-Turns-to-NonPhysicians (accessed 11/1/12).

ACOs: Risk or Reward? Mark Hagland.,July 2011. Online at: http://www.healthcare-informatics.com/article/acos-risk-or-reward (accessed 07/07/11).

ACOs and Meaningful Use to Go Hand in Hand. Diana Manos, March 31, 2011. Online at: http://www.healthcareitnews.com/news/acos-and-meaningful-use-go-hand-hand (accessed 7/5/11).

Advanced Health IT Needed for ACO Initiates. Nicole Lewis, *InformationWeek*, May 26, 2011. Online at: http://www.informationweek.com/news/healthcare/clinical-systems/229700076 (accessed 07/15/2011).

Aetna Official: Get the Technology Right on ACOs. Sherry Sanderford. *ACO Business News*, Atlantic Information Services, Inc., vol. 2, no. 4, April 2012.

AHRA: Rads Need to Carve a Role in ACOs. HealthImaging, August 17, 2011. Online at: http://www.healthimaging.com/index.php?option=com_articles&article=29100 (accessed 10/13/2011).

America's Rural Hospitals Are Charting a Collaborative Path to Healthcare IT Success. Alan Morgan, 2011.

Beneficiary Communication Is Rudimentary in Medicare ACOs. *ACO Business News*, Atlantic Information Services, Inc., vol. 2, no. 10.

Benefits of Evidence-Based Medicine in EHR Systems, The.Tom Doerr, *EHR Scope*. Online at: http://www.ehrscope.com/the-benefits-of-evidence-based-medicine-in-ehr-systems.

Benefits of Health Information Technology, The: A Review of the Recent Literature Shows Predominantly Positive Results. Melinda B. Butin, Matthew F. Burke, Michael C, Hoaglin, and David Blumenthal, vol. 30, no. 3, 2011.

Big Data: The Next Frontier for Innovation, Competition, and Productivity.

Building a Healthcare Information System to Integrate the Healthcare System. Jim Pesce, McKessen, San Francisco, 2011.

Can a National Healthcare Information Network Work? Booz Allen Hamilton, Tysons Corner, VA, June 15, 2005.

Can Electronic Medical Record Systems Transform Health Care? Potential Health Benefits, Savings, and Costs. Richard Hillestad, James Bigelow, Anthony Bower, Federico Girosi, Robin Meili, et al., vol. 24, no. 5, September/October 2005.

Case Study: Becoming Accountable to Patients. Healthcare Financial Management Association. Online at: http://www.hfma.org/Templates/Print.aspx?id=26368 (accessed 7/7/2011).

Case Study of a Primary Care-Based Accountable Care System Approach to Medical Home Transformation. Robert L. Phillips, Svetlana Bronnikov, Stephen Petterson, Maribel Cifuentes, and Bridget Teevan, Vol. 34, no. 1, Lippincott Williams & Wilkins, 2010. Online at: http://journals.lww.com/ambulatorycaremanagement/Abstract/2011/01000/Case_Study_of_a_Primary_Care_Based_Accountable.9.aspx (accessed 5/2011).

Choosing the Best of Both Worlds: Functionality and Affordability. Robin LaBonte, McKesson Corporation, San Francisco, 2011.

CIGNA and Piedmont Physicians: Partnership Keeps Patients on Healthy Track. Tricia Molloy, vol. 21, no. 2, Piedmont Healthcare, Spring 2011. Online at: http://newsroom.CIGNA.com/KnowledgeCenter/ACO (accessed November 16, 2011).

CIO's Guide to Implementing EHRs in the HITECH Era, The. College of Healthcare Information Management Executives, 2010.

Clinical Registries: The Opportunity for the Nation. Don Berwick, Sachin Jain, and Michael Porter, Project Hope, May 11, 2011. Online at: http://healthaffairs.org/blog/2011/05/11/clinical-registries-the-opportunity-for-the-nation/ (accessed 5/15/2011).

CMS, Private Payers Prepare for CPCI Rollout with Data, Care Collaboration. *ACO Business News*, Atlantic Information Services, Inc., vol. 2, no. 10.

Defining Key Health Information Technology Terms. Karen M. Bell, National Alliance for Health Information Technology, April 28, 2008.

Dictionary of Health Information Technology and Security. David E. Marcinko and Hope R. Hetico (eds.), New York: Springer Publishing Company, 2007.

Electronic Health Record. Healthcare Information and Management Systems Society. Online at: http://www.himss.org/ASP/topics_ehr.asp (accessed 6/22/09).

Electronic Medical Record at Mayo Clinic, The. Online at: http://www.mayoclinic.org/emr/ (accessed 11/18/2011).

Electronic Medical Record (EMR) Proves Profitable for Multispecialty Practice. Jonathan S. Batchelor, *Imaging Technology News*.

Electronics Health Records Overview. National Institutes of Health National Center for Research Resources, MITRE Corporation. Online at: http://www.ncrr.nih.gov/publications/informatics/ehr.pdf.

Emergence of National Electronic Health Record Architectures in the United States and Australia, The: Models, Costs, and Questions. Tracy D. Gunter and Nicolas P. Terry, *Journal of Medical Internet Research*, vol. 7, no. 1, 2005.

EMR Success: Training Is the Key: Plan Your Computer Education as Carefully as You Picked Your System. Robert Lewis, Advanstar Communication Inc., May 7, 2004.

Financial Position and Adoption of Electronic Health Records: A Retrospective Longitudinal Study. Jay J. Shen and Gregory O. Ginn, *Journal of Healthcare Finance*, vol. 38, no. 3.

Finding the Right Fit: Montefiore's ACO Solutions. Jennifer Dennard, Billian Publishing Inc., January 19, 2011. Online at: http://www.billianshealthdata.com/news/SiteNews/news_items/2011/January/Montefiore_News.html (accessed 01/21/11).

Findings Brief: The Effect of Health Information Technology on Quality in U.S. Hospitals. Christina Zimmerman, Changes in Healthcare Financing & Organization, April 2012.

Follow the Money: Our Experts Believe Federal Seed Capital Is the Best Way to Move the ACO Program Forward. *Inside Healthcare*, January 2011.

Fostering Accountable Health Care: Moving Forward in Medicine. Elliot S. Fisher, Mark B. McClellan, John Bertko, Steven M. Lieberman, Julie J. Lee, et al., Project Hope, vol. 28, no. 2, February 2009. Online at: http://content.healthaffairs.org/content/30/3/439.full.html (accessed 6/16/2011).

Future of Medicine, The: Squeezing out the Doctor. Bangalore Framingham, *The Economist*. Online at: http://www.economist.com/node/21556227.

Health Information Exchange. Health Information Management Systems Society. Online at: http://www.himss.org/asp/topics_focusdynamic.asp?faid=419 (accessed 5/21/2012).

Health Information Technology: Benefits and Problems. Devon M. Herrick, Linda Gorman, and John C. Goodman, Policy Report No. 327, April 2010.

Health Information Technology Is a Vehicle Not a Destination: A Conversation with David J. Brailer. Arnold Milstein, vol. 26, no. 2, February 7, 2007.

Health Reform Maze, The: A Blueprint for Physician Practices. Richard L. Reece, Phoenix, MD: Greenbranch Publishing Inc., 2011.

Healthcare Services: Revenue Cycle Management. Duff & Phelps Corporation, New York, July 2011.

Healthcare Technology & Management Consulting. Santa Rosa Consulting. Online at: http://www.santarosaconsulting.com/.

HHSC Aims to Optimize Expertise of Specialists and Pediatric Subspecialists. July/August 2010. Online at: http://www.hhsc.state.tx.us/stakeholder/July_Aug10/2.html (accessed 02/17/2012).

HITECH Programs. January 27, 2011. Online at: http://healthit.hhs.gov/....pt?open=512&objID=1487&parentname=CommunityPage&parentid=58&mode=2&in_hi_userid=11113&cached=true (accessed 7/7/2011).

Home Health Care and Predictive Modeling: Reducing Unplanned Rehospitalizations. Tessie Ganzsarto and Dan Hogan, *Accountable Care News*, Health Policy Publishing, vol. 2, no. 5.

Horizon Healthcare Innovations. Online at: http://www.horizonhealthcareinnovations.com/ (accessed 11/17/2011).

iMBA Healthcare Information Technology: Introduction to Healthcare Information Technology. Medical Business Advisors, Inc. Online at: http://www.medicalbusinessadvisors.com/services-information.asp (accessed 5/27/2010).

Implementing Patient Access to Electronic Health Records under HIPAA: Lessons Learned. Tiffany Wang, Lisa Pizziferri, Lynn A. Volk, Debra A. Mikels, and Karen G. Grant, vol. 1, no. 11, December, 2004.

Importance of Health Information Technology for Accountable Care Organizations, The. Amy K. Fehn, Wachler and Associates, P.C., Royal Oak, MI, June 1, 2011.

Intelligent Solutions for Achieving Clinical Integration & Accountable Care: Case Study: Advocate Physician Partners. Paul Katz, Intelligent Healthcare.

Internet Personal Health Record Services Slow to Catch on. John Przybys, September 18, 2011. Online at: http://www.lvrj.com/health/internet-personal-health-record-services-slow-tocatch-on-130098668.html?ref=668 (accessed 9/21/2011).

Is Your Hospital Wasting Money on the Wrong Capital Technology Purchases? ECRI Institute White Paper Offers Unbiased Help Setting Priorities. ECRI Institute, April 19 2010. Online at: https:www.ecri.org/Press/Pages/Spending_Scare_Resources.aspx (accessed 04/27/2011).

It Ain't Necessarily So: The Electronic Health Record and the Unlikely Prospect of Reducing Health Care Costs. Jaan Sidorov, vol. 25, no. 4.

IT and Accountable Care—The Big Challenge Ahead: An Overview of the Mission and IT Requirements of Next-Generation Providers. James L. Field and David E. Garets, Advisor Board Company, January 21, 2011. Online at: https://himss.webex.com/ec0605lc/eventcenter/recording/recordAction.do;jsessionid=ZpktN4vTgvtTpJRGrkynjkHYYnryqwthCv2j10vL62JmnSDpTryX!478173253?theAction=poprecord&actname=%2Feventcenter%2Fframe%2Fg.do&apiname=lsr.php&renewticket=0&renewticket=0&actappname=ec0605lc&entappname=url0107lc&needFilter=false&&isurlact=true&entactname=%2FnbrRecordingURL.do&rID=47605692&rKey=254f794bd3a31b07&recordID=47605692&rnd=8946070091&siteurl=himss&SP=EC&AT=pb&format=short (accessed 1/21/2011).

Keep Your Eye on the IT Prize. Mary Kelly. Online at: http://www.hfma.org/templates/Print.aspx?id=18731 (accessed 7/7/2011).

KLAS: ACOs Will Be the Future of Healthcare. CMIO, September 22 2011. Online at: http://www.cmio.net/index.php?option%3Dcom_articles%26view%3Darticle%26id%3D2 9612 (accessed 10/13/11).

Loose-Knit Physician Group Seek Advice on How to Form "Virtual" ACOs. *ACO Business News*, Atlantic Information Services, Inc., vol. 2, no. 2, February 2011.

Managing Your Health Information Online. Online at: http://www.medicare.gov/navigation/manage-your-health/personal-health-records/personal-health-records-overview.aspx?AspxAutoDetectCookieSupport=1 (accessed 9/21/2011).

Mayo Clinic Electronic Health Records System. Mayo Clinic. Online at: http://www.mayoclinic.org/emr/ (accessed 11/18/11).

Meaningful Use of Health Information Technology: From Public Policy to Changing Care. Paul Tang, *Healthcare Trends and Implications,* Futurescan, Society for Healthcare Strategy and Market Development.

Medical Device Makers to CMS: Make Sure ACOs Protect Innovation. Brendon Nafziger, December 6, 2010. Online at: http://www.dotmed.com/news/story/14929/.

Message for Health CIOs: Quicken EMR Pace to Capture, Manage Data That Drives Business Value. Accenture. Online at: http://www.accenture.com/SiteCollectionDocuments/PDF/Accenture_Quicken_EMR_Pace_to_Capture.pdf (accessed 3/2/2012).

Milliman: Care Management Tools Are Crucial Building Block. *ACO Business News*, Atlantic Information Services, Inc., vol. 2, no. 2. February 2011.

The National Alliance for Health Information Technology Report to the Office of the National Coordinator for Health Information Technology on Defining Key Health Information Technology Terms. April 28, 2008.

Nursing Homes Vital to ACO? Depends on Whom You Ask. Jennifer Dennard, Billian's HealthDATA Group, Billian Publishing Inc., July 8, 2011. Online at: http://www.billianshealthdata.com/news/SiteNews/news_items/2011/July/ACO_Feature.ht ml (accessed 10/13/2011).

Optimizing Enterprise-Wide Capital Resource Allocation in Hospitals and Health Systems. Don M. Kleinmuntz, Strata Decision Technology LLC, Chicago, 2009.

Patients and Health Care Providers' Concerns about the Privacy of Electronic Health Records: A Review of the Literature. Nicola T. Shaw, Anjali Kulkarni, and Rebecca L. Mador, *Journal of Health Informatics*, vol. 6, no. 1, 2011.

Paying for Electronic Health Records (EHRs). *MD Buyline*, vol. 3, no. 1, January 2010.

Physicians in Nonprimary Care and Small Practices and Those Age 55 and Older Lag in Adopting Electronic Health Record Systems. Sandra L. Decker, Eric W. Jamoom, and Jane E. Sisk, *Health Affairs*, May 3, 2012.

Population: Health IT for ACOs: A Patchwork Quilt. Ron Parton, vol. 3, no. 3, March 2012.

Predictive Analytics Can Support the ACO Model: Using Data to Identify Trends and Patterns Can Help Drive Better Outcomes. Paul Bradley, Healthcare Financial Management Association, Chicago, April 2012.

Preparing for Accountable Care: The Role of Health IT in Building Capability. Jordan Battani, CSC Healthcare Group, September 2011. Online at: http://assets1.csc.com/health_services/downloads/CSC_Preparing_for_Accountable_Care_The_Role_of_Health_IT_in_Building_Capability.pdf (accessed December 27, 2011).

Proposed Data Requirements for ACOs Pose Burdens for Providers, Panel Says. Bureau of National Affairs, Inc. (BNA), vol. 20, no. 988, June 30, 2011.

Proposed Rules for ACOs Push EHR Adoption. Robert Lowes, *New England Journal of Medicine* (NEJM), March 31, 2011.

Q&A: HIT's Critical Role in Rural Hospital of the Future. Gienna Shaw, August 9, 2011. Online at: http://www.healthleadersmedia.com/page-1/TEC-269560/QA-HITs-Critical-Rolein-Rural-Hospital-of-the-Future (accessed 10/13/11).

ROI of EMR-EHR, The: Productivity Soars, Hospitals Save Time and, Yes, Money. 2006. Online at: http://www.featherly-jossi.com/whitepapers/Pat%20White%20Papers/ROI.pdf (accessed 3/9/2012).

Running IT Like a Business in the Healthcare Industry. Craig Mindrum, Accenture, no. 1, April 2011.

Running the Numbers on an EHR: Applying Cost-Benefit Analysis in EHR Adoption. Tiankai Wang and Sue Biederman, vol. 81, no. 8, August 1, 2010. Online at: http://library.ahima.org/xpedio/groups/public/documents/ahima/bok1_047866.hcsp?dDocName=bok1_047866 (accessed 7/8/2011).

Rural Iowa Hospital Uses IT to Create a Connected Regional Community. Brenda Tiefenthaler, McKesson Corporation, 2011. Online at: http://www.strategiestoperform.com/volume5_issue1/index.html (accessed 2011).

Six Key Technologies to Support Accountable Care. John Glaser, *Hospitals & Health Networks Daily.* Online at: http://www.hhnmag.com/hhnmag/HHNDaily/HHNDailyDisplay.dhtml?id=8910003663.

Small, Nonteaching, and Rural Hospitals Continue to Be Slow in Adopting Electronic Health Record Systems. Catherine M. DesRoches, Chantal Worzala, Maulik S. Joshi, Peter D. Kralovec, and Ashish K. Jha, Health Record Systems, *Health Affairs*, May 3, 2012.

Solving a Piece of the Readmissions Problem. Maureen G. McElhinney, Dorland Health, New York.

Supply Chain Management: IT-Powered Procurement and Payment Saves Time, Money. Richard Haugh, vol. 5, no. 3, Summer 2006.

Surviving a Revenue Cycle System Conversion. Online at: http://www.hhnmag.com/hhnmag/HHNDaily/HHNDailyDisplay.dhtml?id=1000006474.

Systematic Reviews: CRD's Guidance for Undertaking Reviews in Health Care. York, U.K.: University of York, January 1, 2009.

Tackling the Capital Aspect of Your EHR Implementation. Shawn McBride, June 3, 2011. Online at: http://blogs.ajc.com/health-flock/2011/06/03/tackling-the-capital-aspect-of-your-ehr-implementation/ (accessed 3/13/2011).

Tech Platforms Improve, but Face Technical, Legal Challenges. Johnson, *ACO Business News*, Atlantic Information Services, Inc., vol. 2, no. 4, April 2012.

Technology a Key Driver to ACO Adoption. Gienna Shaw, HealthLeaders Media, February 1, 2011. Online at: http://www.healthleadersmedia.com/print/TEC262031/Technology-a-Key-Diver-to-ACO-Adoption (accessed 3/28/11).

Technology Fundamentals for Realizing ACO Success. September 2010.

Three-Facility Ohio Health System Uses Advanced HIT to Meet Challenges. Greg Slattery, vol. 5, no. 1, 2011.

Training Family Doctors: Musings of an Academic Family Physician (and Department Chair) about This (Dysfunctional) Healthcare World and How to Fix It. Ezekiel Emanuel, *Wordpress*, April 5, 2011. Online at: http://usafamilymedicine.wordpress.com/2010/09/05/accountable-care-organizations/ (accessed 10/10/2011).

Transformative Role of Healthcare IT in Accountable Care Frameworks, The. Keith J. Figlioli. Online at: http://www.hfma.org/Templates/Print.aspx?id=27539 (accessed 07/07/11).

Typical Electronic Health Record Use in Primary Care Practices and the Quality of Diabetes Care. Jesse C. Crosson, Pamela A. Ohman-Strickland, Deborah J. Cohen, Elizabeth C. Clark, and Benjamin F. Crabtree, *Annals of Family Medicine*, vol. 10, no. 3.

US Pharmacists' Effect as Team Members on Patient Care: Systematic Review and Meta-Analysis. Marie A. Chisholm-Burns, Jeannie K. Lee, Christina A. Spivey, Marion Slack, Richard N. Herrier, et al., *Medical Care*, 2010.

Use of Electronic Health Records in U.S. Hospitals. Ashish K. Jha, Catherine M. DesRoches, Eric G. Campbell, Karen Donelan, Rao R. Rao, et al., *The New England Journal of Medicine*, April 16, 2009,

Version 5010 and ICD-10 Readiness Assessment: Conducted among Health Care Providers, Payers, and Vendors for the Centers for Medicare and Medicaid Studies. Center for Medicare and Medicaid Studies, Ketchum Inc., New York. Online at: http://www.cms.gov/Medicare/Coding/ICD10/Downloads/ReadinessAssessmentSummary.pdf, December, 2011.

What to Consider When Purchasing an EHR System. Joe Swab and Vince Ciotti. Healthcare Financial Management. Online at: http://www.hfma.org/Publications/hfm-Magazine/Archives/2010/May/What-to-Consider-When-Purchasing-an-EHR-System/ (accessed 07/07/11).

Why Care Management Matters to ACOs: Techniques and Technologies Converge to Help ACOs "Individualize" Care for Entire Populations. Nandini Rangaswamy. *Accountable Care News*, vol. 2, no. 6, Health Policy Publishing, LLC, June, 2012.

Working Group 6: The Role of Technology to Enhance Clinical and Educational Efficiency. Steven E. Nissen, Abdulla M. Abdulla, Bijoy K. Khandheriam Michael G. Kinezle, and Carol A. Zaher, *Journal of the American College of Cardiology*, vol. 44, no. 2, July 21, 2004.

Glossary

501(c)(3) Organization: An organization that is exempt from taxation.

Academic Medical Center (AMC): A group of related institutions including a teaching hospital or hospitals, a medical school and its affiliated faculty practice plan, and other health professional schools.

Accountability: In the context of ACOs, the treatment outcomes of a patient population for which data are gathered determines whether the ACO is eligible for shared savings. Commercial ACOs have the flexibility to adjust the scope of accountability to either a specific patient population or all patients seen by the ACO.

Accountable Care Organization (ACO): A healthcare organization where a set of otherwise independent providers, usually physicians and hospitals, willingly integrate to become responsible for the cost, quality, and overall care delivered to a specified patient population.

ACO Culture: An environment that emphasizes the importance of collaboration and quality as a means of lowering costs.

ACO Operations: A collection of Medicare-enrolled TINs (Tax Identified Numbers) of which the ACO must identify their individual participants on the CMS application and update this list of participants as needed throughout the life of the ACO.

ACO Participant: An individual or group of ACO provider(s)/supplier(s), identifiable by a Medicare-enrolled tax identification number (TIN), that alone or together with one or more other ACO participants comprise an ACO.

ACO Professional: Any provider of healthcare services within an ACO.

ACO Provider/Supplier: An individual or entity that (1) is a provider or a supplier, (2) is enrolled in Medicare, (3) bills for items and services it furnishes to Medicare fee-for-service beneficiaries, and (4) is included on the list of ACO providers/suppliers.

Adjustable Mortgage Rate: A mortgage whose interest rate adjusts with movements in an underlying market index interest rate. Attributed as a partial cause of the recent housing market collapse that began in 2006.

Ambulatory Care: Outpatient medical care for an injury or illness.

Annuity Services: Continuity services provided on an annual basis.

Anti-Kickback Statute: Legislation enacted to prevent industries from having an unfair advantage in obtaining government contracts.

Antitrust: Legislation preventing trade restrictions or price fixing of particular organization's goods and services.

Attestation Services: A certified audit.

Auction Rate Security (ARS): A debt security that is sold through a Dutch auction. The auction rate security (ARS) is sold at an interest rate that will clear the market at the lowest yield possible. This ensures that all bidders on the ARS receive the same yield on the debt issue.

Benchmark: Derived from similar processes or services in an industry, competitors, or internal organization in order to set a level of care as a goal to be attained.

Beneficiary: Someone who receives benefits or is covered by an insurance policy or other healthcare financing program.

Best Practices: Providers can use ACO comparative analyses to evaluate strengths and weaknesses of practices in order to develop best practices, which lead to greater efficiencies.

Bundled Payment: Often based on a specific episode of care or over a specific period of time. A bundled payment may include a single payment for multiple provider entities. This method apportions the bundled payment to each entity that provided service.

Capital Expenditures: The cash outflows a firm incurs to acquire long-lived assets, both tangible (e.g., buildings, equipment, furniture, and fixtures) and intangible (e.g., computer software, patents, work product).

Capital Structure: The mix of the various debt and equity capital maintained by a firm. Also called financial structure. The composition of a corporation's securities used to finance its investment activities; the relative proportions of short-term debt, long-term debt, and owners' equity.

Capitation: Method of payment for health services in which an individual or institutional provider is paid a fixed amount for each person served.

Case Management: Monitoring and coordination of treatment rendered to patients with specific diagnosis or requiring high-cost or extensive services.

Case-Based Payment: A case-based payment system reimburses the healthcare entity based on a predetermined and fixed rate per case treated by the entity.

Centers for Medicare and Medicaid Services (CMS): An agency within the U.S. Department of Health and Human Services responsible for the administration of Medicare, Medicaid, and other programs.

Chronic Care: Care and treatment rendered to patients with long-term health problems.

Civil Monetary Penalties Law: Some guidelines regarding civil monetary penalties have been codified into this federal law, which specifically prohibits, among other things, payments by hospitals to physicians in return for reducing or limiting care.

Civil Monetary Penalty (CMP): A fine imposed on an organization that has engaged in illegal or unethical activity to gain higher profits.

Clinical Dashboard: A toolset developed to improve quality of care by providing clinicians with information that is needed to make daily decisions.

Clinical Integration: The confidential communication of patient information, clinical and administrative, with all appropriate healthcare parties or decision makers.

Collateralized Debt Obligation (CDO): A way of packaging credit risk. Several classes of securities (known as *tranches*) are created from a portfolio of bonds, and there are rules for determining how the cost of defaults are allocated to classes.

Commercial ACO: An ACO where the contracting payor is a private insurer. These are monitored and regulated through general healthcare laws.

Commercial Reasonableness: An arrangement that makes commercial sense "if entered into by a reasonable entity of similar type and size and a reasonable physician (or family member or group practice) of similar scope and specialty, even if there were no potential DHS (designated health services) referrals."

Continuity Consulting Services: Services provided on an ongoing basis.

Corporate Practice of Medicine (CPOM) Prohibitions: These prohibitions, which exist in several states, bar a business corporation from practicing medicine or employing a doctor for the purposes of practicing medicine.

Cost Control or Cost Containment: The practice of managing and/or reducing business expenses.

Critical Access Hospital (CAH): A rural hospital providing both inpatient and outpatient services located more than 35 miles from the nearest facility. The hospital must provide emergency services 24 hours a day, contain fewer than 25 inpatient beds, and have an average length of stay of less than 96 hours.

Debt: Loan agreement that is a liability on the firm. An obligation to repay a specified amount at a particular time.

Department of Health and Human Services (HHS): An agency of the U.S. government that protects health and provides essential human services, especially for those who are least able to help themselves.

Designated Health Services (DHS): Enumerated services that physicians are prohibited from providing under the Stark Law. They include: (1) clinical laboratory services; (2) physical therapy, occupational therapy, and outpatient speech-language pathology services; (3) radiology and certain other imaging services; (4) radiation therapy services and supplies; (5) durable medical equipment and supplies; (6) parental and enteral nutrients, equipment, and supplies; (7) prosthetics, orthotics, and prosthetic devices and supplies; (8) home health services; (9) outpatient prescription drugs; and (10) inpatient and outpatient hospital services.

Diabetes Physician Recognition Program (DPRP): A voluntary program for physicians or physician groups that provide care to people with diabetes.

Discharge: Release of a patient from a provider's care, usually referring to the date at which a patient checks out of a hospital.

Discounted Payback Period Method: An investment decision rule in which the cash flows are discounted at an interest rate and the payback rule is applied on these discounted cash flows.

Electronic Health Record (EHR): A longitudinal collection of electronic health information about individual patients and populations.

Electronic Prescribing or E-prescribing: Incorporates the writing and sending of prescriptions electronically to a pharmacy.

End-of-Life Care: The care provided to individuals in the final stages of their life. It is also known as hospice care, comfort care, supportive care, palliative care, or symptom management.

Episodic Consulting Services: Services provided on a discrete engagement basis, wherein each project has separate deliverables and timetables, and often a different engagement agreement detailing the terms of each.

Equity Ownership: Interest of common and preferred shareholders in a corporation. Also, total assets minus total liabilities, or net worth.

Evidence-Based Decision Making: Using the best available scientific evidence to make medical treatment decisions or changes in the healthcare delivery system.

Extended Hospital Medical Staff: A multispecialty group associated with a hospital that provides the hospital with direct and indirect referrals.

Fair Market Value: The most probable price that the subject interest should bring if exposed for sale on the open market.

Federal Accountable Care Organization (ACO): ACO where the contracting payor is CMS. These ACOs are monitored and regulated through the MSSP and general healthcare laws.

Federal Funds Rate: The rate at which depository institutions trade balances at the Federal Reserve.

Federal Open Market Committee: A major component of the federal reserve system. The FOMC oversees open market operations, which is the main tool used by the Federal Reserve to influence overall monetary and credit conditions.

Federal Reserve Bank: The central bank of the United States, which provides the nation with a safer, more flexible, and more stable monetary and financial system.

Federal Rule of Evidence 702 (i.e., Daubert Rule): State testimony must adhere to the following: (1) be based on sufficient facts or data, (2) be the product of reliable principles and methods, and (3) that the consultant has applied the principles and methods reliably to the facts of the case.

Fee-for-Service (FFS): A method of billing for health services where each patient is charged differently from the physician or other practitioner.

Financial Feasibility Services: Services that either develop or evaluate a sustainable financial model that will provide adequate funding for the initial capital investment related to the ACO, as well as the ongoing working capital and operational costs required of the ACO going forward.

Gainsharing: When hospital or healthcare organization gives physicians a particular percentage of cost reduction that the physician was responsible for due to efficient patient care.

Geriatrics: Healthcare given to individuals over the age of 65. This population represents the Medicare population.

Government Accountability Office (GAO): The department of the U.S. government that monitors and audits how the legislative and executive branches use tax dollars.

Gross Domestic Product (GDP): The total value of all goods and services produced domestically by a nation during a year. It is equivalent to gross national product minus net investment income from foreign nations.

Group Practice: An association between three or more physicians or health professionals that varies in size, composition, and financial arrangements, and provides healthcare services.

Group Purchasing Organization (GPO): An entity that obtains discounts from vendors through collective buying power of the organization's members.

Health Information Exchange (HIE): The infrastructure for data sharing between providers and supporting access to the complete patient record across providers in many geographic regions of the country

Health Information Technology (HIT): Associated with improving the health of individuals and the performance of providers, yielding improved quality, cost savings, and greater engagement by patients in their own healthcare.

Health Information Technology for Economic and Clinical Health (HITECH) Act: Federal legislation that provides financial incentives for proper EHR implementation and utilization

Health Insurance Portability and Accountability Act (HIPAA): Sets minimum standards for regulation of particular groups in health insurance markets in the area of portability and availability.

Health Maintenance Organization (HMO): An organization providing an agreed-upon set of basic and supplemental health maintenance and treatment services that are reimbursed through a predetermined fixed period prepayment made by each person or family unit that is voluntarily enrolled.

Health Status: An individual, group, or population's state of health.

Incentive-Based Payment: Payments made to influence prevalence of certain activities, generally among providers.

Independence: Being free from the influence or control of another.

Independent Physician/Practice Association (IPA): A form of prepaid medical practice where the physicians see both enrollees and private-pay patients and are reimbursed through fee-for-service or capitation basis.

Integrated Delivery System (IDS): A network of physicians, hospitals, and other medical services combined with a health plan to provide a spectrum and organized continuum of services to a particular population.

Integrated Health System: A managed care system in the United States that includes a hospital organization that provides acute patient care, a multispecialty medical care delivery system, the capability of contracting for any other needed services, and a payer. Services are provided to enrollees of the health plan.

Internal Rate of Return (IRR) Method: A discount rate at which the net present value of an investment is zero. The IRR is a method of evaluating capital expenditure proposals.

International Monetary Fund (IMF): An organization of 188 countries with the stated goal of ensuring the stability of the international monetary system—the system of exchange rates and international payments that enables countries to transact with one another.

Joint Venture: When two or more companies enter into a business enterprise together sharing investment, risks, and profits.

Managed Care: Strategies to control healthcare provider costs while increasing quality care.

Market Share: Total sales proportion of a particular company's product or service.

Medicaid: A healthcare program paid for by federal and state dollars for individuals who meet specific income and other requirements.

Medical Home: Continuous and coordinated patient-centered, team-based care led by an individual's physician, commonly referred to as a patient-centered medical home (PCMH).

Medicare: A federal healthcare program offered for individuals 65 and over or who have certain disabilities.

Medicare Payment Advisory Commission (MedPAC): Created by the Balanced Budget Act of 1997 to review Medicare Part A, B, and C, and to evaluate the effects of payment policies.

Medicare Physician Group Practice (PGP) Demonstration Project: A five-year demonstration project beginning in April 2005. Medicare's first physician pay-for-performance initiative. Designed to assess if care management initiatives would improve quality in order to ultimately lower cost for providers.

Medicare Shared Savings Program (MSSP): The legislation that established the formation and operational requirements for ACOs.

Medicare Trust Fund: U.S. Department of Treasury accounts created for the receipt of revenues, maintenance of reserves, and disbursement of payments for Medicare programs.

Medicare, Medicaid, and SCHIP Benefits Improvement and Protection Act: A bill created to provide benefits improvements and beneficiary protections in the three programs.

Merger: The combination of a single firm from two or more existing firms.

Mortgage-Backed Security (MBS): A security that entitles the owner to a share in the cash flows realized from a pool of mortgages

Multispecialty Physician Group (MSPG): Group practice with physicians practicing in more than one specialty.

National Committee for Quality Assurance (NCQA): Founded in 1979 to accredit and coordinate quality assurance programs in managed care organizations.

Net Present Value (NPV) Method: The present value of future cash returns, discounted at the appropriate market interest rate, minus the present value of the cost of the investment.

One-Sided Risk Model: Savings determination is calculated on whether the ACO's expenditures from the performance are below the benchmark determined by § 425.602.

Opportunity Cost: Most valuable alternative that is given up. The rate of return used in NPV computation is an opportunity interest rate.

Organizational Structure: Institutional policies that coordinate work roles, responsibilities, and information.

Patient Protection and Affordable Care Act (ACA): Landmark healthcare reform legislation passed on March 23, 2010.

Patient-Centered Care: Coordinated, efficient, and considerate care given to patients.

Patient-Centered Medical Home (PCMH): An enterprise that approaches the delivery of healthcare services through coordinated, centralized patient care, with an emphasis on the primary care physician as manager of the patient's treatment.

Payback Period: An investment decision rule that states that all investment projects with payback periods equal to or less than a particular cutoff period are accepted, and all of those that pay off in more than the particular cutoff period are rejected. The payback period is the number of years required for a firm to recover its initial investment required by a project from the cash flow it generates.

Pay-for-Performance (P4P): A payment system that incentivizes healthcare organizations and professions to achieve healthcare quality objectives.

Pediatric Accountable Care Organization (PACO) Demonstration Project: Federal ACO program involving pediatric medical providers.

Performance Measures: Estimating or monitoring the actions of healthcare providers in conforming to practice guidelines, medical review criteria, or standards of quality.

Physician Group Practice (PGP): An association of physicians who share premises and resources.

Physician Quality Reporting Initiative (PQRI): A quality reporting incentive program authorized by the Medicare Improvements and Extensions Act of 2006.

Physician–Hospital Organization (PHO): A formally organized, contractual, or corporate arrangement between physicians and hospitals to contract with managed care organizations.

Pioneer Accountable Care Organization Program: A program designed for healthcare organizations and providers that already have experience in coordinating care for patients.

Positive Externalities: Positive effects or benefits on third parties (e.g., society, providers, or payors).

Preferred Provider Organization (PPO): A contracted network of medical providers and an insurer who provide healthcare services at prenegotiated fees.

Preventive Care: Healthcare services that aim at preventing health problems by promoting healthy behavior through the use of education, immunizations, early disease detection, health evaluations, and follow-up care.

Primary Care Physician Practice: Practice that provides the patient with services, including health promotion, disease prevention, health maintenance, counseling, etc., beginning at the first point of entry.

Primary Care Physician/Provider (PCP): A physician who provides primary care services.

Process Improvement: Using techniques and strategies to improve implemented processes in the healthcare organization.

Provider: A healthcare organization or professional that provides health-related services to patients.

Qualified Domestic Relations Order (QDRO): An order by a judge that creates, recognizes, or assigns to an alternate payee the right to receive a percentage of benefits payable to a participant under a retirement plan.

Quality Metrics: The comparison of criterion using instruments that assign a quantity to the quality of care.

Readmission: When a patient must be admitted to a hospital for a diagnosis that is the same or similar to recent admission.

Referral: The sending of a patient from one provider to receive healthcare service from a different provider.

Report Card: An assessment on the quality of health services published by states, healthcare organizations, consumer groups, or health plans to provide practitioner and organizational performance information to patients.

Resource Planning: Identifying, quantifying, and scheduling the resources needed to accomplish a particular task.

Revenue Cycle: All administrative and clinical functions that contribute to the capture, management, and collection of patient service revenue.

Risk Sharing: The distribution of the chance of incurring financial loss by healthcare organizations.

Risk Adjustment: The correcting of capitation or fee rates based on certain factors that cause medical costs to rise.

Safe Harbors: Exceptions to federal fraud and abuse laws that identify criteria that must be met to shield an arrangement from liability.

Securities Exchange Commission's Consolidated Supervised Entity (CSE) Program: A program created in 2004 designed to regulate global investment bank conglomerates. These conglomerates that lack a supervisor under law could voluntarily submit to regulation. The program ended in 2008.

Sherman Antitrust Act: Prohibits monopolies, contracts, combinations, and conspiracies that unreasonably restrain trade. Antitrust liability is analyzed using two standards: (1) per se illegality and (2) the rule of reason.

Standard of Care: An expected level and type of care provided by a healthcare professional in a particular set of circumstances.

Stark Law: The physician self-referral law that prohibits referrals to an organization in which that physician or his/her family has a financial relationship.

Subprime Loan: A type of loan that is offered at a rate above prime to individuals who do not qualify for prime rate loans. Usually, subprime borrowers are often turned away from traditional lenders because of their low credit ratings or other factors that suggest they have a reasonable chance of defaulting on the debt repayment.

Third-Party Payer: Any entity that is paying for the healthcare of the patient.

Two-Sided Risk Model: Each performance year, CMS will determine whether the ACO's expenditures are above or below the appropriate benchmark previously calculated under §425.602. In order to receive savings payments or be responsible for losses, the expenditures must be above (to receive shared payment) or below (to share in losses) by at least the minimum savings or loss rate.

Utilization: The use patterns of a particular type of healthcare service.

Utilization Review: The evaluation of appropriateness and effectiveness of healthcare services and facilities.

Value-Based Purchasing: The notion that purchasers hold healthcare providers accountable for both the quality and cost of care.

Value Metrics Services: Services that consider the potential value of an ACO investment in the current healthcare marketplace.

Variable Rate Demand Bond (VRDB): A bond with a floating interest rate.

Venture Capital: Early stage financing of young companies seeking to grow rapidly.

Weighted Average Cost of Capital (WACC): The average cost of capital on the firm's existing projects and activities. The weighted average cost of capital for the firm is calculated by weighting the cost of each source of funds by its proportion of the total market value of the firm. It is calculated on a before- and after-tax basis.

Literature Review

Since the early 1930s, beginning with the *Cost of Medical Care,* sources have been produced that discuss the need for accountable care. However, it was after the term "*accountable care organization*" was officially coined by Elliott Fisher in 2005, that the number of published works on the subject soared. As healthcare industry stakeholders have been preparing to move away from current volume-focused operational and reimbursement models toward more value and patient-focused models of care, the interest in the ACO topic has been sustained, which has provided ample material for writers and publishers to add to the available sea of information.

These emerging organizations have received both praise and skepticism, resulting in a wide array of literature, with each source focusing on various aspects of ACO development and operation. This literature review identifies a selection of seminal works, including legislation, government reports, books, studies, surveys, peer-reviewed journal articles, and white papers, as well as other related works. These works have been pivotal to the evolution, development, regulation, and understanding of ACOs and have given rise to a multitude of derivative works. Below is a description of key foundational documents. Please note that these seminal works are also included within the assembled Bibliography.

2011 *Benchmarks in Accountable Care Organizations: Metrics from Early ACO Adopters.* Healthcare Intelligence Network, Sea Girt, NJ: 2011.

This is a report published in 2011 by the Healthcare Intelligence Network (HIN) summarizing and examining the results of the 2011 HIN Benchmark Survey on Accountable Care Organizations. This 2011 survey focuses on the healthcare industry's capability to form ACO structures, and includes 228 healthcare organization respondents. Written for healthcare analysts, policy makers, and future ACO participants, the report indicates that the healthcare industry is in the process of incorporating many ACO tenets; a process that began even prior to the issuance of the Proposed Rule governing ACOs. This report also identifies the primary barriers to ACO engagement, and concludes that, while hospitals are currently the drivers of ACO formation, leadership will shift to physician organizations and physician–hospital organizations. The HIN survey report was one of the first published surveys of healthcare leaders regarding their progress toward ACO implementation.

2012 Standards and Guidelines for the Accreditation of Accountable Care Organizations. National Committee for Quality Assurance, Washington, D.C.: 2011.

The National Committee for Quality Assurance (NCQA), in collaboration with stakeholders, developed the *2012 Standards and Guidelines for the Accreditation of Accountable Care Organizations,* a book that provides clear criteria and standards for ACO development. This manuscript sets forth eligibility requirements, outlines the accreditation process, and details policies and procedures necessary to ensure quality of care in commercial ACOs. The published guidelines serve as the final regulation for NCAQ ACO accreditation and evaluate ACO programs in seven categories: ACO structure and operations, access to needed providers, patient-centered primary care, care management, care coordination and transitions, patient rights and responsibilities, and performance reporting and quality improvement. Under these guidelines, ACOs can achieve one of three accreditation levels that represent their degree of ability in the seven categories. These accreditation guidelines are the first published ACO specific regulations within the commercial ACO market and offer potential ACOs detailed information on the accreditation process.

Accountable Care Organizations: 10 Things You Need to Know about Accountable Care. Eleanor Burton and Virginia Traweek, Institute for Health Technology Transformation, 2011.

This was published by the Institute for Health Technology Transformation in 2011 and is a white paper derived from public and private sources, which discusses ACO structure and required healthcare information technology (HIT). The association report provides a summary of 10 crucial concepts to understand regarding ACOs and offers six recommendations for potential ACO participants. The report highlights the necessity of HIT for accountable care development and specifies the characteristics necessary for such technology. It also provides an analysis of the accuracy and significance of various cost estimates from CMS and the American Hospital Association (whose work also is considered seminal within this literature review). While the white paper may be a tool for potential ACO participants aiming to understand the history and structure of ACOs, the report's focus on HIT and, more notably, the analysis of cost estimations is what distinguishes the source.

Accountable Care Organizations: A Roadmap for Success (Guidance on First Steps). Bruce Flareau, Joe Bohn, and Colin Konschack, Virginia Beach, VA: Convurgent Publishing, LLC, 2011.

The book is derived from numerous industry sources, including legislation, regulations, and key foundational literature. Focusing on ACO structure and provider payment incentives, the book summarizes the critical issues for healthcare industry stakeholders (e.g., providers, insurers, consultants, lawyers, and other interested parties) regarding ACO development. The book is intended for potential ACO participants and provides some guidelines for successful ACO implementation. The authors also include hypothetical models that are intended to foster a smooth transition into the ACO era. This source was one of the first books specifically about ACOs, published after the passage of the Patient Protection and Affordable Care Act, which introduced the Medicare Shared Savings Program (MSSP) that regulates federal ACOs. Since the publication of the MSSP Final Rule, the authors released a second edition to *A Roadmap for Success*, entitled, *Clinical Integration: A Roadmap to Accountable Care*, published at the end of 2011.

The Accountable Care Organization: Whatever Its Growing Pains, the Concept Is Too Vitally Important to Fail. Francis Crosson, *Health Affairs,* vol. 30, no. 7, July 1, 2011.

This article addresses potential barriers to ACO implementation and market competition. Specifically, it discusses ACOs' potential negative influence on innovation and government regulation as well as other industry stakeholders' concerns. This article was written to quell criticisms of the ACO model and stress its critical importance to the healthcare field.

ACOs beyond Medicare. Victoria Boyarsky, et al., Milliman Inc., April 2011. Online at: http://publications.milliman.com/publications/healthreform/pdfs/acos-beyond-medicare.pdf (Accessed on: 4/20/2011).

ACOs beyond Medicare is a healthcare reform issue brief written by Victoria Boyarsky, Howard Kahn, David Mirkin, and Rob Parke, and published in April 2011. Focusing on ACO structure and provider payment regulation, this paper discusses the pressures facing physicians and hospitals related to value-based care standards, which emphasize lower costs and higher quality care, in contrast to the fee-for-service (FFS) payment system. Milliman concludes that, in the future, operating a practice will be difficult for individual providers that do not become part of a large integrated health system due to industry changes. The authors also explain that, under the Proposed Rule, ACO formation is a less attractive option than partnering with a health plan. This paper was published for policy makers as well as providers and industry analysts to inform them of current healthcare trends.

Commercial ACO Market Research Findings. MedeAnalytics, February 2011.

MedeAnalytics, a provider of performance management solutions for healthcare entities, developed a summary report of its *Commercial ACO Market Research Findings* in February 2011. Focusing on ACO structure and competition, the information presents primary research by a third-party market research firm regarding the commercial ACO marketplace. The report summarizes the top 10 findings for payors and providers and details how their perspectives intersect. Both payors and providers agreed that the MSSP and competition, rather than employers' pressure, were leading to commercial ACO formation. The objectives of this research were to assess providers' and payors' perceptions, needs, and challenges related to ACO formation.

Contemplating the ACO Opportunity: An HFM Compendium. Healthcare Financial Management Association, November 2010.

Contemplating the ACO Opportunity is a compendium of ACO articles compiled by the Healthcare Financial Management Association. The compendium presents articles on ACOs from a variety of perspectives, including the MSSP, provider integration, the application of value-based purchasing (VBP), and related issues. While most authors encourage ACO development, some still acknowledge that VBP could be a better alternative. This compendium was directed at leaders of healthcare organizations with the goal of providing useful resources and identifying critical points to consider as these organizations decide whether to pursue ACO formation and are in the process of developing their own ACO strategies.

Creating Accountable Care Organizations: The Extended Hospital Medical Staff. Elliott S. Fisher, et al., *Health Affairs,* vol. 26, no. 1, December 5, 2006.

This is a peer-reviewed journal article written by Elliott S. Fisher, Douglas O. Staiger, Julie P.W. Bynum, and Daniel J. Gottlieb and published as a Web exclusive for the peer-reviewed health policy journal *Health Affairs* in December 2006. This Web exclusive details the issue of physician–hospital integration as a barrier to ACO implementation. Fisher discusses the coordination of care provided to Medicare beneficiaries through local healthcare delivery systems. Further, it examines ACOs' potential to utilize empirical data to improve quality and lower cost at the "extended hospital medical staff" level, which is comprised of physicians and the hospital to which they refer patients. The paper was published to provide support for the idea of using the extended hospital medical staff as a "locus of accountability" for quality and costs of medical care and to evaluate ACO policy initiatives on whether or not they strengthen accountability and collaboration at this organizational level.

Fostering Accountable Care: Moving Forward in Medicare. Elliot S. Fisher, et al., *Health Affairs* vol. 28, no. 2, January 27, 2009.

This peer-reviewed journal article was written by Elliot S. Fisher, Mark B. McClellan, John Bertko, Steven M. Lieberman, Julie J. Lee, Julie L. Lewis, and Jonathan S. Skinner. The article primarily discusses provider payment incentives. The authors propose a new approach to integrated care via local organizational accountability that aims to develop ACOs under the Medicare shared savings concept. This source was one of the first since the passage of the ACA to provide an outline for payment reform within the healthcare industry and to discuss shared savings techniques.

Growth and Dispersion of Accountable Care Organizations. David Muhlestein, et al., Leavitt Partners, November 2011.

Growth and Dispersion of Accountable Care Organizations is a report that examines data from an ongoing national study, which identifies 164 healthcare organizations that have implemented some form of an ACO model. The paper identifies commonalities between organizations identifying themselves as ACOs and addresses the geographic growth of ACOs across the United States. By studying the varying approaches to ACO formation that these organizations have taken, this paper identifies which approaches have been the most successful at improving the value of health care. An update to the November 2011 report was published in June, 2012, and tracks the activities of 221 different ACOs across 45 states and concludes that ACO approaches to care coordination and payment vary depending on the organization's composition and its regional market.

High Performance Accountable Care: Building on Success and Learning from Experience. Stuart Guterman, et al., The Commonwealth Fund, April 2011.

This report was written by Stuart Guterman, Stephen C. Schoenbaum, Karen Davis, Cathy Schoen, Anne-Marie J. Audet, Kristof Stremikis, and Mark A. Zezza, and was published in April 2011 by The Commonwealth Fund. The report provides recommendations for executing and growing ACOs to maximize their potential to develop into a high-performance health system. Specifically, this source discusses strengthening the primary care foundation, emphasizing accountability for quality of care, informing and engaging patients, making a commitment to serve the community, implementing multipayer alignment, creating payment incentives that reinforce and reward high performance, creating innovative payment methods, balancing physician compensation incentives, and utilizing data feedback and technical support for improvement. The goal of this report is to help promote the growth of ACOs to achieve a high-performance, low-cost healthcare system.

Report to the Congress: Improving Incentives in the Medicare Program. Medicare Payment Advisory Commission, Washington, D.C., June 2009.

The *Report to Congress: Improving Incentives in the Medicare Program* was published by the Medicare Payment Advisory Commission (MedPAC) in June of 2009. The report is concentrated on reimbursement policy and regulation within the Medicare program with respect to how Medicare must overcome the problems of the current payment system. Specifically, it discusses incentives used to prioritize the value of services over the volume of services. The report also focuses on reforming the system used to deliver efficient healthcare. This source discusses restructuring medical education to better support the future needs of the Medicare program and how to efficiently utilize ACOs in order to deliver more coordinated care at a lower price, as well as other future spending issues. This report was published for the purpose of making recommendations to Congress about issues affecting the Medicare program.

Lessons from Medicare's Demonstration Projects on Disease Management, Care Coordination, and Value-Based Purchasing. Congressional Budget Office, January 2012.

This document is a government issue brief by the CBO, published in January 2012. It reviews the outcomes of 10 major Medicare demonstration projects that have been evaluated by independent researchers—six related to disease management and care coordination, and four related to value-based payment. The report concludes that most of the programs' reimbursement methods have not significantly reduced Medicare spending.

Medicare Program; Final Waivers in Connection with the Shared Savings Program. 76 *Federal Register* 212, 42 C.F.R. Chapter V (November 2, 2011).

On November 2, 2011, in conjunction with the publication of the MSSP Final Rule, an interim final rule with comment period was released in the *Federal Register* by CMS, the Office of Inspector General (OIG), and HHS establishing five specific waivers for the Physician Self-Referral Law (i.e., Stark Law, the Federal Anti-Kickback Statute, and certain civil monetary penalty (CMP) laws). These waivers are designed to facilitate integration and care coordination for federal ACOs meeting specific qualifications. These waivers received a mixed reaction from the industry concerning whether or not they will provide broad enough protection for ACOs against potential violations of the applicable laws and about what type of safeguards are appropriate. However, due to the short time frame since the waivers' implementation, the waivers' effects have yet to be determined.

Medicare Program; Medicare Shared Savings Program: Accountable Care Organizations and Medicare Program: Waiver Designs in Connection with the Medicare Shared Savings Program and the Innovation Center; Final Rule. 76 *Federal Register* 212, 42 C.F.R. 425 (November 2, 2011).

On November 2, 2011, the Final Rule regarding ACOs and the Medicare Shared Savings Program was officially published in the *Federal Register.* The Final Rule included modifications to the Proposed Rule meant to reduce cost and burden for participating entities. The Final Rule decreases the number of quality measures from 65 to 33 measures, incorporates a flexible application process and provides additional incentives by allowing entities to share in savings from the first dollar. Since the publication of the Final Rule, 32 entities have been approved as federal ACOs, but it is still unclear whether the Rule's provisions will help or hinder ACOs in achieving their cost and quality goals.

Medicare Program; Medicare Shared Savings Program: Accountable Care Organizations and Medicare Program: Waiver Designs in Connection with the Medicare Shared Savings Program and the Innovation Center; Proposed Rule and Notice. 76 *Federal Register* 67, 42 C.F.R. 425, (April 7, 2011).

In the April 7th issue of the *Federal Register*, CMS released a Proposed Rule regarding the Medicare Shared Savings Plan (MSSP). The Proposed Rule includes the definition of an ACO, requirements for ACO formation and eligibility as well as proposed methodology. The rule also expands past restrictions to allow other Medicare enrolled entities, such as Critical Access Hospitals (CAHs), to become ACOs. Healthcare policy makers and providers published numerous comments that vehemently opposed many of the provisions of the Proposed Rule and argued that it was cost-prohibitive; in response, CMS later released the Final Rule to address these concerns.

Next Steps for ACOs: Will This New Approach to Health Care Delivery Live Up to the Dual Promises of Reducing Costs and Improving Quality of Care. Robert Wood Johnson Foundation, *Health Affairs,* January 31, 2012.

This is a peer-reviewed article authored by the Robert Woods Johnson Foundation for the January 31, 2012 issue of *Health Affairs.* Focusing on ACO regulation and competition, this health policy brief summarizes the history of ACOs and the current status of ACO adoption by both Medicare and private health insurers. In particular, the brief provides information regarding the Pioneer ACO Program, which is a three-year pilot program incorporating 32 healthcare organizations. The document reflects on potential issues that may arise from ACOs, such as those dealing with health disparities and antitrust laws. Further, the authors summarize the findings of a larger analysis, *Accountable Care Organizations in Medicare and the Private Sector: A Status Update*, by the Urban Institute that was published in November 2011. Meant for industry analysts, policy makers, and potential ACO entities, this brief effectively summarizes the current nature of the healthcare environment in regard to ACOs.

Notice Regarding Participation in the MSSP through an ACO. Internal Revenue Service, 2011-12 I.R.B. (April 18, 2011).

On March 31, 2011, the IRS issued a *Notice Regarding Participation in the MSSP through an ACO,* which solicited comments to determine whether sufficient guidance existed for tax-exempt organizations planning to participate in the MSSP. Specifically, the IRS focused on those 501(c)(3) tax-exempt organizations that would be ACO participants, either with shared savings arrangements solely within the ACO, or arrangements both within the ACO and with commercial healthcare insurers outside of their ACO. The purpose of this source is to provide information on the potential application of tax-exempt status to ACOs and other healthcare programs participating in an MSSP.

Patient Protection and Affordable Care Act, Pub Law 111-148, 124 STAT 119 (March 23, 2010).

Signed into law on March 23, 2010, the *Patient Protection and Affordable Care Act* (ACA) is a massive, 906-page legislative work, published as Public Law 111-148, which along with its amendment, the Health Care and Education Reconciliation Act (Pub Law 111-152), is commonly referred to as *healthcare reform.* The regulation contains many provisions affecting access, quality, and cost of healthcare (also referred to as the *triple aim* of healthcare reform), including section 3002, the first reference to the Medicare Shared Savings Program (MSSP) that governs federal ACOs. The ACA is one of the most transformative pieces of legislation introduced to the healthcare industry in this decade. Its provisions include: the formation of risk pools, increased transparency through publication of outcomes and fraud and abuse audits, expanded access to affordable insurance, and expanded access to care (especially preventative services and primary care providers). The acceptance of the ACA has been widely contested, with several states refusing to enact several of its provisions, namely the individual mandate. On June 28, 2012, the Supreme Court of the United States (SCOTUS), in a 5-4 decision, affirmed the constitutionality of the ACA (despite removing the requirement that States had to participate in the *Medicaid Expansion* program), ensuring that the ACA's provisions that had gone into effect to date would stand, and that the remaining provisions would be implemented as scheduled.

Providers' Perceptions: Accountable Care Organizations. Billian's HealthDATA/Porter Research, February 2012.

Providers' Perceptions: Accountable Care Organizations is a white paper written and published by Billian's HealthDATA/Porter Research in February 2012. This paper discusses issues pertaining to the structure of ACOs, specifically the importance of provider participation, funding, and technology for successful ACO implementation. Written with ACO participants in mind, the paper provides guidance for internal HIT systems. The paper discusses several key findings. For example, providers recognize the need for solid HIT, but are still struggling to maintain profit revenues, while simultaneously keeping costs low and quality high. In addition, hospitals and hospital-employed physicians will be key drivers of ACO formation and, finally, that coordination of care is among the most important provider initiatives for improving patient health outcomes within the ACO model.

Report to Congress: Physician Group Practice Demonstration Evaluation Report. Kathleen Sebelius, September 2009.

Kathleen Sebelius, the Secretary of Health and Human Services, delivered the *Physician Group Practice Demonstration Evaluation Report* to Congress in September 2009. Section 412 of the Medicare, Medicaid, and SCHIP Benefits Improvement and Protection Act of 2000 (BIPA) mandated the Physician Group Practice (PGP) Demonstration. BIPA specified the basic features of the Demonstration model, which began on April 1, 2005 and ran for five years through March 31, 2010. BIPA also required the submission of four reports to Congress that assessed the impact of the Demonstration on expenditures, access, and quality. This report is the last of these mandated reports and uses data (collected by Research Triangle Group) from the 10 participating practices from the first two years of the Demonstration. The report specifically delves into the impact on access, quality, and expenditures among PGPs.

Statement of Antitrust Enforcement Policy Regarding Accountable Care Organizations Participating in the Medicare Shared Savings Program. 76 *Federal Register* 209 (October 28, 2011).

This statement is a Final Policy Statement published by the Federal Trade Commission (FTC) and the Department of Justice (DOJ). It focuses on the effect of ACOs participating in the Medicare Shared Savings Program (MSSP) on competition between providers in the healthcare industry and the guidelines by which these ACOs should abide to avoid violating antitrust laws. This statement was published in order to provide guidance to ACOs that wish to participate in both the Medicare and commercial markets, including enumerating exceptions to antitrust laws, clarifying conduct to avoid antitrust violations, and explaining the antitrust review process. Although the goal of this policy statement was to clarify the government's position regarding ACOs and antitrust laws, it does not incorporate many of the comments submitted by stakeholders in response to the Proposed Policy Statement. The industry is still generally dissatisfied with the level of guidance given and the number of questions left unanswered regarding the level of scrutiny from antitrust enforcement.

The History and Principles of Managed Competition. Alain C. Enthoven, *Health Affairs,* vol. 12, no. Suppl. 1, January 1993.

This peer-reviewed article focuses primarily on insurance and the healthcare market. Enthoven discusses the history and principles of managed competition as well as the effect that sponsors, such as employers, government entities, or purchasing cooperatives, have in this arena. Specifically, the article discusses how sponsors create price-elastic demand, such as employer/sponsor contributions, standardized coverage contracts, quality-related information, or choice of plans at individual levels. This article also discusses Health Insurance Purchasing Cooperatives (HIPC), which are formed when small employers join together to purchase health coverage, thus capitalizing on economies of scale and lowering their overall fixed costs per unit. The goal of this article is to provide a concise yet comprehensive understanding of managed competition and how it can be used to reform the U.S. healthcare system.

The Work Ahead: Activities and Costs to Develop an Affordable Care Organization. Keith Moore and Dean Coddington, American Hospital Association, April 2011.

This is an association paper prepared by Keith Moore and Dean Coddington of McManis Consulting. This report analyzes case studies to identify activities and costs relevant to ACO organizers. Though prepared for the AHA, this whitepaper is meant to help all ACO organizers understand the potential costs of capital formation and clinical integration associated with ACO formation. This paper was utilized by many providers and policy makers to show the ineffective nature of the Proposed Rule as well as in their own financial analyses regarding ACO formation. In response to these analyses, many providers and policy makers wrote disparaging letters regarding the Proposed Rule to CMS, which eventually led to CMS releasing the Final Rule.

Toolkit. Accountable Care Organization Learning Network, The Brookings Institution, January 2011.

The *ACO Toolkit* is a multipart primer that was published in 2011 by the Brookings Institution and was written for the Accountable Care Organization Learning Network and the Engelberg Center for Health Care Reform. The *Toolkit* addresses issues concerning ACOs' structure, specifically organization and governance, accountability for performance, infrastructure, changes in healthcare delivery, and legal issues surrounding ACO formation. This source was one of the first to provide concise guidance to potential ACO participants regarding how to successfully implement an ACO.

Valuing Health Care: Improving Productivity and Quality. Kauffman Task Force on Cost-Effective Health Care Innovation, April 2012.

Valuing Health Care: Improving Productivity and Quality is an association report written by the Kauffman Foundation's Task Force on Cost-Effective Health Care Innovation. The report focuses on improving the cost-benefit balance in the U.S. healthcare system through incremental "workable" reforms that do not require massive expenditures and can be implemented independently or in conjunction with ACA reform implementation. Major themes of these reform efforts include making better, more efficient use of existing resources; executing effective local changes; and understanding and using incentives to improve productivity. Specific policy recommendations include harnessing information through systematic gathering and sharing of data, improving research, and implementing legal and regulatory reforms.

OTHER RELEVANT WORKS

Some works have influenced the public understanding of the healthcare industry to such a degree that, although they do not directly discuss ACOs and have not directly impacted ACO evolution, they have been included within this literature review.

Competitive Strategy: Techniques for Analyzing Industries and Competitors. Michael D. Porter, New York: The Free Press, 1980.

Michael D. Porter developed his "competitive strategy" in the 1980s as a model to analyze the attractiveness of a market to new entrants. *Competitive Strategy: Techniques for Analyzing Industries and Competitors* provides a useful framework for understanding the five fundamental forces of competition in a market: (1) potential entrants, (2) suppliers, (3) buyers, (4) substitutes, and (5) rivalry among existing competitors. This framework is particularly relevant and applicable today, as scope of practice and types of providers grows and changes. This book uses Porter's five forces to project how ACOs may compete within the healthcare field as new entrants.

Financial Valuation: Applications and Models, 3rd ed. James R. Hitchner, Hoboken, NJ: John Wiley & Sons, 2011.

Financial Valuation: Applications and Models was first written in 2003 by James R. Hitchner and published by John Wiley & Sons. Now in its third edition, the book gathers extensive contributions from valuators to provide a comprehensive overview of methodologies for financial analysis. Accompanied by a workbook, it serves as an educational tool for providers supplying guidance on how to apply financial valuation theory. ACO integration has increased the need for financial assessments of provider practices and entities, so this book will be useful to new practitioners as they proceed.

Medical Care for the American People. Committee on the Costs of Medical Care, Chicago: The University of Chicago Press, 1932.

This is a book published in 1932 by the members of the Committee on the Costs of Medical Care, a group sponsored by several educational and charitable U.S. organizations, including the Rockefeller and the Carnegie Foundations and the Julius Rosenwald and Milbank Memorial Funds, which collectively donated almost $1 million dollars. This book represents the culmination of the Committee's five-year study of the U.S. healthcare system and describes the majority consensus, which includes five key recommendations for reducing waste, decreasing costs, and improving quality and access to healthcare. Though its recommendations for the restructuring of the healthcare delivery system were initially considered controversial, recognition of their significance has grown immensely. Many of the issues identified by the Committee are perceived as foreshadowing problems within the current healthcare system.

Physician Characteristics and Distribution in the U.S. American Medical Association, Chicago, 2012.

Since 1963, the American Medical Association has published *Physician Characteristics and Distribution in the U.S.*, an annual report of demographic information on all physicians in the United States and its territories. These reports track year-to-year trends in the physician workforce in order to forecast and plan for future healthcare needs. The predictive ability, offered through this annual report, has become increasingly important as a result of healthcare reform legislation, which relies heavily upon sufficient physician supply, especially primary care providers. The detailed statistical information provided by this survey report allows for comparisons by physician characteristics, distribution, self-designated specialty, geographic region, primary care specialty, osteopathic physicians, and other physician trends. This report is intended for a broad audience (e.g., hospitals, medical societies, medical schools, specialty boards, and government agencies), all of whom rely upon this data when researching healthcare issues regarding physician services.

The Social Transformation of American Medicine: The Rise of a Sovereign Profession and the Making of a Vast Industry. Paul Starr, New York: Basic Books, 1982.

The Social Transformation of American Medicine is a book written by Paul Starr and published in 1982 by Basic Books. The book provides a comprehensive history of the development of medicine, as both a profession and an industry, by detailing the public's growing trust in physicians. Starr chronicles major concepts currently under contention, such as the development and establishment of hospitals as centerpieces of the U.S. healthcare delivery system, the rise of public and private healthcare providers and payors, the shift from the avoidance of corporate healthcare to its current integral role, and, ultimately, the fragmentation of modern healthcare. Starr's book has been widely circulated and cited, and is often considered required reading for many professionals in the healthcare industry.

To Err Is Human: Building a Safer Health System. Linda Kohn, Janet Corrigan, and Molla Donaldson (eds.), Washington, D.C.: National Academy Press, 2009.

To Err is Human: Building a Safer Health System is a production of the Quality of Health Care in America Project under the aegis of the Institute of Medicine. This book is the first publication of this project, which researches issues and recommends changes in the U.S. healthcare industry. In this volume, the editors establish a national agenda for the design of a safer health system in order to reduce medical errors and improve patient safety. Recommendations for improving patient safety encompass the areas of leadership, data collection and analysis, as well as the development of effective systems. By applying these concepts to a case study, the book provides a concrete explanation concerning why errors occur. The book is meant for all participants of the healthcare industry including policy makers, providers, and patients, and has been cited numerous times to indicate the startling incidence of medical errors in the healthcare delivery system and the need for change.

The Valuation of Property: A Treatise on the Appraisal of Property for Different Legal Purposes. James C. Bonbright, Buffalo, NY: William S. Hein & Co., Inc., 1937.

This book was originally written by James C. Bonbright and published by William S. Hein & Co., Inc., in 1937. Written under the auspices of the Columbia University Council for Research in the Social Sciences, the book is a foundational source within the property valuation genre. Healthcare finance analysts rely upon its principles when valuing physician practices, hospitals, and other healthcare businesses that are in the stages of selling, acquiring, or merging with other entities *inter alia*. This practice is becoming especially commonplace during the current shift toward ACOs, as provider entities, such as hospitals and physician practices, integrate.

Valuing a Business: The Analysis and Appraisal of Closely Held Companies, 5th ed. Shannon P. Pratt, Robert F. Reilly, and Robert P. Schweihs, New York: McGraw Hill, 2008.

This book, now in its fifth edition, is intended to serve the needs of a wide audience, from students to seasoned business appraisers. It provides guidance on how to formulate solid assessments that avoid common pitfalls and can stand up to intense scrutiny. The instruction offered in the book is useful to valuators of healthcare businesses, especially as hospital–physician alignments increase within the context of ACO integration.

The above list of seminal sources contains a wide variety of different documents types, written for diverse audiences, that contribute to an understanding of the evolution of ACOs. It is the aim of this literature review to give deference to these works and present a cogent and distilled review of the immense assemblage of applicable sources for the reader. Accountable care, while not a new concept, has continually transformed the way in which healthcare has been delivered. These works provide a thorough comprehension of how accountable care has evolved within various eras of healthcare, and what aspects of the current healthcare environment have driven the emergence of ACOs.

Index

D

E

F

G

K

L

M

Q

R

S

T

U

V

W